THE LEGAL
RESEARCH
AND WRITING
HANDBOOK

SECOND EDITION

THE LEGAL RESEARCH AND WRITING HANDBOOK

A BASIC APPROACH FOR PARALEGALS

ANDREA B. YELIN
Loyola University, Chicago

HOPE VINER SAMBORN
Loyola University, Chicago

 ASPEN LAW & BUSINESS
A Division of Aspen Publishers, Inc.
Gaithersburg   New York

Permissions
Aspen Law & Business
1185 Avenue of the Americas
New York, NY 10036

Printed in the United States of America.

ISBN 0-7355-0296-x

1 2 3 4 5 6 7 8 9 0

Library of Congress Cataloging-in-Publication Data
Yelin, Andrea B.
  The legal research and writing handbook: a basic approach for paralegals / Andrea B. Yelin, Hope Viner Samborn.—2nd ed.
     p.   cm.
  Includes index.
  ISBN 0-7355-0296-x
  1. Legal research—United States.   2. Legal composition.
I. Samborn, Hope Viner.   II. Title.
KF240.Y45   1999
340′.07′2073—dc21   99-13631
                                                          CIP

ABOUT ASPEN LAW & BUSINESS
LEGAL EDUCATION DIVISION

In 1996, Aspen Law & Business welcomed the Law School Division of Little, Brown and Company into its growing business—already established as a leading provider of practical information to legal practitioners.

Acquiring much more than a prestigious collection of educational publications by the country's foremost authors, Aspen Law & Business inherited the long-standing Little, Brown tradition of excellence—born over 150 years ago. As one of America's oldest and most venerable publishing houses, Little, Brown and Company commenced in a world of change and challenge, innovation and growth. Sharing that same spirit, Aspen Law & Business has dedicated itself to continuing and strengthening the integrity begun so many years ago.

ASPEN LAW & BUSINESS
A Division of Aspen Publishers, Inc.
A Wolters Kluwer Company

To David, Rachel and Henry, with all my love
ABY

To my youngest students and teachers, Eve, Sarah,
and Benjamin,
and to my favorite teacher and friend, Randy.
You have all of my love and thanks.
HVS

SUMMARY
OF CONTENTS

PART 1   LEGAL RESEARCH

CHAPTERS

CONTENTS

LIST OF
ILLUSTRATIONS

PREFACE

As paralegals, you can be invaluable members of the attorney-paralegal team when you have adequately mastered the skills of legal research and writing. This book is a step-by-step guide that explores the twists and turns of legal research and writing, teaching you how to avoid the dead ends and conquer obstacles along the way. Examples, exercises, and checklists help make it a smooth and enjoyable road.

Part I features an introduction to the legal system and legal authorities: the state and federal legislatures, the courts, and administrative agencies. It explains the relationship between state and federal governments, and between other governing bodies.

The research component of Part I begins with hardcopy resources—which are still more readily available to students than computer resources. Proficiency in hardcopy research will bring you greater success when performing research using a computer. You will also learn how to use Internet and CD-ROM sources. All available resources will be explored, and you will learn how they are interrelated and how to find the best sources for your particular project. Points from legal writing are integrated throughout the research chapters where relevant.

Part II focuses on basic legal writing, with a focus on legal memoranda and letters—the most common documents that paralegals draft. Objective memos inform the attorney of all of the relevant law, both for and against the client's position. Having paralegals brief cases expedites the research process. Delegating research and writing tasks to the paralegal is cost effective for the attorney, and saves the client money.

Part II also guides you step-by-step through the legal writing process. You will be introduced to the case brief, the legal memorandum, the questions presented statement, the brief answer, and the facts statement. You will learn how to identify the legal issues and relevant facts of a case, and how to organize and present them in a written brief or memorandum. As the culmination of your legal writing skills, you will learn to synthesize—to distill a general legal concept that applies to a case, and then state it in writing (citing more than one case or statute). Synthesis is essential to writing most case-related documents. A clear methodology—IRAC—will introduce you to the important components of synthesis: Issue, Rule, Application, and Conclusion. Using IRAC, you will learn to synthesize effectively and consistently.

A valuable reference tool, *The Legal Research and Writing Handbook* reviews letter writing, grammar, and editing—all essential skills you will use every day as a paralegal.

The Legal Research and Writing Workbook gives you hands-on exercises that reinforce the concepts in your textbook and provide you with practical applications for future work experiences.

You should view *The Legal Research and Writing Handbook* as a launching point from which to begin developing your research and writing skills. You will want to refer to the guidelines and concepts in this book throughout your career as you continue to expand in knowledge and experience.

April 1999   *Andrea B. Yelin*
                                                Hope Viner Samborn

ACKNOWLEDGMENTS

We would like to acknowledge all of the people who have helped us create this text and who have shaped its contents.

Thank you to Betsy Kenny for helping us to hone our revisions of the text, the workbook, and the teacher's manual. Thanks to Lisa Wehrle for her great job copyediting this edition as well as the first edition. Thanks to Peggy Rehberger, Melody Davies, Ellen Greenblatt, and Dave Herzog for their help with the text.

Thanks to the U.S. Attorney's office library in Chicago, Loyola University Law School Library in Chicago, West Group, the U.S. District Court in Toledo, and Premark Corporation for assistance in obtaining illustrations for this book.

Thanks also to Bob Doyle, Sherman Lewis, Julia Wentz, and Elizabeth Cooper of Loyola University Law School for all of your help.

Thanks to our families and friends, whose continued support has helped us to revise this text.

We continue to be indebted to the people whose assistance, direction and support led to the first edition of this text and ultimately this revised text as well as individuals who helped with our text, *Basic Legal Writing for Paralegals,* a project that led to some of the revisions in this text.

To that end, we thank Jean Hellman, Director of the Loyola University of Chicago, Institute for Paralegal Studies, who encouraged us to write our first book and who introduced us to Carolyn

O'Sullivan of Little, Brown and Company, the predecessor of Aspen Law & Business. We cannot thank Carolyn O'Sullivan, Betsy Kenny, Lisa Wehrle, Joan Horan, John Lyman, and Katie Byrne Butcher enough for their assistance with our books.

We also thank our students who have helped us to hone the text and the exercises. Their writing and use of the exercises helped form the skeleton for the book and then mold its contents. Their continued use of the book assisted us in revising the text. Our students have taught us more than we ever could teach them, and we appreciate all that they have done. Some students who deserve special thanks for their critiques, suggestions, and encouragement include Kelly Barry, Amy Berezinski, Nanette Boryc, Mara Castello, Patricia Cochran, Jessie Cohen, Nan Crotty, Beverly Dombroski, Stephen Gromala, Susanne Grant, Chris Harrigan, Marion Kahle, Michael Luckey, Mitchell McClure, Brenda Mondul, Cheryl Morgan, Patricia Naqvi, Melissa Pederson, Shay Robertson, Louise Tessitore, and Amy Widmer.

Thanks to Terri Rudd for your insightful ideas and assistance.

We would also like to thank the reviewers listed below. Their careful review of the first manuscript and the *Basic Legal Writing for Paralegals* manuscript produced many valuable comments and suggestions. We greatly appreciate their efforts.

Jonathan H. Barker
George Washington University

Laura Barnard
Lakeland Community College

Suzanne Cascio
Manhattanville College

Charles E. Coleman
New York City Technical College

Holly L. Enterline
State Technical Institute at Memphis

Andrew T. Fede
Montclair State College

William J. Heimbuch
Montclair State College

Patricia Hohl
Boston University

Mary Holland
Manchester Community College

Helene Kulczycki
Briarcliffe, The College for Business and Technology

Cynthia B. Lauber
Denver Paralegal Institute

Judith M. Maloney, Esq.
Long Island University

Joan M. McAuliffe
Quincy College

Elaine Puri
University of North Florida

Gina-Marie Reitano
St. John's University

Julia O. Tryk
Cuyahoga Community College

Sue K. Varon
National Center for Paralegal Training

Brenda L. Rice, J.D.
Johnson County Community College

Joy O'Donnell
Pima Community College

Eric Olson
Barry University

Holly L. Enterline
State Technical Institute at
  Memphis

Kay Y. Rute
Washburn University

Sy Littman
Platt College

Paul Klein
Duquesne University

Adelaide Lagnese
University of Maryland

Robin O. McNeely
McNeese State University

Lastly, we would like to thank the following publishers for allowing us to reprint the illustrations listed below.

Illustration 3-2. Reprinted with permission from *The United States Law Week,* Vol. 66. No. 49 (June 23, 1998). Copyright © 1998 by The Bureau of National Affairs, Inc. (800-372-1033) *http://www.bna.com*

Illustration 3-4. Reprinted with permission from LEXIS Law Publishing.

Illustration 3-5. Use of this material approved by LEXIS Law Publishing.

Illustrations 3-6, 3-7, 3-10, and 3-12. Reprinted with permission from West Group.

Illustration 3-13. Reprinted from *A Uniform System of Citation, Sixteenth Edition,* (1996), with permission of the Columbia Law Review Association, the Harvard Law Review, the University of Pennsylvania Law Review, and the Yale Law Journal.

Illustrations 3-14, 3-15, 3-16, 3-17, and 3-18. Reprinted with permission from West Group.

Illustrations 4-1, 4-2, 4-3, 4-5, 4-6, 4-7, 4-8, 4-9, 4-10, and 4-12. Reproduced by permission of *Shepard's.* Further reproduction of any kind is strictly prohibited.

Illustration 4-13. Reprinted by permission from West Group.

Illustration 4-14. Reprinted with permission from LEXIS Law Publishing.

Illustrations 5-1, 5-2, 5-3, 5-4, 5-5, 5-6, 5-7, 5-8, 5-9, 5-10, 5-11, 5-12, 5-13, and 5-14. Reprinted with permission from West Group.

Illustration 5-15. Reproduced by permission of LEXIS/NEXIS. Further reproduction is strictly prohibited.

Illustrations 5-16 and 5-17. Copyright © by the American Law Institute. Reprinted with permission from the American Law Institute.

Illustration 6-1. Reproduced by permission of LEXIS/NEXIS. Further reproduction is strictly prohibited.

Illustration 6-7. Reprinted with permission of LEXIS/NEXIS. Further reproduction is strictly prohibited.

Illustrations 6-6, 6-8, and 6-13. Reprinted with permission from West Group.

Illustration 6-9. Reprinted with permission from LEXIS/NEXIS. Further reproduction is strictly prohibited.

Illustration 6-10. Reprinted with permission from West Group.

Illustrations 6-11, 6-12, and 6-15. Reprinted with permission from LEXIS/NEXIS. Further reproduction is strictly prohibited.

Illustration 6-14. Reprinted by permission of Shepard's

Illustration 6-16. Reprinted with permission from West Group.

Illustration 6-18. Reprinted from *A Uniform System of Citation, Sixteenth Edition,* (1996), with permission of the Columbia Law Review, the Harvard Law Review, the University of Pennsylvania Law Review, and the Yale Law Journal.

Illustrations 7-1 and 7-2. Reprinted with permission from West Group.

Illustration 10-4. Reprinted with permission of Yahoo!, Inc.

Illustration 10-5. Copyright © Compaq Corporation. Used with permission.

Illustrations 11-3 and 11-4. Reprinted with permission from LEXIS/NEXIS. Further reproduction is strictly prohibited.

Illustration 12-1. Reprinted by permission of ABA Publishing.

Illustrations 13-1, 13-2, and 13-3. Reprinted with permission of West Group.

Illustrations 13-4 and 13-5. Copyright © 1998-1999 Martindale-Hubbell Law Directory, a division of Reed-Elsevier, Inc. All rights reserved.

THE LEGAL
RESEARCH
AND WRITING
HANDBOOK

LEGAL
RESEARCH

INTRODUCTION TO LEGAL RESEARCH

CHAPTER OVERVIEW

Before you begin to research and to write about a legal problem, you must understand your role as a paralegal. You are an important member of a team. To function effectively, you must know which legal system governs and how that system operates. This chapter first considers your role in researching a legal program. Next, it discusses the legal system. It focuses on the organization of the U.S. federal government, which is divided into three separate branches: the legislative, the executive, and the judicial. It also provides a general explanation of how state governments are structured. Finally, the role of major governmental bodies is explored.

A. INTRODUCTION TO LEGAL RESEARCH

1. The Role of the Paralegal in Legal Research and Writing

Legal research and legal writing are among the tasks paralegals can perform efficiently and cost-effectively for law firms and their clients. But to do so effectively, paralegals must understand the legal system and a variety of legal concepts. They must be able to use all of the research tools available to lawyers and their staffs, including the computer. Paralegals retrieve information regarding the law as well as nonlegal information, such as financial information and test results.

▼ Why Do Paralegals Perform Research?

Often research is done to determine whether a client has a case. Other times, you must research a particular issue raised after a case has been filed. Some research is done to support motions to be filed with courts. Research also may be done when a client is involved in a transaction and the attorney needs to determine the law and the steps to take in the transaction.

▼ What Is the Research Strategy?

Try to analyze the problem using the authorities you have found and discuss the issue and research with the assigning attorney. Many times you will not find a legal authority concerning the issue you have been asked to research. Do not despair.

▼ After a Research Project Is Completed, What Is the Next Step?

You must communicate your research results to an attorney effectively. To do this, you must understand the fundamentals of legal writing and be able to write detailed, clear, and thoughtful memoranda.

2. The Importance of Paralegals as Researchers

In practice, paralegals act as an arm of a lawyer. The amount of research and the type of assignments paralegals perform vary throughout the country. In some law offices, paralegals undertake all of the research in preparation for the filing of motions. In others, paralegals research and prepare rough drafts of judicial decisions. Paralegals often are asked to prepare memoranda that summarize their research results. This book is designed to help you complete these tasks.

ETHICS ALERT

Attorneys are required to supervise paralegals. Attorneys can be sanctioned for providing invalid case law to the courts. Therefore, attorneys could be liable for any mistakes you might make.

When you are assigned a research problem, you are expected to work as a professional. You should complete the assignment in a timely fashion. More important, however, the research results must be accurate, complete, and current. This book teaches you how to approach a research problem, about the resources available to uncover the legal standards, and about the various methods for ensuring that those standards are current, complete, and valid.

▼ What Are You Trying to Accomplish with Your Research?

In completing your tasks, you are looking for legal standards that will apply to the legal problem you must research. The ideal standards of authorities would be ones that are based on facts and circumstances identical to those posed in your legal problem. This quest is difficult. Do not be discouraged if you do not find such standards easily or at all.

B. INTRODUCTION TO THE U.S. LEGAL SYSTEM

1. The Organization of the Legal System

The United States consists of a multitiered system of government. The **federal government** and the **state governments** are the top two tiers. See Illustration 1-1.

ILLUSTRATION 1-1.   U.S. and State Government Systems

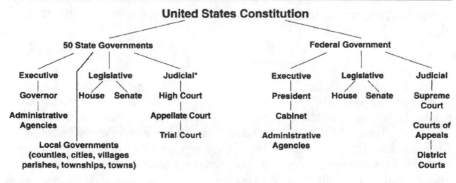

United States Constitution

50 State Governments — Federal Government

Executive	Legislative	Judicial*	Executive	Legislative	Judicial
Governor	House Senate	High Court	President	House Senate	Supreme Court
Administrative Agencies		Appellate Court	Cabinet		Courts of Appeals
		Trial Court	Administrative Agencies		District Courts

Local Governments
(counties, cities, villages
parishes, townships, towns)

*Most, but not all, state courts consist of three tiers.

Several lower-tier governmental bodies, including **city** and **county governments,** exercise authority over the citizens of the United States. For the most part, your research will concern either federal or state law. Therefore, this book focuses its discussion on the federal and state systems and how to find the law they generate. The knowledge of these systems, the types of laws they adopt, and how to find legal standards for these systems later can be applied to any research you plan to do concerning other government bodies and the law they generate.

▼ How Did the Federal and State Systems Originate?

Representatives of the states adopted a **constitution** for the United States that is the framework for the operation of this federal/state system of government. To that end, the U.S. Constitution creates three branches of government and defines their powers. You can think of the Constitution as an umbrella over all of the United States' governing bodies as it covers the question of not only federal government powers, but state powers as well. The Constitution reserves for the states all of the remaining powers not specifically designated to the federal government bodies. In addition, the Constitution establishes the rules for the relationship between the federal and state governments. The U.S. Constitution is the supreme law of the United States. For example, Congress, the legislative body of the federal government, cannot enact a law that is contrary to the U.S. Constitution. The state legislatures similarly are prevented from adopting laws that violate provisions of the U.S. Constitution.

2. Components of the Federal System and Governing Law

The federal government consists of three branches of government: the legislative, the executive, and the judicial. The U.S. Constitution created each branch and defines the relationship between them. The Constitution establishes a system in which each branch of government can monitor the activities of the other branches to prevent abuses.

a. The Legislative Branch

The **legislative branch** of the federal government is called the **Congress.** It is comprised of two houses or chambers called the **Senate** and the **House of Representatives.** Both houses are comprised of individuals who are elected. The Congress creates laws called **statutes.** Some statutes are new rules of law. Other statutes supersede or adopt court-made law, commonly referred to as **case law** or the **common law.** When Congress adopts common law as its own, the process is called **codification.** The statutes and the U.S. Constitution comprise a body of law called **enacted law.**

▼ How Is a Law Created?

Anyone can propose that Congress adopt a new law, and either chamber can introduce a law for consideration. When a proposed law is introduced, it is called a **bill.** Before the bill can become a law, both chambers must approve it. If both houses approve the same version of the bill, it is sent to the President. The President can sign or veto the bill or withhold action on it. If the President signs the bill, it becomes law. If the President does not act within ten days and the legislative session is still in progress, the bill becomes law. If the President vetoes the bill, Congress may override the veto by a two-thirds majority vote of each house.

If the President fails to act on the bill within the ten days and the legislature is out of session, the bill does not become law. This action is called a **pocket veto.**

b. The Executive Branch

The **executive branch** of the government includes the President as well as some federal administrative agencies. See Illustration 1-2.

The **President** is the country's top executive. The President has the authority to control many administrative agencies.

Administrative agencies enforce many of the laws of the United States. These agencies are responsible for the daily regulation of activities controlled by federal law. For a listing of some of the many administrative agencies, see Illustration 1-2.

Congress creates the agencies and delegates some of its own power to them because it alone is unable to handle the day-to-day enforcement of the overwhelming number of federal laws. Agencies, however, have the staff and often the technical expertise to deal with the daily enforcement of Congress's enacted laws. To do this, agencies often make rules that explain in detail how individuals should act to comply with congressional mandates. In some cases, agencies hold hearings to enforce the law.

For example, Congress enacted the Consumer Product Safety Act and delegated its enforcement power to the U.S. Consumer Product Safety Commission. Congress charged the commission with the responsibility for the daily enforcement of that act. As part of the commission's duties, it adopts rules or regulations. It also has administrative hearings, which often result in decisions.

c. The Judicial Branch

The third branch of government is the **judicial branch**. The judicial system includes three levels of courts that resolve disputes. See Illustration 1-3.

ILLUSTRATION 1-2. The Government of the United States

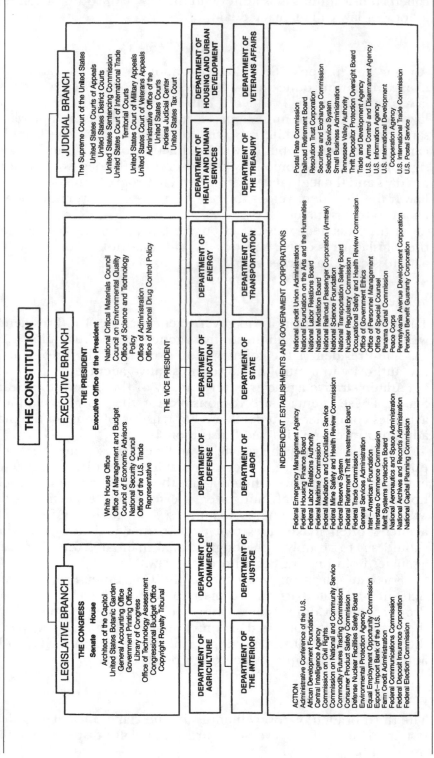

ILLUSTRATION 1-3. Federal Judicial System

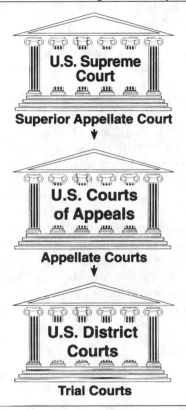

The entry-level court is the **trial court.** In that court, disputes are heard and decided by either a judge or a jury. This court also hears appeals from some administrative agencies and the federal bankruptcy courts. Some administrative agency decisions, however, are appealed directly to the **appellate courts.**

▼ Who Can Bring an Action in Federal Court?

A court can only consider a case if it has **jurisdiction** to hear it, that is, if the court is authorized to consider such cases. The federal court can consider all cases involving issues of federal law. In addition, it may hear cases involving disputes between parties of different states. Such cases are called **diversity cases.** Cases in which both the plaintiff, who is the party bringing the lawsuit, and the defendant are citizens of different states are examples of diversity cases. Diversity cases often involve issues of state law. For these cases that involve state law questions, the amount in dispute must exceed $75,000.

PRACTICE POINTER

Courts can decide issues of state or federal law.

i. The Trial Courts

The **trial court** is the court that hears the facts concerning a dispute. It is generally the first place in which a party can seek a remedy in federal court. Known as the **district courts,** these courts decide disputes when a party (which can be a person, corporation, or other entity) brings an action against another party. In such cases, the trial courts often are asked to interpret congressional enactments such as statutes, ordinances, charters, or executive branch–created laws, including agency rules or decisions. When a court interprets a statute or regulation, it is overseeing the actions of other government branches. Courts often consult a body of law called the **common law** before rendering any decisions. Common law is court-created law found in the judicial opinions or cases; it is not found in the statutes.

ii. The Appellate Courts

The federal trial courts' decisions can be appealed to one of the 13 **federal appellate courts** known as the **U.S. Courts of Appeals.** See Illustration 1-3. This second tier of federal courts is broken into numbered **circuits.** The circuits are geographic, except for the Federal Circuit. See Illustration 1-4. These courts only decide issues of law posed in appeals of trial court decisions. These courts do not consider new factual evidence. An excellent source of information about the federal courts, their boundaries, and the names and phone numbers of the courts and their officials is *BNA's Directory of State and Federal Courts, Judges and Clerks,* published and regularly updated by the Bureau of National Affairs.

Decisions of the federal appellate courts can be appealed to the U.S. Supreme Court.

iii. The Supreme Court

The **U.S. Supreme Court** is the highest court in the United States. See Illustration 1-3. The U.S. Constitution establishes this court. Today nine justices, appointed by the President and confirmed by the U.S. Senate, sit on this tribunal. The U.S. Supreme Court has discretion to consider many issues. This discretion is called **certiorari.** If the court decides not to hear an issue, it denies certiorari; if the court decides to hear an issue, it grants certiorari. By law, this court alone has the authority to hear appeals of a state court of last resort

ILLUSTRATION 1-4.   Circuit Map of the U.S. Courts of Appeals

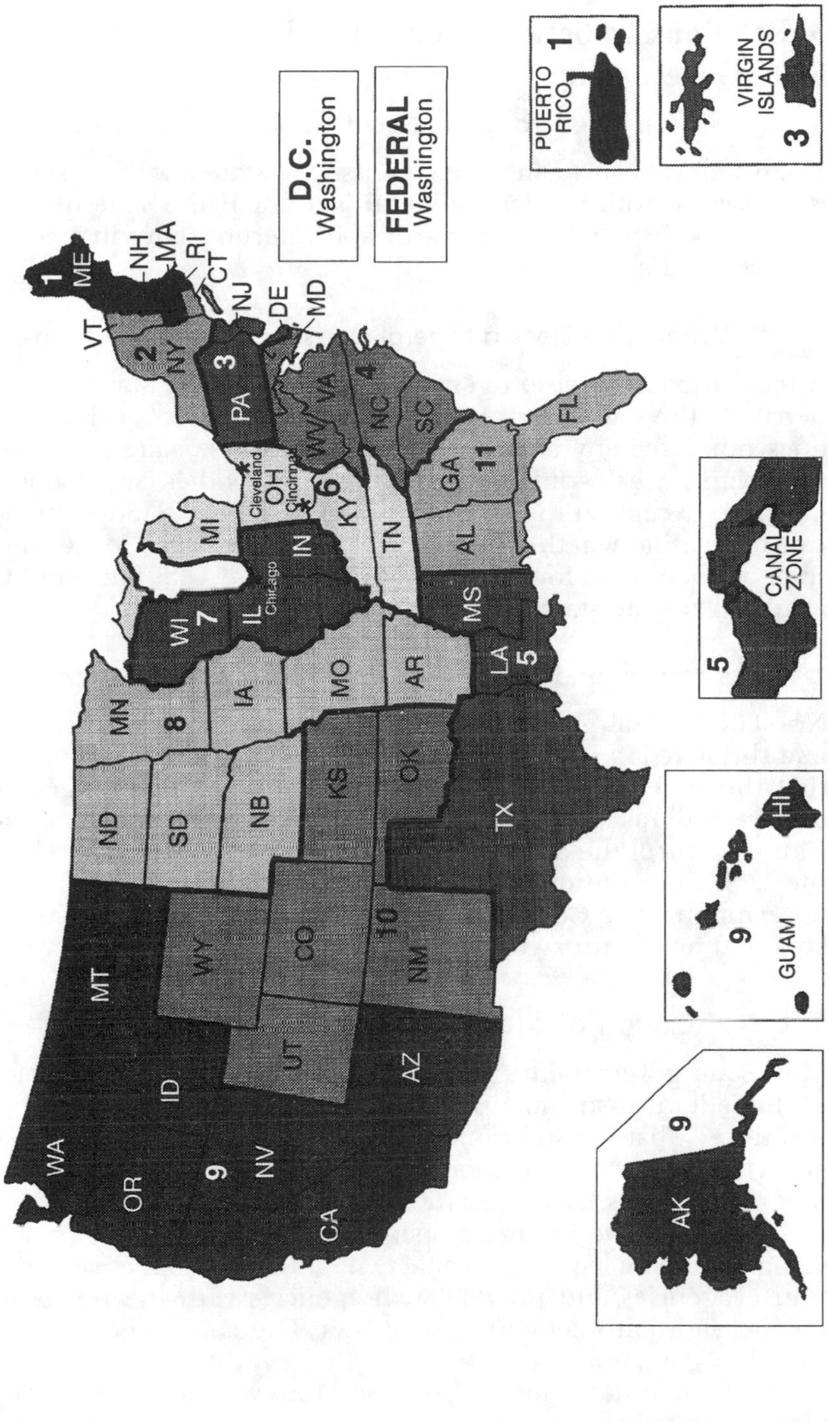

decision when a substantial federal constitutional issue is presented. The U.S. Supreme Court also may hear a dispute between two states.

3. Relationship between Federal and State Governments

▼ Can a Federal Court Decide an Issue of State Law?

Yes. A federal court can decide an issue of state law if the state issue is presented with a related federal issue or if the state question is raised in a dispute between parties of different states in a complete diversity action.

▼ What Effect Does a Federal Decision Have on State Law?

A federal court decision generally cannot change state law. It may persuade the state courts to review state law, but its decision usually does not force any change in the law. Because states are separate sovereigns, usually only the state governing bodies can change state law. One exception to this rule does exist. The U.S. Supreme Court can determine whether state law violates the U.S. Constitution. If such a violation is found, the decision of the U.S. Supreme Court would invalidate state law.

▼ Are Federal and State Agencies Part of One Governing Body?

No. The federal government is one sovereign or governing body and the state is a separate governing body or sovereign. That means that the state cannot control the federal government agencies or change federal law. In general, the federal government branches cannot control the state government or change state law. However, the U.S. Constitution, the umbrella, can limit actions of the state government. The Constitution prohibits the states from making any laws that are contrary to its provisions.

4. Organization of State Governments

Most state governments are organized in a manner similar to that of the federal government. State governments are governed by constitutions. That constitution defines the organization of the state's government and the relationship between the branches of government. The states have legislative, executive, and judicial branches.

The legislative branches operate in a manner similar to that of Congress. Some legislatures enact enabling laws that create administrative agencies and provide such agencies with the responsibility for the daily enforcement of state laws. The chief executive in each state is a governor.

Each state has a judicial system. However, not all state systems mirror the federal government's three-tier court system. Each state establishes which courts can hear different disputes. Some states have a three-tier system similar to that of the federal judicial branch. In some states, the intermediate appellate court is eliminated. The following systems do not include an intermediate appellate court: Delaware, District of Columbia, Maine, Mississippi, Montana, Nevada, New Hampshire, Rhode Island, South Dakota, Vermont, West Virginia, Wyoming, and Puerto Rico.

PRACTICE POINTER

The Supreme Court may not be the highest court in a state. This is the case in New York.

▼ What Are the Duties of the State Courts?

In most state court systems, a trial court determines the facts and legal issues of a case. This court might include a family court and a municipal or small claims court. The jurisdiction of these courts is generally limited, sometimes according to the amount of money in dispute.

The next level generally is an appellate level court. However, as noted above, some states do not have this level. As in the federal court system, this court does not hear new facts or evidence. Instead, it decides whether the lower court erred in deciding substantive law or procedural issues. Finally, most states have another appellate level court, similar to the U.S. Supreme Court, which is the final arbiter of disputes.

PRACTICE POINTER

An appellate court may hear facts and evidence if it is the court of original jurisdiction. That is the court charged with first hearing the case.

▼ Can State Courts Decide Issues of Federal Law?

Yes, state courts can decide issues of federal law. However, a state court decision concerning federal law does not change the federal law. It, however, may persuade federal governing bodies to change federal law. The state court decision's impact is limited to the case in which the federal issue was presented.

The federal government controls all issues of federal law. The state governments exercise authority over all issues of state law. These areas are not always well defined. In some areas, both the state and federal governments, exercise authority. For example, both the state and federal governments control how industries dispose of their wastes. Do not be discouraged if you have difficulty separating state and federal issues in some cases.

CHAPTER SUMMARY

In this chapter, you learned about the branches of the U.S. government and their functions, as well as the general structure of the state governments. The United States has three branches of government: the legislative, the executive, and the judicial. All of these branches were created by the U.S. Constitution, which guides their activities. In addition, administrative agencies enforce the laws created by the legislature.

The legislature, which consists of the House of Representatives and the Senate, creates laws called statutes.

The executive branch enforces the laws of the United States, and the judicial branch resolves disputes and interprets the laws.

The judicial branch is comprised of a three-tier court system. The highest court is the U.S. Supreme Court; the middle courts are the U.S. Courts of Appeals; the trial or lowest courts are the U.S. District Courts. All three branches of government create law.

KEY TERMS

administrative agencies	federal administrative agencies
appellate courts	federal appellate court
bill	federal government
case law	House of Representatives
certiorari	judicial branch
circuits	jurisdiction
city government	legislative branch
codification	pocket veto
common law	President
Congress	Senate
constitution	state governments
county government	statutes
district courts	trial court
diversity cases	U.S. Courts of Appeals
enacted law	U.S. Supreme Court
executive branch	

EXERCISES

HOMEWORK EXERCISES

1. Draw a diagram of your state government.
2. How many houses does your legislature have?
3. Diagram your state court system. Is there an intermediate court?
4. Draw a flow chart of the bill process.

WHAT LAW GOVERNS

CHAPTER OVERVIEW

In researching legal issues, you must have goals and understand the value of the legal authorities you find. This chapter explains the concept of legal authority and the determination of governing law. It discusses the value of various authorities and how authorities interrelate with each other. You will learn which authorities should determine the outcome of a case and which authorities merely provide persuasive support for a case.

15

A. DETERMINATION OF GOVERNING LAW

To determine what law controls your case, you must first determine the jurisdiction. Next, you must identify the current law that applies to your case by examining the hierarchy of authorities. Looking at relevant precedent and dicta completes your strategy for determining the governing law.

1. Jurisdiction

Jurisdiction is a complex concept that has several different definitions. It is the authority of a government body to exercise control over a conflict. In the broadest sense, jurisdiction is the right of a state or of the federal government to apply its laws to a dispute. It also is the right of a court to interpret and apply the law to a particular case. When a court or a governing body has jurisdiction over a case or situation, it has the authority to control the case or outcome of the situation.

▼ **What Factors Determine Which Jurisdiction Governs Your Case?**

A variety of factors affect which jurisdiction governs a claim in a particular case, including where the dispute arose, the parties involved in the case, and the nature of the dispute. Sometimes making this determination is a complex task. Ask the assigning attorney to assist you in making this determination.

2. Hierarchy of Authorities

Once you have determined the jurisdiction, you then must identify the current law that applies to the case. To determine what law applies to your case, you must determine the **hierarchy of authorities**. This is a system in which legal authorities such as court decisions, statutes, administrative rules and decisions, and constitutions are ranked according to the effect they have in controlling the law of a governing body. Determining the hierarchy of authorities is based in part on the nature of the case, the currency of an authority, and the structure of the court system.

a. Currency

You must first determine which authority is most current. Suppose you find that the law governing your case is a federal law and the case involves a question of federal constitutional law. At first glance the highest legal authority would appear to be the U.S. Constitution because it is the supreme law of the United States and because the legal issue in question is constitutional in nature. However, if the U.S. Supreme Court has interpreted the Constitution on the issue presented in your case, its decision is more current and would therefore be the highest legal authority.

In another case that does not involve a constitutional issue, a federal statute might be the highest authority. This would depend on whether a court had interpreted the statute. If a federal court had interpreted the statute's language and that language affected the issue involved in your case, you would need to determine whether the court decision or the statute is more recent. The most current authority is the highest authority.

EXAMPLE OF THE HIERARCHY QUESTION BETWEEN A STATUTE AND A CASE

Your case involves a statute that was enacted on December 1, 1997. All of the court cases you have found that may have a bearing on the issue involved in this case were decided before December 1, 1997. Therefore, the statute—the most current authority—is the highest authority concerning this issue.

b. Levels of Court

Next, you must consider the level of each authority, that is, where the court or government body ranks in order of its authority. The trial courts, appellate courts, and U.S. Supreme Court do not carry the same weight. For example, a decision of the highest court, the U.S. Supreme Court, would be at the top of the hierarchy of authorities of court decisions.

Except for the U.S. Supreme Court, all of the federal courts are within defined groups called **circuits**. Within each circuit is a group of district courts and one circuit court of appeals. The key to the relationship between the federal courts is that the district courts, which are the entry-level courts, must follow decisions of the U.S. Circuit Court of Appeals within its circuit. A district court does not have to follow decisions of appellate courts that are outside of its circuit.

PRACTICE POINTER

Making a chart of authorities if you have multiple authorities to consider is often helpful.

Two examples of how such a hierarchical ranking would work in practice follow.

EXAMPLES OF HIERARCHY BETWEEN COURTS

The U.S. District Court for the Northern District of Illinois, which is in Chicago, falls in the Seventh Circuit. See Illustration 1-4, page 11. If the federal district court in Illinois was asked to determine whether federal law permitted a union to charge a fee to nonmembers for activities that benefit nonmembers, it would be bound to follow any U.S. Seventh Circuit Court of Appeals decision concerning this issue. This is because this appellate court is a higher court than the district court. But the Illinois district court would not have to follow decisions of the U.S. Sixth Circuit Court of Appeals in Cincinnati concerning the above issue.

The U.S. District Court for the Northern District of Ohio, based in Cleveland, falls within the Sixth Circuit. See Illustration 1-4. That district court must follow decisions of the Sixth Circuit appellate court, not those of the Seventh Circuit Court of Appeals in Chicago.

c. Conflicting Decisions between Circuits

Each circuit is independent of the other circuits. Therefore, their decisions may conflict. Each appellate court can make its decision independent of any decision concerning the same issue rendered by another appellate court. Often, however, one appellate court is guided in its decision by the decision of another appellate court. If two appellate courts have conflicting decisions concerning the same issue, how can you, as a researcher, decide what law governs? You must determine what circuit court authority is mandatory for your case. (If the question is a particularly significant issue, check if the U.S. Supreme Court has decided the issue or is about to render a decision concerning such an issue. If so, a decision of the Supreme Court—the highest level of court—will be at the top of the hierarchy of authority.)

d. State and Federal Decisions Concerning an Issue

What happens if the issue in your case involves both state and federal decisions? How do you make sense of the hierarchy of authorities in such cases? The key is to determine which court has jurisdiction or the right to hear the case. The court systems of the state and federal governments operate in tandem. As explained above, the federal courts may decide issues of both federal or state law. For example, a federal diversity case may involve a negligence issue—a state law issue.

Next, you must determine whether federal or state law applies. If you find this difficult, ask the assigning attorney. The federal courts must look to decisions of the highest court of the state to make a determination of state law.[1] The federal court decision, however, does not bind later state court decisions.

State courts also may decide issues of either federal or state law. The state court decisions concerning federal law are merely persuasive, however. For instance, a plaintiff may bring an age discrimination case based on both the state and federal age discrimination in employment statutes. State courts will look to federal courts for guidance in deciding issues of federal law. However, they are not bound to follow those decisions.

e. Conflicts in Federal and State Authority

Although the federal and state governments are independent governments, they sometimes regulate some of the same areas, such as environmental pollution and securities. In some cases, the federal government by congressional action will control an area extensively, and a state will attempt to monitor the same area. Who controls varies. Often, this determination is made by reviewing the Constitution.

The federal courts sometimes are asked to decide who controls. The courts may look to the Constitution for guidance or may consider what has pervasively regulated an area. For example, if a case involves a section of the U.S. Constitution, the U.S. Supreme Court is the final authority. In other cases, it depends on the area being regulated.

f. State Court Decisions

Each group of state courts is a separate court system. State courts of one state do not have to follow decisions made by courts of other states. Often, however, state courts consider other states' court decisions for guidance in how to decide a case. Decisions of one state's courts are merely advisory or persuasive decisions for another state's courts, not decisions that control the law of the first state.

3. Precedent

You already have learned that the courts generate decisions or cases that become law. The basic rule of law decided by the court is the **holding**. If the court is presented with more than one issue, the decision includes more than one holding. The holding also is called the **precedent**.

Theoretically, the lower courts must follow decisions or precedents of the higher courts in their jurisdiction. This theory is called **stare decisis**. The idea behind it is that parties should be able to rely

---

[1]For a more complete discussion of this point, see Charles A. Wright, *The Law of Federal Courts* (4th ed. 1983).

on what the courts have done in the past. Doing so allows parties to predict how a court is likely to rule in their cases.

The doctrine of stare decisis makes your job as a researcher important. You must determine what the courts have decided in the past to assist the attorneys in predicting what the court is likely to do, or likely to be persuaded to do, in your case. Sometimes a court will not follow precedent. Even though stare decisis and precedent are the controlling doctrines, courts decide cases based on the facts before them and the changes in society. This allows the law, through the holdings, to evolve and to meet contemporary needs.

4. Dicta

Often a court addresses an issue that is not directly presented by the parties. In such cases, a court states what it would do if it was presented directly with the issue. When the court makes such statements, they are called **dicta**. Dicta do not have the same force and effect as holdings. They are not authoritative, and lower courts are not bound to follow such statements.

You might use dicta when no court has ever been asked directly to decide the issue addressed. The dicta explain how the court would decide the issue if it was directly presented to the court. Because of this, the dicta might help you to predict how a court might decide an issue. Dicta also can be used to persuade a court to decide an issue in a certain manner. Although dicta may be helpful, finding dicta is not the goal of your research.

B. GOAL OF YOUR RESEARCH

Your task is to find primary authority "on point" or "on all fours" with your case, in other words, cases that are similar in fact and in legal issue to your case and whose holdings address an issue presented in your case.

1. Primary Authority

Primary authority is law generated by a government body. Cases decided by any court are primary authority. Legislative enactments such as constitutions, statutes, ordinances, or charters are primary authorities. See Illustration 2-1. Administrative agency rules and decisions are primary authorities.

These authorities often are published chronologically. However, statutes are arranged by subject. Some sources of primary authorities will be more appropriate for your research than others. In some cases, primary authority is **mandatory** or **binding authority** because

ILLUSTRATION 2-1. Authorities and Finding Tools

Primary Authorities	Secondary Authorities	Finding Tools
Court decisions	Encyclopedias	Digests
Statutes	*American Law Reports*	Citators
Agency rules and regulations	Periodicals and law reviews	Updaters
Constitutions	Dictionaries	Annotated statutes
Charters	Thesauri	
Ordinances	Model codes	
Adopted pattern jury instructions	Unadopted uniform laws	
	Treatises	
Court rules	Restatements of the Law	

a government body must follow that authority when it makes future decisions. The words *mandatory* and *binding* are interchangeable.

▼ How Do You Determine Whether a Case Is Mandatory or Binding?

To determine whether a case is mandatory or binding, you must consider the rank of the authorities. Follow the steps below.

1. Determine the jurisdiction that applies to your case. Then, look to the hierarchy of the courts within that jurisdiction.
2. Note what court decided the case you are reviewing.
3. Determine whether this is a court within the jurisdiction that applies to your case.
4. If the court is within the appropriate jurisdiction, you must determine the level of that court within the court system. Is it a trial court or an appellate court? Is it the highest court of the system? States often have rules that specify the effect of a court decision on other courts within the same system. In general, the lower courts in a system must follow the decisions of the highest court in the system. The rules concerning which courts must follow the decisions of the intermediate-tier courts vary by jurisdiction. Consult the rules for that jurisdiction.

An authority is only mandatory if it controls or shapes the law of a particular jurisdiction, for example, an opinion from a state appellate court or an applicable state statute.

An authority is **persuasive** when it is made by a court outside of a particular jurisdiction. For example, decisions of one state court are not binding on courts of other states. Decisions of the Illinois Supreme Court are mandatory or binding on the lower courts in Illinois, but these decisions are merely persuasive primary authority in Michigan.

A decision is also persuasive rather than mandatory if it is made by a court whose decisions according to the law do not bind other courts. For example, decisions of the federal trial courts do not have to be followed by other federal courts.

2. Secondary Authority

Another type of authority is **secondary authority**. Such authority is not generated by government bodies. Instead, secondary authority includes commentary of attorneys or other experts. Secondary authority is persuasive only, and it is never binding or mandatory. In general, an attorney would not base an argument to a court on a secondary authority.

Secondary sources are helpful in understanding an issue of law, in determining other issues, and in finding primary authorities. Sometimes secondary authorities help to interpret primary authority for you and the court. Secondary sources include treatises, Restatements of the Law, dictionaries, encyclopedias, legal periodicals, *American Law Reports*, books, and thesauri. See Illustration 2-1. Often these sources direct you to cases, statutes, and other primary authorities.

Some secondary authorities are more persuasive than others. Many restatements and treatises are authoritative and can be noted in court documents and legal reports called memoranda addressed to attorneys. However, most secondary authorities should not be noted in these reports.

PRACTICE POINTER

If you have a primary authority on point, do not cite a secondary authority to make the same point.

---

3. Finding Tools

To find primary and secondary resources, often you need to consult **finding tools**, such as digests and citators. See Illustration 2-1. These finding tools are neither primary nor secondary authority. They should never be noted or cited in memoranda or court documents. Among the finding tools are **digests**, which are books containing case abstracts arranged according to publisher-assigned topics rather than in chronological order. **Annotated statutes** also include case abstracts written by the publishers. **Citators**, such as *Shepard's*, provide you with listings of cases and some secondary authorities.

PRACTICE POINTER

Attorneys do not look favorably on paralegals who cite finding tools as authority.

4. Hybrid Sources of Authority

Hybrid sources of authority contain primary authorities, secondary authorities, regulations, cases, and finding tools. Hybrid sources of authority include looseleaf services, formbooks, and proof of facts.

5. Nonlegal Sources

You often must consult nonlegal sources, such as newspapers or corporate information statements. These sources are not authoritative. Never use nonlegal sources to determine the law that governs a case. However, they can assist you in your work. These sources often provide insight into the purpose behind a court decision or the enactment of a law.

CHAPTER SUMMARY

In this chapter, you learned that determining governing law involves examining jurisdiction and the hierarchy of authorities. You also learned how precedent and dicta influence governing law. As a researcher, your goal is to find cases that are similar to yours in fact and legal issue and whose holdings address an issue presented in your case. In reaching this goal, you first seek primary authorities because these authorities carry more weight with the courts than secondary authorities. Primary authorities include court decisions, statutes, court rules, constitutions, and administrative rules and regulations.

Some primary authorities are binding. If an authority is binding, a court must follow that authority. Other authorities are merely persuasive. Such authorities provide guidance to the courts and often are followed by the decision-making tribunal.

As you are researching, you often will refer to secondary authorities. Secondary authorities provide you with information to understand primary authorities. Generally, secondary authorities are commentaries prepared by experts in a particular field. These authorities often include citations to primary authorities. Secondary authorities are persuasive only. Therefore, you would rely on a primary authority rather than a secondary authority. Secondary authorities include encyclopedias, treatises, and legal periodicals.

Finding tools are designed to assist you in your research, but they are not considered authorities. These tools provide you with citations to primary and secondary authorities. Finding tools include annotated statutes, digests, and citators.

KEY TERMS

annotated statutes

binding authority

circuits

citators

dicta

digests

finding tools

hierarchy of authorities

holding

hybrid sources of authority

jurisdiction

mandatory authority

persuasive authority

precedent

primary authority

secondary authority

stare decisis

EXERCISES

Court Systems
IN-CLASS EXERCISES

1. What is the highest court of your state?
2. Within your state's court system, what type of authority are decisions made by the highest court named in question 1?
   a. primary binding
   b. primary persuasive
   c. secondary binding
   d. secondary persuasive
3. What is the name of the trial court of your state?
4. Are the trial court's decisions binding on the highest court of the state?
5. What is the highest court of the federal system of government?
6. Within the federal system of government, what type of authority are decisions made by the highest court named in question 5?
   a. primary binding
   b. primary persuasive
   c. secondary binding
   d. secondary persuasive
7. What is the name of the trial court of the federal government?
8. Are decisions of any federal trial court binding on any federal appellate court?

Homework Exercises
RESEARCH STRATEGY

9. You are a paralegal assigned to research the components necessary to create a valid will in your state. List in order the types of authorities you would consult and why. Next, rank the authorities according to whether they are primary mandatory, primary persuasive, or secondary.
10. You are a paralegal who has just researched what constitutes a breach of contract in a case involving the delivery of dairy products in Wiscon-

sin. Rank the following authorities and list whether each is a primary binding, primary persuasive, or secondary authority.

   a. a Wisconsin Supreme Court case involving a breach of contract dispute.

   b. a Wisconsin statute that defines breach of contract.

   c. a Wisconsin statute that defines the term *delivery* in a contract.

   d. a Wisconsin trial court case involving a breach of contract dispute.

   e. an Illinois Supreme Court case involving a breach of contract dispute.

   f. a Uniform Commercial Code section concerning breach of contract. (The Wisconsin statute is derived in part from this section but does not adopt it in total.)

11. You are researching the question of whether a company that employs 50 individuals is an employer under the federal law regulating age discrimination in employment. Your case is pending in the federal district court in Toledo, Ohio. You learn that the definitions in the age discrimination statute were derived from those already in the sex discrimination statute. Rank the following authorities and list whether each is a primary binding, primary persuasive, or secondary authority.

   a. the federal age discrimination in employment statute that defines the term *employer*.

   b. the federal sex discrimination in employment statute that defines the term *employer*.

   c. a U.S. Supreme Court case that interprets the definition of *employer* contained in the federal age discrimination in employment statute.

   d. a U.S. Supreme Court case that interprets the definition of *employer* contained in the federal sex discrimination in employment statute.

   e. a decision of the Northern District Court of Ohio, Western Division, concerning the definition of *employer* under the federal age discrimination in employment statute.

   f. a law review article in the *University of Toledo Law Review* concerning the definition of *employer* contained in the federal age discrimination in employment statute.

   g. a section of an employment law treatise that explains the definition of *employer* under the federal age discrimination in employment statute.

   h. an Ohio Supreme Court case that explains the definition of *employer* under the federal age discrimination in employment statute.

12. You are asked to research the validity of a New York statute that bars high school students from wearing t-shirts bearing antigovernment slogans. Your case is pending in the state court of New York. Rank the following authorities and list whether each is a primary binding, primary persuasive, or secondary authority.

   a. the New York statute in question.

   b. the U.S. Constitution's First Amendment regarding free speech.

   c. a U.S. Supreme Court case that prohibits states from banning the wearing of symbols by high school students because such a ban violates the U.S. Constitution.

   d. a case decided by the highest court in New York that holds that the statute is invalid.
   e. a California case involving an identical statute adopted in California that holds that the statute is valid.
   f. an encyclopedia entry that states that such bans are invalid.
   g. a newspaper article in *The National Law Journal* that predicts that the U.S. Supreme Court will invalidate the New York statute.

COURT DECISIONS

CHAPTER OVERVIEW

In Chapters 1 and 2, you learned about our system of government and were introduced to the concept of legal authorities. This chapter focuses on one of those legal authorities—case law, which is a primary authority. The chapter describes where to find U.S. Supreme Court cases and other federal court decisions as well as the location of many state court opinions. It also explains where you can find the most recent court decisions. You are then introduced to a topical system for locating cases and are shown how to use this system.

A. REPORTERS

Court decisions are often referred to as **case law**. Case law is one of the primary sources of our law, on both the state and the federal levels. Finding and reading past court decisions is therefore vital to any lawyer or paralegal working on a client's case.

Several publishers publish court decisions in various forms. These publishers have devised **reporting systems** for organizing these court decisions. The major reporting system is called the **National Reporter System** and is published by West Group. It includes books called **reporters** that contain many federal and state decisions in chronological order. Several other companies and government agencies also publish court decisions in chronologically arranged reporters.

1. Slip Opinions

The first printed version of a judge's decision is generally a set of typed pages called a **slip opinion**. See Illustration 3-1. In some cases, the slip opinion is the only report of a court's action because the case is never published in a reporter or looseleaf service or placed in a computer database. This is often the case with trial court decisions.

▼ Where Can You Get a Slip Opinion?

Slip opinions are obtained from the courts. All you need is the name of the case. Sometimes you can locate the slip opinion with the name of only one of the parties involved in the case. Some courts widely distribute slip opinions in printed form. In addition, WESTLAW and LEXIS, two computerized legal research services, include many slip opinions online. The Internet is increasingly offering court opinions free of charge. A list of some of the sources of these opinions is included in Chapter 10. Computer bulletin boards also allow for easy and immediate access to some court slip opinions. To use these, you must use a computer modem and a telephone line. You dial directly into the computer that stores the court opinions. Most bulletin boards are free; however, most require that users be registered and pay phone access charges. Many courts are placing decisions on the Internet rather than on bulletin boards daily. Newspaper reports of court cases also are quickly available, although these should never be quoted in a memorandum for an attorney or in a motion to the court because such reports have no force within the law. In addition, they may be incorrect. Only quote or cite information that comes directly from an opinion.

ILLUSTRATION 3-1. Slip Opinion Page from *Gillespie v. Willard City Board of Education,* **No. 87C-7043 (N.D. Ohio September 29, 1987)**

IN THE UNITED STATES DISTRICT COURT
FOR THE NORTHERN DISTRICT OF OHIO
WESTERN DIVISION

MARIANNA GILLESPIE et al.,)	No. C87-7043
)	
Plaintiff(s),)	
)	
-vs-)	MEMORANDUM AND
)	ORDER
WILLARD CITY BOARD)	
OF EDUCATION et al.,)	
)	
Defendant(s).)	

* * * * *

This case presents challenges to the constitutionality of the procedures established by various union organizations and the Willard School Board for collecting and determining agency fees. Agency fees are assessed by unions against non-members who receive the benefits of union bargaining and contract administration. These challenges are being considered in light of the standards the Supreme Court set forth in Chicago Teachers Union v. Hudson, ____U.S. ____, 106 S. Ct. 1066, 89 L. Ed.2d 232 (1986) ("Hudson"), and the ruling of the Sixth Circuit Court of Appeals in Tierney v. Toledo, No. 85-3016/3290 (6th Cir. July 27, 1987). Plaintiffs contend that the Ohio law permitting such agency fee collections violates the U.S. Constitution. Furthermore, plaintiffs have brought this action under 42 U.S.C. §1983. . . .

---

a. Supreme Court Slip Opinions

For the U.S. Supreme Court, you can retrieve decisions from the court clerk or from the Internet. However, retrieving them may be difficult. For specific search techniques and resources that contain these decisions, see Chapter 10. In addition, *United States Law Week,* a service of the Bureau of National Affairs, publishes opinions within days of a decision. See Illustration 3-2. It contains a list of all of the cases argued, docketed, or reviewed by the U.S. Supreme Court. *U.S. Law Week*'s Supreme Court Today provides daily updates of

ILLUSTRATION 3-2.   *U.S. Law Week* Sample Page

 BNA

The United States Law Week

♦ CASE ALERT
♦ LEGAL NEWS
♦ SUPREME COURT TODAY

VOL. 66, NO. 49   *A NATIONAL SURVEY OF CURRENT CASE LAW*   JUNE 23, 1998

SUMMARY AND ANALYSIS OF SIGNIFICANT COURT OPINIONS

HIGHLIGHTS

School Districts Aren't Liable for Teacher-Student Harassment Unless Responsible Official With Actual Knowledge Fails to Act

A school district can be held liable in damages under Title IX of the 1972 Education Amendments for a teacher's sexual harassment of a student only if a district official with authority to remedy the discrimination has actual knowledge of the misconduct and is deliberately indifferent to it, the U.S. Supreme Court holds in a 5–4 ruling. The federal government and a number of federal appeals courts have imposed less demanding standards.

Because Title IX merely conditions the receipt of federal education funds on the recipient's agreement not to discriminate, the court finds it unlikely that Congress intended to impose damages liability absent the recipient's actual knowledge of noncompliance. The court also rejects the federal government's argument that, as under Title VII of the 1964 Civil Rights Act, principles of respondeat superior and constructive notice should apply. **Page 1780**

Presence of Claims Barred by Eleventh Amendment Doesn't Spoil Removal of Otherwise Removable Case

An Eleventh Amendment defense to some claims in an otherwise removable case does not bar removal or require remand of the entire case, the U.S. Supreme Court holds. Resolving a circuit split, the court says state sovereign immunity is an affirmative defense that may be waived by the state or ignored by a court if not asserted, and thus does not automatically deprive a federal court of "original jurisdiction" within the meaning of the federal removal statute.

The court further rules that the statute requiring remand of a removed case "[i]f at any time before judgment it appears that the district court lacks subject matter jurisdiction" does not apply when the Eleventh Amendment bars only some claims, rather than the entire case. **Page 1773**

Supreme Court Strikes Down Currency Reporting Fine As Violation of Eighth Amendment's Excessive Fines Clause

In an important 5–4 ruling under the Eighth Amendment's Excessive Fines Clause, the Supreme Court decides that the government cannot constitutionally require a defendant who was convicted of failing to report the transport of more than $10,000 in currency out of the country to forfeit the entire amount transported—$357,144.

Such a forfeiture constitutes punishment and is thus a "fine" within the meaning of the clause, the court says. It then articulates for the first time a standard for determining excessiveness in this context, concluding that a punitive forfeiture violates the Excessive Fines Clause if it is grossly disproportional to the gravity of a defendant's offense. That being the case here, the court says full forfeiture of the defendant's currency would violate the clause. **Page 1775**

IN THIS ISSUE

A complete topical index of Case Alert.

ANTITRUST: A city that fears an electric utility merger will deprive it of the opportunity to obtain lower rates through competition lacks antitrust standing, the Third Circuit determines. **Page 1771**

CIVIL PROCEDURE: The cash-free nationwide class settlement of product liability claims involving rear liftgate latches on Chrysler minivans satisfies Rule 23 class action and fairness standards, the Ninth Circuit finds. **Page 1772**

CIVIL PROCEDURE: The availability of an Eleventh Amendment defense to some claims in an otherwise removable case does not preclude removal or require remand of the entire case, the U.S. Supreme Court holds. **Page 1773**

CONSUMER CREDIT: Condominium fee obligations are "debts" subject to the Fair Debt Collection Practices Act, the Tenth Circuit rules. **Page 1773**

CRIMINAL LAW: A felon whose pardon or restoration of civil rights under state law continues to restrict his possession of some firearms remains subject to federal statutes barring and punishing possession of any firearm by one previously convicted of a felony, the U.S. Supreme Court concludes. **Page 1774**

Reprinted with permission from *The United States Law Week,* Vol. 66, No. 49 (June 23, 1998). Copyright 1998 by The Bureau of National Affairs, Inc. (800-372-1033) 〈*http://www.bna.com*〉

cases at its Web home page, http://www.bna.com. *U.S. Law Week* also provides some synopsis of arguments and analysis of significant opinions complete with headnotes and electronic links.

United States Supreme Court slip opinions also can be found on WESTLAW and LEXIS within 24 to 48 hours after the decision.

Some decisions are electronically transmitted from the Court to these services within hours of the decision's release and are available to users on the day that they are released.

b. Other Slip Opinions

Slip opinions for other federal courts can be secured from the court, the Internet, or WESTLAW and LEXIS. State court slip opinions are most easily accessible from WESTLAW, LEXIS, or the Internet. However, not all of these court decisions are available on the computer. WESTLAW and LEXIS have many court decisions, but the coverage is not complete. Several of these resources are just being added to the Internet and, therefore, may not be available. Contact the state court if you cannot find its opinion elsewhere.

▼ How Are Slip Opinions Cited?

Slip opinions are cited according to Rule 10.8.1 of *A Uniform System of Citation* (16th ed. 1996) (the Bluebook). You should provide the docket number, the court, and the full (but abbreviated) date of the most recent disposition of the case.

slip opinion cite: Gillespie v. Willard City Bd. of Educ., No. C87-7043 (N.D. Ohio Sept. 28, 1987)

with page cite: Gillespie v. Willard City Bd. of Educ., No. C87-7043, slip op. at 3 (N.D. Ohio Sept. 28, 1987)

2. Advance Sheets

After a slip opinion is released, it is published in **advance sheets**. Advance sheets, often distributed as pamphlets, contain the full text of a decision and are paginated using the same page numbers that will be used when the decision is published in the bound reporter. Many advance sheets contain publisher's notes called **headnotes** that are designed to assist readers. These notes summarize points of law in a case and have a topic and number assigned to them. These topics and numbers assist you in finding additional cases. After decisions appear in advance sheets, they are published in the bound reporters.

3. Bound Reporters

a. U.S. Supreme Court Decisions

A U.S. Supreme Court case is first published as a slip opinion, then as an advance sheet, and finally as a report in a bound volume. For U.S. Supreme Court cases, the official, government-printed reporter is *United States Reports*. See Illustration 3-3. This reporter, however, is not published quickly, nor does it contain any research aids. Because of this delay, commercial publishers have created reporter systems that contain the same decisions as those published in *U.S. Reports*.

Commercial publishers produce these decisions as well. One commercial publisher, West Group, publishes all U.S. Supreme Court decisions in its reporter called the **Supreme Court Reporter**. LEXIS Law Publishing Co. prints the same full text of U.S. Supreme Court decisions in its reporter called *United States Supreme Court Reports, Lawyers' Edition*. Most people simply call it the **Lawyers' Edition**. These reports were once published by Lawyers Cooperative Publishing Co. The cases are identical to the decisions that appear in the official *U.S. Reports*, except that they also contain references prepared by the publishers to assist you in your research. These references direct you to other sources that may help you understand a point of law. For example, a publisher may direct you to a treatise that contains commentary about a point of law raised in the case reported.

▼ Are Supreme Court Decisions Available on CD-ROM?

Yes. You can use CD-ROM libraries, for example, to consult opinions found in *West's Supreme Court Reporter*. CD-ROM libraries are compact discs that contain collections of cases or other materials. The CD-ROM libraries can be searched by citation. Within a CD-ROM library you can perform electronic word searches of relevant documents.

▼ What Happens If the Language of a Decision in the Commercial Reporters Varies from the Language in *U.S. Reports?*

If the report contained in either the *Supreme Court Reporter* or the *Lawyers' Edition* varies from the official, government-printed report, the language in *U.S. Reports* governs.

▼ Why Use the Commercial Reporters Rather Than the Official Reports?

You should review U.S. Supreme Court cases in either the *Supreme Court Reporter* or in the *U.S. Supreme Court Reports, Lawyers' Edition*. First, these reporters are published sooner than the official, government-printed version. In addition, they contain a variety of publisher's headnotes or case abstracts that assist you in your research. These headnotes summarize points of law found in a case. They also include a publisher's topic designation and number. These topics and numbers tie into the commercial publisher's indexes of legal issues called **digests**. These digests are organized by topic and numbers.

The *Lawyers' Edition*, now in its second series, contains a list of references. Older volumes reference Lawyers Cooperative Publishing Co. materials such as encyclopedias or commentaries. This reference box is called the Total Client-Service Library References. See Illustra-

ILLUSTRATION 3-3. Pages from *U.S. Reports, United Paperworkers Intl. Union, AFL-CIO, et al. v. Misco, Inc.,* 484 U.S. 29 (1987)

PAPERWORKERS *v.* MISCO, INC.   29

Syllabus

UNITED PAPERWORKERS INTERNATIONAL UNION, AFL–CIO, ET AL. *v.* MISCO, INC.

CERTIORARI TO THE UNITED STATES COURT OF APPEALS FOR THE FIFTH CIRCUIT

No. 86–651. Argued October 13, 1987—Decided December 1, 1987

Respondent employer's collective-bargaining agreement with petitioner union authorizes the submission to binding arbitration of any grievance that arises from the interpretation or application of the agreement's terms, and reserves to management the right to establish, amend, and enforce rules regulating employee discharge and discipline and setting forth disciplinary procedures. One of respondent's rules listed as causes for discharge the possession or use of controlled substances on company property. Isiah Cooper, an employee covered by the agreement who operated a hazardous machine, was apprehended by police in the backseat of someone else's car in respondent's parking lot with marijuana smoke in the air and a lighted marijuana cigarette in the frontseat ashtray. A police search of Cooper's own car on the lot revealed marijuana gleanings. Upon learning of the cigarette incident, respondent discharged Cooper for violation of the disciplinary rule. Cooper then filed a grievance which proceeded to arbitration on the stipulated issue whether respondent had just cause for the discharge under the rule and, if not, the appropriate remedy. The arbitrator upheld the grievance and ordered Cooper's reinstatement, finding that the cigarette incident was insufficient proof that Cooper was using or possessed marijuana on company property. Because, at the time of the discharge, respondent was not aware of, and thus did not rely upon, the fact that marijuana had been found in Cooper's own car, the arbitrator refused to accept this fact into evidence. However, the District Court vacated the arbitration award and the Court of Appeals affirmed, ruling that reinstatement would violate the public policy "against the operation of dangerous machinery by persons under the influence of drugs." The court held that the cigarette incident and the finding of marijuana in Cooper's car established a violation of the disciplinary rule that gave respondent just cause for discharge.

Held:

    1. The Court of Appeals exceeded the limited authority possessed by a court reviewing an arbitrator's award entered pursuant to a collective-bargaining agreement. Pp. 36–42.

ILLUSTRATION 3-3.   *Continued*

framed under the approach set out in *W. R. Grace*, and the violation of such policy must be clearly shown. Here, the court made no attempt to review existing laws and legal precedents, but simply formulated a policy against the operation of dangerous machinery under the influence of drugs based on "general considerations of supposed public interests." Even if that formulation could be accepted, no violation of the policy was clearly shown, since the assumed connection between the marijuana gleanings in Cooper's car and his actual use of drugs in the workplace is tenuous at best. It was inappropriate for the court itself to draw that inference, since such factfinding is the task of the arbitrator chosen by the parties, not the reviewing court. Furthermore, the award ordered Cooper's reinstatement in his old job or an equivalent one for which he was qualified, and it is not clear that he would pose a threat to the asserted public policy in every such alternative job. Pp. 42–45.

768 F. 2d 739, reversed.

WHITE, J., delivered the opinion for a unanimous Court. BLACKMUN, J., filed a concurring opinion, in which BRENNAN, J., joined, *post,* p. 46.

David Silberman argued the cause for petitioners. With him on the briefs were *Lynn Agee, Michael Gottesman,* and *Laurence Gold.*

A. Richard Gear argued the cause and filed a brief for respondent.*

JUSTICE WHITE delivered the opinion of the Court.

The issue for decision involves several aspects of when a federal court may refuse to enforce an arbitration award rendered under a collective-bargaining agreement.

I

Misco, Inc. (Misco, or the Company), operates a paper converting plant in Monroe, Louisiana. The Company is a party to a collective-bargaining agreement with the United Paperworkers International Union, AFL–CIO, and its union local (the Union); the agreement covers the production and main-

---

*David E. Feller and *William P. Murphy* filed a brief for the National Academy of Arbitrators as *amicus curiae* urging reversal.

Philip A. Lacovara and *William R. Stein* filed a brief for Northwest Airlines, Inc., et al. as *amici curiae* urging affirmance.

tion 3-4. However, newer volumes are expected to guide you to LEXIS Law Publishing Co. materials, and the name of the reference guide is expected to change.

The *Lawyers' Edition* also includes headnotes, or the publisher's summaries of points of law presented in each case. See Illustration 3-5. The headnote in this illustration includes the text of the publisher's case abstract of a point of law as well as references to the topic Labor and a section number, 125. These headnotes are arranged by publisher-designated topics and numbers in a series of volumes called *United States Supreme Court Digest, Lawyers' Edition*. Headnotes and digests are explained in detail later in this chapter. You should not quote from these headnotes because they are not authoritative. Another value of the *Lawyers' Edition* is that annotations or articles about some noteworthy cases are included in the reporters, as are some case briefs. The annotations assist you in understanding the points of law raised in a particular case.

Cases published in the *Supreme Court Reporter* also contain headnotes. See Illustration 3-6. Similar to the cases published in the *Lawyers' Edition*, the *Supreme Court Reporter* cases include topics and numbers, which West calls "**key numbers**." In Illustration 3-6, the first headnote includes the topic Arbitration and the key number 73.7(3). Also included in the text is the publisher's case abstract of a point of law. West has devised a system of organizing federal and state cases according to topics coupled with key numbers. See Section B of this chapter for a more detailed explanation of this system. Across the top of the page in Illustration 3-6 is the citation to the *Supreme Court Reporter*. Above the name of the case is the official citation to the *U.S. Reports* and a citation to the *Lawyers' Edition* report of this case. In addition to the official syllabus of the court, West provides a summary of each case called a **syllabus**. This syllabus should not be cited because it is not authoritative.

Note in Illustration 3-6 the small numbers in front of some words. Those numbers indicate the page number in which that text would appear in the official reports.

▼ How Do You Locate a Reported Case?

Cases have citations that are similar to addresses. For example, "581 N.E.2d 885" is a citation. The number "581" indicates the volume that contains the case. "N.E.2d" is the abbreviation for the reporter, the *North Eastern Reporter Second Series*. The last number, "885," is the first page of the case. This citation identifies the case, *Thompson v. Economy Super Marts*. See Illustration 3-7.

At the top of Illustration 3-7, next to the circled "1" is this same *West's North Eastern Reporter* citation. Above the name of the case, you can find the official (that is, state government-printed) citation and a citation to *West's Illinois Decisions Reporter*.

ILLUSTRATION 3-4.   Total Client-Service Library References within *U.S. Supreme Court Reports, Lawyers' Edition*

UNITED PAPERWORKERS v MISCO
484 US 29, 98 L Ed 2d 286, 108 S Ct 364

TOTAL CLIENT-SERVICE LIBRARY® REFERENCES

5 Am Jur 2d, Arbitration and Award §§ 167-189; 48A Am Jur 2d, Labor and Labor Relations §§ 1986-1988

22 Federal Procedure, L Ed, Labor and Labor Relations § 52:2080

12 Federal Procedural Forms, L Ed, Labor and Labor Relations § 46:123

2 Am Jur Pl & Pr Forms (Rev), Arbitration and Award, Form 144

2 Am Jur Legal Forms 2d, Arbitration and Award §§ 23:361, 23:362

4 Am Jur Proof of Facts 2d 709, Bias of Arbitrator

11 Am Jur Trials 327, Arbitration of Labor Dispute—Management Representation

13 RIA Employment Coordinator ¶¶ LR 44,740 to LR 44,746

US L Ed Digest, Arbitration § 2; Labor and Employment § 125

Index to Annotations, Arbitration and Award; Discharge from Employment or Office; Labor and Employment

VERALEX®: Cases and annotations referred to herein can be further researched through the VERALEX electronic retrieval system's two services, **Auto-Cite®** and **SHOWME®.** Use Auto-Cite to check citations for form, parallel references, prior and later history, and annotation references. Use SHOWME to display the full text of cases and annotations.

ANNOTATION REFERENCES

Construction and application of Section 10(a-d) of United States Arbitration Act of 1947 (9 USCS § 10(a-d)), providing grounds for vacating arbitration awards. 20 ALR Fed 295.

What constitutes corruption, fraud, or undue means in obtaining arbitration award justifying avoidance of award under state law. 22 ALR4th 366.

Setting aside arbitration award on ground of interest or bias of arbitrators. 56 ALR3d 697.

Comment Note.—Power of court to resubmit matter to arbitrators for correction or clarification, because of ambiguity or error in, or omission from, arbitration award. 37 ALR3d 200.

Power of arbitrator to correct, or power of court to correct or resubmit, non-labor award because of incompleteness or failure to pass on all matters submitted. 36 ALR3d 939.

*Reprinted with permission from LEXIS Law Publishing.

ILLUSTRATION 3-5.   Headnote from *U.S. Supreme Court Reports, Lawyers' Edition*

U.S. SUPREME COURT REPORTS   98 L Ed 2d

HEADNOTES
Classified to U.S. Supreme Court Digest, Lawyers' Edition

Labor § 125 — arbitration award — judicial review

1a-1f. A Federal Court of Appeals errs in affirming the vacation of an arbitration award which orders the reinstatement of an employee who was dismissed after the employer learned that the employee had been apprehended by police in the back seat of a car in the employer's parking lot with marijuana smoke in the air and a lighted marijuana cigarette in the front-seat ashtray, in violation of a rule of the employer against the bringing of controlled substances on company premises— where (1) under the applicable collective bargaining agreement, any grievance arising from the interpretation or application of the terms of the agreement is to be submitted to final and binding arbitration, and management has the right to establish, amend, and enforce rules regulating employee discharge and discipline and setting forth disciplinary procedures, (2) the arbitrator found that the marijuana cigarette incident was insufficient proof that the employee was using or possessed marijuana on company property, and (3) the arbitrator refused to consider evidence that marijuana gleanings were later found in the employee's car in the company parking lot, such evidence not having come to the employer's knowledge at the time of the employee's dismissal—in that (1) the Court of Appeals exceeds its limited authority to review the award, since, in the absence of fraud by the parties or dishonesty by the arbitrator, the Court of Appeals cannot overturn the arbitrator's findings of fact and refuse to enforce the award because (a) it considers the employee's presence in the car where the lighted marijuana cigarette was found ample proof that the employer's rule against bringing drugs on plant premises was violated, and (b) it concludes that the arbitrator erred in refusing to consider evidence unknown to the employer at the time the employee was fired, where, even assuming that the arbitrator so erred, his error was not in bad faith or so gross as to amount to affirmative misconduct; (2) in holding that the evidence of marijuana in the employee's car requires that the award be set aside because to reinstate a person who brought drugs to company propery is contrary to the public policy against the operation of dangerous machinery by persons under the influence of drugs or alcohol (the employee's job being to operate a hazardous machine), the Court of Appeals makes no attempt to review existing laws and legal precedents in order to demonstrate that they establish a well-defined and dominant policy against the operation of dangerous machinery while under the influence of drugs; and (3) even if the Court of Appeals' formulation of public policy is to be accepted, no violation of that policy is clearly shown, where the assumed connection between the marijuana gleanings found in the employee's car and his actual use of drugs in the workplace is tenuous at best and provides an insufficient basis for holding that his reinstatement would actually violate the public policy identified by the Court of Appeals.

Labor § 125 — arbitration award — judicial review

2a, 2b. The courts play only a

ILLUSTRATION 3-6. Pages from *Supreme Court Reporter,* *United Paperworkers Intl. Union, AFL-CIO, et al., v. Misco, Inc.,* 108 S. Ct. 364-365, 370 (1987)

①

② 364   **108 SUPREME COURT REPORTER**   484 U.S. 29

③   ④
484 U.S. 29, 98 L.Ed.2d 286

⑧ **1. Arbitration** ⟜73.7(3) ⑨

UNITED PAPERWORKERS INTERNA-TIONAL UNION, AFL-CIO, et al., Petitioners

⑤

v.

MISCO, INC.

⑥   No. 86-651.

Argued Oct. 13, 1987.

Decided Dec. 1, 1987.

⑦ After arbitrator determined that employee did not violate employer's rule regarding use or possession of marijuana on company property, and ordered reinstatement of employee, the United States District Court for the Western District of Louisiana, Tom Stagg, Chief Judge, vacated arbitration award. On appeal, the Court of Appeals for the Fifth Circuit, Gee, Circuit Judge, 768 F.2d 739, affirmed, and determined that reinstatement would violate public policy against operation of dangerous machinery by persons under influence of drugs. On writ of certiorari, the Supreme Court, Justice White, held that: (1) Court of Appeals was not free to refuse enforcement of arbitrator's award on basis that it found arbitrator's fact-finding improvident; (2) arbitrator was entitled to refuse to consider evidence unknown to company at time employee was fired; (3) formulation of public policy set up by Court of Appeals did not comply with requirement that such policy must be ascertained by reference to laws and legal precedence and not from general considerations of supposed public interests; and (4) even if Court of Appeals' formulation of public policy was accepted, no violation of that policy was clearly shown.

Reversed.

Justice Blackmun filed concurring opinion in which Justice Brennan joined.

Courts play only limited role when asked to review decision of arbitrator; courts are not authorized to reconsider merits of award even though parties may allege that award rests on errors of fact or on misinterpretation of collective bargaining contract.

2. Labor Relations ⟜416.1

Courts have jurisdiction to enforce collective bargaining contracts, but where contract provides grievance and arbitration procedures, those procedures must first be exhausted and courts must order resort to private settlement mechanism without dealing with merits of dispute.   ⑩

3. Labor Relations ⟜485

To resolve disputes about application of collective bargaining agreement, arbitrator must find facts and court may not reject those findings simply because it disagrees with them.

4. Labor Relations ⟜462, 479

Arbitrator may not ignore plain lan-

1 *Supreme Court Reporter* volume number
2 *Supreme Court Reporter* page number
3 Citation to official reporter
4 Citation to unofficial reporter
5 Case name
6 Docket number
7 Syllabus by reporter editor
8 West topic
9 West key number
10 West headnotes
11 Number of page of official reports

ably construing or applying contract and acting within scope of its authority, fact that court is convinced that he committed serious error does not suffice to overturn decision.

ILLUSTRATION 3-6. *Continued*

7. Labor Relations ☞479

Arbitral decisions pertaining to collective bargaining agreements which are procured by parties through fraud or through arbitrator's dishonesty need not be enforced.

8. Labor Relations ☞479

Arbitrator's decision, which was rendered pursuant to collective bargaining agreement, that evidence was insufficient to prove that discharged employee had possessed or used marijuana on company property in contravention of company's rule could not be reversed on basis that appellate court found fact-finding by arbitrator to be improvident.

9. Labor Relations ☞479

Appellate court could not refuse to enforce arbitrator's award which required company to reinstate employee who had been discharged for allegedly violating company rule pertaining to use of marijuana on company property because arbitrator, in deciding whether there was just cause to discharge, refused to consider evidence unknown to company at time of discharge; arbitrator's approach was consistent with collective bargaining agreement, and with practice followed by other arbitrators, and further, even if arbitrator erred in refusing to consider disputed evidence, error was not in bad faith so as to justify setting aside award. 9 U.S.C.A. § 10(c).

10. Labor Relations ☞479

Court's refusal to enforce arbitrator's award under collective bargaining agreement because it is contrary to public policy is specific application of more general doctrine, rooted in common law, that court may refuse to enforce contracts that violate law or public policy.

11. Labor Relations ☞264

Courts may only refuse to enforce collective bargaining agreement when specific terms contained in agreement violate public policy.

12. Labor Relations ☞479

Formulation of public policy based only on general considerations of supposed public interest is not type of public policy that permits court to set aside arbitration award that was entered in accordance with valid collective bargaining agreement.

13. Master and Servant ☞47

Even if public policy considerations against operation of dangerous machinery while under influence of drugs existed, no violation of that policy was shown in case where traces of marijuana had been found in terminated employee's car; assumed connection between marijuana gleanings and employee's actual use of drugs in workplace provided insufficient basis for holding that his reinstatement would actually violate public policy.

14. Labor Relations ☞483

Appellate court's conclusion that since marijuana had been found in terminated employee's car, employee had ever been or would ever be under influence of marijuana while he was on job and operating dangerous machinery was improper exercise in fact-finding about employee's use of drugs and his amenability to discipline, which exceeded authority of court which was asked to overturn arbitration award; parties did not bargain for facts to be found by court, but rather, fact-finding was to be made by arbitrator chosen by parties who had more opportunity to observe employee and to be familiar with workplace and its problems.

Syllabus *

Respondent employer's collective-bargaining agreement with petitioner union authorizes the submission to binding arbitration of any grievance that arises from the interpretation or application of the agreement's terms, and reserves to management the right to establish, amend,

---

* The syllabus constitutes no part of the opinion of the Court but has been prepared by the Reporter of Decisions for the convenience of the reader. See *United States v. Detroit Lumber Co.,* 200 U.S. 321, 337, 26 S.Ct. 282, 287, 50 L.Ed. 499.

ILLUSTRATION 3-6.   *Continued*

370   108 SUPREME COURT REPORTER   484 U.S. 36

peals but alternatively argues that the judgment below should be affirmed because of erroneous findings by the arbitrator. We deal first with the opposing alternative arguments.

A

[1] Collective-bargaining agreements commonly provide grievance procedures to settle disputes between union and employer with respect to the interpretation and application of the agreement and require binding arbitration for unsettled grievances. In such cases, and this is such a case, the Court made clear almost 30 years ago that the courts play only a limited role when asked to review the decision of an arbitrator. The courts are not authorized to reconsider the merits of an award even though the parties may allege that the award rests on errors of fact or on misinterpretation of the contract. "The refusal of courts to review the merits of an arbitration award is the proper approach to arbitration under collective bargaining agreements. The federal policy of settling labor disputes by arbitration would be undermined if courts had the final say on the merits of the awards." *Steelworkers v. Enterprise Wheel & Car Corp.*, 363 U.S. 593, 596, 80 S.Ct. 1358, 1360, 4 L.Ed.2d 1424 (1960). As long as the arbitrator's award "draws its essence from the collective bargaining agreement," and is not merely "his own brand of industrial justice," the award is legitimate. *Id.*, at 597, 80 S.Ct., at 1361.

"The function of the court is very limited when the parties have agreed to submit all questions of contract interpretation₃₇ to the arbitrator. It is confined to ascertaining whether the party seeking (11) tration is making a claim which on its face is governed by the contract. Whether the moving party is right or wrong is a question of contract interpretation for the arbitrator. In these circumstances the moving party should not be deprived of the arbitrator's judgment,

when it was his judgment and all that it connotes that was bargained for.

"The courts, therefore, have no business weighing the merits of the grievance, considering whether there is equity in a particular claim, or determining whether there is particular language in the written instrument which will support the claim." *Steelworkers v. American Mfg. Co.*, 363 U.S. 564, 567–568, 80 S.Ct. 1343, 1346, 4 L.Ed.2d 1403 (1960) (emphasis added; footnote omitted).

See also *AT & T Technologies, Inc. v. Communications Workers*, 475 U.S. 643, 649–650, 106 S.Ct. 1415, 1418–1419, 89 L.Ed.2d 648 (1986).

[2–7] The reasons for insulating arbitral decisions from judicial review are grounded in the federal statutes regulating labor-management relations. These statutes reflect a decided preference for private settlement of labor disputes without the intervention of government: The Labor Management Relations Act of 1947, 61 Stat. 154, 29 U.S.C. § 173(d), provides that "[f]inal adjustment by a method agreed upon by the parties is hereby declared to be the desirable method for settlement of grievance disputes arising over the application or interpretation of an existing collective-bargaining agreement." See also *AT & T Technologies, supra*, at 650, 106 S.Ct., at 1419. The courts have jurisdiction to enforce collective-bargaining contracts; but where the contract provides grievance and arbitration procedures, those procedures must first be exhausted and courts must order resort to the private settlement mechanisms without dealing with the merits of the dispute. Because the parties have contracted to have disputes settled by an arbitrator chosen by the (11) ther than by a judge, it is the arbitrator's view of the facts and of the meaning₃₈ of the contract that they have agreed to accept. Courts thus do not sit to hear claims of factual or legal error by an arbitrator as an appellate court does in reviewing decisions of lower courts. To resolve disputes about the application of a collective-bargaining agree-

---

*Reprinted with permission from West Group.

ILLUSTRATION 3-7. *West's North Eastern Reporter, Thompson v. Economy Super Marts, Inc.,* 581 N.E.2d 885 (Ill. Ct. App. 1991)

THOMPSON v. ECONOMY SUPER MARTS, INC. ① Ill. **885**
Cite as 581 N.E.2d 885 (Ill.App. 3 Dist. 1991)

provided for both of them on the instrument. Therefore, the defendant argues, since the intention of the Bank was to obtain a mortgage of the premises from both joint tenants and only one joint tenant signed the mortgage, the instrument should be found to be unenforceable as was the contract in *Dineff.*

Dineff is clearly distinguishable from the instant case. In *Dineff,* the plaintiff was attempting to enforce an agreement to convey the entire interest in the jointly held property without the signatures of both cotenants. The court pointed out that there was no prayer for partial performance against the cotenant who had signed the agreement. (*Dineff,* 27 Ill.2d at 482, 190 N.E.2d at 311.) It is well established that one cotenant cannot convey the interest of another cotenant without proper authority.

Here, however, the plaintiff is not attempting to foreclose on the entire interest in the property. The foreclosure complaint is against only the undivided one-half interest of the joint tenant who signed the mortgage.

[4] We disagree with the defendant's argument that the clear intention of the parties required the defendant's signature

1 Citation to *West's North Eastern Reporter*
2 Citation to official reporter
3 Citation to unofficial reporter
4 Case name
5 Docket number
6 Syllabus by reporter editor
7 West key numbers and headnotes
8 *Ward* case cited in Illustration 4-2

that the names of both husband and wife appear in the body of the instrument and in the acknowledgment. The rule seems to be general that a deed naming two or more parties as grantors, executed by only a portion of them, is valid as to

those executing it." *Heckmann,* 283 Ill. at 513, 119 N.E. at 642.

It is clear that Mr. Stauffenberg intended to mortgage the real estate. There is nothing in the mortgage to indicate that it was not to be binding unless the defendant signed it also. We see no reason to deviate from the established rule that when a property owner attempts to convey a greater interest in the property than he actually has, that the conveyance is valid to the extent of his interest and void only as to the excess.

For the reasons stated above, the order of the trial court dismissing the complaint is reversed. This cause is remanded for further proceedings.

Reversed and remanded.

GORMAN and McCUSKEY, JJ., concur.

221 Ill.App.3d 263 ②
163 Ill.Dec. 731 ③

Cherryl E. THOMPSON,
Plaintiff–Appellant,

v.

ECONOMY SUPER MARTS, INC., a Division of Weems & Bruns Corp., a Corporation, and Weems & Bruns Corp., a Corporation, Defendants–Appellees. ④

No. 3–90–0662. ⑤

Appellate Court of Illinois,
Third District.

Nov. 8, 1991.

Customer allegedly injured when she slipped on lettuce leaf in produce section of grocery store brought negligence action against store owners. The Circuit Court, 12th Judicial Circuit, Will County, Michael H. Lyons, J., granted defendants' posttrial motion for judgment notwithstanding verdict after jury found customer to be 55% contributorily negligent and awarded her ⑥

ILLUSTRATION 3-7. *Continued*

886 Ill.   581 **NORTH EASTERN REPORTER, 2d SERIES**

damages. the Appellate Court, Haase, J., held that: (1) where foreign substance causing slip of business invitee is on premises due to negligence of proprietor or his servants, it is not necessary to establish their actual or constructive knowledge of the substance, but if substance is on premises through acts of third persons, time element during which substance was present is material factor to establish ⑥ knowledge of, or notice to, proprietor; (2) even where there is proof that foreign substance causing slip of business invitee was related to defendant's business, where no further evidence is offered other than presence of substance and occurrence of injury, defendant is entitled to directed verdict, as such evidence is insufficient to support necessary inference of negligence; and (3) evidence of negligence of grocery store was not sufficient to permit customer to recover from store owners.

Affirmed.

⑦ **1. Negligence** ⟨⇒⟩32(2.8)

Defendant owes business invitee on defendant's premises duty to exercise ordinary care in maintaining premises in reasonably safe condition.

2. Negligence ⟨⇒⟩44, 48

Where business invitee is injured by slipping on premises, liability may be imposed if substance causing slip was placed by negligence of proprietor or his servants; or if substance was on premises through acts of third persons or there is no showing how it got there, liability may be imposed if it appears that proprietor or his servant knew of presence of substance, or that substance was there sufficient length of time so that in exercise of ordinary care its presence should have been discovered.

3. Negligence ⟨⇒⟩48

Where foreign substance causing slip of business invitee is on premises due to negligence of proprietor or his servants, it is not necessary to establish their actual or constructive knowledge of the substance, but if substance is on premises through acts of third persons, time element during which substance was present is material

factor to establish knowledge of, or notice to, proprietor.

4. Negligence ⟨⇒⟩136(22)

Where there is proof that foreign substance causing slip of business invitee was product sold or related to defendant's operations and invitee offered some further evidence, direct or circumstantial, however slight, such as location of substance or business practices of defendant from which it could be inferred that it was more likely that defendant or his servants, rather than a customer, dropped the substance on the premises, trial court should allow negligence issue to go to jury.

5. Negligence ⟨⇒⟩121.1(8)

Even where there is proof that foreign substance causing slip of business invitee was related to defendant's business, where no further evidence is offered other than presence of substance and occurrence of injury, defendant is entitled to directed verdict, such evidence being insufficient to support necessary inference of negligence.

6. Negligence ⟨⇒⟩134(5)

Evidence of negligence of grocery store was not sufficient to permit customer allegedly injured when she slipped on lettuce leaf in produce section of store to recover from store, even though leaf was described as wilted and was found near unsupervised produce section where vegetables were packed on ice; no direct or circumstantial evidence made it more likely that store's servants, rather than customer, dropped the leaf, and customer presented no evidence that ice which packed produce was directly above water spot or any evidence regarding how ice was packed or how easy it might have been to jar ice loose and spill it to the floor.

James J. Morici, Jr., argued, Anesi, Ozmon & Rodin, Ltd., Chicago, for Cherryl E. Thompson.

Kenneth T. Garvey, Robert Spitkovsky, Jr. and Kevin P. O'Connell, argued, Bresnahan & Garvey, Chicago, for Economy Super Marts, Inc.

ILLUSTRATION 3-7. *Continued*

THOMPSON v. ECONOMY SUPER MARTS, INC.   Ill. **887**
Cite as 581 N.E.2d 885 (Ill.App. 3 Dist. 1991)

Justice HAASE delivered the opinion of the Court.

The plaintiff, Cherryl E. Thompson, brought this negligence action against the defendants, Economy Super Marts, Inc. and Weems & Bruns Corp., to recover damages for personal injuries she sustained when she slipped on a lettuce leaf in the produce section of the defendants' grocery store. A jury awarded the plaintiff $12,974.96 in recoverable damages after finding that she was 55% contributorily negligent. Thereafter, the trial court granted the defendants' post-trial motion for a judgment notwithstanding the verdict. The plaintiff appeals from that decision.

The plaintiff testified at trial that on July 3, 1986, she picked up a watermelon in the produce section of the defendants' store and began to walk through the produce aisle. At that point, she slipped and fell on a lettuce leaf and water. She had not seen the leaf or the water before her fall and did not know how long they were there. She noted that the lettuce leaf was green and brown, had dirt on it, and appeared beat up. According to the plaintiff, her fall occurred about two or three feet to the left of the produce aisle. She also stated that the fruits and vegetables in the produce aisle were kept on ice.

Terida Thompson, the plaintiff's daughter, substantially corroborated the plaintiff's testimony. Additionally, she stated that the lettuce leaf looked old and like it had been there awhile. She further stated that she had walked through the produce aisle once before the accident occurred and did not see any water or a lettuce leaf on the floor prior to the plaintiff's fall.

Gene Pesavento, the assistant store manager, testified that it was his duty to make sure that all areas in the grocery store were clear and free of debris. He agreed that the produce department requires constant surveillance to ensure that debris is not left on the floor. He also agreed that debris poses a tripping hazard.

Pesavento further testified that no one was specifically charged with the responsibility of constantly monitoring the floor of the produce department. He explained

that the defendants' employees knew that they were supposed to keep an eye on the entire store, and not specifically one area.

Phil Woock, the store's general manager, testified that he was not working at the time of the plaintiff's accident. He stated that the store's floor was dry mopped and swept every night in July, 1986. In addition, the floors were swept during the day as needed, and spills were cleaned as needed. The floors were professionally mopped and waxed every Wednesday night, and the plaintiff's accident occurred on a Thursday. Woock further testified that a part-time employee was on duty in the produce department at the time of the accident, but he could have been working in the back room when it occurred. Woock also testified that all store workers have the responsibility of keeping the floor clean if no one is working in the produce department at a particular time.

Donald Schreiner and Rubin Amazan each testified that they were working at the store at the time of the plaintiff's accident, but did not witness the fall. They both stated that they did not observe a lettuce leaf on the floor after inspecting the floor following the accident.

Based on the foregoing evidence, the jury found that the plaintiff suffered $28,833.24 in damages, but it awarded her only $12,974.96 because it found that she was 55% contributorily negligent. Thereafter, the defendants filed a post-trial motion requesting that the trial court enter a judgment notwithstanding the verdict. The trial court subsequently granted the defendants' motion, finding that: (1) no evidence was presented that the defendants had actual or constructive notice of the lettuce leaf and water for a sufficient length of time that its presence should have been discovered; and (2) the jury's award of damages was a compromise verdict and could not be sustained.

On appeal, the plaintiff initially argues that the trial court erred in granting a judgment notwithstanding the verdict. She contends that the court mistakenly found that she did not present any evidence that

ILLUSTRATION 3-7.   *Continued*

the defendants had actual or constructive notice of the lettuce leaf.

⑧ [1–3] It is well-settled that a defendant owes a business invitee on the defendant's premises a duty to exercise ordinary care in maintaining the premises in a reasonably safe condition. (*Ward v. K Mart Corp.* (1990), 136 Ill.2d 132, 143 Ill.Dec. 288, 554 N.E.2d 223; *Perminas v. Montgomery Ward & Co.* (1975), 60 Ill.2d 469, 328 N.E.2d 290.) Where a business invitee is injured by slipping on the premises, liability may be imposed if the substance was placed there by the negligence of the proprietor or his servants, or, if the substance was on the premises through acts of third persons or there is no showing how it got there, liability may be imposed if it appears that the proprietor or his servant knew of its presence, or that the substance was there a sufficient length of time so that in the exercise of ordinary care its presence should have been discovered. (*Olinger v. Great Atlantic & Pacific Tea Co.* (1961), 21 Ill.2d 469, 173 N.E.2d 443; *Wroblewski v. Hillman's, Inc.* (1963), 43 Ill.App.2d 246, 193 N.E.2d 470.) Thus, where the foreign substance is on the premises due to the negligence of the proprietor or his servants, it is not necessary to establish their knowledge, actual or constructive; whereas, if the substance is on the premises through acts of third persons, the time element to establish knowledge or notice to the proprietor is a material factor. *Blake v. Dickinson* (1975), 31 Ill.App.3d 379, 332 N.E.2d 575.

[4, 5] Where there is proof that the foreign substance was a product sold or related to the defendant's operations, and the plaintiff offers some further evidence direct or circumstantial, however slight, such as the location of the substance or the business practices of the defendant, from which it could be inferred that it was more likely that the defendant or his servants, rather than a customer, dropped the substance on the premises, the trial court should allow the negligence issue to go to the jury. (*Donoho v. O'Connell's, Inc.* (1958), 13 Ill.2d 113, 148 N.E.2d 434.) However, even where there is proof that the foreign substance was related to the defendant's business, but no further evidence is offered other than the presence of the substance and the occurrence of the injury, the defendant is entitled to a directed verdict, such evidence being insufficient to support the necessary inference. *Olinger v. Great Atlantic & Pacific Tea Co.* (1961), 21 Ill.2d 469, 173 N.E.2d 443; *Wroblewski v. Hillman's, Inc.* (1963), 43 Ill. App.2d 246, 193 N.E.2d 470.

[6] The plaintiff argues that she satisfied the requirements set forth in *Donoho* of introducing "further evidence, however slight, such as the location of the substance or the business practice of the defendant, from which it could be inferred that it was more likely that the defendant or his servants, rather than a customer, dropped the substance on the premises." She contends that evidence of the wilted lettuce leaf and the fact that it was found near the unsupervised produce section where vegetables were packed on ice was sufficient to allow the case to go to the jury under *Donoho*.

We disagree. The Illinois Supreme Court in *Donoho* undertook an extensive analysis of the circumstances under which negligence could be inferred from the conduct of the defendant when it was uncertain who was responsible for the foreign substance dropped on the premises. In *Donoho*, the plaintiff slipped and fell on an onion ring at the defendant's restaurant. It was unknown who dropped the onion ring. Yet, the court found that from the circumstantial evidence, it could be reasonably inferred that it was more likely that the onion ring was on the floor through the acts of the defendant's servants rather than a customer. The court based its decision on the additional circumstantial evidence that the onion ring on which the plaintiff slipped was located by a table cleared by a bus boy, under the bus boy's practice of clearing tables food particles could drop to the floor, and testimony that after the bus boy cleared the table in question no one else ate there before the plaintiff fell.

In the present case, however, there was no direct or circumstantial evidence indicating that it was more likely that the defendants' servants dropped the item than a customer. Furthermore, the plaintiff did not present any evidence that the ice, which

ILLUSTRATION 3-7.   *Continued*

PEOPLE v. SOLANO

Cite as 581 N.E.2d 889 (Ill.App. 3 Dist. 1991)

Ill.   **889**

packed the produce, was directly above the water spot. Nor did she present any evidence regarding how the ice was packed or how easy it might have been to jar it loose spilling it to the floor. Moreover, there was no specific evidence that the plaintiff's business practice was unusual or created any special hazard.

The plaintiff also relies on *Perminas v. Montgomery Ward & Company* (1975), 60 Ill.2d 469, 328 N.E.2d 290, in support of her position. In *Perminas*, the plaintiff slipped on a skateboard-like object in an aisle of the defendant's store. There, one of the defendant's employees actually had knowledge that the object was creating a dangerous condition. The court imposed liability on the defendant because the defendant, after receiving notice through its employee that its product was creating a dangerous situation, failed to return its premises to a safe condition or warn its customers.

We find that the plaintiff's reliance on *Perminas* is misplaced. In the present case, unlike *Perminas*, the defendants did not have actual or constructive knowledge of the situation. Furthermore, the record in the instant case does not contain any evidence regarding the length of time the substance was on the floor from which it could be inferred that the defendants had constructive notice.

After reviewing the evidence in the aspect most favorable to the plaintiff, we conclude that the evidence so overwhelmingly favored the defendants that no contrary verdict could ever stand. Accordingly, we find that the trial court properly granted the defendants' motion for a judgment notwithstanding the verdict. Our resolution of the foregoing issue renders the parties' remaining issues moot.

The judgment of the circuit court of Will County is affirmed.

Affirmed.

McCUSKEY, J., and STOUDER, P.J., concur.

221 Ill.App.3d 272

163 Ill.Dec. 735

The PEOPLE of the State of Illinois, Plaintiff-Appellee,

v.

Juan SOLANO, Defendant-Appellant.

No. 3-91-0067.

Appellate Court of Illinois, Third District.

Nov. 8, 1991.

Sixteen-year-old defendant was convicted of reckless homicide and driving under the influence of alcohol by the 13th Judicial Circuit Court, LaSalle County, James Lanuti, J., and he appealed. The Appellate Court, McCuskey, J., held that: (1) degree of harm to passenger in defendant's car was aggravating factor that trial judge could consider in imposing sentence, and (2) trial judge could likewise consider defendant's prior underage drinking and level of alcohol in defendant's blood.

Affirmed.

1. **Criminal Law** ⟨⟩1147, 1208.2

Sentencing is matter of judicial discretion and, absent abuse of discretion by trial court, sentence may not be altered on review.

2. **Criminal Law** ⟨⟩986.2(1)

Defendant's history, character and rehabilitative potential, along with the seriousness of defendant's offense, need to protect society, and need for deterrence and punishment, must be equally weighed at sentencing.

3. **Criminal Law** ⟨⟩986(3), 1144.17

Sentencing judge is presumed to have considered mitigating circumstances before court, and there is no requirement that judge recite and assign value to each circumstance presented.

4. **Automobiles** ⟨⟩359

Trial judge sufficiently considered motorist's rehabilitative potential, young age,

---

*Reprinted with permission from West Group.

▼ How Are U.S. Supreme Court Cases Cited?

Cite U.S. Supreme Court cases according to Bluebook Rule 10; see especially Bluebook Rule 10.4 and Table T.1. Once a U.S. Supreme Court case is published in an advance sheet of the *U.S. Reports,* the *U.S. Reports* citation, and only the *U.S. Reports* citation, is the proper citation. Do not include parallel citations with the official *U.S. Reports* cite.

correct: Erie R.R. v. Tompkins, 304 U.S. 64 (1938)

incorrect: Erie R.R. v. Tompkins, 304 U.S. 64, 58 S. Ct. 817, 82 L. Ed. 1188 (1938)

However, if a Supreme Court opinion has been published in the *West's Supreme Court Reporter* but not yet in the *U.S. Reports,* the *Supreme Court Reporter* citation should be used. See Bluebook Table T.1.

If a Supreme Court opinion has not yet been published in *U.S. Reports,* the *Supreme Court Reporter,* or *Lawyers' Edition,* then you should cite to *United States Law Week.* See Bluebook Table T.1.

U.S.L.W. cite: UAW v. Johnson Controls, 59 U.S.L.W. 4209 (U.S. Mar. 20, 1991)

Place the court designation for U.S. Supreme Court, "U.S.," in parentheses with the full date following. See Bluebook Rules 10.4 and 10.5.

b. Other Federal Case Reports

▼ Where Do You Find Decisions of Other Federal Courts?

Many published opinions of the U.S Courts of Appeals can be found in *West's* **Federal Reporter,** now in its third series. In addition to printing the decisions of the U.S. Courts of Appeals, the current series contains some decisions of the U.S. Claims Court, Court of Customs and Patent Appeals, and the Temporary Emergency Court of Appeals. In the past, the *Federal Reporter* also contained decisions of the U.S. Circuit Courts, the Commerce Court of the United States, the U.S. District Courts (until 1932), the U.S. Court of Claims, the former U.S. Circuit Courts of Appeals, the U.S. Court of Customs and Patent Appeals, and the U.S. Emergency Court of Appeals. See Illustration 3-8 for specific years of coverage.

West's **Federal Supplement,** a publication started in 1932 to connect with the *Federal Reporter Second* and *Third* series, includes decisions of the U.S. District Courts, the U.S. Court of Claims from 1932 to 1960, the U.S. Court of International Trade (formerly known as the U.S. Customs Court), and the Judicial Panel on Multidistrict Litigation. See Illustration 3-8. This publication is now in its second series.

ILLUSTRATION 3-8. *West's Federal Reporter* and *Federal Supplement Coverage*

West's Federal Reporter **Coverage (F. and F.2d)**

U.S. Circuit Courts	1880 to 1912
Commerce Court of the United States	1911 to 1913
U.S. District Courts	1880 to 1932
U.S. Court of Claims (1960 to 1982)	1929 to 1932
U.S. Court of Appeals (formerly United States Circuit Court of Appeals)	1891 to date
U.S. Court of Customs and Patent Appeals	1929 to 1982
U.S. Emergency Court of Appeals	1943 to 1961
Temporary Emergency Court of Appeals	1972 to date

West's Federal Supplement **Coverage (F. Supp.)**

U.S. District Courts	1932 to date
U.S. Court of Claims	1932 to 1960
U.S. Court of International Trade (formerly U.S. Customs Court)	1956 to date
Judicial Panel on Multidistrict Litigation	1968 to date

PRACTICE POINTER

Some courts have special rules concerning the use of unpublished decisions. Check all applicable rules, whenever you plan to use an unpublished case as an authority for a point of law.

Not all federal appellate court or district court decisions are published. In some instances, the judges of these courts determine whether to submit their decisions to the publishers. In other cases, the publishers selectively print decisions. Unpublished opinions are always available from the courts.

▼ Are *Federal Reporter* and *Federal Supplement* Decisions Available on CD-ROM?

Yes. West has released CD-ROM libraries for the *Federal Reporter* and the *Federal Supplement*. Check your library.

▼ Are Federal Trial Court and Appellate Court Decisions Available on the Internet?

Yes. You may access these decisions through the Internet. However, some are not proofread, and many do not contain the research aids available from the commercial publishers. In addition, searching for a case by topic is difficult. For more information about accessing cases from the Internet, see Chapter 10.

▼ How Are *Federal Reporter* and *Federal Supplement* Decisions Cited?

Cite *Federal Reporter* and *Federal Supplement* decisions according to Bluebook Rules 10.1 to 10.6 and Table T.1 Note that for the *Federal Reporter,* the abbreviation is "F." If the *Federal Reporter* cited belongs to the second or third series, "2d" or "3d" should be placed next to the "F." For the *Federal Supplement,* the reporter is abbreviated "F. Supp." In parentheses you should place an abbreviation that denotes the appropriate court and then the date of the decision. Be certain to include a geographic designation for the district courts.

Federal Reporter **case:** Zimmerman v. North Am. Signal Co., 704 F.2d 347 (7th Cir. 1983)

Federal Supplement **case:** Musser v. Mountain View Broad., 578 F. Supp. 229 (E.D. Tenn. 1984)

▼ Are Decisions Published in Any Other Reporters?

Several publishers of looseleaf services and specialized reporters also publish some federal decisions. Sometimes they duplicate opinions found in the West series. West also publishes some specialized reporters, such as the ***Federal Rules Decisions*** (F.R.D.). This reporter contains decisions in which a federal rule of civil or criminal procedure is at issue. *Federal Rules Decisions* includes not only cases but speeches, articles, and reports of judicial conferences. During court sessions, advance sheets are available weekly.

West Group's Lawyers Cooperative Publishing Co. publishes some noteworthy federal and state decisions in its *American Law Reports* (A.L.R.) series. For information about this series, see Chapter 5. Some decisions are found only in looseleaf services or specialized reporters. For a discussion of looseleaf services, see Chapter 8. For a listing of some specialized reporters, see Illustration 3-9.

4. Computerized Reporting

▼ Can You Find Decisions on the Computer?

Yes. Many published and unpublished federal and state decisions are online on WESTLAW and LEXIS. See Illustration 3-10. These cases are organized into databases or files and can be accessed

ILLUSTRATION 3-9.   West's Specialized Reporters

West's Bankruptcy Reporter (B.R.)

Contains reprints of bankruptcy decisions from U.S. Bankruptcy Courts, U.S. Supreme Court, U.S. Courts of Appeals, U.S. District Courts. Publishes bankruptcy decisions not published in F. Supp.

West's Federal Rules Decisions (F.R.D.)

Contains U.S. District Court cases construing Federal Rules of Civil Procedure not published in F. Supp. (1939–present) and cases construing Federal Criminal Rules of Procedure not published in F. Supp. (1946–present)

West's Military Justice Reporter (M.J.)

Contains cases decided by U.S. Court of Military Appeals (1975–present) and Courts of Military Review (1975–present)

West's Veterans Appeals Reporter (Vet. App.)

Contains cases decided by U.S. Court of Veterans Appeals (1991–present)

West's United States Claims Court Reporter (Cl. Ct.)

Contains cases decided by U.S. Claims Court (October 1, 1982–present), U.S. Courts of Appeals (1982–present), and U.S. Supreme Court (reprints of claims decisions; 1982–present)

through keyword and other searches. Unlike cases that may be found on the Internet, these cases contain publishers' research aids.

▼ How Do You Know Whether a Case Is Published or Only Available Online?

WESTLAW and LEXIS provide the print citations for all cases that are published in hardcopy. In Illustration 3-10, note that at the top, the publisher indicates that the case is not reported in the *Federal Supplement*. Instead, WESTLAW provides its own citation for this case. Because of the high costs of computer research, it is often best to review the cases in print if they are available. However, use the computer whenever cases are not available in your library or the opinion you are seeking is an unpublished opinion. Note that some courts have special rules for the use of unpublished cases.

ILLUSTRATION 3-10. Case Available on WESTLAW

FOR EDUCATIONAL USE ONLY
Not Reported in F.Supp.
(Cite as: **1985 WL 2917 (N.D.Ill.)**)

CLARK EQUIPMENT COMPANY, Plaintiff-
Counterdefendant,

v.

LIFT PARTS MFG. CO., INC., Defendant-
Counterclaimant.

No. 82 C 4585.

United States District Court, N.D. Illinois, Eastern
Division.

October 1, 1985.

MEMORANDUM OPINION AND ORDER

JAMES F. HOLDERMAN, District Judge:

*1 Like the Sorcerer's apprentice, counsel here appear to have conjured up a litigation monster that threatens to devour counsel, the parties and the Court. During the past year alone, more than 70 depositions were taken consuming 120 days of testimony. Hundreds of document requests and interrogatories have been propounded. Non-expert discovery mercifully came to an end in this matter on April 15, 1985.

Now the Court is confronted with five fully briefed motions, which have required the review of over 500 pages of briefs and thousands of pages of exhibits.

BACKGROUND
Plaintiff-counterdefendant Clark Equipment Company ('Clark') is a manufacturer and distributor of lift trucks and replacement parts for Clark lift trucks. Defendant-counterplaintiff Lift Parts Manufacturing Co., Inc. ('LPM'), is a competitor of Clark in the sale and distribution of replacement parts for lift trucks.

Clark has made various claims against LPM involving LPM's allegedly unlawful conduct respecting Clark's 'Master Parts System', including its 'Master Parts Book' ('MPB') and 'Master Assembly Lists.'

Basically, Clark alleges as follows:

With a large volum of trucks and parts to manufacture, order, stock and sell, Clark developed a parts identification system that would be comprehensive, compact, changeable and efficient. Clark had previously used a system of publishing a

separate book for each lift truck. That method proved unsatisfactory because the books took up significant dealer shelf space, generated dealer complaints, and could not easily be updated. In 1962 Clark instituted the 'Master Parts System', whereby each type of part or assembly was assigned a 'key number' which would remain the same for all lift trucks. All trucks, key numbers and part numbers were then consolidated in to a single reference source, called the 'Master Parts Book' (the 'MPB'). The MPS first appeared in 1962 in hard copy form and later, in 1973, in microfilm form.

Included in the Master Parts System are diagamatic illustrations, which comprise, together with the assembly parts list, the 'Master Assembly Lists' (the 'MAL'). The 'MAL' contains pictorial illustrations for virtually every Clark parts assembly and sub-assembly, such as carburetors, transmissions, axles and so on. Each assembly or sub-assembly is a composite of numerous separate component parts. Clark graphically 'broke down' each assembly and sub-assembly, photographed the individual constituents of these assemblies and sub-assemblies, and employed technical artists to illustrate each drawing. Clark then added noun names, key numbers, part numbers, and additional information to the pictorial illustrations. The illustrations were then correlated into the entire Master Parts Sysetm.

From these graphic illustrations, a Clark dealer, Clark parts man, or Clark service man could open a complex assembly or sub-assembly, identify the particular part in need of replacement, physically substitute the new part for the old, and then reassemble the entire composite.

*2 The MAL appeared in hard copy from 1964 until 1973. Thereafter, it appeared in microfilm cartridge form. It is alleged that each page of the Master Parts System, including each MAL illustration page, has always contained the Clark trademark and logo.

Clark's Dealer Marketing Plans contain, among other things, Clark parts sales figures and lift truck population within each of the independent Clark dealer's area of principal responsibility. Clark compiles and anaylzes these marketing materials and maintains them in the strictest confidence.

Clark claims that LPM has acquired Clark's MAL assembly illustrations, removed Clark's trademarks,

---

*Reprinted with permission from West Group.

▼ How Are Decisions Reported Only on WESTLAW or LEXIS Cited?

Bluebook Rule 10.8.1(a) explains how you should cite an unpublished decision found only on either WESTLAW or LEXIS. (If a decision is published in a hardcopy reporter, you should not use the WESTLAW or LEXIS citation.)

After the case name is the docket number. In the example that follows, that number is "No. 82-C-4585." Next is the year of the decision, followed by "WL" for WESTLAW. The WESTLAW number assigned to the case follows that. If a spot cite is provided, precede the screen or page number with an asterisk. Finally, in the parentheses, place the court and the full date.

WESTLAW cite: Clark Equip. Co. v. Lift Parts Mfg. Co., No. 82-C-4585, 1985 WL 2917, at *1 (N.D. Ill. Oct. 1, 1985)

For LEXIS citations, state the name of the case, the docket number, the year of the decision, the name of the LEXIS file that contains the case, the name "LEXIS" to indicate that the case is found on LEXIS, and the document number. Last, place the court and the full date in parentheses.

LEXIS cite: Barrett Indus. Trucks v. Old Republic Ins. Co., No. 87-C-9429, 1990 U.S. Dist. LEXIS 142, at *1 (N.D. Ill. Jan. 9, 1990)

5. State Reporters

▼ Where Can You Find State Court Decisions?

Many states continue to publish state decisions in their own reporters. In those states, the state publication is the official reporter. Some states authorize private publishers to publish the official reports.

▼ Are There Any Unofficial Reports of State Cases?

Yes. In addition to its publication of some states' official reporters, West Group publishes seven **regional reporters** that contain state cases. See Illustrations 3-11 and 3-12. The regional reporters are not based on actual geographic regions. For example, Illinois is in the American Midwest region, but the regional reporter that contains Illinois decisions is the *North Eastern Reporter.*

The regional reporters contain decisions from several different states. Some states, such as Minnesota, have designated the West regional reporter as the official reporter of their state decisions.

PRACTICE POINTER

In theory, the text of a case published in the state reporter should be identical to that in the regional reporter. If the two differ, then the language of the official version governs.

ILLUSTRATION 3-11.   West's Regional Reporters Coverage

Regional Reporter	States Covered
West's Atlantic Reporter (A. or A.2d)	Connecticut, Delaware, Maine, Maryland, New Hampshire, New Jersey, Pennsylvania, Rhode Island, Vermont, and the District of Columbia
West's North Eastern Reporter (N.E. or N.E.2d)	Illinois, Indiana, Massachusetts, New York, and Ohio
West's North Western Reporter (N.W. or N.W.2d)	Iowa, Michigan, Minnesota, Nebraska, North Dakota, South Dakota, and Wisconsin
West's Pacific Reporter (P. or P.2d)	Alaska, Arizona, California, Colorado, Hawaii, Idaho, Kansas, Montana, Nevada, New Mexico, Oklahoma, Oregon, Utah, Washington, and Wyoming
West's South Eastern Reporter (S.E. or S.E.2d)	Georgia, North Carolina, South Carolina, Virginia, and West Virginia
West's South Western Reporter (S.W. or S.W.2d)	Arkansas, Kentucky, Missouri, Tennessee, Texas, and Indian Territories
West's Southern Reporter (So. or So. 2d)	Alabama, Florida, Louisiana, and Mississippi

▼ Why Would You Use the Regional Reporter Rather Than the Official State Reporter?

The regional reporter contains the publisher's headnotes designed to assist you. These notes guide you to the publisher's topical index of cases called a digest. You also might use the regional reporter because it is published sooner than the official reporter.

▼ How Are State Cases Cited?

Cite a state case according to Bluebook Rule 10. Note especially Bluebook Rule 10.3.1 and Table T.1 (excerpted in Illustration 3-13), which instruct on which state reporter to cite and when.

If you are citing a state case in a document submitted to a court in the same state, you should provide both the official citation, if

ILLUSTRATION 3-12. West National Reporter System

Section 1/In the Beginning: Case Law Research

National Reporter System® Map
Showing the States included in each Reporter group

Pacific | North Western | South Western | North Eastern | Southern | South Eastern | Atlantic

35

*Reprinted with permission from West Group.

one exists, and the regional citation. The official citation should be listed first.

When you cite a state case in a memorandum addressed to a federal court or to a court of a different state, you should include only the regional citation. If you are only using the regional citation, you must remember to place the abbreviation for the deciding court in parentheses. See Bluebook Rule 10.4. You can remember this if you consider the reasoning behind it. Most libraries outside of the state have no need to purchase materials that are merely persuasive because of the cost involved and the space necessary to store the reports. Therefore, they are likely only to have the regional reporter—a more economic version of out-of-state cases.

The following are examples of how an Illinois Appellate Court case would be cited in a brief prepared for the Illinois Supreme

ILLUSTRATION 3-13. Table T.1, *A Uniform System of Citation, Sixteenth Edition*

Illinois

Supreme Court (Ill.): In documents submitted to Illinois state courts, cite to Ill. or Ill. 2d, to N.E. or N.E.2d if therein, and to Ill. Dec. if therein. In all other documents, cite only to N.E. or N.E.2d, if therein; otherwise, cite to one of the Illinois Reports listed below.

Illinois Reports		
11 Ill. to date	1849–date	Ill., Ill. 2d
Gilman	1844–1849	e.g., 6 Ill. (1 Gilm.)
Scammon	1832–1843	e.g., 2 Ill. (1 Scam.)
Breese	1819–1831	1 Ill. (Breese)
North Eastern Reporter	1886–date	N.E., N.E.2d
Illinois Decisions	1976–date	Ill. Dec.

Appellate Court (Ill. App. Ct.): In documents submitted to Illinois state courts, cite to Ill. App., Ill. App. 2d, or Ill. App. 3d; to N.E.2d if therein; and to Ill. Dec. if therein. In all other documents, cite only to N.E.2d, if therein; otherwise, cite to an Illinois Appellate Court Report.

Illinois Appellate Court Reports	1877–date	Ill. App., Ill. App. 2d, Ill. App. 3d
North Eastern Reporter	1936–date	N.E.2d
Illinois Decisions	1976–date	Ill. Dec.

Court of Claims (Ill. Ct. Cl.): Cite to Ill. Ct. Cl.

Illinois Court of Claims Reports	1889–date	Ill. Ct. Cl.

Statutory compilations: Cite to ILL. COMP. STAT. if therein.

Illinois Compiled Statutes	x ILL. COMP. STAT. x/x-x (West 19xx)
West's Smith-Hurd Illinois Compiled Statutes Annotated	x ILL. COMP. STAT. ANN. x/x-x (West 19xx)

Session laws: Cite to Ill. Laws if therein.

Laws of Illinois	19xx Ill. Laws xxx
Illinois Legislative Service (West)	19xx Ill. Legis. Serv. xxx (West)

Administrative compilation

Illinois Administrative Code	ILL. ADMIN. CODE tit. x, § x (19xx)

Administrative register

Illinois Register	Ill. Reg.

*Reprinted from *A Uniform System of Citation, Sixteenth Edition* (1996), with permission of the Columbia Law Review Association, the Harvard Law Review, the University of Pennsylvania Law Review, and the Yale Law Journal.

Court and in one prepared for the U.S. District Court for the Northern District of Illinois.

Illinois Supreme Court brief:	Thompson v. Economy Super Marts, 221 Ill. App. 3d 263, 581 N.E.2d 885, 163 Ill. Dec. 731 (1991)
U.S. District Court (N.D. Ill.) brief:	Thompson v. Economy Super Marts, 581 N.E.2d 885 (Ill. Ct. App. 1991)

Some states now have adopted so-called public domain citations as their official cites. These cites allow readers to find their case in a computerized system that does not rely on commercial publishers. Cites to commercial reporters such as West's may be used to augment public domain citations.

Cite public domain citations according to Bluebook Rule 10.3.1, as follows: case name, followed by the year of the decision, the deciding court, and the sequential number of the decision. To cite to a specific portion of the decision, you may add a reference to the paragraph.

public domain citation: State v. Kienast, 1996 S.D. 111 ¶ 2

B. DIGESTS

1. Overview

▼ What Are Digests, and What Do They Contain?

Publishers have developed systems called **digests** that index the law by topics or legal issues. For example, West's digests contain hundreds of topics. See Illustration 3-14, which contains some of those topics. In the digest you find **headnotes** or case abstracts in which the publishers assign a topic and number to a point of law. The headnotes assist you in finding other cases that are relevant to the issues presented in your case. Cases are read by editors, and each issue is put into a topic category. The specific legal issue is then assigned a number to accompany the topic. This enables you to match cases discussing the same issues of law. Digests also contain references to the publisher's other resources and law review articles.

The most comprehensive digest system is published by West Group. The **West key number system** is divided into seven main divisions of the law and then into digest topics, such as negligence, civil rights, treason, states, and damages. LEXIS Law Publishing Co. publishes a digest for U.S. Supreme Court cases and a series covering state cases. Other publishers also prepare state digests. West's state digests contain references to decisions of federal courts sitting within

ILLUSTRATION 3-14.   West's Digest Topics

APPENDIX A
Digest Topics

Digest Topics Arranged by Seven Main Divisions of the Law

1. Persons
2. Property
3. Contracts
4. Torts
5. Crimes
6. Remedies
7. Government

1. PERSONS

RELATING TO NATURAL PERSONS
IN GENERAL
Civil Rights   78
Dead Bodies   116
Death   117
Domicile   135
Drugs and Narcotics   138
Food   178
Health and Environment   199
Holidays   201
Intoxicating Liquors   223
Names   269
Poisons   304
Seals   347
Signatures   355
Sunday   369
Time   378
Weapons   406

PARTICULAR CLASSES OF NATURAL PERSONS
Absentees   5
Aliens   24
Chemical Dependents   762
Children Out-of-Wedlock   76H
Citizens   77
Convicts   98
Indians   209
Infants   211
Mental Health   257A
Paupers   292
Slaves   356
Spendthrifts   359

PERSONAL RELATIONS
Adoption   17
Attorney and Client   45
Employers' Liability   148A
Executors and Administrators   162
Guardian and Ward   196
Husband and Wife   205
Labor Relations   232A
Marriage   253
Master and Servant   255
Parent and Child   285
Principal and Agent   308
Workers' Compensation   413

ASSOCIATED AND ARTIFICIAL PERSONS
Associations   41
Beneficial Associations   54
Building and Loan Associations   66
Clubs   80
Colleges and Universities   81
Corporations   101
Exchanges   160
Joint-Stock Companies and Business
   Trusts   225
Partnership   289
Religious Societies   332

PARTICULAR OCCUPATIONS
Accountants   11A
Agriculture   23
Auctions and Auctioneers   47
Aviation   48B
Banks and Banking   52
Bridges   64
Brokers   65
Canals   68
Carriers   70
Commerce   83
Consumer Credit   92B
Consumer Protection   92H
Credit Reporting Agencies   108A
Detectives   125
Electricity   145
Explosives   164
Factors   167
Ferries   172
Gas   190
Hawkers and Peddlers   198
Innkeepers   213
Insurance   217
Licenses   238

Manufactures   251
Monopolies   265
Physicians and Surgeons   299
Pilots   300
Railroads   320
Seamen   348
Shipping   354
Steam   362
Telecommunications   372
Theaters and Shows   376
Towage   380
Turnpikes and Toll Roads   391
Urban Railroads   396A
Warehousemen   403
Wharves   408

2. PROPERTY

NATURE, SUBJECTS, AND INCIDENTS OF
OWNERSHIP IN GENERAL
Abandoned and Lost Property   1
Accession   7
Adjoining Landowners   15
Confusion of Goods   90
Improvements   206
Property   315

PARTICULAR SUBJECTS
AND INCIDENTS OF OWNERSHIP
Animals   28
Annuities   29
Automobiles   48A
Boundaries   59
Cemeteries   71
Common Lands   84
Copyrights and Intellectual Property   99
Crops   111
Fences   171
Fish   176
Fixtures   177
Franchises   183
Game   187
Good Will   192
Logs and Logging   245
Mines and Minerals   260
Navigable Waters   270
Party Walls   290
Patents   291
Public Lands   317
Trade Regulation   382
Waters and Water Courses   405
Woods and Forests   411

67

that state that pertain to the state's legal issues. West's regional digests do not contain federal cases. In addition to these digests, West and other publishers print topical digests, such as *West's Education Law Digest*.

The ***West American Digest System*** is a comprehensive set of all of West's reported federal and state cases. See Illustration 3-15. This

ILLUSTRATION 3-15. Digests

American Digest System

West's General Digest: contains all state and federal cases reported by West
Century Digest: cases from 1658 to 1897
Decennial Digests: cases from 1897 to 1986 (nine digests)
General Digests: cases from 1986 to date (published annually)

Digests that Abstract All U.S. Supreme Court Cases

U.S. Supreme Court Digest (West)
U.S. Supreme Court Digest

Other Federal Court Digests

Federal Digest
Modern Federal Practice Digest
West's Federal Practice Digest 2d
West's Federal Practice Digest 3d
West's Federal Practice Digest 4th: contains all of the federal court cases reported by West, including U.S. Supreme Court cases
U.S. Court of Appeals Digest—5th Circuit (West)
U.S. Court of Appeals Digest—11th Circuit (West)

State Cases

West Regional Digests: indexes cases reported in the reporter bearing the same name and some cases published in the state reporter before West reporter system started
   North Western Digest
   South Eastern Digest
   Pacific Digest
   Atlantic Digest
West does not publish a digest for the *North Eastern Reporter*, the *Southern Reporter*, or the *South Western Reporter*
Individual State Digests: West publishes digests for all states and the District of Columbia; however, it publishes a combined digest for South Dakota and North Dakota and a combined digest for West Virginia and Virginia.

Specialized Digests

West's Bankruptcy Digest
West's Military Justice Digest
West's U.S. Claims Court Digest
West's Education Law Digest
West's United States Merit Systems Protection Board Digest
California Personal Injury Digest

system includes the *Century Digest,* which contains cases decided between 1658 and 1897. It does not contain key numbers. However, a West index allows you to cross-reference cases in the first and second *Decennial Digest* to convert them to the equivalent key number.

The *Decennial Digests* contain all of the abstracts from West's regional, state, and federal digests during the 9 decennials from 1897 to 1986. The current *Decennial Digests* are published in five-year intervals. *General Digests,* printed annually, also are included in this system.

United States Supreme Court opinions are indexed in a digest called the *United States Supreme Court Digest,* in *West's Supreme Court Digest,* and in *West's Federal Practice Digest series.*

▼ How Are Digest Systems Organized?

Most digest systems are organized by topic. Case abstracts of points of law are prepared by the publisher, and these points of law are then assigned topics. Within each topic, points of law are assigned numbers. In the West system, this match of a topic and a number is called a "key number." Key numbers are the cornerstones of the West system. Key numbers correspond to specific points of law presented in a case. See Illustration 3-7. The case abstracts are not authoritative and should never be cited. These case abstracts contain a publisher's summary of a point of law, the case name, and a citation. See Illustration 3-16.

Illustration 3-16 is a page from the *West's Illinois Digest.* The *Thompson* case is noted in the second column by an arrow. Note that the case abstract contained on this digest page is identical to the first headnote contained in Illustration 3-7. At the top of Illustration 3-16 is the word *Negligence.* This indicates the topic. Next to it is a key and the number 32(2.8). This is the key number. The deciding court and the year of the decision are noted at the beginning of the abstract.

The theory of the key number system is that if you have a good case on point and you want to find similar cases on point, you look under the topic and the key number assigned to the point in your case. The case abstracts listed under that topic and key number should be similar to your case. A case generally has multiple key numbers because a case abstract and a corresponding topic and key number prepared for each point of law raised in a case.

PRACTICE POINTER

The same West digest system is used for all states. Therefore, you can find a good case in one state and look up the relevant key number in another state's digest. That will lead you to cases that are similarly decided in the second state.

ILLUSTRATION 3-16. *West's Illinois Digest*

ed by owner.—Stypinski v. First Chicago Bldg. Corp., 158 Ill.Dec. 604, 574 N.E.2d 717, 214 Ill. App.3d 714.

Ill.App. 1 Dist. 1990. Person is classified as "invitee" on land of another if he or she enters by invitation, express or implied, his or her entry is connected with owner's business or with activity owner conducts or permits to be conducted on his or her land and there is mutuality of benefit or benefit to owner.—Lutz v. Goodlife Entertainment, Inc., 153 Ill.Dec. 519, 567 N.E.2d 477, 208 Ill. App.3d 565.

Ill.App. 1 Dist. 1990. "Business invitee" is one who enters land of another by express or implied invitation, in connection with other's business or activities, with resulting benefit to other and invitee.—B.C. v. J.C. Penney Co., Inc., 150 Ill.Dec. 3, 562 N.E.2d 533, 205 Ill.App.3d 5, appeal denied 153 Ill.Dec. 370, 567 N.E.2d 328, 136 Ill.2d 541.

Ill.App. 1 Dist. 1989. Store owner owed customer the duty of exercising ordinary care in maintaining the premises in a reasonably safe condition.—Palumbo v. Frank's Nursery and Crafts, Inc., 130 Ill.Dec. 744, 537 N.E.2d 1073, 182 Ill.App.3d 283.

Ill.App. 1 Dist. 1989. Property owner owes business invitee a general duty to use reasonable and ordinary care to keep the property reasonably safe.—Courtney v. Allied Filter Engineering, Inc., 129 Ill.Dec. 902, 536 N.E.2d 952, 181 Ill.App.3d 222.

Ill.App. 1 Dist. 1988. General rule regarding duty of business occupier of any premises is that it must provide reasonably safe means of ingress to and egress from premises, but ordinarily it will not be held liable for any injuries incurred on public sidewalk under control of municipality, even though sidewalk may also be used for ingress or egress to premises; however, if occupier of premises appropriates sidewalk for its own use, it then has duty to insure that sidewalk is safe.—Dodd v. Cavett Rexall Drugs, Inc., 127 Ill.Dec. 614, 533 N.E.2d 486, 178 Ill.App.3d 424.

Ill.App. 1 Dist. 1987. A tavern operator, while not an insurer of his patron's safety, has duty to take reasonable action to protect its invitees from foreseeable dangers caused by third persons.—Badillo v. DeVivo, 113 Ill.Dec. 696, 515 N.E.2d 681, 161 Ill.App.3d 596, appeal denied 115 Ill.Dec. 397, 517 N.E.2d 1083, 117 Ill.2d 541.

Ill.App. 1 Dist. 1987. Under Florida law, distinction between commercial visitors and social guests upon premises has been eliminated, and single standard for determining duty owed by landowner to them is one of reasonable care under circumstances; however, landowner's duty to trespasser is limited to avoiding harming trespasser wilfully and wantonly.—Rosett v. Schatzman, 109 Ill.Dec. 900, 510 N.E.2d 968, 157 Ill.App.3d 939.

Ill.App. 1 Dist. 1987. "Special relationships" which give rise to duty to protect another from harm are carrier-passenger, innkeeper-guest, business invitor-invitee, and voluntary custodian-protecting under certain limited circumstances.—Serritos v. Chicago Transit Authority, 106 Ill.Dec. 243, 505 N.E.2d 1034, 153 Ill.App.3d 265, appeal denied 113 Ill.Dec. 318, 515 N.E.2d 127, 116 Ill.2d 576.

Ill.App. 1 Dist. 1985. Owner and operator of restaurant owed business invitee a duty of reasonable care to provide for his safety.—Welsh v. White Castle Systems, Inc., 88 Ill.Dec. 924, 479 N.E.2d 944, 133 Ill.App.3d 957, appeal denied.

Ill.App. 1 Dist. 1985. Owner and lessees of self-service gasoline station owed customer, as business invitee, duty of exercising reasonable care for her safety.—Anderson v. Woodlawn Shell, Inc., 87 Ill. Dec. 871, 478 N.E.2d 10, 132 Ill.App.3d 580, appeal denied.

Business proprietor is not insurer of his customer's safety.—Id.

Ill.App. 2 Dist. 1992. Property owner generally owes no duty to its customers to remove snow or ice that accumulates naturally on its premises, but where property owner undertakes to remove snow or ice, it must exercise ordinary care in doing so.—Madeo v. Tri–Land Properties, Inc., 179 Ill.Dec. 869, 606 N.E.2d 701, 239 Ill.App.3d 288.

Neither store owner nor snowplowing company was liable for injuries sustained by customer in slip and fall on patch of ice in store parking lot, absent proof that customer slipped on ice that had accumulated unnaturally.—Id.

Ill.App. 2 Dist. 1988. Owner of business premises is not an insurer of the safety of the patrons on his premises, but owes a duty toward them to exercise ordinary care in maintaining the premises in a reasonably safe condition.—Rutzen v. Pertile, 123 Ill.Dec. 140, 527 N.E.2d 603, 172 Ill.App.3d 968.

Ill.App. 2 Dist. 1987. Owner of business premises has a duty to his invitees to exercise ordinary care in use and maintenance of his property and to warn of dangerous latent conditions.—Burns v. Addison Golf Club, Inc., 112 Ill.Dec. 672, 514 N.E.2d 68, 161 Ill.App.3d 127.

Ill.App. 2 Dist. 1985. Particular standard of care is imposed on those involved in one of four "special relationships", which are: carrier-passenger, innkeeper-guest, business invitor-invitee, and voluntary custodian-protectee under certain limited circumstances.—Garrett by Garrett v. Grant School Dist. No. 124, 93 Ill.Dec. 874, 487 N.E.2d 699, 139 Ill.App.3d 569.

Ill.App. 3 Dist. 1993. Person is "business invitee" on land of another if that person enters land by express or implied invitation, if entry is connected with owner's business or with activity conducted by owner on land, and if owner receives benefit.—Leonardi v. Bradley University, 192 Ill.Dec. 471, 625 N.E.2d 431, 253 Ill.App.3d 685.

Ill.App. 3 Dist. 1991. Defendant owes business invitee on defendant's premises duty to exercise ordinary care in maintaining premises in reasonably safe condition.—Thompson v. Economy Super Marts, Inc., 163 Ill.Dec. 731, 581 N.E.2d 885, 221 Ill.App.3d 263.

Ill.App. 3 Dist. 1987. A "business invitee" is one who enters upon the premises of another in response to an express or implied invitation for the purpose of transacting business in which the parties are mutually interested.—Simmons v. Aldi-Brenner Co., 113 Ill.Dec. 594, 515 N.E.2d 403, 162 Ill.App.3d 238, appeal denied 119 Ill.Dec. 398, 522 N.E.2d 1257, 119 Ill.2d 575.

Liability of a storekeeper to his customers must be founded on fault.—Id.

The owner or occupier of land owes to persons present on the premises as business invitees the duty of exercising ordinary and reasonable care to see that the premises are reasonably safe for use by the business invitees.—Id.

Ill.App. 3 Dist. 1985. Storekeeper is not insurer of customer's safety.—Nicholson v. St. Anne Lanes, Inc., 91 Ill.Dec. 9, 483 N.E.2d 291, 136 Ill.App.3d 664, appeal denied.

Ill.App. 3 Dist. 1983. Since motorcycle gangs are not illegal and since there was no evidence of actions of one gang member of which bar owner was aware, or should have been aware, which would have compelled a reasonably prudent person to conclude that it was likely gang members might endanger an invitee, danger of criminal attacks was not foreseeable, and thus bar did not violate any duty to patrons who were stabbed outside of bar by motorcycle gang members and could not be held liable for their injuries in negligence action.—Getson v. Edifice Lounge, Inc., 72 Ill.Dec. 826, 453 N.E.2d 131, 117 Ill.App.3d 707.

Once fight began between motorcycle gang members and patrons of bar, bar owner acted reason-

2. Step-by-Step Guide to the Digest System

▼ How Do You Use a Digest System?

You might use one of several methods for finding cases within a digest: the descriptive word index method, the topic outline method, and the one good case method.

▼ What Is the Descriptive Word Index Method?

One method you might use is the **descriptive word index method.** This index is included in each West digest. Other digest series have similar indexes. Before you review the digest, brainstorm for words that might be indexed. You must separate the facts into various categories. These categories will assist you in brainstorming.

To categorize the materials, first review the facts. Select only the important or relevant facts. How do you determine which facts are relevant? Facts are relevant if they might have a bearing on the outcome of a case. These are facts that the courts will look at to make their determinations of the law.

Let's suppose that you are asked to research the claims a client might have against a supermarket for a slip and fall accident in a grocery store. In this case, your client slipped on a banana peel in the produce section of the supermarket while she was speaking on a portable telephone.

First, determine what facts are legally relevant. How do you as a researcher make this determination? You must first determine the legal issues presented. Negligence is one theory. The question posed is, Was the store owner negligent? The second question to consider is, Was the woman also negligent? Negligence is a broad area of the law.

Next, you should brainstorm to develop a list of possible words to review in the digest. Brainstorming is important because a publisher might index a subject differently than you would index it. For example, slip and fall accidents at hotels or motels are not indexed under hotel or motel in the West digest. Instead, they are found under the topic Innkeepers.

Consider the people, the places, and the things involved in your case, as well as the basis for any action and any defenses. These are manageable categories. Consider also the relationships between people. In this case, we have a grocer and a patron. Next, think about the location of the incident. Where did the accident occur? It occurred in the produce section of a grocery store. Finally, determine what happened. A woman slipped on a banana peel while talking on a portable telephone.

Next, develop a relationship between the facts to one another. For example, does the grocer owe a duty to his patron to prevent the patron from slipping and falling inside his store? Does the patron owe a duty to herself to ensure that she does not fall?

Once you have determined these relationships, you should find synonyms for the words you plan to research. Use a thesaurus or an encyclopedia to find synonyms and other additional search words. For example, *grocer* might be indexed. But other words might be used in its place. Try *store owner, market owner, shopping center owner.* For *patron,* an index might contain the words *customer, shopper,* or *invitee,* a legal term of art. Cases may have dealt with a shop owner's liability for a slip and fall accident, but banana peels may not have been involved. Research slip and fall accidents that occurred on surfaces covered with food or other slippery items such as snow or water as well as those that occurred on dry surfaces.

Now frame the legal issues: Did the owner clean the floor? If so, did he do it in a timely fashion? Did the owner ensure his patrons' safety? Was the woman negligent because she walked while talking on the telephone?

The results of your brainstorming session for the grocery slip and fall might be recorded as follows.

People or Parties	Place	Things
Customer	Grocery store	Banana peel
Patron	Shopping center	
Buyer	Supermarket	
Purchaser	Shop	
Shopper	Store	
Grocer		
Supermarket		
Grocery store		
Store		
Shop		
Shopping center		

Activity	Action	Defense
Slip	Negligence	Contributory negligence
Fall	Negligence	Comparative negligence

Once you have brainstormed, review the descriptive word index. Look under the most obvious topics first, such as negligence, slip and fall, customer, or grocery store. Once you have reviewed these words, the digest will lead you to topics and key numbers. See Illustration 3-17.

Illustration 3-17 is a sample page from *West's Illinois Digest* Descriptive Word Index. Under the word *stores* and *storekeepers,* you see a variety of subtopics such as Injuries and Patrons. Many of these subtopics refer you to the Negligence topic with the designation "Neglig." The number next to the topic designation is the key

ILLUSTRATION 3-17.   *West's Illinois Digest* Descriptive Word Index

57 Ill D 2d—599

STORES

References are to Digest Topics and Key Numbers

STORES AND STOREKEEPERS—Cont'd

HEALTH regulations, difficulties, newspaper articles, libel and slander. **Libel 42(2)**

INJUNCTIVE relief against interference with business as property right. **Inj 54**

INJURIES to child carried by customer, care owing. **Neglig 32(4)**
  Contributory negligence of child, age. **Neglig 85(3)**

INJURIES to customers—
  By falling fixture repaired by independent contractor. **Mast & S 315**
  Care required as to persons invited. **Neglig 32(1)**
  Contributory negligence as question for jury. **Neglig 136(26)**
  Evidence. **Neglig 134(5)**
  Instructions in action for injuries—
    App & E 1068(3)
    Neglig 139(1)
    Trial 229
  Instructions on weight of evidence. **Trial 194(16)**
  Presence of vomitus as question for jury. **Neglig 136(16)**
  Question for jury. **Neglig 136(22)**
  Reviewing court's finding that verdict was against weight of evidence. **App & E 1003**

INSTRUCTIONS to jury—
  Burden of proof in action for injuries by railroad fire. **R R 485(1)**
  False imprisonment of person in store. **False Imp 40**

ISSUES and proof in action for injuries to customer. **Neglig 119(1)**

JUDICIAL notice, purchases. **Evid 5(2)**

KNOWLEDGE of defect as affecting liability to customer. **Neglig 48**

LANDLORD and tenant—
  Acceptance of lease. **Land & Ten 25(5)**
  Clerk's authority to accept surrender by receiving key. **Land & Ten 109(5)**
  Conditions precedent to action for rent. **Land & Ten 220**
  Damages for trespass by forcibly entering store. **Land & Ten 132(3)**
  Evidence in action for trespass in forcibly entering store. **Land & Ten 132(2)**
  Injuries to—
    Customer in hallway. **Land & Ten 167(8)**
    Third person for injuries from defective condition of steps. **Land & Ten 167(2)**
  Injuries to tenant's invitee from dangerous or defective condition. **Land & Ten 167(8), 169(11)**
  Landlord's failure to construct runways under lease for automobile showroom as eviction affecting liability for rent. **Land & Ten 190(1)**
  Lessee's liability for breach of contract. **Land & Ten 49(2)**
  Lessee's right to restrain adjoining owner from erecting structure interfering with free passage. **Land & Ten 133(3)**
  Property included in lease of building for store. **Land & Ten 123**
  Recovery of payments of rent on failure to occupy premises. **Land & Ten 213(5)**
  Relation created by contract for floor space. **Land & Ten 1**
  Right of entry and possession by tenant. **Land & Ten 127**
  Trustee's management in leasing store building to numerous tenants as ground for removal. **Trusts 166(2)**
  Use and occupation by person leasing vacant store to prevent competition. **Impl & C C 58**

LARCENY from. **Larc 21, 38**
  Evidence of value of property stolen. **Larc 59**

LEASES, see Landlord and tenant, ante

STORES AND STOREKEEPERS—Cont'd

LETTUCE, dropped leaf, employes as only possible source, customer slipping and falling. **Neglig 136(22)**

LIBEL and slander—
  Evidence. **Libel 112(1)**
  Newspaper articles, difficulties with health department. **Libel 42(2)**
  Presumption and burden of proof. **Libel 101(1)**
  Words tending to injure business. **Libel 9(7)**

LIGHT, power disconnected by store owner, policeman killed on security check. **Neglig 111(1)**

LOTTERIES, "split dollar" game. **Lotteries 3**

MANAGEMENT trainee, hiring by the year. **Mast & S 8(2)**

MONEY back guarantee, false advertising, defenses. **Trade Reg 777**

MONOPOLIES, limiting marketing hours, restraint of interstate commerce. **Monop 28(6.6)**

MUNICIPAL regulations. **Mun Corp 615**

NEGLIGENCE, candy maker injured making delivery. **Neglig 136(24, 25, 26)**

OUTSIDE terrazzo floor, slipperiness, unsafe condition, knowledge, jury question. **Neglig 136(16, 24)**

PARKING lot—
  Customer falling, natural conditions causing. **Neglig 32(1)**

PATRONS, injuries to. **Neglig 32(2.8)** ◄

  Condition of building or structure. **Neglig 44, 136(22)**
  Duties as to patrons. **Neglig 32(1)**
  Evidence as to storekeeper's negligence. **Neglig 134(5)**
  Evidence in action for. **Neglig 134(11), 135(1)**
  Exterior entrance way, slip and fall, concrete incline in slippery conditions. **Neglig 136(22)**
  Falling in terrazzo surfaced entryway, questions for jury. **Neglig 136(24, 26)**
  Hand injuries sustained while opening door, liability of store owner, applicability of test for negligence rather than for products liability—
    Neglig 44
    Torts 14.1
  Hand truck pushed by store employee striking patron. **Neglig 136(22)**
  Illumination of steps, evidence. **Neglig 134(5), 135(1)**
  Knowledge of proprietor of defect or danger. **Neglig 48**
  Matters to be proved in action for injuries. **Neglig 119(1)**
  Obstruction on sidewalk in front of store causing injury. **Mun Corp 808(2)**
  Pins on floor, proprietor's constructive notice. **Neglig 134(7)**
  Proximate cause, evidence. **Neglig 134(11)**
  Questions for jury—
    Condition of building or structure. **Neglig 136(22)**
    Contributory negligence. **Neglig 136(26)**
  Slipping and falling on awning crank, negligence as question for jury. **Neglig 136(22)**
  Stepping on drill bit on floor near counter where bits were displayed. **Neglig 134(5), 138(2)**

PLATE glass doors, inherently dangerous. **Neglig 22**

PLAYROOMS, see this index **Playrooms**

POLICEMAN, burglar killing during security check, store owner creating area of darkness. **Neglig 111(1)**

PRESUMPTIONS and burden of proof, see Evidence, ante

PRIZE drawings, lottery. **Lotteries 3**
  Television advertisement, offense. **Lotteries 22**

PROOF required, injuries to customer. **Neglig 119(1)**

QUESTIONS for jury—
  Assault and battery. **Assault 42**
  False imprisonment. **False Imp 39**

Reprinted with permission from West Group.

number. Under the subtopic Patrons, the notation is "Neglig 32(2.8)." This topic and key number should have cases that are relevant. After reviewing this page, you would retrieve the volume with the Negligence topic (each volume's binding gives an alphabetical range of topics) and follow the numbers to the key numbers suggested in the descriptive word index. In this case, you would review Negligence key number 32(2.8). Reading the case abstracts (such as those found in Illustration 3-16), you could determine the cases relevant to your own. Each digest case abstract contains a notation of the deciding court, a publisher's statement concerning the issue of law, and a citation. Under key number 32(2.8), you would find a case abstract that refers to headnote 1 of the *Thompson v. Economy Super Marts* case. See Illustrations 3-16 and 3-7.

▼ What Is the Topic Outline Method?

Another method you can use to locate cases is the **topic outline method**. If you were asked to research a slip and fall problem similar to the one noted above, you might already suspect that negligence is the designated topic. You then would find the negligence topic in the appropriate volume of the digest series. At the beginning of the topic, you would review a topic outline, which is similar to a table of contents. See Illustration 3-18. Scan the outline and note the key numbers that might be relevant to your case. Note any related topics. You might want to consider them if you decide that this topic is not appropriate. Note that in Illustration 3-18, key number 32(2.8) is the "business visitors, and store and restaurant patrons" key number. Note that number 44 pertains to "buildings and other structures." Both key numbers are relevant to the issue you are researching.

▼ What Is the One Good Case Method?

You also can use the **one good case method** to find cases when you already have found a case on point. If you have a West report of the case, the report will contain headnotes or abstracts with topic and key number designations. See Illustration 3-7. Note the topic and key number designations for the points contained in the case that are relevant to your research; next, go to the relevant digest. For example, if you were researching an issue of federal law, you would review the *Federal Practice Digest, 4th* first. However, if you are researching a question of Arizona law, you should review the Arizona digest. Next, go to the topic and find the key number. Review the case abstracts. The case abstracts contained in the digests are identical to the headnotes. Compare Illustrations 3-7 and 3-16.

▼ Are There Any Other Ways to Find Cases in the Digests?

Yes. If you have the name of a case on point but you do not have information about the key numbers contained in the case, you can

ILLUSTRATION 3-18. *West's Illinois Digest* Topic Outline

NEGLIGENCE

SUBJECTS INCLUDED

Failure to use due care, either in respect of acts or of omissions, in performance or observance of a duty not founded on contract, which failure is the proximate cause of unintended injury to the person to whom such duty is owing

Nature and extent of liability for such injuries in general

Nature and effect of negligence or other fault on the part of the person injured contributing to his injury

Comparison of negligence of the parties

Imputation to the person injured of others' negligence

Civil remedies for such injuries

Criminal responsibility for such negligence in general, and prosecution and punishment thereof as a public offense

(1) **SUBJECTS EXCLUDED AND COVERED BY OTHER TOPICS**

Death, actions for damages for, see DEATH

Manslaughter by negligence, see AUTOMOBILES, HOMICIDE

Particular kinds of property, negligence in care and use of, see MINES AND MINERALS, WATERS AND WATER COURSES, ANIMALS, SHIPPING, COLLISION, and other specific topics

Particular kinds of works, public improvements, etc., negligence in construction and use of, see RAILROADS, BRIDGES, HIGHWAYS, MUNICIPAL CORPORATIONS, and other specific topics

Particular personal relations, occupations, employments, contracts, etc., negligence in respect of duties incident to, see ATTORNEY AND CLIENT, EMPLOYERS' LIABILITY, PHYSICIANS AND SURGEONS, CARRIERS, LANDLORD AND TENANT, BAILMENT and other specific topics

For detailed references to other topics, see Descriptive-Word Index

(2) (C) CONDITION AND USE OF LAND, BUILDINGS, AND OTHER STRUCTURES.
     ⟺28. Care required in general.
     29. Duty to use care.

1 Related subjects
2 Topics and key numbers

ILLUSTRATION 3-18. *Continued*

NEGLIGENCE 38 Ill D 2d—36

I. ACTS OR OMISSIONS CONSTITUTING NEGLIGENCE.—Continued.
    (C) CONDITION AND USE OF LAND, BUILDINGS, AND OTHER STRUCTURES.
        —Continued.
        30. Customary methods and acts.
        31. Requirements of statutes or ordinances.
        32. Care as to licensees or persons invited.
            (1). In general.
            (2). Who are licensees, and status of person going on land of another in
                general.
            (2.1). Classes of licensees, and distinction between them in general.
            (2.2). Bare licensees.
            (2.3). Invitees in general.
            (2.4). Implied invitation in general.
            (2.5). Automobile service stations and parking service.
            (2.6). Bill collectors.
            (2.7). Buildings in process of construction, alteration, or demolition.
➤   (2.8). Business visitors, and store and restaurant patrons.
            (2.9). Deliverymen and haulers.
            (2.10). Employees and contractors.
            (2.11). Frequenters.
            (2.12). Gratuitous licensees.
            (2.13). Guests in private homes.
            (2.14). Meter readers.
            (2.15). Persons accompanying invitees.
            (2.16). Postmen.
            (2.17). Public officials in general.
            (2.18). Firemen and policemen.
            (3). Exceeding or abusing license or invitation.
            (4). Children and others under disability.
        33. Care as to trespassers.
            (1). In general.
            (2). Who are trespassers.
            (3). Children.
        34. Care as to persons on adjacent premises.
        35. Care as to persons on adjacent highway.
        36. Private grounds in general.
        37. Places open to public; recreational use.
        38. Places abutting on or near highways.
        39. Places attractive to children.
        41. Streams, ponds, and wells.
        42. Excavations.
        43. Embankments and piling of materials.
        44. Buildings and other structures.
        45. Elevators, hoistways, and shafts.
        46. Use of property.
        47. Traps, pitfalls, and harmful devices.
        48. Knowledge of defect or danger.
        49. Precautions against injury.
        50. —— In general.
        51. —— Barriers, or covering or guarding dangerous places.
        52. —— Notices and warnings.

look up the case name in the table of cases. It will list the case name and any applicable key numbers.

A single volume included in West's digest series called *Words and Phrases* also can be used to find cases. In it, you will find a case citation definition of a word or phrase taken from that case. (This *Words and Phrases* volume, however, is not part of a West-published series entitled *Words and Phrases*.)

▼ Once You Have a Relevant Topic or Key Number, What Comes Next?

Once you find a relevant topic and key number using any of these methods, then you must be certain to check that topic and key number in the bound volume of the digest, in any pocket parts, and in any supplemental pamphlets.

▼ What Are Pocket Parts?

Pocket parts are pamphlets that are usually inserted in a slot at the back of a bound book. If the pocket part is too thick, the publishers often will print it as a small pamphlet. These pamphlets contain the most current cases and publisher references to related sources.

▼ How Do You Use the Pocket Parts?

To find cases in the pocket parts or in the pamphlets, you should find the topic that is listed alphabetically and then locate the appropriate key number.

▼ Can Digests Be Searched Online?

You can search online for topics and key numbers on WESTLAW only. Because WESTLAW is a West product, it has exclusive access to the key number system. Key number searches are invaluable when you do not have a digest for a particular state. Suppose you are presented with the same slip and fall issue noted above. You need to find Ohio law, but you only have the Illinois digest or an Illinois case on point. You could use a key number search on the computer to find similar cases decided in Ohio.

To do this search, you could review the *Illinois Digest* for an appropriate key number or you could use a key number you found in a case. Map out your key number search or searches. Each West topic is assigned a number to facilitate computerized key number searches. To find the number assigned to a topic on WESTLAW, click on topic search and find the topic sought. For negligence, the topic number is 272. The key number search should start with the topic number, 272. Next, place a "k" (for key number) next to the topic number. Finally, list the appropriate key number found in the digest or case. In the above case, key number 44 was helpful. This search, then, would be 272k44.

Now you can get online. Find the appropriate database. In this case, the database is Oh-CS, which contains Ohio cases. Type **Oh-CS** and push **[enter]**. At the search screen, type **272k44** and **[enter]**. You will find all of the West-reported Ohio cases that contain that topic and key number.

You also can search cases by topic or by case abstract. To perform a topic search, enter the appropriate database. Then type **to** and the topic in parentheses or click on the topic search button and follow the instructions. When you begin to research an unfamiliar topic, try multiple methods for searching the digest. You may come across an issue or topic you had not found in the descriptive word index.

CHAPTER SUMMARY

In this chapter, you learned about case law and about the reporters that contain supreme court, federal, and state decisions.

Case law consists of court-adopted decisions. These decisions are primary authorities. These authorities generally are organized chronologically. Several publishers have established case reporters that are books, usually in series format, which contain court decisions.

Decisions are first published in slip opinions, generally a typed set of pages. Next, advance sheets are published. These decisions usually look similar to the final case reporter version of a decision.

Next, bound reporters that carry the case decision reports are published. For the Supreme Court decisions, three reporters are available. The *United States Reports* is published by the government. The *United States Supreme Court Reports, Lawyers' Edition* is published by LEXIS Law Publishing Co. The *Supreme Court Reporter* is published by West Group. The commercial publishers' reports include publishers' notes and annotations such as headnotes designed to assist you in your research.

Many other federal court decisions are published in *West's Federal Supplement* and *West's Federal Reporter.* State court decisions often are found in a state-published case reporter and in West's regional reporters. Some looseleaf publishers also report decisions, and West reports some opinions in specialized reporters such as the *West Bankruptcy Reporter.* These commercial reporters have headnotes that assist you in your research. These headnotes contain case abstracts concerning a point of law raised in a case and a topic and number that refer you to a topical system for finding additional similar cases. West Group has established the National Reporter System that ties federal reporters and those for a number of states into a unified topical digest system. This system enables a researcher to find an applicable topic in one state and review the same topic in a different state digest to find similar cases on point.

When you research a legal issue, the digests assist you in locating similar cases on point. You can review the digest's index to find a relevant topic and number that direct you to cases on point. In the West system, these numbers are called key numbers. Another method for using the digest is to review the outline presented before each topic. You also might find a good case on point and locate other similar cases by using the digest topic and numbers listed in the publisher's notes that appear at the beginning of the case report.

In the next chapter, you will learn how to ensure that the cases you found are good law.

KEY TERMS

advance sheets
American Digest System
case law
descriptive word index method
digests
Federal Reporter
Federal Rules Decision
Federal Supplement
headnotes
Key numbers
Lawyers' Edition
National Reporter System

one good case method
pocket parts
regional reporter
reporters
reporting systems
slip opinion
Supreme Court Reporter
syllabus
topic outline method
U.S. Law Week
U.S. Reports
West key number system

EXERCISES

REPORTER EXERCISES

1. What reporter would you use to find a published U.S. Claims Court decision decided in 1983?
2. What reporter or reporters would you look in to find a published Illinois Supreme Court decision?
3. What reporter or reporters would you look in to find a published U.S. Court of Appeals decision decided in 1991?
4. What reporter or reporters would you look in to find a U.S. District Court decision from 1930?
5. What is contained in the *Federal Rules Decisions*?
6. What sources would you look in to find a U.S. Supreme Court decision one to two weeks after the case was decided by the Court? (List at least four sources.)
7. What is the advantage of using the *Lawyers' Edition* to review a Supreme Court case?
8. What is the advantage of using a West's regional reporter in researching rather than the *Illinois Reports*?
9. When you are beginning a research assignment, what is the first thing that you should determine? How is this determined?
10. Are headnotes cited? Why, or why not?

TREASURE HUNT

11. Find 507 F. Supp. 1091. What is the key number and topic for the second headnote?
12. Find 825 F.2d 257. What court decided this case?
13. Find 819 F.2d 630. What is the docket number for this case? List the names of the attorneys who argued this case.
14. Find 373 N.E.2d 1371. List the presiding judge and the date the case was decided.
15. Find 432 N.E.2d 1123. List the official citation for this case, the name of the plaintiff, and the name of the defendant.
16. Find 222 N.E.2d 561. List the name of the judge who wrote the opinion.

COMPUTER EXERCISE

17. On the WESTLAW system, prepare a key number search for Weapons, key number 18(1), to be run in the Illinois database. Do any of the headnotes state that parents of a child who shot a police officer with a stolen handgun could not be held liable to the officer on theory of negligent entrustment? That a child had purchased a gun two weeks prior to shooting and parents were unaware of its existence? If so, list the case or cases.

DIGEST RESEARCH

18. Research the following issue in the appropriate digest.

    Your firm's client was fired from her job because she was 69 years old. She had worked for 40 years in this position. When she was fired, she was replaced with a 25-year-old woman. Your firm's client has a master's degree; the 25-year-old has a bachelor's degree.

    You only need to consider what federal law claims she might have against her former employer. Her case would be brought in the U.S. District Court for the Northern District of Ohio.

Brainstorm: What words would you review? What topics and key numbers did you find? List them. List two relevant cases.

    You must determine whether a former employee can assert the attorney-client privilege in your state when a third party, not the former employee, brings an action against the former employer.

Brainstorm: What words would you review? What topics and key numbers did you find? List them. List two relevant cases.

Portfolio Assignment for Digest Research

19. Read the following fact situation. Answer the questions following the situation.

FACTS

Nate Late, a business owner, has two partners in the operation of Loose Cannon Manufacturing in Gurnee, Illinois. He owns 33 1/3 percent of a

$3 million company. Late is ill, but not dying. He is grooming a 26-year-old, Ivan T. All, to run the business. He tells his family he likes All and wants to teach him the business. Nate Late dies.

The most current will leaves Late's estate to his wife of 24 years, Shirley Late, and his only son, Lou Sier. Mr. All tells Mrs. Late that her husband told All he intended to give the 26-year-old his one-third interest in Loose Cannon. This conversation took place in front of a bank president. No written record exists concerning Late's intention to give his stock to All. However, family members knew that Late intended for All to run the business and for All to get something if the business was sold. None of the family believed that Late intended to give the business to newcomer Ivan T. All. Late's shares of stock were never given to All. The shares were in the safe deposit box shared by Late and his wife.

Mrs. Late said that Mr. Late planned to give her the shares. He told her this when he opened the joint safety deposit box and gave her the key.

You work for a firm that has been retained by Mrs. Late. She would like to know if All can prove that Mr. Late gave All Mr. Late's interest in the company.

DIGEST QUESTIONS

a. What digest is appropriate for this problem?
b. How would you find the appropriate digest topics? Note in detail two methods for finding the appropriate digest topics. Next, review two topics.
c. What topics did you review?
d. Did you find additional topics that should be reviewed? If so, review those now.
e. What topics and key numbers are relevant to this problem?
f. Review the case abstracts listed under one of the topics and key numbers. Which cases are relevant? Note two below. Copy the case abstract or photocopy the case abstracts. Review two cases.

Computer Exercises for Digest Topics

20. Search for Master and Servant, key number 30(6.35), cases in all 50 states. Print the search and the first page of the citation list of the cases.
21. Using the computer, prepare and list a headnote search of topic Hospitals, key number 8, in Minnesota. Print your search and the first page of the list of cases you find.

SHEPARDIZING

CHAPTER OVERVIEW

This chapter teaches you how to ensure that a case that you find is good law and how to find additional cases using citators. To ensure that a case is current or is still good law, you must validate or update your research findings. A case is good law if its ruling has not been reversed or overruled by another court's decision. Validating or Shepardizing, as it is commonly called, is one of the most important tasks you must do as a researcher. To do this, you must review citators.

A. *SHEPARD'S*

▼ What Is a Citator?

Citators are services that note when a court has mentioned or relied on a case. The citator may be found on the computer or in print.

The **Shepard's citator system** is the most pervasive. It is found in printed form, on the Internet, and on legal computer systems such as LEXIS. Citators are used to validate a case. In addition, you can use them to locate relevant primary authorities, such as cases and statutes, and secondary authorities, such as law review articles and *American Law Reports*. You also can review citators to determine the direct history of a case. This history describes the progress and all of the decisions made by different courts about a specific case.

▼ What Do You Learn from Reviewing *Shepard's* Citations?

Shepard's provides the history of the case you are reviewing and a list of parallel citations. When you **Shepardize** a court case, you find the history of the case. If it is a trial court case, *Shepard's* indicates whether it was appealed and lists the appellate citation. For state cases such as the *Thompson* case (discussed in Chapter 3), *Shepard's* contains parallel citations in parentheses. See Illustration 4-1. The parallel citations are reported the first time *Shepard's* reports a case; they are not reported in subsequent *Shepard's* reports.

Shepard's lists any cases that mention or cite the case you are Shepardizing. For example, the *Thompson* case cites *Ward v. K Mart Corp.,* 136 Ill. 2d 132, 554 N.E.2d 223 (1990). See Illustration 3-7, page 44. The *Shepard's* listing for the *Ward* case includes a notation that it is cited in the *Thompson* case, 581 N.E.2d 885, on page 888. See Illustrations 3-7 and 4-2.

Shepard's also references West's headnote system. In Illustration 4-2, the small raised 7 between the N.E.2d symbol and 888 in the *Thompson* notation of the *Ward Shepard's* report indicates that the citing case, *Thompson,* refers to the text found within the portion of the *Ward* case the publisher designated as headnote 7. See the arrow in Illustration 4-2.

For some citing authorities, *Shepard's* provides additional information about the decision of the citing case. For example, the *Shepard's* citation may include the letter *a* at the front of the citations list. See Illustration 4-3. That letter indicates that the case was affirmed on appeal. *Shepard's* may indicate with other abbreviations whether a case has been dismissed, modified, reversed, criticized, explained, followed, limited, questioned, or overruled. See Illustration 4-3. In this way you can find the negative history of a case, which tells you how other courts have viewed it. Not all of these court cases, however, have a direct relationship to the cited case.

Shepard's can be used to research almost every federal and state case reported in the past 200 years. *Shepard's* publishes a variety of citation books for federal and state authorities. See Illustration 4-4. Among the authorities that can be Shepardized are cases, statutes, constitutions, codes, jury instructions, administrative decisions,

ILLUSTRATION 4-1. *Shepard's North Eastern Reporter Citations, Thompson v. Economy Super Marts, Inc.,* 581 N.E.2d 885

NORTHEASTERN REPORTER, 2d SERIES (Illinois Cases)				Vol. 582
f 600NE³461	598NE⁸1012	—901—	—1208—	593NE²136
	604NE443			597NE⁵657
—842—		Mirly v Basola	In the Matter	f 597NE³813
	—877—	1991	of McMahon	f 597NE⁴813
Estate of			v McMahon	f 597NE⁸813
Stanford	Holmstrom	(163IID747)	1991	f 597NE⁷813
1991	v Kunis			f 597NE⁹813
	1991	—904—	(163IID785)	599NE⁸⁹935
(163IID688)				j 599NE938
Cert Den	(163IID723)	Illinois v Gold	—1213—	605NE⁴498
in 587NE1015	596NE⁴711	1991		e 605NE⁸575
591NE947	596NE720		Hany v General	606NE⁸817
c 591NE¹948	605NE³1083	(163IID750)	Electric Co.	Cir. 7
	606NE⁴275	Cert Den	1991	965F2d1425
—849—		in 591NE26		975F2d³331
	—882—	597NE³935	(163IID790)	
In re D.D.H.		602NE1373	Cert Den	—114—
1991	Cadle Company		in 587NE1015	
	II Inc. v	—907—	592NE¹²682	Bochantin
(163IID695)	Stauffenberg			v Petroff
	1991	Illinois v	—1219—	1991
—852—		Rolland		
	(163IID728)	1991	In re the	(163IID848)
Illinois v			Marriage	s 555NE1066
Saucier	—885—	(163IID753)	of Joerger	590NE²499
1991			v Joerger	
	Thompson v	—911—	1991	—120—
(163IID698)	Economy Super			
	Marts Inc.	In re	(163IID796)	Harris Trust
—857—	1991	Application of	608NE⁵623	and Savings
		Multimedia		Bank v
Trettenero v	(163IID731)	KSDK Inc.	**Vol. 582**	Donovan
Civil Service		1991		1991
Commission	—889—		—71—	
of Aurora		(163IID757)		(163IID854)
1991	Illinois v Solano	Cir. 7	Illinois v	s 560NE1175
	1991	805FS32	Seuffer	596NE¹725
(163IID703)			1991	605NE¹1053
	(163IID735)	—914—		4PPR(4)10
—860—			(163IID805)	4PPR(7)11
	—892—	Cosey v Metro-	582NE1381	
Lindholm		East Sanitary	589NE1120	—125—
v Holtz	Illinois v Ocon	District	592NE²153	
1991	1991	1991	594NE²³241	Illinois v
				Jackson
(163IID706)	(163IID738)	(163IID760)	—89—	1991
		Cir. 7		
—864—	—895—	f 790FS³1388	Illinois v Gosier	(163IID859)
			1991	580NE1375
Illinois v Haun	Illinois v	—1189—		586NE489
1991	Mika Timber		(163IID823)	587NE¹²546
	Company Inc.	Illinois v Ford	592NE²⁷1025	592NE¹54
(163IID710)	1991	1991	f 603NE²⁷546	592NE671
Cert Den			604NE²⁷292	594NE⁴⁵290
in 602NE463	(163IID741)	(163IID766)	609NE303	f 594NE⁴⁴291
c 585NE¹⁹140		Cert Den		594NE⁴⁵301
c 592NE1114	—898—	in 587NE1019	—108—	594NE¹¹1172
604NE428		592NE¹97		594NE1174
f 604NE¹⁴496	Selph v North		Gouge v	597NE²719
f 604NE¹⁶496	Wayne	—1202—	Central	600NE418
604NE¹⁸499	Community		Illinois Public	602NE949
f 606NE¹⁹665	Unit School	In the Interest	Service Co.	606NE1092
	District	of C.R. v	1991	608NE231
—873—	1991	Richardson		f 608NE¹⁴232
		1991	(163IID842)	f 610NE50
In re Marriage	(163IID744)		s 552NE1304	60USLW4542
of Salata		(163IID779)	f 582NE³250	10A³797n
1991		598NE475	f 582NE⁵250	
(163IID719)				

—164—
Pape v Byrd
1991
(163IID898)
s 555NE428
29COA431§ 11
—173—
Illinois v Szabo
1991
(163IID907)
cc 447NE193
cc 497NE995
f 582NE183
f 589NE¹699
591NE³928
591NE⁴928
593NE941
601NE¹860
e 602NE¹1318
608NE548
f 608NE¹552
609NE⁴309
—177—
Cesena v Du
Page County
1991
(163IID911)
US cert den
in 60USLW3780
s 558NE1378
j 588NE390
594NE1370
598NE374
j 610NE70
—183—
Case 1
Illinois v
Washington
1991
(163IID917)
s 568NE1279
s 608NE546
589NE698
601NE860
—183—
Case 2
Illinois v Blake
1991
(163IID917)

1047

ILLUSTRATION 4-2. *Shepard's North Eastern Reporter Citations, Ward v. K-Mart Corp.,* 554 N.E.2d 223 (Ill. 1990)

Vol. 554		NORTHEASTERN REPORTER, 2d SERIES (Illinois Cases)			
577NE1297	596NE⁷653	588NE⁴1091	566NE⁴243	f 600NE³876	**—244—**
577NE1358	598NE⁷976	588NE¹⁰1092	567NE426	f 600NE⁴876	
577NE¹1359	598NE⁷983	595NE⁶1332	f 567NE⁸427	d 600NE⁹880	Schackleton
d 578NE⁹31	e 599NE⁸952	f 597NE²244	569NE215	j 600NE884	v Federal
580NE⁴1310	599NE⁷1050	f 597NE³244	d 569NE⁷216	f 600NE²¹1252	Signal Corp.
581NE122	601NE858	f 597NE⁶244	d 569NE⁹216	600NE⁴1281	1989
584NE⁴465	604NE⁷391	598NE¹1385	569NE²583	602NE²21	
e 584NE546	605NE⁸594	598NE²1385	569NE³583	602NE³22	(196Il∎437)
586NE¹¹281	89Æ715s	598NE⁴1385	570NE³¹1222	f 602NE²57	(143IlD309)
586NE¹²281	1Æ673s	598NE⁶1388	e 571NE⁴481	f 602NE³57	568NE908
e 586NE282		599NE³1148	571NE817	d 602NE58	571NE²1092
586NE²290	**—206—**	599NE⁵1148	d 571NE⁵818	602NE⁴58	571NE³1092
586NE⁷746		607NE¹216	f 571NE²1112	602NE³899	c 598NE437
587NE⁷1110	Condon v	607NE²216	f 571NE³1112	602NE⁴899	603NE737
587NE⁸1110	American	607NE⁴216	f 571NE⁴1112	e 602NE⁶901	Cir. 7
f 590NE⁸554	Telephone and	609NE¹808	572NE²989	603NE²17	d 796FS⁷1129
590NE⁴556	Telegraph	609NE⁴808	578NE²602	d 603NE¹18	
590NE⁵557	Company Inc.	609NE⁵808	579NE1020	603NE²819	**—251—**
593NE³949	1990	609NE⁸808	d 580NE⁸167	603NE³819	
593NE1129		610NE821	d 580NE⁹167	605NE³502	Northbrook
593NE¹1129	(136Il2d95)	610NE²822	581NE23	d 605NE725	National
593NE³¹1129	(143IlD271)	76Æ22s	581NE⁷888	j 605NE727	Insurance
594NE⁴228	s 569NE518		582NE³300	606NE388	Co. v Nehoc
594NE¹²1259	564NE¹1205	**—216—**	583NE¹705	606NE³635	Advertising
594NE¹¹1260	564NE²1205		584NE¹161	606NE753	Service Inc.
e 594NE²1285	585NE1158	Illinois v Brown	585NE170	e 606NE1281	1989
d 596NE¹113	600NE¹914	1990	585NE173	607NE²274	
d 596NE²113	607NE¹1381		585NE⁴173	f 607NE⁴1286	(196Il∎448)
599NE⁴1039		(136Il2d116)	585NE¹228	609NE⁸924	(143IlD316)
599NE⁷1039	**—209—**	(143IlD281)	f 586NE²378	Cir. 7	570NE³872
f 601NE1279		s 553NE455	f 586NE⁴379	945F2d959	
602NE¹849	Griffith v	556NE901	e 587NE⁵13	e 965F2d⁹1423	**—257—**
606NE352	Mitsubishi	556NE¹902	588NE⁵382	f 773FS²113	
606NE⁹369	Aircraft	f 565NE¹1353	j 588NE383	f 778FS²957	O'Brien
608NE203	International	f 565NE²1354	588NE441	f 778FS³957	v Meyer
608NE358	Inc.	f 565NE³1354	d 588NE⁹442	f 789FS²942	1989
f 608NE²359	1990	587NE²1189	589NE²572		
f 609NE¹²917		587NE³1189	589NE³572	**—235—**	(196Il∎457)
8Æ16s	(136Il2d101)	588NE¹1179	589NE⁹575		(143IlD322)
	(143IlD274)	593NE³1017	589NE⁴578	Illinois v	Cert Den
—192—	f 556NE¹1287	f 599NE²948	f 592NE³366	Morris	587NE60
	f 556NE²1287	f 599NE³948	f 592NE⁴366	1990	587NE70
Illinois v	f 556NE³1287	f 603NE²599	f 592NE⁷366		597NE⁴784
Foskey	f 556NE⁴1287	606NE³284	f 592NE367	(136Il2d157)	Cir. 7
1990	558NE135	608NE606	593NE²607	(143IlD300)	e 984F2d218
	f 558NE⁶136	610NE166	j 593NE616	563NE²1244	
(136Il2d66)	558NE²703		d 593NE994	566NE¹989	**—263—**
(143IlD257)	558NE705	**—223—**	594NE³318	576NE¹398	
s 529NE1158	565NE²288		594NE⁴318	576NE399	Illinois v Smith
557NE²⁰1280	565NE²288	Ward v K-	e 594NE⁹319	582NE¹742	1989
563NE⁷1116	565NE⁷289	Mart Corp.	595NE³46	584NE²1043	
563NE²1183	566NE³721	1990	f 595NE⁷47	595NE²547	(197Il∎226)
564NE²²1265	566NE⁵721		595NE⁹49	598NE¹1375	(143IlD328)
565NE¹⁸642	566NE⁶722	(136Il2d132)	f 595NE50	598NE²1375	Cert Den
566NE713	568NE³886	(143IlD288)	595NE⁵582	599NE²554	d 577NE1299
568NE⁷912	j 568NE893	s 540NE1036	f 595NE¹624	607NE¹152	d 577NE²1300
568NE⁸912	575NE246	560NE²23	595NE²667	608NE141	
571NE⁸187	575NE⁵247	560NE1102	595NE⁵667		**—266—**
e 571NE¹⁴191	d 575NE⁷247	f 561NE²324	595NE⁴667	**—240—**	
d 573NE²²1356	576NE¹1128	562NE⁴403	595NE668		Mondelli v
578NE¹⁶247	576NE²1128	f 562NE⁹1060	e 595NE⁹1103	In re Marriage	Checker Taxi
578NE¹⁸247	576NE⁴1128	563NE²1122	f 596NE⁶98	of Fowler	Company Inc.
581NE²220	576NE⁸1129	563NE³1122	598NE²343	1990	1990
585NE²184	f 576NE⁶1159	563NE⁴1228	598NE⁴344		
587NE1193	579NE⁴859	j 563NE1229	598NE⁷344	(197Il∎95)	(197Il∎258)
f 587NE¹⁷1194	586NE³1292	f 563NE⁵1229	599NE¹1014	(143IlD305)	(143IlD331)
f 587NE¹⁸1194	587NE¹1165	565NE³689	599NE1142		567NE1365
592NE⁷308	588NE²1091	f 566NE241	f 600NE²876		576NE²¹1077

940

---

*Reproduced by permission of *Shepard's*. Further reproduction of any kind is strictly prohibited.

ILLUSTRATION 4-3.   *Shepard's* Abbreviations—Analysis, in *Shepard's Citations*

ABBREVIATIONS—ANALYSIS
CASES

History of Case

a	(affirmed)	Same case affirmed on appeal.
cc	(connected case)	Different case from case cited but arising out of same subject matter or intimately connected therewith.
D	(dismissed)	Appeal from same case dismissed.
m	(modified)	Same case modified on appeal.
r	(reversed)	Same case reversed on appeal.
s	(same case)	Same case as case cited.
S	(superseded)	Substitution for former opinion.
v	(vacated)	Same case vacated.
Cert Den		Certiorari or Appeal Denied or Dismissed by Illinois Supreme Court.
US	cert den	Certiorari denied by U.S. Supreme Court.
US	cert dis	Certiorari dismissed by U.S. Supreme Court.
US	reh den	Rehearing denied by U.S. Supreme Court.
US	reh dis	Rehearing dismissed by U.S. Supreme Court.

Treatment of Case

c	(criticized)	Soundness of decision or reasoning in cited case criticized for reasons given.
d	(distinguished)	Case at bar different either in law or fact from case cited for reasons given.
e	(explained)	Statement of import of decision in cited case. Not merely a restatement of the facts.
f	(followed)	Cited as controlling.
h	(harmonized)	Apparent inconsistency explained and shown not to exist.
j	(dissenting opinion)	Citation in dissenting opinion.
L	(limited)	Refusal to extend decision of cited case beyond precise issues involved.
o	(overruled)	Ruling in cited case expressly overruled.
p	(parallel)	Citing case substantially alike or on all fours with cited case in its law or facts.
q	(questioned)	Soundness of decision or reasoning in cited case questioned.

ABBREVIATIONS—COURTS

Cir. DC–U.S. Court of Appeals, District of Columbia Circuit
Cir. (number)–U.S. Court of Appeals Circuit (number)
Cir. Fed.–U.S. Court of Appeals, Federal Circuit
CCPA–Court of Customs and Patent Appeals
CIT–United States Court of International Trade
ClCt–Claims Court (U.S.)
CtCl–Court of Claims (U.S.)
CuCt–Customs Court
ECA–Temporary Emergency Court of Appeals
ML–Judicial Panel on Multidistrict Litigation
RRR–Special Court Regional Rail Reorganization Act of 1973

ILLUSTRATION 4-4.   *Shepard's Citations*

United States Citations
Reports citations to decisions of the U.S. Supreme Court, the U.S.C., and the U.S. Constitution

Shepard's Federal Citations, Parts One and Two
Reports citations to decisions of the U.S. Courts of Appeal, the U.S. District Court, and the U.S. Court of Claims

State, Puerto Rico, and District of Columbia cases
Each state has a *Shepard's* citator, as does Puerto Rico and the District of Columbia

Shepard's Regional Citators
Cases of all 50 states divided into nine regions

Topical Citators
Shepard's Banking Law Citations
Reports citations to federal and state cases and statutes dealing with banking law

Shepard's Bankruptcy Citations
Reports citations to West's Bankruptcy Reporter decisions

Shepard's Federal Merit System Citations
Reports citations to the *United States Merit Systems Protection Board Reporter*

---

copyrights, trademarks, patents, and regulations as well as secondary authorities including Restatements and *American Law Reports.*

The list of citing references to each will vary because different *Shepard's* divisions and citators include different citing sources. For example, if you reviewed the *Thompson* case under the Illinois division of the *Shepard's Illinois Citator,* you might find a listing for an attorney general opinion or a law review article. However, the attorney general opinion and the law review citations would not be listed under the *Thompson* case in the *North Eastern Reporter* division of that citator. Also, under the regional citation for the *Thompson* case in the Illinois *Shepard's,* you would find the *North Eastern Reporter* citations for the Illinois cases that cite the *Thompson* case, the parallel citations, and persuasive authorities from other states on point rather than the Illinois citations for the case. You would find that the citators contained in *Shepard's North Eastern Citations* differ from the report in the *Shepard's Illinois Citations, Illinois Appellate Third Series* cases because each citator includes a review of a different group of citing authorities. Each citator contains a list at the front of a volume of the sources that have been consulted to determine whether a case has been referred to within that source. See Illustrations 4-5 and 4-6. You will see that these two citators draw from different sources.

▼ How Do You Use *Shepard's* in Print?

First, you must determine which *Shepard's* series is the appropriate one to consult. *Shepard's* has multiple citators that might contain a particular case. For example, a state citator and a regional citator would contain the *Shepard's* for a state case. For the *Thompson* case, you would look in the Illinois citator if you knew it was an Illinois case. Next, you must review the front cover of the most current pamphlet that accompanies the *Shepard's* citations. See Illustration 4-7. In Illustration 4-7, you can see the heading "What Your Library Should Contain." This lists all of the *Shepard's* volumes and supplements you must consider to complete your review of the *Shepard's* citations for a particular case. After you view this cover, gather each of the volumes and supplements mentioned on the cover. The case citations are organized by reporter, volume, and page number. Find the appropriate reporter section. For the *Thompson* case, the *North Eastern Reporter Second Series* is the correct division. Locate the volume number. In bold at the top corner of the page you will find a volume number. Other volumes may be contained on the same page. If the volume you wish to review is not listed in the corner, scan the page for your volume. Find the page number for the case. See Illustration 4-1. You then must repeat this procedure in each of the *Shepard's* volumes and pamphlets.

Review Illustrations 4-8 and 4-9. These are additional pages from a pamphlet that must be reviewed to completely Shepardize the *Thompson* citation. In Illustration 4-8, the volume number appears on the top of the page in the corner. The page numbers are found in bold in the middle of the page. In Illustration 4-9, the volume number appears boxed in the middle of the page. You then must read down until you would find "885," the number referencing the first page of the *Thompson* case. Cases that cite to *Thompson* would be listed below that number as they are in Illustration 4-8. However, in this example, no new cases cite to the *Thompson* case in Illustration 4-9 because "885" does not appear.

Note that the *Shepard's* citations are not Bluebook abbreviations for the reporters and that the number for each series is placed on top of the reporter abbreviations. See Illustration 4-1.

You also can review cases by either official or parallel citations. For example, you can find the *Thompson* citation under the listings for *North Eastern Reporter Second Series, Illinois Appellate Reports Third Series,* or *Illinois Decisions.* A U.S. Supreme Court decision can be found based on its citation in *U.S. Reports, U.S. Supreme Court Reports,*

ILLUSTRATION 4-5.   List of Sources Reviewed for *Shepard's Illinois Citations*

THE CITATIONS INCLUDED IN THIS VOLUME

APPEAR IN

Illinois Supreme Court Reports, Vols. 1 Ill–142 Il2d
Illinois Appellate Court Reports, Vols. 1 IlA–212 IlA
Illinois Court of Claims Reports, Vols. 1–43
Illinois Circuit Court Reports, Vols. 1–3
Northeastern Reporter (Illinois Cases), Vols. 1 NE–610 NE
Illinois Decisions, Vols. 1–182
United States Supreme Court Reports, Vols. 18–489
Lawyers' Edition, United States Supreme Court Reports, Vols. 5 LE–111 LE
Supreme Court Reporter, Vols. 1–108
Federal Cases, Vols. 1–30
Federal Reporter, Vols. 1 F–984 F2d
Federal Supplement, Vols. 1–811
Federal Rules Decisions, Vols. 1–144
Bankruptcy Reporter, Vols. 1–149
Claims Court Reporter, Vols. 1–26
Military Justice Reporter, Vols. 32–35
Illinois Law Review, Vols. 1–46
Northwestern University Law Review, Vols. 47–86
University of Chicago Law Review, Vols. 1–59
University of Illinois Law Forum, 1949–1980
University of Illinois Law Review, 1981–1992
Chicago-Kent Law Review, 1931, Vols. 8–67
Illinois Bar Journal, Vols. 20–80
Illinois Law Bulletin, Vols. 1–3
Illinois Law Quarterly, Vols. 4–6
De Paul Law Review, Vols. 11–41
John Marshall Journal of Practice and Procedure, Vols. 1–13
John Marshall Law Review, Vols. 14–25
Loyola University of Chicago Law Review, Vols. 1–23
California Law Review, Vols. 45–80
Columbia Law Review, Vols. 57–92
Cornell Law Quarterly, Vols. 44–52
Cornell Law Review, Vols. 53–77
Georgetown Law Journal, Vols. 61–80
Harvard Law Review, Vols. 71–105
Law and Contemporary Problems, Vols. 22–55
Michigan Law Review, Vols. 56–90
Minnesota Law Review, Vols. 43–77
New York University Law Review, Vols. 34–66
Stanford Law Review, Vols. 11–44
Texas Law Review, Vols. 37–70
University of California at Los Angeles Law Review, Vols. 20–37
University of Pennsylvania Law Review, Vols. 106–140
Virginia Law Review, Vols. 44–78
Wisconsin Law Review, 1973–1992
Yale Law Journal, Vols. 67–101
American Bar Association Journal, Vols. 41–77

and in annotations of

Lawyers' Edition, United States Supreme Court Reports, Vols. 93 LE–111 LE
American Law Reports, Vols. 1 AR–10 A5
American Law Reports, Federal, Vols. 1–112

---

*Reproduced by permission of *Shepard's*. Further reproduction of any kind is strictly prohibited.

ILLUSTRATION 4-6.   List of Sources Reviewed for *Shepard's North Eastern Reporter Citations*

THIS ISSUE, COMPILED BY THE PUBLISHER'S EDITORIAL STAFF, INCLUDES

CITATIONS IN

Northeastern Reporter, Second Series, Vols. 615–626 p. 1033
United States Supreme Court Reports, Vols. 490–498 pp. 1–570, 801–1130, 1301–1307
Lawyers' Edition, United States Supreme Court Reports, Second Series, Vols. 111–125 p. 750
Supreme Court Reporter, Vols. 109–114 p. 296
Federal Reporter, Second Series, Vols. 990–999 p. 1584
Federal Reporter, Third Series, Vols. 1–3 p. 1525
Federal Supplement, Vols. 817–829 p. 1400
Federal Rules Decisions, Vols. 147–149 p. 685
Bankruptcy Reporter, Vols. 153–159 p. 373
Federal Claims Reporter, Vols. 28–29 p. 179
Military Justice Reporter, Vol. 37 pp. 1–494, 501–1119
Atlantic Reporter, Second Series, Vols. 626–635 p. 1219
California Reporter, Second Series, Vols. 13–27 p. 315
New York Supplement, Second Series, Vols. 584–606 p. 578
Northwestern Reporter, Second Series, Vols. 503–510 p. 843
Pacific Reporter, Second Series, Vols. 854–865 p. 631
Southeastern Reporter, Second Series, Vols. 431–439 p. 639
Southern Reporter, Second Series, Vols. 619–630 p. 55
Southwestern Reporter, Second Series, Vols. 854–868 p. 31

and in annotations of

Lawyers' Edition, United States Supreme Court Reports, Second Series, Vol. 111
American Law Reports, Fifth Series, Vol. 14

---

*Reproduced by permission of *Shepard's*. Further reproduction of any kind is strictly prohibited.

Lawyers' Edition, and *U.S. Supreme Court* reporter. For your research to be complete, you must consult multiple citation services whenever possible. This ensures that you will review the different sources *Shepard's* reviewed to compile a citation list.

▼ Which Citator Should You Consult for State Cases?

For state cases, you should begin with the state *Shepard's,* if available.

Find the official citation, if one exists, and review it. Then review the regional citation. Next, if available, review the regional *Shepard's* citator that includes that state. If you have access to a relevant topical citator, review that citator.

PRACTICE POINTER

Update any print *Shepard's* with the most current online information.

ILLUSTRATION 4-7. Cover of *Shepard's Illinois Citations* Pamphlet

VOL. 93   OCTOBER 1998   NO. 10A

Shepard's
Illinois
Citations

EXPRESS UPDATE
CASES AND STATUTES

(USPS 656810)

Log onto
http://helpcite.shepards.com

WHAT YOUR LIBRARY SHOULD CONTAIN

1993 Bound Volume, Cases (Parts 1–10)*
1995 Bound Volume, Cases (Parts 11 and 12)*
1993 Bound Volume, Statutes (Parts 1–3)*
1993-1997 Bound Supplement, Cases and Statutes
     (Parts A and B)*
Supplemented with:
  —October 1998 Cumulative Supplement Vol. 93 No. 10
  —October 1998 Express Update Vol. 93 No. 10A

DESTROY ALL OTHER ISSUES

RECYCLE YOUR
OUTDATED
SUPPLEMENTS
When you receive new supplements and are instructed to destroy the outdated versions, please consider taking these paper products to a local recycling center to help conserve our nation's natural resources. Thank you.

Shepard's

ILLUSTRATION 4-8. Page from *Shepard's Illinois Citations*

NORTHEASTERN REPORTER, 2d SERIES (Illinois Cases)   Vol. 582

—786—
(221Ill𝔞140)
645NE[2]559

—788—
(221Ill𝔞143)
665NE[5]1317

—793—
(221Ill𝔞25)
629NE[8]156
638NE[8]298
j 669NE1278

—800—
(220Ill𝔞1093)

—804—
(221Ill𝔞35)
627NE[2]273
e 655NE923

—809—
(221Ill𝔞222)
672NE864

—817—
(221Ill𝔞234)
617NE841
617NE[1]843
d 626NE1388
c 628NE219
e 628NE220
d 636NE1106
655NE[1]955

—819—
(221Ill𝔞241)
s 623NE841
612NE[7]1011
615NE[7]1157
627NE376
633NE[8]854
664NE[3]317
664NE[6]317
677NE[6]442

—822—
(221Ill𝔞219)

—824—
(221Ill𝔞47)
613NE319
f 613NE321
638NE[2]1146
654NE[3]611
654NE[4]611
662NE136
668NE[1]1121
668NE[2]1121
668NE[3]1121

—831—
(221Ill𝔞44)

—833—
(221Ill𝔞275)

—837—
(221Ill𝔞295)
s 632NE335
618NE1164

—839—
(221Ill𝔞298)
612NE[6]1353
622NE[2]886
j 658NE1261
666NE877
669NE[2]1239

—842—
(221Ill𝔞154)
630NE809
645NE355

—849—
(221Ill𝔞150)

—852—
(221Ill𝔞287)
f 615NE[3]751
625NE126
656NE442

—857—
(221Ill𝔞326)

—860—
(221Ill𝔞330)
662NE[9]601

—864—
(221Ill𝔞164)
613NE743
625NE1140
625NE[18]1144
626NE[9]756
j 665NE1344

—873—
(221Ill𝔞336)

—877—
(221Ill𝔞317)
616NE[4]1012
616NE[5]1012
622NE[4]101
628NE[5]207
631NE[5]265
636NE[5]1149
658NE[5]505

—882—
(221Ill𝔞267)

➡ **—885—**
(221Ill𝔞263)
648NE[3]100
j 648NE101
650NE[1]262

—889—
(221Ill𝔞272)

—892—
(221Ill𝔞311)
614NE873

—895—
(221Ill𝔞192)
d 614NE1292
614NE[3]1293
668NE[1]1022

—898—
(221Ill𝔞177)

—901—
(221Ill𝔞182)
642NE[1]1266
645NE[3]240

—904—
(221Ill𝔞187)

—907—
(221Ill𝔞195)

—911—
(221Ill𝔞199)
Cir. 7
883FS1142
12𝔞³171n

—914—
(221Ill𝔞205)
Cir. 7
882FS724

—1189—
(221Ill𝔞354)
cc 104F3d926
cc 888FS909
613NE387
631NE841

—1202—
(221Ill𝔞373)
615NE[6]1351
633NE34
634NE1309
634NE[1]1312
649NE[4]1000
652NE424
672NE[3]409

—1208—
(221Ill𝔞383)
627NE[5]58
653NE[5]441

—1213—
(221Ill𝔞390)
615NE[7]28
625NE1052
f 657NE[4]1035
657NE[5]1035

—1219—
(221Ill𝔞400)
625NE938

j 659NE447

Vol. 582

—71—
(144Ill2d482)
614NE[10]12
622NE781
622NE[7]782
628NE490
631NE382
641NE[7]318
d 641NE319
641NE[6]319
649NE599
651NE149
658NE[19]402
658NE[14]403
665NE1281
665NE1304
670NE618
670NE648

—89—
(145Ill2d127)
US cert den
119LE590
US cert den
112SC2970
US cert den
116SC194
cc 649NE364
f 616NE329
620NE[7]337
620NE351
626NE[7]156
631NE[4]413
f 637NE1015
f 643NE[27]810
645NE856
f 645NE[22]876
651NE92
658NE[19]410
665NE[6]793
670NE[17]660
675NE933

—108—
(144Ill2d535)
615NE[2]51
618NE[2]976
619NE767
620NE[4]666
621NE[3]54
j 621NE912
623NE[4]843
623NE[5]843
623NE[9]845
623NE[6]846
630NE[4]1175
630NE[6]1329
j 632NE680
633NE[3]989
634NE[2]308
634NE[4]391

634NE[6]391
637NE[2]1200
638NE[2]222
639NE1289
641NE914
643NE[4]1328
644NE[2]35
646NE[4]933
646NE[5]933
657NE[6]671
660NE[4]224
665NE[4]1267
669NE[4]652
674NE1275
Cir. 7
f 884FS1177
950FS[4]1389
950FS[5]1389

—114—
(145Ill2d1)
612NE1053
614NE1201
627NE[2]41
627NE[3]41
631NE[1]1306
e 638NE[4]1192

—120—
(145Ill2d166)
f 617NE[7]858
617NE[2]875
617NE[1]1246
625NE[3]716
625NE[5]717
637NE[2]556
638NE[1]665
642NE[6]851
642NE[1]886
j 651NE132
660NE[3]1313
660NE[4]1313
666NE[3]55

—125—
(145Ill2d43)
v 121LE5
v 113SC32
615NE784
f 621NE20
626NE[4]1156
628NE495
628NE[12]1065
629NE581
630NE[8]1274
631NE[8]1324
636NE452
q 636NE502
f 636NE[11]661
f 636NE[12]661
f 636NE[13]661
645NE269
645NE[12]394
661NE519
663NE[8]147
665NE[12]1305
665NE[131]1305

665NE[41]1312
665NE[39]1316
504US724
119LE500
112SC2227

—164—
(145Ill2d13)
626NE1213
32𝔞³679n

—173—
(144Ill2d525)
US cert den
121LE59
US cert den
113SC99
625NE768
628NE1023
637NE1038
640NE1342
655NE[2]887
e 656NE[4]757
659NE946
19𝔞³359n

—177—
(145Ill2d32)
US cert den
118LE557
US cert den
112SC1953
613NE287
617NE[2]249
619NE227
625NE1064
628NE[6]173
d 632NE1013
640NE944
640NE977
j 642NE1246
d 650NE982
657NE646
663NE1121
668NE580
Cir. 7
158BRW742

—183—
Case 1
657NE1093

—183—
Case 2
(221Ill𝔞586)
617NE501

—185—
(221Ill𝔞858)
613NE[2]830

—189—
(221Ill𝔞574)

—192—
(221Ill𝔞280)
f 638NE[3]331
Continued

ILLUSTRATION 4-9.   Page from *Shepard's Illinois Citations*

NORTHEASTERN REPORTER, 2d SERIES (Illinois Cases)   Vol. 582

—137—
Case 1
s 1998
[IllAppLX194
s 693NE426

—139—
683NE[18]520

—191—
680NE[16]422
Cir. 7
d 1998USDist
[LX3988
1998USDist
[LX5095

—586—
1998IllAppLX
[[2]236
693NE[2]510

—619—
682NE435

—655—
1997IllAppLX
[539
681NE[9]149
684NE[9]820

—887—
f 678NE[4]1044

—903—
c 687NE[3]530
j 687NE532

—1198—
Cir. 7
962FS[5]1053
966FS749
d 1996Bankr LX
[1202

—1220—
682NE1213
682NE[3]1215
57ÆZ315n

—1246—
687NE900

—1274—
e 682NE[25]1119

—1342—
683NE153
683NE1010

Vol. 581

—1—
f 1998IllAppLX
[320

—19—
Cir. 7
1998USDist
[LX2459

—44—
689NE359
689NE379
Cir. 7
f 1998USDist
[LX1048

—67—
691NE832

—73—
689NE[2]408

—90—
1998IllAppLX
[[2]138
692NE[2]798
Cir. 7
1998USDist
[LX2878
967FS[2]1048
967FS[3]1048

—118—
1998IllAppLX
[314
f 678NE[6]362
691NE[4]83

—138—
684NE[1]801
685NE[1]875
685NE[2]875

—145—
1998IllAppLX
[274

—154—
d 690NE159

—158—
682NE99
682NE303
f 691NE[3]45
691NE[5]46

—175—
1998IllAppLX
[[3]103
679NE[3]434
692NE[3]717

—180—
f 683NE[2]1259
Cir. 7
979FS[4]739

—191—
f 682NE1140

—196—
683NE[5]519

—236—
1998IllAppLX
[[3]191
1998IllAppLX
[[4]191
c 1998
[IllAppLX191
c 693NE436

—275—
691NE[8]116

—288—
Cir. 7
127F3d[1]579

—293—
cc 1998USDist
[LX4907

—329—
1998IllAppLX
[[5]302

—367—
1998IllAppLX
[[2]171
692NE[2]1290

—383—
1998IllAppLX
[156
692NE1226

—426—
686NE[3]621
f 686NE622

—637—
Cir. 1
954FS[1]436

—644—
683NE[2]932
683NE1271

—648—
1998IllAppLX
[130
685NE427
691NE98
693NE869

—651—
681NE[1]547
681NE[2]601

—656—
1998IllAppLX
[[5]325
678NE[2]1105
f 688NE[3]84

—664—
1998IllAppLX
[[4]297
682NE[4]104
682NE[3]1142
682NE[2]1198
686NE[5]64
Cir. 3
976FS[4]296
Cir. 7
121F3d[3]1105
1998USDist
[LX1726
1998USDist
[LX6188
979FS[2]654

—669—
Cir. 7
956FS[6]818
211BRW280

—678—
f 1997IllAppLX
[527
f 682NE[1]749
682NE[2]749
f 682NE750
682NE[4]750
682NE[6]752

—715—
683NE1000

—716—
683NE[2]457
683NE[8]457
683NE[9]457
690NE[9]1029

—728—
682NE218

—730—
f 688NE148
688NE[8]148

—739—
687NE[3]875

—759—
681NE[10]567
f 681NE568
c 681NE568

—819—
684NE[9]828

—860—
Cir. 7
1997Bankr LX
[1258
215BRW168
215BRW[5]374

—864—
689NE[12]676

689NE[14]676

—877—
678NE[5]379
686NE[5]1253

—882—
684NE1038
687NE[1]1198
687NE[2]1198
687NE[3]1198

—895—
f 1998IllAppLX
[[1]184
f 693NE[1]393

—911—
691NE[2]128

—1202—
691NE106
691NE[1]107

Vol. 582

—89—
US cert den
516US872
680NE[8]306
j 685NE907

—108—
h 1998
[IllAppLX[4]216
1998IllAppLX
[[7]216
1998IllAppLX
[[8]216
j 1998IllAppLX
[216
1998IllAppLX
[[2]302
678NE[3]28
678NE[3]52
678NE[4]52
678NE[5]52
680NE[4]434
681NE[5]1068
f 682NE[4]1243
f 688NE[6]84
688NE[2]1175
690NE[4]622
j 693NE500
Cir. 7
1998USDist
[LX743
1998USDist
[LX2829

—120—
682NE[3]289
682NE[4]289

—125—
s 1998Ill LX
[361
1998Ill LX353
1998IllAppLX
[[4]7314
685NE906
688NE[4]7663
j 688NE666

—173—
e 685NE895
687NE[4]1075

—196—
682NE169

—200—
f 688NE[4]690
Cir. 7
1998USDist
[LX600

—227—
691NE[3]152

—265—
689NE[2]230

—271—
f 679NE[3]430

—274—
681NE[2]558
681NE[4]563

—281—
685NE1043

—296—
678NE[2]377
679NE[2]94
680NE[2]434
681NE[2]92
684NE[2]171
687NE[2]546
689NE[2]261
690NE[2]1050
691NE[2]397

—308—
688NE[3]128

—317—
e 1998
[IllAppLX[2]177
e 692NE[2]831

—685—
Case 2
681NE162
691NE30

—690—
687NE1123
f 687NE1124
690NE[3]139

459

B. *SHEPARD'S* ONLINE

▼ How Do You Use *Shepard's* Online?

You can access *Shepard's* online at its Web site or with LEXIS during any point in your research. Your access to Shepard's and other online citators and updating services depends upon the software version you are using and whether you are using the *Shepard's* Web site. For newer Windows software, you merely click on the **SH** button. A box will appear and you type in the citation you wish to Shepardize. If you are using older software and you are at the main directory or you are reviewing a document other than the case you plan to Shepardize, you should type **sh,[space]**, and then the citation (without punctuation). For example, to access the *Thompson* case, type **sh 581 NE2d 885.** For older LEXIS software, you should type **shep 581 NE2d 885** and retrieve the same result. If you are viewing the case on LEXIS, you need only type **sh.**

The *Shepard's* Web site allows you to log on with a password and to follow its instructions for Shepardizing a citation. The site is http://www.shepards.com.

▼ Is *Shepard's* Online More Current
than *Shepard's* in Print?

The online *Shepard's* at its Web site and on LEXIS are more up to date than the print *Shepard's*. You can receive daily updates through these services. The publisher, however, does not assign a treatment, such as "reversed," to the citing case.

▼ How Is *Shepard's* Different Online
than in Hardcopy?

First, the online document provides you with a *Shepard's* listing only for the case you are reviewing. See Illustration 4-10. It provides the parallel citations in parentheses and notes that they are the same text. However, it provides the parallel Illinois citations. Compare Illustrations 4-1 and 4-10. See also Illustration 4-11. This illustration explains the advantages of using the computerized *Shepard's* citations. The computer record of the *Shepard's* search is easier to read. Listing only one case eliminates the possibility of confusion, which often

ILLUSTRATION 4-10. *Shepard's* Computerized Report, *Thompson v. Economy Super Marts, Inc.,* 581 N.E.2d 885

Ret. No.	Analysis	Citation	Headnote No.
1	Shep Same Text	(221 III.App.3d 263)	
2	Shep Same Text	(163 III.Dec. 731)	
3		648 N.E.2d 98, 100	3
4	J Dissenting Opin	648 N.E.2d 98, 101	
5		650 N.E.2d 258, 262	1

*Reproduced by permission of *Shepard's*. Further reproduction of any kind is strictly prohibited.

occurs with the print *Shepard's* materials. Computerized *Shepard's* also facilitates notetaking because the *Shepard's* can be printed, often on a single page, and does not involve the painstaking task of writing each notation. This also minimizes notetaking errors. One of the other advantages of *Shepard's* online is that the computer automatically reviews all of the *Shepard's* volumes and provides one complete list of all of the *Shepard's* citations. See Illustration 4-10. A print search of the same citation would require you to review multiple volumes. The computer system is much easier to use because you only need to push a few buttons. It also is much quicker. In addition, the computer search will find *Shepard's* citations contained in different *Shepard's* citators. For example, a search online of the *Thompson* case produces the reports of the *Shepard's Illinois Citator* and the *Shepard's North Eastern Reporter Citations* because the computer searches multiple citators at one time. See Illustration 4-10. The publisher's *Shepard's* treatments also are easier to understand online because the publisher includes a full word to tell you the value of a case. Another advantage is that you often can immediately access the citing cases online with the push of a number and the enter key. The cases will be displayed in kwic, full or cite format similar to other Lexis cases. After you retrieve the Shepard's cases, you will be able to perform word searches to narrow your results. The computer system allows you to design your *Shepard's* research so that you retrieve only the cases that have a negative impact on your case. You also can retrieve cases that contain only a particular headnote or are decided by a specific court. With LEXIS, you would perform a focus search. You also may restrict your search to a particular jurisdiction or headnote.

In addition, *Shepard's* added a new aid, the Signal feature, which tells you either to proceed in using an authority, to use the authority

ILLUSTRATION 4-11. Advantages of Computerized Citations

Easier to Use

- — simple push of a few buttons
- — searches multiple volumes in seconds
- — searches multiple citators at the same time

Easier to Read

- — only one case is displayed at one time
- — eliminates the confusion that often occurs with the print *Shepard's* materials

Shepard's Treatments Easier to Understand

- — explained with a word; for example, the letter "E" found in the print materials is listed as "Explained" in the computerized *Shepard's* listing

Printing Function Saves Time

Allows User Immediate Access to Citing Cases Online

Shepard's Allows the User to Limit the Search of Citing References According to the User's Needs

- — LEXIS: *Shepard's* searches can be limited to a particular history, treatment, or headnote number

---

with caution, or to not use the authority. A red stop sign indicates that the case is no longer good law.

ETHICS ALERT

Some courts may sanction attorneys if they provide cases that are no longer good law to support their claims.

C. *SHEPARD'S* ON CD-ROM

▼ Are *Shepard's* Available on CD-ROM?

Yes. CD-ROM editions of *Shepard's* are distributed biweekly or monthly, depending upon the publication.

The CD-ROM service is presented in a Windows or DOS display format. See Illustration 4-12.

▼ What Does the CD-ROM *Shepard's* Provide?

CD-ROM *Shepard's* citations provide any cases that cite to the *Thompson* case and provide an indication of whether these cases are good law. See Illustration 4-12. In addition, the headnote references are noted as well as the name of the case. *Shepard's* also displays any parallel citations, the deciding court, and the names of the judges, if available. The service provides concise editorial summaries that explain the effect of significant citing references; it may also provide editorial summaries explaining the reason behind a designated treatment code, such as "distinguished." The treatments are listed in complete words rather than in letter abbreviations. All CD-ROM searches can be done without accessing an online service, thereby saving a client money.

From the CD-ROM, you can print the *Shepard's* citations and treatments for a single case, or you can save the information onto a disk to insert into a document later. *Shepard's* also builds in a feature that creates a record of the time spent Shepardizing using the CD-ROM edition.

▼ How Do You Use the *Shepard's* CD-ROM Edition?

1. Select the proper CD-ROM and place it in the drive.
2. Type in the citation you want to Shepardize.
3. You will receive the *Shepard's* display of the citation. You will not need to review multiple volumes.

If you do not have the citation, you can enter the name of the case and the CD-ROM service will display the case for you. You also can

ILLUSTRATION 4-12.   *Shepard's* **CD-ROM Page**

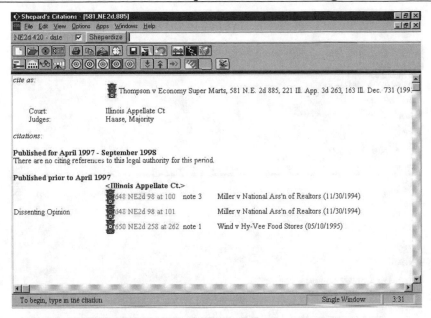

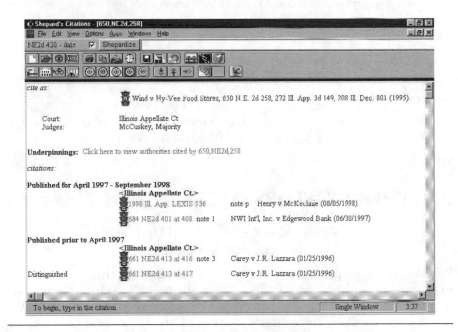

ILLUSTRATION 4-12. *Continued*

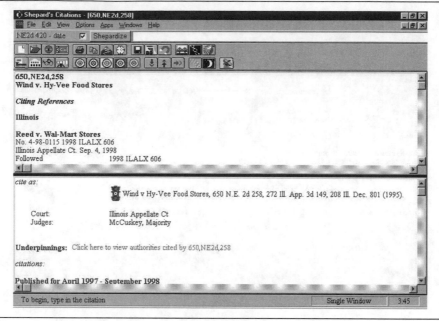

*Reproduced by permission of *Shepard's*. Further reproduction of any kind is strictly prohibited.

target your display for negative treatments or other items. CD-ROM subscribers also have access to a daily update service.

D. OTHER CITATORS ONLINE

▼ What Other Computerized Updating
Services Are Available?

WESTLAW now provides a service called **KeyCite** that is designed to compete with *Shepard's*. See Illustration 4-13. With it you can retrieve all citing references that are contained within WESTLAW, including cases and secondary sources. This includes thousands of unpublished decisions. In addition, you can view the case histories and be alerted to possible court actions that may affect the validity of an authority.

    KeyCite uses a system of colored flags to alert you to the history. A red case flag warns that the case is no longer good law for at least one of the points of law. A yellow flag warns that there is some

ILLUSTRATION 4-13. WESTLAW KeyCite of *Thompson v. Economy Super Marts, Inc.*, 581 N.E.2d 885

History of the Case
(Showing 1 document)

➜ 1 **Thompson v. Economy Super Marts, Inc.,** 221 Ill.App.3d 263, 581 N.E.2d 885, 163 Ill.Dec. 731 (Ill.App. 3 Dist. Nov 08, 1991) (NO. 3-90-0662)

Citations to the Case
(Showing 4 documents)

★ ★ ★ **Discussed**

1 Miller v. National Ass'n of Realtors, 648 N.E.2d 98, 100+ (Ill.App. 1 Dist. 1994) ❯❯

★ ★ **Cited**

2 Wind v. Hy-Vee Food Stores, Inc., 650 N.E.2d 258, 262 (Ill.App. 3 Dist. 1995)

Non-Cases

3 Liability of operator of grocery store to invitee slipping on spilled liquid or semiliquid substance, 24 A.L.R.4th 696, §11b (1983)

4 Store or business premises slip-and-fall: Modern status of rules requiring showing of notice of proprietor of transitory interior condition allegedly causing plaintiff's fall, 85 A.L.R.3d 1000, §4b (1978)

*Reprinted with permission from West Group.

negative history, but that the case has not been overruled or reversed. If the case has history that is neither not negative, it will have a blue II.

In addition, WESTLAW has developed a star system for noting the depth of the treatment a court provides to a case. Four stars means that the case was examined. Three stars means it was discussed, and two stars indicate it was cited. One star means that the case was mentioned.

WESTLAW's headnotes and topics and key numbers also are incorporated into the KeyCite display. You can tailor your KeyCite search to focus on key numbers, topics, or jurisdictions.

LEXIS offers an updating service called **Auto-Cite** that provides the most current direct case history and negative prior history of a case. The direct history shows the case from the trial court through the appellate process. This history also includes information about related references to a case involving the same parties and facts. The negative direct history includes cases that are not in the chain of the case viewed. See Illustration 4-14. The Auto-Cite report shown in Illustration 4-14 provides the full case name, all parallel citations, and the date of the decision. Both services allow you to access most of the cases referenced in the reports.

▼ What Is the Difference between *Shepard's* and KeyCite?

KeyCite includes unpublished cases; *Shepard's* does not. In addition, KeyCite only cites to cases contained in the WESTLAW database. *Shepard's* includes other materials. *Shepard's* also is available for authorities other than cases.

ILLUSTRATION 4-14.   LEXIS Auto-Cite of *Thompson v. Economy Super Marts, Inc.*, 581 N.E.2d 885

PAGE   1

581 NE2D 885:

CITATION YOU ENTERED:

Thompson v. Economy Super Marts, Inc.*1, 221 Ill. App. 3d 263, 163 Ill. Dec.
731, 581 N.E.2d 885, 1991 Ill. App. LEXIS 1898 (3d Dist. 1991)

ANNOTATIONS CITING THE CASE(S) INDICATED ABOVE WITH ASTERISK(S):

*1   Liability of operator of grocery store to invitee slipping on spilled
     liquid or semiliquid substance, 24 A.L.R.4th 696, supp sec. 11.

     Store or business premises slip-and-fall: Modern status of rules requiring
     showing of notice of proprietor of transitory interior condition allegedly
     causing plaintiff's fall, 85 A.L.R.3d 1000, supp sec. 4.

     Liability of proprietor of store, office, or similar business premises for
     injury from fall due to presence of litter or debris on floor, 61 A.L.R.2d
     6, supp sec. 6.

To search for collateral annotations referring to the annotation(s) above, type
the citation and press the ENTER key.

*Reprinted with permission from LEXIS Law Publishing.

▼ Why Would You Use KeyCite and Auto-Cite as Well as *Shepard's?*

These services provide an additional check on the accuracy of the
citation. Another advantage of using KeyCite or Auto-Cite is that
they provide references to secondary sources that might assist you
in your research. For more information about secondary sources,
consult Chapter 5.

▼ How Do I Access KeyCite?

From any WESTLAW screen, point your mouse at the KeyCite, click
the **check a citation** button, type your citation, and press **[enter]**. If
you are already viewing a case, you merely click the **status** flag or **H**
or click the **KeyCite** button on the main screen.

▼ How Would You Access an Auto-Cite Report?

You can access an Auto-Cite report from any point in your LEXIS
research by clicking on the **Auto-Cite** button and entering the citation. Alternatively, you may type **ac, [space]**, and the citation (without

punctuation). To retrieve the *Thompson v. Economy Super Marts, Inc.,* 581 N.E.2d 885, Auto-Cite report, type **ac 581 NE2d 885**. You can type the official cite or the regional cite for state cases and still retrieve the Auto-Cite report. If you are viewing a case for which you want an Auto-Cite report, you only need type **ac**.

▼ Can WESTLAW Be Used as a Citator?

You can search the WESTLAW databases, which are files, and use WESTLAW as a citator. WESTLAW had offered a service called **QuickCite**. This service is essentially being superseded by KeyCite.

▼ Does LEXIS Have a Comparable Service?

LEXIS has a similar service called **LexCite**. However, it is more difficult to use. To use it, you must access a library and then access a file. Next, you would type **lexcite**, and type the citation (without punctuation) in parentheses. This search asks the computer to find all references to that citation contained in that file. These references will include short citations such as *id.* LEXIS is modifying this service. For a quick review of LEXIS and WESTLAW services, see Illustration 4-15.

CHAPTER SUMMARY

In this chapter, you learned that you must ensure that the law or authority you are citing is still current or valid. To determine this, you must validate or update your research findings. This process often is called Shepardizing. Citators not only assist you in validating the law but also provide you with citations to other authorities. You can validate an authority in both print and online. WESTLAW and LEXIS have provided special online citators such as KeyCite and Auto-Cite that describe the direct and negative history of a case.

The next chapter discusses resources called secondary authorities that help you understand legal issues and find primary authorities.

KEY TERMS

Auto-Cite	Shepardize
citators	*Shepard's* citator system
KeyCite	
LexCite	

ILLUSTRATION 4-15.   Computerized Citators of WESTLAW and LEXIS and Print Equivalents

Print		Computer
Shepard's	=	*Shepard's* all citing cases, law reviews, A.L.R.s, etc. *Shepard's* treatments history of the case headnote relationship

None		Auto-Cite (LEXIS)
		 Direct history of case
		 Cites only to cases bearing directly on
		     precedential value or those that criticize
		     or overrule the case

None		Lexcite
		 LEXIS
		 Retrieves references to cases parallel citations,
		     id. and *supra* references within LEXIS case
		     law documents, law reviews, etc.
		 User must select library, file then enter:
		     Lexcite (citation)

None		LEXIS as a citator User must formulate search
None		KeyCite

EXERCISES

Computer Exercises

LEXIS

1. Shepardize and do an Auto-Cite of the following citations:
   a. 64 N.W.2d 38
   b. 150 Ill. App. 3d 21
   c. 326 U.S. 310
2. Access the GENFED library on LEXIS and perform a LexCite search for 326 U.S. 310.

WESTLAW

3. Shepardize and perform a KeyCite search for 64 N.W.2d 38.

COMPUTER VALIDATING EXERCISES

4. Shepardize, Auto-Cite, and KeyCite, all of the following cases on the computer. Print out the first page of each result.
   a. *Consolidation Coal Co. v. Bucyrus-Erie Co.*, 89 Ill. 2d 103, 432 N.E.2d 250 (1982)
   b. *United States v. Upjohn*, 449 U.S. 383 (1981)
   c. *People v. Adam*, 51 Ill. 2d 46, 280 N.E.2d 205 (1972)
   d. *Cox v. Yellow Cab Co.*, 61 Ill. 2d 416, 337 N.E.2d 15 (1975)
   e. *Archer Daniels Midland Co. v. Koppers Co.*, 138 Ill. App. 3d 276, 485 N.E.2d 1301 (1985)

Hardcopy Validation Exercises

5. Shepardize the citations listed below. Photocopy the *Shepard's* pages. List any missing volumes. Be certain to Shepardize all citations for each case or statute.
   a. 361 N.E.2d 325
   b. 80 Ill. App. 3d 315
   c. 571 F. Supp. 1012
   d. 8 U.S.C. §1449
6. Shepardize the following citations in the *Shepard's* citators and provide the official citations. Do not use the computer. Photocopy all of the relevant *Shepard's* pages. Also photocopy the list that details the *Shepard's* bound volumes and supplements you should have consulted for each citation. For each photocopy, carefully note where you found the page, for example, "1990-1991 Illinois bound volume." For each case, highlight in yellow one headnote notation. Then select one case that has a *Shepard's* notation and highlight the case in pink or blue on the photo-

copy and note on the page the meaning of the *Shepard's* notation. (If you prefer to hand copy each *Shepard's* page, that is acceptable too.)

a. 129 F.R.D. 515
b. 432 N.E.2d 250
c. 449 U.S. 383
d. 51 Ill. 2d 46
e. 138 Ill. App. 3d 276
f. 423 F.2d 487
g. Ill. S. Ct. Rule 201

SECONDARY AUTHORITY

CHAPTER OVERVIEW

Secondary authorities are used to understand, analyze, and tie together primary authorities, or the law. Cases, statutes, and administrative regulations—all primary authorities—are frequently cited in secondary sources. Secondary authorities are useful tools for finding citations to law supporting a legal issue.

This chapter details the many sources of secondary authority, how to use the sources, and how to update them. Citation information is given for each source.

A. SECONDARY AUTHORITY: WHAT IT IS AND WHERE TO FIND IT

▼ What Is Secondary Authority?

Secondary authority describes, analyzes, and comments on primary authority. Secondary authority provides commentary on the law. Any analytical or critical discussion of the law is considered secondary authority. Generally, individuals, institutions, and publishers create secondary sources.

Secondary authority compares and contrasts judicial opinions and indicates how the law is evolving. Also, a secondary source will often tell the researcher which cases are most important and which have little merit. Secondary sources discuss statutes and administrative materials expounding on the policy motivations for enacting legislation and the accompanying regulations.

▼ Why and When Do You Use a Secondary Source?

Secondary sources are used to explain the law or a particular legal concept. Secondary sources discuss the legal rules directly without requiring the reader to unearth the issues and the holdings from the texts of judicial decisions. Secondary authority provides insight into a legal topic by discussing the most important relevant cases and statutes and by explaining how that law is applied to the facts. Because secondary sources comment on, describe, and analyze primary sources, a researcher obtains citations to primary authority. By providing access to citations, secondary sources are great finding tools. A researcher uses secondary authority to gain insight into a legal topic as well as to obtain citations to primary sources.

Paralegals use secondary sources when they are unfamiliar with a legal issue or topic and need a broad overview of the concepts written in a text format that is easily understandable. Using secondary authority provides access to primary sources because of the great number of footnotes and citations found in the secondary source.

▼ What Are the Sources of Secondary Authority?

Generally, any source that comments on, analyzes, criticizes, describes, or projects the status of the law is a secondary source. Any source that states what the law should be is a secondary source. Some secondary sources are considered more prestigious and carry more persuasive authority than others. For instance, the Restatements of Law are very well respected, as are scholarly law review articles. The major sources of secondary authority are dictionaries, thesauri, encyclopedias, *American Law Reports* (A.L.R.), hornbooks, treatises, Restatements, legal periodicals, and newspapers. We will discuss each source separately, give examples, and illustrate which research situation would mandate their respective use.

PRACTICE POINTER

Secondary sources are great finding tools for primary authority, particularly case law. Use the secondary source to understand how case law fits together and to obtain citations. Always read the primary source, that is, the case or the statute, yourself to see if it is applicable to your research. Also, never forget to Shepardize any primary source before you rely on it as a source of authority.

B. DICTIONARIES

▼ What Is a Legal Dictionary?

The **legal dictionary** provides the legal definition of a word or term. Sometimes a case is mentioned that contains the judicial definition of that word. The two most common legal dictionaries are *Black's Law Dictionary* and *Ballentine's Law Dictionary*.

▼ When Would a Legal Dictionary Be Used?

Researchers use a legal dictionary when they do not understand the **legal meaning** of a word or term. The emphasis is on the legal meaning because the legal definition of a word often differs from its lay meaning. Sometimes you will be assigned a research project where you cannot answer or resolve the issue without first figuring out what the terms mean.

EXAMPLE

Ms. Associate asks you if Mr. Blackacre can obtain an easement by necessity to access his farm from the road by crossing his neighbor's property. You do not know what an easement is, nor do you know what an easement by necessity is. To research the issue effectively, you would use a legal dictionary to look up easement and easement by necessity.

Examples of dictionary entries of the word *easement* are provided in Illustration 5-1. The entries in the legal dictionary are in alphabetical order. Under the word *easement* are the various types of easements.

▼ How Would You Cite to a Legal Dictionary?

The correct citation format for dictionaries is found in Bluebook Rule 15.7.

Ballentine's Law Dictionary 1190 (3d ed. 1969)
Black's Law Dictionary 712 (6th ed. 1990)

▼ Are Legal Dictionaries Available Online?

Black's Law Dictionary is available on WESTLAW. The Directory screen, which changes constantly, indicates exactly where the dictionary is located within the WESTLAW database. The contents of *Black's* online is identical to the hardcopy version. To search for a definition online, enter the word that you want to be defined. In our example, you would enter the word *easement.*

C. THESAURI

▼ What Is a Thesaurus?

A **thesaurus** provides synonyms and antonyms for words. A legal thesaurus provides synonymous terms and opposite terms for legal words. A thesaurus is the same type of source for legal and nonlegal materials.

Common legal thesauri are *Legal Thesaurus* by William C. Burton (N.Y.: Macmillan, 2d ed. 1992) and *West's Legal Thesaurus/Dictionary* by William Statsky (St. Paul, Minn.: West Publishing 1986).

▼ Why Would You Use a Thesaurus?

A paralegal uses a thesaurus when drafting a memo about a single topic, like easement. The memo becomes very dull if the term *easement* is used over and over again. After a while you lose the reader's attention. Substituting a synonymous term makes reading the memo much more interesting. Occasionally substituting *right of way* for *easement* keeps the reader's interest.

Unfortunately, the Bluebook does not have an entry for citing thesauri. A writer does not cite to *Roget's Thesaurus* when using a synonym found in that work, so the same principle applies with legal thesauri.

ILLUSTRATION 5-1.   Definition of *Easement* in *Black's Law Dictionary*

Earnings. Income. That which is earned; *i.e.*, money earned from performance of labor, services, sale of goods, etc. Revenue earned by an individual or business. Earnings generally include but are not limited to: salaries and wages, interest and dividends, and income from self-employment. Term is broader in meaning than "wages." *See also* Commissions; Compensation; Dividend; Gross earnings; Income; Premium; Real earnings; Retained earnings; Salary; Wages.

Gross earnings. Total income from all sources without considering deductions, personal exemptions, or other reductions of income in order to arrive at taxable income. *See also* Gross income.

Net earnings. Net earnings (income) is the excess of gross income over expenses incurred in connection with the production of such income. For tax purposes, net earnings is the number used to determine taxable income. For accounting purposes, net earnings is generally determined after deduction of income taxes. *See also* Net income.

Surplus earnings. See Surplus.

Earnings and profits. A tax concept peculiar to corporate taxpayers which measures economic capacity to make a distribution to shareholders that is not a return of capital. Such a distribution will result in dividend income to the shareholders to the extent of the corporation's current and accumulated earnings and profits. *See also* Accumulated earnings tax; Accumulated taxable income.

Earnings per share. One common measure of the value of common stock. The figure is computed by dividing the net earnings for the year (after interest and prior dividends) by the number of shares of common stock outstanding.

Earnings report. Businesses' statement of profit and loss; commonly issued quarterly by publically-held companies.

Earth. Soil of all kinds, including gravel, clay, loam, and the like, in distinction from the firm rock.

Ear-witness. In the law of evidence, one who attests or can attest anything as heard by himself. *See also* Voiceprint.

Ease. Comfort, consolation, contentment, enjoyment, happiness, pleasure, satisfaction.

Easement. A right of use over the property of another. Traditionally the permitted kinds of uses were limited, the most important being rights of way and rights concerning flowing waters. The easement was normally for the benefit of adjoining lands, no matter who the owner was (an easement appurtenant), rather than for the benefit of a specific individual (easement in gross). The land having the right of use as an appurtenance is known as the dominant tenement and the land which is subject to the easement is known as the servient tenement.

A right in the owner of one parcel of land, by reason of such ownership, to use the land of another for a special purpose not inconsistent with a general property in the owner.

An interest which one person has in the land of another. A primary characteristic of an easement is that its burden falls upon the possessor of the land from which it issued and that characteristic is expressed in the statement that the land constitutes a servient tenement and the easement a dominant tenement. Potter v. Northern Natural Gas Co., 201 Kan. 528, 441 P.2d 802, 805. An interest in land in and over which it is to be enjoyed, and is distinguishable from a "license" which merely confers personal privilege to do some act on the land. Logan v. McGee, Miss., 320 So.2d 792, 793.

See also Affirmative easement; Non-continuous easement; Prescriptive easement.

Access easement. See Access.

Affirmative easement. One where the servient estate must permit something to be done thereon, as to pass over it, or to discharge water on it.

Apparent easement. One the existence of which appears from the construction or condition of one of the tenements, so as to be capable of being seen or known on inspection.

Appendent easement. See Appurtenant easement, below.

Appurtenant easement. An incorporeal right which is attached to a superior right and inheres in land to which it is attached and is in the nature of a covenant running with the land. Fort Dodge, D. M. & S. Ry. v. American Community Stores Corp., 256 Iowa 1344, 131 N.W.2d 515, 521. There must be a dominant estate and servient estate. An easement interest which attaches to the land and passes with it. First Nat. Bank of Amarillo v. Amarillo Nat. Bank, Tex.Civ.App., 531 S.W.2d 905, 907. An "incorporeal right" which is attached to and belongs with some greater and superior right or something annexed to another thing more worthy and which passes as incident to it and is incapable of existence separate and apart from the particular land to which it is annexed.

Discontinuing easement. Discontinuous, non-continuous, or non-apparent easements are those the enjoyment of which can be had only by the interference of man, as, a right of way or a right to draw water.

Easement by estoppel. Easement which is created when landlord voluntarily imposes apparent servitude on his property and another person, acting reasonably, believes that servitude is permanent and in reliance upon that belief does something that he would not have done otherwise or refrains from doing something that he would have done otherwise. U. S. v. Thompson, D.C. Ark., 272 F.Supp. 774, 784.

Easement by implication. Easement created by law and grounded in court's decision in reference to particular transaction in land where owner of two parcels had so used one parcel to the benefit of other parcel that on selling the benefited parcel purchaser could reasonably have expected, without further inquiries, that these ben-

D. ENCYCLOPEDIAS

1. Generally

▼ What Is a Legal Encyclopedia?

Just as *Encyclopedia Britannica* and *World Book* divide the realm of knowledge into subjects and discuss each subject broadly (for example, the subjects Insects and Cities), a **legal encyclopedia** divides the law into topics and offers a broad coverage of the legal rules pertaining to each topic. The discussion is thorough but not too detailed and is oriented to the reader with legal knowledge, though not necessarily of the particular subject in question. Encyclopedias provide generalized commentary on the law.

There are legal encyclopedias such as the *Encyclopedia of the American Constitution* that cover specialized subject areas. There are encyclopedias such as *American Jurisprudence* and *Corpus Juris Secundum* that are national in scope. Finally, there are state law encyclopedias such as *Illinois Law and Practice*.

▼ Why Would You Use an Encyclopedia?

An encyclopedia is very helpful when beginning research in an area of the law in which you have no basic knowledge of the subject or the issues. Encyclopedias divide the law into topics and subtopics and provide a generalized, clearly written discussion of the issues and the general rules. A working vocabulary and a knowledge of the general rules are obtained when using an encyclopedia. In addition, encyclopedias give credit to every tenet mentioned, so they are a marvelous source for citations.

After reading the encyclopedia entry, you must always read for yourself the cases cited in the references to determine if they are relevant to your problem.

▼ When Do You Cite an Encyclopedia as Authority?

As a general rule, encyclopedias should never be cited as authority. Encyclopedias are not scholarly sources, and authorship is institutional rather than individual. This does not detract from their helpfulness in providing a broad overview of the legal topic and in providing citations to primary source materials.

A researcher should use primary source references, even from other jurisdictions, obtained from the encyclopedia rather than cite to the encyclopedia's text. Always read the case or statute that the encyclopedia cites and rely on the primary source for authority. It is better to analogize to the law from another jurisdiction than to use an encyclopedia as authority.

The two predominant encyclopedias that are national in scope are *American Jurisprudence,* common referred to as Am. Jur. and Am. Jr. 2d (second series), and *Corpus Juris Secundum,* known as C.J.S.

Both encyclopedias cover the individual legal disciplines in a generalized manner. Discussion is thorough but not overly detailed. The footnotes and citations included in the sections provide citations to primary authorities. You must always read the primary source that you rely on, not only the encyclopedia's interpretation of it.

State encyclopedias also exist. In Illinois, *Illinois Law and Practice* is the encyclopedia that deals with issues of state law. *Illinois Law and Practice* is published by West Group and contains references to many other West publications, particularly the digests with the topics and key numbers. Check with your librarian for the encyclopedia in your state.

2. American Jurisprudence

▼ What Is Contained in *American Jurisprudence?*

American Jurisprudence, commonly called Am. Jur., is published by West Group and references other publications such as the *American Law Reports* (A.L.R.). The encyclopedia is in the second edition. The entire set is divided into topics, and the topics are arranged alphabetically.

Illustration 5-2 shows the topic outline for Easements and Licenses in Am. Jur. 2d. Notice that under the topics of Easements are various subtopics. The initial discussion of the subtopic Easements in Gross begins with a category entitled Generally, where the general rule of law is explained.

The editors attempt to divide the entire body of American law into labeled topics. This gives the reader a subject approach to the law and permits the gathering of legal information, allowing the researcher to find out the general legal rules without reading the actual cases and statutes from which the rules are derived. The text explores each legal topic by providing the most important law that is relevant or the controlling legal doctrine, then discusses the exceptions to the general rules. The encyclopedia is considered to be a secondary source because it offers discussion and commentary on the law and synthesizes, or puts together, many cases. Of course, there is extensive footnoting to give proper credit or attribution to the authority discussed. This makes the encyclopedia a great finding tool, although not a substitute for reading the primary source material. The encyclopedia is a good place to begin research when you do not understand the topic and need a broad overview of the discipline. By virtue of reading about the topic, you will acquire case and statute citations to relevant materials.

Am. Jur. is organized by topic, and the volumes are updated with pocket parts. The pocket parts are called **Cumulative Supplements** and are generally published annually. Each volume of Am. Jur. is numbered, and the topics and sections contained within the volume are listed on the spine; for example, Volume 25 of Am. Jur. contains Domicil to Elections §§1-206. At the beginning of each topic is an

ILLUSTRATION 5-2. Topic Outline for Easements and Licenses at 25 Am. Jur. 2d 567 (1996)

25 Am Jur 2d   EASEMENTS AND LICENSES

VI.   TRANSFER OF EASEMENT

A. EASEMENTS IN GROSS

→ § 102.   Generally

B. APPURTENANT EASEMENTS

§ 103.   Generally
§ 104.   On transfer of dominant tenement
§ 105.   On division of dominant tenement
§ 106.   On transfer of servient tenement; requirements as to notice
§ 107.   —What constitutes notice

VII.   DURATION, TERMINATION, AND REVIVAL

A. DURATION

§ 108.   Generally
§ 109.   Necessity of words of inheritance or limitation to create perpetual easement

B. TERMINATION OR EXTINGUISHMENT

§ 110.   Generally
§ 111.   Occurrence of stated event or violation of conditions
§ 112.   Abandonment
§ 113.   —Acts inconsistent with easement
§ 114.   —Nonuse; use of other way
§ 115.   Completion of purpose; change of conditions
§ 116.   Misuse
§ 117.   Merger of dominant and servient estates
§ 118.   Release; license
§ 119.   Adverse possession
§ 120.   Destruction or alteration of building or structure
§ 121.   Foreclosure of mortgage or trust deed
§ 122.   Sale for taxes; enforcement of special assessment

C. REVIVAL

§ 123.   Generally

VIII.   ACTIONS TO ESTABLISH, ENFORCE, OR PROTECT EASEMENTS

A. IN GENERAL

§ 124.   Generally
§ 125.   Persons entitled to maintain action; parties
§ 126.   —Action by owner of servient estate or his lessee

567

*Reprinted with permission from West Group.

outline listing every related subtopic. Each section within a topic refers to a subtopic; for example, under the topic of Easements and Licenses, captions indicate categories within the topics such as VI. Transfer of Easement. Under Transfer of Easement, §102 is entitled Generally. The text of Am. Jur. 2d repeats the topic and subtopic heading. See Illustration 5-3.

Notice that the topic or subtopic is first discussed generally, then the subissues are explored. To update the information found in the main volume, refer to the pocket part, or supplement, under the topic and then under the section. See Illustration 5-4. In our example, the supplement has no additional material to update §102.

Narrative text generally is omitted in the pocket part, but new and updating citation references are included. This means that citations to new cases published that support the legal premises discussed in the main text are listed so that you can find the most recent authority for the legal premise.

Am. Jur. updates its topics with a looseleaf volume entitled *New Topic Service* in which current topics, complete with text and footnotes, are contained. The looseleaf volume is updated with great speed so that when a new topic appears, it can be included quickly rather than waiting for a published volume to be printed and bound. An example of a new topic is the Americans with Disabilities Act.

Am. Jur. also published the *Desk Book*, which contains facts, charts, tables, statistics, and court rules of interest to attorneys. The *Desk Book* is published annually.

▼ How Do You Use Am. Jur.?

One approach to using Am. Jur. is the topic outline. In this method you review the topics outlined at the beginning of each topic section. See Illustration 5-2.

The index approach is more efficient than the topic outline method. At the end of the set is a multivolume index that is printed annually. Entries are organized by descriptive word and topic and include subtopics as well as cross-references. The index entries for Easement by Necessity are shown in Illustration 5-5.

If you have a statutory cite, the most efficient method is to use the separate Am. Jur. volume entitled *Table of Statutes, Rules, and Regulations Cited.* If you have a relevant *United States Code* (U.S.C.) or U.S.C.S., *Code of Federal Regulations,* or uniform law citation, the tables will indicate the precise topic and section where it is discussed. See Illustration 5-6.

▼ What Is the Citation Format for Am. Jur.?

Bluebook Rule 15.7 discusses citation style for legal encyclopedias. A citation to the discussion of easements in §102 would be as follows:

25 Am. Jur. 2d Easements and Licenses §102 (1996 & Supp. 1998)

ILLUSTRATION 5-3. Portion of Easements Entry at 25 Am. Jur. 2d §102 (1996)

| 25 Am Jur 2d | EASEMENTS AND LICENSES | § 103 |

VI. TRANSFER OF EASEMENT [§§ 102–107]

A. EASEMENTS IN GROSS [§ 102]

Research References
ALR Digest: Easements § 59.7
ALR Index: Easements
15 Am Jur Legal Forms 2d, Pipelines §§ 203:84, 203:85

§ 102. Generally

As a general rule, an easement in gross, as a right personal to the one to whom it is granted, cannot be assigned or otherwise transmitted by him to another.[3] Easements in gross may be made assignable, however, by the terms of the instrument creating the right, particularly where the easement is of a commercial character, such as an easement for a pipeline, telegraph and telephone line, or railroad right of way.[4]

B. APPURTENANT EASEMENTS [§§ 103–107]

Research References
ALR Digest: Easements §§ 2, 57-59
ALR Index: Easements

§ 103. Generally

An appurtenant easement cannot be separated from, or transferred independently of, the land to which it is appurtenant.[5] Such an easement cannot be converted into an easement in gross.[6]

§ 104. On transfer of dominant tenement

Unless expressly excepted, a transfer of real property passes all easements

3. Hanson v Fergus Falls Nat'l Bank, 242 Minn 498, 65 NW2d 857, 49 ALR2d 1379; Gross v Cizauskas (3d Dept) 53 App Div 2d 969, 385 NYS2d 832; Maw v Weber Basin Water Conservancy Dist., 20 Utah 2d 195, 436 P2d 230.

As to what constitutes an easement in gross, see § 11.

Law Reviews: Hegi, The Easement in Gross Revisited: Transferability and Divisability since 1945. 39 Vand LR 109 (January 1986).

4. Johnston v Michigan Consol. Gas Co., 337 Mich 572, 60 NW2d 464 (ovrld in part on other grounds by Morris v Metriyakool, 418 Mich 423, 344 NW2d 736); Sandy Island Corp. v Ragsdale, 246 SC 414, 143 SE2d 803.

The fact that the instrument creating an easement in gross conveys the rights in question to the grantee and "his heirs and assigns" indicates an intention to attach the attribute of assignability to the privileges. Miller v Lutheran Conference & Camp Ass'n, 331 Pa 241, 200 A 646, 130 ALR 1245.

Forms: Assignment of pipeline easement permitted—Exception of right to construct additional pipelines. 15 Am Jur Legal Forms 2d, Pipelines § 203:84.

Assignment of pipeline easement prohibited—Exception of certain subsidiaries. 15 Am Jur Legal Forms 2d, Pipelines § 203:85.

5. Mancini v Bard, 42 NY2d 28, 396 NYS2d 621, 364 NE2d 1313; William S. Stokes, Jr., Inc. v Matney, 194 Va 339, 73 SE2d 269.

As a general rule, an easement appurtenant to one parcel of land may not be extended by the owner of the dominant estate to other parcels owned by him, whether adjoining or distinct tracts, to which the easement is not appurtenant; if an easement is appurtenant to a particular parcel of land, any extension thereof to other parcels is a misuse of the easement. Brown v Voss, 105 Wash 2d 366, 715 P2d 514.

6. Mancini v Bard, 42 NY2d 28, 396 NYS2d 621, 364 NE2d 1313; William S. Stokes, Jr., Inc. v Matney, 194 Va 339, 73 SE2d 269.

675

*Reprinted with permission from West Group.

ILLUSTRATION 5-4. Pocket Part for the Easements Entry at 25 Am. Jur. 2d §79 (1996 & Supp. 1998)

§ 72 Attorney's fees

Cases

District court erred in denying intervenor's motion requesting permission to file application for attorney's fees under 42 USCS § 1973l, where intervenor intervened on behalf of defendant United States in action brought by county under 42 USCS § 1973c to get preclearance of redistricting plan, where court had dismissed action without prejudice, and intervenors were not required to file application for fees withing 14 days of court order, where case had not yet concluded on merits, and before that time parties' status and amount of fees incurred remained uncertain. Castro County, Tex. v. Crespin, 101 F.3d 121, 36 Fed. R. Serv. 3d (LCP) 518 (D.C. Cir. 1996).

§ 73 Request for three-judge court

Cases

Generally, actions by private individuals seeking declaratory and injunctive relief against violations of Voting Rights Act preclearance requirement must be referred to three-judge court for determination of whether political subdivision has adopted a change covered by Act without first obtaining preclearance. League of United Latin American Citizens (LULAC) of Texas v. State of Tex., 113 F.3d 53 (5th Cir. 1997).

§ 79 Designation of members of court

Cases

Justice Department's preclearance of recodification of election code of State of Texas did not operate to preclear county's use of partisan considerations in selecting election judges, pursuant to section of Voting Rights Act requiring political subdivisions to obtain preclearance prior to enacting voting practices different from those in effect on November 1, 1972; neither recodified statute nor State's explanations said anything about using specific, partisan-affiliation methods for selecting election judges. Foreman v. Dallas County, Tex., 117 S. Ct. 2357, 138 L. Ed. 2d 972 (U.S. Sup. Ct. 1997).

§ 80 Orders granting or denying request for three-judge court

Cases

Party objecting to new state senate district created by redistricting plan approved by federal district court had preserved issue for appellate review; party had argued before district court that existing plan should be declared unconstitutional before any new plan was approved, and had asked that state legislature and Supreme Court have opportunity to redistrict following finding of liability. Voting Rights Act of 1965, §§ 2 et seq., as amended, 42 USCA § 1973 et seq. Lawyer v. Department of Justice, 117 S. Ct. 2186, 138 L. Ed. 2d 669 (U.S. 1997).

When state takes opportunity to make its own legislative redistricting decisions, re-

view discretion of federal court is limited except to extent that redistricting plan itself runs afoul of federal law. Voting Rights Act of 1965, §§ 2 et seq., as amended, 42 USCA §§ 1973 et seq. Lawyer v. Department of Justice, 117 S. Ct. 2186, 138 L. Ed. 2d 669 (U.S. 1997).

§ 84 Appeal of order granting or denying interlocutory or permanent injunction; stay

Cases

District court determination that redistricting plan for state legislature did not subordinate traditional districting principles to race was subject to review for clear error. Voting Rights Act of 1965, § 2 et seq., as amended, 42 USCA § 1973 et seq. Lawyer v. Department of Justice, 117 S. Ct. 2186, 138 L. Ed. 2d 669 (U.S. 1997).

Preliminary injunction to prevent city officers election unless ballot includes referendum calling for citizens' police review board will not be granted, even though plaintiffs contend that city and its clerk have violated § 1983 by their unconstitutional denial of ballot access, because clerk tabulated signatures and found there to be too few to make petition for placement of referendum valid, and plaintiffs fail to demonstrate likelihood of success on merits or irreparable harm. Lee v. Smith, 927 F. Supp. 205 (E.D. Tex. 1996).

§ 103 Generally

Research References

Indirect effect of direct election: A structural examination of the Seventeenth Amendment, 49 Vand LR 6:1346 (1996).

Cases

The right to an undiluted vote, that is, the right to cast a ballot equal among voters, under the equal protection clause of the Federal Constitution's Fourteenth Amendment does not belong to a minority as a group, rather than to the group's individual members. Shaw v Hunt (1996, US) 135 L Ed 2d 207, 96 CDOS 4215, 96 Daily Journal DAR 6793, 9 FLW Fed S 686.

Voting irregularites arising from human error in conduct of elections did not rise to level of constitutional violation under 42 USCS § 1983 in absence of willful action by state officials intending to deprive individuals of their constitutional right to vote, where fair and adequate state law remedy existed to remedy election irregularities. Gold v. Feinberg, 101 F.3d 796 (2d Cir. 1996).

In fairness hearing at which district court heard objections to proposed settlement of Voting Rights Act case, court erred in inferring from fact that only two members of black community objected to proposed settlement that settlement was unobjectionable, since notice of proposed settlement was printed in very small type and couched in legalese at times so dense that even lawyer would have had difficulty determining settle-

Cumulative Supplement

---

*Reprinted with permission from West Group.

ILLUSTRATION 5-5. General Index Entry for Easements at 25 Am. Jur. 2d 985 (1998)

GENERAL INDEX

EASEMENTS—Cont'd
Highways and streets—Cont'd
  turnpikes and toll roads and bridges, **Highways § 612, 625, 627**
Hostile use. Prescriptive easements, infra
Implied easements
  general discussion, **Ease § 23-44**
  manner and extent of use, **Ease § 91, 92**
  map or plat, conveyance with reference to, **Ease § 25, 26**
  necessity, ways of, infra
  pre-existing uses, implication of easement from, infra
  severance of property. creation of easement on, generally, **Ease § 27-44**
  streets, alleys, parks and other open areas, extent of easement in, **Ease § 26**
  way or street, conveyance of land bound by, **Ease § 24**
Infants
  disaffirmance of easements, **Inf § 88**
  guardian and ward, **Guar & W § 110, 140**
In gross or appurtenant easements, generally, **Ease § 10-12, 102-107**
Inheritance, creation of perpetual easement, **Ease § 109**
Injunctions (this index)
Insurance, **Ins § 169**
Interference with easements. Obstructions and interference, infra
Interruption of use, acquisition of prescriptive easement, **Ease § 68-70**
Intoxicating liquors, covenant not to sell liquor as creating negative easement, **Intox L § 539**
Irrigation (this index)
Judgments, **Decl J § 164, 165, 229, 231**
Judicial sales, **Jud S § 248**
Knowledge. Notice, infra
Landlord and Tenant (this index)
Licenses in Real Property (this index)
Liens and encumbrances
  mechanics' liens, **Mech L § 40**
Life tenants and remaindermen, **Ease § 108; Life Ten § 2, 3, 17**
Light, Air, or View (this index)
Limitations, **Ease § 81, 133**
Location
  general discussion, **Ease § 74-80**
  agreement or acquiescence, location of way by, **Ease § 77**
  change of location, **Ease § 79**
  court, location by, **Ease § 78**
  deviation from route, **Ease § 80**
  effect of designation, **Ease § 79**
  existing way as that impliedly intended, **Ease § 75**
  right of parties to designate location, **Ease § 76, 77**
Logs and Timber (this index)
Maintenance and repairs, **Ease § 94, 95**
Manner of use, generally, **Ease § 81-93**
Mechanics' liens, **Mech L § 40**

EASEMENTS—Cont'd
Merger of estates, **Ease § 117; Estates § 379**
Misuse of easement, **Ease § 116**
Modification. Change or modification, supra
Monopolies, restraint of trade, and unfair competition, **Monop § 990**
Mortgages
  general discussion, **Mort § 816**
  termination of easement by foreclosure of trust deed, **Ease § 121**
Municipal Corporations and Other Political Subdivisions (this index)
Natural rights, compared and distinguished, **Ease § 6**
Nature, **Ease § 2, 137**
Navigable water, way of necessity where land borders on, **Ease § 44, 93**
Necessity, ways of
  general discussion, **Ease § 36-44**
  basis, **Ease § 37**
  burden of proof, **Ease § 135**
  deeds, **Deeds § 81**
  degree of necessity required, **Ease § 42**
  manner and extent of use, **Ease § 92**
  manner of severance, **Ease § 40**
  navigable water, land bordering on, **Ease § 44, 93**
  necessity, requirement of, **Ease § 41-44**
  other way, effect of existence of, **Ease § 43**
  pre-existing uses, implication of easement from, infra
  prior use, distinction from easement implied by, **Ease § 38**
  requisites, **Ease § 39-44**
  unity and subsequent severance of ownership or title, **Ease § 39**
Negative easements
  general discussion, **Ease § 8**
  eminent domain, **Em Dom § 175**
Nonapparent or apparent easements, **Ease § 9, 32**
Notice or knowledge
  acquisition of prescriptive easement, **Ease § 72, 73**
  revocation of license, **Ease § 147**
  transfer of easement on transfer of servient tenement, **Ease § 106, 107**
Notorious use, acquisition of prescriptive easement, **Ease § 60**
Nuisances (this index)
Obstructions and interference
  general discussion, **Ease § 98-101**
  pipelines, **Pipe § 30, 36, 37**
Oil. **Gas and Oil** (this index)
Open use, acquisition of prescriptive easement, **Ease § 60**
Operation, generally, **Ease § 81-101**
Owner of fee or lesser estate, creation of easement by, **Ease § 14**
Parking, **Decl J § 164**
Parks, Squares, and Playgrounds (this index)

EASEMENTS—Cont'd
Parol and extrinsic evidence, will, showing nature and extent of easement accompanying real property in connection with construction of, **Wills § 1314**
Partition (this index)
Party walls, **Party W § 21-23**
Penal and correctional institutions, **Penal Inst § 9**
Permanency of use, implication of easement from pre-existing uses, **Ease § 33**
Permissive use, effect on acquisition of prescriptive easement, **Ease § 65, 66**
Perpetual easement, necessity of words of inheritance or limitation to create, **Ease § 109**
Perpetuities and restraints on alienation, **Perp § 49**
Persons who may create easements, **Ease § 13-15**
Pipes and Pipelines (this index)
Place. Location, supra
Pleading, generally, **Ease § 132; Plead § 21**
Pollution, **Poll Cont § 569-570**
Possession. Adverse possession, supra
Powers of appointment and alienation, **Powers § 47, 55**
Pre-existing uses, implication of easement from
  general discussion, **Ease § 27-35**
  apparentness of use, **Ease § 32**
  basis or rationale of rule, **Ease § 29**
  continuousness of use, **Ease § 34**
  implied reservation, **Ease § 28**
  manner of severance, **Ease § 30**
  necessity, distinction from way of, **Ease § 38**
  necessity of use, **Ease § 35**
  permanency of use, **Ease § 33**
  presumptions, **Ease § 29**
  quasi-easement, **Ease § 31**
  requisites, **Ease § 30-35**
  unity and subsequent severance of title, **Ease § 30, 31**
Premises Liability (this index)
Prescriptive easements
  general discussion, **Ease § 45-73**
  adverse or hostile use, generally, **Ease § 61-67**
  adverse possession, relation to, **Ease § 57**
  burden of proof, **Ease § 136**
  claim of right, **Ease § 63**
  color of title, **Ease § 64**
  common use with adjacent owners, acquisition of, **Ease § 52**
  continuous and uninterrupted use, **Ease § 68-70**
  definite line of travel with respect to way, **Ease § 59**
  dominant and servient tracts in same ownership, **Ease § 49**
  drains, pipes and sewers, **Ease § 55**
  exclusive use, **Ease § 71**
  knowledge and acquiescence of servient owner, **Ease § 72, 73**
  manner and extent of use, **Ease § 93**
  open, visible and notorious use, **Ease § 60**

For assistance using this Index, call 1-800-527-0430 **985**

*Reprinted with permission from West Group.

3. *Corpus Juris Secundum*

▼ What Is Contained in *Corpus Juris Secundum*?

Corpus Juris Secundum, commonly known as C.J.S., is the other predominant encyclopedia that is national in scope. C.J.S. is a West

ILLUSTRATION 5-6. Table of Statutes, Rules, and Regulations Cited at Am. Jur. 2d 748 (1996)

TABLE OF STATUTES

UNITED STATES CODE SERVICE—Continued

Title and section 49 USCS	Am Jur 2d title and section
	Public Utilities § 207*
10707(a)	Carriers § 34*, 67*
10707a	Public Utilities § 225*
10708	Carriers § 105*, 140*; Public Utilities § 211*
10709	Carriers § 82*, 137*; Railroads § 36*
10712	Carriers § 105*; Public Utilities § 211*
10713 ...	Carriers § 177*; Freedom of Information Acts § 3; Public Utilities § 211*
10721	Carriers § 105*, 117*, 118*
10721 to 10724	Carriers § 22*, 57*, 107*, 113*, 117*, 209*, 341*, 792*, 844*, 845*
10721(a)(1)	Post Office § 76
10726	Carriers § 205*, 206*; Public Utilities § 214*, 215*
10729	Carriers § 191*
10730 ...	Carriers § 264*, 518*, 539*, 549*, 555*, 579*, 600*, 601*, 640*, 700*, 701*, 702*, 703*, 705*, 706*, 707*, 708*, 1237*, 1310*; Public Utilities § 211*
10730(a)	Carriers § 539*
10730(c)	Public Utilities § 211*
10731(e)	Carriers § 67*
10741 ...	Carriers § 107*, 139*, 177*, 180*, 187*, 202*, 209*
10741 to 10744	Carriers § 473*, 474*, 672*; Public Utilities § 212*; Railroads § 216*, 255*
10743	Carriers § 473*, 474*
10744	Carriers § 473*, 474*
10747	Carriers § 144*, 470*
10761	Carriers § 107*, 113*, 341*
10761(a)	Carriers § 107*
10762	Carriers § 107*, 113*, 341*
10762(a)(1)	Carriers § 107*

Title and section 49 USCS	Am Jur 2d title and section
10764	Carriers § 35*, 791*
10766	Carriers § 180*
10767	Carriers § 108*
10781 to 10786	Mandamus § 16*; Public Utilities § 208*
10901	Railroads § 69*
10903	Carriers § 142*; Railroads § 69*, 82*, 185*, 188*
10903(a)	Railroads § 185*
10904	Carriers § 35*, 48*; Railroads § 185*, 188*
10905	Railroads § 185*, 188*
10906	Eminent Domain § 939; Railroads § 185*
10908	Carriers § 34*, 47*, 48*; Public Utilities § 222*, 254*; Railroads § 188*, 344*
10909	Carriers § 34*, 47*, 48*; Public Utilities § 222*, 254*; Railroads § 188*, 344*
10910	Labor and Labor Relations § 121; Railroads § 188*
10921	Carriers § 77*, 78*, 80*, 86*, 791*
10921 et seq	Carriers § 100*
10922	Carriers § 42*, 77*, 78*, 80*, 81*, 82*, 83*, 84*, 86*, 87*
10922(a)(1)	Carriers § 82*
10923	Carriers § 87*, 99*, 100*, 102*, 104*
10924	Carriers § 77*, 791*
10925	Carriers § 90*, 96*, 97*
10926	Carriers § 90*, 96*, 97*
10927	Automobiles and Highway Traffic § 164, 166*; Carriers § 34*, 45*, 421*, 791*; Labor and Labor Relations § 927
10927(b)	Automobiles and Highway Traffic § 166*; Carriers § 421*

*Designates supplement references

Am Jur 2d

---

*Reprinted with permission from West Group.

publication, and other West materials are referred to in its text. The most notable reference in C.J.S. is to the West topics and key numbers, thereby tying the encyclopedia to the West National Reporter system and the West Digests. See Illustration 5-7. This attribute makes C.J.S. a very powerful research tool.

C.J.S. is organized by titles, which are the individual legal subjects. At the beginning of each title is a section analysis that outlines the legal issues and subissues within the subject. The volumes are numbered and contain the various titles in alphabetical order; for example, Volume 28A contains the titles Drugs and Narcotics 224 to End to Election of Remedies or Rights or Theories of Recovery. Easements is one of the titles within the volume because it falls alphabetically after Drugs but before Election. Footnotes within the text refer the reader to case citations. Each volume of C.J.S. is updated by a pocket part that contains subsequent citations and references to support the legal premises discussed in the main volume. See Illustration 5-8. The pocket parts also have Library References at the beginning of various sections that indicate the correlating topic and key number in the West Digest system. C.J.S. is updated in the same manner as Am. Jur.

C.J.S. has a multivolume general index that is replaced annually. The general index is located in the last volumes of the set.

▼ How Do You Use C.J.S.?

There are two methods of using C.J.S. In the title analysis method, you review the title outline at the beginning of the subject or title and read the entry under the appropriate section.

In the general index method you look up the appropriate subject in the book's general index just as you would in any book's index to obtain references to titles and section. If nothing is relevant, you may be given a *See also* instruction, indicating that you should look up the subject using a different word.

C.J.S. is particularly helpful if you want to obtain relevant topics and key numbers to use the West Digest system. See Illustration 5-7.

▼ How Is C.J.S. Cited?

Bluebook Rule 15.7 discusses citation style for legal encyclopedias. A citation to the discussion of easements in §18 would be as follows:

28A C.J.S. Easements §18 (1996 & Supp. 1998)

4. State Law Encyclopedias

▼ Are There Any Legal Encyclopedias for State Law?

Yes, almost every jurisdiction has a legal encyclopedia. Illinois, for example, has *Illinois Law and Practice,* commonly known as I.L.P.

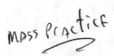

Mass Practice

ILLUSTRATION 5-7. Easements Entry at 28A C.J.S. §18 (1996 & Supp. 1998)
Note 1. References to West topics and key numbers
Note 2. References to case citations

28A C.J.S.   EASEMENTS § 18

presumed grant;[63] and members of the general public cannot, by routine and regular use, create a prescriptive easement on behalf of the landholder.[64] However, the state may, upon a proper showing, successfully claim an easement by prescription on behalf of the public;[65] and a public easement such as a public footway in connection with a railroad bridge,[66] a ford,[67] or a landing,[68] provided it is connected with a public street or road extending to the river,[69] have been spoken of as arising by prescription.

For purposes of establishing a prescriptive easement, public usage will not give any one person or entity any property right in the disputed area; if the public's adverse use continues long enough to establish a public easement, all members of the public will have equal usage rights.[70]

Association or club.

Prescriptive use of property by members of an association or club for purposes of the association or club may serve as a basis for the acquisition of an easement by the club or association, or by its individual members.[71]

§ 18. Against Whom Prescription Runs and Property Subject Thereto

    a. Government and governmental subdivisions

    b. Persons capable or incapable of making grant or resisting use

    c. Property subject to prescription

a. Government and Governmental Subdivisions

Unless allowed by statute an easement, ordinarily, cannot be acquired by prescription against the government, federal or state, or a subdivision thereof.

Library References

Easements ⬦—4, 5.

An easement by prescription cannot be acquired against the government,[72] nor against a subdivision thereof, as to property held for the public.[73]

United States.

In the absence of enabling statutes no prescriptive rights can be acquired against the United States;[74] and where land is owned by the United States, adverse user of an easement over such land cannot begin until the title has passed to a private grantee.[75]

States.

While there is authority apparently to the contrary,[76] it is generally held an easement cannot be acquired, in real property, by prescription against a state, its subdivisions, or persons holding thereunder,[77] at least where the real property is held in fee

---

63. Conn.—Turner v. Selectmen of Hebron, 22 A. 951, 61 Conn. 175.

64. Ind.—Greenco, Inc. v. May, App. 1 Dist., 506 N.E.2d 42.

65. Tex.—Villa Nova Resort, Inc. v. State, App.–Corpus Christi, 711 S.W.2d 120.

66. Ky.—Kentucky Cent. Ry. Co. v. City of Paris, 27 S.W. 84, 95 Ky. 627.

67. Tex.—City of Austin v. Hall, 58 S.W. 1038, 24 Tex.Civ.App. 412.

68. Mass.—Coolidge v. Learned, 8 Pick. 504.

S.C.—State v. Randall, 32 S.C.L. 110.

69. Del.—State v. Reybold, 5 Harr. 484, 5 Del. 484.

S.C.—State v. Randall, 32 S.C.L. 110.

70. Access drive

Ohio—J.F. Gioia, Inc. v. Cardinal American Corp., 491 N.E.2d 325, 23 Ohio App.3d 33, 23 O.B.R. 76.

71. Easement in gross

Utah—Crane v. Crane, 683 P.2d 1062.

Right to use beach

Where members of club believed their right to use beach derived from their membership and participation in club and was not right which they had as individuals or by reason of their residence, where this use was in the presence of defendant's predecessors in title and acts performed indicating right to use of beach were acts done by club and not independent acts done by members in their individual capacities, and where defendants were forewarned in their deed that predecessors in title recognized adverse claims relative to use of beach area,

trial court did not err in finding prescriptive right in the use of beach by club.

Conn.—Sauden Point Ass'n, Inc. v. Cannon, 418 A.2d 70, 117 Conn. 413.

72. Ind.—Randall v. Board of Com'rs of Tippecanoe County, 131 N.E. 776, 77 Ind.App. 320, error dismissed 43 S.Ct. 252, 261 U.S. 252, 67 L.Ed. 556.

73. Ind.—Randall v. Board of Com'rs of Tippecanoe County, 131 N.E. 776, 77 Ind.App. 320, error dismissed 43 S.Ct. 252, 261 U.S. 252, 67 L.Ed. 556.

Municipality or municipal corporation

N.Y.—Firsty v. De Thomasis, 3 Dept., 576 N.Y.S.2d 454, 177 A.D.2d 839.

Wash.—City of Benton City v. Adrian, 748 P.2d 679, 50 Wash.App. 330, reconsideration denied.

74. Cal.—Smith v. Hawkins, 42 P. 453, 110 C. 122.

Or.—Miser v. O'Shea, 62 P. 491, 37 Or. 231.

75. U.S.—Union Mill & Mining Co. v. Ferries, C.C.Nev., 24 F.Cas. No. 14,371, 2 Sawy. 176.

N.M.—Herbertson v. Iliff, App., 775 P.2d 754, 108 N.M. 552, certiorari denied 775 P.2d 251, 108 N.M. 485.

76. Tex.—City of Austin v. Hall, 58 S.W. 1038, 24 Tex.Civ.App. 412.

77. Alaska—Classen v. State, Dept. of Highways, 621 P.2d 15.

N.M.—Matthews v. State, App., 825 P.2d 224, 113 N.M. 291.

197

---

*Reprinted with permission from West Group.

ILLUSTRATION 5-8. Pocket Part for Easements Entry at 28A C.J.S. §18 (1996 & Supp. 1998) Note that pocket part updates main volume entry. Pocket part is organized by topic and section.

28A CJS 5

§ 10. —— Easements Appurtenant in General

page 182

3. Ind.—Consolidation Coal Co. v. Mutchman, App. 1 Dist., 565 N.E.2d 1074, transfer den., reh. den. 589 N.E.2d 1163, app. after remand 666 N.E.2d 461, reh. den., transfer den.

9. Benefit in physical use
Ind.—Consolidation Coal Co. v. Mutchman, App. 1 Dist., 565 N.E.2d 1074, transfer den., reh. den. 589 N.E.2d 1163, app. after remand 666 N.E.2d 461, reh. den., transfer den.

page 183

§ 11. —— Easements in Gross in General

21. Not incident of possession
Ind.—Consolidation Coal Co. v. Mutchman, App. 1 Dist., 565 N.E.2d 1074, transfer den. reh. den. 589 N.E.2d 1163, app. after remand 666 N.E.2d 461, reh. den., transfer den.

page 184

24. Ind.—Consolidation Coal Co. v. Mutchman, App. 1 Dist., 565 N.E.2d 1074, transfer den., reh. den. 589 N.E.2d 1163, app. after remand 666 N.E.2d 461, reh. den., transfer den.
25. Va.—Hise v. BARC Elec. Co-op., 492 S.E.2d 154 (Va. 1997).

§ 12. —— Determination Whether Easement is Appurtenant or in Gross

page 186

44. Right to haul coal
Ind.—Consolidation Coal Co. v. Mutchman, App. 1 Dist., 565 N.E.2d 1074, transfer den., reh. den. 589 N.E.2d 1163, app. after remand 666 N.E.2d 461, reh. den., transfer den.

page 189

75. Ind.—Consolidation Coal Co. v. Mutchman, App. 1 Dist., 565 N.E.2d 1074, transfer den., reh. den. 589 N.E.2d 1163, app. after remand 666 N.E.2d 461, reh. den., transfer den.

§ 13. General Considerations

page 191

Language in a deed which provides that upon the occurrence of a stated event the conveyor shall have the power to terminate the estate so created does not create an easement in the property.[95.5]

95.5 Neb.—State, Dept. of Roads v. Union Pacific R. Co., 490 N.W.2d 461, 241 Neb. 675, 242 Neb. 97, mod., overruling George v. Pracheil, 137 N.W. 880, 92 Neb. 81.

page 192

§ 14. General Considerations

Noncontiguousness does not bar the establishment of a prescriptive easement.[10.5]

10.5 Direct and apparent correction with dominant tenement sufficient
Tenn.—Pevear v. Hunt, App., 924 S.W.2d 114.

§ 15. Time Requisite for Acquisition of Easement by Prescription

page 194

29. Miss.—Rutland v. Stewart, 630 So.2d 996, overruling McIntyre v. Harvey, 128 So. 572, 158 Miss. 16, to the extent that it hold that tacking may not be applied to establish an easement by prescription.

§ 21. In General

page 200

9. Proof required
Prescriptive easement cannot be acquired without proof of adverse use, a claim of right under color of title or claim of right, use of such a kind as to put the owner of a subservient estate on notice of claim, and use that is continuous and uninterrupted adverse use for at least ten years.
Wyo.—A.B. Cattle Co. v. Forgey Ranches, Inc., 943 P.2d 1184 (Wyo. 1997).

page 203

§ 23. With Knowledge and Acquiescence of Owner

66. Mere acquiescence insufficient
Landowners' acquiescence in mere use by neighbors of road on their property for seven years, without notice of adverse use in the form of making repairs or otherwise, did not authorize grant of prescriptive easement to neighbors; owners' acquiescence in mere use of road established, at most, a revocable license.
Ga.—Eileen B. White & Associates, Inc. v. Gunnells, 434 S.E.2d 477, 263 Ga. 360, overruling Rizer v. Harris, 354 S.E.2d 660, 182 Ga.App. 31, and Fine v. Strauss, 71 S.E.2d 580, 86 Ga.App. 354.

§ 32. —— Claim of Right as Element

page 211

78. Use of private roadway
Conn.—Gioielli v. Mallard Cove Condominium Ass'n, Inc., 658 A.2d 134, 37 Conn.App. 822.

§ 57. Construction and Operation of Grant

page 238

19. La.—Gravolet v. Board of Com'rs for Grand Prairie Levee Dist., App. 4 Cir., 598 So.2d 1231, app. after remand 676 So.2d 199, 95–2477 (La. App. 4 Cir. 6/12/96).

§ 60. Reservations, Exceptions, and Conditions

page 244

13. Wis.—Matter of Parcel of Land Located on Geneva Lake, Town of Linn, Walworth County, App., 477 N.W.2d 333, 165 Wis.2d 235, app. after remand 552 N.W.2d 898, 204 Wis.2d 109, review den. 555 N.W.2d 815, 205 Wis.2d 135.

§ 94. Unity of Title

page 277

87. Okl.—DeWitt v. Cavender, App., 878 P.2d 1077.

§ 98. —— Access by Waterway

page 282

41. Sea
Access to landowner's land was not cut off such that property was landlocked as would support creation of

EASEMENTS § 117
Page 300

easement by necessity over adjoining parcel of land where there was evidence that land could be reasonably reached by sea.
Me.—Amodeo v. Francis, 681 A.2d 462.

page 287

§ 106. In General

3. Right of review
Condemnees could appeal condemnation of easement of necessity, even though condemnees had cashed check representing amount of commissioners' award, where condemnees made no application to court for disbursing funds, and condemnors did not move that funds stay with court clerk.
Okl.—McMillian v. Holcomb, 907 P.2d 1034.

§ 111. As Appurtenant to Dominant Estate

page 292

72. Ind.—Consolidation Coal Co. v. Mutchman, App. 1 Dist., 565 N.E.2d 1074, transfer den., reh. den. 589 N.E.2d 1163, app. after remand 666 N.E.2d 461, reh. den., transfer den.
73. Vertical privity required
Wis.—Matter of Parcel of Land Located on Geneva Lake, Town of Linn, Walworth County, App., 477 N.W.2d 333, 165 Wis.2d 235, app. after remand 552 N.W.2d 898, 204 Wis.2d 109, review den. 555 N.W.2d 815, 205 Wis.2d 135.
Horizontal privity
Wis.—Matter of Parcel of Land Located on Geneva Lake, Town of Linn, Walworth County, App., 477 N.W.2d 333, 165 Wis.2d 235, app. after remand 552 N.W.2d 898, 204 Wis.2d 109, review den. 555 N.W.2d 815, 205 Wis.2d 135.
74. Wis.—Matter of Parcel of Land Located on Geneva Lake, Town of Linn, Walworth County, App., 477 N.W.2d 333, 165 Wis.2d 235, app. after remand 552 N.W.2d 898, 204 Wis.2d 109, review den. 555 N.W.2d 815, 205 Wis.2d 135.

page 295

§ 113. Continuous and Apparent Easements and Notice

8. Constructive notice from deed of direct predecessor in title
N.Y.—Breakers Motel, Inc. v. Sunbeach Montauk Two, Inc., 2 Dept., 638 N.Y.S.2d 135, 224 A.D.2d 473, app. dism. 672 N.E.2d 608, 88 N.Y.2d 1016, 649 N.Y.S.2d 382.

§ 114. —— Requisites and Sufficiency of Notice

page 296

17. Minn.—Petition of Willmus, 568 N.W.2d 722 (Minn. Ct. App. 1997), review denied, (Oct. 21, 1997).

page 298

32. Inquiry in exercise of ordinary diligence
Ga.—Carroll v. Pierce, 472 S.E.2d 560, 221 Ga.App. 805.

page 300

§ 117. Termination in General

70. Consent, prescription, abandonment, or merger
Or.—Cotsifas v. Conrad, 905 P.2d 851, 137 Or.App. 468.

---

*Reprinted with permission from West Group.

I.L.P. is published by West and refers the reader to the other West resources such as the key numbers and the digests. West publishes many state encyclopedias.

5. Online Encyclopedia Services

▼ Are Legal Encyclopedias Available on LEXIS or WESTLAW?

Legal encyclopedias are available online. Am. Jur. is on LEXIS. Selected portions of C.J.S. are on WESTLAW. Am. Jur. is on WESTLAW as well.

E. *AMERICAN LAW REPORTS*

▼ What Are *American Law Reports?*

The *American Law Reports* (A.L.R.), formerly published by Lawyers Cooperative Publishing Co. and new produced by West Group, contain annotations on narrow, well-defined legal topics. Each volume contains at least a half dozen annotations, or in-depth articles, about a legal issue and the pivotal case that prompted the examination of the issue. Subjects common to A.L.R. are torts, property, contracts, sales, and criminal law. Federal and state law are combined in A.L.R. until 1969. A.L.R. Federal (A.L.R. Fed.) began to be published in 1969. A.L.R. is in its 5th series. In print and updated with pocket part supplements are A.L.R., A.L.R.2d, A.L.R.3d, A.L.R.4th, and A.L.R.5th. A.L.R. is published sequentially, just like case reporters, so that when a number of annotations are written, although they may bear no subject relationship to one another (just as with opinions), a volume of A.L.R. is published. A new volume is published about every six weeks.

Each volume of A.L.R. contains cases and annotations. The first section in each volume is a list entitled Subjects Annotated in this Volume. This provides a cross-reference for the annotations in the volume. The next section is *Table of Cases Reported,* which lists the full text decisions in the volume. Because every annotation is developed from a pivotal legal decision, A.L.R. reprints the full text of that decision before the annotation. A.L.R.5th puts the decisions in the back of each volume. Researchers can also find the decisions by using the *American Law Reports Digest.* The Digest has synopses of the case opinions, and the cases themselves are cross-referenced and in A.L.R. volumes to the Digest headnotes. Following the text of each decision is the annotation, for example, the annotation entitled Locating Easement of Way Created by Necessity. The first page containing library references leads you to many other relevant practice

ILLUSTRATION 5-9. Total Client-Service Library References at 36 A.L.R.4th 769 (1985)

ANNOTATION

LOCATING EASEMENT OF WAY CREATED BY NECESSITY

by

William B. Johnson, J.D.

TOTAL CLIENT-SERVICE LIBRARY® REFERENCES

25 Am Jur 2d, Easements and Licenses §§ 64–69

Annotations: See the related matters listed in the annotation, infra.

9 Am Jur Pl & Pr Forms (Rev), Easements and Licenses, Forms 41–48

3 Am Jur Proof of Facts 2d 647, Abandonment of Easement; 5 Am Jur Proof of Facts 2d 621, Intent to Create Negative Easement; 33 Am Jur Proof of Facts 2d 669, Extent of Easement Over Servient Estate

22 Am Jur Trials 743, Condemnation of Easements

L Ed Index to Annos, Real Property; Trespass

ALR Quick Index, Access; Adjoining or Abutting Landowners; Easements; Ingress and Egress; Place or Location; Right of Way; Trespass; Way by Necessity

Federal Quick Index, Adjoining Landowners and Property; Easements and Right of Way; Ingress; Place and Location; Trespass

Auto-Cite®: Any case citation herein can be checked for form, parallel references, later history, and annotation references through the Auto-Cite computer research system.

---

*Reprinted with permission from West Group.

aids. See Illustration 5-9. The next entry is a detailed outline of the annotation so that if you are interested in only a portion of the discussion, you can focus your research efforts. There is also an index so that you can see which subjects are discussed by section. See Illustration 5-10. Following the index is the Table of Jurisdictions Represented. See Illustration 5-11. The Table of Jurisdictions Represented makes A.L.R. a unique resource because the annotation includes every relevant statute or case from all of the appropriate jurisdictions. This is a windfall for the researcher.

▼ How Do You Use A.L.R.?

There are four basic methods of using A.L.R.

1. **The index method.** A.L.R. has a subject index for A.L.R.2d

ILLUSTRATION 5-10.   Outline of Annotation at 36 A.L.R. 4th 770 (1985)

EASEMENT OF WAY BY NECESSITY—LOCATION   36 ALR4th
36 ALR4th 769

Locating easement of way created by necessity

INDEX

*Reprinted with permission from West Group.

ILLUSTRATION 5-11.   Table of Jurisdictions Represented at 36 A.L.R.4th 771 1985)

TABLE OF JURISDICTIONS REPRESENTED
Consult POCKET PART in this volume for later cases

I. Preliminary matters

§ 1. Introduction

[a] Scope

This annotation[1] collects and analyzes the state and federal cases in which the courts have determined, or discussed how to determine, the location[2]—initially or on relocation—of an easement of way created[3] by necessity.[4]

This annotation includes cases in-through A.L.R.4th, A.L.R. Fed., and *U.S. Supreme Court Reports, Lawyers' Edition*. See Illustration 5-12. It also contains a *Table of Statutes, Rules, and Regulations*. A.L.R. (first series) has a separate index entitled the *Quick Index*. See Illustration 5-13. The index method requires that you find descriptive words for the issue or topic you are researching in one of A.L.R.'s indexes. This is a very efficient method.

2. **The digest method.** The A.L.R. Digest is organized like any other digest in topics and sections. See Illustration 5-14. Each section stands for a point of law. Under the digest entry is an encyclopedia reference to Am. Jur., if relevant, and to the case that stands for that premise of law. If a case is given a digest entry, then you may assume that an annotation will follow the case in the A.L.R. volume. This is a very good way to find multiple cases and multiple annotations dealing with related legal issues. This method is best when you find a good case that forms the basis for an annotation.

3. **The computerized method.** This is the best method of accessing A.L.R. annotations when available. LEXIS has the full text of A.L.R. online, and WESTLAW has A.L.R.3d-5th and A.L.R. Fed. Using online access permits you to search for relevant annotations using the words that you think would appear in an annotation on point.

4. *Shepard's.* This is also an excellent way to find A.L.R. annotations. *Shepard's* lists any A.L.R. citations in which the opinion is cited. See Illustration 5-15.

▼ Why Would You Use A.L.R.?

A.L.R. is best consulted when you are researching a narrow, well-defined issue, similar to how you might use a law review article. The major difference between A.L.R. and a law review article is that A.L.R. provides you with indexed terms, an outline, a table of law from other jurisdictions, and library references to encyclopedias, form books, and digest topics. A.L.R., however, is not considered nearly as scholarly as a law review article.

It is best not to cite A.L.R. annotations and to not rely on them as authority unless absolutely necessary. Cite to the primary source materials that A.L.R. annotations provide.

▼ How Do You Cite to an A.L.R. Annotation?

Citation style for A.L.R. is found in Bluebook Rule 16.5.5. An example would be the following:

> William B. Johnson, Annotation, Locating Easement of Way Created by Necessity, 36 A.L.R.4th 769 (1985 & Supp. 1997)

▼ How Do You Update an A.L.R. Annotation?

A.L.R. (first series) Volumes 1 to 175 are updated in the *Blue Book of Supplemental Decisions*. This is a separate set of books that comes

ILLUSTRATION 5-12. A.L.R. Index Entry for Easements in A.L.R. Index

ALR INDEX

EARTHQUAKES—Cont'd

Property insurance, construction and effect of provision excluding loss caused by earth movement or earthquake, 44 ALR3d 1316

Res ipsa loquitur as applicable in actions for damage to property by the overflow or escape of water, 91 ALR3d 186, § 3[b]

EASEMENTS

For digest treatment, see title **Easements in ALR Digest**

Abstract of title, liability of one preparing abstract of title, for deficiencies therein, to one other than person directly contracting for abstract, 34 ALR3d 1122, §§ 2[b], 4, 5, 10

Access roads
- grant which does not specify location, 24 ALR4th 1053, §§ 5, 8, 13[b]
- inadequate access, way of necessity where a means of access does exist, but is claimed to be inadequate, inconvenient, difficult, or costly, 10 ALR4th 447
- locating easement of way created by necessity, 36 ALR4th 769
- part of land is inaccessible, 10 ALR4th 500

Access, scope of prescriptive easement for access (easement of way), 79 ALR4th 604

Adverse possession
- building, adverse possession based on encroachment of building or other structure, 2 ALR3d 1005, §§ 3[a, b], 8-11
- loss of private easement by, 25 ALR2d 1265
- prescriptive easements, see group Prescriptive easements in this topic
- presumptions and evidence respecting identification of land on which property taxes were paid to establish adverse possession, 36 ALR4th 843, § 6[a]

Alleys
- location, easement of way created by grant which does not specify location, 24 ALR4th 1053, § 9[a]
- maps, conveyance with reference to map or plat as giving purchaser rights in indicated streets, alleys, or areas not abutting his lot, 7 ALR2d 607

EASEMENTS—Cont'd

Alleys—Cont'd
- tacking as applied to prescriptive easements, 72 ALR3d 648, §§ 49, 9 10, 12[a], 15[b], 18, 19

Animals, liability of person, other than owner of animal or owner or operator of motor vehicle, for damage to motor vehicle or injury to person riding therein resulting from collision with domestic animal at large in street or highway, 21 ALR4th 132, §§ 3[a], 5, 6

Arbitration, contract containing arbitration as subject to the stay and enforcement provisions of United States Arbitration Act, federal cases 18 L Ed 2d 1685, § 12

Automobiles and highway traffic, parking on private way, 37 ALR2d 944

Beaches and shores
- location, easement of way created by grant which does not specify location, 24 ALR4th 1053, § 9[a]
- tacking as applied to prescriptive easements, 72 ALR3d 648, §§ 9[a] 11[a]

Boating, fishing, wading or recreational rights of public in inland streams the bed of which is privately owned 6 ALR4th 1030, § 6[b]

Bridges
- accessibility, way of necessity over another's land where a means of access does exist, but is claimed to be inadequate, inconvenient, difficult, or costly, 10 ALR4th 447, §§ 6, 7[a], 9[b]-11[a], 12, 13
- locating easement of way created by necessity, 36 ALR4th 769, §§ 7[a] 9[a]

Cemeteries
- eminent domain, unsightliness of powerline or other wire, or related structure, as element of damages in easement condemnation proceeding, 97 ALR3d 587, §§ 3[b] 6
- locating easement of way created by necessity, 36 ALR4th 769, §§ 7[a] 8[a]

Change or modification
- acquisition of right of way by prescription as affected by change of location or deviation during prescriptive period, 80 ALR2d 1095

*Reprinted with permission from West Group.

ILLUSTRATION 5-13. A.L.R. First Series Quick Index Entry for Easements

Construction contract: construction and application of provision of construction contract as regards retention of percentage of current earnings until completion, 107 ALR 960

Damages—

earnings or income, other than railroad earnings as proper matters for consideration in fixing damages under Federal Employers' Liability Act, 102 ALR 560

measure of damages for loss of earning capacity of person engaged in business for himself, 9 ALR 510, supp 27 ALR 430, 63 ALR 142, 122 ALR 297

on account of loss of earnings or impairment of earning capacity due to wife's personal injury as recoverable by her or by her husband, 151 ALR 479

Employer's right to earnings or profits made by employee, 13 ALR 905, supp 71 ALR 933

Future earnings, see **Future Matters or Acts**

Municipality: disposition of revenues from operation of revenue-producing enterprise owned by municipal corporation, 103 ALR 579, supp 165 ALR 854

Profits, see **Rents and Profits**

Public officer or employee: earnings or opportunity of earning from other sources as reducing claim of public officer or employee wrongfully excluded from his office or position, 150 ALR 100

Wills: right of specific or demonstrative legatee or devisee (or general legatee for the payment of whose legacy there is a direction to set aside or a setting aside of property) to earnings, dividends, and accretions between time of testator's death and payment of the legacy, 116 ALR 1129

Workmen's compensation—

construction, application, and effect of provisions of workmen's compensation acts that made one's status as employee dependent upon amount of earnings, 87 ALR 958

crediting employer or insurance carrier with earnings of employee re-employed, or continued in employment, after injury, 175 ALR 725, supp 84 ALR2d 1108

Workmen's compensation—Cont'd

deductions allowable in computing earnings as basis of compensation, 22 ALR 864

duty of injured employee to submit to operation or to take other measures to restore earning capacity, 6 ALR 1260, supp 18 ALR 431, 73 ALR 1303, 105 ALR 1470

expense money as a factor in computing one's earnings, salary, or compensation as regards his status as an employee within the workmen's compensation act or the amount of compensation under the act in event of his injury or death, 94 ALR 763

right to take rise or fall in wages since date of accident into account in fixing workman's compensation, 2 ALR 1642, supp 92 ALR 1188

time as of which earnings are to be considered in computing compensation for an injury or incapacity ultimately resulting from causes not immediately operative, 86 ALR 524

EARTHQUAKE

Injury during earthquake as within workmen's compensation act, 54 ALR 1396

EASEMENTS

For correlative topic, see **Right of Way**

§ 1. **Creation or acquisition, generally**
§ 2. **Prescription**
§ 3. **Extent of easement, and rights and duties, generally**
§ 4. **— Easement of way; streets**
§ 5. **— Light, air, and view; water**
§ 6. **Termination**

---

§ 1. **Creation or acquisition, generally.**

Building: implied easement upon severance of tract where building is near or encroaches upon the dividing line, 9 ALR 488, supp 41 ALR 1210, 53 ALR 910

Commencement and duration of express easement as affected by provision in instrument creating it, 154 ALR 5

Dedication, see **Dedication**

Deed as conveying fee or easement, 136 ALR 379

*Reprinted with permission from West Group.

ILLUSTRATION 5-14. A.L.R. Digest of Decisions and Annotations with Related Total Client-Service References

Consult pocket part for later cases

The remote grantees of an alleged dominant estate, which had been conveyed from the larger alleged servient estate, have a right of way by necessity over the servient estate also owned by remote grantees, where the dominant estate was landlocked except for being bounded on one side by a navigable creek. *Hancock v Henderson (1964) 236 Md 98, 202 A2d 599, 9 ALR3d 592.*

[Annotated]

In an action by holders of an easement by necessity to enjoin a landowner from interfering with their use of a way across the land of the owner, the trial court erred in entering a judgment of injunction since the easement holders did not meet their burden of proof as to why their acquisition of adjoining property that abuts a public road did not extinguish their easement by necessity. At most, the evidence showed that their continued use of the way was more convenient and would spare them the expense of building their own road. If one has a way through his own land, he cannot impose a way of necessity through his neighbor's land unless his own way is not reasonably adequate or its cost is prohibitive. Mere inconvenience or mere cost, as the basis for using another's land to get access to one's own property, falls short of meeting this test. The burden of proof is upon the one that seeks to impose a way of necessity irrespective of which party initiates the proceedings. *Oyler v Gilliland (1980, Ala) 382 So 2d 517, 10 ALR4th 443.*

[Annotated]

In an action by plaintiff-landowners to establish a private road of necessity over an adjacent landowner's property for ingress to and egress from their own property, the trial court erred in granting a judgment that established the private road of necessity, where a part of the tract that comprised plaintiffs' property abutted upon a public road. The statute authorized the establishment of a private road only for the purpose of providing egress and ingress to land that does not abut upon a public road. *Hollars v Church of God of Apostolic Faith, Inc. (1980, Mo App) 596 SW2d 73, 10 ALR4th 495.*

[Annotated]

§ 38.7 —Necessity of unity of derivation of title
Text References:
25 Am Jur 2d, Easements and Licenses § 35

In order to establish a right of way by necessity, it must be demonstrated that the land for the benefit of which the easement is claimed and that over which it is claimed belonged to the same person at the same time. *Stair v Miller (1982) 52 Md App 108, 447 A2d 109, 36 ALR4th 764.*

Although all the properties involved in a dispute over a way by necessity were at one time owned by a single owner, there can be no right of way over a particular parcel where this parcel was sold prior to that of the lands of the remaining parties to the action, and at the time the first parcel was sold all the parcels had road frontage. *Stair v Miller (1982) 52 Md App 108, 447 A2d 109, 36 ALR4th 764.*

§ 39 —On, over, or to, railroad property
Text References:
65 Am Jur 2d, Railroads §§ 91-100

§ 41 Conveyance with reference to street or alley
Text References:
25 Am Jur 2d, Easements and Licenses § 25

§ 41.5 Miscellaneous easements
Text References:
25 Am Jur 2d, Easements and Licenses §§ 24-38

The provision of the Cable Communications Policy Act which grants governmentally franchised cable companies a right to access public rights-of-way and easements which have been dedicated for compatible use (47 USCS § 541(a)(2)) will be construed to authorize such access only when the private property owner has dedicated those easements for the general use of any utilities where such a construction is compatible with the court's precedent and avoids constitutional problems arising under the takings clause. *Cable Holdings of Georgia, Inc. v McNeil Real Estate Fund VI, Ltd. (1992, CA11 Ga) 953 F2d 600, 113 ALR Fed 817, 6 FLW Fed C 18, cert den (US) 121 L Ed 2d 127, 113 S Ct 182, reh, en banc, den (CA11 Ga) 988 F2d 1071, 7 FLW Fed C 233.*

[Annotated]

Where it is clear that a private property owner has not dedicated easements within its buildings for the general use of all utilities, the provision of the Cable Communications Policy Act which grants governmentally franchised cable companies a right to access public rights-of-way and easements which have been dedicated for compatible use (47 USCS § 541(a)(2)) does not afford such a franchisee with a right to access and occupy the property owner's private apartment buildings. *Cable Holdings of Georgia, Inc. v McNeil Real Estate Fund VI, Ltd. (1992, CA11 Ga) 953 F2d 600, 113 ALR Fed 817, 6 FLW Fed C 18, cert den (US) 121 L Ed 2d 127, 113 S Ct 182, reh, en banc, den (CA11 Ga) 988 F2d 1071, 7 FLW Fed C 233.*

[Annotated]

The provision of the Cable Communications Policy Act which grants governmentally franchised cable companies a right to access public rights-of-way and easements which have been dedicated for compatible use (47 USCS § 541(a)(2)) does not provide a right to access wholly private easements granted by property owners in favor of particular utilities, but only a right to access easements on private property

239

out every two years that updates the annotations in Volumes 1 to 175. It also indicates where annotations have been superseded or supplemented in later editions or series of the A.L.R. Entries are organized by volume and page numbers.

A.L.R.2d is updated by using the separate set entitled the *A.L.R.2d Later Case Service.* All entries are found by volume and page numbers.

The best way to update A.L.R.3d, 4th, 5th, or Fed. annotations is to consult the pocket part supplement to the volume to see if additional annotations and new statute and case law references are mentioned. Pocket parts are issued at least annually.

Last, always use the Annotation History Table in the Tables volume to see if the annotation is superseded.

▼ Can A.L.R. Annotations Be Shepardized?

There is a *Shepard's Citations* for A.L.R. annotations. See Illustration 5-15. In it you can Shepardize reported opinions to see where they are cited within the A.L.R. You can also Shepardize annotations to see where they are cited in reported opinions. This is a valuable research tool.

F. TREATISES AND HORNBOOKS

▼ What Are Treatises and Hornbooks?

Both hornbooks and treatises are secondary sources because they provide commentary, analysis, and criticism of the law and are written by private parties. Treatises and hornbooks help the researcher to understand the topic and, through cited references, provide citations to cases and statutes. **Treatises** are scholarly works, generally multivolume sets, that examine one legal topic, such as contracts, in great detail and with very broad coverage. **Hornbooks,** also scholarly but designed for the student of law, are generally one-volume works providing an overview of a single legal topic. The authors of hornbooks and treatises are legal scholars.

▼ How Do You Find a Thorough Treatise or Hornbook?

The best place to look for a hornbook or treatise is in the law library. The librarian will be able to refer you to the treatises that are best for the legal topic you are researching. There is a treatise for almost every legal subject. Many hornbooks are published by West Publishing Co. At the beginning of a West hornbook is a list entitled *Hornbook Series and Basic Legal Texts,* which provides all of the hornbooks categorized by legal subject.

ILLUSTRATION 5-15.   Sample Page from *Shepard's Citations* for *Annotations*

SOUTHWESTERN REPORTER, 2d SERIES   **Vol. 203**

-115-	-631-	**Vol. 200**	-608-	-1004-	-441-	-1019-	-681-
(184Ten404)	(303Ky864)		(239MA1092)	(150TxCr368)	(356Mo276)	(211Ark645)	(150TxCr524)
31A331n	65A3322n	-80-	44A3370n	14A3747n	68A3720n	24A4153n	34A3808n
31A3124n	-662-	1A3112n	44A3438n		68A3781n		-767-
31A3189n	40A4891n	1A3293n	-699-	**Vol. 201**	68A3801n	**Vol. 202**	(211Ark814)
31A3265n	-665-	59A3226n	49A3963n		30A4584n		58A3508n
-164-	17A4544n	-84-	-709-	-1-	-475-	-7-	23A4914n
(150TxCr158)	-689-	1A3157n	43A367n	(184Ten428)	2A3303n	(356Mo435)	-795-
46A31173n	53A3682n	1A3200n	43A398n	62A3672n	2A3507n	60A3246n	(356Mo558)
-168-	53A3691n	-120-	-757-	-7-	-492-	-50-	24A41131n
(150TxCr161)	53A3712n	67A442n	(304Ky296)	(304Ky456)	7A31019n	29A3941n	35A4609n
21A429n	-745-	-133-	20A3346n	13A3212n	-531-	-75-	-827-
-172-	(211Ark185)	(304Ky127)	16A441n	13A3258n	(239MA1247)	(356Mo514)	(30TnA14)
(150TxCr148)	89A3562n	18A3520n	44A436n	24A4653n	80A3170n	93A3648n	21A31183n
43A31094n	89A3613n	-174-	-775-	-17-	-561-	-92-	-869-
-202-	98A3704n	(150TxCr264)	(211Ark403)	(211Ark519)	(304Ky528)	35A4515n	(356Mo602)
47A31358n	-747-	67A3843n	7A31306n	1A3267n	3A3220n	-163-	1A3579n
-210-	(211Ark189)	67A3866n	7A31331n	1A3467n	3A3315n	(304Ky686)	-887-
67A3937n	92A3879n	-187-	-782-	-21-	-583-	16A31163n	44A4457n
-288-	-754-	(150TxCr277)	(211Ark280)	(211Ark499)	(211Ark577)	-212-	-900-
37A3803n	(211Ark177)	100A3316n	5A3524n	19A31183n	31A3469n	(146Tex37)	(356Mo627)
-298-	95A3513n	-265-	5A3550n	-46-	-643-	67A3937n	68A3720n
31A336n	-780-	7A3942n	-789-	(150TxCr378)	40A4891n	-238-	69A3169n
31A3151n	(150TxCr57)	7A3946n	(211Ark362)	50A3826n	-691-	(150TxCr406)	69A3282n
-344-	76A3179n	43A3613n	60A31085n	50A394n	(184Ten563)	8A31241n	71A3301n
(355Mo924)	76A3271n	13A4375n	60A31102n	-61-	19A425n	-293-	71A3432n
51A31260n	-819-	-283-	60A31109n	32A31243n	37A4219n	28A41059n	-921-
30A4326n	34A3311n	(304Ky167)	-804-	32A31259n	-723-	-311-	(150TxCr500)
-421-	-853-	35A3539n	(211Ark460)	-73-	(304Ky551)	65A3138n	8A3760n
(239MA749)	30A31449n	-290-	30A31005n	44A3495n	9A3638n	94A3409n	8A3790n
40A3616n	35A4611n	(304Ky172)	30A31022n	44A3517n	-731-	-341-	-947-
40A3624n	-858-	26A426n	-820-	-77-	Case 2	16A31337n	56A4978n
-435-	7A3800n	-311-	(145Tex575)	56A4962n	(304Ky565)	-394-	-985-
(303Ky772)	-866-	(211Ark349)	26A31069n	-100-	2A3451n	(304Ky708)	(30TnA25)
37A393n	(240MA376)	7A476n	26A31097n	56A4683n	2A3531n	(172AR546)	9A3583n
-457-	78A3650n	-316-	28A31273n	-144-	-748-	53A41225n	9A3591n
(303Ky789)	78A3680n	(211Ark205)	-865-	35A4579n	(211Ark440)	-429-	51A4259n
50A334n	-872-	1A3370n	13A31166n	-158-	36A4871n	(305Ky172)	51A4285n
50A365n	26A4496n	23A3339n	-869-	29A4721n	-753-	70A3359n	-1001-
-461-	-899-	23A372n	95A3762n	-176-	(211Ark568)	-433-	(305Ky48)
(29TnA602)	(239MA801)	32A31242n	-890-	(356Mo55)	1A3267n	60A4807n	20A3203n
28A3525n	20A4201n	32A31252n	42A31264n	61A3560n	59A3219n	60A4875n	
28A3544n	-931-	-326-	-900-	-197-	-775-	-448-	**Vol. 203**
-503-	(29TnA651)	(355Mo1196)	(304Ky509)	(304Ky498)	34A3429n	(146Tex46)	
(145Tex528)	70A3396n	3A3131n	8A4237n	96A3548n	34A3433n	47A3105n	-2-
95A3762n	70A3431n	-343-	-923-	-305-	34A3444n	56A4568n	(305Ky111)
-510-	70A3516n	(355Mo1222)	(304Ky438)	(356Mo95)	34A3449n	-462-	66A3923n
Case 2	-940-	(170AR391)	58A3250n	-320-	-784-	(150TxCr467)	-30-
(150TxCr95)	(211Ark222)	33A3188n	-926-	20A3271n	43A3564n	21A3137n	(305Ky270)
8A3802n	57A31096n	33A3220n	Case 2	-327-	43A3569n	21A3152n	8A31248n
21A3137n	57A31112n	48A3406n	(304Ky359)	(356Mo210)	43A3572n	-474-	-78-
21A3152n	-943-	-352-	100A3294n	-330-	43A3582n	39A31319n	(305Ky235)
-547-	(211Ark229)	(355Mo1236)	100A3332n	39A326n	43A3587n	-500-	5A3532n
50A3934n	66A3604n	47A3941n	-930-	39A361n	-820-	25A326n	-89-
-560-	-954-	-375-	(304Ky398)	-336-	(150TxCr397)	25A361n	(240MA278)
4A4567n	(210ArkI092)	(240MA355)	59A3177n	(356Mo125)	74A3285n	25A3105n	46A3216n
7A41224n	56A31345n	33A4169n	-946-	(172AR344)	-561-	-561-	-100-
-571-	-955-	-400-	(304Ky416)	28A3998n	1A3418n	16A3296n	23A3395n
(211Ark99)	(211Ark132)	(150TxCr215)	26A3338n	-395-	-901-	-612-	-115-
18A3110n	31A324n	8A3760n	26A3297n	(356Mo258)	(304Ky650)	(305Ky31)	(240MA307)
-591-	31A347n	8A3784n	-949-	85A366n	24A3239n	65A3302n	44A31250n
(211Ark159)	-990-	13A4819n	(304Ky409)	85A386n	-935-	65A3333n	44A31255n
77A31322n	(304Ky58)	-421-	96A3588n	-416-	(356Mo382)	-620-	-143-
-598-	52A31045n	21A3497n	-953-	95A337n	49A3959n	(304Ky783)	(240MA932)
(211Ark80)	52A31062n	-469-	(304Ky422)	95A3116n	-952-	6A3543n	61A3665n
59A31179n	-994-	(304Ky223)	49A3958n	95A3160n	(356Mo372)	-623-	100A31147n
-602-	(304Ky73)	1A3138n	-965-	-423-	56A3778n	(304Ky798)	-147-
(211Ark88)	93A31146n	1A3165n	(211Ark489)	(240MA18)	-958-	21A324n	61A333n
3A3273n	-1000-	-519-	7A31103n	31A3536n	(356Mo412)	21A363n	-158-
3A3355n	40A4891n	(211Ark322)	-981-	-434-	47A3944n	-637-	(239MA901)
-620-		17A367n	(29TnA675)	(240MA325)	45A4741n	(304Ky811)	57A3567n
(303Ky819)		-546-	22A3386n	12A323n	-964-	3A4246n	-170-
66A3754n		46A3690n	22A3423n		97A3361n		(30TnA40)
66A3762n					97A3391n		
66A3782n							*Continued*

1035

*Reproduced by permission of LEXIS-NEXIS. Further reproduction is strictly prohibited.

▼ Which Treatises Are Most Noteworthy?

The following treatises are well known and respected.

Corbin, *Contracts*

Hazan, *Securities Regulation*

Herzog, *Bankruptcy*

Kratovil and Werner, *Real Estate Law*

LaFave and Scott, *Criminal Law*

McCormick, *Evidence*

Nowak, Rotunda, and Young, *Constitutional Law*

Prosser, *Torts*

White and Summers, *Uniform Commercial Code*

Wright and Miller, *Federal Practice and Procedure*

▼ Why Do You Use a Treatise?

There are a few approaches to using a treatise. Because the treatise covers a single legal topic and is written like a text, rather than like a case opinion, it is easy to find relevant information. The amount of relevant information may present the only problem when using a treatise: so much detail is provided that you may lose sight of the focus of your research. A treatise is used to find a very detailed analysis of a point of law or a legal rule. A hornbook is used to find an overview of a point of law or a legal rule. Both sources provide the general rules of law, its exceptions, and information on how the law is evolving. Often, a treatise or hornbook offers discussion of how the legal rules are applied in specific situations or in specific factual scenarios. You should use a treatise or a hornbook to educate yourself in a legal discipline or when an encyclopedia does not offer adequate detail in the discussion of a topic.

▼ How Do You Use a Treatise or Hornbook?

There are three methods of using a treatise or a hornbook.

1. **The table of contents method.** Treatises and hornbooks have detailed tables of contents that serve as outlines of the legal topics covered. A chapter or a subchapter often discusses the area you are researching.

2. **Table method.** Hornbooks and treatises contain tables of cases and tables of statutes. Use the relevant table when you have an excellent case or statute on point and want to understand the significance of the primary source in the context of the subject as a whole.

3. **Index method.** A subject index is found at the end of every treatise and hornbook. The index is a good place to start if you have

found a word like *easement* and want to find out its relevance in property law.

▼ Are Treatises Ever Relied on as Authority?

Treatises are occasionally relied on as authority in a document when no primary authority is available on point and when it is necessary to show the progression or evolution of the law. Because scholars write treatises, they are considered to be very prestigious sources of secondary authority. Hornbooks should not be relied on for authority because they are designed for the student and are diluted versions of treatises.

▼ How Do You Cite to a Hornbook and a Treatise?

Bluebook Rules 15.1.1 and 3.4 cover citation style for treatises and hornbooks.

Roger A. Cunningham et al., The Law of Property §8.5 (1993)

▼ Are Treatises Available Online?

More and more treatise titles are appearing online. WESTLAW, because it is part of West Group, makes a number of treatise titles available online, and its list is growing. LEXIS also has an expanding number of treatises available. The benefit of using a treatise online is that you can perform full text searching whereby you construct a query and retrieve relevant information with your own selection of terms rather than relying on any of the traditional research methods.

▼ How Are Treatises and Hornbooks Updated?

Treatises are updated in two ways: pocket parts of supplements, which are published at least annually, and new editions. Always check to see that you are working with the most recent edition available and to see if there is a pocket part or updating supplement.

G. RESTATEMENTS OF THE LAW

▼ What Are Restatements?

Restatements of the Law, published by the American Law Institute, are the most prestigious source of secondary authority. The subjects covered are agency, conflict of laws, contracts, foreign relations, judgments, property, restitution, security, torts, and trusts. There is a Restatement on Security, but this set is only in the first edition. Each of the legal disciplines mentioned comprises a separate set of the Restatements. The authors of the Restatements write every rule of law from these legal disciplines in a form that resembles a code and not a judicial opinion. The drafters of the Restatements are "restating" the law. The purposes are to codify the common law holdings so that a researcher does not have to unearth the legal rule from the text of an opinion and to make common law principles straightforward and succinct, like statutes. The Comments and the Illustrations are most helpful in understanding the application of the rule. The Reporter's Note, following the Illustrations, contains case references in which the Restatement section has been cited. See Illustration 5-16.

▼ How Are the Restatements Updated?

Most of the Restatements are in their second series. The rules, the codified-type versions of the legal principles, are updated in the appendix. Additional case references are also included in the appendix. The appendix is organized by section in the same order as the main text. The appendix is updated annually by pocket part supplements that are organized in the same manner as the main volume, by section, Also, semiannually a pamphlet is published called the *Interim Case Citations to the Restatements of Law.*

▼ How Do You Use the Restatements?

1. **The table of contents method.** Every set of the Restatements begins with a table of contents. See Illustration 5-17. The table of contents is an outline of the entire legal discipline, by topic and then within the topic, by rule. This is not a very efficient method, but it gives the researcher insight into where the section fits into the legal discipline. For instance, §174 of the Restatement (Second) of Contracts is entitled When Duress by Physical Compulsion Prevents Formation of a Contract. This section falls under Topic 2, Duress and Undue Influence, which is part of Chapter 7, Misrepresentation, Duress and Undue Influence.

2. **The index method.** Use the index at the end of the set by looking up various descriptive words pertaining to your issue. Under Duress is Physical Compulsion §174. This method is moderately efficient.

3. **The table of cases method.** When you have an excellent case on point, use the table of cases, organized in alphabetical order by plaintiff, to find references in the Restatements. This is the most efficient method when you have a specific case on point.

4. **The online method.** The Restatements are available on LEXIS and WESTLAW. This is an efficient method to use when you know the significant vocabulary words that describe the subject. If you are unfamiliar with the terminology or the words used to describe the

ILLUSTRATION 5-16. Sample Pages from Restatement (Second) of Contracts

on Illustration 6 to former § 267. Beach v. First Fed. Sav. & Loan Ass'n, 140 Ga. App. 882, 232 S.E.2d 158 (1977). Illustration 5 is adapted from Illustration 7 to former § 267.

Comment c. See former § 272. Illustration 6 is based on Illustration 1 to former § 268 and on Kane v. Hood, 30 Mass. (13 Pick.) 281 (1832). Illustration 7 is based on Illustration 2 to former § 268.

Comment d. This Comment replaces former § 273. See 3A Corbin, Contracts § 689 (1951); 6 Williston, Contracts § 887C (3d ed. 1962). Illustration 8 is based on Illustration 2 to former § 273 and on Beecher v. Conradt, 13 N.Y. (3 Kern.) 108 (1855); see also Kennelly v. Shapiro, 222 A.D. 488, 226 N.Y.S. 692 (1928).

Comment e. On the origin of the principle, see 6 Williston, Contracts §

830 (3d ed. 1962); Murray, Contracts § 162 (2d rev. ed. 1974). That a substantial failure to make timely progress payments is a material breach when the payments are required by a construction contract, see United States ex rel. Micro-King Co. v. Community Science Technology, Inc., 574 F.2d 1292, 1295 n.3 (5th Cir. 1978).

Comment f. Illustration 9 is based on Stewart v. Newbury, 220 N.Y. 379, 115 N.E. 984 (1917). See also Illustration 1 to former § 270. Illustration 10 is based on Clark v. Gulesian, 197 Mass. 492, 84 N.E. 94 (1908). The facts in Illustration 11 are taken from New Era Homes v. Forster, 299 N.Y. 303, 86 N.E.2d 757 (1949). Illustration 12 is based on Comment *a* to former § 270 and Illustration 1 to former § 268.

TOPIC 2.   EFFECT OF PERFORMANCE AND NON-PERFORMANCE

§ 235.   Effect of Performance as Discharge and of Non-Performance as Breach

(1) Full performance of a duty under a contract discharges the duty.

(2) When performance of a duty under a contract is due any non-performance is a breach.

Comment:

a. Discharge by performance. Under the rule stated in Subsection (1), a duty is discharged when it is fully performed. Nothing less than full performance, however, has this effect and any defect in performance, even an insubstantial one, prevents discharge on this ground. The defect need not be wilful or even negligent. Although a court may ignore trifling departures, performance that is merely substantial does not result in discharge under Subsection (1). See Comment *d* to § 237. A duty may, of course, be discharged on some other ground. See Chapter 12. For example, a duty that has not been fully

ILLUSTRATION 5-16. *Continued*

performed may be discharged on the ground of impracticability of performance. See Chapter 11.

Illustration:

 1. A contracts to build a house for B for $50,000 according to specifications furnished by B. A builds the house according to the specifications. A's duty to build the house is discharged.

 b. Effect of non-performance. Non-performance is not a breach unless performance is due. Performance may not be due because a required period of time has not passed, or because a condition has not occurred (§ 225), or because the duty has already been discharged (Chapter 12) as, for example, by impracticability of performance (Chapter 11). In such a case non-performance is justified. When performance is due, however, anything short of full performance is a breach, even if the party who does not fully perform was not at fault and even if the defect in his performance was not substantial. Non-performance of a duty when performance is due is a breach whether the duty is imposed by a promise stated in the agreement or by a term supplied by the court (§ 204), as in the case of the duty of good faith and fair dealing (§ 205). Non-performance includes defective performance as well as an absence of performance.

Illustrations:

 2. The facts being otherwise as stated in Illustration 1, A builds the house according to the specifications except for an inadvertent variation in kitchen fixtures which can easily be remedied for $100. A's non-performance is a breach.

 3. A contracts with B to manufacture and deliver 100,000 plastic containers for a price of $100,000. The colors of the containers are to be selected by B from among those specified in the contract. B delays in making his selection for an unreasonable time, holding up their manufacture and causing A loss. B's delay is a breach. His duty of good faith and fair dealing (§ 205) includes a duty to make his selection within a reasonable time.

 4. A contracts with B to repair B's building for $20,000, payment to be made "on the satisfaction of C, B's architect, and the issuance of his certificate." A makes the repairs but does not ask C for his certificate. B does not pay A. B's non-performance is not a breach. It is justified on the ground that performance is not due because of the non-occurrence of a condition. See Illustration 5 to § 227.

ILLUSTRATION 5-17.   Table of Contents from Restatement (Second) of Contracts

TABLE OF CONTENTS

Chapter 7

MISREPRESENTATION, DURESS AND UNDUE INFLUENCE

Introductory Note

TOPIC 1.   MISREPRESENTATION

TOPIC 2.   DURESS AND UNDUE UNFLUENCE

Volume 2

Chapter 8

UNENFORCEABILITY ON GROUNDS OF PUBLIC POLICY

Introductory Note

XIV

legal principles, then the online method is very costly and not very efficient.

▼ Can the Restatements Be Shepardized?

Yes, the Restatements can be Shepardized in the *Shepard's Restatement of Law Citations.* The *Shepard's* for the Restatements does not in any way validate the authority because the Restatements are secondary sources. *Shepard's,* in this instance, is a citator telling the researcher which cases contain citations to the Restatements.

▼ Are the Restatements Available Online?

Yes, as mentioned earlier, the Restatements are available online on both LEXIS and WESTLAW. The advantage of searching the Restatements online is that you do not have to rely on indexing terms. However, using the Restatements online can be very expensive if you are unfamiliar with the legal terms used.

▼ How Are the Restatements Cited?

Bluebook Rule 12.8.5 indicates that Restatements are cited as follows:

Restatement (Second) of Contracts §235 (1979)

Note that the year is the year that the Restatement section was adopted. This information is given on the title page of every volume of the Restatements.

When you are citing to a Comment of Illustration that follows the Restatement section, Rule 3.5 of the Bluebook applies.

Restatement (Second) of Contracts §235 cmt. a, illus. 2 (1979)

H. LEGAL PERIODICALS

▼ What Are Legal Periodicals?

Legal periodicals are secondary sources ranging from very prestigious to very practical forms of authority. Scholarly law review articles are considered the most prestigious, and bar journals and commercial publications are considered the most pragmatic. The major categories of legal periodicals are

1. academic law reviews
2. bar journals and practitioner's periodicals
3. commercial journals and newsletters
4. legal newspapers

Every conceivable subject is covered in a legal periodical. Some legal periodicals focus on a particular practice area, like estate planning. The different forms of legal periodicals have different attributes.

▼ Why Would You Use a Legal Periodical?

Legal periodicals are published quickly and keep abreast of new legal issues and laws. They are a terrific place to obtain articles discussing the impact of a Supreme Court decision or the enactment of new legislation because such information is published very quickly, far faster than any text could be printed. Also, certain legal periodicals (for example, the practitioner's journals, the journals that pertain to specific bar association sections, the commercial journals, and newsletters) cover discrete legal subject areas and enable paralegals, practitioners, and researchers to keep up with all of the new developments in their respective practice areas.

The legal newspapers provide up-to-date information about the legal profession, the courts and significant opinions, the federal and state legislatures and significant laws, and information about law firms and the business of law. Legal newspapers also write about major and interesting cases and clients. Legal newspapers provide great insight into the realities of legal practice.

Academic law review articles are very scholarly and are excellent finding tools because of the voluminous number of cited references in each article. Academic law review articles are often theoretical and discuss the application of a particular legal doctrine or a trend in the law. Sometimes authors of law review articles suggest how the law should hold on certain issues. Because the academic law reviews are a very prestigious source of secondary authority, sometimes these resources are relied on for persuasive purposes when no primary authority is available on point.

▼ How Do You Obtain Relevant Legal Periodical Articles?

First, the researcher must decide the type of information needed. For example, is scholarly material required, or is practical information on drafting a will needed? After deciding on the type of information required for the project, the source should be selected accordingly. If scholarly material is required, then an academic law review would be appropriate. If practical information is needed, then a practitioner's journal, bar association section newsletter, or commercial publication dealing with the legal discipline is appropriate. If the researcher needs information about a law firm, a client, or a very recent (two-week-old) Supreme Court decision, then a legal newspaper is the ideal source.

Almost all legal periodicals, regardless of format, are indexed. The major indexes are:

Current Law Index (1980 to present): the most comprehensive hard-copy index; the contents are included in the CD-ROM product entitled *Legal Resource Index*.

LegalTrac: a CD-ROM format index covering 1985 to present; LegalTrac is like the *Current Law Index* in CD-ROM format.

Index to Legal Periodicals (1908 to present): goes back farther than *Current Law Index* and contains sections on book reviews, statutes, and cases.

Kindex: includes articles related to juvenile law.

Index to Foreign Legal Periodicals (1960 to present): index to federal tax articles.

▼ Are Legal Periodicals Available Online?

Yes, legal periodicals are available online on both LEXIS and WESTLAW and on Dialog and NEXIS. LEXIS has the LAWREV library, which contains the full text articles, cover to cover, of an increasing number of law reviews. Also, the NEWS library on LEXIS contains the full text copies of legal newspapers. WESTLAW has the full text articles from an increasing number of law reviews.

▼ How Do You Cite to a Law Review or Law Journal?

Bluebook Rule 16 and Table 13 indicate the citation form as follows:

Thomas W. Merrill, Property Rules, Liability Rules, and Adverse Possession, 79 Nw. U. L. Rev. 1122 (1985)

A legal newspaper is cited according to Bluebook Rule 16.4.

David Bailey, Call for Video Reenactment of Jury Rejected, Chi. D. L. Bull., Nov. 1, 1993, at 1

CHAPTER SUMMARY

Secondary authorities describe, analyze, and criticize primary sources. You use secondary authorities to educate yourself about a legal topic and to find citations to primary sources.

The major sources of secondary authority are dictionaries, thesauri, encyclopedias, *American Law Reports* (A.L.R.), hornbooks, treatises, Restatements of the Law, and legal periodicals.

Dictionaries and thesauri are used to find definitions and synonyms. Encyclopedias are used to educate yourself about a legal topic. *American Law Reports* contain articles called annotations that explore a legal issue in depth. Hornbooks are written for the student of law and cover a single legal subject. Treatises cover a single legal subject but go into great detail. Restatements of the Law, produced by the American Law Institute, attempt to organize common law holdings from cases into a format resembling statutes. Legal periodicals include academic law reviews, bar association and legal specialty publications, and legal newspapers. Law reviews are the most scholarly form of legal periodicals. Law review articles contain many citations to primary authority and are known for research accuracy.

Updating and correctly citing secondary authorities are important in your research process. Generally, it is best to rely on primary authority when writing a memo or a brief. Rely on secondary authority when there is no primary authority on point.

KEY TERMS

American Law Reports   legal periodicals
Cumulative Supplements   Restatements of the Law
hornbooks   secondary authority
legal dictionary   thesaurus
legal encyclopedia   treatises
legal meaning

EXERCISES

COMPARING SECONDARY AUTHORITIES

1. Look up the word *easement* in a legal dictionary. Now look up the same word in a thesaurus. Compare the two sources and the information provided. What is different?

   Now look up the word *easement* in your state legal encyclopedia (if you do not have a state legal encyclopedia available, use Am. Jur. or C.J.S.). How is the term treated in an encyclopedia? How is this different from a dictionary?

ENCYCLOPEDIA RESEARCH

Use *Corpus Juris Secundum* for Exercises 2 and 3.

2. Go to the index and look up *Landmarks—Removal of, Civil Liability* and find the appropriate section that the index refers you to. Look at that title and section. What is the title and section?

   Now you must update your research by checking the pocket part. When you check the pocket part, you will see a Library Reference referring you to a West topic and key number. What is the topic and key number?

   Using this topic and key number, check the *West Digest* that includes cases from your state and the *West Federal Digest* for additional case annotations. List two annotations from the digest that you consulted.

3. Go to the index and look up *Telecommunications—creation of an easement to maintain lines over the land of another.* Look at the title and section. What is the title and section?

   Now you must update your research by checking the pocket part.

When you check the pocket part, you will see a Library Reference referring you to a West topic and key number. What is the topic and key number?

Use this topic and key number and check the *West Digest* containing cases from your jurisdiction and the *West Federal Digest* for additional case annotations. List two case annotations.

Use *American Jurisprudence* for Exercises 4 and 5.

4. Use the index to look up *Landmarks, Boundaries* and the subcategory of *Trees—as monuments*. Find the topic and section. What is the topic and section?

   When reading the information, a footnote will refer you to an A.L.R. annotation. What is the full citation to the annotation?

5. Use the index to look up *Easements for Telecommunications Lines and Acquisition of a right of way*. Find the topic and section. What is the topic and section?

   Are there any references to A.L.R. annotations? If so, what are they?

Assignment for Encyclopedia Research

Read the following fact situation, which you first encountered in Chapter 3. Answer the questions following the situation.

FACTS

Nate Late, a business owner, has two partners in the operation of Loose Cannon Manufacturing in Gurnee, Illinois. He owns 33 ⅓ percent of a $3 million company. Late is ill, but not dying. He is grooming a 26-year-old, Ivan T. All, to run the business. He tells his family he likes All and wants to teach him the business. Nate Late dies.

The most current will leaves Late's estate to his wife of 24 years, Shirley Late, and his only son, Lou Sier. Mr. All tells Mrs. Late that her husband told All he intended to give the 26-year-old his one-third interest in Loose Cannon. This conversation took place in front of a bank president. No written record exists concerning Late's intention to give his stock to All. However, family members knew that Late intended for All to run the business and for All to get something if the business was sold. None of the family believed that Late intended to give the business to newcomer Ivan T. All. Late's shares of stock were never given to All. The shares were in the safe deposit box shared by Late and his wife.

Mrs. Late said that Mr. Late planned to give her the shares. He told her this when he opened the joint safety deposit box and gave her the key.

You work for a firm that has been retained by Mrs. Late. She would like to know if All can prove that Mr. Late gave All Mr. Late's interest in the company.

6. What topics might be relevant to this question?
7. How would you determine where to find those topics?
8. List the steps that you would take.
9. Take those steps. Note what you find.

10. Select two topics for review. Review those topics. Which topics were most relevant?
11. What additional information did you find to determine the answer to Mrs. Late's question?
12. Where did you find that information?
13. List the two most relevant cases that address this problem.

6

CONSTITUTIONS AND STATUTES

CHAPTER OVERVIEW

Constitutions and statutes occupy the highest rung in the hierarchy of authority. Constitutions are the highest form of legal authority, only to be followed by statutes. In ordinary legal dilemmas, statutes are often the controlling law. In our society statutes govern relationships like marriage and adoption, transactions like banking, and behavior like criminal acts. Learning how to find relevant statutes and constitutional provisions is very important for effective legal research.

    This chapter details the research methods used to find, to cite, and to validate constitutions and statutes. The legislative process that charts the path that a statute takes from initial sponsorship through codification is outlined. This chapter gives you the skills you need to perform constitutional and statutory research.

A. CONSTITUTIONS

▼ What Is a Constitution?

A **constitution** is a document that establishes the legal structure of a state or nation and the basic legal principles that control the operation of the government and the conduct of its citizens.

▼ What Is the Relationship between the Federal Constitution and the State Constitutions?

The U.S. Constitution is, in essence, the supreme law of the land. The state constitutions are the supreme law of each particular state. The federal constitution takes precedence over any state constitution. What does this mean? Only the U.S. Congress can repeal or redraft legislation or amend the U.S. Constitution. If a federal court determines that a state constitutional provision violates the U.S. Constitution, then the court must deem that section of the state constitution unconstitutional.

▼ Who Determines Whether a Statute Violates the U.S. Constitution?

Federal courts determine whether a statute violates the U.S. Constitution, and state courts determine if their respective state constitutions are being violated. Although courts determine if a statute violates the constitution, courts cannot rewrite or repeal statutes; only legislatures can. ?

▼ Can Federal and State Constitutions Be Shepardized?

Yes, federal and state constitutions can be Shepardized. *Shepard's United States Citations* indicates if a court of law has interpreted or applied a section of the U.S. Constitution in question. *Shepard's* serves to validate the authority and is a finding tool to obtain relevant case law decisions applying the constitutional section or amendment at issue in your research. See Illustration 6-1. Illustration 6-2 is the page from one decision cited in *Shepard's* mentioning the Fourth Amendment (see arrow in Illustration 6-1). State constitutions are Shepardized in the particular state code *Shepard's*. For a full discussion of how to Shepardize, see Chapter 4.

ILLUSTRATION 6-1. Sample Page from *Shepard's United States Citations*

UNITED STATES CONSTITUTION — **Amend. 4**

Cir. 5	49ABA634	87SC429	346FS396	161US479	302US324	367US738	393US410
48F85	50ABA918	87SC439	380FS1381	161US616	302US383	367US776	393US821
441F2d1136	51ABA554	88SC507	582FS360	166US668	307US498	370US141	393US1090
446F2d486	51ABA665	90SC1922	Cir. 9	167US187	308US326	371US346	393US1110
532F2d505	52ABA162	91SC384	501F2d420	168US544	316US120	371US403	394US165
11FS216	54ABA785	91SC1491	576F2d166	176US607	316US130	371US471	394US224
31FS790	18LE1395n	92SC2327	713F2d1413	180US86	321US725	372US337	394US244
252FS250	18LE1400n	96SC1753	48FS45	181US302	322US489	373US274	394US280
414FS1347	20LE1464n	97SC881	95FS363	187US101	322US694	373US427	394US313
543FS210	28A845s	98SC1679	230FS180	192US587	324US416	373US647	394US317
571FS198	28A849n	Cir. DC	Cir. 10	194US45	325US150	374US23	394US325
Cir. 6	28A852n	74F2d559	706F2d1076	194US385	327US186	376US364	394US448
78F478	13ARF116n	724F2d172	12FRD87	201US80	327US678	376US488	394US569
349F2d603	33ARF830n	745F2d1543	5MJ15	201US92	328US582	377US203	394US721
423F2d706	33ARF832n	333FS481	15MJ549	201US120	328US624	378US4	394US1016
440F2d144	37ARF696s	Cir. 1	41ABA811	207US301	330US604	378US74	395US752
440F2d1069	37ARF699n	186FS954	46ABA599	207US542	331US145	378US108	395US814
529F2d103	37ARF703n	338FS574	49ABA639	211US123	332US585	378US254	395US818
530F2d103	37ARF711n	Cir. 2	50ABA918	212US352	333US10	378US497	396US103
633F2d1248	37ARF718n	237F2d807	51ABA554	213US111	333US189	378US518	396US239
368FS729	43ARF343n	579F2d180	52ABA162	217US598	333US651	379US89	397US77
435FS452	43ARF349n	601F2d1238	52ABA624	220US112	334US270	379US460	397US249
555FS1301		677F2d958	53ABA1033	221US362	334US700	379US476	397US383
Cir. 7	Amends.3 to 5	724F2d28	54ABA785	221US603	335US29	380US105	397US707
427F2d259	Cir. 6	36FS916	61ABA830	221US612	335US425	380US412	398US223
444F2d1038	424F2d213	261FS110	65ABA1181	226US484	335US451	380US693	399US30
446F2d133	Cir. 9	270FS666	18LE1395n	232US58	336US796	381US484	399US43
504F2d1288	319FS369	342FS805	43LE876n	232US383	338US25	381US568	399US131
695FS264		365FS66	43LE895n	234US94	338US75	381US655	400US129
727F2d637	Amend. 3	428FS899	32A1274n	235US227	338US160	382US413	400US309
769F2d415	48US67	433FS471	82A774n	236US328	338US633	382US1024	400US522
174FS801	176US607	505FS931	96A245n	239US1	339US1	383US77	400US1212
313FS1331	256US165	522FS59	§2	241US75	339US56	384US520	401US160
340FS147	343US644	525FS797	Cir. 2	245US295	339US784	384US759	401US224
363FS322	351US366	533FS1049	217FS167	247US7	341US66	385US206	401US564
419FS471	354US29	572FS45	Cir. 5	249US48	342US48	385US293	401US653
532FS1171	373US274	52FRD361	217FS517	251US385	342US119	385US323	401US672
556FS738	376US4	83FRD95		255US298	342US176	385US413	401US745
Cir. 8	378US254	Cir. 3	Amends. 4 to 10	255US314	343US176	385US497	401US797
96F361	381US481	44F2d985	333US640	256US465	343US285	385US967	401US997
389F2d381	385US341	246FS179	92LE986	262US591	343US467	386US44	402US211
420F2d308	389US350	321FS1109	68SC763	262US147	343US747	386US58	402US381
438F2d765	399US131	353FS1308		262US151	344US201	386US301	402US965
446F2d164	400US314	419FS573		263US151	346US555	386US950	402US980
448F2d476	402US255	557FS431	Amends. 4 to 8	264US299	347US65	386US955	403US233
460F2d34	425US561	586FS540	264US299	265US57	347US134	386US1019	403US388
558F2d893	429US608	81FRD745	Cir. 6	267US132	348US420	387US82	403US443
579F2d1093	436US63	Cir. 4	721F2d1065	267US499	350US220	387US294	403US577
675F2d220	12LE609	490F2d375	315FS696	268US435	352US432	387US523	404US325
26FS1002	44LE607	254FS598	Cir. 8	269US20	354US9	387US541	404US479
309FS142	65LE875	334FS209	385FS1150	272US532	355US102	388US41	404US1235
328FS675	96LE1204	Cir. 5	Cir. 10	273US1	355US111	388US130	405US169
522FS904	100LE1258	410F2d733	540F2d1044	273US29	357US378	388US249	405US966
Cir. 9	1LE1148	714F2d528	Amends. 4 to 6	273US95	357US480	388US265	406US311
253F234	10LE343	21FS627	Cir. 2	273US162	357US493	389US114	406US356
258F2d783	12LE654	217FS466	399F2d611	273US605	358US308	389US347	406US935
454F2d176	12LE874	250FS227	437F2d297	274US559	358US813	389US560	407US71
501F2d420	14LE512	252FS250	Cir. 4	275US112	359US363	390US235	407US145
547F2d1076	17LE405	269FS529	203FS752	275US192	361US100	390US377	407US297
581F2d1357	19LE578	325FS572	Cir. 5	275US310	362US217	390US616	407US345
606F2d873	26LE471	377FS542	328FS137	276US140	362US273	391US141	407US494
731F2d1383	27LE412	430FS54	388F2d843	276US610	364US206	391US148	408US64
155FS929	28LE753	446FS833	Amend. 4	277US439	364US235	391US214	408US227
608FS730	33LE164	Cir. 6	48US67	279US293	364US253	391US220	408US435
Cir. 10	48LE167	653F2d1087	59US71	282US345	364US272	391US390	408US737
564F2d384	51LE78	745F2d1033	59US272	282US694	364US377	391US545	409US35
695F2d1357	56LE118	506FS929	71US119	284US441	365US167	392US2	409US322
706F2d1076	20SC494	19BRW449	96US733	285US37	365US384	392US42	409US1013
506FS87	41SC463	Cir. 7	116US616	285US452	365US460	392US109	409US1065
549FS299	72SC874	253F108	123US138	286US1	365US505	392US364	409US1091
12FRD87	76SC931	695F2d279	142US552	287US124	365US613	392US379	409US1219
15MJ549	77SC1223	330FS159	149US733	287US206	366US156	392US603	409US1233
41ABA811	83SC1126	603FS1555	153US87	290US41	366US262	392US924	409US1238
44ABA88	84SC1491	Cir. 8	153US536	293US411	367US110	393US6	410US1
45ABA594	84SC1829	572F2d155		295US400	367US549	393US81	*Continued*
	85SC1679	346FS97		300US139	367US646	393US166	

97

---

*Reproduced by permission of LEXIS-NEXIS. Further reproduction is strictly prohibited.

ILLUSTRATION 6-2. Page from Decision in *U.S. Reports* That Discusses the Fourth Amendment

344   OCTOBER TERM, 1930.

Syllabus.   282 U. S.

to do business within a state. In those cases the judgment of this Court in no way restricts the further exercise of the legislative power of the state in any constitutional manner. Here the Commission is ousted from the exercise of power which Congress has given it, and an order is sanctioned authorizing an issue of securities which it cannot be said the Commission has approved, and which this Court does not purport to say is appropriate under the statute.

MR. JUSTICE HOLMES and MR. JUSTICE BRANDEIS concur in this opinion.

GO-BART IMPORTING COMPANY ET AL. *v.* UNITED STATES.

CERTIORARI TO THE CIRCUIT COURT OF APPEALS FOR THE SECOND CIRCUIT.

No. 111. Argued November 25, 1930.—Decided January 5, 1931.

1. A warrant issued by a United States Commissioner, addressed only to the Marshal and his deputies, and based upon, and reciting the substance of, a complaint that was verified merely on information and belief and that did not state an offense,—*held* invalid on its face, and no authority to prohibition officers to make an arrest. P. 355.
2. Acting under color of an invalid warrant of arrest, and falsely claiming to have a search warrant, prohibition agents entered the office of a company, placed under arrest two of its officers, and made a general search of the premises. They compelled by threats of force the opening of a desk and safe, and seized therefrom and from other parts of the office, papers and records belonging to the company and its officers. The officers of the company were arraigned before a United States Commissioner, and by him held on bail further to answer the complaint (U. S. C., Title 18, § 591), while the seized papers were held under the control of the United States Attorney in the care and custody of the prohibition agent in charge. The company, and its two officers individually, before

ILLUSTRATION 6-2. *Continued*

GO-BART CO. *v.* UNITED STATES. 345

an information or indictment had been returned against them, applied to the District Court for an order to enjoin the use of the seized papers as evidence and directing their return. On a rule against the United States to show cause, the United States Attorney appeared and opposed the motion and an affidavit of the agent in charge was also filed in opposition. The applications were denied. *Held:*

(1) In the proceedings before him, the Commissioner acted merely as an officer of the District Court in a matter of which it had authority to take control at any time. P. 353.

(2) Notwithstanding the order to show cause was addressed to the United States alone, the proceeding was in substance and effect against the United States Attorney and the prohibition agent in charge, the latter being required by the Prohibition Act to report violations of it to the former and being authorized by the statute, subject to the former's control, to conduct such prosecutions; and both these officers were subject to the proper exertion of the disciplinary powers of the court. P. 354.

(3) The District Court had jurisdiction summarily to determine whether the evidence should be suppressed and the papers returned to the petitioners. P. 355.

(4) The company being a stranger to the proceedings before the Commissioner, the order of the District Court as to it was final and appealable. P. 356.

(5) There being no information or indictment against the officers of the company when the application was made, and nothing to show that any criminal proceeding would ever be instituted in that court against them, it follows that the order was not made in or dependent upon any case or proceeding pending before the court, and therefore the order as to them was appealable. *Id.*

(6) The Fourth Amendment forbids every search that is unreasonable, and is to be liberally construed. P. 356.

(7) Assuming that the facts of which the arresting officers had been previously informed were sufficient to justify the arrests without a warrant, nevertheless the uncontradicted evidence requires a finding that the search of the premises was unreasonable. *Marron* v. *United States*, 275 U. S. 192, distinguished. P. 356.

(8) The District Court is directed to enjoin the United States Attorney and the agent in charge from using the papers as evidence and to order the same returned to petitioners. P. 358.

40 F. (2d) 593, reversed.

▼ Where Are Federal and State Constitutions Found?

The full text of the current version of the U.S. Constitution as well as all the amendments are contained in the first volume of the annotated versions of the *United States Code* (U.S.C.), the *United States Code Service* (U.S.C.S.), and the *United States Code Annotated* (U.S.C.A.). Encyclopedias are also sources of unannotated versions of the U.S. Constitution.

State constitutions are located in the first volume of the respective state code. Both the unannotated and the annotated state codes contain the state constitutions.

▼ How Do You Cite Federal or State Constitutions?

Bluebook Rule 11 outlines the citation format. A citation to the U.S. Constitution includes the particular article, section, and clause being used.

U.S. Const. art. II, §2, cl. 1

This cite is used when you are referring to the body of the Constitution. A special citation format is required when you are referring to an amendment.

U.S. Const. amend. II

State constitutions are indicated by the name of the state in the Bluebook abbreviated format. Table 1 in the Bluebook indicates the accepted state name abbreviation; this is not necessarily the postal abbreviation. For example, the state of Washington's postal abbreviation is WA, but the Bluebook abbreviation is Wash. A section of the Washington state constitution would be cited as follows:

Wash. Const. art. I, §2

Years or dates are not included in citations to federal or state constitutions that are current. Parenthetical notations after the citation indicate the year only if a constitutional provision was repealed or amended. An example is the Eighteenth Amendment to the U.S. Constitution prohibiting the sale of liquor. This amendment was later repealed by the Twenty-First Amendment. Bluebook Rule 11 provides the following example using the Prohibition amendment:

U.S. Const. amend. XVIII (repealed 1933)

▼ Are Constitutions Available on LEXIS and WESTLAW?

The full text of the U.S. Constitution, in its current format, is available on LEXIS in the GENFED library in the USCNST file. WESTLAW has the full text of the current U.S. Constitution in the U.S.C.A. database, which can be viewed after completing the following search: **pr,ca** (constitution) and **amendment 2** (if you want to view the text of the Second Amendment). (**Pr** and **ca** are search fields in WEST-LAW. After selecting a WESTLAW database, you can type in **fields** and find out the various fields available in the database. The fields are components of the document. An example of a field is the citation, abbreviated **cf. Pr** stands for Prelim, the "headings that precede the caption." **Ca** is the abbreviation for Caption, which is "the section, rule, or canon number and heading." Field searches help you f .... ble to locate documents .... areas, like a citation.)

The inc .... ugh the state code datab

▼ Are Ther .... ls That Assist
.... ?

Yes, the *Su* .... n of how to use digests, ... *ations.* There are annota .... *American Law Reports Fede*

Do not .... lent treatises on constitu

Constitution
American Constitutional Law by Laurence Tribe.

A treatise is the best place to start researching a constitutional law issue. Treatises explain the legal issues and indicate which cases are the most important. Treatises are particularly helpful in the area of constitutional law because the issues are very complex and require a high level of analysis. For more information on secondary sources, see Chapter 5.

B. STATUTES

▼ What Are Statutes?

Statutes are the laws enacted by either a federal or a state legislature. The business of the legislature is to enact laws. Statutes, both state and federal, as well as municipal and county ordinances and charters, are primary authority.

1. THE LEGISLATIVE PROCESS

▼ How Is a Statute Created through the Federal Legislative Process?

Anyone can propose **legislation.** Very often special interest groups and law firms propose legislation. Once the legislation is proposed, a **sponsor** in the ranks of Congress must be found to introduce the legislation.

Legislation is generally introduced in the U.S. House of Representatives, but it can be introduced in the U.S. Senate. For purposes of our discussion, assume the legislation is introduced in the House. Once introduced, it is called a **slip bill.** The slip bill is given a numerical designation and is referred to the appropriate **House committee** and then often referred to a **subcommittee.** A committee print of the bill is created. Hearings are conducted on the bill to determine its impact and effectiveness. Various experts may testify at the hearings to give input as to the possible effects of the legislation or to offer insight as to the purpose the legislation will serve. The tangible result of the hearings is the transcript of the testimony. This records the testimony of experts and lobbyists and their exhibits.

The next stage is the presentation of the committee's report. The **committee report** is a very informative resource because it generally includes the purpose of the bill and the public policies that the bill addresses. The bill is then debated on the floor of the House. The *Congressional Record,* which prints all activity occurring on the floor of both the House and the Senate, prints the transcripts of the debates. More policy information can be gathered from the debates. Flaws in the legislation can also be discerned from the text of the debates. The bill must pass by vote in the chamber of Congress in which it was initiated. In our example, the bill began in the House, so it would have to pass in the House before going to the Senate for approval.

what happens
not when.

When a bill is passed by the House and sent to the Senate, it must be referred to the appropriate committee and follow the identical route as it did in the first chamber. When the Senate passes its version of the bill, it may differ from the original House bill. Before the bill can become law, both chambers must pass the same version of the bill. If the House and the Senate pass different versions of the bill, the bill is referred to a **conference committee,** which issues a conference committee report and the conference committee version of the bill. The conference committee version is then submitted for votes in both chambers.

If both congressional chambers approve the same version, the bill is sent to the president for signing. If the president signs the bill, it becomes a slip law. If the president **vetoes** the bill, that is, refuses to approve it, the bill goes back to the Congress, and Congress may override the veto by a two-thirds majority vote in both the House and the Senate. If the president does not sign or veto the bill within ten days and the legislature is still in session, the bill automatically becomes law. Occasionally, the president uses a **pocket veto.** This occurs when there are fewer than ten days left in the legislative session and the president neither signs nor vetoes the bill, but merely waits for the session to expire. If the session expires before the president acts on the bill, the bill dies because it did not survive the legislative session. If the sponsors are still interested in passing this legislation, it must be reintroduced, in either chamber, at the beginning of the next legislative session. If both chambers pass the bill in the same exact version, then it is sent again to the president for signing. The president has the same choices: sign or veto. If the president signs the bill, it becomes a slip law.

▼ What Are Slip Laws?

Slip laws are the first written presentation of enacted laws from a legislative body. Slip laws are identified by numbers, for example, Pub. L. No. 104-145. This cite is for a federal session law, or **public law,** for the popularly named statute called Megan's Law. The 104 indicates the congressional or legislative session, in this case the 104th Congress. The 145 indicates that it is the 145th law passed by the 104th Congress.

Slip laws can be obtained at federal government depository libraries (many university and large city libraries are government depository libraries) or purchased from the U.S. Government Printing Office. Slip laws can also be obtained from the law's sponsor in Congress. The annotated versions of the *United States Code* and the *United States Code Congressional and Administrative News* have advance services that publish the slip laws. Advance services are paperbound volumes that contain updated information published in advance of the bound volume or supplement.

▼ What Are Session Laws?

At the end of a congressional session, all of the laws created during the course of the session are numbered and given the designation of **session laws.** Session laws on the federal level, also known as public laws, are added to the *Statutes at Large* and receive a *Statutes at Large* citation. See Illustration 6-3 for Megan's Law in the *Statutes at Large* at 110 Stat. 1345. The text for Megan's Law in the *Statutes at Large* is identical to what is found in the earlier slip law.

▼ What Are the *Statutes at Large*?

The *Statutes at Large* are the compilation of the slip laws from the session of Congress that just ended. After each congressional session

ILLUSTRATION 6-3. Sample Session Law Published in *Statutes at Large*

Public Law 104–145
104th Congress

An Act

To amend the Violent Crime Control and Law Enforcement Act of 1994 to require the release of relevant information to protect the public from sexually violent offenders.

May 17, 1996

[H.R. 2137]

Be it enacted by the Senate and House of Representatives of the United States of America in Congress assembled,

SECTION 1. SHORT TITLE.

This Act may be cited as "Megan's Law".

Megan's Law.

42 USC 13701 note.

SEC. 2. RELEASE OF INFORMATION AND CLARIFICATION OF PUBLIC NATURE OF INFORMATION.

Section 170101(d) of the Violent Crime Control and Law Enforcement Act of 1994 (42 U.S.C. 14071(d)) is amended to read as follows:

"(d) RELEASE OF INFORMATION.—

"(1) The information collected under a State registration program may be disclosed for any purpose permitted under the laws of the State.

"(2) The designated State law enforcement agency and any local law enforcement agency authorized by the State agency shall release relevant information that is necessary to protect the public concerning a specific person required to register under this section, except that the identity of a victim of an offense that requires registration under this section shall not be released.".

Approved May 17, 1996.

---

ends, the slip laws from that session are bound into at least one volume to form the *Statutes at Large*. The laws are published in chronological order rather than codified like the statutes because they document all legislation enacted during the congressional session. Unfortunately, the *Statutes at Large* volumes are not produced immediately after a congressional session. The *Statutes at Large* contain the public laws, or slip laws, as well as presidential proclamations and private laws. The wording of the session laws in the *Statutes at Large* is identical to the public law. The federal codes have tables indicating the *Statutes at Large* citation for a public law. See Illustration 6-3 for a reprint of the *Statutes at Large*.

▼ What Is Codification?

Finally, the session laws are codified. **Codification** means that the session laws are grouped by subject and placed in the statutes according to their titles, which contain particular subject areas of the law. Unlike cases, which are published as the opinions are written, federal statutes are arranged by a defined group of 50 subject categories called titles. See Illustration 6-4 for the list of titles. Statutes are

ILLUSTRATION 6-4.　Table of U.S.C. Titles

*1. General Provisions.
2. The Congress.
*3. The President.
*4. Flag and Seal, Seat of Government, and the States.
*5. Government Organization and Employees: and Appendix.
†6. [Surety Bonds.]
7. Agriculture.
8. Aliens and Nationality.
*9. Arbitration.
*10. Armed Forces; and Appendix.
*11. Bankruptcy; and Appendix.
12. Banks and Banking.
*13. Census.
*14. Coast Guard.
15. Commerce and Trade.
16. Conservation.
*17. Copyrights.
*18. Crimes and Criminal Procedure; and Appendix.
19. Customs Duties.
20. Education.
21. Food and Drugs.
22. Foreign Relations and Intercourse.
*23. Highways.
24. Hospitals and Asylums.
25. Indians.
26. Internal Revenue Code.

27. Intoxicating Liquors.
*28. Judiciary and Judicial Procedure; and Appendix.
29. Labor.
30. Mineral Lands and Mining.
*31. Money and Finance.
*32. National Guard.
33. Navigation and Navigable Waters.
‡34. [Navy.]
*35. Patents.
36. Patriotic Societies and Observances.
*37. Pay and Allowances of the Uniformed Services.
*38. Veterans' Benefits.
*39. Postal Service.
40. Public Buildings, Property, and Works.
41. Public Contracts.
42. The Public Health and Welfare.
43. Public Lands.
*44. Public Printing and Documents.
45. Railroads.
*46. Shipping; and Appendix.
47. Telegraphs, Telephones, and Radiotelegraphs.
48. Territories and Insular Possessions.
*49. Transportation; and Appendix.
50. War and National Defense; and Appendix.

*This title has been enacted as law. However, any Appendix to this title has not been enacted as law.
†This title was enacted as law and has been repealed by the enactment of Title 31.
‡This title has been eliminated by the enactment of Title 10.

updated during the course of a legislative session if the legislature proposes amendments or revisions. The best finding tools for the appropriate statute on point is a good index. A new version of the *United States Code* appears approximately every six years. In the interim, the Code is updated by slip laws and session laws.

2. Reading and Understanding Statutes

▼ How Do You Read a Statute?

Each word of a statute is read for its plain meaning. Statutes are drafted using as few words as possible to state the law. Any ambiguities that arise when applying a statute are resolved by the courts. The text of the statute does not discuss policy issues.

The focus of statutory analysis is that legislation is adopted to apply to situations that will arise after the legislation goes into effect. An activity existing prior to passing of legislation is **grandfathered** if the legislation includes language that does not prohibit this existing activity from continuing. For instance, suppose a city passes an ordinance forbidding the operation of commercial businesses in residentially zoned neighborhoods. Under a grandfather clause, an existing business would be permitted to continue its operation; the legislation would apply only to businesses opened after the legislation took effect.

▼ What Type of Legal Authority Are Statutes?

Statutes are primary authority because codes and statutes are the laws created by the legislature. Statutes are the authority to rely on when researching. If there is a relevant statute on point, the statute takes precedence over case law holdings that were decided prior to the statute's enactment. Statutes are enacted to control conduct like criminal acts, relationships like marriage and adoption, and transactions like banking that occur frequently in our society. Court decisions applying and interpreting statutes already enacted must be consulted to assess how a statute has been applied and analyzed.

▼ What Is the Relationship between Statutes and Case Law?

Most cases today revolve around the application or the interpretation of a statute. Courts determine whether an individual or an institution—public, private, or government—violated a statute or whether the statute itself is unconstitutional. People, institutions, municipalities, and even state governments go to court to determine if a statute is unconstitutional.

3. How to Find Federal Statutes

▼ Where Are Federal Statutes Found?

The official, government-issued compilation of the federal statutes is the *United States Code,* or U.S.C. See Illustration 6-5, the 1994 version of 42 U.S.C. §14071(d). The U.S.C. contains most of the laws created by the U.S. Congress. The U.S. Government Printing Office publishes the U.S.C.

The U.S.C. is organized by title. Each title covers a specific subject area over which the U.S. Congress has authority to draft legislation. For example, Title 42 contains all statutes dealing with public health and welfare. When a new piece of legislation is enacted that pertains to public health and welfare, which includes crime prevention, it is placed in Title 42. When new statutes are enacted that replace existing statute sections, the older sections are then superseded. This differs from case law because new decisions overrule prior decisions' holdings; they do not supersede them. Sometimes only a portion of an existing statute changes when a new public law is enacted. In this case, the new public law amends the existing statute. Megan's Law amended 42 U.S.C. §14071(d). The 1994 version of the *United States Code* in Illustration 6-5 was amended by Pub. L. 104-145, which was passed in 1996.

▼ How Often Is the U.S.C. Updated?

An official version of the U.S.C. is published every six years. Supplements updating the existing Code are published annually. During the course of the six years, new legislation is passed all of the time. It is not included in the official code until the annual supplement is published. There may be a great time lag between the law's enactment and the production of the annual supplement. New legislation retains the slip format until it becomes a session law and gets a *Statutes at Large* citation. It is important to check to see if the legislation has been repealed or superseded by a slip law or a session law in the intervening years between publications of the official code and during the time between publications of the annual supplements.

▼ Is the U.S.C. the Only Codified Version
of the Federal Statutes?

No. There are two unofficial versions of the U.S.C., the *United States Code Annotated* (U.S.C.A.) published by West Group and the *United*

ILLUSTRATION 6-5. Sample Page Showing 42 U.S.C. §14071(d)

---

violent crime or drug emergency assistance under this section, the chief executive officer of a State or local government shall—

(1) take appropriate action under State or local law and furnish information on the nature and amount of State and local resources that have been or will be committed to alleviating the major violent crime- or drug-related emergency;

SUBCHAPTER V—CRIMINAL STREET GANGS

§ 14061. Juvenile anti-drug and anti-gang grants in federally assisted low-income housing

Grants authorized in this Act to reduce or prevent juvenile drug and gang-related activity in "public housing" may be used for such purposes in federally assisted, low-income housing.

---

may extend the provision of Federal assistance for not more than an additional 180 days.

(i) Regulations

Not later than 120 days after September 13, 1994, the Attorney General shall issue regulations to implement this section.

(j) No effect on existing authority

Nothing in this section shall diminish or detract from existing authority possessed by the President or Attorney General.

(Pub. L. 103–322, title IX, § 90107, Sept. 13, 1994, 108 Stat. 1988.)

SUBCHAPTER VI—CRIMES AGAINST CHILDREN

§ 14071. Jacob Wetterling Crimes Against Children and Sexually Violent Offender Registration Program

(a) In general

(1) State guidelines

The Attorney General shall establish guidelines for State programs that require—

(A) a person who is convicted of a criminal offense against a victim who is a minor or who is convicted of a sexually violent offense to register a current address with a designated State law enforcement agency

---

(iii) The verification form shall be signed by the person, and state that the person still resides at the address last reported to the designated State law enforcement agency.

(iv) If the person fails to mail the verification form to the designated State law enforcement agency within 10 days after receipt of the form, the person shall be in violation of this section unless the person proves that the person has not changed the residence address.

(B) The provisions of subparagraph (A) shall be applied to a person required to register under subparagraph (B) of subsection (a)(1) of this section, except that such person must verify the registration every 90 days after the date of the initial release or commencement of parole.

(4) Notification of local law enforcement agencies of changes in address

(d) Release of information

The information collected under a State registration program shall be treated as private data expect that—

(1) such information may be disclosed to law enforcement agencies for law enforcement purposes;

(2) such information may be disclosed to government agencies conducting confidential background checks; and

(3) the designated State law enforcement agency and any local law enforcement agency authorized by the State agency may release relevant information that is necessary to protect the public concerning a specific person required to register under this section, except that the identity of a victim of an offense that requires registration under this section shall not be released.

(e) Immunity for good faith conduct

States Code Service (U.S.C.S.) published by LEXIS-NEXIS. Both the U.S.C.A. and the U.S.C.S. contain the text of the laws found in the U.S.C. and also include case law annotations and excellent updating services. Unlike case law where the official and the unofficial reporters have different volume numbers and different pagination for the same case, the citations for the unofficial codes have the same title and section designations as the U.S.C. cite. For example, the following are citations to the identical statute:

26 U.S.C. §61 (1994)

26 U.S.C.A. §61 (West 1994)

▼ What Do the Unofficial Codes Contain?

The unofficial codes contain references to cases that construe and apply the code section. See Illustrations 6-6 and 6-7. They are called annotated codes because they contain these case law annotations. The codes also contain references to law review articles dealing with the particular code section. The U.S.C.A. and U.S.C.S. are excellent research tools. See Illustrations 6-5, 6-6, and 6-7 for a comparison of the official and the unofficial codes.

The U.S.C.A., because it is published by West Group, ties the researcher into all of the other West publications. See Illustration 6-6. References are given to topic and key numbers so that the subject covered by the code section can be examined in the *West Digests* to find pertinent case law. (See Chapter 3 for a detailed discussion of digests.) References to legal encyclopedias are given as well. (See Chapter 5.) Electronic search queries for WESTLAW are provided. References to the *United States Code Congressional and Administrative News* (U.S.C.C.A.N.), published by West and containing compilations of legislative histories for public laws since the 1950s, are contained in the U.S.C.A. (The U.S.C.C.A.N. is discussed fully in Chapter 7.)

The U.S.C.S., formerly published by Lawyers Cooperative and recently acquired by LEXIS-NEXIS, provides references to other publications that are relevant to the particular code section. See Illustration 6-7. Electronic search queries to be used on LEXIS are printed. Pertinent *American Law Reports* (A.L.R.) cites are given as well as *American Jurisprudence* (Am. Jur.) and *American Jurisprudence Legal Forms* references. U.S.C.S. has consistent references to the *Code of Federal Regulations*. (See Chapter 8.)

Aside from providing case law annotations and law review citations, the annotated or unofficial federal codes provide the researcher with an entry into the entire research network created by the respective publisher.

ILLUSTRATION 6-6. Sample Pages Showing 42 U.S.C. §14071(d)

SUBCHAPTER VI—CRIMES AGAINST CHILDREN

§ 14071. Jacob Wetterling Crimes Against Children and Sexually Violent Offender Registration Program

(a) In general

(1) State guidelines

The Attorney General shall establish guidelines for State programs that require—

(A) a person who is convicted of a criminal offense against a victim who is a minor or who is convicted of a sexually violent offense to register a current address with a designated State law enforcement agency for the time period specified in subparagraph (A) of subsection (b)(6) of this section; and

(B) a person who is a sexually violent predator to register a current address with a designated State law enforcement agency unless such requirement is terminated under subparagraph (B) of subsection (b)(6) of this section.

713

(d) Release of information

The information collected under a State registration program shall be treated as private data except that—

(1) such information may be disclosed to law enforcement agencies for law enforcement purposes;

717

---

42 § 14071   VIOLENT CRIME CONTROL   Ch. 136

(2) such information may be disclosed to government agencies conducting confidential background checks; and

(3) the designated State law enforcement agency and any local law enforcement agency authorized by the State agency may release relevant information that is necessary to protect the public concerning a specific person required to register under this section, except that the identity of a victim of an offense that requires registration under this section shall not be released.

ILLUSTRATION 6-6. *Continued*

(Pub.L. 103–322, Title XVII, § 170101, Sept. 13, 1994, 108 Stat. 2038.)

HISTORICAL AND STATUTORY NOTES

(1) **Revision Notes and Legislative Reports**
1994 Acts. House Report Nos. 103–324 and 103–489, and House Conference Report No. 103–711, see 1994 U.S. Code Cong. and Adm. News, p. 1801.

LIBRARY REFERENCES

(2) **American Digest System**

Criminal prosecutions under laws for protection of children, see Infants ⊂20.
Discharge of prisoner by prison authorities in general, see Prisons ⊂14.
Parole conditions; status, rights, and supervision of parolee, see Pardon and Parole ⊂64 et seq., 66, 68.
Prevention and investigation of crime generally; criminal records, see Criminal Law ⊂1222 et seq., 1226(1 to 5).

(3) **Encyclopedias**

Criminal prosecutions under laws for protection of children, see C.J.S. Infants §§ 92 et seq., 100 et seq.

718

Ch. 136   **RURAL CRIME**   **42 § 14081**

Discharge of prisoner by prison authorities in general, see C.J.S. Prisons and Rights of Prisoners §§ 154, 155.
Parole conditions; status, rights, and supervision of parolee, see C.J.S. Pardon and Parole §§ 55 et seq., 58.
Prevention and investigation of crime generally; criminal records, see C.J.S. Criminal Law § 1724 et seq.

(4)   **WESTLAW ELECTRONIC RESEARCH**

Criminal law cases: 110k[add key number].
Infants cases: 211k[add key number].
Pardon and parole cases: 284k[add key number].
Prisons cases: 310k[add key number].
See, also, WESTLAW guide following the Explanation pages of this volume.

> **1 Citation to legislative history**
> **2 West topics key numbers in digest**
> **3 Encyclopedia**
> **4 WESTLAW searches**

Reprinted with permission of West Group.

ILLUSTRATION 6-7. Sample Page Showing 42 U.S.C.S. §14071(d)

42 USCS § 14071   PUBLIC HEALTH AND WELFARE

(5) Registration for change of address to another state. A person who has been convicted of an offense which requires registration under this section shall register the new address with a designated law enforcement agency in another State to which the person moves not later than 10 days after such person establishes residence in the new State, if the new State has a registration requirement.

(6) Length of registration. (A) A person required to register under subparagraph (A) of subsection (a)(1) shall continue to comply with this section until 10 years have elapsed since the person was released from prison, placed on parole, supervised release, or probation.

(B) The requirement of a person to register under subparagraph (B) of subsection (a)(1) shall terminate upon a determination, made in accordance with paragraph (2) of subsection (a), that the person no longer suffers from a mental abnormality or personality disorder that would make the person likely to engage in a predatory sexually violent offense.

(c) **Penalty.** A person required to register under a State program established pursuant to this section who knowingly fails to so register and keep such registration current shall be subject to criminal penalties in any State in which the person has so failed.

(d) **Release of information.** (1) The information collected under a State registration program may be disclosed for any purpose permitted under the laws of the State.

(2) The designated State law enforcement agency and any local law enforcement agency authorized by the State agency shall release relevant information that is necessary to protect the public concerning a specific person required to register under this section, except that the identity of a victim of an offense that requires registration under this section shall not be released.

(e) **Immunity for good faith conduct.** Law enforcement agencies, employees of law enforcement agencies, and State officials shall be immune from liability for good faith conduct under this section.

(f) **Compliance.** (1) Compliance date. Each State shall have not more than 3 years from the date of enactment of this Act [enacted Sept. 13, 1994] in which to implement this section, except that the Attorney General may grant an additional 2 years to a State that is making good faith efforts to implement this section.

(2) Ineligibility for funds. (A) A State that fails to implement the program as described in this section shall not receive 10 percent of the funds that would otherwise be allocated to the State under section 506 of the Omnibus Crime Control and Safe Streets Act of 1968 (42 U.S.C. 3765).

(B) Reallocation of funds. Any funds that are not allocated for failure to comply with this section shall be reallocated to States that comply with this section.

(Sept. 13, 1994, P. L. 103-322, Title XVII, Subtitle A, § 170101, 108 Stat.

742

▼ Is There Any Difference between the U.S.C.S. and the U.S.C.A.?

The U.S.C.S. provides references to relevant *Code of Federal Regulations* (C.F.R.) citations; the U.S.C.A. does not consistently include administrative law citations. Overall, then, the U.S.C.S. is better for researching administrative issues. The U.S.C.A. provides key numbers and topics relating to the West Digest System as well as electronic searching tips for WESTLAW query formulation.

▼ Why Would You Use an Annotated Set of the U.S.C.?

As mentioned earlier, the annotated codes offer a host of references to secondary source publications produced by the respective code's publisher as well as case law annotations. You would use an annotated, or unofficial code, because the updating through pocket parts, bound supplements, and advance session law pamphlets is very timely. Between publication of the official statutes every six years, consult an unofficial version of the U.S.C. to determine if a statute has been updated, modified, or superseded. The unofficial versions contain references to any new legislation that relates to the code section, even if it is a session law. The indexes of the unofficial codes are also superior to the index of the U.S.C.

▼ How Useful Are Annotated Statutes as Finding Tools?

Annotated codes are excellent finding tools for retrieving cases that interpret the statute section in question. You do not cite to the research points and abstracts following the code section, although they are very helpful in your research. When using an annotated code section on point, you are also linked to many other resources produced by the particular code's publisher. For example, within the U.S.C.A. you would find citations to encyclopedia sections. In addition, because of the excellent updating services, the annotated codes allow you to find subsequent legislation that relates to the statute section.

▼ What Are the Research Methods Used to Find Relevant Statutes?

The research methods are the same for the U.S.C., the U.S.C.A., and the U.S.C.S.

1. Index method. First try to find the relevant code section by using the index. You can also find a relevant statute by checking under some of the significant terms from the act. Very often a word from the popular name of the statute is cited in the index. The index is in alphabetical order. In Illustration 6-8, our example focuses on finding Megan's Law in the U.S.C.A. Megan's Law amends an earlier statute on the same subject. Note that the index entry contains some of the terms describing the subject matter of the statute.

2. **Title outline.** If you know the particular title where the statute section is located but don't know the section number, you can look at the title outline to see if any entry in the particular title is appropriate. Illustration 6-9 shows the outline of every subchapter and section in U.S.C.S. Title 42. You must have a very clear idea of what you are looking for and knowledge about the statute's language to use the title outline method effectively. Use this method only if you cannot find a statute section by any other means.

Megan's law

3. **Popular name table.** The popular name table is found in the last index volume. Almost every statute passed in Congress has a popular name, usually a last name of the sponsor or a description of the act's intent. If you have a popular name but not a title and section number, you can use the popular name table. See Illustration 6-10. All of the popular names for all of the code sections are listed in alphabetical order with the corresponding title and section numbers of the act, the public law numbers, and the *Statutes at Large* citations. The popular name table is an excellent research tool for finding public law numbers quickly. In Illustration 6-10, the public law number for Megan's Law is Pub. L. No. 104-145.

4. **Conversion table.** The conversion table is also at the end of the U.S.C. set, in the tables volume, and lets you find the U.S.C. citation if you have a *Statutes at Large* citation. In Illustration 6-11, our example focuses on Megan's Law using the tables in the U.S.C.S. Using the conversion table in the U.S.C.S., you are able to convert the public law number into a *Statutes at Large* citation. For example, you would obtain the citation of 110 Stat. 1345 from Pub. L. No. 104-145. The table also converts the public law number into a U.S.C.S. citation. (The public law number helps you find the legislative history of the act in the U.S.C.C.A.N. also. See Chapter 7 for more information on the U.S.C.C.A.N.)

Another excellent resource that helps you find relevant federal and state statutes is *Shepard's Acts and Cases by Popular Names—Federal and State.* As the title indicates, all of the acts and cases are organized by popular name. It is handy to use this source when you are not certain if the act is state, federal, or both and do not know which statutory compilation will have the correct statute. When using the popular name table of a code, you must know the jurisdiction and the date of enactment, but *Shepard's Acts and Cases by Popular Names* lists all acts and cases in alphabetical order regardless of jurisdiction. Look up Megan's Law in Illustration 6-12. Notice that there are both

ILLUSTRATION 6-8.   U.S.C.A. General Index

CRIMES   1022

*Reprinted with permission from West Group.

ILLUSTRATION 6-9.   Outline of Sections in Title 42 U.S.C.S., Public Health and Welfare, §§12301–end

645

*Reprinted with permission from LEXIS-NEXIS.

ILLUSTRATION 6-10.   U.S.C.A. Popular Name Table

POPULAR NAME TABLE   1364

Medicare Catastrophic Coverage Act of 1988—Continued
Pub.L. 101–476, Title IX, § 901(a)(2), Oct. 30, 1990, 104 Stat. 1142 (20 §§ 238, 244, 1087ee, 1203a, 1206a, 1400 note, 1402 note, 1412 note, 1415 note, 1419 note, 2323, 2334, 2372, 2421, 2744, 2782, 2791, 2792, 2794, 2796, 3227, 3291, 3441, 4311, 4321, 4342, 4356, 4907; 25 §§ 2503, 2504; 29 §§ 721, 774, 777a, 795m, 796d, 2215; 42 §§ 1396b, 1396n, 5117c, 6022, 6024, 9835, 9886)

Medicare Catastrophic Coverage Repeal Act of 1989
Pub.L. 101–234, Dec. 13, 1989, 103 Stat. 1979 (5 § 8902 note; 26 §§ 59B, 59B notes, 6050F, 6050F note; 42 §§ 401, 401 note, 1305 note, 1320a–7a, 1320a–7a notes, 1320c–3, 1395b note, 1395b–1 notes, 1395b–2 notes, 1395c, 1395c note, 1395d, 1395e, 1395e notes, 1395f, 1395h, 1395h note, 1395i, 1395i–1a, 1395i–1a note, 1395k to 1395m, 1395m note, 1395n, 1395r, 1395r note, 1395s, 1395t, 1395t note, 1395t–1, 1395t–2, 1395u, 1395u notes, 1395w, 1395w–2, 1395w–3, 1395x, 1395x notes, 1395y, 1395z, 1395aa to 1395cc, 1395*ll*, 1395*ll* note, 1395mm, 1395mm note, 1395ss, 1395ss notes, 1395tt, 1395ww, 1395ww notes, 1396a, 1396b, 1396n)

Medicare-Medicaid Anti-Fraud and Abuse Amendments
Pub.L. 95–142, Oct. 25, 1977, 91 Stat. 1175 (42 §§ 254e, 1301, 1305 note, 1320a, 1320a–3 to 1320a–5, 1320c–1, 1320c–3, 1320c–4, 1320c–6, 1320c–7, 1320c–9, 1320c–12, 1320c–15 to 1320c–17, 1320c–20 to 1320c–22, 1395f to 1395h, 1395*l*, 1395u, 1395x, 1395y, 1395cc, 1395*ll* note, 1395nn, 1396a, 1396b, 1396b–1, 1396h, 1396k, 1397a, 1397b, 3524)
Pub.L. 95–292, § 8(e), June 13, 1978, 92 Stat. 316 (42 § 1396b note)

Megan's Law
Pub.L. 104–145, May 17, 1996, 110 Stat. 1345 (42 §§ 13701 note, 14071)

Mellon Art Gallery Act
Mar. 24, 1937, ch. 50, 50 Stat. 51 (20 §§ 71 to 75)

Membrane Processes Research Act of 1992
Pub.L. 102–490, Oct. 24, 1992, 106 Stat. 3142 (42 § 10341, 10341 note, 10342 to 10345)

Menominee Restoration Act
Pub.L. 93–197, Dec. 22, 1973, 87 Stat. 770 (25 §§ 903 to 903f)

Mental Health Amendments of 1967
Pub.L. 90–31, June 24, 1967, 81 Stat. 79 (42 §§ 225a, 2681, 2684, 2687, 2688a, 2688d, 2691)

Mental Health Amendments of 1990
Pub.L. 101–639, Nov. 28, 1990, 104 Stat. 4600 (42 §§ 201 note, 290cc–13, 299a, 300x–3, 300x–10 to 300x–12)

Mental Health Parity Act of 1996
Pub.L. 104–204, Title VII, Sept. 26, 1996, 110 Stat. 2944 (29 § 1185a, 1185a note; 42 §§ 201 note, 300gg–5, 300gg–5 note)

Mental Health Study Act of 1955
July 28, 1955, ch. 417, 69 Stat. 382 (42 § 242b)

Mental Health Systems Act
Pub.L. 96–398, Oct. 7, 1980, 94 Stat. 1564 (42 §§ 210, 225a, 229b, 242a, 246, 289k–1, 300*l*–2, 300m–2, 1396b, 2689a to 2689c, 2689c, 2689g, 2689h, 2689q, 9401, 9411, 9412, 9421 to 9423, 9431 to 9438, 9451, 9452, 9461 to 9465, 9471 to 9473, 9481, 9491 to 9493, 9501, 9502, 9511, 9512, 9521 to 9523)
Pub.L. 97–35, Title IX, § 902(e)(1), (f)(1), (20), Aug. 13 1981, 95 Stat. 560 (42 §§ 2689, 2689a to 2689*l*, 2689n to 2689p, 2689r to 2689z, 2689aa, 9412, 9511)
Pub.L. 99–646, § 87(d)(2) to (7), Nov. 10, 1986, 100 Stat. 3624 (42 § 9511)
Pub.L. 99–654, § 3(b)(3) to (7), Nov. 14, 1986, 100 Stat. 3663, 3664 (42 § 9511)

Mental Retardation Amendments of 1967
Pub.L. 90–170, Dec. 4, 1967, 81 Stat. 527 (20 § 617; 42 §§ 2661, 2665, 2671, 2672, 2674, 2677 to 2678d, 2698 to 2698b)

Mental Retardation Facilities and Community Mental Health Centers Construction Act of 1963
Pub.L. 88–164, Oct. 31, 1963, 77 Stat. 282 (20 §§ 611 to 613, 617, 618, 676; 42 §§ 291k, 295 to 295e, 2661 to 2665, 2671 to 2677, 2681 to 2687, 2691 to 2696, 6000 to 6009, 6021 to 6030, 6041 to 6043, 6061 to 6064, 6081 to 6083)
Pub.L. 89–105, §§ 2 to 5, Aug. 4, 1965, 79 Stat. 427 to 430 (20 § 618; 42 §§ 2672, 2682 to 2688d, 2692, 2697)

ILLUSTRATION 6-11. U.S.C.S. *Statutes at Large* and Public Law Numbers Table

| 110 Stat | | | STATUTES AT LARGE | | | | | | 104th Cong | | |

Pub. L.	Section	Stat. Page	USCS Title	Section	Status	Pub. L.	Section	Stat. Page	USCS Title	Section	Status
1996 May 2—Cont'd						1996 May 2—Cont'd					
104-140 —Cont'd						104-140 —Cont'd					
			20	5895(b)(2)	Amd.				12	1715l(g)(4)	Amd.
			20	5895(b)(3)	Amd.				12	1710(a)	Amd.
			20	5895(b)(4)	Amd.				12	1715u nt.	New
			20	5895(c)(2)	Amd.				12	1715u(d)	Rpld.
			20	5895(f)	Amd.				12	1710 nt.	New
			20	5896	Rpld.				12	1710 nt.	Rpld.
			20	5897(d)(4)	Amd.				12	1710 nt.	Amd.
			20	5897(e)(2)	Amd.				42	5305(a)(4)	Amd.
			20	5897(e)(3)	Rpld.				42	5305(a)(13)	Amd.
			20	5897(e)(3) [(4)]	Redes.				42	5305(a)(19)	Rpld.
			20	5933(b)(1)	Amd.				42	5305(a)(24)	Amd.
			20	5933(b)(2), (3), (5)	Amd.				42	5305(a)(25)	Amd.
			20	5933(b)(2)	Amd.				42	5305(a)(19)-(24) [(20)-(25)]	Redes.
			20	5933(b)(4)	Amd.				42	5305(a)(25) [(21)]	Redes.
			20	5933(b)(5)	Amd.				12	1715z-1(f)(1)	Amd.
			20	5933(e)(1)	Amd.				12	1715z-1(g)	Amd.
			20	5933(e)(2)	Amd.				36	121b	Re-peat
			20	5934(f)	Rpld.				36	122	Re-peat
			20	5934(f) [(g)]	Redes.				36	122a	Re-peat
			20	6311(b)(8)	Amd.				12	4703 nt.	Re-peat
			20	6311(f)	Amd.				33	1281 nt.	New
			20	6311(g)	Rpld.				33	1281 nt.	New
			20	6311(g) [(h)]	Redes.			(b)-(e)			Appn.	Un-class.
			20	6317(c)(2)	Amd.							
			20	6317(c)(5)	Amd.	1996 May 6					
			20	6317(d)(4)	Amd.	104-141	1	1328	20	1063b nt.	New
			20	6317(d)(6)	Amd.		2		20	1063b(b)	Amd.
			20	6491(a)(2)	Amd.						
			20	8001(b)(1)	Amd.	1996 May 13					
			20	8941(b)(1)	Amd.	104-142	1	1329	42	14301 nt.	New
			20	1228b	Amd.		2		42	14301	New
			25	2001(b)	Amd.		3		42	14302	New
			20	5884(e)	Added		4	1330	42	14303	New
			20	5886(n)(4)	Added		5	1331	42	14304	New
			20	5885(c)(2)	Amd.		6	1332	42	14305	New
			20	5887(b)(1)	Amd.		7		42	14306	New
			20	5892(a)	Amd.		8		42	14307	New
			20	5900	Added		Title I				
			12	4101 nt.	New		101		42	14301 nt.	New
			42	5305 nt.	New		102		42	14321	New
			42	5306 nt.	New		103		42	14322	New
			42	1437l(q)	Amd.		104	1335	42	14323	New
			42	1437l nt.	New		Title II				
			42	1437aa nt.	New		201	1336	42	14301 nt.	New
			42	1437c nt.	Amd.		202		42	14331	New
			42	1437p(f)	Amd.		203		42	14332	New
			42	1437aa nt.	New		204		42	14333	New
			42	1437l nt.	New		205		42	14334	New
			42	1437f(t)	Rpld.		206		42	14335	New
			42	1437f(c)(8)	Amd.		207		42	14336	New
			42	1437f(c)(9)	Amd.	1996 May 15					
			42	1437f(d)(1)	Amd.						
			42	1437f nt.	New	104-143	1—7	1338		Spec.	Un-class.
			42	1437f nt.	New						
			12	1707 nt.	Amd.	1996 May 16					
			12	1707 nt.	Amd.	104-144	1	1342		Spec.	Un-class.
			42	1437f(bb)	Added						
			12	1715n nt.	New	1996 May 17					
			42	1437f nt.	New	104-145	1	1345	42	13701 nt.	New
			12	4516(b)(2)	Amd.		2		42	14071(d)	Amd.
			42	4852(a), (c) (4), (d)(1), (e)(1)-(3), (7), (9)	Amd.	1996 May 20					
			42	4852(a)	Amd.						
			42	1437g(a)(3)	Amd.	104-146	1	1346	42	201 nt.	New

614

ILLUSTRATION 6-12.   Sample Page from *Shepard's Acts and Cases by Popular Name*

Medicinal Drug Use Clarification Act (Animal)
U.S. Code Title 21, § § 331, 360b, 343-1, 371
U.S., P.L. 103-396, 108 Stat. 4153

Medicine and Dentistry Flexibility Act (University)
N.J. Stat. Anno., 18A:64G-1 et seq.

Meditation in Public Schools Act
N.M. Stat. Anno. 1978, 22-27-1 et seq.

▶ **Megan's Law**
U.S. Code Title 42, § 14071, Subsec. d
May, 17, 1996, P.L. 104-145, 110 Stat. 1345
Ala. Code 1975, § § 13A-11-200 to 13A-11-203
Alk. Stat. 1962, § § 11.56.840, 12.63.010 to 12.63.100, 18.65.087, 28.05.048, 33.30.035
Az. Rev. Stat., § § 13-3821 to 13-3825
Ark. Code 1987, 12-12-901 to 12-12-909
Cal. Penal Code § § 290 to 290.4
Colo. Rev. Stat., 18-3-412.5
Conn. Gen. Stat. 1983, § § 54-102a to 54-102r
Del. Code of 1974, Title 11, § 4120
Fla. Stats., 775.13, 775.22
Ga. Official Code Anno., 42-9-44.1
Haw. Session Laws 1995, Act 160
Ida. Code 1947, 9-340, Subd. 11, Para. f, 18-8301 to 18-8311
Ill. Comp. Stat. 1992, Ch. 730, § § 150/1 to 10
Ind. Code 1982, 5-2-12-1 to 5-2-12-13
Kan. Stat. Anno. 22-4901 to 22-4910
Ky. Rev. Stat. 1971, 17.500 to 17.540
La. Rev. Stat. Anno. 15:540 to 15:549
Me. Rev. Stat. Anno. 1964, Title 34-A, § § 11001 to 11004
Md. Laws 1995, Ch. 142
Mich. Public Acts 1994, No. 295
Min. Stat. 1986, 243.166
Mis. Code 1972, § § 45-33-1 to 45-33-19
Mo. Rev. Stat. 1986, 566.600 to 566.625
Mont. Code Anno., 46-23-501 to 46-23-507
Nev. Rev. Stat. (1987 Reprint), 207.080, 207.151 to 207.157
N.H. Rev. Stat. 1955, 632-A:11 to 632-A:19
N.J. Stat. Anno., 2C:7-1 to 2C:7-11
N.M. Stat. Anno. 1978, 29-11A-1 to 29-11A-8
N.Y. Correction Law (Consol. Laws Ch. 43) § § 168 to 168V
N.C. Gen. Stat. 1943, § § 14-208.5 to 14-208.10
▶ N.D. Century Code, 12.1-32-15
Ohio Rev. Code 1953, 2950.01 to 2950.08
Okla. Stat. 1991, Title 57, § § 581 to 587
Ore. Rev. Stat., 181.507 to 181.519
Pa. 1995 Pamph. Laws, No. 24
R.I. Gen. Laws 1956, 11-37-16
S.D. Codified Laws 1967, 22-22-30 to 22-22-41

Ten. Code Anno., 40-39-101 to 40-39-108
Tex. Rev. Civ. Stat., Art. 6252-13c-1
Utah Code Anno. 1953, 53-5-212.5, 77-27-21.5
Va. Code 1950, § § 19.2-298.1 to 19.2-390.1
Wash. Rev. Code, 4.24.550, 9A.44.130, 9A.44.140, 10.01.200, 70.48.470, 72.09.330
W.Va. Code 1966, § § 61-8F-1 to 61-8F-8
Wis. Stat. 1989, 175.45
Wyo. Stat. 1977, § § 7-19-301 to 7-19-306

Meigs Field Airport Act
Ill. Comp. Stat. 1992, Ch. 620, § 60/1 et seq.

Melrose Park and Chicago South Civic Center Act
Ill. Comp. Stat. 1992, Ch. 70, § 245/0 01 et seq.

Membership Camping Act
N.C. Gen. Stat. 1943, § 66-220 et seq.

Membrane Processes Research Act of 1992
U.S. Code Title 42, § 10341 et seq.
Oct. 24, 1992, P.L. 102-490, 106 Stat. 3142

Memorial Auditorium Authority Act (Upper Mohawk Valley)
N.Y. Public Authorities Law (Consol. Laws Ch. 43A) § 1940 et seq.

Memorial Day Act (Coal Miners)
Ill. Comp. Stat. 1992, Ch. 5, § 490/30

Memorial Monument Permanent Trust Act (First Special Service Force)
Mont. Code Anno., 35-21-901 to 35-21-903

Mendocino County Flood Control and Water Conservation District Act
Cal. Water Code, Appendix, § 54-1 et seq.

Mental Health Act (Community)
Ill. Comp. Stat. 1992, Ch. 405, § 20/0.01 et seq.

Mental Health, Alcohol, Drug Abuse and Developmental Disabilities Act
Wis. Stat., 51.001 et seq.

Mental Health and Developmental Disabilities Act (Children's)
N.M. Stat. Anno. 1978, 32A-6-1 et seq.

Mental Health and Developmental Disabilities Administrative Act
Ill. Laws 1997, P.A. 90-423

Mental Health Compact (Interstate)
Iowa Code 1991, 221.1 et seq.
Me. Rev. Stat. Anno. 1964, Title 34-B, § 9001 et seq.

federal and state versions of Megan's Law. *Shepard's Acts and Cases by Popular Name* provides the date of codification and, for federal statutes, the *Statutes at Large* citation.

▼ How Do You Cite Federal Statutes?

Always cite to the official statutory compilation. The first entry in the citation is the title number, then the abbreviation for the statutory compilation, and then the section or paragraph number. Bluebook Rule 12 details all of the various rules pertaining to citing statutes and codes, state or federal. For example, Title 12, §211 of the U.S.C. would be cited as:

> 12 U.S.C. §211 (1994)

You always cite to the official code, the U.S.C., unless you are relying on an unofficial code for updating purposes.

The year included in the citation is the year that the code volume was published, not the year that the statute was enacted. The publication date is printed either on the title page of the bound volume or on the back of the title page. If a pocket part supplement is used, include that date as well.

> 42 U.S.C.A. §14071(d) (West 1995 & Supp. 1998)

In this example, the first year mentioned, 1995, is the year that the particular volume of the code was published. The second date, 1998, is the year of the pocket part supplement that updates the code volume.

If a code section is well known by a popular name, then include the name in the citation:

> Strikebreaker Act, 18 U.S.C. §1231 (1994)

4. Shepardizing and Updating Statutes

▼ How and Why Would You Shepardize Federal Statutes?

Remember, it is important to validate and update statutes. *Shepard's* provides the analytical treatment indicating how a court of law interprets or applies a statute section. *Shepard's* contains analysis that tells you whether the statute is constitutional, unconstitutional, valid, or invalid. See Illustration 6-13 for a portion of a case applying a statute and Illustration 6-14 for the corresponding *Shepard's* entry indicating the analytical treatment. See also Illustration 6-15 for the *Shepard's* abbreviations for the analytical treatment of statutes by courts. Validating, by Shepardizing, indicates whether a court deems the statute constitutional or unconstitutional, valid or invalid.

ILLUSTRATION 6-13. Pages from Decision in the *Federal Supplement* that Cites to 42 U.S.C. §14071(d)

DOE v. PATAKI   **603**

Cite as 940 F.Supp. 603 (S.D.N.Y. 1996)

John DOE, Richard Roe and Samuel Poe, individually and on behalf of all other persons similarly situated, Plaintiffs,

v.

Hon. George E. PATAKI, in his official capacity as Governor of the State of New York, et al., Defendants.

No. 96 Civ. 1657 (DC).

United States District Court, S.D. New York.

Sept. 24, 1996.

3. Constitutional Law ⬱203

To determine whether government measure constitutes punishment, for purposes of applying constitutional prohibition against ex post facto laws, one must analyze totality of circumstances by grouping them in four areas: (1) intent, (2) design, (3) history, and (4) effects. U.S.C.A. Const. Art. 1, § 10, cl. 1.

4. Constitutional Law ⬱203

In determining whether government measure constitutes punishment, for purposes of applying constitutional prohibition against ex post facto laws, court cannot transform the factors it considers into rigid

---

(N.Y.Sup.Ct.N.Y.Co.1996) (citing statutes). The statutes resulted from growing public concern over the substantial threats presented by sex offenders and a belief that sex offenders as a group are more likely to repeat their crimes. In enacting these laws, legislatures have articulated two goals: (i) enhancing law enforcement authorities' ability to fight sex crimes and (ii) protecting

1. In 1994, Congress enacted the Jacob Wetterling Crimes Against Children and Sexually Violent Offender Registration Program, 42 U.S.C. §§ 14071(a)–(f) (the "Federal Act"). The Federal Act initially encouraged states, through funding incentives, to enact laws requiring individuals convicted of crimes against children or sexually violent offenses to register with state law enforcement agencies. The Federal Act also permitted law enforcement authorities to release certain information in certain limited circumstances. *Id.* at § 14071(d). Congress recently amended the Federal Act to provide, as an additional requirement of funding, that state and local law enforcement agencies "*shall* release relevant information that is necessary to protect the public concerning a specific person required

2. *Registration*

Under the Act, a "sex offender" is any person convicted of a "sex offense" or a "sexually violent offense." § 168–a(1), (2), (3). These designations encompass 36 offenses, including attempts. Seven of the designated offenses are misdemeanors. (Stip. ¶ 16).[2]

to register." Pub.L. No. 104–145, 110 Stat. 1345 (emphasis added) (to be codified at 42 U.S.C. § 14071(d)(2)).

2. References to "Stip." are to the parties' "Stipulation of Undisputed Facts," dated August 22, 1996.

"Sex offenses" include, for example, convictions for rape in the second or third degree, sodomy in the second or third degree, or sexual abuse in the second degree, and convictions for attempt thereof. § 168–a(2) (*citing* N.Y. Penal Law §§ 130.25, 130.30, 130.40, 130.45, 130.60 (McKinney 1987 & Supp.1996)). "Sexually violent offenses" include, for example, convictions for rape in the first degree, sodomy in the first

ILLUSTRATION 6-14. Sample Pages from *Shepard's* Showing Treatment of U.S.C. References

①UNITED STATES CODE			②TITLE 43 §§ 270-1 to 270-3
Cir. 6 922FS1216△1996 Cir. 7 940FS1244△1996 959FS907△1997 Cir. 9 957FS197△1997 Cir. 10 108F3d1321△1997 926FS1015△1996 929FS1359△1996 936FS1580△1996 959FS1391△1997 Cir. 11 i) 99F3d1073△1996 **§ 12203(b)** Cir. 2 923FS50△1996 Cir. 7 959FS907△1997 Cir. 8 95F3d684*1994 **§ 12203(c)** Cir. 6 922FS1219△1996 Cir. 9 957FS197△1997 **§ 12204** Cir. 6	**§ 12206(a)** Cir. 2 931FS236△1996 **§ 12206(c)** Cir. 2 931FS236△1996 **§ 12206(c)(3)** Cir. 9 931FS694△1996 Cir. 11 86F3d196△1996 **§ 12208** Cir. 6 952FS529△1997 **§ 12209** Cir. 1 957FS9△1997 **§ 12210(a)** Cir. 5 929FS981△1996 Cir. 6 952FS529△1997 **§ 12210(b)** Cir. 2 931FS231△1996 **§ 12210(c)**	**§ 12741 et seq.** Cir. 1 958FS690△1997 **§ 13041** Cir. 7 110F3d407△1997 **§ 13041(c)** Cir. 7 110F3d407△1997 **§ 13701 et seq.** 137L**E**441*1994 117SC1224*1994 **§ 13710** Cir. DC 114F3d1225△1997 **§ 13791** Cir. 9 115F3d664△1997 **§ 13801** Cir. 9 115F3d664△1997 **§ 13861** Cir. 9 115F3d664△1997 **§ 13868** Cir. 9 115F3d664△1997 **§ 13951(a)** Cir. 9 961FS1329*1996 **§ 13951(c)**	**§ 13981(c)** Cir. 4 112F3d765△1997 935FS790△1996 958FS249△1997 **§ 13981(d)(1)** Cir. 4 935FS784△1996 **§ 13981(d)(2)(A)** Cir. 4 935FS790△1996 **§ 13981(e)(4)** Cir. 2 929FS616△1996 Cir. 4 935FS793△1996 **§ 14071** Cir. 1 954FS427*1994 **§ 14071(a to f)** Cir. 2 940FS606△1996 ③ **§ 14071(d)** Cir. 2 919FS694 ④ 0FS606△1996 **§ 14071(d)(2)** Cir. 2 940FS606△1996 **§ 14131(a)** Cir. 1 954FS415△1997 957FS339*1995 **§ 14151** Cir. 9 115F3d664△1997

> **1 The code name**
> **2 Title**
> **3 Section**
> **4 Case where section is cited**

Reprinted with permission of *Shepard's*.
1 The Code name.
2 Title.
3 Section.
4 Case where section is cited.

Shepardizing statutes no longer yields information indicating whether the statute has been repealed or amended. You must update statutory authority by using the code's pocket part supplement and advance sheets. Most important, *Shepard's* for codes indicates the judicial treatment or interpretation of a statute, meaning how courts of law have looked at a statute's application and at whether its application was discriminatory or affected too broad or too narrow a group of people. Judges then determine if the statute has been complied with or if the statute is unconstitutional or constitutional in whole or in part. See Illustration 6-14 for Shepard's treatment of 42 U.S.C. §14071(d) and Illustration 6-13 where 42 U.S.C. §14071(d) is cited in a case listed in *Shepard's*.

ILLUSTRATION 6-15. *Shepard's* **Abbreviations**

ABBREVIATIONS—ANALYSIS

Form of Statute

Amend.	Amendment	Proc.	Proclamation
App.	Appendix	Pt.	Part
Art.	Article	Res.	Resolution
Ch.	Chapter	§	Section
Cl.	Clause	St.	Statutes at Large
Ex. Ord.	Executive Order	Subch.	Subchapter
H.C.R.	House Concurrent	Subcl.	Subclause
	Resolution	Subd.	Subdivision
No.	Number	Sub ¶	Subparagraph
¶	Paragraph	Subsec.	Subsection
P.L.	Public Law	Vet. Reg.	Veterans' Regulations
Pr.L.	Private Law		

Operation of Statute
Judicial

C	Constitutional.		V	Void or invalid.
U	Unconstitutional.		Va	Valid.
Up	Unconstitutional in part.		Vp	Void or invalid in part.

*Reproduced by permission of LEXIS-NEXIS. Further reproduction is strictly prohibited.

▼ How Do You Update Statutes with Print Resources?

To update statutes to ensure that you have the most recent version, you must take the following steps.

1. Rely on an unofficial code, the U.S.C.A. or the U.S.C.S. After finding the appropriate code section, consult the pocket part supplement at the end of the volume or the separately published pamphlet that updates the particular volume. For example, 42 U.S.C.A. §14071(d) is viewed in the main volume. See Illustration 6-6. Then turn to the back of the volume containing the initial entry and open the pocket part supplement, to see if §14071(d) is included. The entries in the supplement are in numerical order just as they are in the main volume. If a section is not affected, it is just skipped over and the next affected section, in sequential order, is mentioned. Section 14071(d) is included, so you know that the code section has been modified. See Illustration 6-16. Note that sometimes the material updating the code volume contains too many pages to be included in a pocket part so that a supplementary pamphlet, a separate paperback bound pamphlet, is published.

2. To further update a federal code section, scan the *United States Code Service Advance Service,* the U.S.C.C.A.N. advance sheets (the paperbound pamphlets that are issued monthly containing the ses-

ILLUSTRATION 6-16. Pocket Part Entry for 42 U.S.C.A. §14071(d)

(5) Registration for change of address to another State

A person who has been convicted of an offense which requires registration under this section and who moves to another State, shall report the change of address to the responsible agency in the State the person is leaving, and shall comply with any registration requirement in the new State of residence. The procedures of the State the person is leaving shall ensure that notice is provided promptly to an agency responsible for registration in the new State, if that State requires registration.

(6) Length of registration

A person required to register under subsection (a)(1) of this section shall continue to comply with this section, except during ensuing periods of incarceration, until—

   (A) 10 years have elapsed since the person was released from prison or placed on parole, supervised release, or probation; or

   (B) for the life of that person if that person—

      (i) has 1 or more prior convictions for an offense described in subsection (a)(1)(A) of this section; or

      (ii) has been convicted of an aggravated offense described in subsection (a)(1)(A) of this section; or

      (iii) has been determined to be a sexually violent predator pursuant to subsection (a)(2) of this section.

(7) Registration of out-of-State offenders, Federal offenders, persons sentenced by courts martial, and offenders crossing State borders

As provided in guidelines issued by the Attorney General, each State shall include in its registration program residents who were convicted in another State and shall ensure that procedures are in place to accept registration information from—

      (A) residents who were convicted in another State, convicted of a Federal offense, or sentenced by a court martial; and

      (B) nonresident offenders who have crossed into another State in order to work or attend school.

(c) Registration of offender crossing State border

Any person who is required under this section to register in the State in which such person resides shall also register in any State in which the person is employed, carries on a vocation, or is a student.

(d) Penalty

A person required to register under a State program established pursuant to this section who knowingly fails to so register and keep such registration current shall be subject to criminal penalties in any State in which the person has so failed.

(e) Release of information

(1) The information collected under a State registration program may be disclosed for any purpose permitted under the laws of the State.

(2) The State or any agency authorized by the State shall release relevant information that is necessary to protect the public concerning a specific person required to register under this section, except that the identity of a victim of an offense that requires registration under this section shall not be released.

(f) Immunity for good faith conduct

Law enforcement agencies, employees of law enforcement agencies and independent contractors acting at the direction of such agencies, and State officials shall be immune from liability for good faith conduct under this section.

30

*Reprinted with permission from West Group.

ILLUSTRATION 6-16. *Continued*

Protection and treatment: Permissible civil detention of sexual predators. John Kip Cornwell, 53 Wash. & Lee L.Rev. 1293 (1996).

Sex offender registration and community notification: Protection, not punishment. 30 New Eng.L.Rev. 183 (1995).

NOTES OF DECISIONS

Equal protection rights 3
Privacy interests 2
Remedial nature of state laws 1

1. Remedial nature of state laws

Statutes for registration and community notification of convicted sex offenders were totally remedial in purpose, and any deterrent effect from offenders' loss of anonymity was merely inevitable consequence, which thus supported conclusion that statutes did not impose punishment for purposes of constitutional challenges under ex post facto, double jeopardy, bill of attainder, and cruel and unusual punishment clauses; statutes were designed solely to enable public to protect itself from danger posed by sex offenders who were widely regarded as having highest risk of recidivism. Doe v. Poritz, N.J. 1995, 662 A.2d 367, 142 N.J. 1.

2. Privacy interests

State interest in public disclosure of sex offender's name, home address, appearance, and crime as required by convicted sex offender community notification statute substantially outweighed offender's limited privacy interest under Federal Constitution, in light of public nature of information, express public policy of protecting public from danger of recidivism posed by sex offenders, and calibration of degree and scope of disclosure by need for disclosure and risk of reoffense. Doe v. Poritz, N.J. 1995, 662 A.2d 367, 142 N.J. 1.

3. Equal protection rights

Statutory registration and community notification requirements for convicted sex offenders were rationally related to legitimate state interest of protecting public from risk from recidivist offenders and, thus, did not violate offender's federal equal protection rights even though he, unlike most convicted sex offenders, had successfully completed treatment program and had been released on parole. Doe v. Poritz, N.J. 1995, 662 A.2d 367, 142 N.J. 1.

§ 14072. FBI database

(a) Definitions

For purposes of this section—

(1) the term "FBI" means the Federal Bureau of Investigation;

(2) the terms "criminal offense against a victim who is a minor", "sexually violent offense", "sexually violent predator", "mental abnormality", "predatory", "employed, or carries on a vocation", and "student" have the same meanings as in section 14071(a)(3) of this title; and

(3) the term "minimally sufficient sexual offender registration program" means any State sexual offender registration program that—

(A) requires the registration of each offender who is convicted of an offense in a range of offenses specified by State law which is comparable to or exceeds that described in subparagraph (A) or (B) of section 14071(a)(1) of this title;

(B) participates in the national database established under subsection (b) of this section in conformity with guidelines issued by the Attorney General;

(C) provides for verification of address at least annually;

(D) requires that each person who is required to register under subparagraph (A) shall do so for a period of not less than 10 years beginning on the date that such person was released from prison or placed on parole, supervised release, or probation.

(b) Establishment

The Attorney General shall establish a national database at the Federal Bureau of Investigation to track the whereabouts and movement of—

(1) each person who has been convicted of a criminal offense against a victim who is a minor;

(2) each person who has been convicted of a sexually violent offense; and

(3) each person who is a sexually violent predator.

(c) Registration requirement

Each person described in subsection (b) of this section who resides in a State that has not established a minimally sufficient sexual offender registration program shall register a current address, fingerprints of that person, and a current photograph of that person

34

sion laws from the Congress), or the U.S.C.A. statutory supplement to find relevant slip laws from recent congressional sessions. Look for entries that are similar in name to the code section you are updating. This can also be done for state statutes by using the state session law reporter.

3. If a state statute is being updated, review the session law reporter for the legislature to see if any new session laws modify, repeal, supersede, or amend existing legislation.

4. You can track pending legislation for the 50 states on LEXIS and on WESTLAW in the respective state bill tracking files.

5. Review the U.S.C.A. statutory supplement for federal statutes. This pamphlet indicates whether a section of the U.S.C. has been amended, repealed, or created. See Illustration 6-16.

PRACTICE POINTER

Always read a statute according to its plain meaning; that is, interpret the language just as it is written. After reading a statute, summarize the language in a few sentences, in your own words. This will help when you then want to use the statute in a written document. Your language and the statutory language won't contrast so sharply. Remember to cite to all statutory authority that you rely on, even if it is written in your own language.

---

5. How to Find State Statutes

▼ How Does State Statutory Research Compare with Federal Statutory Research?

State statutory research closely parallels federal statutory research. To perform state statutory research, you would use the index method, the title outline method, the popular name table, or the conversion table approach, just as you would with the federal materials. Even the precise, succinct language of the state statutes is similar to the federal statutes because of the canons of construction and models of statutory parallelism that are adopted by drafters of legislation. Compare North Dakota's version of Megan's Law, shown in Illustration 6-17, to the federal version, shown in Illustration 6-6. See also Illustration 6-12 for other state statutes for Megan's Law.

State statutes are enacted by the state legislatures and appear in the slip law format first, then become session laws, and finally are codified and incorporated into the state statutory codes. For example, in Ohio the session laws are called the Laws of Ohio and can be found in the *Ohio Legislative Bulletin* published by Anderson or Banks-Baldwin's *Legislative Service*. Current state legislation also can be found in state bar bulletins and legal newspapers.

ILLUSTRATION 6-17.   Sample Page Showing North Dakota Century Code §12.1-32-15

12.1-32-15.   Offenders against children and sexual offenders — Sexually violent predators — Registration requirement — Penalty.
1. As used in this section:
    a. "A crime against a child" means a violation of chapter 12.1-16, 12.1-17, 12.1-18, or 12.1-29, or an equivalent ordinance, in which the victim is a minor or is otherwise of the age required for the act to be a crime or an attempt to commit these offenses.
    b. "Department" means the department of corrections and rehabilitation.
    c. "Mental abnormality" means a congenital or acquired condition of an individual that affects the emotional or volitional capacity of the individual in a manner that predisposes that individual to the

360

11. Relevant and necessary registration information shall be disclosed to the public by a law enforcement agency if the agency determines that the individual registered under this section is a public risk and disclosure of the registration information is necessary for public protection. The department, in a timely manner, shall provide law enforcement agencies any information the department determines is relevant concerning individuals required to be registered under this section who are about to be released or placed into the community. A law enforcement agency, its officials, and its employees are not subject to civil or criminal liability for disclosing or for failing to

363

▼ How Can You Tell Whether a State Code Is the Official or the Unofficial Statutory Compilation?

Bluebook Table T.1 provides the answer to this question. Under each state in Table T.1 is the boldface heading **Statutory compilations.** Immediately following this heading is information indicating the official format of the state code. For example, under Wisconsin you find:

Statutory compilations: Cite to Wis. Stat. if therein.

This indicates that Wis. Stat., the Bluebook abbreviation for the *Wisconsin Statutes,* is the official statutory compilation for Wisconsin. Under the **Statutory compilations** heading, the names of the state

ILLUSTRATION 6-17.   *Continued*

12.1-33-01   CRIMINAL CODE

disclose information as permitted by this section. Nonregistration information concerning an offender required to register under this section consisting of the name of the offender, the last known address of the offender, the offense or offenses as defined in subsection 1 to which the offender pled guilty or of which the offender was found guilty, the date of the judgment or order imposing a sentence or probation and the court entering the judgment or order, the sentence or probation imposed upon the offender, and any disposition, if known, of a sentence or probation may be disclosed to the public. The attorney general shall compile nonregistration information concerning offenders required to register under this section from criminal history record information maintained pursuant to chapter 12-60 or from an agency or department of another state or the federal government and shall provide the information upon request at no cost.

Source: S.L. 1991, ch. 136, § 1; 1993, ch. 129, § 3; 1995, ch. 139, § 1; 1997, ch. 124, § 5; 1997, ch. 128, § 2; 1997, ch. 136, § 1; 1997, ch. 137, § 1.

Effective Date.
The 1997 amendment of this section by section 5 of chapter 124, S.L. 1997 became effective August 1, 1997.
The 1997 amendment of this section by section 2 of chapter 128, S.L. 1997 became effective August 1, 1997.
The 1997 amendment to this section by section 1 of chapter 136, S.L. 1997 became effective August 1, 1997.
The 1997 amendment of subsection 1 of this section by section 1 of chapter 137, S.L. 1997 became effective August 1, 1997.

Note.
Section 12.1-32-15 was amended four times by the 1997 Legislative Assembly. Pursuant to section 1-02-09.1, the section is printed above to harmonize and give effect to the changes made in section 1 of chapter 136, S.L. 1997, section 1 of the chapter 137, S.L. 1997, section 5 of chapter 124, S.L. 1997, and section 2 of chapter 128, S.L. 1997.

Withdrawal of Guilty Plea.
Trial court abused its discretion in denying defendant's withdrawal of his guilty plea, because its failure to inform him he was required to register as a sexual offender upon conviction of engaging in a sexual act with a minor caused a manifest injustice, unless he knew of the need to register when he pled. State v. Breiner, 1997 ND 71, 562 N.W.2d 565 (1997).

Collateral References.
State statutes or ordinances requiring persons previously convicted of crime to register with authorities, 36 A.L.R.5th 161.

code, in the official and the unofficial format, are listed along with the Bluebook abbreviation.

Sometimes a state has more than one statutory compilation, or there is not official compilation. When this occurs, follow the Bluebook for guidance when citing. See Illustration 6-18. Sometimes a state, such as West Virginia, has only one statutory compilation, the

ILLUSTRATION 6-18.   Bluebook Table T.1 Showing West Virginia and Wisconsin Statutory Compilations

West Virginia

Statutory compilation

West Virginia Code — W. Va. Code § x (19xx)

Session laws

Acts of the Legislature of West Virginia — 19xx W. Va. Acts xxx

Wisconsin

Statutory compilations: Cite to Wis. Stat. if therein.

Wisconsin Statutes (1975 and biannually) — Wis. Stat. § x (19xx)

West's Wisconsin Statutes Annotated — Wis. Stat. Ann. § x (West 19xx)

Session laws: Cite to Wis. Laws if therein.

Laws of Wisconsin — 19xx Wis. Laws xxx

Wisconsin Legislative Service (West) — 19xx Wis. Legis. Serv. xxx (West)

*Reprinted from *A Uniform System of Citation, Sixteenth Edition* (1996) with permission of the Columbia Law Review, the Harvard Law Review, the University of Pennsylvania Law Review, and the Yale Law Journal.

West Virginia Code, so it is automatically the official compilation. See Illustration 6-18.

6. Researching Statutes Online

▼ Are the Federal Statutes Available on LEXIS and WESTLAW?

Yes, the complete texts of the U.S.C. and the U.S.C.A. (published by West) are available on WESTLAW. The U.S.C.A. is in the USCA database, and the U.S.C. is in the USC database. The U.S.C.S., but not the U.S.C., is available on LEXIS. The U.S.C.S. is available in full text on LEXIS, in the GENFED library, USCS file, and is updated on a monthly basis.

Both LEXIS and WESTLAW have added the browse enhancement to the statutes databases, enabling you to view the code sections preceding and following the code section that you retrieved. The browse feature emulates researching code sections in a hardbound format because you often look at related code sections when you find the section of the statutes with information on point.

▼ Are State Statutes Available on LEXIS and WESTLAW?

Yes, the full text of all 50 state statutory compilations are available on both WESTLAW and LEXIS. On LEXIS, you can search all 50 state codes simultaneously in the CODE library, ALLCDE file. Slip laws are available for all 50 states on LEXIS and WESTLAW in the respective state legislative service file.

▼ Can Statutes Be Shepardized on LEXIS and WESTLAW?

Shepard's for all statutes is now available on LEXIS but not on WESTLAW.

▼ How Do You Update Federal Statutes Online?

Updating statutory authority online is achieved through the point-and-click method. Once you have the relevant statutory provision on the screen, there will be a caption indicating that the statute is current through a particular date or session law. Citations to any slip laws or session laws updating the statute will be given. If the updating documents are available online, WESTLAW marks the updating document with a jump marker, and LEXIS marks it with an equal sign followed by a number. Merely point and click the identifying icon and you will link to the updating document. Before you perform this on either LEXIS or WESTLAW, call customer service for guidance.

▼ Are Statutes Available on the Internet?

Yes, the U.S.C. is available on the Internet at www.thomas.loc.gov. Updating is not guaranteed to be current, so you must Shepardize and update any federal statute that you find on the Net. Most state statutes are also available on the Internet, but once again, you must Shepardize and update any state statutory authority retrieved on the Internet.

CHAPTER SUMMARY

This chapter led you through the legislative process, where you learned the steps a bill goes through to become law. Also, this chapter detailed constitutional and statutory research on the state and federal levels. You learned how to find, to cite, and to Shepardize pertinent constitutional provisions. You learned about the different ways to perform statutory research and how to update, validate, and cite statutes.

KEY TERMS

codification

committee report

conference committee

constitution

grandfathered

House committee

legislation

pocket veto

public laws

session laws

slip bill

slip laws

sponsor

statutes

Statutes at Large

subcommittee

United States Code

United States Code Annotated

United States Code Service

veto

EXERCISES

RESEARCHING BY POPULAR NAME

To answer questions 1-9, look up the Americans with Disabilities Act of 1990.

1. What date was the act enacted originally? Where is the information? List at least two places.
2. List the names of the four substantive titles of the act. What are they called in the codified version?
3. Provide the public law number for the act. List at least two places where this information is found.
4. Explain what the numbers included in the public law number mean.
5. Provide the U.S.C. citation for the act. List the steps you followed to find this information.
6. Provide the *Statutes at Large* citation for the act. List at least two places where this information is found.
7. What is the definition of *employer* under the act?
8. Does the definition of *employer* under Title I of the act differ in the U.S.C.A. from the definition found in the *Statutes at Large* when the law was originally enacted? If so, how?
9. Find the *United States Code* section for the Americans with Disabilities Act on the Internet at www.thomas.loc.gov.

For questions 10-16, look up the Energy Conservation and Production Act in the U.S.C.'s popular name table. Note in particular the section discussing State Utility Regulatory Assistance.

10. Write the U.S.C. citation in Bluebook format. (Remember to look at the most recent amendments.)
11. After you find the U.S.C. cite, look up the U.S.C.A. entry for the code section. Compare the entries and the annotations. Note the research enhancements that a West publication provides. Write down any key numbers and any U.S.C.C.A.N. references.
12. Look up the U.S.C.S. entry for the code section. Note the research

aids that U.S.C.S. provides. Note that you see administrative regulation references in the U.S.C.S.

13. What C.F.R. citation is referred to in the code section? (Remember to use the supplements and the pocket parts to ensure that you are looking at the most current version of the statute.)
14. Are there any cases that discuss or interpret the statute? If so, look up two cases and see how the statute is treated in the opinions.
15. Shepardize the statute citation.
16. Find the statute on the Internet at www.thomas.loc.gov.

Illinois Statutes

For questions 17-18, use the *Illinois Compiled Statutes* to find the sections that pertain to pawnbrokers and moneylenders.

17. Write the *Illinois Compiled Statute* cite in correct Bluebook format. Next, write the Smith-Hurd Annotated cite. Compare the entries.
18. Are there any cases that discuss or interpret the statute? If so, look them up and see how the statute is treated in the opinion. Use the tables to find the *Illinois Compiled Statute* citation. Finally, Shepardize the statute citation.

Appendix
STATE LEGISLATIVE REFERENCE LIBRARIES

Alabama	Director Legislative Reference Service Rm. 613, State Capitol Montgomery, AL 36130 (334) 242-7627 House (334) 242-7825 Senate
Alaska	Librarian Division of Legal Services Legislative Affairs Agency P.O. Box 7 Juneau, AK 99811 (907) 465-4648
Arizona	Director Library, Archives & Public Records 1700 West Washington State Capitol Phoenix, AZ 85007 (602) 542-4221 House (602) 542-3559 Senate
Arkansas	Librarian Bureau of Legislative Research Room 315, State Capitol Little Rock, AR 72201 (501) 682-7771 House (501) 682-2902 Senate
California	Librarian California State Library Capitol Branch Room 2019 State Capitol

Sacramento, CA 95814
(916) 445-3614 Assembly
(916) 445-4251 Senate

Director
Office of Research
1100 J Street, Room 535
Sacramento, CA 95814
(916) 445-1638

Colorado

Principal Analyst II
Legislative Council
Room 029, State Capitol Bldg.
Denver, CO 80203
(303) 866-3521

Connecticut

Legislative Librarian
Legislative Library
Section, State Library
231 Capitol Avenue
Hartford, CT 06106
(860) 566-5736

Delaware

Librarian
Division of Research
Legislative Council
Legislative Hall
Dover, DE 19901
(800) 282-8545

District of Columbia

Legislative Services Division
Room 714, 414 Fourth Street, N.W.
Washington, D.C. 20004
(202) 724-8050

Florida

Director
Division of Legislative Library Services
Joint Legislative Management Committee
Room 701, The Capitol
Tallahassee, FL 32399-1400
(800) 342-1827

Georgia

Director
Senate Research Office
Room 204, Legislative Office Building
Atlanta, GA 30334
(800) 282-5800

Executive Director
House Research Office
Suite 458, East Tower, Floyd Building
2 Martin Luther King Jr. Drive
Atlanta, GA 30334

	Legislative Council Legislative Services Committee Room 316, State Capitol Atlanta, GA 30334
Hawaii	Head Research Librarian Office of the Legislative Reference Bureau Room 004, State Capitol Honolulu, HI 96813 (808) 587-0700
Idaho	Legislative Librarian Legislative Council State Capitol Boise, ID 83720 (208) 334-3175
Illinois	Librarian Legislative Information System Room 705, Stratton Building Springfield, IL 62706 (217) 782-3944
Indiana	Office of Legislative Information Room 230, State House Indianapolis, IN 46204-2789 (317) 232-9856
Iowa	Legislative Librarian Legislative Service Bureau Room 16, State Capitol Des Moines, IA 50319 (515) 281-5129
Kansas	Legislative Reference Division State Library Third Floor, State House Topeka, KS 66612 (800) 432-3924
Kentucky	Legislative Research Commission Room 300, State Capitol Frankfort, KY 40601 (502) 564-8100
Louisiana	Legislative Research Library Thirteenth Floor, State Capitol Baton Rouge, LA 70804 (800) 256-3793
Maine	Legislative Information Office Room 314, State House Augusta, ME 04333 (207) 287-1692

Maryland	Information Desk, Library Division Department of Legislative Services Basement, Legislative Services Building 90 State Circle Annapolis, MD 21401 (410) 841-3810 (800) 492-7122
Massachusetts	Clerk of the House Room 145, State House Boston, MA 02133 (617) 722-2356 Clerk of the Senate Room 335, State House Boston, MA 02133 (617) 722-1276
Michigan	Legislative Service Bureau Fourth Floor, 124 W. Allegan Lansing, MI 48909 (517) 373-0169
Minnesota	House Index Room 211, State Capitol St. Paul, MN 55155 (612) 296-6646 Senate Information Office Room 231, State Capitol St. Paul, MN 55155 (612) 296-0504
Mississippi	Bill Status Center (sessions only) First Floor, New Capitol Jackson, MS 39201 (601) 359 –3729
Missouri	Legislative Library State Capitol Jefferson City, MO 65101 (573) 751-4633
Montana	Legislative Services Division Room 138, State Capitol Helena, MT 59620 (406) 444-3064
Nebraska	Legislative Hotline (sessions only) Room 2018, State Capitol Lincoln, NE 68509 (402) 471-2709 (800) 742-7456

Nevada	Research Librarian Research Division Legislative Counsel Bureau Legislative Building, Capitol Complex Carson City, NV 89710 (702) 687-6827 (between sessions) (800) 367-5057 ext. 5545 (sessions only)
New Hampshire	Director Government Information Service State Library 20 Park Street Concord, NH 03301 (603) 271-2239
New Jersey	Legislative Information and Bill Room Room B01 State House Annex Trenton, NJ 08625 (609) 292-4840 (800) 792-8630
New Mexico	Legislative Council Service Room 311, State Capitol Santa Fe, NM 87501 (505) 986-4600
New York	Legislative Bill Drafting Commission 55 Elk Street Albany, NY 12207 (518) 455-7545 (800) 342-9860
North Carolina	Legislative Library Rm. 2226, State Legislative Building Raleigh, NC 27601 (919) 733-7779
North Dakota	Research Librarian Legislative Council State Capitol Bismark, ND 58505 (701) 328-2916
Ohio	Legislative Information Office State House Columbus, OH 43215 (614) 466-8842 (800) 282-0253
Oklahoma	Senate Records and Information Room 309, State Capitol Oklahoma City, OK 73105 (405) 521-5642

Oregon	Legislative Publications and Distribution Services Room 49, State Capitol Salem, OR 97310 (800) 332-2313
Pennsylvania	Legislative Reference Bureau Room 648, Main Capitol Building Harrisburg, PA 17120 (717) 787-2342
Puerto Rico	Michie of Puerto Rico, Inc. P.O. Box 9066550 San Juan, PR 00906-6550 (787) 721-1349
Rhode Island	Legislative Data Systems Room 1, State House Providence, RI 02903 (401) 751-8833
South Carolina	Information Desk Legislative Information Systems Second Floor, Carolina Plaza 937 Assembly Street Columbia, SC 29208 (803) 734-2060 (800) 922-1539
South Dakota	Reference Librarian Legislative Research Council Third Floor, State Capitol Pierre, SD 57501-5070 (605) 773-4498
Tennessee	Office of Legislative Services Upper Level, Legislative Plaza Nashville, TN 37243-0080 (615) 741-3511
Texas	Legislative Reference Library (during sessions) Room 2N.3, State Capitol Austin, TX 78701 (512) 463-1251
Utah	Legislative Bill Room Room 419, State Capitol Salt Lake City, UT 84114 (801) 538-1588
Vermont	Legislative Council First Floor Annex, State House Montpelier, VT 05633 (802) 828-2231

Virginia	Legislative Information Office First Floor, State Capitol Richmond, VA 23219 (804) 698-1500
Washington	Director Legislative Bill Room Room 120, Legislative Building Olympia, WA 98504 (800) 562-6000
West Virginia	Legislative Reference and Information Center Room MB27, State Capitol Charleston, WV 25305 (304) 347-4836 (800) 642-8650
Wisconsin	Legislative Hotline Lower Level, 1 E. Main Street Madison, WI 53702 (608) 266-9960 (800) 362-9472
Wyoming	Bill Status Desk (sessions only) Basement, State Capitol Cheyenne, WY 82002 (800) 342-9570

7

LEGISLATIVE HISTORY

CHAPTER OVERVIEW

Paralegals are called on to monitor the status of bills and proposed legislation currently being considered on the federal and state levels and to compile legislative histories of laws already passed and codified to ascertain the policy or intended effect of the legislation. The process of compiling all of the components of the legislative process leading to the enactment of a statute, called **legislative history**, is growing in importance as the need for the interpretation of statutes in litigation increases.

A. LEGISLATIVE INFORMATION

Researching a legislative history requires that you retrace the law making process of enacted law from the initial bill through the committee reports through the various versions of the bill to the final version and the enacted law. Legislative histories are very informative because the information gathered from the committee reports and the speeches or legislative debates given on the floor of the legislative body provides insight into the purpose and intent of the legislation.

1. Finding the Text of Pending Legislation

Bills currently going through the process of being enacted into law are classified as **pending legislation.** Paralegals are called on to monitor pending legislation and to make sure that the information is as current as possible. The legislative hotline telephone numbers for all of the jurisdictions at the end of Chapter 6 may be of assistance. You can call the particular jurisdiction's legislative hotline telephone number with the bill name, number, or sponsor and obtain the most recent status of the pending legislation.

LEXIS and WESTLAW have current federal and state bills online. LEXIS has the text of current pending federal bills in the LEXIS library, BLTEXT file. The CMTRPT file in the LEGIS library on LEXIS contains the full text of federal committee and conference reports dating back to January 1990. The text of most pending state bills is available in the CODES library; the files are the state postal abbreviation followed by "TEXT." For example, the CATEXT file contains the text of pending California bills.

WESTLAW has current pending federal bills online and Billcast, which has the summaries of pending legislation from all 50 states and the U.S. Congress. Billcast also contains statistical odds of passage in each chamber. WESTLAW also has state pending legislation and the text of bills for states online.

On the state level, each state has a legislative library from which you can request the copy of the particular bill in question. If the librarian cannot provide a copy of the bill, he or she will generally direct you to the member of the state House or Senate who sponsored the bill or to the appropriate committee. Pending legislation for all 50 states can be tracked on LEXIS and WESTLAW.

2. Tracking Pending Legislation

On the federal level, Commerce Clearing House publishes a two-volume set called *Congressional Index* that monitors the status of every bill currently pending in the U.S. House of Representatives and the U.S. Senate. A new set is published for each Congress. The first volume covers the Senate, and the second volume covers the House. The *Congressional Index* is updated weekly when Congress is in session and provides information on voting records and the status of bills during the prior week. The status of the bill means where the bill in question is in the legislative process, whether it is in committee or subcommittee hearings, or whether it is being debated on the floor. Note that *Congressional Index* does not print the text of the bills.

Another source in tracking pending federal legislation is the *Congressional Quarterly Weekly Report.* This source is helpful for policy information regarding bills currently being considered in Congress and for voting records.

On the state level, almost every state has either a state legislative hotline, a state bar association, or a state legislative library that provides information as to the status of bills that are currently being created and considered. See the list of state legislative hotline numbers at the end of Chapter 6.

B. LEGISLATIVE HISTORIES

▼ Where Do You Find Copies of Public Laws?

Public laws, which are the federally enacted laws, can be obtained by contacting the law's sponsor in the House or the Senate. Also, the U.S. Government Printing Office issues pamphlets for each public law passed. These can be obtained at a government depository library. (Many university libraries and large city libraries are government depository libraries.) See Ilustration 6-3, page 142. The *United States Code Service* (U.S.C.S.) publishes paperback advance sheets with the public laws enacted during the prior month. The *United States Code Annotated* (U.S.C.A.) also prints paperback advance sheets each month that contain all of the public laws enacted during the prior month.

Public laws starting with the 103d Congress are available online at www.thomas.loc.gov.

▼ How Do You Research Legislative Histories of Laws That Are Already Enacted?

Commercial publishers compile the most accessible sources of legislative histories for laws that are already enacted. The easiest source of commercially compiled federal legislative histories is the *United States Code Congressional and Administrative News* (U.S.C.C.A.N.). U.S.C.C.A.N., which began publication in the 1950s, is published by West Group, and references to U.S.C.C.A.N. are provided in the U.S.C.A. Often a U.S.C.A. entry to a statute enacted since U.S.C.-C.A.N.'s publication will contain a reference to the U.S.C.C.A.N. citation, which outlines the legislative process that the statute underwent prior to enactment.

U.S.C.C.A.N. is organized by congressional session; the congressional session is indicated on the spine of each volume. Each session's public laws, also indicated on the spine of each volume, and the legislative history of the public laws are arranged in numerical order according to public law number. See Illustrations 7-1 and 7-2.

U.S.C.C.A.N. is a good place to find legislative history and a copy of a public law, provided it is not too recent. For copies of recent public laws (one-month old), consult the pamphlets at the end of the U.S.C.A., U.S.C.S., and U.S.C.C.A.N. sets.

Legislative histories are also available on WESTLAW in the LH database. The coverage begins in 1948.

▼ How Do You Use U.S.C.C.A.N. in Conjunction with the U.S.C.A.?

In Illustration 6-6, pages 148-149, look at the reprint of 42 U.S.C.A. §14071(d) from the main code volume of the U.S.C.A. Notice the heading that follows the text of the statute: Historical and Statutory Notes. It is in this part of the U.S.C.A. that you obtain references to the public laws that created the statute and to the appropriate U.S.C.C.A.N. cite that contains the legislative history for the public law that was codified in the U.S.C.

▼ What Are Other Ways to Find Relevant Legislative History in U.S.C.C.A.N.?

The popular name tables in the U.S.C., U.S.C.A., and U.S.C.S. provide references to the public law numbers for the statutes. If you have the public law number of a statute, then you can find the legislative history in U.S.C.C.A.N. because it is organized by public law number.

▼ Is Legislative History Primary Authority?

Legislative history is not primary authority but is considered to be secondary authority because it provides material to interpret the statutes. In the legislative branch of our government, primary authority is limited to constitutions, statutes, codes, charters, and ordinances.

▼ How Do You Cite Legislative History Found in U.S.C.C.A.N.?

Legislative history materials found in U.S.C.C.A.N. are cited according to Bluebook Rule 13.4. The correct cite for a U.S. Senate Report reprinted in U.S.C.C.A.N. is:

S. Rep. No. 13, 102d Cong., 2d Sess. 111 (1991), <u>reprinted in</u> 1991 U.S.C.C.A.N. 12

ILLUSTRATION 7-1. Sample Pages from U.S.C.C.A.N. Showing Pub. L. No. 104-145

PUBLIC LAW 104–145 [H.R. 2137]; May 17, 1996

MEGAN'S LAW

For Legislative History of Act, see p. 980.

An Act to amend the Violent Crime Control and Law Enforcement Act of 1994 to require the release of relevant information to protect the public from sexually violent offenders.

Be it enacted by the Senate and House of Representatives of the United States of America in Congress assembled,

SECTION 1. SHORT TITLE.

This Act may be cited as "Megan's Law".

SEC. 2. RELEASE OF INFORMATION AND CLARIFICATION OF PUBLIC NATURE OF INFORMATION.

Section 170101(d) of the Violent Crime Control and Law Enforcement Act of 1994 (42 U.S.C. 14071(d)) is amended to read as follows:

"(d) RELEASE OF INFORMATION.—

"(1) The information collected under a State registration program may be disclosed for any purpose permitted under the laws of the State.

"(2) The designated State law enforcement agency and any local law enforcement agency authorized by the State agency shall release relevant information that is necessary to protect the public concerning a specific person required to register under this section, except that the identity of a victim of an offense that requires registration under this section shall not be released.".

Approved May 17, 1996.

Megan's Law.

42 USC 13701 note.

LEGISLATIVE HISTORY—H.R. 2137:

HOUSE REPORTS: No. 104–555 (Comm. on the Judiciary).
CONGRESSIONAL RECORD, Vol. 142 (1996):
    May 7, considered and passed House.
    May 9, considered and passed Senate.
WEEKLY COMPILATION OF PRESIDENTIAL DOCUMENTS, Vol. 32 (1996):
    May 17, Presidential remarks.

110 STAT. 1345

---

*Reprinted with permission from West Group.

ILLUSTRATION 7-2. Sample Pages from U.S.C.C.A.N.
Showing the Legislative History of Pub. L. No. 104-145

MEGAN'S LAW

P.L. 104–145, see page 110 Stat. 1345

DATES OF CONSIDERATION AND PASSAGE

House: May 7, 1996

Senate: May 9, 1996

Cong. Record Vol. 142 (1996)

**House Report (Judiciary Committee)
No. 104–555, May 6, 1996
[To accompany H.R. 2137]**

No Senate Report was submitted with this legislation.

HOUSE REPORT NO. 104–555

[page 1]

The Committee on the Judiciary, to whom was referred the bill
(H.R. 2137) to amend the Violent Crime Control and Law Enforcement Act of 1994 to require the release of relevant information to
protect the public from sexually violent offenders, having considered the same, report favorably thereon with an amendment and
recommend that the bill as amended do pass.

*   *   *   *   *

[page 2]

PURPOSE AND SUMMARY

This bill would amend a provision enacted as part of the Violent
Crime Control and Law Enforcement Act of 1994 (Public Law 103–
322). Title XVII of that Act, the "Jacob Wetterling Crimes Against
Children and Sexually Violent Offender Registration Act" (42
U.S.C. 14071), requires States to implement a system where all
persons who commit sexual or kidnapping crimes against children
or who commit sexually violent crimes against any person (whether
adult or child) are required to register their addresses with the
State upon their release from prison. The 1994 Act also provides
that law enforcement agencies may release "relevant information"
about an offender if they deem it necessary to protect the public.
This bill will require the release of such information when law enforcement officials deem it to be necessary to protect the public.
While the 1994 Act does not mandate that States comply with its
provisions, a State's failure to implement such a system by September 1997 will result in that State losing part of its annual federal
crime-fighting funding.

ILLUSTRATION 7-2.   *Continued*

MEGAN'S LAW
P.L. 104-145

BACKGROUND AND NEED FOR THE LEGISLATION

Perhaps no type of crime has received more attention in recent years than crimes against children involving sexual acts and violence. Several recent tragic cases have focused public attention on this type of crime and resulted in public demand that government take stronger action against those who commit these crimes.

In partial response to this demand, Congress passed Title XVII of the Violent Crime Control and Law Enforcement Act of 1994 (Public Law 103–322). That title, the "Jacob Wetterling Crimes Against Children and Sexually Violent Offender Registration Act," attempted to address the concerns about these crimes by encouraging States to establish a system where every person who commits a sexual or kidnapping crime against children or who commit sexually violent crimes against any person (whether adult or child) would be required to register his or her address with the State upon their release from prison. As a further protection, the 1994 Act required States to allow law enforcement agencies to release "relevant information" about an offender if they deemed it necessary to protect the public.

The 1994 Act provision with respect to notification only required States to give law enforcement agencies the discretion to release offender registry information when they deemed it necessary to protect the public. It has been brought to the attention of the Committee, however, that notwithstanding the clear intent of Congress that relevant information about these offenders be released to the public in these situations, some law enforcement agencies are still reluctant to do so. This bill would amend the 1994 Act to mandate that States require their law enforcement agencies to release "relevant information" in all cases when they deem it "necessary to protect the public."

The bill also amends the 1994 Act to provide that information collected under a State registration program may be disclosed for any purpose permitted under the laws of that State. The 1994 Act required that information collected by the registration program be

[page 3]

kept confidential. In some instances this requirement limited public access to what had been public records before the 1994 Act became law. H.R. 2137 will correct this unintended consequence of the 1994 Act by allowing each State to determine the extent to which the public may gain access to the information kept by the State.

HEARINGS

The Committee's Subcommittee on Crime held one day of hearings on H.R. 2137 on March 7, 1996. Testimony was received from two witnesses, Representative Dick Zimmer of New Jersey, the sponsor of H.R. 2137, and Kevin Di Gregory, Deputy Assistant Attorney General, Department of Justice, with no additional material submitted.

981

▼ How Do You Cite to a Legislative History of a Statute?

Bluebook Rule 13 details the citation format for all of the components of the legislative process: the bill, the committee report, the debates, and the transcripts of the hearings.

▼ What Are Some Other Sources of Legislative Information?

Congressional Information Service (CIS) has been produced since 1970. CIS is a source of detailed compiled legislative histories. CIS has an index, which is published annually, that allows you to find the reference to the relevant public law. After you find the reference to the relevant legislation, you are instructed to consult the abstracts detailing the components of the legislative history for the relevant public law. The abstracts are very informative and should be consulted because you can find out if the information you need is found in the complete document. CIS is exhaustive in its coverage of legislative history information for public laws. Unfortunately, to obtain the full text of the document, you must have access to the microfiche set and to a microfiche reader/printer. After consulting the abstracts and finding the appropriate information, ask the librarian for assistance you in obtaining the microfiche card that contains the full text document.

The CIS index is also available online on LEXIS and Dialog (a commercial database service concentrating on nonlegal information).

The *Congressional Record* contains the text of all of the proceedings from the floor of the U.S. Congress. It is published every day that Congress is in session. The *Congressional Record* has been in print since the 1870s. It is currently available on LEXIS and WESTLAW. On LEXIS, it is organized by topic. The coverage goes back as far as 1978 for bankruptcy information but generally begins in 1985. The *Congressional Record* is also on WESTLAW in the CR database. Coverage begins in 1985 with the 99th Congress.

Sometimes it is necessary to consult a privately published legislative history. You should see your law librarian for this or contact the sponsor of the public law to find out more detailed information.

▼ How Do You Research State Legislative Histories?

Each state compiles legislative resources in a different manner, which complicates the task of research. Most states do not have commercially compiled legislative histories in hardcopy format. Some states have printed indexes, but the actual documents are on microfiche. Each state has a legislative library that you can call for more information. Large public libraries and university libraries, particularly law school libraries, are good places to obtain state legislative history information. Commerce Clearing House publishes a session law reporter for every state.

▼ What Additional Resources Are Available for Researching Legislative Information?

The following sources provide additional assistance in researching legislative information.

Congressional Staff Directory, New York: Monitor Leadership Directories

Congressional Yellow Book, New York: Monitor Leadership Directories

Introduction to United States Government Information Sources by Joe Morehead and Mary Fetzer, Englewood, Colo.: Libraries Unlimited, Inc. (1992)

Sources of Compiled Legislative Histories by Nancy Johnson, Littleton, Colo.: F. B. Rothman (1988)

State Yellow Book, New York: Monitor Leadership Directories; who's who in the executive and legislative branches of the 50 state governments

---

PRACTICE POINTER

Researching legislative histories can be time-consuming. Ask the attorney that you are working for about a time budget for the project before performing a legislative history. Also, contact a librarian at a large academic law library for assistance when performing legislative histories.

CHAPTER SUMMARY

This chapter defined pending legislation and provided the tools to monitor pending legislation. U.S.C.C.A.N. is highlighted as the best tool for compiling a legislative history of a federal statute. You are also introduced to other resources to perform more detailed legislative histories, both federal and state.

KEY TERMS

Congressional Index
Congressional Information
  Service
Congressional Quarterly Weekly Report
Congressional Record

legislative history
pending legislation
public laws
United States Code Congressional and Adminstrative News

EXERCISES

1. Find the legislative history of the Brady Handgun Violence Prevention Act. This is a federal act. Cite the legislative history of the act in Bluebook format.
2. Find the legislative history of the Depository Library Act of 1964. This is a federal act. Cite the legislative history of the act in Bluebook format.
3. Name two components of a typical legislative history.
4. Why would you perform a legislative history of an act?
5. What information would you gather when performing a legislative history?

8

ADMINISTRATIVE MATERIALS AND LOOSELEAF SERVICES

CHAPTER OVERVIEW

In Chapter 6 you learned about the enactment of statutes and how to research them. Some statutes create administrative agencies and provide these agencies with a variety of powers. In this chapter, you learn about the creation of administrative agencies, the powers of these agencies, and the authority that they generate. You are shown how to locate these authorities as well as how to update and validate them. By the chapter's end, you will know how to use administrative materials and will understand their importance and relationship to other primary and secondary sources.

A. INTRODUCTION

▼ What Is Administrative Law?

Administrative rules and regulations are essential to the practice of law in a variety of areas, such as taxation, environmental law, education, and health care law. Federal and state administrative agencies regulate many aspects of our lives ranging from the safety of the products we purchase to the amount of hazardous wastes that can be placed in our landfills. Although administrative law governs many facets of daily life, appointed, rather than elected, individuals create this law.

▼ How Can Administrative Agencies Create Law When This Is the Job of Congress?

Congress and other legislative bodies delegate their power to create law to **administrative agencies** by enacting **enabling statutes.** Delegating authority to the agencies relieves Congress of the daily enforcement of detailed regulations.

▼ How Do Administrative Agencies Operate?

On the federal level, administrative agencies fall under the control of the executive branch of the government.[1] Although every cabinet post has an agency beneath it, some agencies are not associated with cabinet posts, such as the National Aeronautics and Space Administration (NASA). Often, agency staff members, other than those who hold cabinet posts, are hired because of their expertise and qualifications in an area of law. These experts do not leave their posts at the end of a legislative term.

Agencies often are called bureaus, boards, commissions, corporations, or administrations. All agencies create law in the form of **rules** or **regulations.**[2] Agencies function in an **adjudicatory** or **quasi-judicial** manner when they hear cases involving the application of a particular regulation and then issue written opinions of their findings.

Agencies create rules or regulations regularly, conduct hearings concerning particular issues, make decisions, and enforce Congress's mandates. The agency regulations adopted, or promulgated, are similar to statutes except that they are far more detailed. The administrative regulations explain how to apply the laws briefly outlined by Congress in the enabling legislation.

[1] To determine which executives control a particular agency, several sources should be consulted. The *United States Government Manual* provides information about all federal government agencies. This information includes a brief description of the agency's functions, how it was created, and how it is controlled. The National Archives publishes this manual annually. Washington Monitor Publishing Co. publishes "yellow directories" that provide the names of individuals working within the government. However, they do not offer any other information about a particular agency. The *American Jurisprudence 2d Desk Book* contains a variety of charts that detail the structure of various government agencies.

[2] Rules and regulations are synonymous. 1 C.F.R. §1.1 (1994).

For example, Congress delegates to the U.S. Food and Drug Administration (FDA) authority to deal with the daily concerns regarding food products. FDA regulates the labeling of all consumer food products based on a Congress-adopted law that created that FDA. The regulations are very specific. Among the details specified is the definition of *principal display panel* and the fact that it should be "large enough to accommodate all the mandatory label information required to be placed thereon."[3] See Illustration 8-1.

B. REGULATIONS

▼ How Are Regulations Adopted?

The process for adoption of regulations varies. The agency or the legislature determines what procedures must be followed before a regulation is adopted. In general, the agency requests comments from the public, conducts one or more hearings, and then decides whether to adopt a regulation. The agency concerns itself with the details. Agency regulations are revised, repealed, and created daily.

▼ What Type of Authority Is an Administrative Regulation or Rule?

The regulations and other documents adopted by federal agencies and published in the *Federal Register* and the *Code of Federal Regulations* (see next section) are primary authority because they are issued by a government body acting in its official law-making capacity.

C. FINDING ADMINISTRATIVE LAW

1. Generally

▼ Where Do You Find Federal Administrative Law?

Federal regulations are found in two official sources: the **Code of Federal Regulations** and the **Federal Register.** The *Code of Federal Regulations,* or the C.F.R. as it is known, contains all of the final administrative regulations. The C.F.R. is published annually, and different titles are published during different quarters of the year. For instance, the Treasury regulations are issued in the first quarter and the environmental regulations are published in the third quarter. The *Federal Register* is the daily newspaper for our administrative agencies and for our executive branch of the government. The *Federal Register* contains all of the proposed and final administrative regulations as well as executive orders and proclamations often issued by the president.

[3]21 C.F.R. §101 (1994).

ILLUSTRATION 8-1.   Sample Page from *Code of Federal Regulations*

---

§ 101.1

101.72 Health claims: calcium and osteoporosis.
101.73 Health claims: dietary lipids and cancer.
101.74 Health claims: sodium and hypertension.
101.75 Health claims: dietary saturated fat and cholesterol and risk of coronary heart disease.
101.76 Health claims: fiber-containing grain products, fruits, and vegetables and cancer.
101.77 Health claims: fruits, vegetables, and grain products that contain fiber, particularly soluble fiber, and risk of coronary heart disease.
101.78 Health claims: fruits and vegetables and cancer.
101.79 Health claims: folate and neural tube defects.

Subpart F—Specific Requirements for Descriptive Claims that are Neither Nutrient Content Claims nor Health Claims

101.95 "Fresh," "freshly frozen," "fresh frozen," "frozen fresh."

Subpart G—Exemptions From Food Labeling Requirements

101.100 Food; exemptions from labeling.
101.103 Petitions requesting exemptions from or special requirements for label declaration of ingredients.
101.105 Declaration of net quantity of contents when exempt.
101.108 Temporary exemptions for purposes of conducting authorized food labeling experiments.
APPENDIX A TO PART 101—MONIER-WILLIAMS PROCEDURE (WITH MODIFICATIONS) FOR SULFITES IN FOOD, CENTER FOR FOOD SAFETY AND APPLIED NUTRITION, FOOD AND DRUG ADMINISTRATION (NOVEMBER 1985)
APPENDIX B TO PART 01—GRAPHIC ENHANCEMENTS USED BY THE FDA

AUTHORITY: Secs. 4, 5, 6 of the Fair Packaging and Labeling Act (15 U.S.C. 1453, 1454, 1455); secs. 201, 301, 402, 403, 409, 701 of the Federal Food, Drug, and Cosmetic Act (21 U.S.C. 321, 331, 342, 343, 348, 371).

SOURCE: 42 FR 14308, Mar. 15, 1977, unless otherwise noted.

Subpart A—General Provisions

§ 101.1 Principal display panel of package form food.

The term "principal display panel" as it applies to food in package form and as used in this part, means the part of a label that is most likely to be dis-

21 CFR Ch. I (4-1-94 Edition)

played, presented, shown, or examined under customary conditions of display for retail sale. The principal display panel shall be large enough to accommodate all the mandatory label information required to be placed thereon by this part with clarity and conspicuousness and without obscuring design, vignettes, or crowding. Where packages bear alternate principal display panels, information required to be placed on the principal display panel shall be duplicated on each principal display panel. For the purpose of obtaining uniform type size in declaring the quantity of contents for all packages of substantially the same size, the term "area of the principal display panel" means the area of the side or surface that bears the principal display panel, which area shall be:

(a) In the case of a rectangular package where one entire side properly can be considered to be the principal display panel side, the product of the height times the width of that side;

(b) In the case of a cylindrical or nearly cylindrical container, 40 percent of the product of the height of the container times the circumference;

(c) In the case of any otherwise shaped container, 40 percent of the total surface of the container: *Provided, however, That where such container* ... display ... gular ... area ... face. ... prin- ... bot- ... ns of ... bot- ... rical ... nfor-

1 Title
2 Sections
3 Authority
4 *Federal Register* citation
5 Text

mation required by this part to appear on the principal display panel shall appear within that 40 percent of the circumference which is most likely to be displayed, presented, shown, or examined under customary conditions of display for retail sale.

§ 101.2 Information panel of package form food.

(a) The term "information panel" as it applies to packaged food means that part of the label immediately contiguous and to the right of the principal display panel as observed by an individ-

14

▼ Where Do You Find State Administrative Law?

States have agencies similar to those of the federal government. Most states have administrative materials that are organized and published in the same manner as those of the federal government. The major differences between the state systems and that of the federal government are that the state materials are not published as frequently and are not updated as often. For example, in Illinois, the *Illinois Register* is published weekly rather than daily, and the *Illinois Administrative Code* is updated only once a year.

The amount of administrative materials states publish sometimes is quite voluminous. Some states, such as Mississippi, have an administrative register but do not publish an administrative compilation. Other states, such as Nevada, have an administrative compilation but do not publish an administrative register.

The best way to determine whether a state has an administrative compilation or an administrative register is to consult *A Uniform System of Citation* (16th ed. 1996) (the Bluebook). Bluebook Table T.1, United States Jurisdictions, lists the administrative materials and the citation format for each state. By reviewing a particular state in Table T.1, you also can determine whether a state has an administrative compilation. For example, Idaho does not have an administrative compilation, but Illinois does. Not only does the Bluebook Table T.1 assist you in determining the type of administrative material available within a state, it also instructs you concerning how to cite these materials.

The major obstacle you face when researching state administrative law is the lack of uniformity among the 50 states' administrative materials in their format, scope, and editing. The indexes to the state publications are often difficult to use, and commercial publishers generally do not publish additional indexes. Also, some states publish their administrative materials only on an irregular basis.

Some of the state administrative codes overlap materials covered in the federal code. For example, both the federal government and the state of Illinois regulate food labeling.

The coverage of state administrative regulations on LEXIS and WESTLAW is constantly changing. Therefore, check the directories. Using codes online, especially codes from other states, can be easier than trying to access print copies of the codes.

The Internet also offers access to various state regulations. Try accessing a state's home page to find its administrative regulations.

2. Specific Sources

a. Federal Register

The *Federal Register,* a pamphlet published Monday through Friday except on legal holidays, contains all of the regulations adopted by the federal agencies, any regulations the agencies are considering adopting, and any agency notices. It often includes agency policy statements and discussions of comments received concerning agency actions. Executive orders and presidential proclamations also are found in the *Federal Register.* Documents are published in chronological order and are not codified. The *Federal Register* is available in print and on both WESTLAW and LEXIS as well as on the Internet.

▼ How Do You Use the *Federal Register?*

To use the *Federal Register,* you could review the table of contents or the index. The table of contents is found at the beginning of each volume of the *Federal Register* and is organized alphabetically by agency name. The index is published monthly and cumulated for 12 months. The index can be difficult to use because it is arranged by agency rather than by subject. Because of this organization, you first must determine what agency is responsible for regulating the conduct or activity you are researching. A review of the enabling statute should provide you with this information. Next, you should find the agency listing in the index and review any topics under each agency heading that are relevant to your research. Illustration 8-2 is an index page from the *Federal Register* that covers the period from January 1993 through March 1993. For example, if you are researching regulations concerning food labeling of fat content and fat claims, circled number 1 indicates the regulating agency, the U.S. Food and Drug Administration. You should note that subheadings under the agency include "Rules," "Proposed Rules," and "Notices." The subtopic "Food labeling" might be of importance to you. The index provides you with the *Federal Register* citation. It states that the regulation concerning food labeling and health claims is found on page 2478 of the most current *Federal Register* volume. You also must check multiple indexes even if they appear to overlap because some citations may be omitted in one of the indexes.

Next, consult the *Federal Register* pages listed in the indexes. The *Federal Register* begins a new volume each year. The issues are consecutively paginated from the first day that the government offices are open during the year through the last day that the government offices are open during the year. For example, a March 1 *Federal Register* might contain pages 2600–4200. The March 2 *Federal Register* would begin on page 4201. It is not uncommon for the page number in the last issue to be 60,000.

Page numbers are not listed on the outside binding of the *Federal Register.* However, dates are listed. Therefore, you must determine the date of the *Federal Register* publication that contains the page that you are seeking. To do this, use the index table entitled Federal Register Pages and Dates. This table provides you with the date of the *Federal Register* that contains the relevant information.

You can consult either a commercially prepared index or the government-published index to the Federal Register. Review the

ILLUSTRATION 8-2. Sample Page from *Federal Register* Index

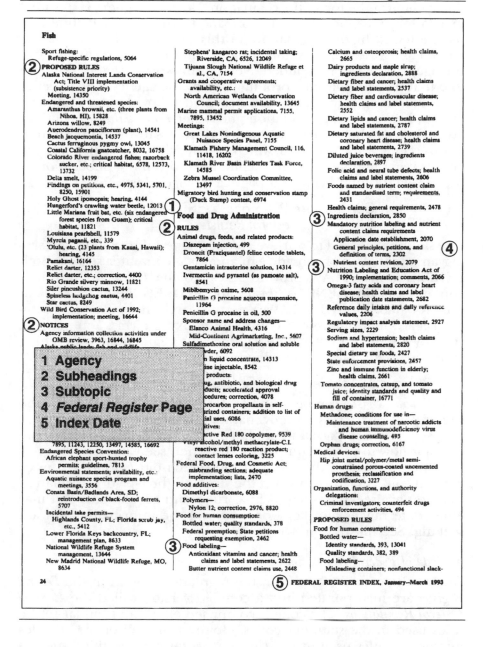

Fish

Sport fishing:
    Refuge-specific regulations, 5064
② PROPOSED RULES
Alaska National Interest Lands Conservation
    Act; Title VIII implementation
    (subsistence priority)
    Meeting, 14350
Endangered and threatened species:
    Amaranthus browaii, etc. (three plants from
        Nihoa, HI), 15828
    Arizona willow, 8249
    Auerodendron pauciflorum (plant), 14541
    Beach jacquemontia, 14537
    Cactus ferruginous pygmy owl, 13045
    Coastal California gnatcatcher, 8032, 16758
    Colorado River endangered fishes; razorback
        sucker, etc.; critical habitat, 6578, 12573,
        13732
    Delta smelt, 14199
    Findings on petitions, etc., 4975, 5341, 5701,
        8250, 15901
    Holy Ghost ipomopsis; hearing, 4144
    Hungerford's crawling water beetle, 12013 ①
    Little Mariana fruit bat, etc. (six endangered
        forest species from Guam); critical
        habitat, 11821   ②
    Louisiana pearlshell, 11579
    Myrcia paganii, etc., 339
    'Olulu, etc. (23 plants from Kauai, Hawaii);
        hearing, 4145
    Pamakani, 16164
    Relict darter, 12353
    Relict darter, etc.; correction, 4400
    Rio Grande silvery minnow, 11821
    Siler pincushion cactus, 13244
    Spineless hedgehog cactus, 4401
    Star cactus, 8249
Wild Bird Conservation Act of 1992;
    implementation; meeting, 16644
② NOTICES
Agency information collection activities under
    OMB review, 3963, 16844, 16845
Alaska public lands; fish and wildlife

1 Agency
2 Subheadings
3 Subtopic
4 *Federal Register* Page
5 Index Date

    7895, 11243, 12250, 13497, 14585, 16692
Endangered Species Convention:
    African elephant sport-hunted trophy
        permits; guidelines, 7813
Environmental statements; availability, etc.:
    Aquatic nuisance species program and
        meetings, 3556
    Conata Basin/Badlands Area, SD;
        reintroduction of black-footed ferrets,
        5707
    Incidental take permits—
        Highlands County, FL; Florida scrub jay,
            etc., 5412
        Lower Florida Keys backcountry, FL;
            management plan, 8633
    National Wildlife Refuge System
        management, 13644
    New Madrid National Wildlife Refuge, MO,
        8634

24

Stephens' kangaroo rat; incidental taking;
    Riverside, CA, 6526, 12049
Tijuana Slough National Wildlife Refuge et
    al., CA, 7154
Grants and cooperative agreements;
    availability, etc.:
    North American Wetlands Conservation
        Council; document availability, 13645
Marine mammal permit applications, 7155,
    7895, 13452
Meetings:
    Great Lakes Nonindigenous Aquatic
        Nuisance Species Panel, 7155
    Klamath Fishery Management Council, 116,
        11418, 16202
    Klamath River Basin Fisheries Task Force,
        14585
    Zebra Mussel Coordination Committee,
        13497
Migratory bird hunting and conservation stamp
    (Duck Stamp) contest, 6974

Food and Drug Administration

② RULES
Animal drugs, feeds, and related products:
    Diazepam injection, 499
    Droncit (Praziquantel) feline cestode tablets,
        7864
    Gentamicin intrauterine solution, 14314
    Ivermectin and pyrantel (as pamoate salt),
        8541
    Miblbemycin oxime, 5608
    Penicillin G procaine aqueous suspension,
        11964
    Penicillin G procaine in oil, 500
    Sponsor name and address changes—
        Elanco Animal Health, 4316
        Mid-Continent Agrimarketing, Inc., 5607
    Sulfadimethoxine oral solution and soluble
        ... wder, 6092
        ... n liquid concentrate, 14313
        ... ine injectable, 8542
    ... products:
        ...ug, antibiotic, and biological drug
            ...ducts; accelerated approval
            ...cedures; correction, 4078
        ...rocarbon propellants in self-
            ...rized containers; addition to list of
            ...ial uses, 6086
        ...itives:
            ...ctive Red 180 copolymer, 9539
    Vinyl alcohol/methyl methacrylate-C.I.
        reactive red 180 reaction product;
        contact lenses coloring, 3225
Federal Food, Drug, and Cosmetic Act;
    misbranding sections; adequate
    implementation; lists, 2470
Food additives:
    Dimethyl dicarbonate, 6088
    Polymers—
        Nylon 12; correction, 2976, 8820
Food for human consumption:
    Bottled water; quality standards, 378
    Federal preemption; State petitions
        requesting exemption, 2462
③ Food labeling—
    Antioxidant vitamins and cancer; health
        claims and label statements, 2622
    Butter nutrient content claims use, 2448

Calcium and osteoporosis; health claims,
    2665
Dairy products and maple sirup;
    ingredients declaration, 2888
Dietary fiber and cancer; health claims
    and label statements, 2537
Dietary fiber and cardiovascular disease;
    health claims and label statements,
    2552
Dietary lipids and cancer; health claims
    and label statements, 2787
Dietary saturated fat and cholesterol and
    coronary heart disease; health claims
    and label statements, 2739
Diluted juice beverages; ingredients
    declaration, 2897
Folic acid and neural tube defects; health
    claims and label statements, 2606
Foods named by nutrient content claim
    and standardized term; requirements,
    2431
Health claims; general requirements, 2478
③ Ingredients declaration, 2850
Mandatory nutrition labeling and nutrient
    content claims requirements
        Application date establishment, 2070
        General principles, petitions, and   ④
            definition of terms, 2302
        Nutrient content revision, 2079
③ Nutrition Labeling and Education Act of
    1990; implementation; comments, 2066
Omega-3 fatty acids and coronary heart
    disease; health claims and label
    publication date statements, 2682
Reference daily intakes and daily reference
    values, 2206
Regulatory impact analysis statement, 2927
Serving sizes, 2229
Sodium and hypertension; health claims
    and label statements, 2820
Special dietary use foods, 2427
State enforcement provisions, 2457
Zinc and immune function in elderly;
    health claims, 2661
Tomato concentrates, catsup, and tomato
    juice; identity standards and quality and
    fill of container, 16771
Human drugs:
    Methadone; conditions for use in—
        Maintenance treatment of narcotic addicts
            and human immunodeficiency virus
            disease counseling, 495
    Orphan drugs; correction, 6167
Medical devices:
    Hip joint metal/polymer/metal semi-
        constrained porous-coated uncemented
        prosthesis; reclassification and
        codification, 3227
Organization, functions, and authority
    delegations:
    Criminal investigators; counterfeit drugs
        enforcement activities, 494
PROPOSED RULES
Food for human consumption:
    Bottled water—
        Identity standards, 393, 13041
        Quality standards, 382, 389
    Food labeling—
        Misleading containers; nonfunctional slack-

⑤ FEDERAL REGISTER INDEX, January–March 1993

government-published Federal Register index found in Illustration 8-2. Under the subtopic "Mandatory nutrition labeling and nutrient content claims requirements" is another subtopic, "General principles, petitions, and definition of terms." Following that subtopic is the notation "2302." That is the *Federal Register* page number that contains that information.

Illustration 8-3 is page 2302 of the *Federal Register.* First, note the department at the top of the regulation. Next, the agency is specified in two locations. You then are provided with the C.F.R. title and parts affected by this regulation: in this case, title 21 of the C.F.R., parts 5 and 101. A brief summary and a more detailed summary of the agency's action is included. Next to the word "Action," you are told that this is a final rule promulgated by the agency. The effective date and an agency contact are provided following the summary. Finally, background information and other *Federal Register* citations are included to help you understand the process involved in adoption of this regulation. Page 2418, which specifically details labeling regulations regarding fat content, is contained within the publication of the regulation that begins on page 2302. See Illustration 8-4.

▼ How Can You Use LEXIS and WESTLAW to Retrieve the *Federal Register?*

The simplest method to retrieve *Federal Register* information concerning an adopted or proposed regulation is a computer search. Both LEXIS and WESTLAW provide access to the *Federal Register.* It is contained in the GENFED library and FEDREG file of LEXIS and the FR database of WESTLAW. You can search these databases without regard to a publisher's choice of indexing terms. You may use your own terms to determine whether any regulations concerning your research topic are contained within the *Federal Register.*

▼ How Do You Search the *Federal Register* on the Internet?

The *Federal Register* can be found at the government-sponsored Web site http://www.access.gpo.gov/nara/#fr or http://www.access.gpo.-gov/su_docs/aces/aces140.html. For complete information concerning how to research using the Internet, see Chapter 10.

Once you access the site, you can search old *Federal Registers* or current volumes. You can select the year and the type of information that you are seeking, such as final rules and regulations. You may enter date ranges and key words to find the information you are seeking. See Illustration 8-5.

b. *Code of Federal Regulations*

During the course of the year, the regulations found in the *Federal Register* are incorporated into a codified version called the **Code of Federal Regulations.** The code is comprised of 50 titles similar to the titles used in the statutory codes. However, not all of the 50 titles mirror the titles used in the *United States Code.* Some titles, such as

---

PRACTICE POINTER

The regulations on the Internet are easy to search and accessible through most public libraries.

ILLUSTRATION 8-3.   Sample *Federal Register* Page

(1) 2302   Federal Register / Vol. 58, No. 3 / Wednesday, January 6, 1993 / Rules and Regulations

(2) **DEPARTMENT OF HEALTH AND HUMAN SERVICES**

(3) **Food and Drug Administration**

(4) **21** CFR Parts 5 and **101** — (6)

(5) [Docket Nos. 91N-0384 and 84N-0153]

RIN 0905-AD08 and 0905-AB68

(7) **Food Labeling: Nutrient Content Claims, General Principles, Petitions, Definition of Terms; Definitions of Nutrient Content Claims for the Fat, Fatty Acid, and Cholesterol Content of Food**

(3) **AGENCY:** Food and Drug Administration, HHS.

(8) **ACTION:** Final rule.

(9) **SUMMARY:** The Food and Drug Administration (FDA) is amending its food labeling regulations to: (1) Provide definitions for specific nutrient content claims using the terms "free," "low," "lean," "extra lean," "good source," "high," "reduced," "light" or "lite," "less," "fewer," and "more" and provide for their use on the food label; (2) provide for the use of implied nutrient content claims; (3) define and provide for the use of the term "fresh;" and (4) address the use of the terms "natural" and "organic." This action is part of the food labeling initiative of the Secretary of Health and Human Services (the Secretary) and in response to the Nutrition Labeling and Education Act of 1990 (the 1990 amendments).

(10) **EFFECTIVE DATE:** February 14, 1994, except §§ 101.10 and 101.13(q)(5) concerning restaurant firms consisting of 10 or less individual restaurant establishments for whom these sections will become effective on February 14, 1995.

(11) **FOR FURTHER INFORMATION CONTACT:** Elizabeth J. Campbell, Center for Food Safety and Applied Nutrition (HFF-312), Food and Drug Administration, 200 C St. SW., Washington, DC 20204, 202-205-5229.

(12) **SUPPLEMENTARY INFORMATION:**

I. Introduction

A. Background

In the Federal Register of November 27, 1991 (56 FR 60421), FDA published a proposed rule (entitled "Food Labeling: Nutrient Content Claims, General Principles, Petitions, Definition of Terms" hereinafter referred to as the general principles proposal) to: (1) Define nutrient content claims (also known as descriptors) and to provide for their use on foods labels; (2) define specific nutrient content claims that

include the terms "free," "low," "source," "reduced," "light" or "lite," and "high"; (3) provide for comparative claims using the terms "less," "fewer," and "more"; (4) set forth specific requirements for sodium and calorie claims; (5) establish procedures for the submission and review of petitions regarding the use of nutrient content claims; (6) revise § 105.66 (21 CFR 105.66), to solely cover foods for special dietary use in reducing or maintaining body weight; (7) establish criteria for the appropriate use of the term "fresh;" and (8) address the use of the term "natural." A document correcting various editorial errors in that proposed rule was published in the Federal Register of March 6, 1992 (57 FR 8189).

In the same issue of the Federal Register (56 FR 60478), FDA also published a proposed rule (entitled "Food Labeling: Definitions of Nutrient Content Claims for the Fat, Fatty Acid, and Cholesterol Content of Food" hereinafter referred to as the fat/cholesterol proposal) to define and provide for the proper use of the nutrient content claims "fat free," "low fat," "reduced fat," "low in saturated fat," "reduced saturated fat," "cholesterol free," "low cholesterol," and "reduced chole[...] correcting various e[...] fat/cholesterol proposal [...] published in the Fe[...] March 6, 1992 (57 F[...] published the fat/ch[...] as a separate docum[...] principles proposal. [...] based the two docu[...] statutory provisions [...] published a tentativ[...] cholesterol content [...] Federal Register of [...] 29456). FDA includ[...] definitions for fat an[...] claims in the fat/cho[...] because of the inter[...] these nutrients and [...] etiology of cardiova[...]

Also in the same i[...] Register (56 FR 605[...] a proposed rule (ent[...] Labeling: 'Cholester[...] Cholesterol,' and '—[...] Free' Claims") to de[...] free" and "low chol[...] provide for the prop[...] and the term "—[...] The proposed rule v[...] ensure on an interim[...] terms are not used [...] misleading to consu[...]

The general principles proposal (56 FR 60421) and the fat/cholesterol proposal (56 FR 60478) were issued as part of the agency's food label reform initiative and in response to the 1990

amendments (Pub. L. 101-535). The food label reform began in 1989 when FDA published an advance notice of proposed rulemaking (ANPRM) that announced a major initiative concerning the use of food labeling as a means for promoting sound nutrition. The following year (November 8, 1990), the President signed the 1990 amendments into law. This legislation clarified and strengthened FDA's legal authority to require nutrition labeling on foods and to establish those circumstances whereby claims can be made about nutrients in foods. Now as FDA prepares to implement the new regulations, the agency reiterates that the 1990 amendments have three basic objectives. They are: (1) To make available nutrition information that can assist consumers in selecting foods that can lead to healthier diets, (2) to eliminate consumer confusion by establishing definitions for nutrient content claims that are consistent with the terms defined by the Secretary, and (3) to encourage product innovation through the development and marketing of nutritionally improved foods. With these goals in mind, the agency believes that the new regulations will reestablish the credibility of the food label.

[...]ded [...]tic

[...]d is

[...]y or [...]any

[...] in

[...]l [...]ents

[...]one

[...]n a [...]ners.

[...]umer

[...]ts

[...]n the

comments addressed issues covered by other proposals that are a part of this overall food labeling initiative and will be addressed in those final documents, while other comments addressed issues

---

1 *Federal Register* page number

2 Department

3 Agency

4 C.F.R. citation

5 Title

6 Part

7 Brief Summary

8 Action

9 More Detailed Summary

10 Effective Date

11 Agency Contact

12 Background Information and Other *Federal Register* Citations

---

26, the Internal Revenue Code, do follow the title of the U.S.C. Title 26 of the C.F.R. contains the Treasury regulations that instruct the researcher on how to apply the relevant statutory code section. The C.F.R. titles are organized by agency, not subjects. The C.F.R. is further divided into chapters, subchapters, parts, and sections. Check the back of each volume for a list of federal agencies and their C.F.R. titles and chapters.

ILLUSTRATION 8-4.   58 Fed. Reg. 2418 (1993)

① ②

2418   **Federal Register** / Vol. 58, No. 3 / Wednesday, January 6, 1993 / Rules and Regulations

(6) The terms "reduced sodium," "reduced in sodium," "sodium reduced," "less sodium," "lower sodium," or "lower in sodium" may be used on the label or in labeling of foods, except meal products as defined in § 101.13(l) and main dish products as defined in § 101.13(m), provided that:

(i) The food contains at least 25 percent less sodium per reference amount customarily consumed than an appropriate reference food as described in § 101.13(j)(1).

(ii) As required for § 101.13(j)(2) for relative claims:

(A) The identity of the reference food and the percent (or fraction) that the sodium has been reduced are declared in immediate proximity to the most prominent such claim (e.g., "reduced sodium —————, 50 percent less sodium than regular —————"); and

(B) Quantitative information comparing the level of the sodium in the product per labeled serving with that of the reference food that it replaces is declared adjacent to the most prominent claim or on the information panel (e.g., "sodium content has been lowered from 300 to 150 mg per serving").

(iii) Claims described in paragraph (b)(6) of this section may not be made on the label or in the labeling of a food if the nutrient content of the reference food meets the definition for "low sodium."

(7) The terms defined in paragraph (b)(6) of this section may be used on the label or in the labeling of meal products as defined in § 101.13(l) and main dish products as defined in § 101.13(m), provided that:

(i) The food contains at least 25 percent less sodium per 100 g of food than an appropriate reference food as described in § 101.13(j)(1), and

(ii) As required in § 101.13(j)(2) for relative claims:

(A) The identity of the reference food and the percent (or fraction) that the sodium has been reduced are declared in immediate proximity to the most prominent such claim (e.g., reduced sodium eggplant parmigiana dinner "30 percent less sodium per oz (or 3 oz) than our regular eggplant parmigiana dinner").

(B) Quantitative information comparing the level of sodium in the product per specified weight with that of the reference food that it replaces is declared adjacent to the most prominent claim or on the information panel (e.g., sodium content has been reduced from 217 mg per 3 oz to 150 mg per 3 oz).

(iii) Claims described in paragraph (b)(7) of this section may not be made on the label or in the labeling of a food if the nutrient content of the reference

food meets the definition for "low sodium."

(c) The term "salt" is not synonymous with "sodium." Salt refers to sodium chloride. However, references to salt content such as "unsalted," "no salt," "no salt added" are potentially misleading.

(1) The term "salt free" may be used on the label or in labeling of foods only if the food is "sodium free" as defined in paragraph (b)(1) of this section.

(2) The terms "unsalted," "without added salt," and "no salt added" may be used on the label or in labeling of foods only if:

(i) No salt is added during processing;

(ii) The food that it resembles and for which it substitutes is normally processed with salt; and

(iii) If the food is not sodium free, the statement, "not a sodium free food" or "not for control of sodium in the diet" appears on the information panel of the food bearing the claim.

(3) Paragraph (c)(2) of this section shall not apply to a factual statement that a food intended specifically for infants and children less than 2 years of age is unsalted, provided such statement refers to the taste of the food and is not otherwise false and misleading.

§ 101.62   **Nutrient content claims for fat, fatty acid, and cholesterol content of foods.**

(a) *General requirements.* A claim about the level of fat, fatty acid, and cholesterol in a food may only be made on the label or in the labeling of foods if:

(1) The claim uses one of the terms defined in this section in accordance with the definition for that term;

(2) The claim is made in accordance with the general requirements for nutrient content claims in § 101.13; and

(3) The food for which the claim is made is labeled in accordance with § 101.9 or § 101.10, where applicable.

(b) *"Fat content claims."* (1) The terms "fat free," "free of fat," "no fat," "zero fat," "without fat," "nonfat," "trivial source of fat," "negligible source of fat," or "dietarily insignificant source of fat" may be used on the label or in labeling of foods, provi[...]

(i) The food contains [...] gram (g) of fat per refer[...] customarily consumed [...] a meal product or main[...] less than 0.5 g of fat pe[...]

(ii) The food contains [...] ingredient that is a fat [...] understood by consume[...] unless the listing of the[...] ingredient statement is [...] asterisk that refers to th[...] below the list of ingred[...] states "adds a trivial am[...]

"adds a negligible amount of fat," or "adds a dietarily insignificant amount of fat;" and

(iii) As required in § 101.13(e)(2), if the food meets these conditions without the benefit of special processing, alteration, formulation, or reformulation to lower fat content, it is labeled to disclose that fat is not usually present in the food (e.g., "broccoli, a fat free food").

(2) The terms "low fat," "low in fat," "contains a small amount of fat," "low source of fat," or "little fat" may be used on the label and in labeling of foods, except meal products as defined in § 101.13(l) and main dish products as defined in § 101.13(m), provided that:

(i)(A) The food has a reference amount customarily consumed greater than 30 g or greater than 2 tablespoons and contains 3 g or less of fat per reference amount customarily consumed; or

(B) The food has a reference amount customarily consumed of 30 g or less or 2 tablespoons or less and contains 3 g or less of fat per reference amount customarily consumed and per 50 g of food (for dehydrated foods that are typically consumed when rehydrated with only water, the per 50 g criterion refers to the "as prepared" form); and

(ii) If the food meets these conditions without the benefit of special processing, alteration, formulation, or reformulation to lower fat content, it is labeled to clearly refer to all foods of its type and not merely to the particular brand to which the label attaches (e.g., "frozen perch, a low fat food").

(3) The terms defined in paragraph (b)(2) of this section may be used on the label and in labeling of meal products as defined in § 101.13(l) or main dish products as defined in § 101.13(m), provided that:

(i) The product contains 3 g or less of total fat per 100 g and not more than 30 percent of calories from fat; and

(ii) If the product meets these conditions without the benefit of special processing, alteration, formulation, or reformulation to lower fat content, it is [...]

③ ④

> 1   **2418 is the page number.**
>
> 2   *Federal Register* **is the publication name, with the volume and date.**
>
> 3   **§ 101.62 begins here.**
>
> 4   **Fat Content Claims are addressed.**

The C.F.R. is prepared and published by the U.S. Government Printing Office. No commercially published complete or annotated version of these regulations is currently available. However, the regulations are available on LEXIS in the GENFED library, C.F.R. file, and on WESTLAW in the CFR database.

ILLUSTRATION 8-5. *Federal Register* **Internet Home Page**

Page 1 of 2

National Archives and
Records Administration

Federal Register
Online via *GPO Access*

Attention: New Federal Register Browse Feature ◀▬▬

Code of Federal Regulations	Federal Register	Privacy Act Issuances	Public Laws	United States Government Manual	Weekly Compilation of Presidential Documents	U.S. Congress Information	GPO Access Search Page

Database for the 1995, 1996, 1997 and 1998 *Federal Register* (Volumes 60, 61, 62 and 63)

The *Federal Register* is the official daily publication for Rules, Proposed Rules, and Notices of Federal agencies and organizations, as well as Executive Orders and other Presidential Documents. Helpful Hints provide instructions for searching the database. Documents may be retrieved in ASCII "TEXT" format (full text, graphics omitted), Adobe Portable Document Format, "PDF" (full text with graphics), and "SUMMARY" format (abbreviated text).

The 1994 Federal Register (Volume 59) database is also available, however, it contains no fields or section identifers.

Federal Register **Volume:**

☑ 1998 Federal Register   ☐ 1997 Federal Register
☐ 1996 Federal Register   ☐ 1995 Federal Register

Federal Register **Sections** (If you select none, all sections will be searched, but you may select one or more sections):

☐ Contents and Preliminary Pages   ☐ Presidential Documents
☐ Final Rules and Regulations   ☐ Sunshine Act Meetings*

http://www.access.gpo.gov/su_docs/aces/aces140.html   9/30/98

▼ How Often Is the C.F.R. Updated?

The C.F.R. titles are updated quarterly. Titles 1 to 16 are updated January 1 of the cover year. Titles 17 to 27 are updated April 1 of that year, and titles 28 to 41 are updated on July 1 of that year. Titles 42 to 50 are updated on October 1 of the cover year.

ILLUSTRATION 8-5. *Continued*

Page 2 of 2

☐ Proposed Rules   ☐ Reader Aids
☐ Notices   ☐ Corrections

* As of March 1, 1996, Sunshine Act Meetings were incorporated into the Notices section of the *Federal Register*.

Issue Date (Enter either a range of dates or a specific date in the format mm/dd/yy):

Date Range: From [   ] to [   ]

OR

⦿ ON � C BEFORE � C AFTER [   ]

Search Terms:

[   ]

[SUBMIT] [CLEAR]

Maximum Records Returned: [40] Default is 40. Maximum is 200.

Enter search terms in the space above. Phrases must be in quotation marks (" "). The operators **ADJ (adjacent)**, **AND**, **OR** and **NOT** can be used, but **must** be in capital letters. For example: "environmental protection agency" **AND** superfund. The page cited as 60 FR 12345 can be retrieved using the search **"page 12345"**. CFR parts should also be searched as phrases; for example: **"40 CFR part 55"**. Word roots can be searched using an asterisk (*) following the word stem. For example: **regulat*** will retrieve both regulation and regulate. Additional instructions and examples.

Browse the Table of Contents of the current issue of the *Federal Register* HTML PDF ◄▄▄

Browse 1998 back issues of the *Federal Register* Table of Contents. ◄▄▄

Cancellation of Legislative Items Pursuant to Line Item Veto Act (as published in the *Federal Register*)

To search the Unified Agenda, return to the list of databases available for simple searches.

━━━━━━━━━━━━━━━━━━━━━

Thi s document is sponsored by the Office of the Federal Register, National Archives and Records Administration on the United States Government Printing Office web site.

Questions or comments regarding this service? Contact the GPO Access User Support Team by Internet e-mail at gpoaccess@gpo.gov; by telephone at (202) 512-1530 or toll free at (888) 293-6498; by fax at (202) 512-1262.

[NARA Home] [Docs Home] [GPO Home] GPO INETservices

Page #ACES/ACES140 March 18, 1998
http://www.access.gpo.gov/su_docs/aces/aces140.html   9/30/98

▼ How Do You Use the C.F.R.?

To use the C.F.R., consult the index that contains listings of subjects, agencies, and references to the regulations codified within the C.F.R. volumes. The index also provides a list of C.F.R. titles, chapters, subchapters, and parts, and an alphabetical list of the agencies in the C.F.R. This index, called the *C.F.R. Index and Finding Aids* volume, is revised once a year as of January 1. The index refers you to parts. Parts contain "the regulations on a single function or specific subject matter under control of the issuing agency."[4] Illustration 8-6 is a page from the 1993 C.F.R. index, published by the U.S. Government Printing Office.

To research a particular topic in the index, you first must locate the name of the agency. Assume that you are looking for regulations concerning the food labeling and fat claims. First, you need to review the enabling statute to determine the agency responsible for such regulation. Once you have made that determination, you are ready to review the index. In this case, the responsible agency is the U.S. Food and Drug Administration. You would find that agency name listed in alphabetical order in the index. Next, you would review the topical listings below the agency name. In this case, the topics of possible interest are "labeling" and "nutritional quality guidelines." See Illustration 8-6. This index page refers you to title 21, part 101 of the C.F.R. for the labeling regulations and title 21, part 104 of the C.F.R. for the nutritional quality guidelines.

The next step is to go to the C.F.R. volumes. The title and part numbers are listed on the binding. Review the appropriate part and chapter. Within the part, you will find a listing of the statutory authority that is the basis for the regulation. If you have not already consulted this statute, find the statute and review it.

Illustration 8-1 is the page of the C.F.R. referred to under the "labeling" topic in the index: title 21, part 101 of the C.F.R. concerning food labeling. You should scan the sections listed to find relevant sections. You should review each relevant section. The C.F.R. part also specifies the enabling statutes. In this case, the enabling statutes are the Fair Packaging and Labeling Act and the Federal Food, Drug, and Cosmetic Act. Citations to the U.S.C. for each act are included. In addition, the citation to the *Federal Register* publication is noted. Finally, the text of the regulation begins under the heading "Subpart A—General Provisions."

Commercial publishers also produce various indexes to the C.F.R. The commercial indexes have many advantages. The indexing terms are not limited to agency names. Information can be retrieved by subject, agency, topic, and key word. The commercial indexes generally are updated and published more frequently than the government index, and they contain better instructions concerning their use.

▼ How Do You Search the C.F.R. on WESTLAW or LEXIS?

Online computer searches may allow easier access to regulations than an index. You can search the full text of the regulations on both the WESTLAW and LEXIS systems and do not need to rely on the terms contained within the index. Current regulations can be searched online as well as many superseded regulations.

[4]*C.F.R. Index and Finding Aids* 1993, Explanation.

ILLUSTRATION 8-6. Sample Page from C.F.R. Index

⑥
CFR Index

① **Food and Drug Administration**

Voluntary filing of cosmetic product experiences, 21 CFR 730

Voluntary filing of cosmetic product ingredient and cosmetic raw material composition statements, 21 CFR 720

Voluntary registration of cosmetic product establishments, 21 CFR 710

Delegations of authority and organization, 21 CFR 5

Employee standards of conduct, supplement, 45 CFR 73a

Employee standards of conduct and conflicts of interest, 21 CFR 19

Enforcement of Federal Food, Drug, and Cosmetic Act and Fair Packaging and Labeling Act, 21 CFR 1

Enforcement policy, recall guidelines, 21 CFR 7

Environmental impact considerations, 21 CFR 25

| 1 Agency |
| 2 Topic |
| 3 C.F.R. Citation |
| 4 Title |
| 5 Part |
| 6 Index Name |

affirmed as
ed as safe
184
CFR 170
adhesives and
tings, 21 CFR

adjuvants, production aids, and sanitizers, 21 CFR 178

Indirect food additives, general, 21 CFR 174

Indirect food additives, paper and paperboard components, 21 CFR 176

Indirect food additives, polymers, 21 CFR 177

Indirect food substances affirmed as generally recognized as safe (GRAS), 21 CFR 186

Permitted for direct addition to food for human consumption, 21 CFR 172

Permitted in food on interim basis or in contact with food pending additional study, 21 CFR 180

Petitions, 21 CFR 171

Prior-sanctioned food ingredients, 21 CFR 181

Secondary direct, permitted in food for human consumption, 21 CFR 173

Substances generally recognized as safe (GRAS), 21 CFR 182

Substances prohibited from use, 21 CFR 189

Food for human consumption
Acidified, 21 CFR 114

Administrative rulings and decisions, 21 CFR 100

Bakery products, 21 CFR 136

Cacao products, 21 CFR 163

Cereal flours and related products, 21 CFR 137

Cheeses and related cheese products, 21 CFR 133

Common or usual name for nonstandardized, 21 CFR 102

Drinking water, processing and bottling of, 21 CFR 129

Eggs and egg products, 21 CFR 160

Emergency permit control, 21 CFR 108

Fish and shellfish, 21 CFR 161

Food dressings and flavorings, 21 CFR 169

Frozen desserts, 21 CFR 135

Fruit butters, jellies, preserves, and related products, 21 CFR 150

Fruit juices, canned, 21 CFR 146

Fruit pies, 21 CFR 152

Fruits, canned, 21 CFR 145

Good practices in manufacturing, packing, or holding human food, 21 CFR 110

Infant formula, 21 CFR 107

Infant formula quality control procedures, 21 CFR 106

Irradiation in production, processing and handling of food, 21 CFR 179

②Labeling, 21 CFR 101 ③

Macaroni and noodle products, 21 CFR 139

Margarine, 21 CFR 166 ④

Milk and cream, 21 CFR 131

②Nutritional quality guidelines, ㉑CFR 104 ⑤

Quality standards for foods with no identity standards, 21 CFR 103

Seafood inspection program, 21 CFR 197

Special dietary use, 21 CFR 105

Standards, general, 21 CFR 130

269

On LEXIS, by accessing the GENFED library, CFR file you automatically retrieve the most current version of the C.F.R. On WEST-LAW, just as on LEXIS, the CFR database has the most current regulations, but older regulations can be accessed as well.

▼ Why Would You Use Old Regulations?

Often a case will turn on a regulation that was in place at the time of the incident involved. For example, suppose you are representing a client involved in a car accident in 1998. The experts say that the accident occurred because the car manufacturer failed to use a safety device—one that was required by federal regulations. The car was manufactured in 1997. You must research the 1997 regulations to determine what safety regulations applied to that manufacturer.

▼ How Do You Update and Validate Regulations?

Updating is one of the most important tasks you must perform when you review agency regulations. This is especially important because the regulations change frequently. Because the C.F.R. is published annually with quarterly updates, you must determine the currentness of the document. The *List of CFR Sections Affected,* or L.S.A., enables you to update a C.F.R. citation. The L.S.A. is published with the C.F.R. and is issued monthly. The L.S.A. identifies which sections have been changed, updated, or removed: in essence, which C.F.R. sections have been affected in any way. The L.S.A. is organized by title and is a single paperback pamphlet. Illustration 8-7 is a page from the *List of CFR Sections Affected* that encompasses changes from April 1, 1992, through March 31, 1993. Changes to regulations are first published in the *Federal Register.* Therefore, you must check not only the monthly L.S.A. pamphlet, but portions of a daily *Federal Register.* Each issue of the *Federal Register* contains a section entitled "CFR Parts Affected in This Issue." At the end of each issue of the *Federal Register* is a section entitled "Reader Aids" that contains a column summarizing the month's changes in various regulations. See Illustration 8-8.

▼ How Is the Updating Performed in Practice?

Assume that you have found the regulation that defines the standard for labeling of a food's fat content in the *Federal Register.* It is 21 C.F.R. §101.62. Assume also that it is April 3, 1993, and you want to determine if this regulation has been changed since it was first published. You want to be certain that you determine whether there have been any changes to the relevant section through the date of your search.

You should now review the current monthly L.S.A. pamphlet. For our purposes, consult Illustration 8-7. This pamphlet discloses any changes to the regulations that occurred between April 1, 1992, and March 31, 1993. Find the title you want to update: in this case,

ILLUSTRATION 8-7.   Sample Page from *List of C.F.R. Sections Affected*

---

50   (4) LSA—LIST OF CFR SECTIONS AFFECTED

(2) CHANGES APRIL 1, 1992 THROUGH MARCH 31, 1993

(1) **TITLE 21 Chapter I—Con.**   Page
and (14) revised; (b)(11)(iv),
(12)(iv) and (16) added.............**56261**
60.10   Revised..............................**56261**
60.22   (b)(1) revised; (d) redesig-
nated as (f); new (d) and (e)
added; new (f) amended......... **56262**
73   Regulation at 57 FR 32173
effective date confirmed..........**61292**
73.1   (a)(3) table amended............. **32175**
73.3121   (a)(8) and (9) amended;
(a)(10) added.............................. 9541
73.3127   Added................................3227
81.1   Regulation at 57 FR 10616
effective date corrected...........**11797**
100   Implementation at 57 FR
56347 revoked.........................2066
Implementation; eff. 5-8-94........2070
Authority citation revised...........2467
Regulatory impact analysis
statement.................................2927
100.1 (Subpart A) Added...............2468
100.2   Added................................2460
101   Implementation at 57 FR
56347 revoked.........................2066
Implementation; eff. 5-8-94........2070
Regulatory impact analysis
statement.................................2927
101.3   (e)(4)(ii) revised; eff. 5-8-
94...2227
101.4   (a)(1) and (b)(2)(i) re-
vised; eff. 5-8-93.....................2875
(b)(20) through (22), (d), (e)
and (f) added, eff. 5-8-94.........2875
101.6   Removed; eff. 5-8-94............2875
101.8   (a) revised; eff. 5-8-94.........2291
101.9   Revised; eff. 2-14-94............2175
(b) revised; eff. 5-8-94...................2291
(c)(7)(iii), (8)(iv) and (9)
added; eff. 5-8-94.....................2227
(k)(1) added; eff. 2-14-94.............2533
101.10   Revised; eff. 2-14-95...........2410
101.12 (Subpart A) Added; eff.
5-8-94......................................2293
101.13   Revised; eff. 2-14-94...........2410
(q)(2) revised; eff. 2-14-95.............2410
101.14   Added; eff. 5-8-93............. 2533
(d)(2)(vii)(B) and (3) added;
eff. 5-8-94................................ 2533
101.22   (h)(7) added; eff. 5-8-
94...2875
(k) added; eff. 5-8-93.....................2875
101.25   Removed; eff. 2-14-94.........2413
101.30   Added; eff. 5-8-93.............. 2925
101.35   Removed; eff. 5-8-94.........2876
(3) 101.54—101.69   (Subpart D)
Added; eff. 2-14-94.....................2413

NOTE: **Boldface page numbers indicate 1992 changes.**

101.67   Added; eff. 5-8-94............... 2455
101.70—101.71   (Subpart   E)
Added; eff. 5-8-93.....................2534
101.71   (Subpart E) Added; eff.
5-8-93......................................2578
(a) added; eff. 5-8-93......................2548
(c) added; eff. 5-8-93......................2620
(d) added; eff. 5-8-93......................2639
(e) added; eff. 5-8-93......................2664
(f) added; eff. 5-8-93......................2714
101.72   Added; eff. 5-8-93.............. 2676
101.73   Added; eff. 5-8-93.............. 2801
101.74   Added; eff. 5-8-93.............. 2836
101.75   Added; eff. 5-8-93.............. 2757
101.76   Added; eff. 5-8-93.............. 2548
101.77   Added; eff. 5-8-93.............. 2578
101.78   Added; eff. 5-8-93.............. 2639
101.95 (Subpart F) Added; eff.
2-14-94....................................2426
101.100—101.108   (Subpart   F)
Redesignated as subpart G;
eff. 2-14-94.............................. 2426
101.100   (d) introductory text
revised; eff. 2-14-94....................2188
(a)(2) revised; eff. 5-8-94.............. 2876
101   Appendix B added; eff. 2-
14-94....................................... 2189
102.22   Added; eff. 5-8-94............. 2876
102.30   Removed; eff. 5-8-94.........2926
102.32   Removed; eff. 5-8-94.........2926
102.33   Revised; eff. 5-8-94...........2926
103.35   (d)(3) added; eff. 7-6-
93.. 381
104.20   (a) amended; (c)(1) and
[...] ...5-8-94.....2228
[...] at 57 FR
[...] 2066
[...] 5-8-94.........2070
[...] analysis
[...]..................... 2927
105.00   Revised; eff. 5-8-94..............2430
130   Implementation at 57 FR
56347 revoked..........................2066
Implementation; eff. 5-8-
94..2070
Regulatory impact analysis
statement.................................2927
130.3   (e) added; eff. 5-8-93............2876
130.9   Added; eff. 5-8-93..................2876
130.10   Added; eff. 5-8-94..............2446
130.11   Added; eff. 5-8-93...............2876
130.110   (f) revised; eff. 5-8-93...... 2890
131.111   (h) revised; eff. 5-8-
93..2890

1 **C.F.R Title**
2 **Dates Included**
3 **C.F.R. Sections**
4 **L.S.A. title**

ILLUSTRATION 8-8. *Federal Register*'s **CFR Parts Affected During April**

---

i

Reader Aids

Federal Register
Vol. 58, No. 62
Friday, April 2, 1993

INFORMATION AND ASSISTANCE

Federal Register

Index, finding aids & general information	202–523–5227
Public inspection desk	523–5215
Corrections to published documents	523–5237
Document drafting information	523–3187
Machine readable documents	523–3447

Code of Federal Regulations

Index, finding aids & general information	523–5227
Printing schedules	523–3419

Laws

Public Laws Update Service (numbers, dates, etc.)	523–6641
Additional information	523–5230

Presidential Documents

Executive orders and proclamations	523–5230
Public Papers of the Presidents	523–5230
Weekly Compilation of Presidential Documents	523–5230

The United States Government Manual

General information	523–5230

Other Services

Data base and machine readable specifications	523–3447
Electronic Bulletin Board	275–1538, 275–0920
Guide to Record Retention Requirements	523–3187
Legal staff	523–4534
Privacy Act Compilation	523–3187
Public Laws Update Service (PLUS)	523–6641
TDD for the hearing impaired	523–5229

FEDERAL REGISTER PAGES AND DATES, APRIL

17081–17320	1
17321–17490	2

> 1 **L.S.A. title and month**
> 2 **C.F.R. title**
> 3 **C.F.R. parts**
> 4 *Federal Register* **page numbers**

CFR PARTS AFFECTED DURING APRIL ①

At the end of each month, the Office of the Federal Register publishes separately a List of CFR Sections Affected (LSA), which lists parts and sections affected by documents published since the revision date of each title.

3 CFR

Executive Orders:
12842	17081

12 CFR
226	17083

② **21 CFR**
Ch. I	17085
1	17085
5	17091, 17093, 17094, 17095, 17096, 17105, 17105
12	17096
14	17095
20	17096, 17097
74	17096
100	17096, 17097
③| 101	17085, 17096, 17097, 17099, 17100, 17101, 17102, 17103, 17104
102	17102, 17103
104	17104
105	17096, 17104
130	17103, 17105
131	17105
133	17105
135	17103, 17105
136	17103
137	17103
139	17103
145	17103
146	17103
150	17103
152	17103
155	17103
156	17103
158	17103
160	17103
161	17103
163	17103
164	17103
166	17103
168	17103, 17105
169	17103
172	17096
177	17096
178	17096
186	17096
189	17096
1308	17106

Proposed Rules:
100	17171
101	17171
102	17171
135	17172
161	17171 |④

24 CFR
50	17164
574	17164
905	17164
3500	17165

Proposed Rules:
125	17172

26 CFR
1	17166

30 CFR

Proposed Rules:
935	17173

34 CFR
377	17308

36 CFR

Proposed Rules:
1191	17175

40 CFR

Proposed Rules:
80	17175

46 CFR
174	17316

47 CFR
61	17166
64	17167

Proposed Rules:
2	17180
80	17180
97	17180

50 CFR
658	17169

Proposed Rules:
226	17181
672	17193, 17196
675	17196, 17200

LIST OF PUBLIC LAWS

Note: No public bills which have become law were received by the Office of the Federal Register for inclusion in today's List of Public Laws.

Last List March 31, 1993

ELECTRONIC BULLETIN BOARD

Free Electronic Bulletin Board Service for Public Law Numbers is available on 202–275–1538 or 275–0920.

---

title 21. Review the sections column and determine whether section 101.62 has been changed. In this case, it has. The L.S.A. indicates that it was added effective February 14, 1994, and is found on page 2413 of the *Federal Register*.

Next, check the title page inside the front cover of the L.S.A. to determine the date when the pamphlet was last revised. As of April 3, 1993, the most relevant pamphlet was revised as of April 1, 1993.

Therefore, the pamphlet will not include any changes to 21 C.F.R. §101.62 made after April 1, 1993. You must determine if any changes occurred to the regulation between April 1, 1993, and April 2, 1993. First, check the *Federal Register* for April 2, 1993. Turn to the "Reader Aids" section in the back and look at the column entitled "CFR Parts Affected During April." See Illustration 8-8. Check to see if your citation is listed there. In this case, several notes indicate that part 101 of title 21 was affected. The *Federal Register* pages are provided. In this example, the notation next to 21 CFR 101 lists *Federal Register* pages 17085, 17096, 17097, 17099, 17100, 17101, 17102, 17103, and 17104. Review those pages to determine if any of the modifications are relevant to your research. Next, review the "CFR Parts Affected in This Issue" listed in the front of the *Federal Register,* which is shown in Illustration 8-9. It directs you to amendments to title 21 on *Federal Register* page 17341, shown in Illustration 8-10. These pages contain changes to page 2418 of the *Federal Register,* shown in Illustration 8-4. Read the text of page 17342 and see how it relates to page 2418.

PRACTICE POINTER

Current "Reader Aids" pages of the *Federal Register* now contain a notation for the relevant Web sites.

Fortunately, on LEXIS and WESTLAW, the changes to the regulations already are incorporated.

▼ How Do You Search a Regulation on the Internet?

You can access the C.F.R. on the Internet at http://www.access.gpo.gov/nara/cfr/cfr-table-search.html. Once you access the C.F.R. page shown in Illustration 8-11, you can search through the titles or you can search by key word for the relevant section. (For a more detailed explanation of how to research using the Internet, see Chapter 10.)

▼ How Do You Validate or Shepardize a C.F.R. Citation?

Cases that construe an administrative regulation are compiled in the *Shepard's Code of Federal Regulations Citations.* The citations are organized by title and then by section. The publisher's analysis is similar to that given to statutes. (For a detailed explanation of how to Shepardize, consult Chapter 4 and Appendix A.) A court cannot repeal or overrule an administrative regulation. Shepardizing, however, indicates whether the regulation continues to be valid. However, Shepardizing an administrative regulation does not replace the need

ILLUSTRATION 8-9. *Federal Register*'s CFR Parts Affected in This Issue

Federal Register / Vol. 58, No. 62 / Friday, April 2, 1993 / Contents   VII

①**CFR PARTS AFFECTED IN THIS ISSUE**

A cumulative list of the parts affected this month can be found in the Reader Aids section at the end of this issue.

10 CFR
2................................17321

14 CFR
71...............................17322
73...............................17323
97 (2 documents)...........17324,
                          17325

17 CFR
200.............................17327
202.............................17327
229.............................17327
230.............................17327
239.............................17327
240.............................17327
249.............................17327
250.............................17327
259.............................17327
270.............................17327
274.............................17327
Proposed Rules:
12...............................17369

②**21 CFR**
③1.......................17328
5........................17341 — ④
101 (3 documents)........17328,
                   17341, 17343
529.............................17346
558.............................17346

30 CFR
Proposed Rules:
935.............................17372

33 CFR
Proposed Rules:
334 (2 documents).........17373,
                          17374

34 CFR
Proposed Rules:
685.............................17472

46 CFR
252.............................17346,

47 CFR
73...............................17349
76...............................17350
Proposed Rules:
97...............................17375

50 CFR
217.............................17364
227.............................17364
675 (2 documents).........17366,
                          17367
Proposed Rules:
17...............................17376

> 1 L.S.A. title and
>   dates included
> 2 C.F.R. title
> 3 C.F.R. parts
> 4 *Federal Register*
>   page number

to update the regulation in the manner discussed in the prior sections. Updating the regulation provides the most current version of the citation. In contrast, Shepardizing the cite reveals the judicial interpretations of the citation. Both tasks, Shepardizing and updating, must be performed for research to be thorough and complete.

▼ How Are the C.F.R. and the *Federal Register* Cited?

Citations to the C.F.R. and the *Federal Register* should follow Bluebook Rule 14.2. Title 21 of the C.F.R., part 101 from 1992 is cited as

21 C.F.R. pt. 101 (1992)

Title 21 of the C.F.R., §101.62 from 1993 would be written as

21 C.F.R. §101.62 (1993)

ILLUSTRATION 8-10.   Sample Pages from 58 Fed. Reg. 17341-17342 (1993)

Federal Register / Vol. 58, No. 62 / Friday, April 2, 1993 / Rules and Regulations   17341 ④

Dated: March 29, 1993.
Michael R. Taylor,
Deputy Commissioner for Policy.
[FR Doc. 93-7672 Filed 3-30-93; 4:07 pm]
BILLING CODE 4160-01-F

① **21 CFR Parts 5 and 101**

[Docket Nos. 91N-0384 and 84N-0153]

RIN 0905-AD06 and 0905-AD68

Food Labeling: Nutrient Content Claims, General Principles, Petitions, Definition of Terms; Definitions of Nutrient Content Claims for the Fat, Fatty Acid, and Cholesterol Content of Food; Correction

AGENCY: Food and Drug Administration, HHS.

② **ACTION:** Final rule; correction.

③ **SUMMARY:** The Food and Drug Administration (FDA) is correcting a final rule that appeared in the Federal Register of January 6, 1993 (58 FR 2302). The document amended the food labeling regulations to: Provide definitions for specific nutrient content claims using the terms "free," "low," "lean," "extra lean," "good source," "high," "reduced," "light" or "lite," "less," "fewer," and "more" and provide for their use on the food label; provide for the use of implied nutrient content claims; define and provide for the use of the term "fresh;" and address the use of the terms "natural" and "organic." The document was published with some inadvertent typographical and editorial errors. This document corrects those errors.

EFFECTIVE DATE: May 8, 1994, except §§ 101.10 and 101.13(q)(5) concerning restaurant firms consisting of 10 or less individual restaurant establishments for whom these sections will become effective on May 8, 1995.

FOR FURTHER INFORMATION CONTACT: Elizabeth J. Campbell, Center for Food Safety and Applied Nutrition (HFS-155), Food and Drug Administration, 200 C St. SW., Washington, DC 20204, 202-205-5229.

In FR Doc. 92-31504, appearing on page 2302 in the Federal Register of Wednesday, January 6, 1993, the following corrections are made:

1. On page 2302, in the first column, under the caption "EFFECTIVE DATE:", in line 1, the date "February 14, 1994" is corrected to read "May 8, 1994"; and beginning in line 6, the date "February 14, 1995" is corrected to read "May 8, 1995"; and under the caption "FOR FURTHER INFORMATION CONTACT:", beginning in line 2, the

mail code "(HFF-312)" is corrected to read "(HFS-155)".
2. On page 2303, in the third column, in the first full paragraph, in line 10, the word "distribution" is corrected to read "distinction".
3. On page 2305, in the third column, in the third full paragraph, in line 6, "(r)(2)(A)(iv)" is corrected to read "(r)(2)(A)(v)".
4. On page 2310, in the second column, in the second full paragraph, in the second line from the bottom, the phrase "III.B.c.vi." is corrected to read "III.B.1.c.vi.".
5. On page 2312, in the third column, in the second full paragraph, in line 8, "(r)(2)(A)(iv)" is corrected to read "(r)(2)(A)(v)"; and in line 12, "or (f)" is corrected to read "or § 101.13(f)".
6. On page 2314, in the third column, in the second full paragraph, in line 9, "i.e.," is corrected to read "e.g.,".
7. On page 2315, in the second column, in the first full paragraph, in line 8, the words "customarily consumed" are added after the word "amount".
8. On page 2323, in the first column, in the fourth full paragraph, in line 8, "§ 101.13(e)" is corrected to read "§ 101.13(d)".
9. On page 2327, in the third column, in the second full paragraph, in line 8, "III.B.c.ii." is corrected to read "III.B.1.c.ii.".
10. On page 2330, in the second column, in the second full paragraph, in line 2, the phrase "no ... is corrected to read " ... free".
11. On page 2335, i... column, in line 29, "§ ... corrected to read "§ 1...
12. On page 2340, i... column, in the second ... line 4, and in the seco... bottom of the third fu... phrase "less than 20 m... read "20 mg or less".
13. On page 2341, in the third column, in the third full paragraph, the first sentence is removed.
14. On page 2345, in the third column, in the fourth full paragraph, in line 9, the phrase "required by" is corrected to read "required in part by"; and the heading "c. *relative claims*" is corrected to read "C. *Relative Claims*".
15. On page 2346, in the third column, in the second full paragraph, in line 10, a period is added after the word "food".

16. On page 2356, in the third column, in the third line from the bottom, "said th" is corrected to read "said that".
17. On page 2361, in the third column, in the fourth full paragraph, in line 9, the word "more" is added before the word "unsaturated".
18. On page 2362, in the second column, beginning in the fifth line from the bottom, the phrase "percent reduction, reductions from a certain class of reference foods," is corrected to read "percentage definitions, differences in the amount of nutrient compared to a certain class of reference foods, i.e.,"; and in the third column, in line 6, the word "reductions" is corrected to read "differences".
19. On page 2365, in the second column, in the fourth full paragraph, in line 11, the phrase "reference the" is corrected to read "the reference".
20. On page 2369, in the second column, in line 1, the words "or no" are removed; and in line 5, the phrase "saturated fat free" is corrected to read "low saturated fat".
21. On page 2370, in the third column, in the second full paragraph, in line 4, the words "made with" are added before the word "corn".
22. On page 2373, in the third column, in the fourth full paragraph, in line 10, the following sentence is added after the second sentence: "Alternatively such statement may not ... ... nt or
... ... d ... ... graph, in ... ... cted to ... ... s ... ... graph in ... ... h, in line 4, the phrase "of sugar and sodium" is corrected to read "of sugar, sodium, and salt".
26. On page 2384, in the first column, in the second full paragraph, in line 7, "185" is corrected to read "183"; in the third column, in line 12, "(§ 101.56(d)(2)(i))" is corrected to read "(§ 101.56(d)(1)(ii)(A))"; and in line 18, "§ 101.56(d)(2)(ii)" is corrected to read "§ 105.56(d)(1)(ii)(B)".
27. On page 2385, in the first column, in line 3, "roducts" is corrected to read

1 C.F.R. parts affected
2 Action taken
3 Summary of change
4 *Federal Register* page number

A *Federal Register* entry from volume 58 beginning on page 26121 from April 30, 1993, would be cited as

    58 Fed. Reg. 26121 (1993)

As you can see, the specific calendar date is not cited, just the year.

ILLUSTRATION 8-10   *Continued*

17342   Federal Register / Vol. 58, No. 62 / Friday, April 2, 1993 / Rules and Regulations

"products"; and in the second full paragraph, in line 3, "o" is corrected to read "to".

28. On page 2388, in the second column, in the first full paragraph, in the last line, the date "February 14, 1995" is corrected to read "May 8, 1995".

29. On page 2392, in the second column, in the first full paragraph, in line 8, the word "*State*" is corrected to read "*States*".

30. On page 2395, in the second column, in line 6, "288–81" is corrected to read "2880–81".

31. On page 2406, in the third column, in the first full paragraph, in line 9, the phrase "in comment 334" is corrected to read "in comment 332".

32. On page 2409, in the second column, in reference 1, in line 2, the word "draft" is added after the word "NCEP"; and in line 5, the date "April 7, 1991" is corrected to read "March 27, 1991".

33. On page 2410, in the first column, in reference 17, in line 5, the words "[Population Panel]" are removed; in reference 21, in line 2, the words "for Proposal," are removed and " No. 3-" is added in their place; in the second column, in reference 24, in line 1, "8–17" is corrected to read "8–18"; in reference 33, in line 3, the phrase "associate ed., 2d ed." is corrected to read "associate ed., Pediatric Nutrition Handbook, 2d ed."; and in Reference 34, in line 3, "p. 254" is corrected to read "pp. 242–245".

§ 101.13 [Corrected]

The following corrections are made in § 101.13 *Nutrient content claims— general principles:*

34. On page 2412, in the first column, in paragraph (i)(1), in line 7, "10 g" is corrected to read "3 g"; in paragraph (i)(2), in the last line, the phrase "of an inch;" is corrected to read "of an inch: or"; and in paragraph (i)(3), in line 6, the phrase "required; or" is corrected to read "required."; and in the second column, in paragraph (j)(2)(i), in line 5, the phrase "the nutrient has been modified" is corrected to read "the nutrient in the labeled food differs"; and in the third column, in paragraph (m)(1)(ii), in line 4, "(i)(1)(ii)(E)" is corrected to read "(m)(1)(ii)(E)".

35. On page 2413, in the first column, in paragraph (p)(1), in line 1, the phrase "specified the" is corrected to read "specified, the"; in the second column, in paragraph (q)(5)(i), beginning in line 4, the citation "(d)(1)(ii)(C)" is corrected to read "(d)(1)(ii)(D)"; and in line 5, the citation "(d)(2)(ii)(C)" is corrected to read "(d)(2)(iii)(C)".

§ 101.54 [Corrected]

The following corrections are made in § 101.54 *Nutrient content claims for "good source," "high," and "more":*

36. On page 2414, in the first column, in paragraph (a), in line 10, the word "and" is corrected to read "or"; in paragraph (b)(1), in line 3, the word "and" is corrected to read "or"; in the second column, in paragraph (e)(1)(i), beginning in line 2, the phrase "for protein, vitamins, or minerals" is corrected to read "for vitamins or minerals"; beginning in line 3, the phrase "for dietary fiber or potassium" is corrected to read "for protein, dietary fiber, or potassium"; in paragraph (e)(1)(iii)(A), in line 3, the phrase "was increased" is corrected to read "is greater"; in the third column, in paragraph (e)(2)(i), beginning in line 2, the phrase "for protein, vitamins, or minerals" is corrected to read "for vitamins or minerals"; and beginning in line 3, the phrase "for dietary fiber or potassium" is corrected to read "for protein, dietary fiber, or potassium".

§ 101.56 [Corrected]

The following corrections are made in § 101.56 *Nutrient content claims for "light" or "lite":*

37. On page 2414, in the third column, in paragraph (a), in line 4, the word "and" is corrected to read "or"; and in paragraph (a)(3), beginning in line 2, the phrase "with § 101.9, § 101.10, or § 101.36, where applicable" is corrected to read "with § 101.9 or § 101.10, where applicable".

38. On page 2415, in the second column, in paragraph (d)(2), the paragraph number "(d)(2)(i)" is corrected to read "(2)(i)"; in the third column, in paragraph (g), beginning in line 10, the phrase "information on the label" is corrected to read "information required to accompany a relative claim shall appear on the label".

§ 101.60 [Corrected]

The following corrections are made in § 101.60 *Nutrient content claims for the calorie content of foods:*

39. On page 2416, in the first column, in paragraph (b)(2), in line 5, the word "and" is corrected to read "or"; paragraphs (b)(2)(ii), (b)(2)(iii), and (b)(2)(iii) are redesignated as paragraphs (b)(2)(ii)(A), (b)(2)(i)(B), and (b)(2)(iii); in newly redesignated paragraph (b)(2)(i)(B), in the bottom line, the phrase "form]; and" is corrected to read "form)."; in the second column, in paragraph (b)(4)(ii)(A), in line 3, the phrase "have been reduced" is corrected to read "differ between the two foods"; and in paragraph (b)(5)(ii)(A), in line 3,

the phrase "have been reduced" is corrected to read "differ between the two foods".

40. On page 2417, in the first column, in paragraphs (c)(4)(ii)(A), in line 3, and in paragraph (c)(5)(ii)(A), in line 3, the phrase "has been reduced" is corrected to read "differs between the two foods".

§ 101.61 [Corrected]

The following corrections are made in § 101.61 *Nutrient content claims for the sodium content of foods:*

41. On page 2417, in the second column, in paragraph (a), in line 1, the word "and" is corrected to read "or"; in paragraph (b)(2), in line 3, the word "and" is corrected to read "or"; in the third column, in paragraph (b)(3), in line 3, the word "and" is corrected to read "or"; in paragraph (b)(4), in line 5, the word "and" is corrected to read "or"; and in paragraph (b)(5), in line 3, the word "and" is corrected to read "or".

42. On page 2418, in the first column, in paragraph (b)(6)(ii)(A), in line 3, the phrase "has been reduced" is corrected to read "differs from the labeled food"; and in paragraph (b)(7)(ii)(A), in line 3, the phrase "has been reduced" is corrected to read "differs from the reference food".

§ 101.62 [Corrected]

The following corrections are made in § 101.62 *Nutrient content claims for fat, fatty acid, and cholesterol content of foods:*

43. On page 2418, in the third column, in paragraph (b)(2), in line 4, the word "and" is corrected to read "or"; and in paragraph (b)(3), in line 3, the word "and" is corrected to read "or".

44. On page 2419, in the first column, in paragraph (b)(4)(ii)(A), in line 3, the phrase "has been reduced" is corrected to read "differs between the two foods"; in paragraph (b)(5)(ii)(A), in line 3, "has been reduced" is corrected to read "differs between the two foods"; in paragraph (b)(6)(ii), in line 1, the phrase "percent of reduction" is corrected to read "percent declared"; in the second column, in paragraph (c), in line 21 "0.5 g or less" is corrected to read "less than 0.5 g"; in the third column, in paragraph (c)(4), in line 7, "§ 101.13(j)(1)(ii)(A)" is corrected to read "§ 101.13(j)(1)(i)(i)"; and in paragraph (c)(4)(ii)(A), in line 3, the phrase "was reduced" is corrected to read "differs between the two foods".

45. On page 2420, in the first column, in paragraph (c)(5)(ii)(A), in line 3, the phrase "has been reduced" is corrected to read "differs between the two foods"; in the second column, in paragraph (d)(1)(ii), in line 4, the phrase "serving,

---

D. DECISIONS

▼ What Else Do Administrative Agencies Do?

Agencies function in a quasi-judicial capacity when they conduct **hearings.** Hearings may resemble court proceedings. However, most hearings are informal. An **administrative law judge** (ALJ) hears cases

ILLUSTRATION 8-11. *Code of Federal Regulations* **Internet Home Page**

Available CFR Titles on GPO Access   Page 1 of 5

National Archives and
Records Administration

CFR Services available online via *GPO Access*

About the CFR online
Establishing HTML links to GPO's CFR WAIS databases
Search the entire set of CFR databases by keyword (current data)
Retrieve CFR sections by citation (current and/or historical data)
Search or browse your choice of CFR titles and/or volumes (current and/or historical
data)
Search the Federal Register for related documents (current and/or historical data)

PARALLEL TABLE OF AUTHORITIES AND RULES   (TXT *992k*)   (PDF *400k*)
  (Extracted from the January 1, 1998, revision of the *CFR Index and Finding Aids* -- pp.
709-817)

- To search or browse a **single** CFR Title for a given year, click on the desired revision date for
  that Title in the table below. ◄■■
                                   - or -
- To search or browse **one or more** CFR Titles, click the appropriate checkbox(es) in the table
  below, then click CONTINUE.

involving the application of a particular regulation. Often these cases involve the violation of a regulation. After the hearing, the ALJ, who may be an agency employee or an independent attorney, issues an opinion that serves as primary authority. However, most agency decisions do not have the same binding effect as court decisions. Some agency decisions can be appealed in the courts if the parties are not satisfied with the results. Often, however, the federal courts follow agency decisions concerning areas in which the agencies have developed expertise. To determine whether a court will follow an agency ruling, you must review court and agency decisions.

The Administrative Procedure Act requires agencies to publish their decisions and to make them available to the public. Researchers

ILLUSTRATION 8-11. *Continued*

Available CFR Titles on *GPO Access*

Title		Revision Date (Unless noted, all parts for a given Title are available)		
		1998	**1997**	**1996**
Title 1	General Provisions		☐ Jan. 1, 1997	
Title 2	[Reserved]			
Title 3	The President	☐ Jan. 1, 1998	☐ Jan. 1, 1997	
Title 4	Accounts		☐ Jan. 1, 1997	
Title 5	Administrative Personnel	☐ Jan. 1, 1998	☐ Jan. 1, 1997	
Title 6	[Reserved]			
Title 7	Agriculture	☐ Jan. 1, 1998	☐ Jan. 1, 1997	
Title 8	Aliens and Nationality	☐ Jan. 1, 1998	☐ Jan. 1, 1997	
Title 9	Animals and Animal Products	☐ Jan. 1, 1998	☐ Jan. 1, 1997	
Title 10	Energy	☐ Jan. 1, 1998	☐ Jan. 1, 1997	
Title 2ʊ	Employees' Benefits	☐ Apr. 1, 1998	☐ Apr. 1, 1997	☐ Apr. 1, 1996 Parts 400-499
Title 21	Food and Drugs	☐ Apr. 1, 1998	☐ Apr. 1, 1997	☐ Apr. 1, 1996
Title 22	Foreign Relations	☐ Apr. 1, 1998	☐ Apr. 1, 1997	
Title 23	Highways	☐ Apr. 1, 1998	☐ Apr. 1, 1997	
Title 24	Housing and Urban Development	☐ Apr. 1, 1998	☐ Apr. 1, 1997	
Title 25	Indians	☐ Apr. 1, 1998	☐ Apr. 1, 1997	
Title 26	Internal Revenue	☐ Apr. 1, 1998	☐ Apr. 1, 1997	

ILLUSTRATION 8-11. *Continued*

Title 43	Public Lands: Interior		☐ Oct. 1, 1997	☐ Oct. 1, 1996
Title 44	Emergency Management and Assistance		☐ Oct. 1, 1997	☐ Oct. 1, 1996
Title 45	Public Welfare		☐ Oct. 1, 1997	☐ Oct. 1, 1996
Title 46	Shipping		☐ Oct. 1, 1997	☐ Oct. 1, 1996
Title 47	Telecommunication		☐ Oct. 1, 1997	☐ Oct. 1, 1996
Title 48	Federal Acquisition Regulations System		☐ Oct. 1, 1997	☐ Oct. 1, 1996
Title 49	Transportation		☐ Oct. 1, 1997	☐ Oct. 1, 1996
Title 50	Wildlife and Fisheries		☐ Oct. 1, 1997	☐ Oct. 1, 1996

This document is sponsored by the Office of the Federal Register, National Archives and Records Administration on the United States Government Printing Office web site.

Questions or comments regarding this service? Contact the GPO Access User Support Team by Internet e-mail at gpoaccess@gpo.gov; by telephone at (202) 512-1530 or toll free at (888) 293-6498; by fax at (202) 512-1262.

Page #nara/cfr/cfr-table-search.html(R) September 2,1998

---

can contact a particular agency to obtain a decision. Administrative rulings are found frequently in the areas of labor, environmental, tax, securities, occupational safety and health, energy, and immigration law.

ETHICS ALERT

Some federal agencies permit paralegals to appear before them without an attorney present.

▼ What Kind of Authority Are Administrative Decisions?

Administrative decisions, like decisions of various courts, are primary authorities. Some of these decisions can be appealed·to the courts after all agency remedies have been satisfied. For example, an ALJ

will determine whether an individual is disabled and qualifies for
social security. This decision is made following a hearing. The ALJ's
decision then can be appealed to the U.S. District Court and subsequently to higher federal courts. The enabling statute defines the
type of review each agency decision will be accorded. However, the
precedential value of the agency's decision varies. Some agencies
do not bind themselves to follow previous decisions. However, the
courts may find that an agency's decision is very persuasive, particularly in areas in which an agency has developed an expertise.

IRS

▼ Can Administrative Agency Decisions Be Shepardized?

Yes, administrative agency decisions can be Shepardized. The citations are contained in *Shepard's United States Administrative Citations.*

▼ Other Than the Agency Itself, Where Can You Find Administrative Agency Decisions?

Sometimes a commercially published service prints administrative
agency decisions. Many agency decisions are also available on WEST-
LAW and LEXIS. Looseleaf services covering a specific legal topic
such as food and drug law or environmental law publish many of
the decisions.

E. LOOSELEAF SERVICES

▼ What Are Looseleaf Services?

Looseleaf services cover one topic thoroughly. The publishers compile administrative decisions, rules, regulations, and editorial comments within a single source. Looseleaf services are published in all
areas covered by administrative law: environmental, labor, energy,
and government contracts law. Many researchers think of looseleaf
services as mini-libraries because they contain a variety of resources
relating to a single legal topic.

Because the looseleafs are not bound volumes but are actually
looseleaf notebooks, they are easily updated by adding and removing
pages. Most looseleaf services are updated weekly, some more frequently. Once you become familiar with a practice area, particularly
a heavily regulated area of the law, you quickly become familiar with
the looseleaf services used in that area.

PRACTICE POINTER

Do not rely on the language of a primary authority you find in a looseleaf.
Check the official version of the authority if one exists.

▼ How Are Looseleaf Services Used?

Although looseleaf services are valuable resources because they contain everything a practitioner needs to research a heavily regulated area of the law, they are quite cumbersome to use. The following instructions should make using looseleaf services easier.

1. Analyze your problem to determine the topic. Is it a tax, environmental, securities, or energy law issue? Select a looseleaf service for that topic area.
2. Determine the type of material you are seeking. Do you need administrative regulations, court decisions, or agency decisions?
3. Review the instructions at the beginning of the looseleaf service that you have selected. Most services are organized by paragraph numbers and not by page numbers. Most services have a section entitled "How to Use This Service."
4. Review the various indexes to locate the specific material you are seeking. In general, you should review the general or topical index and then the current material index. If you are looking for a specific document, such as an agency decision, and you have the citation, use the finding tables or lists to obtain it.
5. Read the texts of the primary materials such as rules, regulations, and decisions and the secondary source commentary.
6. Update and validate your findings by using citators, including *Shepard's* or a service provided by the looseleaf publisher, and by looking through the "Current Materials" section.

▼ Can Looseleafs Be Retrieved Online?

More and more looseleaf services are being used online. Subscriptions to looseleaf services are expensive, require shelf space, and are labor intensive to update and to maintain. Online use eliminates the subscription cost, permits the cost of its use to be charged to the client as online time, and avoids the labor required to update the looseleaf because the computerized version always is current.

Using the looseleaf services online is advantageous for the paralegal. The multiple indexes in the hardcopy are difficult to use. You must use the terms selected by the indexer. In contrast, when accessing the service online, you have the benefit of full text searching. You can enter your query and select your own words. Another advantage of using looseleaf services online is that you can validate your research instantly at the terminal by using *Shepard's* online.

▼ What Type of Authority Are Looseleaf Services?

Looseleaf services as a whole are considered secondary authority because they are not published by a government body in its official law-making capacity. However, looseleaf services contain primary resources such as agency decisions, and frequently a looseleaf service is the only hardcopy resource for the decision. When citing to an agency decision obtained in a looseleaf service, that decision is primary authority.

Researching Administrative Law: A Summary

1. Find the enabling statute.
2. Find judicial opinions concerning the enabling statute.
3. Find agency regulations.
   a. Review the index for the appropriate title or look up title paralleling the statutory title and skim the contents.
   b. Or, look up the agency by name in the index. It will direct you to a C.F.R. part.
4. Find case adjudications. Consult looseleaf services, *Shepard's* and other citators, and the U.S.C.S. annotations.
5. Validate and update your research.

CHAPTER SUMMARY

Administrative agencies and their power and the authority are created by the federal and state legislatures when they enact enabling statutes. These agencies operate on a daily basis to enforce these legislative mandates.

As part of their enforcement duties, the agencies adopt rules and regulations and hold quasi-judicial hearings.

Rules and regulations of the federal administrative agencies can be found in the *Code of Federal Regulations*. These regulations also are available online. A daily paper called the *Federal Register* also reports any new or proposed regulations. States also have codes of regulations and generally a daily record of new and proposed administrative rules and regulations.

Updating these authorities is essential. You must use the *List of C.F.R. Sections Affected* (L.S.A.) to update a C.F.R. citation. These lists are organized by title and section and are included in the daily *Federal Register* publications. You must review both the monthly L.S.A. pamphlets and the *Federal Register* to update a C.F.R. section properly.

Decisions of administrative agencies also can be validated in a manner similar to other case decisions.

Looseleaf services focus on one area of the law. They contain both primary authorities such as statutes, administrative rules, and cases, and secondary authorities such as expert commentary. Some looseleaf services also have digests and citators and some can be found online.

The next chapter will explain how and when to use the computerized legal research systems.

KEY TERMS

adjudicatory

administrative law judge (ALJ)

administrative agencies

Code of Federal Regulations (C.F.R.)

enabling statutes

Federal Register

hearings

List of C.F.R. Section Affected (L.S.A.)

looseleaf services

quasi-judicial

regulations

rules

EXERCISES

FEDERAL REGULATIONS

1. Find a federal regulation that concerns the number of parts of lead allowable in drinking water.
   a. List each source that might contain the regulation.
   b. Map out your search strategy.
   c. List at least two sources and how you would find a regulation in each.
   d. List topics you might consult.
   e. List at least one regulation.
   f. Update the regulation using the hardcopy materials. What steps did you take?
   g. List the citation in proper Bluebook format.
2. Find a federal tax regulation that specifies how the value of estate property will be determined.
   a. List each source that might contain the regulation.
   b. Map out your search strategy.
   c. List at least two sources and how you would find a regulation in each.
   d. List topics you might consult.
   e. List at least one regulation.
   f. Update the regulation using the hardcopy materials. What steps did you take?
   g. List the regulation in proper Bluebook format.

STATE REGULATIONS

3. In your state, where would you look to find state regulations?
4. Find a state regulation that deals with the question of physician licensing.
   a. List each source that might contain the regulation.
   b. Map out your search strategy.
   c. List at least two sources and how you would find a regulation in each.
   d. List topics you might consult.
   e. List at least one regulation.
   f. Update the regulation using the hardcopy materials. What steps did you take?
   g. List the citation in proper Bluebook format.
5. You must find a federal regulation that concerns small toy parts and children under the age of three years old.
   a. List each source that might contain the regulation.
   b. Map out your search strategy.
   c. List at least two sources and how you would find a regulation in each.
   d. List topics you might consult.
   e. List at least one regulation.
   f. Update the regulation using the hardcopy materials. What steps did you take?
   g. List the citation in proper Bluebook format.

COMPUTERIZED LEGAL RESEARCH

CHAPTER OVERVIEW

This chapter explains the basic concepts of WESTLAW and LEXIS use and the way information is organized on the systems. Three fundamental electronic research skills are explored:

1. query formulation,
2. document retrieval, and
3. validation of authority.

Although this chapter focuses exclusively on online services, using computer-assisted legal research in specific research situations is discussed throughout this book. Legal databanks are really just additional, albeit powerful and expensive, research tools.

A. INTRODUCTION

LEXIS is an online research system owned by Reed Elsevier P.L.C., a British-Dutch publishing business. West Group, owned by Thompson, a major legal publisher, also decided to create computerized legal databases and named their system WESTLAW.

A revolution in legal research occurred with the advent of computerized legal research. Researchers can now obtain documents, cases, statutes, bills, regulations, attorney general opinions, slip laws, and many other forms of information, legal and factual, from a myriad of jurisdictions and print it out in full text without leaving the office. In addition, researchers do not have to use an index when obtaining material online. Researchers can select terms or words that need to appear in the ideal document on point. The researcher can then combine the relevant terms in a query, which is used to search the appropriate databank for documents with those words or terms. Computerized research systems continually increase the amount of information and the variety of documents they contain.

1. CD-ROM Resources

CD-ROM (an acronym for compact disc–read only memory) permit searching through thousands of pages of documents stored on a compact disc. CD-ROM searching technique is similar to online searching except that the connect charges do not mount because you are not connected to a database. However, CD-ROMs are not free; subscription fees are needed to keep the material current. The hardware is an expense as well. Sometimes, as is the case with many West CD-ROM products, CD-ROM searching is combined with online access. For example, say you begin your search on the CD drive and find relevant case law. You can then sign on to WESTLAW and update the research. The impact and the role of CD-ROM technology on legal research is growing. CD-ROMs are used in many large law firm libraries because they save valuable shelf space. Many firms have complete sets of reporters on CD-ROM from which researchers access cases and print them as needed.

2. The Internet

Paralegals are using the Internet with increasing frequency. Sources of legal information are growing daily on the Internet. Supreme Court opinions are available within 60 minutes of being handed down. Generally, the only fees incurred to access legal information on the Net are your Internet provider or access fees. Although the information on the Internet comes online quickly and is virtually cost-free, it is not as polished in its presentation as the commercial databases. The documents often are not indexed or cannot be searched by key words. Also, most legal documents on the Net do not date before the 1990s. If you are looking for cases from earlier dates, you must use hardcopy resources or the commercial databases. Nevertheless, the Internet is an excellent source for U.S. government information. Also, LEXIS and WESTLAW have fee-based gateways via the Net. The Internet is only going to grow in importance in the future not only as a searchable resource but as a gateway to commercial databanks. For a detailed discussion of the Internet, see Chapter 10.

don't go to Far back.

▼ What Are the Benefits of Using Computerized Legal Research?

The greatest benefit of computerized legal research is that all sources available through the online vendor, **LEXIS** or **WESTLAW,** are accessible through a single computer terminal. You do not have to travel to various libraries to obtain the information that you need. Also, the material online is never off the shelf or checked out. It is always up-to-date. Currentness is essential in legal research, and the online databases keep everything as current as possible. (See Chapter 4, for example, on how to validate cases on LEXIS and WESTLAW, and Chapter 6 on how to update statutes online.)

▼ What Are the Major Disadvantages of Using Computerized Research Services?

The first major disadvantage is cost. Online research is very expensive, and the charges for searching, connect time, and subscribing add up very quickly. A half-hour search can easily cost well over $100. You can avoid some of the high fees by engaging in a special contract with LEXIS or WESTLAW. Many types of contracts can be negotiated, including contracts for single-state research. Although the vendors have made online research easier and easier by adding many user-friendly features—like menu-driven searching and point-and-click search capabilities when accessing the services via the Internet—many skills must be developed to search online effectively and efficiently.

PRACTICE POINTER

Before using commercial databases to perform any research or cite checking, ask the attorney assigning the project if it is permissible. Sometimes budgets are very low and there isn't any extra money for computerized research.

3. Uses for LEXIS and WESTLAW

Computerized legal research is a very powerful search tool to find cases that discuss unique fact patterns. For example, suppose you want to find cases that deal with a slip-and-fall issue on a shag carpet. An encyclopedia or digest index may have entries under "slip and fall" and possibly under "carpet," but it is very unlikely that there would be an index entry under "shag." LEXIS and WESTLAW permit you to search "shag carpet" to see where those words appear in a document.

With computerized legal research you also can find documents, cases, statutes, and articles when you only have some information from the cite but not the complete cite. Suppose you hear about a promising Florida Supreme Court case on point. You know the case was decided in April 1993 and the judge's name was Murphy, but you do not have a clue as to the case name. Knowing the court, the year, and the judge will lead you to the case on LEXIS or WESTLAW.

4. Additional Uses for Computerized Legal Research

LEXIS and WESTLAW are used very effectively for cite checking, updating, and validating authority. (See Chapter 4 for a full discussion of citators, *Shepard's,* and KeyCite.) The online systems enable you to obtain the subsequent history of a case. Retrieving updated statutory and administrative materials on LEXIS and WESTLAW is another valuable use of the systems' capabilities because you do not have to consult a number of hardcopy sources to find the most current version of a statute or a regulation. Also, administrative and statutory materials have cumbersome and difficult-to-use indexes, and the full text search capabilities of LEXIS and WESTLAW permit you to obtain documents by combining the words and terms relevant to your research problem. Case law and code research from other jurisdictions is also suited to online retrieval because you do not have to find out-of-state primary sources in hardcopy format. A rarely used feature of computerized legal research is to access looseleaf services online; subscription and filing fees are saved and the material is always current.

B. USING WESTLAW AND LEXIS

▼ How Does Computerized Research Work?

WESTLAW and LEXIS work in a similar fashion. Both are **literal searching devices,** meaning that the computer system cannot answer a question but instead searches for the appearance of the words or terms that you select in the text of the document. The information that you retrieve after executing a search is a group of documents *[retrieves]* containing your search terms.

You begin by creating a list of words that would appear in the ideal document on point. (You should educate yourself on the topic before you get online so that you have a research vocabulary that includes synonymous terms.) Then you figure out the relationship between the ideal words or terms. How close together would they appear in the document? Would the words and terms appear in the same sentence? In the same paragraph? Within 100 words of one another? This involves thinking about the context of the words within the document's text and how those words should appear without losing their contextual significance.

LEXIS and WESTLAW have made the process of selecting the terms and determining the terms' contextual relationship simpler by the introduction of **natural language searching** on WESTLAW and **Freestyle** in LEXIS. Both Freestyle and natural language let you search in plain English using sentences and phrases without selecting connectors between the terms. (More on connectors later in the chapter.) The system then selects the significant terms from your search and looks for documents containing those terms. Whether you search using a group of words separated by connectors, or use natural language or Freestyle, computerized legal research scans the databank for the appearance of those words and retrieves the documents for you. *[don't use connector word And, or at, the, there etc]*

Electronic retrieval systems do not replace traditional research sources. LEXIS and WESTLAW are literal searching tools that cannot analyze or reach conclusions, legal or factual. LEXIS and WESTLAW search for terms within the parameters that you specify, the connectors. The systems are excellent for searching terms that are not ordinarily included in traditional indexes. They are also good for searching for specific facts or legal terms. Remember that the most successful searching occurs after some preliminary research has been performed using secondary sources and digests and, if possible, primary authority. Preliminary research makes you aware of the vocabulary used in topic discussions and the wording in on-point opinions. *One warning:* The service is very costly when you are using it at a law firm or a corporation. LEXIS and WESTLAW are not suited to researching broad legal concepts like *breach of contract.* Use your judgment to determine if computerized or hardcopy research is the best route. The best and most effective research uses a combination of hardcopy and computerized sources, drawing on the strengths of both. Computerized research is yet another tool in your arsenal of sources.

1. THE BASICS

▼ How Is Information Organized?

Information is organized in **libraries** on LEXIS and in **databases** on WESTLAW. Libraries and databases are merely synonyms for the same concept: that information is grouped together using the following categories:

1. by jurisdiction: individual states and federal cases and statutes;
2. by topic: for example, bankruptcy, tax, or contracts; or
3. by format: for example, law reviews, looseleaf services, or news articles.

LEXIS further divides the broad categories of information, the libraries, into subcategories called **files.** For example, the GENFED library on LEXIS contains all federal case law, statutory material, and administrative material. You must select what type of federal source you want after you go into the GENFED library. For example, you can choose the US file, which lets you search U.S. Supreme Court opinions after a specific date.

2. Search Formulation

▼ What Is a Search or Query?

LEXIS and WESTLAW are literal searching systems. You must determine the words or terms that you want to appear in a document on point. Your **search** or **query** is the group of terms or words that you select, separated by connectors, that you enter into the system to retrieve on target information. Suppose you want to find cases discussing Seminole Indians in Florida, particularly near St. Augustine, and their water, land, or property rights. The terms that you would select are:

Seminole Indian
St. Augustine
water right
land right
property right

These are the terms that would appear in the ideal opinion. Use a thesaurus to find synonymous terms to expand the number of documents you will retrieve. Next, you must determine the placement of the terms in the document's text. Do you want the terms to be close together and to all fall in the same sentence? Do you want the terms to be anywhere in the document? In the same paragraph? Will the contextual meaning or significance of the terms be lost if they are too far apart? Will you fail to retrieve many documents if you indicate that they should be close together? You indicate the proximity of the terms by using connectors.

a. Connectors

Connectors are the special words or symbols devised by WESTLAW and by LEXIS that link your search terms together to indicate your search terms' physical placement in the document's text. Connectors tell LEXIS and WESTLAW the proximity of the search terms in relation to one another. LEXIS uses the following connectors:

and—indicates that the terms are anywhere in the document but both terms must appear in the document. For example, in typing **seminole and indian,** the word *and* indicates that both terms must appear in the document.

or—indicates that one term or the other term or both terms must appear in the document. A blank space on WESTLAW indicates "or." For example, on LEXIS, typing **seminole or indian** would cause the retrieval system to look for the occurrence of either *Seminole* or *Indian* or both words in the document. To search for these synonymous terms on WESTLAW, input **seminole indian.** The *or* connector is most frequently used for synonymous terms, like *car or vehicle or automobile.* This maximizes the possibility of retrieving a greater number of on-point documents.

w/n—means within *n* number of words. You determine how close the words should appear in relation to one another. In our example, you could use **seminole w/5 indian,** which would tell LEXIS to search for the word *Seminole* to appear within 5 words of *Indian.*

Pre/n— This connector is unique to LEXIS and is identical to *w/n* except that the first word must precede the second. You are able to set the spacing. For example, **seminole pre/5 indian** would search for the word *Seminole* to precede the word *Indian* by 5 words.

w/s—indicates that the two words must appear in the same sentence in any order. You can also use */s* instead of *w/s.* **Seminole w/s indian** would search for the two terms to appear in the same sentence in any order.

w/p—instructs LEXIS to search for the terms within the same paragraph in any order. You can also use */p* instead of *w/p.* **Seminole w/p indian** would search for the appearance of those terms in the same paragraph in any order.

and not—excludes terms. Use it as your last connector. For example, **seminole and indian and not tribe** would retrieve documents with the words *Seminole* and *Indian* anywhere in the document but no documents with the word *tribe* would be retrieved.

WESTLAW's connectors are very similar to those of LEXIS, but as indicated earlier, WESTLAW does have a few unique features:

&—identical to the LEXIS **and.**

[blank space]—typing a blank space between two or more terms indicates *or.* For example, the search **auto car vehicle** translates into *auto or car or vehicle.* The **or** connector is most frequently used to indicate synonymous terms, but it is also used to link antonyms or opposites like *day or night.*

/s—WESTLAW pioneered the within-the-same-sentence connector. It is very handy because you do not have to estimate the proximity of the words to one another. If the words fall in the same sentence, you retrieve the document. Sentences can vary in length, and **/s** approximates written English.

+s—indicates that the two words must appear in the same sentence, but the first term must precede the second. For example, **seminole +s indian** would search for *Seminole* and *Indian* to appear in the same sentence, but *Seminole* must precede *Indian.*

/p—indicates that the two terms appear within the same paragraph. The search **seminole /p indian** would search for those two terms' appearance in the same paragraph in any order.

+p—searches for two terms to appear in the same paragraph, but the first term must precede the second. In our example, **seminole +p indian** would retrieve documents with *Seminole* occurring before *Indian* in the same paragraph.

/n—you can customize the proximity of terms on WESTLAW just as you can on LEXIS. For example, **seminole /5 indian** would search for the word *Seminole* to appear within *5* words of *Indian.*

+n—this connector allows you to establish the number of words between terms, but the first term must appear before the second. For example, **seminole +5 indian** searches for documents with *Seminole* falling *5* words before *Indian.*

%—excludes the term following the connector.

The following table summarizes connectors.

Description	*LEXIS*	*WESTLAW*
terms within the same document	and	&
either or both terms within the same document	or	[blank space]
terms appear within specified number of words of each other	w/n	/n
same as w/n but first term precedes second term	pre/n	+n
terms within the same sentence, any order	w/s	/s
terms within same sentence; first term precedes second term	—	+s
terms within same paragraph, any order	w/p	/p
excludes terms following the connector	and not	%

b. Quotations

Sometimes you want to search for a specific phrase or a complete name. The spaces betwen the words would be interpreted as *or* on WESTLAW. Sometimes you want to search for a phrase that includes articles that are not terms located by either system. In these instances, place the phrase or name in quotations and the system will search for all the terms within the quotes as a unit. For example, you would use quotations to search for cases discussing Megan's Law and the Americans with Disabilities Act. If you do not use quotes, WESTLAW would interpret *Megan's Law* to be *Megan's* or *Law*. To obtain the exact phrase in a document enter it as follows: "Americans with Disabilities Act."

c. Plurals

LEXIS and WESTLAW automatically search for regular plurals. For example, if you enter the word *pattern, patterns* is automatically searched. Irregular plurals like *children* are not automatically searched when the singular term is entered.

d. Irregular Plurals

LEXIS and WESTLAW have two symbols that assist you in searching for irregular plurals and for words that could have various endings stemming from the root word. The symbol * is like a Scrabble blank: You use it to replace a letter in a term. For example, suppose you are searching for articles about women. Documents on point could have the term *woman* or *women,* so your query would be typed as

wom*n to increase the potential of retrieving on-point information. If you want documents about children, you could use the term **child***** and retrieve documents with *child* or *children*. The word *childhood* would not appear, however, because you only reserved three spaces after the root of *child*. If you want all possible endings of a word following its root, regardless of the amount of letters, use ! In our example, **child!** would retrieve *children, childhood, child,* and *childish*.

e. Hyphenated Words

If you place a space between two search terms on LEXIS, the system will automatically search for the hyphenated version of the word. For example, if you are searching for documents containing the term *full-text,* and you enter **full text** as your query, you will retrieve documents with *full-text* as well as *full text.* On WESTLAW, if you use **full-text** as your query, the system will search for the appearance of *full-text* and *full text.* WESTLAW interprets a blank space as an *or,* so you must put phrases in quotes so that the system searches for the existence of the phrase or term. For example, you can enter **"full text"** and WESTLAW will search for *full-text* and *full text.* The quotes are useful for phrases such as *res ipsa loquitor* so that the entire phrase will be searched for as a whole.

f. Noise Words or Articles

LEXIS and WESTLAW do not search for the occurrence of articles. Omit *the, a, an,* and *and* from your search queries. The frequent appearance of articles (or "noise words") in text would slow down the computer system if it had to search for them.

g. Capitalizing Proper Nouns and Other Terms

You do not have to worry about capitalization style. LEXIS and WESTLAW are not case sensitive, meaning that the databases do not discern between upper- and lowercase letters but search by matching words. Your query can be written as **united w/1 states** and you will retrieve relevant documents.

3. Other Ways to Restrict Your Search to Retrieve On-Point Information

a. Date and Court Restrictors

Date and court **restrictors** in your query help to narrow your search. On both LEXIS and WESTLAW, you can limit your search to look for documents from a particular time frame. On LEXIS, you can restrict your search for information on the Seminole Indians to after

1993, before August 31, 1994, or to a specific date. The searches would look as follows: **seminole w/5 indian and date aft 1993** for documents after 1993; **seminole w/5 indian and date bef 8/31/94** for documents before August 31, 1994; or **seminole w/5 indian and date = 10/1/94** for documents pertaining to the date of October 1, 1994. WESTLAW has the equivalent method of restricting the date in the search query. On WESTLAW, you would search for documents after a certain date as follows: **seminole /5 indian and da(aft 1993);** before a certain date: **seminole /5 indian and da(bef 8/31/94);** from a specific date: **seminole /5 indian and da(10/1/94).**

Court restrictors are another method of ensuring that the documents retrieved are pertinent. On WESTLAW, to retrieve cases from Florida courts enter the following: **co(florida).** You can also search by level of court. If you want only Florida Supreme Court cases, your search would include the following on WESTLAW: **seminole /5 indian & co(high).** This search would ensure that you would only receive cases from Florida's highest court.

On Westlaw.com and on some of the newer database software packages, you no longer have to remember these commands, but merely fill in the blanks after clicking a date restriction box. It is important to know that searches can be constructed with specific date parameters to add precision to the information retrieved.

On LEXIS you can limit the courts to only the jurisdictionally relevant ones by using the court segment in the query. An example of this is when you are searching all federal cases and want only those actually decided in Florida. A search using the court segment would look like this: **seminole w/5 indian and court(florida).**

b. Other Restrictors

The following table summarizes the symbols and abbreviations used for search query restriction.

Description	LEXIS	WESTLAW
replaces a letter in a word or term	*	*
unlimited endings following the root of the word	!	!
date after	date aft 1/1/94	da(aft 1/1/94)
date before	date bef 1/1/94	da(bef 1/1/94)
date is	date = 1/1/94	da(1/1/94)
court	court(florida)	co(florida)
level of court		co(high)

c. Fields

Cases and other documents on LEXIS contain **segments** and on WESTLAW contain **fields** that can be searched. Date and court restrictors are examples of segments or fields. LEXIS also has case name, judge, and counsel segments for cases, and WESTLAW has counsel, judge, case name, and topic (from the West Digest topics). Every category of information on each database has different segments or fields. The Internet versions of LEXIS and WESTLAW, Lexis-Nexis Xchange and Westlaw.com respectively, have point, and click captions to indicate segments and fields. Just read the screen, point and click. The newer software packages have menu-driven searching to facilitate segment and field searching if you are unfamiliar with the terms. It is helpful to understand the underlying concepts to achieve more effective searching.

▼ Why Does Integrating Traditional and Computerized Resources Result in the Most Effective Computerized Legal Research?

Beginning your research with traditional sources allows you to become educated in the area of law and to learn the pertinent vocabulary used in decisions and in statutes. (See Chapter 5 for a complete discussion of secondary authorities.) A vocabulary of the words used in on-point opinions lets you construct your search queries most effectively. Online research is very costly, and you cannot afford to use the time online to educate yourself on a topic. It is, in fact, cost-effective to print out the citations and to read sources in hardcopy if they are easily obtained.

EXAMPLE

You are asked to find Florida cases discussing abuse of process. Your first reaction to the assignment is that you do not even know what abuse of process is. This is the strategy that you would follow:

1. Consult secondary source materials to educate yourself and to acquire a research vocabulary for search formulation.

2. Begin the education process with a dictionary. Abuse of process is a tort and occurs when the process of the courts is used for an improper purpose. Here's an example of abuse of process: An individual enters into a contract with another to purchase rare coins. The two parties draw up an installment contract specifying monthly payments for 10 years. After possessing the coins for 2 years and after making the agreed-on monthly payments, the buyer decides that the market value of the coins has fallen and does not want to continue to make the monthly payments. The buyer sues the seller for fraud, claiming that he was deceived as to the true value of the coins. The buyer sues for fraud not because a fraud actually occurred but because he wants to get out of the contract. This is an abuse of process.

3. Decide the jurisdiction that the materials should be from. Consult your hardcopy database directories for the LEXIS library and file name or the WESTLAW database. The supervising attorney

requested Florida cases, so Florida is the appropriate jurisdiction. Determining the appropriate jurisdiction enables you to select a library and a file on LEXIS or a database on WESTLAW. In this instance, you would select the FLA library and the FLCTS file on LEXIS or the FL-CS database on WESTLAW.

4. Determine the terms that would appear in the ideal opinion. *Abuse* and *process* would be the terms in this example.

5. Decide the relationship that the terms would have to one another in the text—the proximity of the terms. It is important to ensure that contextual meaning is not lost. This is where you decide what connectors you will use. We are looking for cases defining abuse of process. *Of* is a noise word, so we ignore it for purposes of listing terms for our query, but we know that it falls between two important words. The terms must be close together to retain their contextual meaning in the document. You select *w/3*. The query would be **abuse w/3 process**.

6. You want to maximize the retrieval of on-point documents. A court can discuss the definition as abusing the process of the courts. To get this decision as well, use a root with a *!*. Your query would be **abus! w/3 process**.

7. To obtain the most recent decisions, add a date restrictor. To search for cases after 1989 on LEXIS would require you to add *and date aft 1989* in the query. On WESTLAW, *& da(aft 1989)* should be added to your query. LEXIS version: **abus! w/3 process and date aft 1989**. WESTLAW version: **abus! /3 process & da(aft 1989)**.

8 If you are frustrated in your attempts to search, call WESTLAW customer service at 1-800-WESTLAW or LEXIS customer service at 1-800-543-6862.

4. Retrieving the Results of Your Research

On LEXIS, the system tells you that there are a certain number of documents containing the information in your query. WESTLAW also indicates that a certain number of documents have been found. How do you bring these documents on to the screen to view? On WESTLAW, the system automatically defaults to **term mode** where you see the appearance of your search terms highlighted in the document's text. A few pages will be skipped, and you will once again see the appearance of your search terms. LEXIS has a parallel method of viewing the document called **KWIC**, which is an acronym for **key word in context.** You see your search terms surrounded by 25 words of the document's text. Term and KWIC are very efficient formats to view documents initially to determine if the material is on point.

Best Mode is WESTLAW's new format to view documents. When your search results appear on the screen, type **B** and enter. The best part of each document appears; this is the place where most of your search terms occur.

On both LEXIS and WESTLAW, you can view the citations of the documents found. On LEXIS, the format is **cite.** On WESTLAW, type in the letter **l,** which stands for list of citations. On the Internet versions and on the new menu-driven software packages, you can select the formats by merely pointing and clicking.

Viewing documents full text is time consuming and costly online. It is best to obtain citations online and go to the hardcopy resources to read the documents. On WESTLAW, **page mode** is the full text format and is obtained by typing **p** and **[enter].** On LEXIS, full text is **full.**

▼ Are There Any Other Ways to Retrieve Documents?

On LEXIS and WESTLAW, you can retrieve a specific statute or a case if you know the citation. On WESTLAW, you would use the FIND command indicated by **fi.** If you want to see the text of 121 So. 2d 319 on WESTLAW, you would type **fi 121 so2d 319** and press **[enter].** To view the text of a statute on WESTLAW, you would type **fi 28 usc 1485** and press **[enter].** On LEXIS, you would use LEXSEE to obtain the text of an opinion. The search would be **lexsee 121 so2d 319** and press **[enter].** To obtain the text of a statute on LEXIS, you would use LEXSTAT. The search would be **lexstat 28 usc 1485** and press **[enter].**

The following chart compares the retrieval options for LEXIS and WESTLAW.

Description	LEXIS	WESTLAW
search terms surrounded by a limited number of words from the document's text (generally 25 words of text)	KWIC	term
full text viewing the entire document	full	page mode (p)
citations to documents retrieved	cite	the letter l
Best Mode		the letter B
finding a case when you know the cite	LEXSEE	fi
finding a statute when you know the cite	LEXSTAT	fi

An important note: You do not have to be in a database on WEST-LAW to use the FIND (for statutes and cases) command or in a library and file on LEXIS to use LEXSTAT (for statutes) or LEXSEE (for cases). You can request a document citation at any point in your research, and it will be retrieved by entering the requisite command.

5. Lexis-Nexis Xchange and Westlaw.com

The Internet is the new on-ramp to access commercial, pay-per-use databanks such as LEXIS and WESTLAW. The advantages of accessing the services via the Internet are that you do not have to install and update proprietary software packages and telephone numbers, and that you can use the commands of your Internet browser combined with point-and-click capability instead of learning the searching nuances of each system. The disadvantages of Internet access are that you cannot customize the programs as you can with the software and that sometimes your Internet connection can be bumped. The Net sites have greatly simplified searching on both systems.

Lexis-Nexis Xchange is at www.Lexis.com. On LEXIS, the source directory has replaced the libraries. Instead of constructing a query at the top of the page, you click on the terms box. Everything is completely menu driven. At the base of the screen are the retrieval formats in little boxes: Cite List, KWIC, and Full Text. You merely click on the format. There is no need to know commands. Also, just as on any other Web site, you can link to other resources. While reading a document you may see a cite to another document in the text. If the cite is highlighted in blue, you can click on the cite and you then go to the text of the cited document. To go back to the original source, just click your Web browser back.

Lexis-Nexis Xchange now has graphics at the beginning of each case to indicate the analysis that case has received. A red stop sign indicates that the case is no longer good law and that there is strong negative analysis. A blue circle means that the available analysis is neutral.

Westlaw.com is just as simple to use as Lexis-Nexis Xchange. WESTLAW also has point-and-click capabilities and hypertext links to cited authorities. WESTLAW developed KeyCite, a new case law validating service with graphics to indicate the strength of the authority. WESTLAW relies on flags as the indicator. Just as on any Net site, instead of paging through the documents, you scroll through them.

6. Accessing Other Online Services

Shepard's is available on LEXIS, and online fees are incurred based on use. The beauty of online cite checking is that you do not have to worry about all of the books being on the shelf or about updating the material. The online services do it. LEXIS permits customized *Shepard's* retrieval by court, jurisdiction, or analysis. Reed-Elsevier, the parent company of LEXIS, now owns *Shepard's,* so *Shepard's* data is updated nightly online. However, *Shepard's* takes at least a week and sometimes as many as four weeks to update their database with case analysis. LEXIS bridges this gap with **LexCite,** which basically uses the document citation as a search term to find references in case law from the past six months.

Online citators are not to be confused with **Auto-Cite** on LEXIS. These services provide subsequent history and significant prior history but do not tell you where your primary authority (case, statute, or regulation) is cited in other cases. Auto-Cite is an update service for case law and is kept current on a daily basis. Auto-Cite is used primarily to find negative subsequent history.

To use LexCite, select the LEXIS library and file where you want to see citing references for the authority that you are checking. Compose the query as follows: **Lexcite(121 f2d 331) and press [enter].** This search will check for any case that cites 121 F.2d 331 in the opinion's text. Basically, you are using LEXIS as a citator. If you know when the *Shepard's* coverage stops, you can fill the gap with LexCite to ensure that the case is still good law. One *important caveat:* You must read the cases yourself to see how the citing court applied the opinion that you are checking. *Shepard's* provides a shortcut by telling you the treatment the citing case gives your opinion, for example, overruled, criticized, or followed. (For a detailed discussion of *Shepard's,* see Chapter 4.)

You can Shepardize and LexCite authority on LEXIS without a LEXIS subscription through the Lexis-Nexis Express service. Dial 1-800-843-6476 to speak to an operator to discuss your research needs. You can charge any fees to your credit card, and the results can be sent via mail, FedEx, e-mail, or fax. Shepardizing costs $15.00 per cite. LEXIS is currently developing a pay-per-use Web site. LEXIS also offers software called CheckCite that extracts the citations from a document and Shepardizes, LexCites, and Auto-Cites the references. Various price plans exist for this service. LEXIS is planning to integrate Shepard's, Auto-Cite, and LexCite into one service. When you Shepardize a citation on LEXIS, you will receive all the information from Auto-Cite and LexCite as well.

WESTLAW also offers the software program WestCheck that Shepardizes all cites in a document. WestCheck costs commercial subscribers $3.75 per cite, but no communications or connect charges are incurred.

The newest case validation service is WESTLAW's KeyCite. Key-Cite is as current as WESTLAW. As soon as a case is placed on WESTLAW, it receives KeyCite analysis and is included in that database. KeyCite includes thousands of unpublished opinions and references to law reviews. You can also customize your KeyCite search by focusing on a particular jurisdiction, date ranges, and court level. Cases receive stars to indicate the level of treatment in the cited case. Four stars indicate that there is more than a page of treatment in the cited case, three stars equal one page of discussion, two stars have up to a paragraph, and one star indicates that your case is included in a string cite. The stars immediately alert you to the depth of treatment in the citing case, which can be a big time saver during research.

A red flag pops up in KeyCite when a case has negative history. This visual clue indicates when a case is no longer good law for one of its points. A yellow flag means that the case has not been overruled but has received some criticism. A blue "H" means that the case has been discussed. Now you can use KeyCite on a pay-per-cite basis via the Internet at www.keycite.com, which is convenient if you do not have a WESTLAW subscription. This service costs $3.75 per cite.

LEXIS has *Shepard's* available online for federal and state materials, which includes cases and statutes from all jurisdictions. You can KeyCite a case by pointing and clicking the KeyCite icon or by typing in **KC.** You can only KeyCite cases now, so keep those *Shepard's* skills. On LEXIS, you can Shepardize a document on the screen by typing **sh** and pressing **[enter].** If *Shepard's* information is available online, it will appear on the screen. (For a full discussion of cite checking, see Chapter 4.) Since Reed Elsevier purchased *Shepard's,* the *Shepard's* database on LEXIS is updated nightly. However, the information that is input is still a bit behind. It is still important to update *Shepard's* on LEXIS by using LexCite. LexCite constructs a search in the library and file that you select and looks to see where your case has been cited. LexCite makes LEXIS a citator. The only drawback is that you do not get the analysis of the treatment by the citing court that *Shepard's* provides. You must read the actual citing decision yourself. An example of a LexCite search is **lexcite(456 so2d 123).** This search would be executed in the FLA library and the FLCTS file if you want to see Florida cases that cited the decision. You must read the text of the citing cases to determine if the citing cases overruled the initial citation, that is, if the citing cases overruled 456 So. 2d 123.

You do not need a document on the screen to Shepardize online with LEXIS. You can enter *Shepard's* at the library screen by typing **.sh** and pressing **[enter].** You can then type in the next citation and press **[enter]** while the *Shepard's* analysis is on the screen, and the information will reflect the analytical treatment of the succeeding document. You can go through entire lists of citations this way without entering a LEXIS library.

7. Obtaining Subsequent Case History on LEXIS and WESTLAW

Subsequent history of a case is obtained in Auto-Cite on LEXIS. The focus is on negative analysis. You can Auto-Cite a decision on the screen by typing **ac** and pressing **[enter].** Auto-Cite gives you any subsequent procedural history. Subsequent procedural history tells you if the case has been appealed or if certiorari has been granted.

You can also Auto-Cite lists of citations after you sign on to LEXIS. At the LEXIS library menu screen, type in **.ac** and you will go into Auto-Cite. Then type in your first cite and press **[enter].** After the

Auto-Cite information appears on the screen, type in the succeeding cite.

The following chart compares the validating and updating methods of LEXIS and WESTLAW.

	LEXIS	*WESTLAW*
Shepard's	.sh	n/a
Shepard's Preview		n/a
Updating *Shepard's* information	LEXITE	n/a
KeyCite		KC
Subsequent history	Auto-Cite AC	n/a

8. Comparing LEXIS and WESTLAW

a. Difference between LEXIS and WESTLAW

LEXIS has the **NEWS library,** which lets you access full text articles from hundreds of periodicals. It is an excellent way to perform factual research.

The Easy Search Library on LEXIS, commonly referred to as Easy, uses menus to make search formulation interactive. The menus help you determine the best LEXIS library and file for the needed information and help you formulate queries by inserting the connectors and universal characters.

Shepard's is now owned by LEXIS, so *Shepard's* searching on LEXIS is updated nightly and covers all cases and statutes from the 50 states and federal government as well as many regulations.

WESTLAW permits you to search the West topics and key numbers online. This is very convenient because you can customize digest searching by adding date and court restrictors.

Another feature of WESTLAW is that you can use WESTLAW as a gateway to **DIALOG;** this means that you can get into DIALOG from the WESTLAW menu screen if you have a DIALOG password. DIALOG is a group of more than 600 databases. Many DIALOG databases only provide citations and abstracts, but there are some full-text databases such as MAG-ASAP. The databases are primarily factual, but there are a few legal databases too. Dow Jones on WESTLAW can be searched as a whole by entering the ALLNEWS database. Dow Jones contains hundreds of newspapers, newsletters, journals, and wire services. WESTLAW has a new case law validation and citing service called KeyCite. KeyCite tells you the status of the case, its analytical treatment by subsequent courts, and the depth of the treatment.

b. Similarities between LEXIS and WESTLAW

Both LEXIS and WESTLAW permit you to research myriad cases, statutes, administrative regulations, articles, factual information, and other documents online using natural language searches that eliminate the cumbersome restrictions imposed by indexes. LEXIS's natural language searching capability is called Freestyle and is accessed by typing **.fr** and pressing **[enter]**. Freestyle enables you to enter questions or phrases instead of queries. WESTLAW's natural language searching capability is entered through a database. When it is time to construct your query, natural language will be an entry at the bottom of the screen. Tab over to natural language and press **[enter]**; you can then construct your query as a phrase or sentence without connectors. Both LEXIS and WESTLAW have menu-driven searching systems and Internet access with point-and-click searching that let you search effectively without becoming very familiar with the system. Both are kept up-to-date and permit you to find documents without having to travel from your keyboard. In summary, LEXIS and WESTLAW are quite similar but competing products that are very powerful when put to use effectively.

▼ How Do You Use the Computer Most Efficiently?

As discussed earlier in the chapter, the most effective and efficient research is performed after you educate yourself on the topic using hardcopy resources. Doing traditional research gives you a vocabulary that you can use to construct your search queries. It is most efficient and cost-effective to obtain citations to relevant documents online and to read the documents in hardcopy format if they are readily available.

▼ What Are the Other Computerized Research Services That Are Available?

LEXIS has the NEWS library, which was called NEXIS until recently. It is an excellent source for full-text news and periodical articles. It is updated daily and is invaluable when performing factual research on an individual, a corporation, or an event.

As mentioned earlier, you can access DIALOG through WESTLAW with an additional DIALOG password. DIALOG is really a group of hundreds of databases that are primarily factual in nature. Each database has its own fee scheme for use. Many of the databases only provide citations and abstracts. DIALOG has some databases that do not have print or hardcopy equivalents, like ABI-INFORM, which is a business news database.

Dow Jones is also available on WESTLAW. Dow Jones consists of wire services and the *Wall Street Journal*, plus hundreds of newspapers and business periodicals.

CHAPTER SUMMARY

Computerized legal research opens up a vast realm of research possibilities for the paralegal. You are no longer limited to the resources available at your firm or school library. This chapter detailed the basic skills and concepts required to use LEXIS and WESTLAW, the two major online legal research systems. LEXIS and WESTLAW were also compared to highlight each system's distinguishing features.

Search query formulation is very important for effective online searching. The skills required to construct queries are used for LEXIS and WESTLAW, as well as for CD-ROM products. Retrieving information in a variety of formats is possible too.

Effective research online comes with careful planning before turning on the computer. Learn the vocabulary for your topic. Evaluate whether the expense of online services warrants their use.

Online research is not a panacea but an additional and powerful research tool.

KEY TERMS

Auto-Cite	libraries
Best Mode	literal searching devices
connectors	natural language searching
databases	NEWS library
DIALOG	query
field	restrictors
files	search
Freestyle	segment
key word in context (KWIC)	term mode
LexCite	WESTLAW
LEXIS	

EXERCISES

1. One fine autumn day, Jim and Jean decide to drive to the country in search of the perfect pumpkin. After driving an hour and a half, they pull

into Pete's Pumpkin Patch, whose sign states "10,000 pumpkins—state's largest pumpkin patch!" Pete's Pumpkin Patch is packed with shoppers. Jim and Jean eye the perfect pumpkin. As Jim is reaching for the pumpkin, Bob reaches for the very same pumpkin. Bob is a little low on patience that day. Instead of offering to look for another pumpkin, Bob punches Jim right in the jaw. Jim wants to sue Bob for battery.

   The problem raises the issue of whether Bob has committed a battery by punching Jim. The attorney that you work for wants you to sign on to LEXIS or WESTLAW and find the statute for battery for your jurisdiction. If your jurisdiction does not have a battery statute, find a case discussing battery.

   a. How would you construct the query?
   b. What sources would you consult before going online to become aware of the terms or words that you would use in your query?
   c. What library and file would you select on LEXIS or what database would you select on WESTLAW?
   d. Print out your document in KWIC on LEXIS or term mode on WESTLAW.

2. Imagine that you are employed as a paralegal at a law firm in Detroit. A partner in the firm has just finished interviewing a client who lives in Munster, Indiana. The partner requests that you find out for him whether the courts of Indiana recognize the "Totten" trust as a valid legal instrument in that state.
   a. How would you educate yourself before going online?
   b. Formulate a search query based on the given information.
   c. What library and file would you select on LEXIS or what database would you select on WESTLAW?
   d. Print the relevant code sections in full format on LEXIS or in page mode on WESTLAW.

3. Mrs. Donahue comes to your firm because she wants to sue her dentist for malpractice. On April 27, 1997, Mrs. Donahue went to her dentist to have a chipped bridge removed and replaced. In removing her bridge, the dentist broke her tooth. Mrs. Donahue had considerable pain due to the broken tooth. In addition, Mrs. Donahue incurred substantial expenses to repair the broken tooth and to replace the bridge with dental implants.

   Now that you have done some research and have read some cases, you are familiar with the vocabulary used in relevant court decisions. You are now best equipped to perform online research economically and efficiently.

   a. Use LEXIS or WESTLAW to find two cases after 1980 that are relevant to Mrs. Donahue's problem.
   b. Print the cases in KWIC format or Best Mode.
   c. Shepardize or KeyCite the cases and print out these results.

4. Use either LEXIS or WESTLAW to find any cases from the U.S. Court of Appeals discussing Megan's Law.
   a. What is your query?
   b. Print out the list of citations.
   c. Shepardize the cites on LEXIS or KeyCite the cites on WESTLAW.

INTERNET RESEARCH

CHAPTER OVERVIEW

This chapter is designed to be a short primer about the Internet, how it can be useful to you as legal researchers, and how to access specific legal as well as other information. It also will point you to resources that may be helpful in your research.

A. INTRODUCTION TO THE INTERNET

▼ What Is the Internet?

The **Internet** is a worldwide network of interconnected computers that you can access from any computer equipped with a modem and connected to a telephone line. The government, universities, and businesses offer both legal and nonlegal resources. The Internet provides a wide array of information. Most people think of the Internet as the World Wide Web—the most often accessed section of the network.

▼ Is the World Wide Web the Same as the Internet?

No. The **World Wide Web** is a collection of computer files, also referred to as home pages, each accessible by an address called a **uniform resource locator (URL).** The Internet is much broader. It includes other information available through gophers. **Gophers,** named for the founding institution's Golden Gophers of the University of Minnesota, are menu-based programs that allow you to access information. To use them, you simply follow the listed instructions. If the address is a gopher, it is located on a part of the Internet that is not within the Web. This is what many universities use; gophers often contain scientific, academic, or government information. Few have graphics. Gophers called Archie and Veronica are the best ways to find gopher sites. However, few people are using gophers with the growing resources available on the Web, and you will most likely be using only the Web for your research. Therefore, the focus of this chapter is the Web because it is the most often used part of the Internet and the one that will be most accessible to you as researchers.

1. Home Pages

▼ What Is a Web Home Page?

A **home page** is a document linked to the Internet. See Illustrations 10-1 and 10-2. You can think of each as an electronic store of information. Stores can range from educational sites to advertisements.

The Web is invaluable because you can easily move from one home page to another site. This is because the pages are linked to other sites by a method called **hypertext.** All you need to do is point and click your mouse on highlighted text words, and you will move to another information page. You can easily travel back to the previous page with the click of a button. Review the home page in Illustra-

ILLUSTRATION 10-1. Thomas Home Page

THOMAS Legislative Information on the Internet

QUICK SEARCH TEXT OF BILLS 105th CONGRESS:

Search by Bill Number:

Ex: *s. 435, H.R. 842*
OR
Search by Word/Phrase:

Ex: *line item veto, tax reform*

Search

Clear

Frequently Asked Questions (FAQs)

105th Congress: House Directories

Senate Directories

Congressional Internet Services: House - Senate Library of Congress GPO - GAO - CBO AOC - OTA - More

Library of Congress Web Links: Legislative Executive Judicial State/Local

CONGRESS NOW

Congress in the News
House and Senate: Floor Activities
House: Latest Floor Actions - Floor Activities This Week
National Bipartisan Commission on the Future of Medicare

BILLS

Bill Summary & Status: 105th (1997-98)
Previous Congresses (1973 - 1996)

Bill Text:
105th (1997-98) - 104th (1995-96) - 103rd (1993-94) - 102nd (1991-92) - 101st (1989-90)

House Roll Call Votes [Help]: 105th - 2nd (1998) - 105th - 1st (1997)
Previous Congresses (1990 - 1996)

Senate Roll Call Votes [Help]: 105th - 2nd (1998) - 105th - 1st (1997)
Previous Congresses (1989 - 1996)

Public Laws By Law Number: 105th (1997-98)
Previous Congresses (1973 - 1996)

Major Legislation: [Definition]
105th: By topic - By popular/short title - By bill number/type - Enacted into law
104th: By topic - By popular/short title - By bill number/type - Enacted into law

CONGRESSIONAL RECORD

Congressional Record Text: Most Recent Issue
105th (1997-98) - 104th (1995-96) - 103rd (1993-94) - 102nd (1991-92)- 101st (1989-90)

Congressional Record Index:
105th - 2nd (1998) - 105th - 1st (1997) - 104th - 2nd (1996) - 104th - 1st (1995) - 103rd - 2nd (1994)

Résumés of Congressional Activity:
105th - 1st (1997) - Previous Congresses (1969 - 1996)

Annals of Congress (Precursor of the *Congressional Record*) [About]
1st Congress (1789-1791) - 2nd Congress (1791-1793)

COMMITTEE INFORMATION

Committee Reports: Congress: 105th (1997-98) - 104th (1995-96)

Committee Home Pages: House - Senate

House Committees: - Schedules and Oversight Plans - Selected Hearing Transcripts

THE LEGISLATIVE PROCESS

How Our Laws Are Made (by Charles W. Johnson, House Parliamentarian)

Enactment of a Law (By Robert B. Dove, Senate Parliamentarian)

HISTORICAL DOCUMENTS

ILLUSTRATION 10-1. *Continued*

Historical documents including the Declaration of Independence, the Federalist Papers, early Congressional documents (Constitutional Convention and Continental Congress broadsides), and the Constitution. <u>U.S. Congressional Documents and Debates: 1774 - 1873.</u>		
The Library of Congress 101 Independence Ave. SE Washington, D.C. 20540	About THOMAS	Feedback

tion 10-1; the list of words on the left side of the page are **links** to other pages that contain more information about each topic.

2. Newsgroups

The Web and Internet also include **newsgroups** that are message boards of topically organized messages. Groups of related messages are called *threads*. You can follow a thread, making it easier to follow a particular discussion if a group is especially active. It is easy for

ILLUSTRATION 10-2.   Federal Judiciary Home Page

What's New | Frequently Asked Questions | For Public Review | About
The U.S. Courts
Publications and Directories | Newsroom | Employment Opportunities
The Federal Judiciary Channel | Links | Search

Search: Match: All   [   ]   Search

This page is maintained by the Administrative Office
of the U.S. Courts on behalf of the U.S. Courts.
The purpose of this site is to function as a clearinghouse for information
from and about the Judicial Branch of the U.S. Government.
This Site contains information about the Federal judiciary, Judge, judges, judicial, judiciary, justice, federal, court, vacancies, judicial vacancies, vacancy, federal judge, judicial reform, federal court, federal judiciary, supreme court, supreme, court, constitution, law, government, bankruptcy, appeals, magistrate, legal system, legal research, opinion, opinions, uscourts.gov, www.uscourts.gov

For information or comments, please contact:
The www.uscourts.gov Webmaster

you to participate in a newsgroup and to find one for almost any topic ranging from legal issues to health information.

3. Chat Groups

Also on the Web and Internet are **chat groups** in which people discuss various topics in real time. You can join the discussions by accessing a home page. Then you will view typed discussions. To enter the discussion, you will type a response and press **[enter]** to send it to the group. Various chat groups meet regularly. Others meet sporadically and will notify members of their meetings. These can be fun and often involve people worldwide. Many are available at various times throughout the day and night. One of the advantages to participating in these chats is that you often get an immediate answer to a troubling question.

4. Online Services

Private **online services** such as CompuServe, America Online, Prodigy, and Microsoft Network provide software for you to access the Internet. In addition, they provide information organized into various groups such as reference materials, legal materials, shopping, and the like. On CompuServe, for example, the groups are called *forums.* In CompuServe's Legal Forum, you can leave messages, review messages to and from attorneys, and often find messages among paralegals in the law-related professionals area. In addition, the forums boast of libraries that store information that you can access at anytime.

5. Listservs

Another messaging system is called a **listserv,** which is a subscription mailing list. Responses to messages are e-mailed to subscribers. For example, you can subscribe to receive U.S. Supreme Court syllabi within hours by e-mailing as follows: listserv@listserve.law.cornell.edu.

B. WHY LEGAL RESEARCHERS USE THE INTERNET

1. Cost and Accessibility

▼ Why Use the Internet When You Can Use WESTLAW and LEXIS?

The Internet is a much cheaper method of retrieving legal information to use than WESTLAW and LEXIS. It also is much cheaper than maintaining print or CD-ROM materials and takes up much less space. Internet access is available for a small monthly cost and the price of a local phone call each time you access the Internet. Access generally runs around $20 or $30 a month, depending on the type of service you request. You also can buy direct access to the Internet from a variety of Internet service providers. In such cases, you need to use a stand-alone browser such as Microsoft's Internet Explorer or Netscape's Navigator.

2. Legal Resources on the Internet

▼ What Legal Resources Are Available on the Internet?

a. Primary Authorities

Court opinions, statutes, government documents, and other primary authorities are readily available on the Internet, and the information is available 24 hours a day. One drawback is that the materials may have been provided directly from the courts without having been proofread. Because there is some concern over the accuracy of the information found on the Net, you may need to double-check it with the official sources. However, often it is reliable and a good place to start.

Some sites allow you to download opinions for free. However, they may be in ASCII format that omits all of the court's formatting. In some cases, you need to know the docket number before you attempt to access the cases. At the end of the chapter is an appendix that lists various court decisions, statutes, and government documents that you can access using the Internet.

b. Pending Legislation

You can track federal bills as well as some pending state legislation on the Web. You can find newly introduced bills, text of enacted laws, and oftentimes information about the progress of the bill. See Illustration 10-1. This chapter's appendix contains a list of some of the federal and state sites that provide you with bills and their status. For example, the California site provides full text of bills for several years in addition to the status, history, and voting record of current legislation. You can search this site by key word or by author.

c. Trademark and Patent Information

Trademark and patent information in full text format is available through the Internet at the government patent office site: http://

www.uspto.gov/web/menu/tm/html. See Illustration 10-3. Access is free.

d. Corporate Information

Corporate information such as U.S. Securities and Exchange Commission filings is available on the Internet. These filings are available usually within 24 hours of filing in an electronic database called EDGAR (Electronic Data, Gathering Analysis and Retrieval System). It is accessible through the Security and Exchange Commission's home page on the Web, www.sec.gov. You can search this database by name, form type, or date. The SEC home page also offers access to commission reports, investor guides, and other securities-related information.

Even WESTLAW and LEXIS, the two legal databases that once could only be accessed with the providers' software, are now available through the Internet.

PRACTICE POINTER

The Internet is still changing, and many resources available on the Internet come and go quickly. Therefore, you should search the Internet for any information you think might be available.

C. SEARCHING THE WEB

▼ Is It Difficult to Use the Web?

Sometimes. You can easily access a variety of resources by using the proper software and by carefully formulating your searches. Related information is found by clicking the mouse on a section of the information already retrieved. This is called a link between one site to another. This makes finding information easy. However, getting to the first home page may be difficult because computer searches often generate either too many results that are not exactly what you are seeking or too few results.

1. Search Engines

▼ How Do You Search the Internet?

The most common method is through **search engines.** There are scores of search engines. Search engines each work differently and

ILLUSTRATION 10-3. Patent and Trademark Office Home Page

General Info
Patents
Trademarks
Databases
Download Forms
Order Copies
PTO Fees
Libraries-PTDLs
Site Index
Organization
About PTO
pto bulletin
Statistics
Acquisitions
Jobs at PTO
Related Web Sites
Public Affairs
FOIA
Document Formats
Privacy Statement
Copyright (LOC)
FTP Raw Data
International

US PATENT AND TRADEMARK OFFICE

New on the PTO site:

- Official Insignia of Native American Tribes: Statutorily Required Study (4Jan99)

- *US Trademark Law -- Rules of Practice & Federal Statutes* Updated (22Dec98)

- *Manual of Patent Examining Procedure, Seventh Edition* Text (22Dec98)

- *Cassis Currents* Optical Disk Publishing Newsletter No. 2 (21Dec98)

- PTO in Maximum Security Mode (21Dec98)

- *PTO Red Book* Definition for Patent Mark-up in SGML (18Dec98)

- Federal Register Notice re: New Fees for Fiscal Year 1999 (8Dec98)

- 1998 Exam Results Notice and General Requirements Bulletin for April 1999 Examination for Registration
  - New PTO/SB/158, *1999 Application for Registration to Practice Before the USPTO* (7Dec98)

- Final Report to the Commissioner on the Conclusion of the Conference on Fair Use (24Nov98)

- US Patent Full Text Database Now Available (20Nov98)

- BPAI: Interference Trial Section Opinions Page (17Nov98)

- Notice re: *Patent Term Extension Info to Be Printed on Notice of Allowance and the Patent* (to be published in OG) (5Nov98)

- Patent Maintenance Fee Page (3Nov98)

- Request for Comments on Proposed Internet Usage Policy (2Nov98)

- 26th Annual Inventors Expo and Conference, March 1999 (26Oct98)

The PTO is not yet equipped to handle general email correspondence. General inquiries should be directed by telephone to 800.786.9199 (800.PTO.9199) or 703.308.4357 (703.308.HELP), or in writing to one of the addresses specified in PTO Information Contacts *.*
Email comments and suggestions concerning server content and operation only to www@uspto.gov

---

General Info | Patents | Trademarks | Weekly Data | Download Forms | Order Copies | PTO Fees | PTDLs | Site Index | Search | Info by Org | About PTO | Legal Materials | Statistics | Acquisitions | Jobs at PTO | Related Web Sites | Public Affairs | FOIA | Document Formats | Privacy Statement | Copyrights (LOC) | Conversations with America | the pto bulletin | Creating Content for this Site (IDO Intranet Server) |

Last Modified: 4 January 1999

often yield different search results from one another. First, there are those that contain a limited number of Web pages that are indexed on each Web site that the search engine reviews. One such search engine is Yahoo! See Illustration 10-4. Yahoo! compiles a list of Web sites under various topics in a directory. One drawback to using Yahoo! and similarly designed search engines is that you rely on their indexing talents for your research results.

Some search engines use software called *spiders* or *crawlers* to review the individual Web pages and find other links. These include AltaVista and HotBot. See Illustration 10-5. They may provide you with broader searches. One such search engine is LawCrawler, a legal search engine.

The remaining search engines search multiple sites for you and display them onto one page. Among these search engines are Dogpile and AskJeeves. This type of search gives you a wider scope if you are looking for a broad range of information.

PRACTICE POINTER

It is best to learn how to use at least two search engines well to successfully search the Web.

---

2. Steps in Using Search Engines

Access a search engine's home page by entering its URL in the search box. If you are using one of the stand-alone browsers, such as Netscape or Internet Explorer, it will have a list of search engines on home page. For most topics, Yahoo! is a good one. Yahoo! has a particularly good collection of legal materials. For more specific searches, other search engines that search for key words of millions of Web pages may be more effective.

When you have the search engine home page on your screen, enter your search words. It generally will retrieve multiple sites to review.

Searching the Web, however, can be challenging. Unlike some of the legal database services such as WESTLAW and LEXIS, the Web is not a well-organized network. Search engines often do not retrieve the sites that you might find the most useful. Therefore, always search using multiple search engines.

With the Web, the key is to be flexible in your searches. A search for *Harvard Law Review,* for example, turned up nothing using Yahoo! But a search using www.harvard.edu turned up the university and then the law school. Unfortunately with the Internet, there is no 24-

ILLUSTRATION 10-4.   Yahoo! Home Page

Yahoo! Mail
free email for life

Know when friends are online!
Click to download Yahoo! Pager

Yahoo! Games
chess, bridge,
spades

Search options

Shopping - Yellow Pages - People Search - Maps - Travel Agent - Classifieds - Personals - Games - Chat
Email - Calendar - Pager - My Yahoo! - Today's News - Sports - **Weather** - TV - Stock Quotes - more...

Arts & Humanities
Literature, Photography...

Business & Economy
Companies, Finance, Jobs...

Computers & Internet
Internet, WWW, Software, Games...

Education
Universities, K-12, College Entrance...

Entertainment
Cool Links, Movies, Humor, Music...

Government
Military, Politics, Law, Taxes...

Health
Medicine, Diseases, Drugs, Fitness...

News & Media
Full Coverage, Newspapers, TV...

Recreation & Sports
Sports, Travel, Autos, Outdoors...

Reference
Libraries, Dictionaries, Quotations...

Regional
Countries, Regions, US States...

Science
Biology, Astronomy, Engineering...

Social Science
Archaeology, Economics, Languages...

Society & Culture
People, Environment, Religion...

In the News
- Midwest digs out
  from storm
- Senate split on
  Clinton trial
- Jesse Ventura sworn
  in
- Euro makes strong
  debut
- NFL playoffs,
  College bowls
                    more...

Inside Yahoo!
- Yahoo! Auctions -
  furbys, beanies...
- Y! Clubs - create
  your own
  community
- Check your credit at
  the Loan Center
                    more...

World Yahoo!s *Americas* : Canada - Spanish
        Europe : Denmark - France - Germany - Italy - Norway - Spain - Sweden - UK & Ireland
        Pacific Rim : Asia - Australia & NZ - Chinese - Japan - Korea

Yahoo! Get Local LA - NYC - SF Bay - Chicago - more...   Enter Zip Code

Other Guides Autos - Computers - **Employment** - Local Events - Net Events - Message Boards
        Movies - Real Estate - Small Business - **Ski & Snow** - Y! Internet Life - Yahooligans!

How to Suggest a Site - Company Info - Privacy Policy - Contributors - Openings at Yahoo!

Reprinted by permission of Yahoo!, Inc.

hour reference person to assist you in completing searches, as may be the case with WESTLAW or LEXIS.

▼ How Do You Refine Your Search?

Some searches return too many documents. It sometimes is frustrating that the item you really want is located at page 8 of the sites

ILLUSTRATION 10-5. Search Engine Home Page

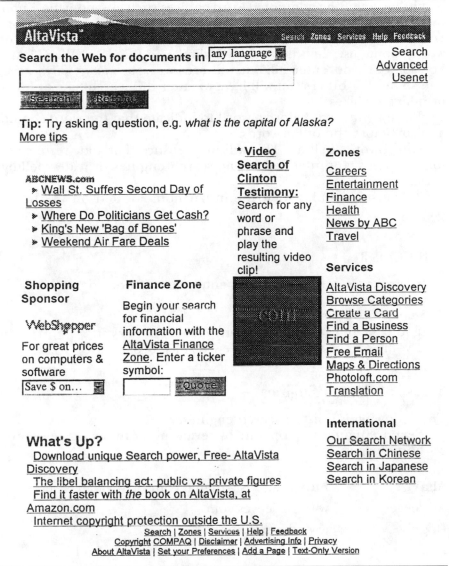

Copyright © Compaq Corporation. Used with permission.

retrieved. Use quotation marks if you want the exact words to be a match. If you don't do this, the search engine may interpret each word listed as separate search references. You also can limit searches by using words such as *and* or *not*. Some search sites, however, use minus signs to eliminate words. Others tell you specifically how to cut down your search choices.

Sometimes using fewer words broadens your search. However, if you are more specific, your search also will be more specific. Broaden your search with words such as *or*. You also can increase your search results by including additional word choices such as synonyms. Enter multiple word choices such as *hike, hiking, hiker, hikes,* and so on. Some search engines will find plurals as well as singular forms of words. Some use the wild character similar to LEXIS or WESTLAW. For some, if you enter **hik***, it will retrieve *hike, hiking, hiker, hikes,* and so on. For others you will have to enter the search **hike or hiker or hiking or hikes.**

Place a plus sign before a word to indicate that the word should appear before the other words.

Check your spelling. This will help ensure that your results are for the items you intended. Some search engines provide spelling assistance.

To be successful, review the instructions located on the home page.

CHECKLIST

1. If you know your site's URL, enter that. If not, locate a search engine.
2. Select your search words.
3. If your search returns too many results, narrow it.
4. If your search brings up too few results, broaden it.

3. List of Search Engines

The following is a list of search engines.

Search Engines that operate by reviewing or indexing key words on home pages:

AltaVista	http://altavista.digital.com or www.altavista.net
AskJeeves	www.askjeeves.com
Dogpile	www.dogpile.com
Excite	http://www.excite.com (formerly Architext)
HotBot	http://www.hotbot.com
Infoseek	http://guide.infoseek.com or www.infoseek.com
Internet Sleuth	www.isleuth.com
LawCrawler	http://www.lawcrawler.com
Lycos	http://www.lycos.com
Magellan	http://www.mckinley.com
Metacrawler	www.metacrawler.com
Northern Light	www.nlsearch.com
Open Text	http://index.opentext.net

WebCrawler   http://webcrawler.com
Yahoo!   www.yahoo.com

Medicine search engines:

Achoo   http://www.achoo.com
HealthAtoZ   http://www.healthatoz.com

D. SEARCHES USING GOPHERS

Gophers can provide a wealth of information. To use a gopher, enter its URL. After you access the gopher, a menu will be displayed that instructs you on how to access information.

E. CITATION

▼ How Do You Cite to an Internet Site?

Bluebook Rule 17.3.3 suggests that you avoid citing Internet resources because of their transient nature. But if the materials are unavailable in print, then cite to the Internet as follows:

Karin Mika, Information v. Commercialization: The Internet and Unsolicited Electronic Mail, 4 RICH. J.L. & TECH. 6 (Spring 1998) <http://www.richmond.edu/~jolt/v4i3/mika.html>

CHAPTER SUMMARY

In this chapter, you learned how to access free legal resources from the Internet. In the next chapter, you will learn how to do a research project from start to finish.

KEY TERMS

chat groups   listserv
gophers   newsgroups
home page   online services
hypertext   search engine
Internet   uniform resource locator (URL)
links   World Wide Web

EXERCISES

In answering some of the following exercises, refer to the appendix at the end of this chapter.

1. Using the Thomas site, find the schedule of congressional committee meetings.
2. Find the Government Printing Office's Supreme Court decisions.
3. Using the U.S. House Law Library site, find a federal regulation dealing with food labeling.
4. Find the *Pennsylvania Law Journal* home page.
5. Access the Ohio Department of Vital Statistics. Find out how you would obtain a death certificate.
6. Find the Michigan home page.
7. Tour the White House.

Appendix
LIST OF HELPFUL WEB SITES

U.S. Courts Generally
   http://www.uscourts.gov
   http://www.cilp.org/Fed-Ct/fedcourt.html
U.S. Supreme Court
   Case Western Reserve University
   Cornell Law School
   http://www.law.cornell.edu/supct
   http://www.access.gpo.gov/sudocs/suport/index.html
   http://wwwfedworld.gov/supcourt/index.htm
   http://www.findlaw.com
First Circuit Court of Appeals
   Emory University School of Law
   http://www.law.emory.edu/1circuit
Second Circuit Court of Appeals
   Touro Law Center
   http://www.TouroLaw.edu/2ndCircuit/
Third Circuit Court of Appeals
   Villanova University School of Law
   http://www.vcilp.org/Fed-Ct/ca03.html
Fourth Circuit Court of Appeals
   Emory University School of Law
   http://www.law.emory.edu/4circuit
Fifth Circuit Court of Appeals
   Fifth Circuit Court of Appeals
   http://www.ca5.uscourts.gov/
   http://www.lawutexas.edu/us5th/us5th/html
Sixth Circuit Court of Appeals
   Emory University Law School
   http://www.law.emory.edu/6circuit
Seventh Circuit Court of Appeals
   Emory University Law School

http://www.law.emory.edu/7circuit
Chicago-Kent College of Law
http://www.kentlaw.edu/7circuit/
Eighth Circuit Court of Appeals
Washington University School of Law
http://www.wulaw.wustl.edu/8th.cir/
Ninth Circuit Court of Appeals
Villanova University Law School
http://www.law.vcilp.org/Fed-Ct/ca09.html
Tenth Circuit Court of Appeals
Emory University Law School
http://www.law.emory.edu/10circuit
Eleventh Circuit Court of Appeals
Emory University Law School
http://www.law.emory.edu/11circuit/index.html
Federal Circuit Court of Appeals
Emory University Law School
http://www.law.emory.edu/fedcircuit
http://www.ll.georgetown.edu/Fed-Ct/cafed.html
U.S. Court of Appeals for the Federal Circuit
http://www.fedcir.gov/
DC Circuit Court of Appeals
Georgetown University Law Center Library
http://www.ll.georgetown.edu/Fed-Ct/cadc.html
Federal Legislation and Information
Generally
www.thomas.gov
U.S. Senate
www.senate.gov
U.S. House
www.house.gov
Other U.S. Government Sites
Consumer Product Safety Commission (Recalls List)
http://www.cpsc.gov
Securities and Exchange Commission
http://www.sec.gov/
Edgar (SEC databases)
http://www.sec.gov/edgar.hp.htm
http://www.law.vil.edu/Fed-Agency/fedwebloc.html
Federal Register
http://www.access.gpo.gov/nara/#fr
Code of Federal Regulations
http://www.access.gpo/gov/nara/cfr/cfr-table-search.html
U.S. Code
http://law.house.gov/usc.html
Justice Department
http://www.usdoj.gov
Department of Labor

http://www.dol.gov
Internal Revenue Service
http://www.irs.ustreas.gov
Patent and Trademarks Office
http://www.uspto.gov/web/menu/tm/html
Occupational Safety and Health Administration
www.osha.gov (free interactive programs)
The Federal Web Locator
http://wwwlaw/vill.edu/Fed-Agency/fedwebloc.html
National Library of Medicine
www.ncbi.nlm.gov/PubMed
Various state codes and rules
http://wwwlaw.house.gov/197.htm
Federal Rules of Evidence
http://www.law.cornell.edu/rules/fre/overview.html

Government Generally

http://www.loc.gov
State Court Locator
http://www.cilp.org/state-Ct/
Alabama
http://www.alalinc.net/
Alaska
Courts
http://www.alaska.net/~akctib
Legislation
http://www.touchngo.com/lglcntr.htm
http://www.legis.state.ak.us
Arizona
Supreme Court and Court of Appeals
http://www.azbar.org
Legislation
http://www.azleg.state.az.us/
Arkansas
Courts
http://www.state.ar.us/supremecourt/
Legislation
http://www.uark.edu/~govinfo/PAGES/WAIS-SEARCH/acts.cgi
California
Courts
http://www.courtinfo.ca.gov/opinions/
Legislation
http://www.leginfo.ca.gov/
http://www.sen.ca.gov
Colorado
Courts
http://www.cobar.org/coappcts/scndx.htm
http://www.courts.state.co.us/ct-index.htm
Legislation

http://www.state.co.us/gov_dir/stateleg.html
http://usa.net/cololaw/research.htm

Connecticut
Courts
http://www.state.ct.us/judic.htm
Legislation
http://www.cslent.ctstateu.edu/statutes/index.htm
http://www.ctstateu.edu/state/public_acts/Public_acts.html

Delaware
Legislation
www.state.de.us.govern/governor/signed.htm

Florida
http://nerp.nerdc.ufl.edu/%7Elawinfo/flsupct/index.html
http://justice.courts.state.fl.us
Legislation
http://www.leg.state.fl.us/

Georgia
Courts
http://www.state.ga.us/Courts/Supreme/
Legislation
http://www.ganet.state.ga.us/services/

Hawaii
Courts
http://www.hsba.org/Hawaii/Court/Cour.htm
Legislation
http://www.hawaii.gov/lrb/dig/digdoc.html

Idaho
Courts
http://www.state.id.us/judicial/scopins.hmtl
Legislation
http://www.state.id.us/legislat/legislat/html

Illinois
Courts
http://www.state.il.us/court/
Legislation
http://housegop.state.il.us/ilconst/menu.htm

Indiana
Courts
Indiana University School of Law with Indiana Supreme Court
http://www.law.indiana.edu/law/incourts/incourts.html
Legislation
http://www.law.indiana.edu/law/research/Indiana.html
http://www.ai.org/legislative/index.html

Iowa
Legislation
http://www2.legis.state.ia.us/Indices/CurrentCode.html

Kansas
Courts
http://www.ukans.edu/kscourts/supreme.html

Legislation
http://www.ink.org/ink-index.cgi?type + byserv&which = legislative
Kentucky
Supreme Court
http://www.state.ky.us/agencies/aoc/supreme.htm
Legislation
http://www.lrc.state.ky.us/lrcindex.htm
Louisiana
Courts
http://www.gnofn.org/~lasc
http://www.lasc.org
Maine
Courts
http://www.courts.state.me.us/
Legislation
http://www.state.me.us/legis/
Maryland
Courts
http://www.mec.state.md.us/mec/mecjudic.htm
http://www.courts.md.us/T40
Massachusetts
Courts
http://www.lweekly.com/sjc.htm
http://www.socialaw.com
http://www.state.ma.us/courts/courts.htm
Legislation
http://www.magnet.state.ma.us/legis/ltform.htm
http://www.state.ma.us/legis/ltform.htm
Michigan
Courts
http://www.icle.org/misupct/
http://www.icle.org/mictapp/
Legislation
http://www.umich.edu/!icle/leg-sums/leglist.htm
Minnesota
Courts
http://www.courts.state.mn.us
Statutes
http://www.leg.state.mn.us/leg/statutes.htm
http://www.library.leg.state.mn.us/leg/statutes.htm
gopher://gopher.revisor.leg.state.mn.us:70/11/.library/statrule
Mississippi
Courts
http://www.mslawyer.com
Legislation
http://www.mslawyer.com
Missouri
Courts
http://www.state.mo.us/sca/mosupct.htm

Legislation
http://www.house.state.mo.us/
Montana
Courts
http://www.lawlibrary.mt.gov/opinions.htm
Legislation
http://www.mt.gov/leg/branch/branch.htm
terra.oscs.montana.edu/msuinfo/gov/mtl/
Nebraska
Courts
http://www.nol.org/legal/index/html
Legislation
http://unicam1.lcs.state.ne.us/
Nevada
http://venus.optimis.com/nrs.htm
New Hamsphire
Courts
http://www.state.nh.us.courts/supreme.htm
Legislation
http://www.state.nh.us/gencourt/gencourt.htm
New Jersey
Legislation
http://www.ngleg.state.nj.us/html/njleg.htm
New Mexico
Legislation
http://www.nm.org/legislature/
http://www.state.nm.us/local/bills/billoc.html
New York
Courts
http://www.law.cornell.edu/ny/ctap/overview/html
Legislation
http://asembly.state.ny.us/ALIS
North Carolina
Courts
http://www.nando.net/insider/supreme.supco.html
http://www.aoc.state.nc.us/www/courts/apppeals/sc/supreme.html
North Dakota
Courts
http://sc3.court.state.nd.us/
Legislation
http://www.state.nd.us/lr/
Ohio
Courts
http://www.sconet.ohio.gov/
Legislation
http://www.avv.com/orc/
http:/winslo.ohio.gov/stgvleg.html
http://www.state.ohio.us

Department of Health and Vital Statistics
http:///www.state.oh.us./doh/heovri.html
Oklahoma
Courts
http://www.onenet.net/oklegal/sample.basic.html
http://www.oc.edu/okgov/
Legislation
http://www.onenet/oklegal/statutes.basic.html
Oregon
Courts
http://www.willamette.edu/law/wlo/caselaw/orcourts.htm
Legislation
http://www.leg.state.or.us/bills.html
Pennsylvania
Courts
http://www.cerf.net/penna-courts
Legislation
http://www.state.pa.us/
Rhode Island
Courts
http://www.ribar.com/courts/courts.html
http://www.state.ri.us/wwwemact.htm
http://www.sec.state.ri.us/pggov.htm
South Carolina
Courts
http://www.law.sc.edu/opinions/opinions.htm
Legislation
http://www.lpitr.state.sc.us/basement.htm
http://www.leginfo.state.sc.us/
South Dakota
Courts
http://www.sdbar.org/opinions/opinopts.htm
Tennessee
Courts
http://www.tsc.state.tn.us/opinions/tsc/oplsttsc.htm
Texas
Courts
http://www.window.state.tx.us/txgovinf/txcoca.html
Legislation
http://lamb.sos.state.tx.us/tax/
Utah
Courts
http://courtlink.utcourt.gov/
Vermont
Courts
http://dol.state.vt.us:70/11GOPHER_ROOT3%3A%5BSUPCT%5D
Legislation
http://dol.state.vt.us:70/11GOPHER_ROOT%3A%5B_LINKS_LEG%5D

Virginia
Courts
http://www.courts.state.va.us/
Legislation
http://leg1.state.va.us
http://senate.state.va.us/
Washington
Courts
http://www.wa.gov/courts
http://www.cdlaw.com/cases.htm
Legislation
http://www.leg.wa.gov/www/ses.htm
http://leginfo.leg.wa.gov/cgi-bin/rcwsearch.pl
West Virginia
Courts
http://www.state.wv.us/wvsca
Legislation
http://www.scusco.wvnet.edu/www/wvleg/htm
Wisconsin
Courts
http://www.wisbar.org/WIS/index.html
Legislation
http://badger.state.wi.us/agencies/wilis/
Wyoming
Courts
http://courts.state.wy.us/OPINION.HTM
Legislation
http://legisweb.state.wy.us/
Medical articles, abstracts, and sites
Medscape
http://www.medscape.com
Healthgate
http://www.healthgate.com
Miscellaneous legal information and information about bar associa-
    tions, courts, statutes, etc.
http://www.legal-pad.com/
American Law Sources Online http://www.lawsources.com/also/
Law Practice Management http://www.seamless.com/jpw/
    manage.hmtl
Internet Legal Resource Guide http://www.ilrg.com
Environmental Law www.toxlaw.com/bookmarks/laws.html
Ethics
http://www.legalethics.com/
Special paralegal sites
NFPA
http://www.paralegals.org/LegalResources/Practice/estate.html
NALA
http://www.nala.campus.com/

PRACTICE RULES

CHAPTER OVERVIEW

This chapter provides an overview of practice rules, the sources that contain these rules, and how to find primary and secondary authorities that explain and interpret these rules. You also learn how to ensure that the rule you are relying on is valid. For our purposes, this chapter focuses on the many rules that surround litigation because these rules are the most comprehensive ones you will review and research as paralegals other than the ethics rules. Most techniques useful for researching these litigation rules also are useful for investigating other rules, such as rules regarding patent and trademark proceedings, workers' compensation, and other administrative law areas.

A. OVERVIEW OF RULES OF PRACTICE

▼ What Are Rules of Practice?

Rules govern the practice of law, especially litigation. Some of these rules also govern the conduct of the lawyers, the litigants, and the judges.

▼ What Rules Govern Procedures in the Federal Courts?

The most extensive set of procedural rules for litigation is the **Federal Rules of Civil Procedure.** These rules direct an attorney on how to conduct himself or herself in a court proceeding. They cover matters such as the filing of a complaint to initiate an action, service of the complaint on the defendant, the answer to the complaint and subsequent motions, and the discovery of information. Postjudgment motions and appeals also are addressed in these rules.

▼ Do the Federal Rules Control Proceedings in State Courts?

The federal rules control the course of a civil case pending in federal court only. They do not govern proceedings in any of the state courts. Within the confines of the federal courts, these rules are primary binding authorities. Many state courts have patterned their procedural rules after the federal rules. Therefore, the decisions interpreting the federal rules that are similar in nature to the state court rules sometimes are very persuasive authorities.

▼ What Federal Courts Follow the Federal Rules of Civil Procedure?

All U.S. trial courts follow the federal rules. These rules are not applicable to the U.S. Bankruptcy courts, the appellate courts, or the U.S. Supreme Court. Nor do these rules generally apply in administrative proceedings. See Illustration 11-1.

▼ Are the Federal Trial Courts Governed by Any Other Rules?

The federal district courts also follow the **Federal Rules of Evidence** for motion practice and trial proceedings, and, in criminal cases, the courts are governed by the **Federal Rules of Criminal Procedure.** In addition, many federal courts have a set of rules called **local rules of court** that dictate the small details of practice before each court. For example, the local rules of the U.S. District Court for the Northern District of Ohio specify the size of the paper on which to file motions or how many interrogatory questions can be asked during discovery. You should carefully review the local rules any time you have an action pending in a federal court. In addition to a set of local rules, some courts have general orders that have the effect of local rules. Be sure to note whether the court you are before has

ILLUSTRATION 11-1.   Courts and the Applicable Rules

U.S. District Courts
Federal Rules of Civil Procedure
Federal Rules of Criminal Procedure
Federal Rules of Evidence
Local Rules and Orders

U.S. Appellate Courts
Federal Rules of Appellate Procedure
Federal Rules of Evidence
Local Rules and Orders

U.S. Supreme Court
Rules of the Supreme Court
Federal Rules of Evidence

U.S. Bankruptcy Courts
Bankruptcy Rules
Federal Rules of Evidence
Local Rules and Orders

such rules. Local rules also can vary among judges within the same court. For example, the Federal Rules of Civil Procedure discovery rules allow local courts to determine whether the courts want to follow the federal discovery rules or adopt their own. In addition, judges within some courts have adopted different rules of discovery than other judges who sit in the same federal district court.

▼ What Rules of Procedure Do Federal Appellate Courts Follow?

The U.S. Courts of Appeals follow the **Federal Rules of Appellate Procedure.** These rules are similar in nature to the Federal Rules of Civil Procedure because they are primary binding authority and can be researched in the federal codes.

▼ What Rules Govern Practice Before the U.S. Supreme Court?

The **Rules of the Supreme Court** control practice before that court. Again, these rules are primary binding authority.

ETHICS ALERT

Courts may sanction attorneys for failing to follow court rules.

PRACTICE POINTER

If you are assisting with litigation, be sure that you know what general and local rules govern your work.

B. RESEARCHING RULES OF PRACTICE

1. Sources

▼ Where Do You Find These Rules in the Print Materials?

All federal rules of civil and criminal procedure, the evidentiary rules, the appellate procedure rules, and the Supreme Court rules, as well as the bankruptcy rules and official forms, are found in the annotated statutory codes, *United States Code Annotated* (U.S.C.A.), published by West Group, and *United States Code Service* (U.S.C.S.), published by LEXIS Law Publishing. See Illustration 11-2. These are the best sources for the most current rules. The rules also are published with the drafters' commentary in the *United States Code* (U.S.C.). However, U.S.C. is not as current as the annotated sources. These codes are discussed in detail in Chapter 6. Several publishers produce the local federal court rules, including West Group, which publishes the Federal Local Court Rules. These rules also can be found in a variety of other sources, including deskbooks and treatises.

Attorney deskbooks, as the name implies, generally are kept at each paralegal's or attorney's desk. These books usually are paperback and contain a full set of the federal rules, local rules, and sometimes the state rules for the state where the deskbook is set. These deskbooks are updated annually and are more convenient to use than a full code.

2. Steps in Researching Rules and Court Decisions

▼ How Do You Research a Federal Rule?

First, review the rule in either the U.S.C., U.S.C.A., or U.S.C.S. See Illustration 11-2 for guidance concerning which source contains the rule you are seeking. Next, you will want to locate court decisions and possibly secondary authorities that explain and interpret the rule.

▼ How Do You Find Cases or Secondary Authorities That Interpret and Explain the Federal Rules?

The annotated codes contain excerpts of cases that explain and interpret the federal rules, as well as references to secondary sources

ILLUSTRATION 11-2.   Where Can You Find the Rules?

U.S. District Courts

Federal Rules of Civil Procedure
28 U.S.C.
28 U.S.C.A.
28 U.S.C.S.

Federal Rules of Criminal Procedure
18 U.S.C.
18 U.S.C.A.
18 U.S.C.S.

Federal Rules of Evidence
U.S.C.
U.S.C.A.
U.S.C.S.

Local Rules and Orders
courts
Federal Rules Service
Federal and local court rules
   book

U.S. Appellate Courts

Federal Rules of Appellate Procedure
28 U.S.C.
28 U.S.C.A.
28 U.S.C.S.

Federal Rules of Evidence
U.S.C.
U.S.C.A.
U.S.C.S.

Local Rules and Orders
courts
Federal Rules Service
Federal and local court rules
   book

U.S. Supreme Court

Rules of the Supreme Court
Federal Rules of Evidence
U.S.C.
U.S.C.A.
U.S.C.S.

U.S. Bankruptcy Courts

Bankruptcy Rules
Federal Rules of Evidence
Local Rules and Orders
U.S.C.
U.S.C.A.
U.S.C.S.

such as encyclopedias, *American Law Reports,* and law review articles. See Illustration 11-3 for a rule and selected annotations.

One of the easiest ways to find cases is to look on the spine of the annotated code volumes for the volume that contains the rules you are researching. Turn to the page that contains the rule. Following the rule is an index of words that lists numbers indicating certain cases. See Illustration 11-4. The research strategy is similar to that involved in researching other statutory materials, explained in Chapter 6. Brainstorm for search words. Find the appropriate topic, then review the case annotations. The annotations also are updated with pocket parts or supplementary pamphlets that should be reviewed for the most current citations to authorities.

ILLUSTRATION 11-3.   Sample Annotated U.S.C.S. Court Rule

VII. JUDGMENT

Rule 60.   Relief from Judgment or Order

(a) Clerical Mistakes. Clerical mistakes in judgments, orders or other parts of the record and errors therein arising from oversight or omission may be corrected by the court at any time of its own initiative or on the motion of any party and after such notice, if any, as the court orders. During the pendency of an appeal, such mistakes may be so corrected before the appeal is docketed in the appellate court, and thereafter while the appeal is pending may be so corrected with leave of the appellate court.

(b) Mistakes; Inadvertence; Excusable Neglect; Newly Discovered Evidence; Fraud, Etc. On motion and upon such terms as are just, the court may relieve a party or his legal representative from a final judgment, order, or proceeding for the following reasons: (1) mistake, inadvertence, surprise, or excusable neglect; (2) newly discovered evidence which by due diligence could not have been discovered in time to move for a new trial under Rule 59(b); (3) fraud (whether heretofore denominated intrinsic or extrinsic), misrepresentation, or other misconduct of an adverse party; (4) the judgment is void; (5) the judgment has been satisfied, released, or discharged, or a prior judgment upon which it is based has been reversed or otherwise vacated, or it is no longer equitable that the judgment should have prospective application; or (6) any other reason justifying relief from the operation of the judgment. The motion shall be made within a reasonable time, and for reasons (1), (2), and (3) not more than one year after the judgment, order, or proceeding was entered or taken. A motion under this subdivision (b) does not affect the finality of a judgment or suspend its operation. This rule does not limit the power of a court to entertain an independent action to relieve a party from a judgment, order, or proceeding, or to grant relief to a defendant not actually personally notified as provided in Title 28, U. S. C., § 1655, or to set aside a judgment for fraud upon the court. Writs of coram nobis, coram vobis, audita querela, and bills of review and bills in the nature of a bill of review, are abolished, and the procedure for obtaining any relief from a judgment shall be by motion as prescribed in these rules or by an independent action.

ILLUSTRATION 11-3. *Continued*

RELIEF FROM JUDGMENT   Rule 60, n 27

District Court has no power to disturb judgment which has been affirmed by appellate court without leave of such court. Wilson Research Corp. v Piolite Plastics Corp. (1964, DC Mass) 234 F Supp 234, 142 USPQ 430, 143 USPQ 116, 8 FR Serv 2d 60b.34, Case 1.

District Court cannot vacate or modify or otherwise disturb judgment after it has been affirmed, reversed, or modified by Court of Appeals, without direction or consent of such court. Rhodes v Houston (1966, DC Neb) 258 F Supp 546, affd (CA8) 418 F2d 1309, cert den 397 US 1049, 25 L Ed 2d 662, 90 S Ct 1382.

3. Review of Rule 60 Rulings

24. Generally

Where not only was there no showing of abuse on the part of trial court in denying debtor's motion for new trial, but it also appeared that the motion was not presented to the trial court until long after the appeal from the order dismissing petition under 11 USCS § 203 had been taken and the appeal perfected in the court of appeals, appeal from denial of motion would be dismissed. Jordan v Federal Farm Mortg. Corp. (1945, CA8 Iowa) 152 F2d 642, cert dismd 328 US 821, 90 L Ed 1601, 66 S Ct 1339, and cert den 328 US 852, 90 L Ed 1624, 66 S Ct 1340.

Where the plaintiff in Oklahoma suit, confronted with plea of res judicata based on dismissal of her complaint, with prejudice, in the District of Columbia district court, moved in that court for order nunc pro tunc excepting from final dismissal order the one defendant subsequently sued in Oklahoma, so as to make the dismissal as to him without prejudice, and such motion was denied, plaintiff's appeal, although stated to be from order denying the motion to amend the final order of dismissal, would be considered to be appeal from denial of motion for relief from a final judgment; and, being predicated on theory that the court lacked authority to dismiss with prejudice as to such defendant while his challenge to its jurisdiction was pending, and as the record did not show whether jurisdiction either in personam or in rem was obtained, judgment as to such defendant would be vacated and case remanded for determination of question. Maben v Norvell (1954) 94 App DC 165, 214 F2d 263.

Appellate court does not pass upon merits of motion for relief from judgment that district court erroneously granted without making evidentiary record; rather, motion is remanded to district court for evidentiary hearing on merits without limitation on district court in its consideration of material which it deems appropriate to proper resolution of issues. Mayberry v Maroney (1976, CA3 Pa) 529 F2d 332, 21 FR Serv 2d

323, on remand (WD Pa) 418 F Supp 669, 22 FR Serv 2d 1046, revd on other grounds (CA3 Pa) 558 F2d 1159, 23 FR Serv 2d 1078.

25. Jurisdiction

Court of appeals had jurisdiction of appeal from order denying motion for new trial filed under Rule 60(b) notwithstanding fact that notice of appeal from the judgment on the merits had been filed prior to the filing of the motion. Serio v Badger Mut. Ins. Co. (1959, CA5 Miss) 266 F2d 418, 2 FR Serv 2d 924, cert den 361 US 832, 4 L Ed 2d 73, 80 S Ct 81.

26. Appealability

The denial of motion under Rule 60(b) is appealable, but denial of such motion does not bring up for review on appeal order sought to be modified. Hines v Seaboard A. L. R. Co. (1965, CA2 NY) 341 F2d 229, 9 FR Serv 2d 60b.35, Case 1; Wilson v Fenton (1982, CA3 Pa) 684 F2d 249.

Order denying motion under Rule 60(b) is final and appealable. Pagan v American Airlines, Inc. (1976, CA1 Puerto Rico) 534 F2d 990, 21 FR Serv 2d 1193.

Generally, trial court lacks jurisdiction pending appeal to enter order under Rule 60(b); proper procedure is for trial court, at movant's request, to indicate whether it would entertain or grant such motion, and where trial court determines that it will not entertain Rule 60(b) motion "at that time," order is generally considered interlocutory in nature and therefore not final and appealable. Craig v M/V Peacock (1985, CA9 Cal) 760 F2d 953.

Order denying relief under Rule 60 is appealable but appeal brings up correctness of order only, thus denial of motion to set aside arbitration award under Rule 60 did not permit appellant to attack arbitration award for error that could have been complained of on direct appeal. Lafarge Conseils Et Etudes, S.A. v Kaiser Cement & Gypsum Corp. (1986, CA9 Cal) 791 F2d 1334.

27. —Particular circumstances

In action on war risk insurance policy by insured's administratrix and against the United States and insured's executrix, order setting aside default entered against individual defendant and allowing her to plead was procedural only and was not appealable final judgment. Kummer v United States (1945, CA6 Mich) 148 F2d 191.

Petition by president of bankrupt corporation to set aside prior proceedings in bankruptcy on ground of alleged errors was not motion for new trial, but a motion to correct judgment on ground of mistake or error; hence, order denying

29

ILLUSTRATION 11-4.   Sample Annotated Code Rules Index

RELIEF FROM JUDGMENT   **Rule 60**

INTERPRETIVE NOTES AND DECISIONS

I. IN GENERAL
  A. General Considerations
    1. Purpose (notes 1, 2)
    2. Construction (notes 3, 4)
    3. Applicability (notes 5-7)
    4. Discretion of Court
      a. In General (notes 8, 9)
      b. Proper Exercise of Discretion (notes 10-12)
      c. Abuse of Discretion (notes 13, 14)
  B. Practice and Procedure
    1. In General (notes 15, 16)
    2. Relief During Appeal (notes 17-23)
    3. Review of Rule 60 Rulings (notes 24-29)
II. CORRECTION OF CLERICAL MISTAKES [RULE 60(a)]
  A. In General (notes 30-33)
  B. Particular Mistakes
    1. Omissions (notes 34-42)
    2. Errors (notes 43-48)
    3. Other Mistakes (notes 49, 50)
III. RELIEF FROM JUDGMENT OR ORDER UNDER RULE 60(b), GENERALLY
  A. General Considerations
    1. In General (notes 51-57)
    2. Construction (notes 59-66)
    3. Factors Considered in Deciding Motion (notes 67-69)
  B. Particular Judgments or Orders
    1. Default Judgments (notes 70-75)
    2. Bankruptcy (notes 76-82)
    3. Other (notes 83-90)
  C. Practice and Procedure
    1. In General (notes 91-100)
    2. Time for Motion
      a. In General (notes 101-103)
      b. One-Year Time Limit (notes 104-109)
      c. "Reasonable" Time (notes 110-119)
    3. Independent Actions (notes 120-127)
IV. MISTAKE, INADVERTENCE, SURPRISE, OR EXCUSABLE NEGLECT [RULE 60(b)(1)]
  A. In General (notes 128-131)
  B. Mistake or Inadvertence
    1. Of Party (notes 132, 133)
    2. Of Attorney (notes 134-138)
    3. Of Court (notes 139-141)
    4. Of Jury (note 142)
  C. Excusable Neglect
    1. In General (notes 143, 144)
    2. Of Party
      a. Failure to Appear, Respond, or File Pleading (notes 145-151)

      b. Other Neglect (notes 152-154)
    3. Of Attorney (notes 155-161)
  D. Other (notes 162-164)
V. NEWLY DISCOVERED EVIDENCE [RULE 60(b)(2)]
  A. In General (notes 165-170)
  B. Particular Types of Evidence (notes 171-178)
VI. FRAUD, MISREPRESENTATION, OR OTHER CONDUCT OF ADVERSE PARTY [RULE 60(b)(3)] (notes 179-188)
VII. VOID JUDGMENT [RULE 60(b)(4)] (notes 189-197)
VIII. SATISFACTION, RELEASE, OR DISCHARGE OF JUDGMENT [RULE 60(b)(5)] (notes 198-207)
IX. OTHER REASONS JUSTIFYING RELIEF [RULE 60(b)(6)]
  A. In General (notes 208-215)
  B. General Factors Affecting Grant or Denial of Relief
    1. Extraordinary Circumstances (notes 216-221)
    2. Failure to Appeal (notes 222-224)
    3. Other Factors (notes 225, 226)
  C. Particular Grounds for Relief
    1. Change in Decisional Law (notes 227-230)
    2. Changed Circumstances (notes 231, 232)
    3. Neglect by Attorney (notes 233-236)
    4. Court's Error (notes 237-239)
    5. Other Grounds (notes 240-253)
X. FRAUD UPON THE COURT (notes 254-262)

I. IN GENERAL

A. General Considerations

1. Purpose

1. Generally
2. Effect on appeal

2. Construction

3. Generally
4. With other rules

3. Applicability

5. Generally
6. To nonfinal orders and rulings
7. To proceedings other than in district court

11

---

*Reprinted with permission of LEXIS-NEXIS.

Although some cases that deal with the federal rules are found in *West's Federal Supplement* or the *Federal Reporter,* many are published in a separate reporter called the ***Federal Rules Decisions.*** This reporter contains federal civil and criminal cases that focus on the federal rules, as well as some conference notes from the sessions that concern the federal rules.

In addition to the annotated codes, selected secondary sources such as looseleaf services and treatises focus on the federal rules. The *Federal Rules Service,* a combination of bound volumes and looseleaf binders published by West Group, contains the text of the federal civil rules, local district and appellate rules, and annotations concerning cases, law review articles, and other secondary sources that interpret and explain the rules.

The service has a topical digest system with headnotes and an index to its digest similar to the digests discussed in Chapter 3.

Decisions of the U.S. Supreme Court, Courts of Appeals, District Courts, Claims Court, Court of Military Appeals, Tax Court, and other federal courts can be found in the service. These cases are published more quickly than other sources, and sometimes the *Federal Rules Service* is the only source of a published opinion. However, this is an unofficial source of a primary authority.

The *Federal Rules of Evidence Service* can assist you in researching the evidence rules. Also published by West, this service includes a digest that includes civil and criminal cases that interpret the Federal Rules of Evidence. Headnotes are used as well as an index system.

The *Federal Local Court Rules* contains the local rules of the individual federal courts.

The *Federal Procedure Rules Service* is a series of volumes published by the West Group. One volume contains the Federal Rules of Civil Procedure, the Federal Rules of Criminal Procedure, the Federal Rules of Evidence, the Rules of Procedure of the Judicial Panel on Multidistrict Litigation, the Federal Rules of Appellate Procedure, the Temporary Emergency Court of Appeals Rules, and the Rules of the United States Supreme Court. Other volumes are divided by circuit and contain the appellate and district court local rules for the circuit. For example, one entire volume is devoted to the Sixth Circuit Court of Appeals rules and the local rules from the district courts that are within the Sixth Circuit. These volumes are replaced annually, and pocket supplements are issued quarterly. This service also includes a federal court procedural guide and checklist as well as a timetable for filing documents. The method for using this treatise is similar to that of the digests or encyclopedias. You can use the index or the table of contents, or you can find the topic by reviewing the selected topics listed on the spines of the volumes.

Two multivolume treatises, *Federal Practice and Procedure,* written by Charles Alan Wright, Arthur R. Miller, and Edward H. Cooper, and *Moore's Federal Practice,* written by James W. Moore et al., are widely regarded and very persuasive secondary authorities that explain the federal rules and provide references to primary and secondary authorities.

Other useful treatises include a one-volume treatise called the *The Law of the Federal Courts,* written by Charles Alan Wright, and *Civil Procedure,* written by Geoffrey C. Hazard Jr. and John Leubsdorf.

For evidence issues, consult the following treatises:

Evidence: Text, Rules, Illustrations and Problems, by Michael H. Graham

McCormick on Evidence

Evidence, by Christopher B. Mueller and Laird C. Kirkpatrick

Weinstein's *Evidence: Commentary on Rules of Evidence for the United States Courts and State Court*

Wigmore on Evidence

If you are dealing with the Seventh Circuit Court of Appeals, a good reference book is the *Practitioner's Handbook for Appeals to the United States Court of Appeals for the Seventh Circuit.* For the Second Circuit, a publication called *Appeals to the Second Circuit* is invaluable. For the Sixth Circuit, a *Practitioner's Handbook* is available. Many of these publications are prepared by local bar federal courts committees. These guides provide you with background and practical information about the courts as well as the time frame and procedure for filing appellate documents.

Another useful resource for you might be the federal rules committee comments concerning any changes in the rules or the committee's commentary regarding the purpose and origin of the rule.

Do not forget to consider resources such as encyclopedias, legal periodicals, and the A.L.R. series. For more information about these sources, see Chapter 5.

Consider a review of the federal digests under the topic Federal Civil Procedure for the federal civil rules and other related topics for other sets of federal rules. These digests provide citations to primary and secondary authorities. For a more detailed explanation of how to use the digests, consult Chapter 3.

▼ Are the Federal Rules Available Online?

Both LEXIS and WESTLAW offer the Federal Rules of Civil Procedure, the Federal Rules of Appellate Procedure, the Federal Rules of Criminal Procedure, the Federal Rules of Evidence, and the Rules of the United States Supreme Court, as well as some local federal court rules.

On WESTLAW, the federal rules are contained in a database called US-RULES. West also has established a federal civil procedure topic area for its federal practice digests (discussed in Chapter 3) and for topic and key number searches of the rules online. (This process is discussed in Chapter 3.) The rules also are found in the USC and USCA database online on WESTLAW.

Local rules for the U.S. Courts of Appeals are available on WEST-LAW in the US-RULES database. Local rules for the U.S. District Courts are found in the databases that contain the state court rules. These can be accessed by typing the postal abbreviation, a hyphen, and the word RULES. For example, the rules for the U.S. District Court for the Southern District of Ohio would be found in the OH-RULES database.

▼ Are Rules Available on the Internet?

A variety of sources provide court rules on the Web and the Internet. For example, you can retrieve the Federal Rules of Evidence by using http://www.law.cornell.edu/rules/fre/overview.html. Some sites are accessible through university gophers. Several sites on the Web provide links to various rule resources such as the Legal Pad. In addition, the U.S. House of Representatives Internet Law Library provides various evidence and procedural rules at http://law.house.gov/197.htm. See Illustration 11-5.

PRACTICE POINTER

Rules found on the Internet, however, may not be relied on. You should always consult the official rule source.

▼ Are Any Federal Rule Treatises Available on CD-ROM?

Yes. Some treatises are now available on CD-ROM, such as *Federal Practice and Procedure,* produced by West. The number of CD-ROM treatises is expected to grow.

However, as there are a limited number of secondary sources online, the print materials may be of more assistance than the computerized sources.

▼ How Would You Cite the Various Federal Rules?

The federal rules should be cited in accordance with Bluebook Rule 12.8.3 as follows:

Fed. R. Civ. P. 56
Fed. R. Crim. P. 1
Fed. R. App. P. 26
Fed. R. Evid. 803

ILLUSTRATION 11-5. U.S. House of Representatives Internet Law Library Home Page

Internet Law Library
Evidence and procedural law

- Alaska Statutes, title 9 (Code of Civil Procedure)
- California Code of Civil Procedure (table of contents)
- California Code of Civil Procedure
- California Evidence Code (table of contents)
- California Evidence Code
- Canada Forensic DNA Analysis Bill (June 22, 1995) and related material (in English and French)
- Chidichimo v. Industrial Commission (Ill. App., 1996) (discovery limits in workers' compensation case)
- Circuit Court (Wise County & the City of Norton, Virginia) local rules and related material
- Degen v. U.S. (U.S., 1996) (Fugative Disentitelment Doctorine)
- Ferreira v. Levin (S. Afr., 1996) (costs)
- Florida Statutes (1993), chapter 45 (Civil Procedure: General Provisions)
- Florida Statutes (1993), chapter 90 (Evidence Code)
- Florida Statutes (1993), chapter 92 (witnesses, records, and documents)
- Frazier v. State (Ark., 1996) (prior consistent and inconsistent statements)
- Henderson v. U.S. (U.S., 1996) (Fed. R. Civ. Pro. superceeds Suits in Admiralty Act procedural provisions)
- Hubbard v. U.S. (U.S., 1995) (unsworn falsehoods to a court)
- Indiana Code, title 34 (Civil Procedure)
- International Criminal Tribunal for Rwanda: Rules of Procedure and Evidence
- International Criminal Tribunal for the former Yugoslavia: Rules of Procedure and Evidence
- Lucas County (Ohio) Common Pleas Court Rules

- "Trial Practice and Procedure" by C. Frederick Overby and Jason Crawford
- "Ten Commandments for a Good Witness" by James McWhinnie
- "Trial Practice and Procedure" by C. Frederick Overby and Teresa T. Abell
- "Domestic Relations" by Barry B. McGough (1996)
- "Trial Practice & Procedure" by Philip W. Savrin (Summer 1995)
- "Trial Practice and Procedure" by Philip W. Savrin (Spring 1996)
- "Using Leading Questions During Direct Examination" by Charles W. Ehrhardt and Stephanie J. Young

- see also Crime
- see also U.S. Federal laws (arranged by original published source)
- see also U.S. Federal laws (arranged by agency)
- see also U.S. state and territorial laws
- see also Laws of other nations
- see also Treaties and international law
- see also Law school library catalogues and services
- see also Attorney and legal profession directories
- See also Law book reviews and publishers

- About the Internet Law Library

■ Internet Law Library Home Page

◆

Your Comments Please!
   Your comments about this service, suggestions for improving the service, and questions about the service, are all welcome. Please include your e-mail address—our address is usc@mail.house.gov.

The local appellate court rules are cited based on the same rule:

7th Cir. R. 1

▼ How Would You Cite a Decision Contained in the *Federal Rules Decisions?*

The abbreviation for the *Federal Rules Decisions* is F.R.D. A case would be cited according to Bluebook Rule 10.2.3 as follows:

<u>Barrett Indus. Trucks v. Old Republic Ins. Co.</u>, 129 F.R.D. 515 (N.D. Ill. 1989)

C. STATE RULES OF PRACTICE

▼ What Rules Control the Conduct of State Proceedings?

Most states have adopted rules of civil and criminal procedure. Many of these rules are patterned after the Federal Rules of Civil or Criminal Procedure. Some states have adopted evidence codes, while others rely on the common law and have not approved any evidentiary codes. Note that some of the states that have not adopted evidence codes rely on the Federal Rules of Evidence for guidance. The rules of the state courts control conduct similar to that dealt with in the federal rules. For example, the federal rules describe the procedure and the requirements for the dismissal of a case. Similarly under state codes, the rules explain the circumstances that would allow a court to dismiss a case and the procedure to follow to obtain such an order. In addition to state codes, many state courts have local rules or orders similar to local rules issued by the federal courts. Again, check with these courts to determine whether such rules exist for each court.

▼ Where Would You Find State Rules and Local Rules for State Courts?

The states often include the rules of criminal and civil procedure and the evidentiary rules in their statutory codes. Deskbooks may contain the statewide and local court rules. Many bar association directories also contain the rules, and several commercially published directories of lawyers, such as Sullivan's, contain the state and local orders of courts in the area covered by the directory.

▼ Are Annotations for State Rules Available?

Yes, many annotated statutory codes contain references to cases and secondary authorities that explain or interpret the state procedural rules. These codes can be used in a manner similar to that of the federal annotated codes. For more information about how to use these annotated codes, see Chapter 6.

▼ Are State Rules Available Online?

Yes, many state codes containing the rules are available online.

Few local rules for state courts are available online on either WESTLAW or LEXIS. For these rules, refer to the hardcopy resources or the courts.

▼ Are There Any Significant State Rule Treatises or Secondary Authorities?

Each state's set of rules varies, as does the type and number of secondary authorities available to you as researchers. Check with your librarian for relevant materials. Consider reviewing the materials discussed above, such as federal treatises, and those discussed below, such as continuing legal education materials. These may be helpful because the states' rules often are patterned after the federal rules.

D. ENSURING CURRENCY

▼ How Do You Ensure That You Are Reviewing the Most Current Version of the Rule?

First, update the rule using the pocket parts and pamphlets that accompany the annotated codes. Next, ensure that the rule is valid and current by Shepardizing it. Shepardizing also helps you to find cases and other authorities that cite the rule. Shepardize both federal and state rules by following the same procedures used for the process for cases and statutes. For a more detailed explanation, consult Chapters 4 and 6.

For the federal rules, *Shepard's United States Citations* should be used because it includes citations for all federal rules. To use this, look for the rule number and set of rules listed at the top of the page. Then find the rule on the page. Citing sources such as cases and A.L.R. annotations will be listed. Note that the rules sometimes have subdivisions and that *Shepard's* lists citations below those subdivisions as well. Some libraries have *Shepard's Federal Rule Citations,* a specialized *Shepard's* devoted entirely to the federal rules and their citing authorities. The process for the use of this citator is similar to that of the other *Shepard's* citators.

▼ Can Federal Rules Be Shepardized Online?

Yes. You can Shepardize rules found in the U.S.C. and U.S.C.A. on WESTLAW and those found in the U.S.C.S. on LEXIS.

▼ Can State Rules Be Shepardized?

Yes. State rules are part of the specific state citator prepared by *Shepard's*. Use these in the same manner as the other *Shepard's* citators noted above.

▼ Can State Rules Be Shepardized Online?

Yes. A growing number of states' rules can be Shepardized online as part of the individual state's codified statutes.

CHAPTER SUMMARY

The rules that govern the conduct of cases brought before courts vary depending on the court in which an action is pending. Federal rules govern proceedings in the federal courts, and state rules control actions in the state courts.

These rules are primary authorities and generally can be found in statutory compilations. They also are contained in reference books called deskbooks. The statutory compilations can direct you to cases that interpret and explain these rules. Secondary authorities such as treatises and legal periodicals often explain these rules and provide you with citations to other primary authorities, including cases, that focus on the rules. Many rules are available online.

These rules are validated in a manner similar to statutes. When you review a *Shepard's* citation for a rule, you also find additional citing authorities.

The next chapter explains ethical rules and how to locate them, as well as how to find cases that interpret these rules. You also learn how to validate the rules.

KEY TERMS

attorney deskbooks	*Federal Rules Decisions*
Federal Rules of Appellate Procedure	Federal Rules of Evidence
Federal Rules of Civil Procedure	local rules of court
Federal Rules of Criminal Procedure	Rules of the Supreme Court

EXERCISES

1. Find Federal Rule of Civil Procedure 12.
    a. What does this rule address?
    b. Where did you find this rule?
2. If the U.S.C.A. was unavailable, where would you look for a Federal Rule of Evidence? List two other sources.

3. What set or sets of rules or orders apply to cases pending in the U.S. District Court in your state or area?
4. What set or sets of rules or orders apply to motions and briefs in a case before the U.S. Circuit Court of Appeals in your state or area?
5. What set or sets of rules or orders apply to a trial in a federal court?
6. What set or sets of rules or orders apply to a trial in your state court?
7. What set or sets of rules apply to attorneys practicing in the Bankruptcy courts generally?
8. What reference books would you use to find such Bankruptcy rules?
9. What federal rule concerns a motion to dismiss for lack of jurisdiction?
10. What federal rule sets forth the criteria for a summary judgment motion?
11. What rules govern practice before the U.S. Supreme Court?
12. What sources contain citations to cases and other authorities that interpret or explain the federal rules?

12

ETHICAL RULES

CHAPTER OVERVIEW

In Chapter 11, you learned about procedural rules. In this chapter, the discussion concerns ethical rules. You learn where to find these rules in print and online and how to retrieve primary and secondary authorities that explain or interpret these rules. You also are shown how to locate ethics opinions, both in print and online. Finally, you are taught about ensuring the currency of these rules.

A. RULES OF PROFESSIONAL RESPONSIBILITY

For the practice of law, individual states determine the rules that regulate the conduct of lawyers. Some of those rules dictate an attorney's **ethical behavior,** while others control an attorney's **ability to practice,** such as state licensing rules.

Each court has rules that govern the conduct of lawyers and litigants. Many state courts also have rules that regulate the activities of lawyers who never appear in court. For example, the high courts in many states have rules concerning licensing and registration of attorneys. You always should consider whether any rules exist that govern your conduct or the litigation process you are involved in.

Paralegals must be able to research ethical rules that control the conduct of attorneys and their staffs.

ETHICS ALERT

Attorneys are responsible for ensuring that paralegals follow the rules that govern attorneys. However, you must know what rules to follow so that you do not jeopardize your attorney or your job.

▼ Is There a National Code of Ethics?

No. Each state has its own set of rules that control the conduct of its lawyers. Lawyers must follow these rules of conduct and must supervise you and ensure that you also follow these rules. Many of these state rules are patterned after the American Bar Association's *Model Code of Professional Responsibility* or the American Bar Association's *Model Rules of Professional Conduct.* These rules govern issues such as conflicts of interest; client confidentiality; communications; fairness; responsibilities of supervisory lawyers, law firms, and associations regarding nonlawyer assistants; unauthorized practice of law; disqualification from a case; and the reporting of professional misconduct. In most cases, the rules require that attorneys ensure that paralegals follow the same rules designed for attorneys. To date, no state has adopted separate ethical rules that control paralegal conduct or that subject the paralegal to disciplinary action rather than the attorney when the paralegal violates the rules. However, several states have advisory rules for paralegals. Paralegals cannot be sanctioned for failing to follow these rules. They merely offer paralegals some direction in how to conduct themselves. Many ask that you follow attorney codes. In addition, many ethics experts believe that the regulation of paralegals will be forthcoming. In addition to the rules of professional responsibility, cases that interpret the rules also govern the conduct of lawyers.

▼ What Type of Authority Are These Rules and Cases?

Rules adopted by a jurisdiction and the subsequent court decisions are primary binding authorities. The *ABA Model Code of Professional Responsibility* and the *ABA Model Rules of Professional Conduct* are secondary authorities, as are any of the drafters' comments about the origin and purpose of these rules. However, these ethics rules and comments are very persuasive secondary authorities because most state ethics codes or rules are drawn from the ABA models.

▼ When Would You Review the Rules for Ethical Conduct and the Applicable Cases?

You will be asked to review the ethical rules whenever issues involving ethics are presented. Self-interest also demands that you be familiar with the rules. You must follow the rules that govern attorneys. As clients, attorneys, and paralegals become more mobile, conflicts of interest have become a frequent topic for research.

B. RESEARCHING ETHICAL QUESTIONS

1. Primary Sources and Annotated Sources

Many rules of professional responsibility are contained within the codifications of the state's statutes. In addition, deskbooks or pamphlets (single-volume references found in most paralegals' and attorneys' offices) often contain the model rules or codes. These are updated annually and are more convenient than reviewing an entire code to find an ethical rule. To find cases, you would use the annotated sources.

▼ What Is the Value of an Annotated Source for the Rules and Codes?

The annotated rule sources are valuable in a manner similar to the annotated codes. These sources provide citations to primary authorities, such as court decisions, that interpret the rules and citations to other secondary authorities, such as the *American Law Reports,* treatises, and law review articles. Some looseleaf publishers also publish ethics cases.

▼ Where Can You Find the *ABA Model Rules of Professional Conduct* and the *ABA Model Code of Professional Responsibility*?

An excellent secondary source for your research are the ABA model rules found in the *Annotated Model Rules of Professional Conduct* published by the ABA Center for Professional Responsibility. The annotated rules book contains the full text of the rules coupled with citations to any interpretations of the rules in court decisions or informal and formal ABA opinions.[1] This source also includes the drafters' commentary about the purpose and design of each rule. The ABA's *Annotated Model Code of Professional Responsibility* focuses on the ABA model code, the predecessor of the model rules. This publication also includes case citations and commentary concerning the model code.

▼ What Other Secondary Sources Are Useful for Ethics Researchers?

In addition to the ABA annotated sources, many states have annotated guides for their rules of professional conduct. For example, the Illinois Institute for Continuing Legal Education publishes a source called the *Annotated Guide to the Illinois Rules of Professional Conduct.* This source also provides the text of the rules and primary and secondary sources. The ABA publishes the *Legislative History of the Model Rules of Professional Conduct: Their Development in the ABA House of Delegates,* which might help you in understanding the rules.

▼ How Do You Use the Annotated Sources?

The methods for using each of these sources generally involves a review of the table of contents or the index. The ABA annotated model rules, for example, lists each rule in the table of contents. This method is useful if you already know what rule you wish to review. Next to the rule is a list of the topics covered by the rule. You could read through each heading to see if the rule applies to your situation. However, it might be more efficient to review the alphabetical index at the back of the annotated rules. Within the index, you will find a variety of topics and cross-references to various subject areas, as well as citations to the rule.

2. Other Useful Authorities

The ABA and many state and local bar associations render **advisory ethics opinions** for attorneys. These opinions are secondary authorities. The ABA issues both formal and informal opinions. Although an **ABA opinion** is a secondary authority that has no force of law, in the ethics area, it is often a very persuasive authority because many ethics rules or codes that govern lawyers are based on the ABA models. The informal and formal opinions generally are issued after a party requests that the ABA provide such an opinion. You also can find these opinions in the ABA's publication *Recent Ethics Opinions* and online on WESTLAW.

---

1. The *Annotated Model Rules of Professional Conduct* also provides a comparison between the model rules and its predecessor, the *ABA Model Code of Professional Responsibility,* a summary of all of the amendments to the model rules and an index to the rules and comments as well as tables that integrate or correlate the provisions of the model code and the model rules.

> *PRACTICE POINTER*
>
> Advisory ethics opinions often are excellent sources of rules and cases.

▼ Do State Bar Associations Publish Ethics Opinions Similar to Those Prepared by the ABA?

Yes. Some organizations publish pamphlets or books that contain their opinions while others can be found by reviewing continuing legal education materials, which are discussed in Chapter 13. Some are accessible through the Internet, and others are available from online services.

3. Research Process

▼ How Would You Research an Ethical Question?

First, you would review the rule. Second, you should review any annotations, especially those found in the annotated codes or the annotated rule books. Next, read the cases and the informal and formal opinions. Shepardize the cases. Sometimes it is necessary to study a secondary authority to better understand an ethical dilemma. If necessary, perform a search of the rule on the computer to see if any additional cases can be found.

▼ Can You Find State Ethical Rules Online?

You can review the ethical rules and perform searches for authorities that discuss these rules on both LEXIS and WESTLAW. Both services have special databases that contain the ethics rules.

▼ How Would You Research an Ethical Issue on WESTLAW?

On WESTLAW the databases are called the LEGAL ETHICS & PROFESSIONAL RESPONSIBILITY databases. These databases contain authorities that relate to the regulation of the practice of law and disciplinary proceedings.

You would search these databases in a fashion similar to searches done in other databases. For a detailed explanation of search formation and use of WESTLAW, see Chapter 9.

First, you should research the cases databases. Next, you might want to search the ethics opinion databases. These databases will provide any informal or formal ethics opinions that may have been released by a state, county, or city bar association.

Next, you might want to review the ABA databases. These databases contain secondary authority that has not been adopted in total by any jurisdiction. However, this secondary authority is very persuasive because most states have patterned their ethics rules according to the ABA model rules or model code.

▼ How Would You Research an Ethical Issue on LEXIS?

For LEXIS, access the ABA library or the ETHICS library at the directory screen. Then, enter the desired file. The focus of the LEXIS ABA library is national bar ethics materials. The ETHICS library on LEXIS contains state-related ethics materials as well as some ABA materials.

▼ Can Ethics Rules Be Shepardized?

Yes. *Shepard's Professional and Judicial Conduct Citations* lists authorities that cite the ABA Model Code sections or the ABA Model Rules. Each ABA rule is listed in bold at the top of the page with a notation about whether it is a model rule or part of the model code.

4. Sample Research Problem

EXAMPLE

You have been asked to research a conflict of interest question. You work for an attorney who represented K. K. Industries in a matter against R. J. Enterprises in a contract dispute in 1993. R. J. Enterprises has now asked your boss to represent its company against Reynolds Wide Haulers in an unrelated contract dispute. Reynolds Wide Haulers, however, is the parent company of K. K. Industries. Your boss wants to know what rules govern such representation. Your firm is located in Illinois, which has adopted the *ABA Model Rules of Professional Conduct*.

First, brainstorm for possible search topics. Next, look in the index to the Illinois statutes. If you don't find any references concerning conflicts of interest, try the *ABA Model Rules*. One source would be the *ABA Annotated Model Rules of Professional Conduct*. You could look in the index under conflict of interest. See Illustration 12-1. Several topics are listed in this illustration, but the most appropriate are "existing client, interest adverse to client" or "former client." The first directs you to Rule 1.7(a) and the second to Rule 1.9. You then would review each rule.

The text of each rule is contained in the annotated resource. After each rule is a comment section that explains the rule. Following the comments is a comparison of the model code and the model rules. Finally, there is a list of authorities, including primary authorities.

Next, you should review the authorities. Finally, you should validate the rule and authorities.

ILLUSTRATION 12-1.   *ABA Annotated Model Rules* Index

▼ How Would You Cite an Ethics Rule Found in the *ABA Code of Professional Responsibility?*

The rules for citation of ethics codes are found in Bluebook Rule 12.8.6. Rule 1.10 of the *ABA Model Rules of Professional Conduct* would be cited as follows:

Model Rules of Professional Conduct Rule 1.10 (1992)

▼ How Would You Cite an ABA Ethics Opinion?

The rules for citation of ethics opinions are contained in Bluebook Rule 12.8.6. A citation of an ABA opinion would be as follows:

ABA Comm. on Professional Ethics and Grievances, Informal Op. 1526 (1988)

CHAPTER SUMMARY

Each state has ethical rules that govern the conduct of lawyers and litigants. Many of these rules are patterned after the *ABA Model Rules of Professional Conduct* or the *ABA Model Code of Professional Responsibility.*

Often these rules are found in state statutory compilations or attorney deskbooks. The statutory codes provide references to other primary authorities, such as cases and related rules, and to secondary sources. A variety of secondary sources, such as treatises, legal periodicals, and A.L.R. annotations, explain and interpret these rules and include citations to primary authorities.

Many ethical rules are available online, as are some secondary sources that explain and interpret these rules.

In addition to state ethics opinions, the ABA and other bar associations issue advisory ethics opinions. These opinions are secondary authorities. However, they may be very persuasive authorities. These can be found in both print and online.

Both the ethics rules and opinions can be validated in print and online. The method for validating these authorities is similar to that used for cases, statutes, and rules governing court proceedings.

The next chapter will focus on practical resources that assist you in your research, such as continuing legal education materials, formbooks, and legal directories.

KEY TERMS

ABA Model Code of Professional
  Responsibility
ABA Model Rules of Professional
  Conduct

ABA opinion
ability to practice
advisory ethics opinion
ethical behavior

EXERCISES

You are working as a paralegal for a firm that is defending a personal injury action against a manufacturer of recreational bikes. The plaintiff, a resident of Findlay, Ohio, was injured while riding one of the bikes in an event known as the Hancock Hill Less Hundred. While working for the defendant's law firm, Cryer, Wolf and Nonnemaker, you attend depositions and strategy conferences between counsel representing the defendant and counsel representing the codefendant. You had many conferences with witnesses, transcribed statements, and prepared letters to clients after reviewing the files. Although you are working hard on this case, billable hours throughout the firm are down, and you are laid off. You are given two weeks to find a job.

A sole practitioner in Findlay, a town of 25,000, tentatively offers you a job, but you first must do some research. This attorney represents the plaintiff in the above mentioned action. Before the practitioner will allow you to begin work, you must research whether his firm can hire you and whether the firm can continue to represent the plaintiff in this action.

1. Map out your research plan. What sources will you consult?
2. For each source, note whether you will find secondary or primary authority or both.
3. As you list each source, note your next step and why you would go to the next source.

PRACTITIONER'S MATERIALS

CHAPTER OVERVIEW

In the preceding chapters, you have learned how to find primary and secondary authorities and how to use the resources that contain these authorities. This chapter focuses on some practical sources, such as formbooks and continuing legal education materials, for you to consider. In addition, you are taught about jury instruction sources and about how and when to use them.

A. FORMBOOKS

Some courts require specific forms. For example, bankruptcy courts require a specific form. Also, some types of legal documents must be drafted in the statutory form established by the state's legislature. For example, in states that have living will statutes, living wills must be drafted using the statute's "magic language" to be valid. To assist you in drafting such documents with the appropriate language, many publishers have compiled **formbooks.** Formbooks can provide you with many federal and state court forms as well as examples of forms that contain the language appropriate for a particular statute. These forms can save you time and help in your drafting. However, you must be careful when using these standardized forms for drafting documents that are not standardized, such as wills. Ideally, these forms properly incorporate the language that would make the document legally valid in your state. Because the form may be out of date, you must know what language the current law requires or double-check with the court if you are using a court form. Do not substitute your independent judgment when you use these forms.

Although generally used only for forms, you might find citations to authorities because some formbooks such as West's provide references to authorities and library sources such as key numbers and encyclopedia materials.

▼ What Formbooks Are Available?

West Group publishes the *Federal Local Court Forms* book, which contains court forms; the *Am. Jur. Legal Forms 2d; West's Legal Forms 2d,* which is separated into 11 topical units; and *West's Federal Forms,* which contains a variety of federal forms. Illustration 13-1 shows a sample West form that is used in the bankruptcy court. At the bottom of the form note the library references to *Corpus Juris Secundum* and West's digests.

In the probate, real estate, and transaction areas, a variety of publishers issue forms. Matthew Bender & Co. publishes several legal form sets, some of which appear on CD-ROM or online and can be downloaded.

Some states have their own forms, occasionally drafted by a state sanctioned body such as the California Judicial Council.

▼ How Do You Use Formbooks?

Included in the set is a page that explains how to use the guide or formbook. Consider starting with the index. Brainstorm to determine what words would be helpful and then look up the forms. You also can use the table of contents method with most formbooks.

▼ Are Formbooks Available Online and on CD-ROM?

Yes, some formbooks are available online and others are found on CD-ROM. The forms often can be downloaded from the computer system directly onto a floppy disk in WordPerfect or in another word

ILLUSTRATION 13-1. Sample Page from *West's Federal Forms*

Ch. 11   OFFICERS AND ADMINISTRATION   § 10386

§ 10385. **Certificate of Authorization to Operate Debtor's Business—11 U.S.C.A. § 1108**

UNITED STATES BANKRUPTCY COURT
for the
_____ DISTRICT OF _____

In re _____,
          Debtor.   Case No. _____
                                       Chapter _____

CERTIFICATE OF AUTHORIZATION TO
OPERATE DEBTOR'S BUSINESS

I hereby certify that _____, trustee, is in possession of debtor's estate and is authorized to operate debtor's business.

_____
Clerk, U.S. Bankruptcy Court

_____
Deputy Clerk

Dated:

Library References:

C.J.S. Bankruptcy § 199.
West's Key No. Digests, Bankruptcy ☜3025, 3026.

*Reprinted with permission of West Group.

processing system. Downloading forms from the computer saves you the time of either photocopying or handcopying forms from the hardcopy materials.

PRACTICE POINTER

Always check if a specific form is required by statute or rule.

ETHICS ALERT

If you use a form and change it substantially, be certain that an attorney reviews it.

B. OTHER PRACTITIONER'S MATERIALS

1. Checklists

▼ Do Any Publications Contain Lists of What Steps You Should Follow to Complete a Project?

Commercial publishers produce **checklists.** The West Group publication *Legal Checklists* features checklists for a variety of topics, such as estate planning, routine corporate matters, or matrimonial matters. See Illustration 13-2. Included in the section for the checklists are citations to authorities. These materials are separated by dividers, and you can turn directly to the section you are interested in because it is tabbed. You can find updates to these materials in the supplements that are regularly provided.

In addition to the commercial checklists, continuing legal education materials often contain checklists and practical information that may be as valuable for paralegals as it is for lawyers.

2. Continuing Legal Education Materials

Continuing legal education (CLE) materials generally explain an area of the law. They tend to be written by individual attorneys who are respected practitioners in a particular area. Within each state, a variety of continuing legal education materials are available. These are secondary authorities and have little or no persuasive value. Therefore, do not cite these materials to a court. However, they can be an invaluable tool in helping you learn about any area of the law. Unfortunately, many states do not update these quickly, and many of the materials lack adequate indexes. You generally must use the table of contents, which may not be comprehensive enough for your needs. However, for new areas of the law, these materials might be your only secondary source of information. Often bar associations present seminars with accompanying CLE materials whenever a major change in the law is made.

▼ Are CLE Materials Available Online?

Some national CLE publications can be found online on WESTLAW, such as those of the Practicing Law Institute (PLI) and the American Law Institute/American Bar Association (ALI/ABA). LEXIS has some CLE materials, such as current course listings, online.

ILLUSTRATION 13-2. West's *Legal Checklists*

CHECKLIST 10–1

ESTATE PLANNING—INFORMATION AND ANALYSIS

10–1.1.	Personal and family information.
10–1.2.	Description of estate assets and their ownership.
10–1.3.	Liabilities of estate owner.
10–1.4.	Estate documents to procure for examination.
10–1.5.	Information with respect to business interests.
10–1.6.	Prospective inheritances.
10–1.7.	Needs of family or dependents.
10–1.8.	Gifts.
10–1.9.	Analysis of estate assets.
10–1.10.	Preliminary analyses to be made.
10–1.11.	Analysis of death costs.
10–1.12.	Use of tools and techniques of estate planning.
10–1.13.	Minimizing exposure to malpractice liability in estate planning.
10–1.14.	Ethical conduct in estate planning.
10–1.15.	Necessity for continual review of will and estate plan.

REFERENCES

Texts and Services

Bittker, Federal Taxation of Income, Estates and Gifts.
Casner, Estate Planning (5th Ed).
Est & Pers Fin Plg
Kess & Westlin, Financial and Estate Planning.
Stephens, Maxfield & Lind, Federal Estate and Gift Taxation (5th Ed).
Westfall, Estate Planning Law and Taxation.

Articles

Armstrong & St. John, Estate Planning Overview: Federal Estate and Gift Taxes, Past, Present and Future, 64 Taxes 634 (1986).
Kelley, After the Disaster: Salvage and Damage Control for the Estate Lawyer, 19 U Miami Inst Est Plan ch 15 (1985).
Perkins, How To Prepare for the First Interview with a Client, and What It Should Cover, 8 Est Plan 91 (1981).

Effective estate planning begins with obtaining all the relevant facts and documents. Analysis of the facts and documents then directs the planner. This checklist deals with the information to be procured and the analyses which should be made.

Checklist 10–1: Page 1

*Reprinted with permission from West Group.

ILLUSTRATION 13-2.   *Continued*

10–1.1. Personal and family information.

With respect to the estate owner, spouse and dependents, the following information should be obtained:

A. Complete name (including maiden name) and any other names which the estate owner and his spouse may use (particularly if any assets are held in such other names).

B. Date and place of birth and citizenship.

C. Social Security number and available benefits.

D. Details of residence and domicile including present address and telephone number. If there are houses or apartments in two or more states, discuss fully the connection of the client to each state. How many days per year does he or she spend in each state. Where does estate owner vote, pay state income taxes, have driver's license, maintain bank accounts, maintain safe boxes? Some jurisdictions have a resident registration, such as in Florida. This information is important for estate tax purposes and for decisions where to probate the will. Consider problems of conflict in determination of legal domicile and possibility of multiple or conflicting jurisdictions over the estate. Discuss any future plans for change in residence or domicile.

E. Occupation.

F. Office address. If the estate owner conducts business activities in more than one state, it is important to select or determine the estate owner's domicile prior to preparing the estate plan. Obtain copies of income tax returns from all states where state taxes are paid and speak to accountant about apportionment determinations for income tax purposes.

G. Marital information.

  1. Married or single.
  2. Date and place of marriage.
  3. Domicile of husband and wife at the time of marriage.
  4. If either husband or wife has been married prior to their present marriage, information should be obtained as to the name of the former spouse, length of the previous marriage, the names, birthdates and present custody rights of any children born of the previous marriage, and the cause of the termination of the prior marriage (death, annulment or divorce). Copies of any divorce decree, property settlement or other relevant documents should be obtained.
  5. A copy of any antenuptial agreement or postnuptial agreement should be obtained. The antenuptial or postnuptial agreement must be examined to see if the agreement provides for full disclosure of assets when the agreement was made and if both

▼ How Do You Find CLE Materials?

Check with the law librarian or the attorney who assigned the project. You also could browse through the card catalog of the library or the library shelves. Finally, you might call the local or state bar associations for guidance about their publications.

3. Handbooks

▼ What Other Valuable Practitioner's Materials Are Available?

Several publishers produce **handbooks** that provide you with special information about a specialized type of practice such as estate planning, real estate, or trial practice. Sometimes they contain research references and case citations as well as trial aids. For example, Robert S. Hunter, a former Illinois judge, writes the *Trial Handbook for Illinois Lawyers Criminal* and the *Trial Handbook for Illinois Lawyers Civil*. These handbooks also include references to research and trial aids.

4. Jury Instructions

Jury instructions are provided to juries just after they are sworn in and before they deliberate in a case. These instructions explain to the jury members their duties and the applicable law in the case they are considering. In general, attorneys representing all litigants have an opportunity to draft jury instructions and work with a judge to develop a fair and accurate statement of the law that the jurors should be told to apply. Paralegals often assist in finding the appropriate instruction or in the drafting of the instructions. Improperly drafted jury instructions can affect the outcome of a case. Some jury instructions reference books are similar to formbooks because they provide you with sample instructions. Others, however, are pattern or approved instructions.

▼ What Are Pattern Jury Instructions, and How Do They Differ from Other Jury Instructions?

Pattern or **approved jury instructions** must be used in many states. For example, Illinois and Michigan practitioners must use their state's pattern instruction if one exists concerning a specific point. See Illustration 13-3. If an instruction does not exist or if it inaccurately states the current law, then an attorney can submit a proposed jury instruction that varies from the pattern instruction. Often criminal pattern jury instructions are out of date even with the regular supplementary pamphlets. In all cases, review the law and the jury instructions in tandem. Some states have "model" or sample jury instructions that they treat similar to pattern or approved instructions. Often verdict forms on which juries enter their findings are included in both the pattern and model jury instructions.

ILLUSTRATION 13-3.   Illinois Pattern Jury Instructions [IPI] Civil

WEIGHT OF EVIDENCE	2.01

2.01   Credibility of Witnesses

You are the sole judges of the credibility of the witnesses and of the weight to be given to the testimony of each of them.   In determining the credit to be given any witness you may take into account his ability and opportunity to observe, his memory, his manner while testifying, any interest, bias or prejudice he may have, and the reasonableness of his testimony considered in the light of all the evidence in the case.

Comment

Lundquist v. Chicago Rys. Co., 305 Ill. 106, 137 N.E. 92 (1922); *People v. Goodrich,* 251 Ill. 558, 96 N.E. 542 (1911); *Schlumbrecht v. Chicago City Ry. Co.,* 153 Ill.App. 254 (1st Dist.1910); *Sommese v. Maling Bros., Inc.,* 36 Ill.2d 263, 222 N.E.2d 468 (1966).

*Reprinted with permission of West Group.

Jury instructions generally contain the text of the instruction and case or statutory authorities from which the instruction was derived. See Illustration 13-3.

PRACTICE POINTER

Always determine whether pattern or approved instructions are required.

▼ Do the Federal Courts Have Pattern Jury Instructions?

No. The federal courts generally are guided by the instructions found in *Federal Jury Practice Instructions Civil and Criminal 4th Edition,* published by West Group. These samples are widely regarded and are available in computerized format. Along with the proposed jury instructions, this source includes citations to relevant authorities and some commentary about the origin of the instruction. Another source of sample federal instructions and citations to authorities is *Modern Federal Jury Instructions: Criminal and Civil,* written by Leonard Sand and published by Matthew Bender.

▼ Are Jury Instructions Available Online?

Yes. WESTLAW has a selection of jury instructions online. For example, the California, Washington, and Illinois pattern jury instructions can be accessed on WESTLAW. The *Federal Jury Practice Instructions Civil and Criminal 4th Edition* also is available on WESTLAW.

▼ What Type of Research Should Be Done Before You Draft Jury Instructions?

First, you should be somewhat familiar with the case and the underlying law of the case. However, if you are just asked to retrieve a jury instruction this may not be necessary. Jury instructions are read to the juries deliberating a variety of cases. Some jury instructions include references to primary authorities that often are the basis for the instruction. Sometimes these sources can be useful in finding primary binding authority. However, you should carefully read the source to ensure that it in fact states the law as described in the jury instruction.

▼ How Do You Find Jury Instructions?

Browse through the online card catalog and library shelves and ask the library staff. Once you locate the proper jury instructions, use the index or table of contents to find the appropriate jury instruction.

5. Other Tools

▼ What Other Tools Might a Paralegal Use in Researching a Problem?

Use your ingenuity when researching any problem. Often you are asked to research factual questions as well as legal questions. For example, your firm may want some information about a corporation one of your clients hopes to acquire, and you have been asked to find as much information as possible. One source would be *Dun & Bradstreet Reports,* which provides information about the corporate officers, the date of incorporation, and capitalization. Additional information often can be obtained from the state's secretary of state.

Also consider reviewing popular press magazines. Many local libraries and law libraries have computerized indexes to such magazines. Some libraries have magazines on CD-ROMs. These indexes allow you to search the CD-ROM index and then insert the CD-ROM that contains the article. Often you can print the article onto a laser printer, a process that is far easier than the microfiche and photocopying that may be necessary if the magazine is not available on CD-ROM.

Brainstorm whenever you are approached about a problem and always consider the sources at the local library.

▼ How Do You Locate Lawyers and Law Firms in Other States or within a State?

The *Martindale-Hubbell Law Directory* lists most attorneys nationwide. This is a voluntary directory, however, so some attorneys have chosen to be excluded. In addition to the free individual listings that include the person's name, address, degrees, and the name of the institute from which the person obtained his or her law degree, some firms pay to publish larger firm directories that list the firm, its areas of expertise, if any, the names of the individual attorneys, and a biography about each attorney. See Illustrations 13-4 and 13-5. In addition,

ILLUSTRATION 13-4. *Martindale-Hubbell Law Directory: Individual Entry*

Typical Subscriber Full Practice Profiles follow:

Firm Subscriber:

Interstate Rating Transfer

Firm Rating

Bar Register Listing Indicator

Firm Name —— **Letterman & Lewandowski, (AV⊤) BR** ←
713 Shady Lane, 94111⊙
Contact Information —— Telephone: 415-555-1313
Email: lawinfo@lettlew.com URL: http://www.lettlew.com
Members of Firm: Mitchell J. Letterman; Marie Lewandowski; — Arlene Catello.
General Practice, Trials, Banking Estate Planning and Probate Law.
Statement of Practice —— Representative Clients: California Home Security, Inc.; American Flight School, Inc.; West Coast Recycling Co.; American Fire Insurance Corp.
Reference: Pacific National Bank.
Clients —— Berkeley, California Office: Suite 3500, Johnson Place. Telephone: 510-555-4563.

Biographical Listing Reference —— *See Professional Biographies, SAN FRANCISCO, CALIFORNIA*

Firm — members, associates, etc.:

College Degree

Year of First Admission

Attorney Rating   College Code   Law School Code

Year of Birth

Attorney Name —— **Bershad, Abe M., (AV)** . . . . '35 '60 C.681 B.S. L.1066 J.D. [Davis & J.]
*PRACTICE AREAS: Insurance Law (68).

Firm Information

Number of Cases

Law School Degree

Individual subscriber:

Year of First Admission   College Degree

Attorney Rating   College Code   Law School Code

Year of Birth

Attorney Name —— **Schetlick, Robert M., (AV) '41 '65 C.816 B.S. L.705 J.D. BR** ←
Suite 3500, Johnson Place, 07974⊙
Bar Register Indicator
Contact Information —— Telephone: 908-555-4563 FAX: 908-555-4972
Email: schetlick@netadd.com URL: http://netadd.com/schetlick
(Also Of Counsel to Aiello & Smertick)
Law School Degree
Additional Firm Information —— *PRACTICE AREAS: Insurance Law (125).
Representative Client: East Coast Recycling Corp.
Approved Attorney For: SMAD Title Insurance Co.
Summit, New Jersey Office: 713 Shady Lane, Telephone: 908-555-1313.

See Professional Biographies, FLANDERS, NEW JERSEY

Biographical Listing Reference   Number of Cases

PATENT AND TRADEMARK PRACTICE PROFILES (BLUE PAGES)

This Section contains the names of subscribing lawyers registered to practice Patent Law and those who practice Trademark Law before the United States Patent and Trademark Office and who devote a considerable portion of their practice or duties to this field of law. It is arranged in the same manner as the Practice Profiles Section.

ILLUSTRATION 13-4. *Continued*

PROFESSIONAL BIOGRAPHIES (WHITE PAGES)

The Professional Biographies Section is arranged alphabetically by state, by city or town, and then by name of attorney or law firm. It provides substantial biographical information on individual attorneys within law firms. Entries in this section include the firm name, contact information, statement of practice, firm profile, individual biographical information, representative clients and references.

A typical entry appears as follows:

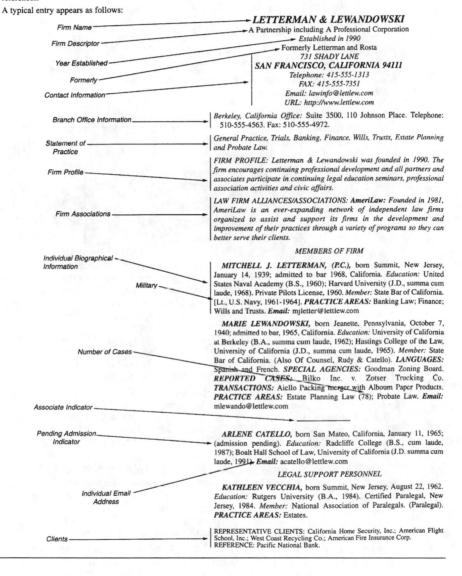

Firm Name — **LETTERMAN & LEWANDOWSKI**

Firm Descriptor — A Partnership including A Professional Corporation

Established in 1990

Formerly Letterman and Rosta

Year Established — *731 SHADY LANE*

SAN FRANCISCO, CALIFORNIA 94111

Formerly — *Telephone: 415-555-1313*

FAX: 415-555-7351

Contact Information — *Email: lawinfo@lettlew.com*

URL: http://www.lettlew.com

Branch Office Information — *Berkeley, California Office:* Suite 3500, 110 Johnson Place. Telephone: 510-555-4563. Fax: 510-555-4972.

Statement of Practice — *General Practice, Trials, Banking, Finance, Wills, Trusts, Estate Planning and Probate Law.*

Firm Profile — *FIRM PROFILE: Letterman & Lewandowski was founded in 1990. The firm encourages continuing professional development and all partners and associates participate in continuing legal education seminars, professional association activities and civic affairs.*

Firm Associations — *LAW FIRM ALLIANCES/ASSOCIATIONS: AmeriLaw:* Founded in 1981, AmeriLaw is an ever-expanding network of independent law firms organized to assist and support its firms in the development and improvement of their practices through a variety of programs so they can better serve their clients.

MEMBERS OF FIRM

Individual Biographical Information — **MITCHELL J. LETTERMAN, (P.C.),** born Summit, New Jersey, January 14, 1939; admitted to bar 1968, California. *Education:* United States Naval Academy (B.S., 1960); Harvard University (J.D., summa cum laude, 1968). Private Pilots License, 1960. *Member:* State Bar of California.

Military — [Lt., U.S. Navy, 1961-1964]. ***PRACTICE AREAS:*** Banking Law; Finance; Wills and Trusts. *Email:* mjletter@lettlew.com

MARIE LEWANDOWSKI, born Jeanette, Pennsylvania, October 7, 1940; admitted to bar, 1965, California. *Education:* University of California at Berkeley (B.A., summa cum laude, 1962); Hastings College of the Law, University of California (J.D., summa cum laude, 1965). *Member:* State Bar of California. (Also Of Counsel, Rudy & Catello). ***LANGUAGES:*** Spanish and French. ***SPECIAL AGENCIES:*** Goodman Zoning Board.

Number of Cases — ***REPORTED CASES:*** Bilko Inc. v. Zotser Trucking Co. ***TRANSACTIONS:*** Aiello Packing merger with Album Paper Products. ***PRACTICE AREAS:*** Estate Planning Law (78); Probate Law. *Email:* mlewando@lettlew.com

Associate Indicator —

Pending Admission Indicator — **ARLENE CATELLO,** born San Mateo, California, January 11, 1965; (admission pending). *Education:* Radcliffe College (B.S., cum laude, 1987); Boalt Hall School of Law, University of California (J.D. summa cum laude, 1991). *Email:* acatello@lettlew.com

LEGAL SUPPORT PERSONNEL

Individual Email Address — **KATHLEEN VECCHIA,** born Summit, New Jersey, August 22, 1962. *Education:* Rutgers University (B.A., 1984). Certified Paralegal, New Jersey, 1984. *Member:* National Association of Paralegals. (Paralegal). ***PRACTICE AREAS:*** Estates.

Clients — REPRESENTATIVE CLIENTS: California Home Security, Inc.; American Flight School, Inc.; West Coast Recycling Co.; American Fire Insurance Corp. REFERENCE: Pacific National Bank.

ILLUSTRATION 13-5. *Martindale-Hubbell Law Directory:* **Firm Entry**

HARRIS KESSLER & GOLDSTEIN ①

A Partnership of Professional Corporations
640 NORTH LA SALLE STREET ②
SUITE 590
CHICAGO, ILLINOIS 60610-3731
Telephone: 312-280-0111
Fax: 312-280-8232
URL: http://www.hkgold.com ③

Waukegan, Illinois Office: 5 South County Street, Suite 200, 60085. ④
Telephone: 847-263-1919. Fax: 847-244-8891.

General Business Practice including Litigation, Secured Lending, Real Estate, ⑤
Health Care and Estate Planning.

⑥*STEVEN M. HARRIS,* born Chicago, Illinois, May 30, 1956; admitted
to bar, 1981, Illinois. Education: Northern Illinois University (B.S., Fi-
nance, magna cum la[...]cago-
Kent College of La[...]rican
Academy of Orthopa[...]ssor,
Practice Management[...]hool,
1988—. Faculty, U[...]88—.
Trustee, 1989—; Tre[...]Park
District Foundation. [...]Law;
Estate Planning. *Em*[...]

> 1 Firm name
> 2 Address
> 3 E-mail address
> 4 Other offices
> 5 Type of practice
> 6 Individual attorney listings
> 7 E-mail address

RICHARD N. KESSLER, born Harvey, Illinois, September 6, 1957;
admitted to bar, 1982, Illinois, U.S. District Court, Northern District of
Illinois and U.S. Court of Appeals, Seventh Circuit. *Education:* University
of Illinois (B.A., 1979); Illinois Institute of Technology; Chicago-Kent Col-
lege of Law (J.D., 1982). Teacher, Business Law, Barat College, 1987.
Assistant State's Attorney, Lake County State's Attorney Office, 1982-1984.
Member: Lake County and Illinois State Bar Associations; Lake County
Volunteer Lawyers Project. *REPORTED CASES:* Poeta v. Sheridan Point
Shopping Plaza, 195 Ill.App.3d 852, 552 N.E.2d 1248 (2d Dist. 1990);
Goldstein v. Mitchell, 144 Ill.App.3d 474, 494 N.E.2d 914 (2d Dist. 1986).
PRACTICE AREAS: Civil Litigation. *Email:* rkessler@hkgold.com

JOHN A. GOLDSTEIN, born Chicago, Illinois, July 27, 1959; admit-
ted to bar, 1984, Illinois and U.S. District Court, Northern District of
Illinois. *Education:* Washington University (A.B., magna cum laude, 1981);
Northwestern University (J.D., 1984). Phi Beta Kappa. *Member:* Chicago
Mortgage Attorneys' Association. *PRACTICE AREAS:* Real Estate Law;
Secured Lending. *Email:* jgold@hkgold.com

RICK L. HINDMAND, born Lincoln, Nebraska, March 23, 1959; ad-
mitted to bar, 1986, Illinois, 1993, Pennsylvania. *Education:* Northwestern
University (B.A., with honors, 1981); University of Michigan (J.D., cum
laude, 1986). *Member:* Chicago Bar Association; American Health Lawyers
Association; Illinois Association of Healthcare Attorneys. *PRACTICE
AREAS:* Health Care; Corporate Law. *Email:* hindmand@hkgold.com

TERRI L. RUDD, born Chicago, Illinois, July 18, 1957; admitted to
bar, 1983, New York; 1984, U.S. District Court, Southern District of New
York; 1993, Illinois and U.S. District Court, Northern District of Illinois.
Education: University of Michigan (A.B., high honors in Political Science,
1979); New York University (J.D., 1982). Phi Beta Kappa. Pi Sigma Alpha.
Recipient, William J. Branstrom Freshman Prize. James B. Angell Scholar.
Moot Court Board, Research Editor. *Member:* Chicago, New York State,
Illinois State and American Bar Associations; Decalogue Society of Law-
yers. *PRACTICE AREAS:* Commercial Litigation. *Email:* trudd@⑦
hkgold.com

Martindale has a rating system for lawyers that is based on solicitations of confidential opinions of members of the bar.

WESTLAW also has the *West's Directory of Lawyers*. Again, this is a voluntary service and not all attorneys choose to be listed.

Many states have a statewide legal directory similar to the *Wisconsin Legal Directory*. This directory and others like it provide the name of federal and state offices, addresses, and phone numbers. In addition, information about the federal, state, and local courts is provided. An alphabetical attorney roster provides information about how to contact an individual attorney.

CHAPTER SUMMARY

Paralegals find that formbooks can be invaluable tools. These commercially published books provide guidance in drafting real estate contracts, court motions, estate plans, and the like. However, these are only guides, and the paralegal should always double-check the accuracy and timeliness of the forms they contain.

Practitioner's materials such as checklists and continuing legal education books can be of great assistance to paralegal researchers. Checklists offer step-by-step guidance for handling a variety of legal matters ranging from a real estate closing to the preparation of a will. CLE materials generally concentrate an individual areas of the law and are particularly good at explaining new or developing legal topics. The type and variety of continuing legal education materials available vary by state.

Jury instructions, including pattern jury instructions, are drafted when a case is presented to a jury. Various books provide sample jury instructions concerning various legal issues. When a state has adopted pattern jury instructions, these instructions must be used.

Legal directories provide information about lawyers, their law firms, and their practices. Some directories also include information about local court phone numbers, rules, and court reporters. There are national and local legal directories.

KEY TERMS

checklists	jury instructions
CLE materials	*Martindale-Hubbell Law Directory*
formbooks	pattern jury instructions
handbooks	

EXERCISES

FORMBOOKS

1. Find a sample power of attorney for your state. What book did you review and why?

CHECKLISTS
2. Find a real estate closing checklist for a residential real estate closing. Where did you look and why?

CLE MATERIALS
3. Find a continuing legal education book that covers estate planning in your state.

HARDCOPY JURY INSTRUCTIONS
4. Locate a civil jury instruction for nominal damages in your state.
5. Find a criminal jury instruction for reasonable doubt.
6. Find a criminal jury instruction for the definition of *recklessly* in your state.

JURY INSTRUCTIONS ONLINE
7. Access the Washington pattern instructions and find the instruction that defines *compensatory damages*.
8. Access the Illinois pattern instructions and find the instruction that defines *punitive damages*.
9. Find the federal jury instructions that explain *retaliatory discharge*.

USING THE *MARTINDALE-HUBBELL LAW DIRECTORY*
10. For attorneys listed in the front section of the *Martindale-Hubbell Law Directory,* what does the abbreviation 851 in the law school code section indicate?
11. What is an AV rating in *Martindale-Hubbell?*

RESEARCH STRATEGY

(— Facts
— Organization)

CHAPTER OVERVIEW

Research involves planning. The more planning, the more effective the research. This chapter gives you step-by-step techniques to use when researching. You begin by educating yourself on a legal topic that pertains to the issue you are researching. You are then advised to note all of the pertinent information that you find during the research process so that you have a complete record of your findings and complete citations to those findings. Finally, you are reminded to update and to validate all of your findings.

Focusing on your issue and knowing when to stop researching are two skills that you must master. As a paralegal, you must always evaluate how much time it takes to research and to weigh cost with accuracy and thoroughness. This chapter helps you achieve the necessary balance required to effectively research a legal topic.

A. DEFINE THE ISSUES AND DETERMINE AREA OF LAW

▼ Where Do You Begin Your Research?

First, gather all facts that are relevant to your problem and define the legal issues. The **facts** and the law guide your research. Ask a lot of questions of the client and of the attorney who assigns the problem. Clarify anything that is unclear. Frame the issue or review the issue framed by the attorney assigning the project.

Discerning the area of law is the second phase in beginning your research. The issues and the facts indicate what area of law is involved in the problem. If you are unclear as to the jurisdiction or the issues, ask the attorney. For example, will the question be resolved by tort law? By constitutional law? By the law of real property?

Make a list of important terms or words that describe the facts and the legal problem. These words help later when you are using an index. You may also want to use a legal dictionary to look up any word or term that sounds unfamiliar. (See Chapter 5 for a discussion on secondary sources.)

B. REFINING RESEARCH

▼ How Do You Refine Your Research Strategy?

After defining the legal issues and determining the area of law to research, you have to devise a systematic approach to the research process.

At times your knowledge of an area of law is not complete. The best way to gain an overview of the subject is by consulting secondary sources. Hornbooks or textbooks about a particular subject are helpful because they explain the law in everyday language and indicate the legal rules and important cases. Generally, treatises are too detailed for the time constraints that you will be under; however, sometimes they may be valuable. (See Chapter 5 for a complete discussion of secondary sources.)

A quick way to find the appropriate legal rule, particularly when the issue involves state law and you do not know whether a statute or a case governs the situation, is to consult a **West Law Finder.** For example, *West's Illinois Law Finder* can be used to find the controlling law relating to dramshops. The appropriate statute citation is indicated. If a case controlled in this instance, a citation to the case would be included.

Once you have educated yourself in the area of law, turn to a legal encyclopedia to obtain case citations. If a statute is involved, use an annotated statute for the relevant jurisdiction. This is particularly helpful when you are performing research for a problem dealing with state law.

For an overview of the law, in a format that is not too scholarly or detailed, use a legal encyclopedia. State legal encyclopedias are helpful in areas of state law research and enable you to find the general legal rule and citations to important cases quickly. Reading the pertinent encyclopedia section also helps you to create a **research vocabulary** that you can use when consulting indexes or constructing search strategies on LEXIS and WESTLAW. Legal encyclopedias can also provide you with citations to primary authority.

Once you find an excellent case or cases, go to the digests and use the one good case method. (See Chapter 3 for a detailed discussion on digest use.)

Most important, once you find pertinent authority to address the issue that you are researching, you must update and validate the authority. Updating and validating authority is performed by using *Shepard's*. *Shepard's* indicates whether the case or the statute that you are relying on is still good law by indicating how subsequent courts viewed the decision. The cited cases in *Shepard's* are also newer cases that interpret the legal rule you are researching. Remember to update your *Shepard's* information by consulting the hardcopy supplements. If you are using LEXIS to validate the authority, Shepardize the cites and use LEXCITE, which indicates where your case has been cited in subsequent decisions. If time and money allow, use all of the updating and citing sources available online.

At this point, reexamine the issue that you formulated when you received the assignment. Review the vocabulary words that you listed to describe the legal issue and the factual scenario. Revise the issue to reflect your enhanced knowledge of the subject. Create an outline of the subissues raised by the problem. Remember three terms— reexamine, review, and revise—when you are performing research to find relevant information. Research involves educating yourself; as you learn more about an issue, your research becomes more focused and more precise.

Remember to stay focused on your issue or issues. While gathering relevant information, it is easy to stray into related but inapplicable areas. Staying focused on your issues also is cost-effective because you do not waste valuable time on irrelevant information.

C. DIAGRAMMING THE RESEARCH PROCESS

▼ What Is the Purpose and Technique for Record Keeping?

Record keeping and **note taking** are essential to effective legal research because they leave a written audit trail of all the sources consulted and the information derived from those sources. Records should also include sources consulted that did not contain pertinent information so that you do not reexamine those sources if you must expand your research at a later time. Another essential component of record keeping is to write the official Bluebook citation for each source that contains information helpful to your research. Establishing the complete citation at the time you are researching means you do not need to retrace your research steps to obtain citation information later on, particularly when you are writing.

Write out the proper Bluebook citation for every source, document, case, and statute that you use. Take notes as you read and indicate in parentheses the page on which you found the information from within the text of the source. For instance, if the case begins on page 1382, but the holding is on page 1389, write out the holding and then indicate parenthetically (1389) so that you know exactly where the information was found within the document.

Make a list of each source that you consult. List sources, citations, and any information obtained from the consulted source on a separate sheet. For example, you may find a useful A.L.R. annotation. Put the A.L.R. annotation at the top of the page in the correct Bluebook format. List all pertinent information relating to your research issue and the pages on which you found that information. Add any pertinent cites to cases and to statutes listed in the source to the sheet. The objective is to create a sheet of information that includes all of the relevant information obtained from the source consulted so that you do not have to go back and review the source again. Also include information indicating whether you Shepardized the document and the date of Shepardizing so that you may redo it if too much time lapses. Note any significant information obtained from *Shepard's* about the document, for instance, if the case was criticized.

EXAMPLE OF RECORD KEEPING

Below is an example of a case brief that supplies the primary authority for a legal memo addressing the topic of the effective rejection of a defective product. Some of the material in the brief has been created for the purpose of the example. Pinpoint citations are noted for all parallel cites.

CITATION
Olson Rug Co. v. Smarto, 55 Ill. App. 2d 348, 204 N.E.2d 838 (1965)

FACTS
On March 16, 1962, Marty and Rose Smarto signed a contract with Olson Rug Company for the purchase of $450.62 worth of carpeting. They paid $120.00 as a down payment and agreed to pay the balance in monthly installments. The contract clearly stated that if the Smartos defaulted on payments, not only did the outstanding balance become immediately due, at Ill. App. 2d 349, 204 N.E.2d 839, but Olson Rug had irrevocable authority to have an attorney represent them and seek to have a judgment confessed against them. At N.E.2d 841. Prior to signing the agreement, Olson Rug assured the Smartos that the color and nap of the carpet would withstand their intended use for it. At Ill. App. 2d 350. Two weeks after installation of the carpet, the color faded and the nap lost its original shape. After two more weeks, the Smartos notified Olson Rug's agent and asked him to take the carpet back. At N.E.2d 842. He refused the request. The Smartos did not return the carpet, continued to use it, and apparently stopped paying installments. At Ill. App. 2d 351. Approximately one year later Olson Rug sought a judgment by confession against the Smartos for the outstanding balance and court costs. At Ill. App. 2d 351 and N.E.2d 842.

ISSUE
Whether buyer's continued use of the carpet for more than one year after discovering that the seller delivered a defective product demonstrates effective rejection. At Ill. App. 2d 351 and N.E.2d 841.

HOLDING
No, buyer's continued use of the carpet for more than one year after having discovered the defects does not indicate a timely rejection of the carpet or defective goods. At Ill. App. 2d 351 and N.E.2d 841.

RATIONALE
A buyer, upon discovering goods to be defective shortly after delivery, should soon thereafter return or offer to return the goods to the seller. The Smartos neither returned the carpeting nor offered to return it. For that reason, the court held that the Smartos, through

their more than one-year-long delay, waived their right to rescind the carpet purchase contract. At Ill. App. 2d 350 and N.E.2d 840.

DISPOSITION

The appellate court affirmed the circuit court's decision to deny the defendants' motion to open or vacate the judgment confessed against them. At Ill. App. 2d 351 and N.E.2d 841.

All of the page numbers, indicating where the information is found within the text of the case, are included. This helps you when you are writing your memo and must include citation references to the case. You will not have to go back to the reporter and review the case again when your brief contains all of the page references and the complete Bluebook citation.

D. EXAMPLE OF RESEARCH STRATEGY

PROBLEM

Mrs. Jones bought a fur coat from John J. Furriers. The coat was labeled 100 percent raccoon. One day Mrs. Jones was smoking a cigarette and a hot ash accidentally fell on the coat while she was wearing it. The ash melted a hole in the coat. Mrs. Jones knew that fur burns, but acrylic melts.

1. How to Phrase the Issue If You Are Researching the Fur Labeling Problem

ISSUE

Whether a furrier is liable to a consumer for mislabeling a product.

2. First Steps

First, perform **background research** using secondary sources to educate yourself about the area of law. This helps you become familiar with the types of legal materials controlling the issue. The background research provides information indicating whether the topic (in our problem, fur labeling) is controlled by statutes, cases, or regulations and whether federal or state law controls. You should develop a research vocabulary from your readings that helps you use the index volumes more effectively.

Start with the descriptive word index of the relevant state statute and the descriptive word index of the *United States Code Annotated* (U.S.C.A.) or the *United States Code Service* (U.S.C.S.) to see if any federal statutes have been violated. The words to check would be

label, fur, and **product mislabeling.** The annotated statutes would be checked to see if any relevant cases are cited discussing or analyzing the issue. Any relevant cases would be Shepardized, and the *Shepard's* citations would be updated by using the paperbound *Shepard's Supplements. Shepard's* indicates the validity of the cases and the statutes and leads you to newer cases that discuss the same issue. *Shepard's* helps you find the on-point decisions that are most recent.

After determining that the relevant cases and statutes are valid, a thorough reading of the decisions is necessary. You should make a list of all of the cites checked at this point and place a check next to the cites that are valid. Add a check next to the cite after you have read the full text of the opinion or statute. This will save you time later if you expand your research. You can merely review your list of cites to see if it is valid and to see if you read the full text of the authority.

3. What Sources to Consult and Why

1. You would consult the U.S.C.A. or the *United States Code Service* (U.S.C.S.) because fur labeling is regulated by the Federal Trade Commission. An annotated code provides recent case references as well as references to administrative material (particularly the U.S.C.S., which provides references to administrative materials; see Chapter 6 for a discussion of statutes). Also, consumer fraud issues could be researched. Use the index to the U.S.C.A. and look up the applicable research terms that you derived from the secondary sources.

2. You would consult the *Code of Federal Regulations* (C.F.R.) to see the particular agency rules pertaining to fur labeling and intentional mislabeling. Use the index to the C.F.R. to find the appropriate titles that discuss furs, fur labeling, labeling, and labeling requirements. The research vocabulary that you generate are the words you look up in the index. (See Chapter 8 for C.F.R. use.)

3. You would consult the *American Law Reports* (A.L.R.) because this is a narrow, well-defined issue and the A.L.R. may have explored this issue thoroughly. The Federal Trade Commission might regulate fur labeling. (See Chapter 5 for a discussion on using the A.L.R.)

4. What to Do after Completing Hardcopy Research

Create a body of information on which to base your memo. Detailed note taking and careful citation to references on sheets of paper for each source are performed here. Also, keep a complete list of all sources consulted, whether a statute, case, regulation, periodical article, or other source. Your list of sources consulted helps later on when you may have to expand your research. You can then check the list to see if you already reviewed a source and to see if it was pertinent.

Remember to Shepardize any primary authority that you use in your memo. *Shepard's* ensures that the authority, whether it is a case, statute, or regulation, is still good or valid law.

Outline the issues that you discuss in your memo or letter. Insert the applicable legal authority under the outline entry.

Review your outline and evaluate whether you have sufficient legal authority to support and to resolve the issues raised by the problem. If you have sufficient authority, begin to write. If you do not have sufficient authority, expand your research. Your notes and list of the materials found help you to avoid duplicating your efforts and wasting time.

5. Combining Computerized Research Methods with Hardcopy Method

The principal difference between the hardcopy method and the combination computerized and hardcopy method is that instead of using indexes to the statutes, C.F.R., and the A.L.R., you construct a search query and search the materials online. You also search legal periodicals online with search queries. The validation, Shepardizing, is performed online as well.

Performing background research using secondary sources is very important for educating yourself in the area of law and for generating a research vocabulary to use later when constructing the research queries for LEXIS or WESTLAW. Secondary source research is still most efficiently and cost-effectively done with hardcopy sources.

Computerized legal research requires you to select precise words to retrieve documents that contain those words and that are on point. Using LEXIS and WESTLAW is most productive after you are versed in the subject and are aware of the words that judges, legislatures, and agencies use when writing about a legal topic.

6. Using Online Services in the Fur Labeling Problem

1. Using LEXIS, first search the U.S.C.S., found in the GENFED library, USCS file, for the appearance of any statutes addressing fur labeling. The query constructed and entered is **fur w/s label!**. *Fur* is an essential factual term. The connector *w/s* (the group of letters indicating to LEXIS the relationship between fur and label!) indicates that *fur* must be within the same sentence as *label*. This connector parallels written English and ensures that the terms keep their significance in the context of the document. For instance, using the connector *and* instead of *w/s* would require LEXIS to search for the appearance of the words fur and label anywhere in the document regardless of their proximity to one another. The exclamation point (!) after *label* indicates to LEXIS to search for all possible endings for the word *label*, so that *labeling* would be picked up as well as

labeled and *labels*. You are using LEXIS instead of the index to the U.S.C.S.

2. Use the same search again to see if any federal administrative regulations are relevant. Go into the GENFED library and CFR file on LEXIS and enter the query **fur w/s label!**. Review the sections of the C.F.R. retrieved to see if any are on point. You are using LEXIS instead of the C.F.R. index. Remember that you can update C.F.R. citations on LEXIS. (See Chapter 8 for a discussion on updating C.F.R. provisions.)

3. Use the same search a third time to find A.L.R. annotations. Use the GENFED library, the ALR file, and type **fur w/s label!**. Once again, your query is a substitute for using the index to the A.L.R. You will find annotations discussing fur labeling and references to primary authority.

Read the text of any material that you found on LEXIS. It is most cost-effective to use the citations to the materials found on LEXIS and read the full text source in hardcopy format, if the hardcopy is available. Take detailed notes. List all of the sources that you consult. Write the Bluebook citation for each source. Update and Shepardize any primary authority on which you will rely. Use *Shepard's* on LEXIS to update and to validate case law. Use either LEXIS or WESTLAW to obtain the C.F.R. section and to make sure that the C.F.R. provision is current.

At this point, you must create an outline of the issues and sub-issues to be addressed. Insert the appropriate legal authority under each outline category. Expand your research if you do not have sufficient authority.

PRACTICE POINTER

Take advantage of any training offered at your firm or through legal publishers. Publishers and online database vendors offer training, very often for free, that will enhance your research skills and help you become familiar with new products. Sometimes existing products are very complex, and training will help you use the resources efficiently.

SUMMARY CHECKLIST

I. When you receive the problem:
   a. Clarify legal issues being researched
   b. Determine relevant jurisdiction
   c. Determine area of the law
   d. Gather all of the facts

      e. Draft a statement of the issue or question that you are researching

  II. Introductory research

      a. Educate yourself in the area of law

      b. Scan a hornbook or textbook on the subject

      c. Learn the relevant vocabulary

      d. Note the major cases

      e. Make an outline of the issues and subissues of your problem

 III. Targeted research

      a. Use a legal encyclopedia or an annotated statute (use descriptive word index), particularly helpful for matters involving state law, to find discussion of legal issue and relevant case and statute citations

      b. Go to the digest for the relevant jurisdiction, and use the one good case method to find other cases

      c. Shepardize to find other cites and to validate your citations before relying on them as authority. Use *Shepard's* in the hardcopy format if the online version is too costly for the assignment's budget or if it is unavailable. Always remember to check the supplements to *Shepard's* to ensure that the references are up-to-date.

      d. Brief cases and relate them to one another (see Chapter 22 on Synthesis)

      e. Review the outline of the issues and subissues that you drafted. Revise the outline to reflect your increased knowledge of the subject.

 IV. Computerized research

      a. Particularly helpful when the facts are unique and the legal issue is narrow (for instance, whether malpractice occurred during the insertion of a chin implant), not broad (for instance, whether a breach of contract occurred)

      b. Best to be thorough and combine computerized and hardcopy methods

  V. Create an audit trail of your research

      a. Take notes of sources and location, including page number, in Bluebook format

      b. Note whether Shepardizing has been completed and date completed

 VI. Organizing your research findings

      a. Review the outline of the issues and the subissues that you created and revise it to reflect any new knowledge

      b. Insert the applicable authority discussing the relevant subissue under the appropriate outline heading

      c. Review the filled-in outline to make sure that you have found adequate authority to address each subissue listed

      d. If you have sufficient legal authority, begin to write. If you do not have sufficient legal authority, expand your research. Always check your list of sources consulted when you are expanding your research to make sure that you do not waste precious time with sources that you have already consulted.

CHAPTER SUMMARY

This chapter led you through the entire research process from initially receiving the project to completing research. Refining the issue at the beginning and focusing on your important sources are as essential as knowing when to stop researching. This chapter and your own experience will guide you through this process. Keep records of all sources consulted and make sure that your citations are accurate; these help when you are ready to write. Also, do not forget to Shepardize all necessary documents and to update all resources. Now you are equipped to write.

KEY TERMS

background research

facts

note taking

record keeping

research vocabulary

West Law Finder

EXERCISES

RESEARCHING IN GENERAL

1. Before you begin a research project, what general questions should you resolve with the assigning attorney?
2. What is the benefit of record keeping when researching?

HARDCOPY RESEARCH

3. You have just received a research project. Outline your research plan using hardcopy resources.
4. Read the following fact pattern and answer the questions.

Facts

John Clark comes to your firm with a question regarding the tax status of his residence. John Clark was just ordained as a Methodist minister. He will be receiving a housing allowance from First Methodist Church, where he will be an assistant pastor. He wants to know if this housing allowance can be excluded from income on his tax return even though the residence is his own.

a. How would you phrase this issue if you were researching this problem using hardcopy resources?
b. What would be your research strategy using hardcopy resources?
c. List three sources that you would consult. Why would you consult them?

HARDCOPY AND ONLINE RESEARCH COMBINED

5. Draw a flow chart of your research strategy using a combination of hardcopy and computerized resources.
6. Read the following fact pattern and answer the questions.

Facts

On November 29, 1993, Michael Jones purchased a used truck from Grimy's Auto and Truck Service. At the time of purchase, Grimy's stated that the engine was completely overhauled and consisted of rebuilt and reconditioned parts, all parts were guaranteed, and invoices for all new parts would be provided. On November 13, 1994, after using the truck for almost one year, Jones discovered that several engine parts were not rebuilt or reconditioned and other engine parts were defective, which caused the truck to break down. This resulted in lost wages and lost profits for Jones. Jones made repairs to the truck on November 13, 1994, December 13, 1994, and December 16, 1994. Jones did not attempt to return the truck and did not notify Grimy's that the truck was defective. The truck is currently disabled in Columbus, Ohio. Jones came to your firm because he wants to sue Grimy's for damages for breach of contract.

Issue

Is Jones entitled to receive damages for breach of contract because the truck does not conform to the terms of the agreement? Remember that Grimy's will assert that Jones continued to use the truck for more than a reasonable time and failed to return the truck or to notify Grimy's of its defects in a timely manner.

a. What would be your research strategy if you were using a combination of hardcopy and computerized resources?
b. How would you educate yourself on the relevant topic so that you could find primary sources?
c. List one secondary source and two primary sources that you would consult. Why would you consult these sources?
d. Use either LEXIS or WESTLAW and formulate a search query that you could use to find primary authority.

LEGAL WRITING

GETTING READY TO WRITE

CHAPTER OVERVIEW

Writing involves planning—the more planning, the more effective the written document. Legal writing has three components: prewriting (which includes researching and planning your written document), drafting, and revising. This chapter explains how to draft documents and how to revise your work so that it is written clearly and concisely. This chapter provides step-by-step techniques to use when preparing to write. You must systematically prepare to write by determining the purpose, audience, and organization of the document and carefully revise your work product to tailor it precisely to the assignment, the client, and the facts. The focus of this chapter is the fundamentals of good writing. Specific tips are provided to improve your drafts.

A. WRITING GOALS AND HOW TO ACHIEVE THEM

The keys to writing well are **clarity** and **organization.** Your readers must understand what you are trying to convey to them. Whether you are writing a letter or a memorandum, your communication must be clear so that it can be understood. Often several proper formats, used at different times, will make your writing easier to read and understand.

▼ How Do You Plan Your Communication and Revise It?

You must think about what you want to say. Outline the communication. Next, write it using correct grammar and spelling, and most important, rewrite it several times. As you rewrite your letters and memos, you will always find that you can eliminate unnecessary words and legalese. Use simple words even though you know more elaborate ones. Doing so makes your writing inviting rather than pompous.

B. THE WRITING PROCESS

Follow a method or format when preparing to write to make the actual drafting process easier. Focus on the mechanics and components of the writing process rather than the finished product. The method that follows is a checklist to ensure thoroughness and to give you confidence in your newly acquired skills. The fundamental components of process writing are assessing the document's purpose and intended audience, drafting a detailed outline before writing, revising your findings into the categories of purpose and audience, and outlining and revising your work.

1. Preparing to Write: <u>Purpose</u> and <u>Audience</u>

▼ How Do You Complete the Research Process and Make the Transition to Writing?

Remember that what we plan as we prepare to write is as important as the final product. The more time you can put into the process, the better the product. Spend at least 50 percent of the time budgeted for writing in the **prewriting stage.** However, time management is crucial with any assignment because time is money and knowing when to stop researching and when to begin writing is important. Therefore, when the project is assigned ask how much time you should spend on the project. What is the budget? A good clue as to when you have completed your research is when you do not retrieve any new information; the same sources keep appearing. Ask your law librarian or another paralegal to briefly review your research strategy and ask if there are any other avenues that he or she would have taken.

Take detailed notes and make careful citations to references for each source. Also, keep a complete list of all sources consulted, whether a statute, case, regulation, periodical article, or other source. Your list of sources consulted helps later on, when you may have to expand your research. You can then check the list to see if you already reviewed a source and to see if it was pertinent.

Shepardize any primary authority that you use in your memo. *Shepard's* ensures that the authority, whether it is a case, statute, or regulation, is still good or valid law. Never start to write using a source of authority without Shepardizing it first.

a. Purpose

▼ What Is the Purpose of the Document?

When you sit down to write, begin by asking yourself: What is the **purpose** of the document that I am preparing? Because a legal document has a variety of goals (to inform, persuade, or advise), you must determine the document's intent before writing. The purpose determines the posture and the format of your work product. If the document is to inform the attorney as to all available law on a particular issue, it is neutral in tone and takes the form of an objective memo. If your goal is to convince another party that your position is correct, then the document may be in the form of a memo for the assigning attorney, a memo for the court, a trial or an appellate brief, and the tone will be persuasive. Sometimes a persuasive document takes the form of a letter that requests an individual or entity to act in a certain way. Examples of persuasive letters are demand letters requesting payment owed, or eviction letters demanding that a tenant vacate the premises. Sometimes you must advise a client as to an action that he or she must take. The document may then be in the form of a letter giving counsel but one that is written as simply as possible; a client usually does not have a legal education. The purpose of the document determines its format and the rhetorical stance: objective, persuasive, or instructive.

b. Audience

▼ To Whom Are You Speaking?

As you prepare to write, determine carefully who the **audience,** or reader, is. Is the reader the assigning attorney? This is often the case when the project is the preparation of an office memo. The memo should be easy for the intended reader to understand; you should insert headings, if necessary, to guide the reader. If the document is intended for a court, then the reader will be a judge and opposing counsel, and your tone will be formal yet persuasive. The assertions or points that you want to prove should be clear and straightforward. The document should always be prepared using language that the reader can comprehend; this is also required when drafting client letters and demand letters.

2. Drafting a Detailed Outline

▼ How Do You Organize Your Ideas?

The next stage is to prepare an **outline** of whatever document you are writing. If it is an office memo, outline the issues and subissues of points that you want to articulate. Make sure that the outline flows logically. See if there are any gaps by reviewing your outline carefully. Organization is crucial to effective legal writing to ensure completeness. Having a complete outline also helps when you have to put your project down for a considerable period of time, or when you must work on more than one matter at a time and easily want to pick up where you left off.

Organize your research findings according to where they are pertinent in your outline. It is best to let your issues or assertions determine where the research should be placed rather than letting the sources determine the placement in the document. Never use your sources as your outline; rely on the issues.

3. Revision: The Final Part of the Process

Rewriting is a continuous part of the writing process and a vital final step. Reread the material after you have reviewed your word choices and eliminated unnecessary words. Rewriting may seem like a tedious waste of time, but it is one of the most important steps in preparing a well-written document.

Review all of the steps you have taken in the prewriting stage. Ask yourself: Is the purpose of the document being prepared according to the assignment, and is it meeting the client's needs? Does the document clearly fulfill its goal of either informing, persuading, or advising? Do the language and format reflect the purpose?

Examine your intended audience. What language is appropriate for the intended reader? What level of sophistication is required? Ask yourself about voice (how it will sound), diction (word choice), and rhetoric (the way you use speech).

Review your outline. Check to see if the outline is well organized, logical, and flows smoothly. At this point, reexamine the issues or assertions that you want to include and make sure that the points are clearly discernible. Insert the appropriate research findings in the relevant place in the outline, as well as the necessary facts and the conclusions that you want to draw. Now you are ready to write.

After you write the first draft, revise and pay attention to the following details.

4. Example of Process Writing Techniques

Ms. Partner calls you into her office and asks that you prepare a client letter to Mrs. Jones advising her as to a course of action that she can take to rectify the problem of her mislabeled fur coat. The facts of the problem are as follows: Mrs. Jones bought a fur coat from John J. Furriers. The coat was labeled 100 percent raccoon. One day Mrs. Jones was smoking a cigarette and a hot ash fell on the coat while she was wearing it. The ash melted a hole in the coat. Mrs. Jones knew that fur burns, but acrylic melts.

First, what is the purpose of the document? The document's goal is to advise Mrs. Jones as to a course of action against the seller, John J. Furriers. The partner specified the document's form, a letter.

Next, you must examine your audience. Who is your reader? Is Mrs. Jones an attorney? Probably not. You can ask the attorney making the assignment some background information about the client. This will help you tailor a document to the reader's precise needs. Mrs. Jones is a stock analyst. She is a sophisticated individual but she does not possess a legal education. The language used in the letter must be understandable to Mrs. Jones. The voice, how the letter sounds, should be instructive and advisory without being condescending. The diction, or word choice, should be simple; avoid legalese.

Now outline the points that you want to address in the letter. Begin by restating the facts as you know them. List the points.

1. The fur coat was mislabeled.
2. The seller misrepresented his product.
3. If the misrepresentation was intentional, there is the possibility of fraud.
4. Mrs. Jones would like to obtain a full refund for the coat that she purchased.
5. If a refund is not given in seven days, court action will proceed.

Insert your research findings, in general language, in the appropriate spot in the outline. In a client letter of this nature there is no need to cite to authority. Use the facts and advise Mrs. Jones as to how she should proceed with the matter. Always remember that an attorney must always review and sign any letter that you prepare that gives legal advice. Only an attorney may sign such a letter.

Revise all of your prewriting steps by checking your purpose, audience, and outline once again. Now you are ready to write.

PRACTICE POINTER

Prewriting preparation is time well spent. Thoroughness and accuracy are so important, and attorneys have little patience for anything besides perfection. Careful note taking, outlining, and citing will provide not only an excellent start to a writing project but ample material if you are called on to discuss a project prior to its completion.

CHECKLIST

I. When you receive the problem
   a. Clarify the legal issues being researched.
   b. Determine the relevant jurisdiction.
   c. Determine the area of the law.
   d. Gather all of the facts.
   e. Draft a statement of the issue or question that you are researching.
II. Introductory research
   a. Educate yourself in the area of the law.
   b. Scan a hornbook or textbook on the subject.
   c. Learn the relevant vocabulary.
   d. Note the major cases.
   e. Make an outline of the issues and subissues of your problem.
III. Process writing
   a. Purpose: Determine the purpose of the document. The document's goal is either to inform, to persuade, or to advise. Select the appropriate rhetorical stance and determine the format (office memo, court memo, brief, or letter).
   b. Audience: Find out who the reader or readers will be. Determine the language that is most comprehensible to the particular reader. Select an appropriate voice for the purpose, format, and reader. Note your diction.
   c. Outline: Outline the issues, assertions, or points that you want to include. Organize research findings according to the outline. Place facts in the appropriate spot and state conclusion.
   d. Revise: Review the purpose and the audience of the intended document and check your outline for appropriateness. Revise your outline to reflect any new knowledge, legal or factual. Reread the outline to ensure that it is complete and flows logically.

CHAPTER SUMMARY

This chapter led you through the writing process. This will ensure thoroughness. Before writing, determine the purpose of your assignment.

This will guide your writing. Also, determine the audience for your work. This will determine the style of your writing. Carefully outline the document before writing and then revise the document by preparing an outline of the material that you prepared, an after-the-fact outline. Review the after-the-fact outline to make sure that it is logically organized and includes all of points that the issues require to be addressed.

The time that you spend in the prewriting stage ensures a better work product that is produced more efficiently than one created by lunging into the writing process. Think about what you want to say, outline it, and write it using good grammar and correct spelling. Then rewrite and edit your work. Prewriting takes planning, but with the methodology outlined in this chapter you will be equipped to write.

KEY TERMS

audience	prewriting stage
clarity	purpose
organization	rewriting
outline	

EXERCISES

PREPARING TO WRITE

1. Why would you use a process method for legal writing?
2. Why would you outline before you write as well as create an outline of your finished document?
3. Why is it important to determine the audience and purpose before writing?

PROCESS WRITING EXERCISE

4. Read the following fact pattern and answer the questions.

Facts

John Clark comes to your firm with a question regarding the tax status of his residence. He has just been ordained as a United Methodist minister and will be receiving a housing allowance from First United Methodist Church, where he will be an assistant pastor. He wants to know if this housing allowance can be excluded from income on his tax return even though the residence is his own.

a. How would you phrase this issue if you were researching this problem?
b. What would be your research strategy?
c. Construct an outline of this problem.

5. The assignment partner requests that you draft a letter of your findings to Rev. Clark. List, in detail, the purpose, audience, and resulting outline of the letter.

6. How would the purpose, audience, and outline change if the assignment partner requests a memo concerning your research findings? Once again, how would the purpose, audience, and outline change if you are requested to prepare a court brief?

EDITING

CHAPTER OVERVIEW

Preparing a first draft of a document can be quite an undertaking, but you have not completed your project until you carefully edit your work. This chapter provides you with guidance in editing and revising your documents and preparing them for clients, courts, and attorneys.

A. PURPOSE OF EDITING

Editing and revising are essential if you want to have well-drafted and organized documents. Few documents are written well after one draft. Good writing entails rewriting. Each time you review your document and revise it, you improve its content and make it more understandable. **Editing** allows you to review your organization, your word choices, and your grammar. It also enables you to determine whether the document you prepared is clear and will be understood by your audience.

B. PROCESS OF EDITING

When you review your draft, you should read it as if you were reading it for the first time. Pretend that you are a stranger to the project and that you don't know anything about it. Ensure that it is understandable.

Next, consider whether each part follows the next. The work should flow in a logical order. Consider whether the organization of the document or of any paragraphs or sentences in it should be revised.

Read your writing aloud. Do you notice anything is missing? Sometimes when you read a work aloud, you find that it is missing something needed to get you from point A to point B. Add any such missing elements.

Next, think about whether you can eliminate unnecessary words, a process called tightening or editing.

Note whether your writing contains transitions and easily flows from one section to the next. If it doesn't, revise it. Add transitional words or sentences where necessary.

Review your grammar. Ensure that your punctuation is correct and that the elements of each sentence and paragraph are correct. Check your citation for errors as well.

C. SPECIFIC ITEMS TO REVIEW WHILE EDITING

1. Diction

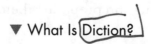
▼ What Is Diction?

Diction means choice of words when writing. Selecting the appropriate words to express your idea precisely is a skill that is developed over time. When you are revising a document, read it over to make sure that the words you selected to convey your ideas do precisely that. Sometimes you must use a dictionary or thesaurus to assist you in selecting the best word.

Select concrete words that allow the readers to visualize what you are saying. Read the following example:

He harmed one of his body parts in the device at issue in the case.

It is better to say:

His arm was severed when the threshing machine stalled and he fell forward in front of the machine.

The second example is clearer because the reader knows what happened and to which body part it happened: The arm was severed. The second sentence also conveys that the device was a threshing machine and that it stalled, throwing the man forward.

▼ What Are Concrete Verbs?

Use **concrete verbs** that exactly describe the action taken. Read the following examples:

The parties entered into an agreement on September 1, 1998.

There was an agreement entered into on September 1, 1998.

The parties agreed to the terms on September 1, 1998.

The last example is the best because it is the simplest and uses the word *agreed* as a verb rather than as a noun. It is the easiest sentence of the three to understand and to visualize.

The first two examples turn the verb *agree* into a noun, a process called **nominalization**. The following illustrates a second example:

The parties entered into an agreement on October 15, 1994, to make a change in the purchase price of the original contract from $1,500 to $2,000.

It is better to say:

The parties agreed to increase the purchase price of the original contract from $1,500 to $2,000.

In the second sentence, *entered into an agreement* becomes *agreed* and *to make a change* becomes *increase*. These changes eliminate the use of verbs as nouns.

▼ How Do You Avoid Legalese or Legalspeak?

Avoid **legalese** or **legalspeak**. What does this mean? Use plain English that your nonattorney clients would use. Consider your audience. Clear writing avoids using unnecessary legal words. For example, do not use the word *scienter* for *intent*. At the end of an affidavit, you often see the term *Further affiant sayeth not,* which means that the person signing the affidavit has nothing further to say. Because that should be clear without the legalistic phrase, skip it (and others like it) that add nothing to your writing.

2. Voice

Voice is the tone of your document. In professional writing, the document's tone is formal. Selecting language that is not colloquial and avoiding slang are ways to ensure that the tone of the document is correct for the law firm or corporate legal department environment. Avoid anything that personalizes the contents; this is achieved by never using the first person. Conjunctions like *can't* are more casual than *cannot*. When revising, be sensitive to the tone of your document; it should have the requisite formal voice.

▼ What Is the Difference between Active Voice and Passive Voice?

Active voice is when the subject of the sentence is doing the action of the verb. Active voice emphasizes the actor. Active voice is the preferred voice because it is clearer, more concise, and more lively.

Active voice: Harold hit a home run.
Diane danced the tango.

Passive voice is when the subject of the sentence is being acted on. Although passive voice has its uses, it is generally wordier and not as strong as active voice.

Passive voice: The home run was hit by Harold.
The tango was danced by Diane.

Often the word *by* is used in a passive voice sentence. When you see the word *by,* consider rewriting the sentence.

Passive example: Their initial quote for heat stamping equipment was rejected by Bailey.

Rewritten example: Bailey rejected their initial quote for heat stamping equipment.

The second example is clearer and more concise.

Passive voice, however, is sometimes acceptable. In some cases, the person or thing performing the action is unknown. For example:

Taxes were not deducted from her paychecks.
Walker received health and life insurance benefits.

In other cases, the actor does not need to be mentioned because he or she is less important than the action. If you believe it advantageous to change the emphasis of the sentence from the person doing the action to the action, use passive voice. For example, if your client is the defendant in a proceeding and you do not want to emphasize her action, you would write a sentence in passive voice, as follows:

> The action stems from a contract dispute in which goods were rejected by the defendant.

This sentence in active voice would emphasize the defendant, as follows:

> The defendant rejected the goods, resulting in a contract dispute.

3. Paragraphs

A **paragraph** is a collection of statements that focus on the same general subject. Effective paragraphs have a unified purpose, a thesis or topic sentence, and transitions between sentences.

The **topic sentence** is generally the first sentence of a paragraph; it tells the reader the subject of the paragraph. This sentence also indicates that a new topic will be discussed. In legal writing, this sentence often introduces the issue or subissues that will be discussed within the paragraph.

You should use **transitions** to guide your reader from one paragraph to the next. Transitions tell the reader that the ideas follow from each other and are related. A transitional sentence ties two paragraphs together. Think of this sentence as a bridge. Whenever you start your new paragraph, think about how you will relate it to the previous paragraph.

4. Sentences

A **sentence** is a statement that conveys a single idea. It generally should be written in active voice and must include a subject and predicate. To avoid confusing your reader, do not place the subject too far from the verb. The focus of your sentence should be the idea you wish to convey. Do not make your readers work too hard to understand your sentence. Be direct and to the point. Keep your sentences short, generally not more than 25 words. As with any rule, you may break this rule about sentence length, but be careful not to make your sentences too complex.

One common mistake in writing sentences is to use a sentence fragment or incomplete sentence.

Incomplete sentence: The extent of the employer's control and supervision over the worker.

Complete sentence: The court will consider the extent of the employer's control and supervision over the worker.

The first example is a sentence fragment. It is incomplete and is missing a verb. The second sentence is a complete thought. It contains both a subject and a verb.

5. Other Key Rules

Do not start your paragraph or sentence with a citation. Instead, start with the rule summarizing the cited authority.

Use quotations sparingly. Most often, you can paraphrase what a court decision or other authority states. Your words convey the concept more clearly to the reader. Direct quotations that are used to convey an idea often are cluttered with unnecessary words or do not effectively explain a concept in the context of your use of the quotation. An added bonus for you when you paraphrase a court decision or other authority is that you are forced to analyze carefully the language of the authority. This ensures that you understand the concepts presented.

REVISION CHECKLIST

1. Does the material make sense?
2. Is it logical?
3. Should the organization of the sentence be changed?
4. Does one sentence follow from the next?
5. Are there any gaps in the sentence?
6. Are there any gaps in the paragraph?
7. Does one paragraph flow into the other?
8. Should the paragraphs be rearranged?
9. Are there any punctuation errors?
10. Are any words misspelled?
11. Are there any typographical errors?
12. Are there any citation errors?

CHAPTER SUMMARY

This chapter led you through the editing process generally and then more specifically. It outlined essential items to check during your editing process.

Choose your words carefully. Select concrete verbs and avoid legalese. Most often, use active voice in which the subject of the sentence is doing the action of the verb.

Make sure your paragraphs focus on a single subject or aspect of a subject and use topic and transition sentences. Use full sentences that are direct and convey the idea you intend.

Use quotations sparingly to effectively convey your messages.

KEY TERMS

active voice	paragraph
concrete verbs	passive voice
diction	sentence
editing	topic sentence
legal speak	transitions
legalese	voice
nominalization	

EXERCISES

1. Eliminate the unnecessary words from the following statement:

At the time when the parties entered into the agreement of purchase and sale it is important to note that neither of them had knowledge of contents of the dresser drawer. Because of the fact that previous to the contract the seller did not own the dresser and the seller's mother had not had many valuable pieces of jewelry despite having a large income, the seller had made the assumption that the dresser did not contain anything. Due to the fact that the seller had made a statement to the buyer of the fact that his mother did not own any jewelry in the buyer's thinking, he had no purpose for to make any further investigation or inspection of the drawers as he might otherwise have considered making. For these reasons, there was no provision in the contract for an upward modification in the payment to be made by the buyer to the seller in the event that the dresser drawer later proved to be filled with jewels.

2. Which is the best sentence? Why?
   a. A modification to the contract occurred on July 8, 1998.
   b. There was a modification of the contract July 8, 1998.
   c. Harry and Morgan modified their contract on July 8, 1998.

WRITING BASICS

CHAPTER OVERVIEW

This chapter reinforces grammar concepts and focuses on problem areas. It provides concrete examples of grammatically correct and incorrect sentences and explains the difference. Because it cannot address all points of grammar that students need to know, it suggests other grammar resources that students can turn to.

A. PUNCTUATION

The punctuation of a sentence, especially the placement of a comma, can change the meaning of that sentence. Therefore, you must carefully place each punctuation mark. The following provides you with some basic rules for checking your punctuation placement.

1. Commas

Commas tell a reader to pause. Use commas to separate a series of items. For example:

> Wally ran to the school, the store, the baseball field, and then home.

Be careful not to use commas to divide run-on sentences. These are sentences that contain two separate sentences.

Incorrect: Tildy's role is merely advisory, although she might be called on to supply facts about the spill, her opinion probably would not form the basis of any final decision.

Correct: Tildy's role is merely advisory. Although she might be called on to supply facts about the spill, her opinion probably would not form the basis of any final decision.

In the second example, the two sentences are correctly separated with a period. You also could use a semicolon. For some run-on sentences, you could divide the sentences with a comma and a conjunction. In the above example, that solution would not cure the problem completely because the second sentence is too long.

Commas also are used to set apart parenthetical phrases. In such a situation, commas should be used in pairs.

> The defendant, Larry Dwyer, filed an answer to the complaint.

The name *Larry Dwyer* is parenthetical because the meaning of the sentence would not be changed if the name was omitted. In contrast, read the following examples:

> Judges who take bribes should be indicted.
> Judges, who take bribes, should be indicted.

In these examples, the phrase *who take bribes* is not parenthetical. If it was omitted, the sentence would say that "judges should be indicted." The phrase *who take bribes* must be part of the sentence to convey the correct meaning. Therefore, it is not parenthetical, and the commas should be omitted.

2. Special Comma Rules

Commas separate a year from the date.

> The plaintiff and the defendant agreed to the settlement on November 15, 1998.

Commas also set off the date from a specific reference to a day of the week.

> The judge decided the summary judgment motion on Monday, November 7, 1998.

Commas separate a proper name from a title that follows it.

> The plaintiff sued RAM Enterprises and Samuel Harris, company president.

Commas and periods should always appear inside quotation marks. This rule is often mistakenly broken.

> "But I wasn't in Toledo on the night of the murder," the defendant protested. "I was in Boca Raton with my elderly mother."

3. Semicolons

Semicolons are similar to commas because they tell a reader to pause and they break apart thoughts. Semicolons are used to separate two independent sentences.

Two sentences: The paralegal's responsibilities are broad.
They include summarization of depositions.

One sentence: The paralegal's responsibilities are broad; they include summarization of depositions.

Semicolons separate clauses of a compound sentence when an adverbial conjunction joins the two.

> The defendants presented a good case; however, they lost.

Semicolons are used to separate phrases in a list.

The committee members were Robert Harris, vice president of Harris Enterprises; Edna Williams, owner of Walworth Products; Barbara Halley, an attorney; and Benjamin Marcus, an accountant.

4. Colons

Colons are marks of introduction: what follow are explanations, conclusions, amplifications, lists or series, or quotations. A colon is always preceded by a main clause, one that can stand alone as a sentence. A main clause may or may not follow a colon.

Help was on the way: Someone had called the police.

Sandra had two assignments: a 5-page paper and a book report.

The mayor stepped to the podium: "I regretfully must submit my resignation."

Colons should appear only at the end of a main clause. They should never directly follow a verb or a preposition.

Incorrect: The hours of the museum are: 10:00 A.M. to 6:00 P.M.

Correct: The hours of the museum are 10:00 A.M. to 6:00 P.M.

Incorrect: Marc loved many sports, such as: soccer, tennis, and softball.

Correct: Marc loved many sports, such as soccer, tennis, and softball.

As with any punctuation mark, use colons only when they best serve your writing purpose. Do not overuse them.

5. Parentheses

Parentheses tell the reader that the idea is an afterthought or is outside the main idea of a sentence.

The tort involved a banana peel (the classic culprit) and a crowded grocery store.

Use parentheses infrequently because they tend to break the flow of the sentence.

6. Double Quotation Marks

These marks enclose direct quotations.

The judge said, "The trial date will not be continued."

Note that the first word of the quotation should be capitalized if it is a complete sentence.

7. Single Quotation Marks

These marks are used to define a quotation within a quotation.

> The client told the lawyer, "My boss said, 'You cannot be a good lawyer and be a good mother,' and then he fired me."

If you end a quotation with quoted words, you place a single quotation mark and follow it with a double quotation mark.

> The witness testified, "The robber said, 'Give me all of your money.'"

B. MODIFIERS

Modifiers provide a description about a subject, a verb, or an object in your sentence. If you misplace a modifier, you might confuse your reader or convey an incorrect message. A modifier should be placed in proximity to the subject, verb, or object it modifies.

Incorrect: Deadlocked for more than two days, the judge asked the jury to continue to deliberate.

Correct: The jury had been deadlocked for two days. Nonetheless, the judge asked the jury to continue to deliberate.

In the first example, the phrase *deadlocked for more than two days* incorrectly modifies the judge rather than the jury. This is a dangling modifier.

C. PARALLEL CONSTRUCTION

Parallel construction is when you make each of the phrases within your sentence follow the same grammatical pattern or number. A plural subject must have a plural verb. A singular subject must have a singular verb. You also must use parallel tenses when you are listing a series of activities. A parallel grammatical pattern makes your writing balanced.

Incorrect: The paralegal association set the following goals: recruitment of new members, educating the community, and improvement of paralegal work conditions.

Correct: The paralegal association set the following goals: recruitment of new members, education of the community, and improvement of paralegal work conditions.

In the correct example, the words *recruitment, education,* and *improvement* are parallel.

D. SUBJECT AND VERB AGREEMENT

Subject and verb agreement, so essential to proper sentence construction, causes great confusion for many writers. The following are sample situations in which errors are most often made.

You must use plural pronouns and verbs when the subjects are plural.

Incorrect: Software Developments Inc. sent Cheryl Faith, a company sales representative, and Mark Gaines, their plant manager, to Bailey's plant.

Correct: Software Developments Inc. sent Cheryl Faith, a company sales representative, and Mark Gaines, its plant manager, to Bailey's plant.

The second example is correct because Software Developments Inc. is a singular subject; therefore, the pronoun before *plant manager* should be the singular possessive *its* rather than *their.*

Incorrect: To assert the attorney-client privilege, the claimant must show that the statements were made in confidence and was made to an attorney for the purpose of obtaining legal advice.

Correct: To assert the attorney-client privilege, the claimant must show that the statements were made in confidence and were made to an attorney for the purpose of obtaining legal advice.

The second example is correct because the verbs must be plural when they have a plural noun. In this example, the word *statements* should have a plural verb.

If you have a singular subject, then each of the pronouns in the sentence that describes that subject should be singular.

Incorrect: To receive this protection in the corporate setting, an individual must show that they were a decision-making employee.

Correct: To receive this protection in the corporate setting, an individual must show that he or she was a decision-making employee.

Collective nouns such as *jury, court, committee,* and *group* often pose a problem for writers. They take a singular verb because they are considered one unit. For example, *jury* is considered one unit; it refers to the group, not to individual jurors.

Incorrect: The jury were to eat lunch at noon.

Correct: The jury was to eat lunch at noon.

Compound subjects also cause confusion. Subjects joined by the word *and* usually use a plural verb, regardless of whether any or all of the individual subjects are singular.

Incorrect: The attorney and the paralegal was available for the client.

Correct: The attorney and the paralegal were available for the client.

When a compound subject is preceded by *each* or *every,* the verb is usually singular.

Incorrect: Each attorney and paralegal in the room have access to the library.

Correct: Each attorney and paralegal in the room has access to the library.

When a compound subject is jointed by *or* or *nor,* it takes a singular verb if each subject is singular. It takes a plural verb if each subject is plural. If one subject is singular and the other is plural, the verb follows the closest subject.

Subjects singular: An apple or an orange is my favorite snack.

Subjects plural: Apples or oranges are my favorite snacks.

Subjects singular and plural: Neither the mother nor the children were happy.

To avoid awkwardness, place the plural noun closest to the verb so that the verb is plural.

Awkward: Neither the dogs nor the cat was anywhere in sight.

Revised: Neither the cat nor the dogs were anywhere in sight.

Indefinite pronouns may also throw up roadblocks for writers. Indefinite pronouns are those that do not refer to a specific person or thing. Some common indefinite pronouns are

all	nobody
any	none
anyone	nothing
each	one
either	some
everyone	something

Most indefinite pronouns refer to singular subjects and therefore take a singular verb.

Incorrect: Everyone are free to go.

Each of the stores were open on Sunday.

Correct: Everyone is free to go.

Each of the stores was open on Sunday.

Some indefinite pronouns (*all, any, none, some*) may take either a singular or plural verb depending on the meaning of the word they refer to.

Singular: All of the library was quiet. (The library was quiet.)

Plural: All of the paralegals were researching the case. (The paralegals were researching the case.)

PRACTICE POINTER

Consult these books for additional guidance:

The Elements of Style, by William Strunk, Jr., and E. B. White

On Writing Well, by William Zinsser

The Careful Writer: A Modern Guide to English Usage, by Theodore Bernstein

---

CHAPTER SUMMARY

This chapter reviewed basic grammar rules concerning punctuation, modifiers, parallel construction, and subject-verb agreement. It emphasized the importance correct grammar plays in legal writing by demonstrating how errors like incorrect punctuation, misplaced modifiers, and faulty subject-verb agreement can affect meaning.

KEY TERMS

collective nouns	modifiers
colons	parallel construction
commas	parentheses
compound subjects	semicolons
indefinite pronouns	

EXERCISES

Edit the following sentences. Name the grammar mistake in each sentence (e.g., misplaced modifier, faulty parallelism, and so forth). Then correct the error by rewriting the sentence.

1. At a time when many law firms and corporations are eliminating jobs for the purpose of elimination from the budget excess expenditures, paralegals may become more of an asset.
2. Because of the fact that paralegals' time is charged at lower rates, paralegals may be employed by law firms and corporations to perform tasks previously performed by lawyers.
3. With specificity, paralegals may be asked to perform legal research of case and statutory materials in the event that a client requests an answer to a problem of a legal nature and is concerned about saving money.
4. In the situation where a paralegal is well trained, that paralegal can be asked by an attorney to perform legal research for the purpose of determining a response to the client's question.
5. With regard to ethical considerations, paralegals can perform legal research under the supervision of an attorney.
6. Subsequent to the research, however, the attorney must be the person who renders the legal opinions that need to be made, the reason being that a paralegal cannot provide legal advice.
7. It is important to note that some states are considering allowing paralegals to practice independently.
8. Try this schedule; shower, eat breakfast, drive to the train, go to work, and come home.
9. There are only one hour and thirty-five minutes left to voir dire, the judge stated.
10. Among the defendants was Craig Fisher, David Michaels, and Mitchell White.
11. The prosecutor will attempt to within the course of the trial persuade you that the defendant committed the crime.
12. The foreman, as well as half of the jury, were late for the afternoon court session.
13. Every one of the councilmen we have named to the commission want to serve.
14. The heart of a trial are the witnesses.
15. None of the players were willing to sign contracts.

16. The substance of Walter Mondale's speeches is more similar to Jimmy Carter.
17. The house was vacated by the tenants.
18. The judge said to the jurors ",please refrain from discussing the case."
19. Four of the five jurors were men (These were Steer, Halsey, Grodsky, and Eirinberg.).
20. In her testimony, the witness said she remembered that the defendant asked her "Do you have an aspirin"?
21. These modems are shared with the other subscribers, so the more people on the connection the slower.
22. Working at a law firm from 8:30 A.M. to 5 P.M. handling high-level paralegal work may seem ideal, especially if you rarely work weekends.
23. The National Association of Paralegals said 12 percent of the law firms responded to their survey.

BRIEFING CASES

CHAPTER OVERVIEW

This chapter teaches you a skill called case briefing. It introduces you to each of the components of a case brief: the issue, the holding, the facts, the rationale or reasoning, and the disposition. It also introduces you to the concept of dicta. You learn what to include in each section of the brief and how to skillfully draft the brief.

Case briefing is a skill that you must master to effectively record your research results and analyze a case. Often attorneys will ask you to summarize a case in the form of a case brief. The key to a good brief is that it must be usable. You must be able to return to the brief months after you have prepared it and still be able to quickly understand the facts, the issues, the holdings, and the reasoning of the court.

A good case brief can be done in a variety of ways. Always ask an attorney if he or she has a preference. If not, you should consider the method discussed in this chapter.

A. PURPOSE OF A CASE BRIEF

The goal in writing a **case brief** is to summarize a court decision. A well-drafted brief saves you time because you do not have to reread the original decision to understand its significance. You are able to review the brief to obtain any necessary information. The next goal in briefing a case is to put the components of a decision in a uniform format. This is why we have specified eight set categories for a brief: citation, procedural facts, issues, holding, facts, rationale, dicta, and disposition. However, many attorneys use their own uniform format, and sometimes that format will depend on why you are briefing a case.

Sometimes you must brief cases in response to a particular legal issue that you are researching. Sometimes you must brief cases just to summarize decisions.

B. DIAGRAM OF A DECISION

Before you begin to write your brief, read the case thoroughly several times. Consider the questions the court was asked to decide. Determine the parties in the action and what each party is seeking. Sometimes this is complicated, and it helps to draw a diagram of the parties. For example, when the parties are involved in a three-way dispute such as a cross-claim, it might take some time to determine what each party is seeking. Make a column for each party in which you list the remedy sought. After you have read the case, you are ready to write the case brief.

Write the brief in your own words and paraphrase rather than quote a court's statements unless the statements are well phrased, concise, and understandable. Paraphrasing helps you analyze a case and allows you to understand the brief quickly when you return to it later.

C. ANATOMY OF A CASE BRIEF

1. Citation

The case brief starts with a **case citation**, which allows you to find the case at a later date. First, note the name of the case, which is generally found at the top of the page. Then add the case citation or docket number of the case. See Illustration 18-1. Be sure to include the date of the decision and the name of the deciding court. Next, you might want to make a note concerning whether the decision is primary binding or primary persuasive authority. (For more information about binding and persuasive authority, see Chapter 2.) You should label the remaining sections of the brief: procedural facts, issue, holding, rationale or reasoning, dicta, and disposition.

ILLUSTRATION 18-1. Sample Case, *King v. Miller*

KING V. MILLER
1000 E.R. 108 (Karen Ct. App. 1998)

Evelyn King, an insurance agent who worked for the defendant, Miller Company, filed a lawsuit claiming that the defendant discriminated against her on the basis of her sex in violation of Title VII, 42 U.S.C. §2000e et seq. Upon a motion for summary judgment, the district court granted the motion in favor of Miller. The district court found that King was not an employee of the defendant. She did not work in a manner consistent with an employee. The court said that King was an independent contractor. As an independent contractor, her discrimination claim was outside the protection of the federal law. King appealed the trial court's decision.

In 1992, King was hired by Miller to work as an "employee agent." As such, she was paid a salary. Income taxes and social security were withheld by Miller. She was promoted to "independent contract agent." King could not remain an employee agent for more than one year. When she was promoted she had to sign an agreement that stated that she was an independent contractor.

As an independent contract agent, King earned a commission on her sales and some bonuses. She did not receive any paid holidays, sick days, or vacation days. She paid for her own health, life, and disability insurance.

Miller, however, provided office space, furniture, file cabinets, rate books, forms, shared secretarial services, stamps, computers, and Miller's stationery. King purchased her own personalized stationery, pens, and business cards. Miller paid her tuition for required special insurance seminars, provided lunch at such programs, and rented the space for the sessions.

King had wanted to work for Miller because Miller had a good

ILLUSTRATION 18-1. *Continued*

reputation. Before coming to Miller's office, King worked for three other insurance companies. King was a single, 30-year-old mother of two children. Before her experience in the insurance industry, she worked as a sales clerk at a local boutique.

While working as an independent contract agent for Miller, King could not sell insurance for any other company. She also could only sell insurance in the county designated by the company manager. She had to work at the Miller office three and one-half days a week and every third Saturday, attend two hour-long meetings each week, and retrieve mail every day.

King was responsible for finding her own customers and deciding which products to offer. She could set the hours she worked and she worked without direct supervision. Miller did not regularly review her work. King was fired in 1993, and a man was hired to take her place.

The district court found that based upon these facts, King was an independent contractor, not an employee. The court focused on the economic realities test. One of the factors it considered as part of its test for determining whether King was an employee or an independent contractor was Miller's right to control King. *Spirides v. Reinhardt,* 613 F.2d 826, 831 (D.C. Cir. 1979), is the leading case regarding the question of whether an individual is an employee under the federal discrimination laws or an independent contractor. The *Spirides* court adopted an 11-part test. These factors are:

> 1) the kind of occupation, whether the work is usually done under the direction of a supervisor or without a supervisor; 2) the skill required; 3) whether the "employer" provides the equipment used and the workplace; 4) how long the individual has worked; 5) how the individual is paid, whether by assignment, piece, or time; 6) how the work relationship is to be terminated, i.e., was notice required; 7) whether vacation is provided; 8) whether retirement benefits are provided; 9) whether the employer deducts social security and income tax payments; 10) whether the work is an integral part of the employer's business; and 11) the intention of the parties.

Id.

The Karen district court focused on five of those factors: 1) the extent of Miller's control and supervision of King concerning scheduling and performance of work; 2) the kind of occupation and the nature of the skill required; 3) the division of the costs of the operation, equipment, supplies, and fees; 4) the method and form of payment and benefits; 5) length of job commitment. Central to its decision was the lack of control Miller exercised over King. The court found that King had a great deal of freedom to select her hours, her clients, and the insurance products she sold.

King must prove that an employment relationship existed between Miller and her in order to maintain a Title VII action against

ILLUSTRATION 18-1.   *Continued*

Miller. Independent contractors are not protected by Title VII. *Spirides*, 613 F.2d at 831. Title VII defines employee "as an individual employed by an employer." 42 U.S.C. §2000e(f). "In determining whether the relationship is one of employee-employer, courts look to the 'economic realities' of the relationship and the degree of control the employer exercises over the alleged employee." See *Unger v. Consolidated Foods Corp.*, 657 F.2d 909, 915-916 n.8 (7th Cir. 1981).

On appeal, King contends that the district court placed too much weight on the "control factor" and the fact the Miller did not supervise King's work and did not dictate King's hours, products or customers. Based upon this emphasis, King argues that the district court's decision was erroneous.

However, this court finds that the district court correctly considered other facts such as that King was paid on commission, did not receive benefits, and provided many of her own supplies, including stationery and business cards.

Although this court was not asked to determine whether the district court should have considered all of the facts that were relevant to each of the 11 factors stated in the *Spirides'* economic realities test, this court finds that the district court should have done so.

Although we think that the district court should have focused its analysis on all 11 factors, we do not think that its decision is clearly erroneous; therefore, we affirm the decision of the district court in granting summary judgment for the defendant, Miller.

2. Procedural Facts

The first section of the case brief should be labeled **procedural facts.** These facts explain the status of the case. See Illustration 18-2. In this section, you note how the case came before the court and what action the court took. For example, if the decision concerns an appeal to a federal appellate court, note that. Also, state whether the court reversed or affirmed the lower court's decision and whether the case was remanded.

ILLUSTRATION 18-2.   Sample Case Brief, *King v. Miller*

KING V. MILLER
1000 E.R. 108 (Karen Ct. App. 1998)

PROCEDURAL FACTS

The case was on appeal from the District Court's grant of summary judgment for the defendant Miller.

ILLUSTRATION 18-2.   *Continued*

ISSUE

Is King, a worker subject to only minimal company control and who was paid commissions rather than a salary and benefits, an employee protected by Title VII or an independent contractor who is outside the protection of the federal law?

HOLDING

King, a worker subject to only minimal company control and who was paid commissions rather than a salary and benefits, was an independent contractor rather than an employee protected by Title VII.

FACTS

King first worked for Miller as an employee agent. During that time, she received a salary and the company withheld income tax and social security payments. King later was promoted to independent contract agent.

As an independent contract agent, King earned a commission and bonuses but did not receive a salary. She signed an agreement that stated that she was an independent contractor. As a contract agent, she did not receive paid holidays, sick days, or vacation days, and she paid for her own health, life, and disability insurance. King supplied her own personalized stationery, business cards, and pens. She found her own customers, decided which products to sell, and set her own hours.

For its contract agents, Miller supplied office space, furniture, file cabinets, forms, shared secretarial services, stamps, computers, and Miller stationery. Miller also paid for required insurance seminars. Miller required that contract agents, such as King, attend weekly meetings, work in the office three and one-half days per week and every third Saturday, check their mail and retrieve messages daily, and sell only Miller insurance. Miller also restricted King's sales area. Miller did not regularly review King's work.

REASONING

In order to determine whether an individual is an employee or an independent contractor, the employment relationship between the parties needs to be evaluated based upon the economic realities and circumstances of the relationship. The court considered the control exercised by the "employer" over the worker; the method of payment; who paid for the individual's benefits, such as life and health insurance; and who paid for the operation. In this case, the court found that King was an independent contractor because she was paid on commission, she paid for her own benefits, she supplied her own supplies, and she controlled her work. The court found that she set her own hours, selected the products she sold, and

ILLUSTRATION 18-2.   *Continued*

generated her own clients. Based upon these facts, the appellate court found that King should be considered an independent contractor rather than an employee.

DICTA

The 11-part test set by the *Spirides* court should be applied to determine whether an individual is an employee or an independent contractor.

DISPOSITION

The Court of Appeals affirmed the district court's judgment in granting summary judgment for the defendant.

After these facts and any other information you note in your brief, you should indicate in parentheses the pages from the case that contain the information noted. This step assists you when you summarize your research results in a memorandum.

3. Issues

Next, list the **issue** or **issues** presented in the case. See Illustration 18-2. Although determining the issues in a case is a difficult process at first, it does get easier with practice.

The issues are the questions the parties asked the court to decide. In most cases, multiple issues are presented. To determine the issues, you must understand the legal rules that govern a particular case. If you are briefing a case and you have not been assigned an issue to research, list all of the issues presented in the case. If you have been given a research assignment, you need only brief the issues that are relevant to your research, listing each one separately.

▼ How Do You Determine the Legal Issue or Issues Presented?

To understand this process, assume you have been asked to research whether your firm's client, Whole In One, will be subject to the federal antidiscrimination laws. Whole In One is a seasonal restaurant and golf course in Glenview, Illinois. Two women, Victoria Vines and Lynda Dogger, brought suit against Whole In One for sex discrimination. Their claims are based on a federal antidiscrimination statute commonly known as Title VII. You have been asked to research whether Whole In One is an employer and whether the women are employees under the definitions included in the federal law. During your research, you find the case of *King v. Miller.* Review Illustration 18-1.

To determine the issue, read the case. Ask yourself, "What did the parties ask the court to determine?" Sometimes, the court will note the issue directly in its opinion. Other times, you must ferret through the opinion to determine the issue. After you have read the *King* case, you should note that it involves a question of sex discrimination. However, your research is limited to the issues that concern the definitions of *employer* and *employee*. Therefore, the case brief should focus on issues that relate to your research problem.

Once you have read the *King* case, you will find that it addresses the question of whether an individual is an employee protected by Title VII. Now you are ready to draft the issue.

▼ How Do You Draft a Statement of the Issue or Issues?

For the *King* case, you might start with this brief issue:

> Is King an employee protected by Title VII or an independent contractor who is outside the protection of the federal law?

Now that the issue is presented in question format, you could leave the issue section here. However, the issue would be more meaningful for your research if you included more information about the legal issue the court focused on in making its determination. In its discussion, the *King* court focused on the amount of control that an employer must exercise before an individual is viewed as an employee rather than an independent contractor. You could incorporate the court's focus on control into the issue as follows:

> Is King, a worker subject to only minimal company control, an employee protected by Title VII, or an independent contractor who is outside the protection of the federal law?

You also should include relevant facts in your issue statement. Again, this will make the issue more meaningful for your research. In this case, for example, you might add some facts about the company's method of payment and its lack of provisions for benefits:

> Is King, a worker subject to only minimal company control who was paid commissions rather than salary and benefits, an employee protected by Title VII or an independent contractor who is outside the protection of the federal law?

The final issue statement is the best because it incorporates the relevant facts that affect a court's decision concerning this issue and the rule of law that will be applied.

You might wonder why the issue did not focus on the appellate court's consideration of the district court's action in granting the motion for summary judgment in favor of the defendant. Students often phrase such an issue as follows:

Did the district court err in granting summary judgment in favor
of the defendant?

However, this issue focuses too heavily on the procedural question
posed in the *King* case and does not include the applicable law or
any of the legally significant facts. Your issue should concern the
legal, not the procedural, questions a court was asked to decide. As
you learned above, the *King* case involved a motion for summary
judgment.

To find the substantive legal issue, determine the legal question
the parties asked the court to answer in the motion for summary
judgment. In the *King* case, the parties asked the court to determine
whether, as a matter of law, King was an independent contractor
rather than an employee. This is the central legal issue. By focusing
on this substantive issue rather than the procedural issue, your brief
will be more useful to you in your research of the Whole In One
case.

Some of you might wonder why you do not focus on the question
of discrimination in your issue section. Remember the issue you
were asked to answer with your research. You were asked to deal
with the issues of the definition of *employee* and *employer.* You should
tailor your brief to address these issues.

4. Holding

The next section should be your **holding.** A holding often is called
the **rule of law.** Essentially a holding is the court's answer to the
issue or question presented. However, it is not a yes, no, or maybe
answer to the issue. The holding should be a full sentence that
responds directly to the issue posed and that incorporates both the
legal standards and the significant legal facts on which the answer
is based. Ideally, the holding should be a nugget you can use later in
a summary of your research. (This summary is called a *memorandum,*
which we will discuss in greater detail in Chapter 19.)

▼ How Do You Draft a Holding?

The process for drafting the holding is similar to the process for
writing your issue statement. First, your holding should be a statement that answers the issue. Assume you selected the first issue
statement considered in this discussion:

Is King an employee protected by Title VII or an independent
contractor who is outside the protection of the federal law?

You might consider answering it as follows:

King is an independent contractor rather than an employee and
therefore is outside the protection of Title VII.

While this statement is simple and direct, similar to the first issue statement, it does not contain any relevant facts or incorporate any legal standards. This holding should be rewritten, incorporating the elements or legal standards that would be considered. Such a change would make the holding more meaningful in the context of this research.

The rewritten issue could read:

> Is King, a worker subject to only minimal company control, an independent contractor or an employee protected by Title VII?

Again, you might want to include additional facts the court considered in determining that King was an independent contractor. For the holding, rewrite the final issue statement drafted above in the form of a statement.

> King, a worker subject to only minimal company control who was paid commissions rather than salary and benefits, was an independent contractor rather than an employee protected by Title VII.

The key to drafting a good issue statement, a holding, or any other type of writing is rewriting and editing. You must make your holding broad enough so that it could be useful for various research projects involving different fact patterns. However, you need to incorporate facts from the case at hand that make it unique and that limit the holding so that you can understand the facts that form the basis for the court's decision. Refine your statements and assess whether they are helpful in your research summary.

Also, be careful to incorporate the facts and the underlying law into your holding statement, as you did in your issue statement. A holding such as

> The district court did not err in granting summary judgment in favor of the defendant.

is not valuable for your research. It does not explain why the court found that the district court's decision was correct.

5. Facts

The next section of the brief should be the facts. Be certain to include the names of the parties, a notation concerning whether the party is a plaintiff, a defendant, an appellant, or appellee, and some details about the party, such as whether it is a corporation or an individual. State the relevant rather than procedural facts in this section. Also, explain why a party sought legal assistance.

▼ What Are the Relevant Facts?

Relevant facts are those facts that may have an effect on the legal issues decided in a particular action. To write this section, you must clearly understand the issues decided by the court. Decide which facts the court relied on to make its decision. Those are the facts that you should include in this section. The facts should be presented in a paragraph rather than in a list. Also, mention any facts that will assist you in understanding the relationship between the parties and the dispute.

In the *King* case, the court relied on facts that explained the relationship between King and the Miller Co. For example, the court considered that King earned commissions and bonuses rather than a salary. That fact should be listed. Before you write your facts statement in paragraph format, make a rough outline of all of the facts that the court considered in making its decision. For the *King* case, your outline might look like this:

King first worked as an "employee" agent
    As an employee agent, was paid salary, company withheld taxes

King later was designated an "independent contract" agent, earned
    commission and bonuses but no salary
        King signed an agreement that she was an independent contractor
        Did not receive paid holidays, sick days, or vacation
        Paid for her own health, life, and disability insurance
        Miller supplied office space, furniture, file cabinets, forms, shared secretarial services, stamps, computers, and Miller stationery
        Miller paid for insurance seminars and lunches at the seminars
        Miller required that King attend weekly meetings, work in the office three and one-half days per week and every third Saturday, check her mail and retrieve messages daily, and sell only Miller insurance
        Miller restricted King's sales area
        Miller did not regularly review King's work
        King supplied her own personalized stationery, business cards, pens
        King found her own customers, decided which products to sell, and set her own hours

The court listed additional facts, such as:
        King had wanted to work for Miller because Miller had a good reputation
        Before coming to Miller's office, King worked for three other insurance companies
        King was a single, 30-year-old mother of two children

> Before her experience in the insurance industry, she worked as
> a sales clerk at a local boutique

Note that for its decision the court did not consider any of the facts contained in the outline under additional facts. Therefore, they are not relevant facts and should not be included in your brief. After you have made your outline and determined which facts are relevant, you should draft your facts statement in a paragraph format. A list is not as helpful as a paragraph when you want to review the brief at a later date.

▼ How Do You Organize Your Facts Statement?

Your facts statement could be written in chronological order, in topical order, or using a combination of the two methods. Chronological order often works best when the case involves facts that need to be placed in order according to when they occurred. For example, in a personal injury action that results from a car accident, a chronological set of facts is best. Start with the first fact that occurred and work forward.

A chronological organization for the facts in the *King* case would read as follows:

> In 1992, King started to work for Miller. King first worked for Miller as an employee agent. During that time, she received a salary and the company withheld income tax and social security payments. King later was promoted to contract agent. King was fired in 1993, and a man was hired to take her place.

A topical organization is the best choice for facts that have no temporal relationship. Instead, these facts are grouped by topic or legal claim. In this case, the topic is the legal question of whether King was an independent contractor. Therefore, you would group together all of the facts that relate to this question.

> As an independent contract agent, King earned a commission and bonuses but did not receive a salary. She signed an agreement that stated that she was an independent contractor. As a contract agent, she did not receive paid holidays, sick days, or vacation days, and she paid for her own health, life, and disability insurance. King supplied her own personalized stationery, business cards, and pens. She found her own customers, decided which products to sell, and set her own hours.

> For its independent contract agents, Miller supplied office space, furniture, file cabinets, forms, shared secretarial services, stamps, computers, and Miller stationery. Miller also paid for required insurance seminars. Miller required that contract agents, such as King, attend weekly meetings, work in the office three and one-half days per week and every third Saturday, check their mail and retrieve messages daily, and sell only Miller insurance. Miller

also restricted King's sales area. Miller did not regularly review King's work.

In the *King* case, a combination of a chronological and topical organization works best. The *King* brief facts statement might read as follows:

> King first worked for Miller as an employee agent. During that time, she received a salary and the company withheld income tax and social security payments. King later was promoted to independent contract agent.

> As an independent contract agent, King earned a commission and bonuses but did not receive a salary. She signed an agreement that stated that she was an independent contractor. As a contract agent, she did not receive paid holidays, sick days, or vacation days, and she paid for her own health, life, and disability insurance. King supplied her own personalized stationery, business cards, and pens. She found her own customers, decided which products to sell, and set her own hours.

> For its contract agents, Miller supplied office space, furniture, file cabinets, forms, shared secretarial services, stamps, computers, and Miller stationery. Miller also paid for required insurance seminars. Miller required that contract agents, such as King, attend weekly meetings, work in the office three and one-half days per week and every third Saturday, check their mail and retrieve messages daily, and sell only Miller insurance. Miller also restricted King's sales area. Miller did not regularly review King's work.

The above facts statement begins with a chronological organization. It explains the beginning of the relationship between King and Miller. Next, it states all of the facts that pertain to King's benefits and her control of her work. The next paragraph explains what Miller provided for the independent contract agents and what Miller required of them. Following this facts section, you should include a reasoning or rationale section in a brief.

6. Rationale

In the **rationale** or **reasoning** section, you should explain the court's thought process and relevant cases or statutes, then apply the law to the facts of the case you are briefing. Essentially, you will explain the law the court relied on in making a decision. For example, the *King* court reviewed the definition of *employee* contained in Title VII and past case precedent, such as *Spirides v. Reinhardt*, 613 F.2d 826, 831 (D.C. Cir. 1979), and *Unger v. Consolidated Foods Corp.*, 657 F.2d 909, 915-916 n.8 (7th Cir. 1981), to determine that independent contractors are not protected by Title VII.

You also must review a decision for any tests a court considered in making its decision. In *King,* the court considered the economic realities test. Finally, note how the court applied the law to the facts of the particular case.

For the *King* case, you might include the following reasoning section in your brief:

> In order to determine whether an individual is an employee or an independent contractor, the employment relationship between the parties needs to be evaluated based on the economic realities and circumstances of the relationship. The court considered the control exercised by the "employer" over the worker; the method of payment; who paid for the individual's benefits, such as life and health insurance; and who paid for the operation. In this case, the court found that King was an independent contractor because she was paid on commission, she paid for her own benefits, she provided her own supplies, and she controlled her work. The court found that she set her own hours, selected the products she sold, and generated her own clients. Based on these facts, the appellate court found that King should be considered an independent contractor rather than an employee.

In the reasoning section, you should include an application of the law to the facts of the case and a miniconclusion that summarizes the court's decision. In the above example, the following section is the application of the court's reasoning to the facts of the case.

> In this case, the court found that King was an independent contractor because she was paid on commission, she paid for her own benefits; she provided her own supplies, and she controlled her work. The court found that she set her own hours, selected the products she sold, and generated her own clients.

In the above example, the following statement is the miniconclusion:

> Based on these facts, the appellate court found that King should be considered an independent contractor rather than an employee.

In some cases, you will find that a court bases its decision on reasons other than statutes or past cases. For example, a court might consider whether its decision would be fair under the circumstances. This type of analysis is called the court's consideration of policy, which sometimes is a question of what would benefit society, such as equal rights in an educational setting. Incorporate this policy into your reasoning section whenever it is useful for your research. After the reasoning or rationale discuss any dicta contained in the court's decision.

7. Dicta

If a court makes a statement concerning a question that it was not asked to answer, this statement is called **dicta.** Although dicta does not have any binding effect, it is often useful to predict how a court might decide a particular issue. Therefore, you want to include any dicta that might affect your case.

In the *King* case, the court stated that it was not asked to decide whether the district court should have considered all 11 factors before it rendered its decision. However, the court stated that the district court should have based its decision on all 11 factors. This statement by the court was dicta. It is helpful for your research problem because it states the factors that this circuit court might consider in determining whether an individual is an independent contractor rather than an employee.

The dicta section for the *King* case might read as follows:

> The 11-part test set by the *Spirides* court should be applied to determine whether an individual is an employee or an independent contractor.

8. Disposition

The final section of your brief is the **disposition.** The disposition of a case is essentially the procedural result of the court's decision. For example, in the *King* case the court found that the district court's decision to grant summary judgment for the defendant was correct. Therefore, the disposition section would state:

> The court of appeals affirmed the district court's judgment in granting summary judgment for the defendant.

Finally, remember to rewrite your brief, but do not spend too much time rewriting it. Use your own words rather than many quotes from the court opinions. Paraphrasing in your own words helps you analyze the case and better understand it when you review your brief in the future.

PRACTICE POINTER

Reread your brief as if you were unfamiliar with the case. If you cannot understand what happened, rewrite your brief.

In-Class Exercise

Sometimes learning to brief can seem like an abstract exercise. The following exercise is designed to hone your brief drafting skills. It is best for students to read the illustrations for this exercise before class. Read the *Molitor* case found in Illustration 18-3. Then read the

ILLUSTRATION 18-3.   *Molitor v. Chicago Title & Trust Co.*

MOLITOR V. CHICAGO TITLE & TRUST CO. et al.

Gen. No. 42960.

Appellate Court of Illinois. First District.
Second Division.

Feb. 13, 1945.

SCANLAN, Justice.

Robert H. Molitor, plaintiff, sued Chicago Title & Trust Company, a corporation, for breach of an employment contract, and also sued Justin M. Dall for damages resulting from the breach of the said contract because of his want of authority, if the evidence should show a want of authority. A jury returned a verdict finding the issues in favor of plaintiff and against Chicago Title & Trust Company and assessing plaintiff's damages at $15,480, and also a verdict finding the issues in favor of defendant Dall. The trial court reserved rulings on motions of defendants for directed verdicts and after verdicts sustained a motion of Chicago Title & Trust Company for judgment in its favor notwithstanding the verdict against it. Plaintiff appeals from that judgment. Judgment was entered upon the verdict in favor of defendant Dall after plaintiff's motion for a new trial had been denied. Plaintiff has not appealed from that judgment. Some days after the entry of the judgment against Chicago Title & Trust Company it entered a motion for a new trial and the trial court entered an order granting the motion, but providing that "this ruling shall not become effective unless and until the order granting the motion for judgment notwithstanding the verdict shall hereafter be reversed, vacated or set aside in the manner provided by law." Plaintiff also appeals from that judgment.

Plaintiff contends that the trial court should not have entertained the motion of defendant Chicago Title & Trust Company for judgment notwithstanding the verdict because no points in writing were filed at any time specifying the grounds upon which such motion was based, as provided by Section 68 of the Civil Practice Act, but we do not deem it necessary to consider this somewhat technical contention in view of the conclusion we have reached as to plaintiff's next contention.

Plaintiff strenuously contends that the trial court erred in sustaining the Chicago Title & Trust Company's motion for judgment notwithstanding the verdict. Neither in the written motion filed by Chicago Title & Trust Company for a directed verdict at the close of the plaintiff's case nor at the close of all the evidence was any attempt made at "specifying the grounds of such motion," as provided by Section 68 of the Civil Practice Act, ch. 110, par. 192, Ill. Rev. Stat. 1943. That section also provides that "if either party may

ILLUSTRATION 18-3. *Continued*

wish to move for . . . a judgment notwithstanding the verdict, he shall, before final judgment be entered, . . . file the points in writing, particularly specifying the grounds of such motion. . . ." The motion for judgment notwithstanding the verdict merely recites that the said defendant "moves the court that judgment be entered for said defendant, Chicago Title & Trust Company, notwithstanding the verdict of the jury."

The complaint alleges that Chicago Title & Trust Company, on or about March 20, 1936, "desiring to continue the service of plaintiff permanently, promised and agreed that in consideration of the plaintiff giving up his residence in the State of New York, and giving up and forgoing all his other engagements and professional connections as aforesaid by moving his family to Cook County, State of Illinois, and thereafter devoting all his time exclusively to the service of the Company, that it would give plaintiff steady, continuous and permanent employment as an examiner of titles; that is to say, for and during the period of his natural life, or so long as said Company required the services of an examiner of titles and plaintiff was willing and able to do such work." Said defendant, in its answer, denies the aforesaid allegations. We may assume from the briefs filed by both parties that the trial court based his ruling upon the assumption that there was no evidence offered by plaintiff that tended to prove an enforceable agreement that plaintiff was to have permanent employment. The following are the settled principles of law that govern a trial court in passing upon a motion for judgment non obstante veredicto:

Rule 22 of the Supreme Court, Ill. Rev. Stat. 1943, c. 110 §259.22, provides: "The power of the Court to enter judgment notwithstanding the verdict may be exercised in all cases where, under the evidence in the case, it would have been the duty of the Court to direct a verdict without submitting the case to the jury."

" 'A motion to instruct the jury to find for the defendant is in the nature of a demurrer to the evidence, and the rule is that the evidence so demurred to, in its aspect most favorable to the plaintiff, together with all reasonable inferences arising therefrom, must be taken most strongly in favor of the plaintiff. The evidence is not weighed, and all contradictory evidence or explanatory circumstances must be rejected. The question presented on such motion is whether there is any evidence fairly tending to prove the plaintiff's declaration. In reviewing the action of the court of which complaint is made, we do not weigh the evidence; we can look only at that which is favorable to appellant. *Yess v. Yess*, 255 Ill. 414, 99 N.E. 687; *McCune v. Reynolds*, 288 Ill. 188, 123 N.E. 317; *Lloyd v. Rush*, 273 Ill. 489, 113 N.E. 122; *Hunter v. Troup*, 315 Ill. 293, 296, 297, 146 N.E. 321, 322." *Mahan v. Richardson*, 284 Ill. App. 493, 495, 1 N.E.2d 100, 101. See also *Wolever v. Curtiss Candy Co.*, 293 Ill. App. 596, 597, 13

ILLUSTRATION 18-3.   *Continued*

N.E.2d 197; *Cooper v. Safeway Lines, Inc.*, 304 Ill. App. 302, 312, 313, 26 N.E.2d 632; *McCarthy v. Rorrison,* 283 Ill. App. 129; *Rose v. City of Chicago,* 317 Ill. App. 1, 12, 45 N.E.2d 717.

Observing these rules we find the following evidence: The Chicago Title & Trust Company is engaged, inter alia, in the business of insuring titles to and interests in real estate in Cook county and elsewhere. It employs a large number of men known as title examiners, who are especially trained and experienced in the law of real property and the validity of real estate titles. It depends upon the ability and integrity of these title examiners to discover defects, if there be any, in real estate titles. In the selection of title examiners it exercises great caution, and applicants for such position go through a long probationary period before they are given "continuous employment." In 1920 plaintiff applied for a position as title examiner and was employed on probation. He had theretofore been engaged in the practice of law in South Dakota. After a number of years of service as a probationer, he was made a regular examiner at a salary of $85 per week. In August, 1927, he quit the services of the defendant company and moved, with his family, to New York to take employment in the office of a former client, the new position paying him twice the salary he was getting as a title examiner. Because of the economic depression, he lost the New York position on February 1, 1933, and he then started to practice his profession in New York—having been admitted to the bar in New York—and by June, 1934, he was commencing to build up a paying practice. About that time one of the departments of defendant company, that was managed by Mr. Dall, was swamped with thousands of HOLC orders for title insurance, and speedy service was demanded. Mr. Dall, in letters and telegrams to plaintiff, asked him to reenter the employ of defendant company. Dall stated that the company was very busy with rush orders from the HOLC but that there was no profit in the business and that the work would probably last about six months. Plaintiff told Mr. Dall that since 1933 conditions had changed for the better for him and his family and that they now had an income; that from time to time he was getting law business which paid substantial fees; that his wife had a music class in New York from which she derived a substantial income every month and that he might have trouble inducing her to give up her work unless plaintiff would have better prospects in Chicago than in New York. Further correspondence followed, and plaintiff finally accepted the offer of employment with the understanding that when the HOLC work gave out that Mr. Dall might be free to dispense with his services. In view of the temporary character of the agreement plaintiff decided not to move his family to Chicago. He came to Chicago on July 23, 1934, and told Mr. Dall, in a conference, that he desired to preserve his business connections in New York and to have his wife retain her music classes there, and

ILLUSTRATION 18-3. *Continued*

that it would be necessary for him to be absent from his work with the defendant company when matters came up in New York that required his presence there. Mr. Dall agreed to this arrangement. Immediately following this conference plaintiff went to work for defendant company and for three or four months thereafter the title examiners were obliged to work four hours overtime every day, all day Saturdays, and some Sundays. Plaintiff spent five days in New York in the following September to attend to a legal matter in which he had been appointed referee. He was also absent from his work during the month of June, 1935, when he was conducting legal business for clients in New York and Philadelphia, and was absent again, upon like work, between December 14, 1935, and February 17, 1936. All of the absences were with the knowledge and consent of Mr. Dall. The HOLC work was tapering off in 1935, and it ended on June 12, 1936. About this time Mr. Dall was preparing for an anticipated improvement in the regular business of defendant company and he became dissatisfied with the arrangement that allowed plaintiff to be absent from his work on trips to New York, and in a conference with plaintiff it was agreed that the trips to New York caused undesirable breaks in plaintiff's work and a new arrangement as to plaintiff's employment was made. The following is plaintiff's evidence as to the agreement: Dall stated to him that the HOLC work would soon be played out but that they were looking for a big boom in regular real estate business, and he asked plaintiff to abandon his New York connections and move his family to Chicago so that he could give the company his continuous service from then on. Plaintiff replied that he would not given up his New York connections so long as there was any uncertainty about his employment in Chicago being continuous. Mr. Dall stated that two of the examiners had died, that there was now a place for plaintiff and that he could depend on the position being permanent. Plaintiff asked him what he meant by that, to which Dall replied, "You can consider yourself employed from now on—the custom here is to retain examiners as long as we can. We have men that have been here all their lives, and there is no reason why you couldn't have a job here the rest of your life." Plaintiff replied that if he could rely on that promise he would buy a house in Chicago and move his family here, that his wife had a big music class in New York and that she would refuse to move unless he had a permanent position in Chicago, to which Mr. Dall replied, "You can rely on it being permanent." Plaintiff then accepted the position and told Mr. Dall that he would abandon his New York connections, buy a house here, and move his family to Chicago. His salary was fixed at $70 per week. Plaintiff thereupon continued in his work with defendant company and began preparations for carrying out his part of the agreement. He abandoned all his business in New York and his wife abandoned her music classes.

ILLUSTRATION 18-3. *Continued*

He bought a home at 7219 Vernon avenue and the family moved to Chicago. The defendant company loaned plaintiff $200 to enable him to move. Plaintiff thereafter continued in the employ of defendant company under the arrangements made with Mr. Dall until March 15, 1938, when he was discharged by defendant company upon the ground that business had fallen off to such an extent that the company could not afford to hold plaintiff any longer. There was evidence tending to show that defendant company about two years prior to plaintiff's discharge employed thirteen new title examiners whose salaries averaged less than $40 per week, and that only one of the thirteen was discharged at the time of plaintiff's discharge.

In passing upon plaintiff's instant contention we must assume that defendant company promised plaintiff "permanent employment" and that plaintiff accepted employment because of that promise, and the question is, What did the parties intend by "permanent employment"? Upon the oral argument counsel for the defendant contended that even under plaintiff's testimony as to the alleged agreement defendant had the right to discharge him at will. This contention is without merit and the cases cited in support of it, *Orr v. Ward,* 73 Ill. 318; *Gunther v. Chicago B. & Q Ry. Co.,* 165 Ill. App. 55, and *Fuchs v. Weibert,* 233 Ill. App. 536, have no application to the facts that must be taken as true in determining the instant contention of plaintiff.

The leading case that bears upon the facts before us is *Carnig v. Carr,* 167 Mass. 544, 46 N.E. 117, 35 L.R.A. 512, 57 Am. St. Rep. 488. We find that that case has been often cited, and always with approval. To quote from the opinion (167 Mass. at pages 546, 547, 46 N.E. at page 117, 35 L.R.A. 512, 57 Am. St. Rep. 488):

"There was evidence tending to show that the defendant agreed that if the plaintiff would give up his business, which was that of an enameler, and enter his service in the same occupation, he would furnish him with permanent employment at stipulated wages; that the plaintiff gave up his business, and entered defendant's employment, and continued therein several months, receiving wages at the rate agreed, when defendant suspended his employment, and finally ceased altogether to employ him, though he had work of the kind which the plaintiff was to do. . . .

"To ascertain what the parties intended by 'permanent employment,' it is necessary to consider the circumstances surrounding the making of the contract, its subject, the situation and relation of the parties, and the sense in which, taking these things into account, the words would be commonly understood; for it fairly may be assumed that the parties used and understood them in that sense. *Schuylkill Navigation Co., v. Moore,* 2 Whart. 477, 491. Looking at the matter in that way, we think that the words would be commonly understood as meaning that so long as the defendant was engaged

ILLUSTRATION 18-3.   *Continued*

in enameling, and had work which the plaintiff could do, and desired to do, and so long as the plaintiff was able to do his work satisfactorily, the defendant would employ him, and that in that sense the employment would be permanent; that is, the plaintiff would be under no necessity of looking for work elsewhere, but could rely on the arrangement thus made. So construed, the contract would be capable of enforcement, and there would be no want of mutuality because the plaintiff might not have bound himself to continue in the defendant's employment. The construction contended for by the defendant, namely, that it was for him to say whether he needed the plaintiff's services or not, would put the plaintiff entirely at the defendant's mercy, and, in view of the fact that the plaintiff was to give up his business to enter the defendant's employment, would be such an agreement as he could not reasonably have been expected to make. See *Russell v. Allerton,* 108 N.Y. 288, 15 N.E. 391. On the other hand, it would be equally unreasonable to hold that the defendant could have intended to bind himself to employ the plaintiff so long as they both lived, regardless of his continuing in the enameling business, or of the plaintiff's rendering satisfactory service. The plaintiff does not, indeed, contend for such a construction. If it is difficult, as the defendant insists that it is, to lay down a rule for estimating the damages arising from the breach of such a contract as we have construed this to be, the difficulty is no greater than exists in many other cases, and does not present an insuperable objection to recovery."

In *Riefkin v. E.I. Du Pont De Nemours & Co.,* 53 App. D.C. 311, 290 F. 286, the plaintiff was induced to resign from a position with the United States government on a promise of permanent employment. After about two and one-half years of service he was discharged without cause although he had rendered satisfactory service to the defendant. In its opinion the Court of Appeals of the District of Columbia stated (290 F. at page 289):

"The circumstances surrounding the making of this contract largely control the interpretation to be given the words 'permanent employment' as used therein, for it must be assumed that the parties, knowing those circumstances, contracted with reference to them. The plaintiff held a position with the United States government, and the defendant agreed that, if he would resign from that position and take charge of the purchase of coal for the defendant, he would be given 'permanent employment in that capacity so long as he rendered satisfactory services and was loyal to its interests.' Relying upon this agreement, plaintiff did resign and perform his part of the contract. May it be said that it was within the contemplation of either party that 'permanent employment,' as used in the contract, meant that the plaintiff, the day following his resignation from his position with the government and the assumption of his new duties,

ILLUSTRATION 18-3.   *Continued*

could have been summarily discharged without any liability on the part of the defendant? Such a result could not have been contemplated by either party. The more reasonable view is that the parties contemplated that, so long as the defendant continued in a business requiring the purchase of coal and the plaintiff performed loyal and satisfactory service, he would continue to be employed in the capacity specified in the contract."

The first case cited in support of the conclusion of the court was *Carnig v. Carr.* The trial court had held as a matter of law that the plaintiff could not recover and awarded judgment upon the special verdict for the defendant. The Court of Appeals reversed that judgment and remanded the cause with directions to enter judgment for the plaintiff in the amount found by the jury. See also *Roxana Petroleum Co. v. Rice,* 109 Okl. 161, 235 P. 502, 507; *Millsap v. National Funding Corporation,* 57 Cal. App. 2d 772, 135 P.2d 407, 409. In *Littell v. Evening Star Newspaper Co.,* 73 App. D.C. 409, 120 F.2d 36, the court approved the rule announced in *Carnig v. Carr* and other cases, but held that the evidence in the case showed that the minds of the parties never met upon a permanent employment agreement. We do not deem it necessary to refer to cases like *Eggers v. Armour & Co. of Delaware,* 8 Cir., 129 F. 2d 729, wherein it appears that the plaintiff suffered injuries in the course of his employment with the defendant and he claimed that the defendant had him sign a written contract that insured him a lifetime job, although we note that the court in the *Eggers* case stated (129 F.2d at page 731): "The rule is that a contract for lifetime employment will be given effect, according to its terms, if the intention of the parties to make such an agreement is clear, even though the only consideration for it, so far as the employer is concerned, is the promise of the employee to render the service called for by the contract."

But the defendant contends (a): "There was no evidence that Dall had authority to enter into the alleged contract to employ plaintiff for life or that defendant company ratified the alleged contract;" and (b) "There was no evidence that defendant company acted in bad faith in discharging plaintiff." All of these contentions involve disputed questions of fact and therefore they cannot be considered in determining the instant contention of plaintiff. After a careful consideration of the question before us we have reached the conclusion that the trial court erred in entering judgment for the defendant company notwithstanding the verdict for plaintiff.

Plaintiff also contends that the trial court erred in entering the order granting the defendant a new trial. The following ground, inter alia, was urged in the motion for a new trial: "The verdict of the jury as to defendant Chicago Title & Trust Company is contrary to the manifest weight of the evidence." As this case may be tried again we refrain from analyzing and commenting upon the evidence

ILLUSTRATION 18-3. *Continued*

that bears upon the instant contention. Suffice it to say that the defendants introduced evidence in support of their claim that Mr. Dall did not promise plaintiff permanent employment. The Appellate Courts of this State, upon an appeal from an order of the trial court granting a new trial, have consistently held that they would not interfere with an order of the trial court granting a new trial unless the record showed a clear abuse of discretion by the trial court in granting the motion. After a careful consideration of all of the evidence, we are satisfied that we would not be justified in holding that the trial court was guilty of a clear abuse of discretion. We have considered the further contention of plaintiff that the trial court should not have entertained the motion for a new trial and find the contention without substantial merit.

The judgment order of the Superior Court of Cook county entered May 13, 1943, entering judgment in favor of the defendant Chicago Title & Trust Company non obstante veredicto is reversed. The judgment order of the Superior Court of Cook county entered June 3, 1943, setting aside the verdict of the jury and granting the defendant Chicago Title & Trust Company a new trial is affirmed. The cause is remanded for a new trial.

Judgment order entered May 13, 1943, entering judgment in favor of the defendant Chicago Title & Trust Company non obstante veredicto is reversed. Judgment order entered June 3, 1943, setting aside the verdict of the jury and granting the defendant Chicago Title & Trust Company a new trial is affirmed. The cause is remanded for a new trial.

SULLIVAN, P.J., and FRIEND, J., concur.

---

case briefs found in Illustrations 18-4 and 18-5. Both are adequate briefs of the case, yet they are different. After reading the case and the briefs, go back to the case and try to find where the issue, facts, holding, and rationale were obtained. This will give you insight into the information that must be gleaned from a case to write a brief.

After reading the *Molitor* case and briefs, read the *Heuvelman* decision found in Illustration 18-6. Although it is also decided by the Illinois Appellate Court and deals with the issue of permanent employment, it was decided 14 years after the *Molitor* case. Read the two briefs following the decision found in Illustrations 18-7 and 18-8. Although the briefs differ, they both are adequate in summarizing the opinions in specific categories. You will notice that *Heuvelman* cites *Molitor;* this is an example of how legal precedent is used and why we perform case law research. Now compare the briefs for the two cases. Since both sets of briefs are drafted with the same categories

ILLUSTRATION 18-4.   Case Brief for *Molitor v. Chicago Title & Trust Co.*

CITE

MOLITOR V. CHICAGO TITLE & TRUST CO.
325 Ill. App. 124, 59 N.E.2d 695 (1945)

PROCEDURE

Plaintiff appeals judgment for defendant non obstante veredicto for breach of employment contract.

ISSUE

Was there an oral contract for permanent employment between plaintiff and defendant?

HOLDING

Contract for lifetime employment is in effect if the intention of the parties is clear even if the only consideration for it is the promise of the employee to render the service called for by the contract.

FACTS

The plaintiff was employed by Chicago Title & Trust as a probationary examiner for seven years before leaving and moving his family to New York to work for a former client. After losing that job, he began to practice law in New York. In June 1934, he was contacted by Mr. Dall of CT&T asking him to reenter their employ temporarily. He and Mr. Dall made arrangement for the plaintiff to work for that period for CT&T while retaining his law practice. He was absent from his work for CT&T to attend to his practice on several occasions with the knowledge of Mr. Dall. In June 1936, Mr. Dall offered the plaintiff a new agreement, asking him to leave his law practice and move his family to Chicago to take permanent employment with CT&T. The plaintiff replied that if he could rely on that promise of permanent employment he would buy a house in Chicago and move his family there. Mr. Dall replied that the position was permanent, whereupon the plaintiff severed his New York connections and moved his family. On March 15, 1938, he was discharged by Mr. Dall.

RATIONALE

To ascertain what is meant by "permanent employment," the circumstances surrounding the making of the contract, the situation, and the relationship of the parties, and the common understanding of the meaning of the words used must be considered.

DISPOSITION

Reversed in part and remanded.

ILLUSTRATION 18-5.   Case Brief for *Molitor v. Chicago Title & Trust Co.*

CITATION

MOLITOR V. CHICAGO TITLE & TRUST CO.
325 Ill. App. 124, 59 N.E.2d 695 (1945)

PROCEDURE

This case is appealed to the First District Appellate Court of Illinois from the Superior Court of Cook County. The trial court gave a judgment in favor of the defendant notwithstanding a jury verdict against Chicago Title. Plaintiff appeals from that judgment.

ISSUE

Was there a breach of employment contract that makes the grant of summary judgment for the defendant in error? Was there also error in granting the defendants a new trial?

HOLDING

The judgment order granting verdict finding for the defendant is reversed. The judgment order granting a new trial is affirmed.

FACTS

Plaintiff Molitor reentered employment of defendant Chicago Title as an examiner. Upon reentry, his employment was of a temporary character in order to maintain his and his wife's business connections in New York. This arrangement ultimately became unsatisfactory with the defendant who asked Molitor to abandon his New York connections so he could give Chicago Title his continuous service. Molitor was unwilling to do so unless he felt this new arrangement was a permanent position. He finally accepted the position, relying on what he believed to be such a promise. He moved his family to Chicago and continued in the employ of Chicago Title until 1938, when he was discharged. Molitor brought suit for breach of an employment contract.

REASONING

The reasonable view is that the parties contemplate employment so long as the defendant continues in the business and the plaintiff performs satisfactory service. The surrounding circumstances in the making of a contract must also be considered to ascertain what the parties intended by "permanent employment." There is evidence to prove the plaintiff's contention of permanent employment. The plaintiff accepted employment with defendant because of a promise. Upon this reliance, he abandoned his work in New York and moved his family to Chicago. He would not have contemplated doing so without clear assurances of a permanent employment agreement.

ILLUSTRATION 18-5.   *Continued*

There is also evidence to support the defendant's claim that permanent employment was not promised. Thus, the order for a new trial is appropriate.

DISPOSITION
   Reversed in part and affirmed in part.

ILLUSTRATION 18-6.   *Heuvelman v. Triplett Elec. Instrument Co.*

Bert W. HEUVELMAN, doing business as Instrument Sales Company (not incorporated), Plaintiff-Appellant,

v.

TRIPLETT ELECTRICAL INSTRUMENT CO., a corporation, Defendant-Appellee.

Gen. No. 47702.

Appellate Court of Illinois.

First District, First Division

Oct. 26, 1959.

Rehearing Denied Nov. 18, 1959.

SCHWARTZ, Justice.

The trial court sustained both defendant's motion for a summary judgment and its motion to strike the amended complaint, and thereupon dismissed the suit with prejudice. From these orders plaintiff has appealed. The principal issue involved turns on an alleged oral agreement for permanent employment.

The amended complaint consists of three counts. Count I seeks a declaratory judgment finding that plaintiff and defendant entered into a contract for the permanent employment of plaintiff as a sales representative for the sale of electrical and radio equipment; that the contract was breached; and that plaintiff suffered damages in the sum of $250,000. Counts II and III are alternatives to Count I. Count II alleges that plaintiff prior to his alleged discharge procured the listing of defendant's products in various catalogs and was entitled to commission on sales obtained through publication and distribution of such catalogs, amounting to a sum in excess of $75,000. Count III alleges that plaintiff although informed that his services were terminated as of November 30, 1955, was called upon for

ILLUSTRATION 18-6. *Continued*

services until the appointment of a new representative in February 1956; that in the interval he serviced the accounts and that his commissions on orders placed with defendant during that time amounted to in excess of $50,000.

The motion for summary judgment was supported by affidavits and depositions of the respective parties. In addition, defendant used the averments of the original complaint which had been sworn to by plaintiff. The amended complaint was not verified. The pertinent facts extracted from these documents follow. From 1925 to January 1933 plaintiff was employed by an agency which served as defendant's sales representative in the midwest. In January 1933 defendant hired plaintiff as its sole sales representative for the territory previously covered by the agency. The agreement specified no definite time of employment. In April 1933 defendant desired to secure the services of another sales representative, Jerome T. Keeney, employed by a competitor of defendant, and defendant brought plaintiff and Keeney together for the purpose of having them become associated as joint representatives for the sale of defendant's products. At that meeting, as plaintiff alleges, defendant agreed that plaintiff's employment would continue as long as defendant manufactured and sold electrical equipment and as long as plaintiff acted as sales representative in that field. Plaintiff charges that it was on the basis of that agreement that he consented to enter into a partnership with Keeney. Instead of a partnership, however, a corporation was formed, the Instrument Sales Corporation, in which plaintiff and Keeney owned stock.

The business association between plaintiff and Keeney continued until 1940, when Keeney left plaintiff to join the Simpson Electric Company, a competitor of defendant. At that time Simpson also made plaintiff an offer. Plaintiff orally discussed with defendant the matter of his leaving and, as stated by plaintiff but denied by defendant, Triplett, president of defendant company, told plaintiff as they walked down State Street in Chicago, that their arrangement was a permanent one. It continued until October 1955, when defendant notified plaintiff that it terminated the relationship effective November 30, 1955.

We will first consider the motion for summary judgment as it applies to Count I. Oral contracts for "permanent employment" (meaning that as long as defendant was engaged in the prescribed work and as long as plaintiff was able to do his work satisfactorily, defendant would employ him) have been sustained, provided such contracts are supported by a consideration other than the obligation of services to be performed on the one hand and wages to be paid on the other. *Molitor v. Chicago Title & Trust Co.,* 1845, 325 Ill. App. 124, 132-133, 59 N.E.2d 695-698; *Carnig v. Carr,* 1897, 167 Mass. 544, 46 N.E. 117, 35 L.R.A. 512; *Riefkin v. E. I. Du Pont, etc., & Co.,* 1923,

ILLUSTRATION 18-6. *Continued*

53 App. D.C. 311, 290 F. 286; *Eggers v. Armour & Co.*, 8 Cir., 1942, 129 F.2d 729; *Roxana Petroleum Co. of Oklahoma v. Rice.*, 1924, 109 Okl. 161, 235 P. 502. In the *Molitor* case the consideration was the giving up by the employee of a profitable law practice in New York in order to move to Chicago in reliance on a promise of permanent employment. The *Molitor* case was supported and approved, but distinguished, in *Goodman v. Motor Products Corp.*, 1950, 9 Ill. App. 2d 57, 77 132 N.E.2d 356, 366. In *Carnig v. Carr*, supra, the plaintiff gave up a going and competitive venture to go with his employer. In *Riefkin v. E. I. Du Pont, etc., & Co.*, supra, the employee gave up his position in government, a position of security and prestige. The case of *Roxana Petroleum Co. v. Rice*, supra, concerned a firm's giving up its whole law practice in order to represent a single client. Where there is no particular detriment to the employee, the act of terminating other employment is not a sufficient consideration to make the new contract binding. *Edwards v. Kentucky Utilities Co.*, 1941, 286 Ky. 341, 150 S.W.2d 916, 135 A.L.R. 642.

In the instant case the time of the first alleged conversation on which permanent employment is based is April 1933. At that time plaintiff was already employed by defendant and the formation of a partnership with Keeney, terminable at will, so far as appears from anything in the record, cannot be considered a detriment but an advantage, Keeney being a man of considerable experience and competence, as was plaintiff in this business. The alleged renewal of the offer in 1940, when plaintiff was being solicited to join Simpson, is presented in such a vague, indefinite way that it is impossible to consider it as an obligation. Plaintiff says Simpson offered him a 25% interest in a new business venture. It does not appear whether this was a gift or a capital contribution. It is not sufficient consideration for a contract of permanent employment to forgo another employment opportunity. *Lewis v. Minnesota Mutual Life Insurance Co.*, 1949, 240 Iowa 1249, 37 N.W.2d 316; *Skagerberg v. Blandin Paper Co.*, 1936, 197 Minn. 291, 266 N.W. 872.

It is our further conclusion that considered in the light of the averments under oath in the complaint and not specifically retracted in the amended complaint, and further considering the deposition of plaintiff, no contract for permanent employment was made, nor was any adequate consideration to support one shown. Such contracts extending for a long duration and resting entirely on parol should have for their basis definite and certain mutual promises. The words and the manner of their utterance should not be of that informal character which expresses only long continuing good will and hopes for eternal association.

We will proceed now to a consideration of the second count, in which plaintiff alleges he was entitled to commission on those sales to distributors induced by the listing of defendant's products in

ILLUSTRATION 18-6. *Continued*

distributors' catalogs. While the court sustained the motion for summary judgment as to that count also, defendant acknowledges that was wrong and that only the motion to strike should have been sustained. The allegations upon which plaintiff relies are that he brought about the listing of defendant's products in various distributors' catalogs; that upon publication of those catalogs and their distribution to customers of distributors, sales would inevitably follow as distributors' inventories would be depleted and they would be required to reorder from defendant. Consequently, plaintiff concludes that when he procured catalog listings, he was the efficient cause of subsequent sales. Defendant in reply states that it is the fact of the sale which fixes the right of a salesman to payment of commission. Therefore a salesman cannot claim commission for sales effected after his term of employment ends, even though he was the efficient cause of the sale subsequently made.

Defendant's contention ignores a principle of law protecting salesmen in a position similar to plaintiff where the salesman is discharged prior to culmination of a sale but after he has done everything necessary to effect the sale. Thus, the general rule recognized in this and other jurisdictions is that an agent or salesman who is the procuring cause of a sale is entitled to commission notwithstanding the fact that the sale was consummated by the principal personally or through another agent. *Atkinson v. New Britain Machine Co.,* 7 Cir., 1946, 154 F.2d 895. See also *Groome v. Freyn Engineering Co.,* 1940, 374 Ill. 113, 28 N.E.2d 274. Cf. Annotation 1950, 12 A.L.R.2d 1361, 1372. We recognize that the usual case within this rule involves an agent who has had some kind of direct personal contact with a prospective customer, and that it is therefore distinguishable from the case at bar. However, each case must be taken in its particular setting. If, as plaintiff alleges, the sales were all but consummated when an article was listed in a distributor's catalog, plaintiff has brought himself within the scope of the general rule. It is our conclusion that the court erroneously sustained the motion to strike Count II.

As to the third count, defendant, as in the case of the second count, acknowledges that the order for summary judgment was improper. The only question therefore with respect to the third count is whether the motion to strike was properly allowed. That count is in the nature of a quantum meruit. It charges that defendant held out plaintiff as its representative after termination of his employment and that plaintiff serviced the accounts until a new representative was appointed. In its motion to strike defendant complains of the use of the phrase "servicing the accounts," that the term "servicing" remains nebulous and undefined. We hold that the term has a common meaning understood not only as a sales term, but by the public generally with relation to those services which a salesman of

ILLUSTRATION 18-6. *Continued*

mechanical appliances is called upon to perform. If defendant desired further clarification, that could easily have been obtained by interrogatories or other liberal discovery procedure.

Defendant charges a further ground for the motion to strike that plaintiff failed to annex to his complaint a copy of a circular which defendant sent to distributors after termination of plaintiff's employment. The provision in Section 36 of the Civil Practice Act, Ill. Rev. Stat. 1959, c. 110, §36, requires the attachment only of those instruments upon which action is brought. It does not contemplate annexation of every paper which may properly be offered in evidence. *H.E. Mueller & Co. v. Kinkead,* 1903, 113 Ill. App. 132.

The allegation that the complaint does not allege the defendant's knowledge of or consent to the services of plaintiff during the period is effectively rebutted by the alleged notice circularized to defendant's customers subsequent to termination of the prior agreement. The notice set forth the fact that plaintiff was still defendant's sales representative.

The order insofar as it sustains the motion to strike Count I and enters summary judgment thereon is affirmed. The order insofar as it sustains the motion to strike Counts II and III and enters summary judgment thereon is reversed and the cause is remanded with directions to vacate the summary judgment and overrule the motion to strike Counts II and III, and for such further proceedings as are not inconsistent with the views herein expressed.

Affirmed in part and reversed in part, and cause remanded for further proceedings.

DEMPSEY, P.J., and McCORMICK, J., concur.

ILLUSTRATION 18-7. **Case Brief for** *Heuvelman v. Triplett Elec. Instrument Co.*

CITE

HEUVELMAN V. TRIPLETT ELEC. INSTRUMENT CO.
23 Ill. App. 2d 231, 161 N.E.2d 875 (1959).

PROCEDURE

The plaintiff appeals summary judgment for the defendant, dismissing his suit for breach of oral contract for permanent employment.

ISSUE

Was there an oral contract for permanent employment between plaintiff and defendant?

ILLUSTRATION 18-7. *Continued*

FACTS

The plaintiff was hired by the defendant as a sales representative in January 1935. The agreement specified no definite time of employment. The defendant brought in another sales rep in April 1933 to act jointly with the plaintiff, who agreed to do so on defendant's promise of permanent employment. A competitor offered plaintiff a job in 1940, which he refused after discussing it with defendant. Plaintiff claims the defendant told him the arrangement was permanent as they walked together down State Street. The defendant denies the claim. In October 1955, the defendant terminated plaintiff's employment as of November 30, 1955.

HOLDING

No contract for permanent employment was made, nor was adequate consideration to support one shown. Contracts extending for long duration resting entirely on parol should have basis on definite and mutual promises. Words should not be of informal character expressing goodwill and hope for eternal association.

RATIONALE

The act of terminating other employment is not sufficient consideration to make a new contract binding if there is no detriment to the employee. Oral contracts have been sustained provided they are supported by consideration other than services for wages. The alleged renewal offer was vague, so it is impossible to consider it an obligation on the part of the defendant.

DISPOSITION

Affirmed in part, reversed in part, remanded.

ILLUSTRATION 18-8. Case Brief for *Heuvelman v. Triplett Elec. Instrument Co.*

CITATION

HEUVELMAN V. TRIPLETT ELEC. INSTRUMENT CO.
23 Ill. App. 2d 231, 161 N.E.2d 875 (1959).

PROCEDURE

This case is appealed by the plaintiff from the circuit court of Cook County to the First District Appellate Court of Illinois. The trial court sustained the defendant's motion for a summary judgment and dismissed the suit with prejudice.

ILLUSTRATION 18-8.   *Continued*

ISSUE
Whether the plaintiff and defendant entered into an oral contract for the permanent employment of the plaintiff.

FACTS
Plaintiff Heuvelman was hired as sole sales representative for the defendant Triplett Electrical. In 1933, defendant brought Heuvelman and a Mr. Keeney together for the purpose of having them become associated as joint representatives for the sale of the company's products. In 1940, Keeney left to join a competitor. Heuvelman also considered leaving to join the competitor but remained with Triplett Electrical after receiving assurances that his arrangment was a permanent one. In 1955, he was then terminated by Triplett Electrical.

HOLDING
It is not sufficient consideration for a contract of permanent employment to forgo another employment opportunity. No contract for permanent employment was made, nor was any adequate consideration to support one shown. Counts relating to commission and compensation for services after termination are not defective.

REASONING
Oral contracts for permanent employment are valid as long as they are supported by a consideration other than the obligation of services to be performed on the one hand and wages to be paid on the other. Where there is no particular detriment to the employee, the act of terminating other employment is not a sufficient consideration to make the new contract binding. When plaintiff was being solicited to join the competitor, the renewal with Triplett Electrical was presented in a vague and indefinite way and cannot be considered as an obligation. A salesman who is the procuring cause of a sale is entitled to commission notwithstanding the fact that the sale was consummated by the principal personally or through another agent. The defendant held the plaintiff as its representative after termination, allowing him to service accounts.

DISPOSITION
Affirmed in part and reversed in part.

(citation, procedure, issue, facts, holding, rationale, and disposition), you can compare and contrast cases easily and quickly. Compare the issues and you will see that they are very similar. Now compare the facts and the holdings and you will notice that they differ.

CHAPTER SUMMARY

A case brief has several components, including a citation, the procedural facts, an issue, a holding, the relevant facts, the reasoning, and the case disposition. These briefs are designed to assist you and sometimes an attorney in understanding a case.

The brief's procedural facts statement should explain briefly how a case came before a court.

The issue statement presents the questions posed by the parties. The holding is the rule of law established by the court. The facts statement should include any relevant facts that affected the court's decision in the case. The reasoning explains how the court developed the rule of law and how it relates to the facts of the case. The disposition is the procedural result of the case.

Dicta often is included in a court decision. It is a statement made by a court concerning an issue other than one the court was asked to decide.

This chapter also provides you with your first exposure to legal writing. You learned the step-by-step process of drafting a case brief. Each component of a case brief relates to the other sections of the brief. For a review, see Illustration 18-9 on page 374.

KEY TERMS

case brief
case citation
dicta
disposition
holding
issue

procedural facts
rationale
reasoning
relevant facts
rule of law

ILLUSTRATION 18-9.   Case Briefing Process

EXERCISES

IN-CLASS EXERCISE

Issues

1. Review the following issues prepared for a case brief of the *King* case. List any problems you find. Which issue of the following five is best, and why?

   Issue 1. Was the district court's decision that King was an independent contractor rather than an employee of the Miller Co. erroneous?

   Issue 2. Whether King was an employee of Miller or an independent contractor for these reasons:

   a. The control factor, in which agents are restricted in the selling of insurance as to whom or where. Agents also have mandatory requirements for working at designated times and dates. In addition, they are expected to attend weekly meetings and engage in daily office tasks.

   b. The economic factor, in which agents are not allowed to sell products for anyone but Miller and that agents are "integral" to Miller's business.

   c. As with employees, services, supplies, and education expenses are provided. Compensation is made in the form of commissions.

   d. Work hours are based on flexibility for prime selling.

   e. Performance evaluations and documents of rules of conduct are customary requirements of an employer-employee relationship.

   Issue 3. Whether, in finding the plaintiff was not an employee under the Title VII definition, the trial court erred by:

   a. failing to properly evaluate the nature of insurance sales;

   b. and failing to evaluate and weigh the integral economic relationship between the defendant and the plaintiff; and

   c. failing to discuss other evidence regarding the "control" criterion used to judge eligibility.

   Issue 4. Whether the district court was clearly erroneous in determining that an insurance agent is an independent contractor rather than an employee when the individual is paid commissions and bonuses rather than a salary and her work is not supervised by the company.

   Issue 5. Does an employer have to exercise control over a worker before that individual is considered an employee under Title VII?

Holdings

2. Review the holdings below that were drafted for a brief in the *King* case, list any problems you see with each, and note which is the best.

   Holding 1. The court of appeals affirmed the lower court's decision that King is an independent contractor rather than an employee of the Miller Co.

   Holding 2. Because the trial court did understand the law and its factual findings are not clearly erroneous, its decision is affirmed.

   Holding 3. The district court's underlying factual findings are not clearly erroneous; therefore, the decision of the district court was affirmed.

   Holding 4. Yes. An employer must exercise control over a worker before that individual is considered an employee under Title VII.

HOMEWORK
Briefing

3. Brief *Kalal v. Goldblatt Bros.*, 368 N.E.2d 671 (Ill. Ct. App. 1977).

THE LEGAL MEMORANDUM

CHAPTER OVERVIEW

This chapter introduces you to the legal memorandum. You learn about your audience and how to write objectively. You are introduced to the components of the memorandum, such as the issues, conclusion or brief answer, facts, and discussion sections. The chapter concludes with a brief overview of the process of writing a memorandum.

A. THE LEGAL MEMORANDUM

▼ What Is an Objective Legal Memorandum?

An **office memorandum**, often called a memo, explains in an objective rather than a persuasive or argumentative manner the current state of the law regarding an issue. It clarifies how that law applies to a client's transaction or legal dilemma. A memo should explain the current law—both favorable and unfavorable—and any legal theories pertaining to the issue.

The balanced approach of a legal memo helps an attorney see the strengths and weaknesses of a transaction or dispute. Only when an attorney can see all sides of an issue can the attorney determine how best to represent a client. Sometimes your research will determine whether the client has a case or not. If in writing a memo you advocate a single position or attempt to persuade an attorney, the attorney cannot make an informed decision about a dispute or transaction. This can be a very costly error in terms of money, time, client loyalty, and court favor.

A memo also assists an attorney in predicting how a court might decide a particular issue. A memo could be drafted to address an issue raised as a case progresses in court. As a paralegal, you might research whether the law provides for the dismissal of an action; your research and memorandum might form the basis for such a motion to dismiss or for subsequent court documents. You might also write a memo to assist an attorney in drafting an appellate brief.

B. AUDIENCE

▼ Who Reads a Memorandum?

Because you usually research a legal question to determine whether a client has a claim or should proceed with a transaction, you generally prepare your memo for an attorney following your research. Your memo also might be sent to the client. Your primary audience, then, is the attorney, and the secondary audience is the client.

Often memoranda are saved in **memo banks** accessible to all firm or corporation attorneys and paralegals, so other attorneys and paralegals might review your memo. These memo banks are a good place for you to start a research project because an attorney or a paralegal already may have researched the topic. These banks often save time and money for a client. After you review a memo from the memo bank, update the research.

C. COMPONENTS OF A MEMORANDUM

▼ What Is Included in a Memorandum?

A memorandum can have a variety of components arranged in different orders. The components and their order often vary from attorney to attorney. Ask the assigning attorney if your firm or corporation has a particular style. Request a sample memo so that you can review the style he or she prefers, or go to the memo bank to review a sample. The format discussed in this chapter is one commonly accepted style. See the sample memo in Illustration 19-1.

ILLUSTRATION 19-1.   Sample Memorandum

MEMORANDUM

To: Benjamin Joyce
From: William Randall
Date: January 28, 1998
Re: *Harris v. Sack and Shop*

QUESTION PRESENTED
Is Sack and Shop, a grocery store, liable for injuries sustained by Harris, a store patron who slipped on a banana peel that had been on the grocery store floor for two days?

BRIEF ANSWER
Probably yes. Sack and Shop, a grocery store, probably will be liable based on negligence for injuries sustained by Harris, a store patron who slipped on a banana peel that had been on the grocery store floor for two days.

FACTS
Our client, Sack and Shop Grocery Store, is being sued for negligence by Rebecca Harris.
Harris went to the store to purchase groceries on July 8, 1997. While she was in the produce section, she slipped on a banana that had been left on the floor by a grocery store employee. The employee had dropped it on the floor two days earlier and had failed to clean it up after a patron asked him to do so.
Harris sustained a broken arm and head injuries as a result of the slip and fall.

DISCUSSION
The issue presented in this case is whether Sack and Shop Grocery Store was negligent when Rebecca Harris slipped in the store's produce section. A grocer will be found negligent if a store employee breached the store's duty of reasonable care to its patrons and, as a result of that breach, the patron was injured. *Ward v. K Mart Corp.,*

ILLUSTRATION 19-1. *Continued*

554 N.E.2d 223 (Ill. 1990). In *Ward,* the grocery store employee failed to clean up a banana peel for two days and that peel caused a patron to be injured. Similarly in our case Sack and Shop failed to remove the banana peel. Therefore, Sack and Shop is likely to be found liable for the injuries Harris sustained.

The first element to consider is whether Sack and Shop owed a duty of reasonable care to Harris. A grocery store owes a duty of care to any patron. *Ward,* 554 N.E.2d at 226. Harris was a customer in the store. Therefore, Sack and Shop owed her a duty of care.

The next question to consider is whether Sack and Shop breached its duty of reasonable care to Harris. A store will be found to have breached its duty of reasonable care to a patron if a store employee fails to properly and regularly clean the floor of the store. *Olinger v. Great Atl. & Pac. Tea Co.,* 173 N.E.2d 443 (Ill. 1961). In *Olinger,* the store was found liable because a store employee failed to clean the floor for one day and a patron slipped on a substance on the floor. 173 N.E.2d at 447. No one had told any store employee about the slippery substance. *Id.* at 447. Nonetheless, the Illinois Supreme Court found the store liable, saying that the store employees had sufficient time to notice the substance if they had used ordinary care. *Id.* In our case, Sack and Shop's employee had two days to clean the floor before Harris fell. In addition, a customer had placed the store employee on notice of the banana. Therefore, Sack and Shop breached its duty of care to Harris.

The plaintiff, however, still must establish proximate cause, that is, that the injury resulted as a natural consequence of Sack and Shop's breach of its duty. A store owner's failure to clear debris from a store floor, resulting in injury to a patron who slipped on the floor, was found to be the proximate cause of the patron's injuries. *Id.* at 449. In this case, Sack and Shop's failure to clean the peel from the floor was a breach of its duty of care to Harris. This breach resulted in injury to Harris. Sack and Shop's breach will be found to be the proximate cause of Harris's injuries.

The final element that must be established is that the plaintiff, Harris, suffered injuries. Harris sustained a broken arm and head injuries as a result of the slip and fall. Therefore, she will be able to show that she was injured.

CONCLUSION

Sack and Shop owed Harris a duty of reasonable care. The store is likely to be found to have breached that duty of reasonable care because an employee failed to remove a banana peel from the grocery store floor during the preceding two days. The injuries Harris sustained were directly caused by a slip on a banana peel. Therefore, Sack and Shop is likely to be found liable to Harris.

ILLUSTRATION 19-2.   Sample Memorandum Heading

MEMORANDUM

To: Sarah E. Lillian
From: Kelsey Barrington
Date: July 8, 1998
Re: Negligence Action between Sack and Shop Grocery Store
    and Rebecca Harris

1. Heading

In Illustration 19-1, the first part of the memo is the **heading**. A sample heading also is shown in Illustration 19-2. The first notation in the heading of either illustration is the word "MEMORANDUM," placed in all capital letters at the top of the page. The next notations in both Illustrations 19-1 and 19-2 tell the reader who the memorandum is written to and from, the date, and the subject. The regarding line, indicated by the "Re:," varies depending on the firm's style. For example, some insurance clients ask that you include claim numbers in the regarding line. Some attorneys prefer court case numbers, and still others prefer clients' billing numbers and file numbers.

2. Questions Presented or Issues

The next portion of the memo seen in Illustration 19-1 is the questions presented section, sometimes called the issues section.

The terms **issues** or **questions presented** are synonymous. For our purposes, we will use the terms "question presented" or "questions presented." The questions presented are the specific legal questions an attorney has asked you to research. The question presented is phrased in the form of a question concerning the legal issue posed, and it includes a reference to the applicable law and some legally significant facts. See Illustration 19-3. The legal issue in Illustration 19-3 is whether the grocery store owner was negligent and whether he owed a duty to the patron. The legally significant facts are that the patron slipped on a banana peel that had been on the grocery store floor for two days. (A detailed explanation of how to draft the questions presented will be provided in Chapter 20.)

ILLUSTRATION 19-3.   Question Presented

Is a grocery store owner liable for injuries sustained by a store patron who slipped on a banana peel that had been on the grocery store for two days?

ILLUSTRATION 19-4.   Brief Answer

Probably yes. A grocery store owner probably will be liable based upon negligence for inquiries sustained by a store patron who slipped on a banana peel that had been on the grocery store floor for two days.

3. Conclusion or Brief Answer

You should follow the questions presented section with a **brief answer** or a **conclusion**. Brief answers and conclusions differ in format, although their purposes are similar. A brief answer is a short statement that directly answers the question or questions presented. See Illustration 19-4.

▼ What Is the Difference between a Conclusion and a Brief Answer?

Some attorneys prefer a brief answer immediately following the question or questions presented and a formal conclusion at the end of the memo. The brief answers should be presented in the same order as the questions they answer.

For other attorneys, a conclusion without a brief answer is sufficient. A conclusion is an in-depth answer to the question presented. There is no set length for a conclusion; it should be a succinct statement that summarizes the substance of the memo. See Illustration 19-5. As you can see in Illustration 19-5, the conclusion is more in-depth than the brief answer. However, note that both the conclusion and the brief answer include references to the legally significant facts: the failure to remove the banana peel from the grocery store floor. In the conclusion, you provide your opinion concerning the case. However, a paralegal should refrain from telling an attorney how to proceed. For example, do not say "I think that we will lose this case, so we should settle it." Instead, say "This case is not likely to be won." Allow the attorney to determine whether the case should be settled. (Drafting conclusions and brief answers will be explained in detail in Chapter 20.)

ILLUSTRATION 19-5.   Conclusion

A grocery store owner owes a patron a duty of reasonable care. The store owner is likely to be found to have breached that duty of reasonable care because he failed to remove a banana peel from the grocery store floor during the preceding two days. The injuries the patron sustained were directly caused by a slip on a banana peel. Therefore, the grocery store owner is likely to be found liable to the patron.

ILLUSTRATION 19-6. Facts Statement

Our client, Sack and Shop Grocery Store, is being sued for negligence by Rebecca Harris.

Harris went to the store to purchase groceries on July 8, 1997. While she was in the produce section, she slipped on a banana peel that had been left on the floor by a grocery store employee. The employee had dropped it on the floor two days earlier and had failed to clean it up after a patron asked him to do so.

Harris sustained a broken arm and head injuries as a result of the slip and fall.

ETHICS ALERT

Refrain from providing a legal opinion. Your memorandum may be given to a client and may be construed as providing legal advice.

4. Facts

Following the conclusion or brief answer, you should include a **facts statement** that explains the status of the case and all of the facts that might have a bearing on the outcome of a client's case. These facts are called **legally significant facts**. You should include facts that cast your client's dispute or transaction in a good light and those that shade it in a negative light. See Illustration 19-6.

5. Discussion

Following the facts, you will include your **discussion** in which you will explain the current state of the applicable law, analyze the law, and apply the law to the legally significant facts noted in the facts statement. Any problems posed in the client's case and counterarguments should be presented here. This should not be an exhaustive review of the history of the law but should be a focused analysis of the current state of the law. The law should be applied to each of the legally significant facts.

Finally, following the discussion, you should include a conclusion if a brief answer rather than a conclusion has been used earlier.

PRACTICE POINTER

Review memos prepared previously for the attorney who assigned the memorandum. Follow that format or ask the assigning attorney what format he or she prefers.

D. STEPS IN DRAFTING A MEMORANDUM

▼ What Steps Should You Take in Drafting a Memo?

1. An attorney will assign a research problem to you. Discuss the problem thoroughly with the attorney. Be certain to ask the attorney questions to clarify the legal issues and the facts of a dispute or transaction. Ask for guidance concerning possible topics to research and resources to consult.

2. Immediately following your meeting, draft a preliminary statement of the legal issues and the relevant facts.

3. Begin your research. To develop an understanding of the issues and the general legal rules applicable to your problem, and to provide you with some search terms, read secondary authorities such as encyclopedias and *American Law Reports*. During your research, you often will discover other issues that may be relevant, and you will find additional facts that are important. If you are uncertain whether to pursue these additional issues, ask the attorney who assigned the case whether the issues are relevant.

4. If you have additional questions about the facts of a case, ask the attorney or the client for additional facts to assist you in determining what authorities are relevant to your research.

5. After you find relevant authorities, validate the authorities and review the citators for more current, valuable authorities. If necessary, review these additional authorities.

6. Prepare case briefs of the relevant cases. (See Chapter 18 for a detailed discussion of case briefing.)

7. After you have completed your research, rewrite the questions presented.

8. Rewrite the facts and then draft the brief answers or conclusions (or both).

9. Next, outline the discussion section. (See Chapter 24 for a discussion of outlining and organizing the memorandum.) While you are preparing your outline, you should synthesize the legal authorities. (This process is explained in Chapter 22.) You should formulate your discussion and paragraphs in a special format called IRAC, which is an abbreviation for the formula Issue, Rule, Application, and Conclusion. (This format is discussed thoroughly in Chapter 23.) You can now begin to write your memorandum.

CHECKLIST FOR DRAFTING A MEMORANDUM

1. Discuss the case with the attorney
   a. Discuss the legal issues presented
   b. Discuss the known facts
   c. Determine whether additional facts should be investigated
   d. Determine what law governs

    e. Check the memo bank to determine firm's style and to learn whether the issue has been researched previously

2. Draft a preliminary statement of the facts
3. Draft a preliminary statement of the legal issues or questions presented
4. Research the legal issue or issues
    a. If you find additional relevant issues, discuss them with the attorney
    b. Determine whether additional facts should be considered in light of the new issues; ask the attorney or client about additional facts
    c. Research the new issues, if necessary
5. Rewrite the issues or questions presented after your research has allowed you to focus them better
6. Draft a brief answer or a conclusion (or both)
7. Rewrite the facts statement of the memo
8. Draft an outline of the discussion section of the memo; organize the discussion
9. Draft the discussion section
10. Reevaluate the facts and rewrite the facts statement to include only legally significant facts
11. Rewrite the conclusion

Memo Drafting Tips

You should be careful to guide your reader through each section of your memo and from issue to issue. To do this, introduce the legal issues in the facts section and again in the discussion section. Also, use headings and transitions to guide your reader into the new sections.

    Your memo should be clearly written, accurate, concise, and thorough. Use everyday language rather than legalese. Write the memo as if the reader is unfamiliar with the law, but do not be condescending. Your memo should not trace the legal history of the law. Instead, it should be a statement of the current state of the law.

    When you approach a legal rule, start with the rule rather than the citation for the authority. Doing so makes your discussion stronger.

    Be certain that your discussion supports your conclusions. Incorporate the relevant facts into your discussion.

CHAPTER SUMMARY

The legal memorandum is composed of issues, conclusions and brief answers, facts, and a discussion section. These are written for attorneys and clients. Memoranda are designed to assist them in determining the current state of the law regarding a legal issue and how that law applies to the facts presented in a particular case.

In the next few chapters, you will learn about each one of the components of a memorandum, the questions presented, the facts, the conclusions, the brief answers, and the discussion.

KEY TERMS

brief answer	issues
conclusion	legally significant facts
discussion	memo banks
facts statement	office memorandum
heading	questions presented

EXERCISES

TRUE OR FALSE

1. A memorandum should be persuasive in its style.
2. A memorandum should present only facts that are favorable to your client's position.
3. A memorandum should inform the attorney and the client about the favorable authorities and known facts as well as the authorities and facts that pose problems for a client's case.
4. Your memorandum will never be read by a client.
5. You should include descriptive words in the facts section that slant the facts in favor of your client's position.

CHAPTER 20

QUESTIONS PRESENTED AND CONCLUSIONS OR BRIEF ANSWERS

CHAPTER OVERVIEW

Chapter 19 introduced you to the legal memorandum and its components. This chapter explains the reasons for drafting questions presented, issues, brief answers, and conclusions and teaches you how to draft these items.

A. QUESTIONS PRESENTED OR ISSUES

The **questions presented** or **issues** are the problems you must research to answer the attorney's or client's questions. These questions provide a preview to the reader about the applicable legal standards and the relevant facts.

▼ Who Reads the Questions Presented Statement?

The questions presented statement often is the first portion of a memorandum an attorney reviews. Many attorneys focus on these questions and the conclusions or brief answers. Some attorneys read these questions and answers without reading the entire memorandum. Therefore, your questions presented statement must be easy to understand and allow the reader to quickly grasp the legal questions that the memo will address.

1. First Draft

The first draft of the questions presented should be done following the receipt of the initial research assignment from the attorney. Draft a simple statement that explains the questions you were asked to research. For example, suppose an attorney provides you with the following facts:

> While driving a car Ronnie Randall struck Janice Kahn's son at 5 P.M. on August 29, 1998. It was bright and clear. No skid marks appeared on the dry street following the accident.

> Janice Kahn was working in her garden about five feet from the accident scene at the time of the accident. Her son was playing a game in the street before Randall's car struck him. Kahn saw the car strike her son. When she first looked up from her garden, she thought her 11-year-old son was dead. He was covered with blood and had several broken bones. However, Kahn's son was conscious after the accident.

> Immediately after the accident, Randall, who had a blood/alcohol level of .11, was cited for drunk driving and driving with a suspended driver's license. Police had charged him with drunk driving and had suspended his license two weeks earlier after the car he was driving struck another child at the same spot. Randall has a drinking history.

> Following the accident, several witnesses said Randall was upset and wobbled as he walked. One witness said that Randall intentionally turned the steering wheel to hit Kahn's son. Kahn stated that Randall often swerved down her street to get her attention.

> Rhonda Albert, Kahn's neighbor, said she heard Randall say he would get even with Kahn after Kahn broke off a 10-year relationship with him. During Kahn and Randall's 10-year relationship, Randall was close to Kahn's son. He took him to ball games, including one in April, and attended the son's baseball games. Randall knew that Kahn's son was the most important person in her life.

Since the accident, Kahn vomits daily and has nightmares about the accident. Dr. Susan Faigen, Kahn's internist, states that the vomiting and nightmares are the result of the accident.

The attorney wants you to research whether Janice Kahn has a claim against Ronnie Randall for intentional infliction of emotional distress. Your first draft of the question presented might be:

> Does Janice Kahn have a valid claim for intentional infliction of emotional distress against Ronnie Randall?

▼ What Are Legally Significant Facts?

This question presented is too vague. To make your question more understandable in the context of Kahn's case, you must incorporate legally significant facts: facts that will have an impact on a jury's or judge's decision concerning Kahn's claim. You might rewrite the question presented with the facts as follows:

> Does Janice Kahn have a valid claim for intentional infliction of emotional distress against Ronnie Randall when Kahn saw Randall strike her 11-year-old child with his car?

By incorporating some **legally significant facts,** you have drafted a question presented that places the issue in perspective for the reader and that clearly identifies the parties in the action. This question presented allows the reader to understand the legal issue in the context of the factual circumstances surrounding the claim.

2. Research the Issue and Revise It

Now you are ready to research the issue. After you complete your research, you determine what law applies to a claim for intentional infliction of emotional distress. Once you determine the legal standard, you rewrite the question presented to incorporate that standard and only the legally significant facts. Your rewrite should frame the questions presented around the applicable legal standard and should present the applicable legal standard in the context of the facts that will affect the determination of a claim.

In the case of Janice Kahn, you learn from a decision of the highest court in your state that intentional infliction of emotional distress is "an act done by a person which is extreme and outrageous, done with intent to cause another to suffer severe emotional distress, and which results in distress and emotional injury to another. The emotional injury must manifest itself with a physical problem." If you rewrite the question presented above to incorporate the legal standard and legally significant facts, it might read as follows:

> Does Janice Kahn have a valid claim for intentional infliction of emotional distress against Ronnie Randall after Kahn saw Randall turn his car to strike Kahn's 11-year-old child in front of her, causing her to suffer from anxiety, headaches, and vomiting?

390 CHAPTER 20 / QUESTIONS PRESENTED AND CONCLUSIONS OR BRIEF ANSWERS

This question presented incorporates legally significant facts and provides these facts in the context of the legal standard. Randall's intention is one of the legal factors or elements in determining whether Kahn has a claim for intentional infliction of emotional distress. The question presented notes the legally significant fact that Randall turned his car to strike the child. Although you should mention legally significant facts and the legal standard, keep the issue short enough for the reader to understand.

3. Specificity and Precision

The facts should be **specific** and your characterization of the parties and the issues should be **precise.** For example, one of the issues posed in the sample memo in Chapter 24's Illustration 24-5 (page 455) involves the question of whether an individual is an independent contractor or an employee. You could pose the question presented as follows:

> Under Title VII, was Walker an employee when she worked exclusively for Whole In One, paid her own taxes quarterly rather than through deductions, and worked with limited company supervision?

The facts in this case are specific: Walker paid her taxes quarterly rather than through payroll deductions. However, the question presented is not precise because it does not characterize the legal issue presented completely. The legal issue is whether Walker is an independent contractor rather than an employee. Therefore, the question presented could be refined as follows:

> Under Title VII, was Walker an independent contractor rather than an employee when she worked exclusively for Whole In One, paid her own taxes quarterly rather than through deductions, and worked with limited company supervision?

You must only ask a question in the questions presented statement, not provide an answer. You will answer the question presented in the brief answer or conclusion section.

If you have more than one issue or question presented, place them in a logical order and make that order consistent throughout the memo. The first question presented, then, should be answered first in the conclusion or brief answer statement and should be the first issue addressed in the discussion. See Illustration 19-1 in Chapter 19.

B. BRIEF ANSWERS AND CONCLUSIONS

1. Brief Answers

Brief answers are the answers to the question or questions presented. A brief answer is a short statement. Some attorneys prefer a brief answer that is later accompanied by a formal conclusion at the end of the memorandum. The brief answer allows an attorney to read a memo in a hurry and determine the legal issues. It is a quick answer to the questions presented. Brief answers should be presented in the same order as the questions presented. See Illustration 20-1. The brief answer should include a brief statement of the applicable

ILLUSTRATION 20-1. Sample Memorandum: Question Presented and Conclusion

QUESTION PRESENTED

Under Title VII, was Whole In One an employer when 14 people, including three full-time and 11 part-time workers, worked on any one day for 24 weeks and when 10 full-time employees were on the payroll when she worked exclusively for Whole In One, paid taxes quarterly rather than through deductions, and worked with limited company supervision?

CONCLUSION

Whole In One was an employer. Under Title VII, an employer has at least 15 employees working for 20 or more weeks during the relevant year. Salaried employees are included in this number for each week they are on the payroll, while hourly workers are only counted on the days they actually work. In 1993, the year of the alleged discrimination, 14 workers, three full-time and 11 part-time people, worked for Whole In One on any day during the 24-week restaurant and golf season. However, 10 full-time workers were on the payroll. As these part-time workers are only counted on the days that they work, the number of part-time individuals included in the count of employees is 11 for each day of the 24-week season. Since full-time workers, however, are counted for each day of a week that they are on the payroll, all 10 of the Whole In One full-time workers would be included in the count of employees. In total, Whole In One had 11 part-time workers and 10 full-time workers "working" for 20 or more weeks during the relevant year, bringing the total count of employees to 21. Therefore, Whole In One was an employer under Title VII.

law and some relevant facts. A brief answer for the question presented above could be presented as follows:

> Yes. Kahn can bring a successful action for intentional infliction of emotional distress against Ronnie Randall because she saw Randall turn his car to strike her 11-year-old son, causing her to suffer severe anxiety, headaches, and vomiting.

In the memorandum, it would appear as follows:

> Question Presented: Does Janice Kahn have a valid claim for intentional infliction of emotional distress against Ronnie Randall after Kahn saw Randall turn his car to strike Kahn's 11-year-old child in front of her, causing her to suffer from anxiety, headaches, and vomiting?
>
> Brief Answer: Yes. Kahn can bring a successful action for intentional infliction of emotional distress against Ronnie Randall because she saw Randall turn his car to strike her 11-year-old son, causing her to suffer severe anxiety, headaches, and vomiting.

2. Conclusions

A **conclusion** also is an answer to the question presented and a summary of the discussion section. For some attorneys, a conclusion without a brief answer is sufficient. However, other attorneys prefer both a brief answer and a conclusion.

▼ How Is a Conclusion Different from a Brief Answer?

A conclusion does not have a set length, but it is generally longer than a brief answer. It is not a detailed or in-depth discussion of the legal issue presented in the case. It is a succinct summary of the substance of the memo. The conclusion should include legally significant facts and the applicable legal standard. In the conclusion, you must answer the question presented and provide your best prediction concerning the outcome of the case. It is acceptable to use terms such as *likely* or *probably* when you think that the outcome of an action is uncertain.

3. Drafting Conclusions

Before you draft your conclusion, review the questions presented and your preliminary facts statement. (A detailed explanation of the facts statement is presented in Chapter 21.)

Next, write the conclusion as an answer to the question presented and incorporate some of the relevant facts contained in the facts section of the memo. Refine the conclusion so that the reader understands the legal standard and the applicable facts. Conclusions often work well when drafted in an IRAC formula: Issue, Rule, Application, and Conclusion. (For a thorough discussion of the IRAC formula, see Chapter 23.)

For the facts and the question presented in the *Kahn* case, the following conclusion might be prepared:

> The central question is whether Janice Kahn has a valid claim for intentional infliction of emotional distress against Ronnie Randall. To successfully prove a claim for intentional infliction of emotional distress, Kahn must show that the act that caused the distress was extreme and outrageous and done with intent. In this case, Kahn saw Randall turn his car to strike her 11-year-old child. Seeing this accident caused Kahn to suffer from anxiety, headaches, and vomiting daily. Several witnesses can testify that Randall said that he intended to harm Kahn, and Kahn states that Randall turned the car to strike her son. Two factors, however, might show that Randall lacked intent: the statement that he made to the police that he did not intend to hit the child and the fact that his blood/alcohol level was .11, possibly preventing him from formulating the needed intent. Kahn probably has a claim for intentional emotional distress.

This conclusion provides a summary of the writer's prediction of the outcome of the case after the legal standards are applied to the legally significant facts:

> Janice Kahn probably has a valid claim for intentional infliction of emotional distress against Ronnie Randall.

Facts such as that Kahn saw Randall turn the car to strike her son and that witnesses can testify concerning what Randall said he intended to do are relevant to the question of whether the act was extreme and outrageous. The legal standard provides that the act must be extreme and outrageous before an individual can be liable for intentional infliction of emotional distress. In addition, the extreme and outrageous act must be done with intent. Randall's intent also is discussed in the conclusion.

Many students include an authority, such as a statute or case, in the conclusion. Most often, however, your analysis of a claim requires that you synthesize a number of authorities to determine the applicable law. It would be misleading, therefore, to include only one authority in your conclusion. You might include an authority if it is the sole authority governing a claim.

PRACTICE POINTER

When you have multiple questions presented, the conclusion section should answer the questions in the same order as they were presented.

In-Class Exercise

Read the questions presented in Illustration 20-1.

1. Discuss the issues and conclusions.
2. After reviewing the questions presented, what legal standards do you think will determine the applicable law?
3. Does the conclusion answer the questions presented? Are the legal standards discussed? What, if any, standards are noted?

Explanation for In-Class Exercise

For the question presented in Illustration 20-1, the issue is whether Whole In One is an employer under Title VII. The legal standards that determine whether Whole In One is an employer center on the definition of employer under Title VII and case law.

Now read the conclusion. It answers the question presented. In the second and third sentences, the conclusion provides the legal standard for determining this issue. These sentences refer to the definition of employer contained in the Title VII statute, which states that an employer "is a person engaged in a business affecting commerce who has fifteen or more employees for each working day in each of 20 or more calendar weeks in the current or preceding calendar year." 42 U.S.C. §2000e(b). The next sentence concerning salaried employees and part-time employees is based on a synthesis of the applicable cases. Next, the relevant facts of this case are discussed and applied to the legal standards. Finally, the writer presents a single sentence summarizing how the issue is likely to be resolved based on the application of the legal standards to the facts presented.

CHAPTER SUMMARY

In this chapter, you learned how to draft questions presented, issues, brief answers, and conclusions. Questions presented or issues should incorporate legally significant facts and the rule of law. Legally significant facts are facts that will affect a decision concerning an issue of law.

Legally significant facts and the current rule of law also should be included in the conclusions or brief answers that answer the questions presented or issues.

Some attorneys prefer both a brief answer and a conclusion, while others require only a conclusion.

The process of writing the questions presented, issues, brief answers, and conclusions requires that you rewrite these components of a memorandum several times. The questions presented or issues should be drafted before you perform your research. They should be rewritten after you complete your research. The conclusions or brief answers also should be rewritten in light of the facts presented in a case.

In the next chapter, you learn how to draft facts statements for your memoranda.

KEY TERMS

brief answers
conclusion
issues
legally significant facts

precise
questions presented
specific

EXERCISES

SHORT ANSWER EXERCISES

1. What is a brief answer?
2. How does a brief answer differ from a conclusion?
3. Is an issue or question presented written as a statement or a question?
4. If you have four questions presented, how many conclusions or brief answers should you have?
5. What is the purpose of a question presented?
6. What is the purpose of a conclusion?

QUESTIONS PRESENTED EXERCISES

Draft questions presented for memos in the following cases.

7. You work as a paralegal for the county prosecutor's office in Houcktown County. One of the assistant prosecutors asks you to research whether Bonnie Bill has committed aggravated burglary under the Houcktown Rev. Code §2911. The attorney has provided you with the following facts:

    Merriweather Halsey and Bonnie Bill were at the Masonic Temple for a fundraiser to fight AIDS. During the fundraiser Bill told a drunken Halsey that she intended to steal the $8,000 fundraiser proceeds from the Masonic Temple after the fundraiser and that she intended to steal a pearl necklace from Alice McKinley.

    Bill, who had helped organize the fundraiser, watched as the chairperson of the fundraiser opened the safe and placed the money in it. She memorized the combination and decided that she would use it later to steal the money.

    After the fundraiser, Bill walked home to get a credit card and a crowbar to open the door if she needed it. Bill went to the Masonic Temple after the fundraiser, wearing a disguise, showed the guard her invitation, and told him that she lost her mother's diamond brooch inside. Although the guard did not remember her, he allowed her to go into the temple. She wandered around the building for about an hour with the brooch inside her purse.

    When the guard decided to eat his supper and call home, Bill went to the safe. She opened it and pulled out all the money, except for $1,000.

    Bill told the guard she found the brooch and then left. She went to Alice McKinley's home, entered the house through an open ground-floor window, took the pearl necklace she had seen Alice wearing earlier, and then left.

The relevant statute is as follows:

§2911 Aggravated Burglary

(A) A person is guilty of aggravated burglary when the person, by force or deception, trespasses in any house, building, outbuilding, watercraft, aircraft, railroad car, truck, trailer, tent vehicle or shelter with the purpose of committing a theft; and

    (1) inflicts or attempts or threatens to inflict physical harm to another; or

    (2) the person has a deadly weapon, which is any instrument, device, or thing capable of inflicting death or designed or specially adapted for use as a weapon; or

    (3) the person has a dangerous ordinance such as any automatic or sawed off firearm, zip gun or ballistic knife, explosive or incendiary device; or

    (4) the structure is the permanent or temporary dwelling of a person.

8. An assistant county prosecutor wants you to research whether Merriweather Halsey committed aggravated burglary based on the following facts:

Merriweather Halsey considered borrowing money from a friend who worked at the local bulb factory. She wandered into the factory around 4:00 A.M., after an AIDS fundraiser. The guard had stepped away from the door for a break. She headed toward her friend's workstation, but she stumbled into an open office where the petty cash was kept. She fell over a secretary's desk. Her leg caught the desk and pulled open a drawer that contained $500. She thought about taking the money, but she passed out before she took it. She woke up the next morning at about 6:00 A.M., when a secretary found her and summoned the security guard.

Halsey then fell onto the security guard, causing him to crash his head into a planter. The guard cut his head and later required six stitches. Halsey thought the security guard was a robber, so she grabbed a letter opener from a nearby desk and told the security guard to back off. The security guard took the letter opener. Halsey's mind was still fuzzy from the alcohol, but she decided to pull a squirt gun out of her pocket to scare the robber.

Draft a question presented for this problem based on the aggravated burglary statute noted in question 1.

CONCLUSIONS EXERCISES

9. Review the conclusion for Illustration 20-1. Analyze the conclusion. What is the applicable law? What are the relevant facts? Which statement summarizes the likely result of this action when the relevant facts are applied to the law?

10. Draft conclusions for a Bonnie Bill and Merriweather Halsey memo.

FACTS

CHAPTER OVERVIEW

This chapter explains the purpose of a facts statement and how to draft one. To do this, you need to learn how to determine which facts are legally significant. The chapter discusses the difference between a fact and a legal conclusion and demonstrates the different organizational structures for the facts section.

A. FACTS STATEMENT

The **facts statement** is a summary of the information that is relevant to the determination of whether a legal claim exists or whether a defense to such a claim can be made. It is also a summary of the status of a pending case.

A fact statement is an integral part of the office memorandum. Often, an attorney reads this statement to refresh his or her memory about the facts of the case before meeting with a client or a judge. The facts detailed in a memorandum also provide a reference point for your research and the framework for the application of the law.

1. Defining *Fact*

A **fact** may be a thing that is known with certainty. It can be an event. It can be an observation. The answer is not clear-cut. Some facts are *pure* facts, which means there is no dispute about them. For example, an individual's birth is a pure fact. Facts in the court document, such as a complaint or an answer, are *asserted* facts, which means the individual is claiming they occurred. Some information can be objectively tested. That is a fact. For the purpose of the facts statement, note all of this information as facts.

2. Legally Significant Facts

▼ What Facts Should Be Included
in the Facts Statement?

All facts that might have an impact on the issues presented in a particular case must be included in the memo. These facts are called **legally significant facts.** A good rule is that if you plan to include a fact in your discussion of the law, it should be mentioned in the facts statement.

Legally significant facts are those facts that may affect how a court would decide a particular legal issue. To determine which facts are legally significant, you must understand the legal issue or issues presented in your case. A **legal claim** is comprised of components called *elements* that must be proven before a claim is successful. Legally significant facts are those facts that might prove or disprove any of those elements.

For example, you are asked to research the factors a court will consider when it decides whether Sack and Shop Grocery Store was liable to Rebecca Harris, a patron, for a slip-and-fall accident that occurred in the store. Ms. Harris was injured when she slipped on a banana peel that had been left on the store floor for two days. Ms. Harris's shopping list included bananas, cherries, and strawberries. You determine that the action or legal claim is based on negligence. You learn that negligence is the breach of a duty of reasonable care that results in an injury to another person. The legal elements of negligence are as follows:

- Existence of a duty
- Breach of that duty
- Injury caused by the breach of the duty

Legally significant facts are those facts that might prove or disprove any of those elements. In this case, the legally significant facts and the legal element that they might prove or disprove would include:

- The slip and fall occurred in the store. (injury, breach)
- Rebecca Harris slipped on a banana peel that had been left on the store floor for two days. (injury, breach)
- Rebecca Harris suffered injuries as a result of the fall. (injury)
- Rebecca Harris shopped daily at the store. (duty)
- Rebecca Harris went to the store to make a purchase. (duty)

A fact that is not necessarily legally significant is:

- Rebecca Harris's shopping list included bananas, cherries, and strawberries.

This fact does not prove or disprove any of the elements.

Do not omit any legally significant facts even if you think that an attorney should remember them from client meetings. Attorneys are responsible for multiple cases, and these statements often are used to refresh their recollection. If a fact is not legally significant, you generally would exclude it. However, if the fact explains how a dispute or transaction arose or explains the relationship between the parties, then that fact should be noted. Such a procedural fact would assist the reader in understanding the status of a case.

Facts statements provide facts that are advantageous for your clients and those facts that are unfavorable to them. Remember that this is an objective memo. The facts should be presented in a neutral manner, devoid of emotion. Compare the following two examples.

EXAMPLE

Our client, Janice Kahn, seeks to sue Ronnie Randall for intentional infliction of emotional distress following a car accident in which Randall brutally struck Kahn's only child while the precious child was playing t-ball in the street with his friends. This brutal act was done in the presence of Ms. Kahn, a caring mother, who was gardening while watching her child play. As a result of the incident, Kahn was devastated and emotionally distraught.

EXAMPLE

Our client, Janice Kahn, seeks to sue Ronnie Randall for intentional infliction of emotional distress following a car accident in which Randall struck Kahn's child while the child was playing t-ball in the street with his friends. After Randall struck the child, he backed up and struck the boy again, running over his head with the rear tire. Ms. Kahn was gardening nearby while watching her child play.

The first example contains several adjectives that slant the statement in favor of Kahn. The statement "Randall brutally struck Kahn's only child" characterizes the action as brutal. This is not a statement of fact. The adjective *brutal* should not be included in a facts statement. The second example is devoid of these **emotional adjectives.** Instead of using the word *brutal,* the second example details the underlying acts that constitute a brutal strike:

> After Randall struck the child, he backed up and struck the boy again, running over his head with the rear tire.

The second example allows readers to draw their own conclusions. The facts statement should not be slanted. Facts such as that Kahn was "a caring mother" or that the child was "precious" should not be incorporated into a facts statement. You should mention only facts, not legal conclusions or definitions of the law.

3. Fact versus a Legal Conclusion

A fact is a piece of information that might explain to the reader what occurred in a particular case. In contrast, a **legal conclusion** is an opinion about the legal significance of a fact. Read the following facts statement:

> Our client, Janice Kahn, seeks to sue Ronnie Randall for intentional infliction of emotional distress following a car accident in which Randall maliciously struck Kahn's only child while the child was playing t-ball in the street with his friends. This malicious and intentional act was done in the presence of Ms. Kahn, a caring mother, who was gardening while watching her child play.

The statements that the act was *malicious* and *intentional* are legal conclusions because the writer makes assumptions about the state of mind of the actor. The term *malicious* is a legal element of many claims; it describes a wicked state of mind. *Intentional* also describes a legal element. You should exclude such characterizations from your facts statements. Instead, describe the acts a person committed that could be considered malicious, or statements that could indicate that an act was intentional. For example:

> Randall struck Kahn's only child after he told a neighbor that he intended to hit the child with his car while the child was playing t-ball. Randall struck the child with his car while the car was traveling at 25 miles an hour.

The information about Randall's comments to the neighbor, coupled with the speed at which he struck the child, could indicate that Randall struck the child maliciously and intentionally. The proper place to discuss whether an act is either malicious or intentional is in the discussion section of the memo. A definition of the law also is not a statement of fact and should be noted only in the memo discussion.

4. Source of Information for a Facts Statement

Most often, information from a client interview is the basis for your facts statement. See the example in Illustration 21-7 later in this chapter. During a court dispute, information for the facts statement can also be found in witness statements, complaints, answers, or discovery materials, such as depositions and interrogatories. For these facts, note the source of the information. For transactions, information might be contained in various business records or contracts.

B. ORGANIZING THE FACTS STATEMENT

A facts statement can be organized in several ways: chronologically, by claim or defense, by party, or according to a combination of these three methods.

▼ What are the Different Methods of
   Organizing a Fact Statement?

1. Chronological Organization

A **chronological organization** is based on the order of events. You start with the event that occurred first and end with the event that occurred last. You can also write the statement in **reverse chronological order,** beginning with the last event and ending with the first. For some claims, such as those stemming from an accident, a contract

---

ILLUSTRATION 21-1.   Chronological Organization

Dr. James Panhandle is suing our client, Hospitality Resorts International, Inc., for negligence stemming from injuries he sustained when he slipped and fell on July 8, 1999, at the Hospitality Resort of Mexico. The doctor seeks $1 million in damages.

On the day of the accident, children were playing in the pool at 8:00 A.M. The children splashed water out of the pool and onto the marble floor near the pool. The floor had not been mopped at any time during the day.

At 8:00 P.M., Dr. Panhandle was walking slowly out of the hotel coffee shop that was adjacent to the pool. He slipped on the wet marble floor next to the pool.

The doctor hit his head on the marble floor, causing him to crack his skull and to bleed.

---

dispute, or a criminal case, chronological organization works well because these concerns often are ordered by time. See Illustration 21-1.

The statement in Illustration 21-1 first introduces the claim. In the succeeding paragraphs, the events are detailed in chronological order from start to finish. Illustration 21-2 starts with the last event and ends with the information about the beginning of the day.

2. Organization by Claim or Defense

Facts statements also can be **organized by claim** or **defense.** In statements of this kind, legally significant facts that relate to a claim or

---

ILLUSTRATION 21-2.   Reverse Chronological Order

Dr. James Panhandle is suing our client, Hospitality Resorts International, Inc., for negligence stemming from injuries he sustained when he slipped and fell on July 8, 1999, at the Hospitality Resort of Mexico. The doctor seeks $1 million in damages.

The doctor hit his head on the marble floor, causing him to crack his skull and to bleed.

At 8:00 P.M., Dr. Panhandle was walking slowly out of the hotel coffee shop that was adjacent to the pool. He slipped on the wet marble floor next to the pool.

On the day of the accident, children were playing in the pool at 8:00 A.M. The children splashed water out of the pool and onto the marble floor near the pool. The floor had not been mopped at any time during the day.

---

a defense are grouped together. See Illustration 21-3. This method is useful when the issue does not concern events that can be organized by time sequence and the information involves individuals who are not parties to the action.

In Illustration 21-3's sample facts statement, the details are organized by claim. The first paragraph introduces the claims—the assertion of attorney-client privilege by Irl and Tildy. The next paragraph includes the facts that are legally significant to Irl's claim of attorney-client privilege. The final paragraph focuses on the facts that are legally significant to Tildy and Tildy's assertion of the attorney-client privilege. Because neither Irl nor Tildy is a party, this organization works well.

3. Organization by Party

Another way to organize the facts is to **organize by party,** grouping the facts according to the party the facts describe. This method is useful when multiple parties are involved in a dispute. See Illustration

ILLUSTRATION 21-3.   Organization by Claim or Defense

Our clients, the Black Hawks, want to know whether the attorney-client privilege can be asserted by a former company president, Debbie Irl, and a current employee, Meredith Tildy, head of the cleaning staff. These questions arose while the plaintiff's attorney was deposing these individuals on July 8, 1998, as part of the discovery in a personal injury lawsuit stemming from a slip and fall at the stadium.

Irl, president of the Hawks at the time of the accident, left the organization in June 1997. During her tenure with the organization, she was a decision maker and she drafted the cleaning policy for the stadium. Irl had spoken with the Hawks' attorney, Ace Rudd, about the accident on July 10, 1997. Irl is not named as a party in the lawsuit and is merely a witness. During the deposition, the plaintiff's attorney asked Irl about her conversation with Rudd. Irl asserted the attorney-client privilege.

Meredith Tildy, the current head of the Hawks' cleaning staff, knew about the accident. Beer had been spilled the night before the accident. A patron told the staff to mop up the beer when it happened. Tildy knew that the cleaning staff had failed to clean up the beer. In her position, Tildy schedules the staff and decides whether the stadium should be cleaned completely each night. On July 10, 1997, Tildy spoke with Rudd, the company attorney, about the accident. The plaintiff's attorney asked Tildy about her conversation with Rudd. Based upon Rudd's advice, Tildy asserted the attorney-client privilege.

21-4, which involves a dispute between three parties: a company and two individuals. The memo focuses on whether Whole In One is an employer under Title VII and whether two individuals are employees or independent contractors.

The first paragraph in Illustration 21-4 introduces the claim. The next paragraph describes one of the parties, Whole In One. The next paragraph describes another party, Walker. The final paragraph tells the reader about Radiant, the third party in the action.

4. Combination of Chronological and Claim or Party Organization

Some facts statements do not lend themselves to one type of organization. Some facts should be arranged by the order of the events, and

ILLUSTRATION 21-4.   Organization by Party

Victoria Radiant and Karen Walker, two former Whole In One Enterprises workers, brought a federal sex discrimination lawsuit, based upon Title VII, against our client, Whole In One Enterprises, owned by Nancy and Craig Black. The lawsuit, filed in the U.S. District Court for the Northern District of Illinois, stems from the dismissal of the two women by the Blacks during 1998.

The Blacks own Whole In One Enterprises, which operates a miniature golf course and restaurant in Glenview, Illinois. During the 24-week 1993 restaurant season, 10 people worked full-time and 14 people worked part-time for Whole In One. However, no more than 14 people worked on any one day. Of those 14 people, only 3 were full-time employees. The other full-time employees regularly took days off during the summer restaurant and golf season.

Among the full-time workers was Karen Walker, who worked as a public relations director for Whole In One. Walker responded to an ad that said that "an employer" sought an individual to perform public relations work. Whole In One hired Walker without a contract and told her she was prohibited from working for other firms. However, Walker worked from home and set her own hours. Whole In One required Walker to attend weekly staff meetings at the company offices, where Whole In One would review and revise Walker's work. The company supplied Walker with paper, pencils, stamps, and telephone service and paid for her life and health insurance. Whole In One did not withhold taxes from Walker's commissions.

Victoria Radiant, who had a two-year employment contract with the company, provided marketing services to Whole In One from October of 1996 until she was fired in 1998. Although Radiant worked in the company office, Whole In One management rarely supervised her work. The company paid for her continued education, provided her with bonuses, and deducted taxes from her weekly salary.

others do not fit neatly into this arrangement. Therefore, you might group facts in chronological order and by party or claim. See Illustration 21-5.

The facts statement in Illustration 21-5 concerns the question of whether Janice Kahn can successfully pursue a claim against Ronnie Randall for intentional infliction of emotional distress after Randall struck Kahn's 11-year-old son with Randall's car. The accident itself is best described in a chronological manner because the events can be explained in a sequential order. However, the witness statements and other "facts" that relate to whether Randall intentionally struck the child and whether Randall intended to cause emotional distress when he struck the child should be organized by issue or claim.

In some instances, your organization should be structured by the sequence of the events and by the parties. See Illustration 21-6.

ILLUSTRATION 21-5. Chronological and Claim Organization

While driving a car, Ronnie Randall struck Janice Kahn's son at 5:00 P.M. on August 29, 1998. It was bright and clear. No skid marks appeared on the dry street following the accident. Janice Kahn was working in her garden about five feet from the accident scene at the time of the accident. Her son was playing a game in the street before Randall's car struck him. Kahn did not see the car strike her 11-year-old son. When she first looked up from her garden, she thought her son was dead. He was covered with blood and had several broken bones. However, Kahn's son was conscious after the accident.

Immediately after the accident, Randall, who had a blood/alcohol level of .11, was cited for drunk driving and driving with a suspended driver's license. Police had charged him with drunk driving and suspended his license two weeks earlier after the car he was driving struck another child at the same spot. Randall has a history of alcohol abuse.

Following the accident, several witnesses said Randall was upset and wobbled as he walked. One witness said that Randall intentionally turned the steering wheel to hit Kahn's son. Kahn stated that Randall often swerved down her street to get her attention.

Rhonda Albert, Kahn's neighbor, said she heard Randall say he would get even with Kahn after Kahn broke off a 10-year relationship with him.

During Kahn and Randall's 10-year relationship, Randall was close to Kahn's son. He took him to ball games, including one in April, and attended the son's baseball games. Randall knew that Kahn's son was the most important person in her life.

Since the accident, Kahn vomits daily and has nightmares about the accident. Dr. Susan Faigen, Kahn's internist, states that the vomiting and nightmares are the result of the accident.

ILLUSTRATION 21-6. Chronological and Party Organization

Merriweather Halsey and Bonnie Bill were at the Masonic Temple for a fundraiser to fight AIDS. During the fundraiser Bill told a drunken Halsey that she intended to steal the $8,000 fundraiser proceeds from the Masonic Temple after the fundraiser and that she intended to steal a pearl necklace from Alice McKinley.

Bill, who had helped organize the fundraiser, watched as the chairperson of the fundraiser opened the safe and placed the money in it. She memorized the combination and decided that she would use it later to steal the money.

After the fundraiser, Bill walked home to get a credit card and a crowbar to open the door if she needed it. Bill went to the Masonic Temple after the fundraiser, wearing a disguise, showed the guard her invitation, and told him that she had lost her mother's diamond brooch inside. Although the guard did not remember her, he allowed her to go into the temple. She wandered around the building for about an hour with the brooch inside her purse.

When the guard decided to eat his supper and call home, Bill went to the safe. She opened it and pulled out all the money, except for $1,000.

Bill told the guard she had found the brooch and then left. She went to Alice McKinley's home, entered the house through an open ground-floor window, and took the pearl necklace she had seen Alice wearing earlier, and then left.

Merriweather Halsey considered borrowing money from a friend who worked at a local bulb factory. She wandered into the factory around 4:00 A.M., after the fundraiser. The guard had stepped away from the door for a break. She headed toward her friend's workstation, but she stumbled into an open office where the petty cash was kept. She fell over a secretary's desk. Her leg caught the desk and pulled open a drawer that contained $500. She thought about taking the money, but she passed out before she took it. She woke up the next morning at about 6:00 A.M., when a secretary found her and summoned the security guard.

Halsey then fell into the security guard, causing him to crash his head into a planter. The guard cut his head and later required six stitches. Halsey thought the security guard was a robber, so she grabbed a letter opener from a nearby desk and told the security guard to back off. The security guard took the letter opener. Halsey's mind was still fuzzy from the alcohol, but she decided to pull a squirt gun out of her pocket to scare the robber.

The question is whether Bill or Halsey can be convicted of aggravated burglary under Houcktown County law.

In Illustration 21-6, the first paragraph introduces both parties, Bonnie Bill and Merriweather Halsey. The facts statement details most of the night's events in chronological order. However, the parties, Bill and Halsey, leave the fundraiser separately. At this point, the organization changes from chronological to one focusing on each party. First, facts that are legally significant to Bill's escapades are explained. These are noted in chronological order from start to finish. After the facts concerning Bill's adventure, the facts related to Halsey's acts at the bulb factory are detailed. These facts also are explained in chronological order. The final paragraph tells the reader the issues that will be considered in the memo.

C. WRITING THE FACTS STATEMENT

1. Prepare a List of Facts and Preliminary Statement

After you meet with an attorney to discuss your research assignment, make a list of the facts and draft a preliminary facts statement. Illustration 21-7 shows an excerpt from a client interview. Following the interview is a list of the facts and a preliminary facts statement, Illustration 21-8, that includes all of the facts provided in the interview.

List of Facts:

Client: Sack and Shop Grocery Store
Plaintiff: Rebecca Harris
   Slip and fall at grocery store on July 8, 1998
   Plaintiff slipped on a banana peel, which had been left on the store floor for two days.
   Harris was walking to the green peppers.
   Another accident happened in the same section when a man slipped on a cantaloupe and broke his finger.
   A patron told the store employee to clean up the banana peel two days earlier.
   The employee kicked it into a corner.
   Somehow the peel got to the middle of the floor again.
   Harris came to the store to purchase cherries, strawberries, and bananas.

2. Research the Issue

After you prepare your list and preliminary facts statement, the next step is to research the legal issue or issues and to determine the applicable law.

ILLUSTRATION 21-7.   Excerpt from a Client Interview

Attorney: What can I do for you today, Mr. Grocer of Sack and Shop?
Grocer: Rebecca Harris, one of my regular customers, is suing me for $1 million.
Attorney: What happened?
Grocer: Ms. Harris came to the store to purchase cherries, strawberries, and bananas. When she was turning the corner in the produce section, she slipped on a banana peel.
Attorney: How long had the banana peel been on the floor?
Grocer: Two days.
Attorney: Did you or any of your employees know about the banana peel on the floor?
Grocer: Yes. One of the patrons told the head of the produce department to clean up the banana peel two days before Ms. Harris fell.
Attorney: Why wasn't it picked up?
Grocer: The produce department head was in a hurry to leave and forgot to do it. The next day, he was very busy and he kicked the banana peel into a corner. Apparently it was knocked out of the corner and to the middle of the floor where Ms. Harris slipped on it.
Attorney: Were there any witnesses?
Grocer: I saw her slip.
Attorney: What was Ms. Harris doing when she slipped?
Grocer: She was walking to the green peppers.
Attorney: What day did the incident occur?
Grocer: July 8, 1998. The same day another accident occurred in the produce section that involved a piece of cut cantaloupe.
Attorney: Was Ms. Harris injured?
Grocer: She claims in the court papers that she hurt her head and broke her arm.
Attorney: Was anyone injured in the second accident?
Grocer: Yes. A man slipped on the cantaloupe and broke his finger.

3. Revise to Include Only Legally Significant Facts

Revise your list so that it includes only the legally significant facts, the facts that will have a bearing on the applicable law. See Illustration 21-9. To draft this list, you must determine the legal elements necessary to establish a claim. In the case of negligence, you would learn that negligence is the breach of a duty of reasonable care that results in injuries to another person. The elements then would be:

• duty of reasonable care
• breach of the duty
• a link between the breach of the duty and the resulting injuries
• injuries

You should review the facts and determine which facts may affect whether the plaintiff can establish one of these elements or whether

ILLUSTRATION 21-8.   Sample Preliminary Facts Statement Based on the Client Interview

Our client, Sack and Shop Grocery Store, is being sued for negligence by Rebecca Harris.

Harris went to the store to purchase cherries, strawberries, and bananas on July 8, 1998.

While Harris was in the produce section, she slipped on a banana peel that had been left on the floor by a grocery store employee. The employee dropped it on the floor two days earlier and had failed to clean it up after a patron asked him to do so. The employee had kicked the peel into the corner two days before the accident. Somehow the peel found its way to the middle of the floor on the date of the accident.

Harris sustained a broken arm and head injuries as a result of the slip and fall. Another man was injured in the produce department that same day when he slipped and fell on some cantaloupe.

---

the defendant would be able to disprove one of the elements—in other words, the legally significant facts. In this case, you should include all of the facts listed in Illustration 21-9. In that illustration, the element of the legal theory is noted in parentheses next to the legally significant fact. The fact that Harris was purchasing cherries, strawberries, and bananas is not legally significant. Similarly, the fact that another patron was injured in the produce section that day did not affect whether Harris was injured and therefore is not legally significant.

4. Organize the Facts

After you have made your list of facts, decide how to organize them. After you select your organizational method, group the legally significant facts together in the organizational style you have selected.

ILLUSTRATION 21-9.   List of Legally Significant Facts

- The slip and fall occurred in the store on July 8, 1998. (breach and duty)
- Rebecca Harris slipped on a banana peel that had been left on the store floor for two days. (breach and duty)
- The store employee dropped the banana peel on the floor two days earlier. (breach and duty)
- A store employee knew about the banana peel on the floor two days before the accident. (breach and duty)
- The employee kicked the peel into the corner after a patron told him to clean it up. (breach and duty)
- Rebecca Harris suffered injuries as a result of the fall. (link and injuries)

PRACTICE POINTER

Sometimes you will use multiple organization methods.

5. Rewrite the Facts Statement

The facts contained in Illustration 21-9 led themselves to a chronological organization because they can be ordered by time. Illustration 21-10 is a rewritten facts statement that includes only the legally significant facts. Finally, remember to introduce the legal issue or issues presented in the facts statement, as shown in the first paragraph of Illustration 21-10.

ILLUSTRATION 21-10.   Sample Facts Statement for Slip-and-Fall Case

Rebecca Harris, a store patron, is suing our client, Sack and Shop Grocery Store, for negligence.

While Harris was in the produce department, on July 8, 1998, she slipped on a banana peel that had been left on the floor by a grocery store employee. The employee dropped it on the floor two days earlier and had failed to clean it up after a patron asked him to do so. When he was told to pick up the peel, the employee kicked the peel into the corner.

Harris sustained a broken arm and head injuries as a result of the slip and fall.

CHAPTER SUMMARY

A facts statement is designed to refresh an attorney's memory about a case or to educate a new attorney about the case. It is a statement of all facts that are legally significant (facts that might affect the outcome of a legal issue). Facts that are not legally significant should be omitted from a facts statement.

Facts statements can be organized in chronological or reverse chronological order, by claim or defense, by party, or any combination of these three.

To draft your statement, make a list of the facts, plan your organization, then write the statement. Next, research the legal issue, then rewrite your facts statement because the legally significant facts may have changed based on your research.

In the next chapter, you will learn how to organize using the IRAC methodology.

KEY TERMS

chronological organization	legal conclusion
emotional adjectives	legally significant facts
fact	organization by claim or defense
facts statement	organization by party
legal claim	reverse chronological order

EXERCISES

SHORT ANSWER EXERCISES

1. What is a facts statement?
2. What are legally significant facts?
3. What facts should be included in the facts statement?
4. What is the difference between a fact and a legal conclusion?
5. Where do you find the information to include in the facts statement?
6. List several methods for organizing a facts statement.
7. Explain two methods of organization.

DRAFTING A LIST OF RELEVANT FACTS

8. Review the following Uniform Commercial Code section and read the list of facts that follows. Make a list of the legally significant facts based on the statute. Next to each fact, list the relevant portion of the statute.

§2-315 Implied Warranty of Fitness for a Particular Purpose

Where the seller at the time of contracting has reason to know any particular purpose for which the goods are required and that buyer is relying on the seller's skill or judgment to select or furnish suitable goods, there is unless excluded or modified under the next section an implied warranty that the goods be fit for such purpose.

FACTS

Your client is Sue A. Buyer. She lives at 3225 Wilmette Avenue, Glenview, Illinois. The defendants are Lee R. Merchant, owner of Mowers R Us, in Glenview, Illinois, and Manny U. Facture, the owner of a manufacturing concern that is not incorporated called Mowers, of Rosemont, Illinois. Ms. Buyer went to the defendant's store, Mowers R Us, to purchase a lawn mower for her new home. She was a first-time homeowner and was unfamiliar with lawn mowers. She had never operated a lawn mower because her brothers had always mowed the lawn when she was a child.

When she went to Mowers R Us, she asked to speak with the owner. She told Mr. Merchant: "I don't know anything about these mowers, and I need to talk with an expert." Mr. Merchant said, "I'm the owner, and you couldn't find a better expert anywhere in the Chicagoland area. I have been in the business of selling mowers for more than 40 years. I only sell mowers and the equipment to clean and repair them. Are you familiar with the type of lawn mower you would like?"

"No, I don't know anything about lawn mowers. I just know that I have to have a lawn mower that will mulch my grass clippings, because I cannot bag the clippings. The village of Glenview does not permit me to bag the clippings, so the clippings must remain on my lawn."

"You're absolutely correct. You must have a mulching mower," Mr. Merchant said. "That type of mower will grind the grass clippings, and you will not notice them on your grass. I have the perfect mower for you. It is a used model that will fit into your price range, only $200. It's a good brand, a Roro, and will mulch the grass as well as any of the new mowers. This one is true blue. You can purchase a separate mulching blade, which will easily attach to it for an additional $50," he added.

"Do you think that I need the mulching blade?" Ms. Buyer asked. "I've never used a lawn mower, so I don't know what to expect, and you appear to be the expert."

"I think that you could do without the mulching blade unless you want the grass ground up very fine."

"I think that I would like it ground up fine. I'll defer to your judgment. If you think a mulching blade is necessary, then I'll buy that with the mower. Do you think that this is the best mower for mulching, or should I go with a new one?"

"Absolutely the used one is best; I told you: it's a true value. It will mulch with the best of them."

"If you think it can do the job, I'll trust your judgment," said Ms. Buyer. "I'll take the mower and the mulching blade. Can you install the mulching blade? I don't know anything about the installation."

"Sure, we can install any blade for another $30."

Ms. Buyer purchased the mower and the blade. She used the mower after Mr. Merchant installed the new mulching blade. It barely cut the grass and certainly didn't mulch the clippings into fine pieces as Mr. Merchant had claimed.

She brought the mower back to Mr. Merchant. He said that he had made no warranties about the mower. He showed her the language on the receipt that said that he did not expressly warranty anything.

Ms. Buyer brought the mower to a Roro dealer. The owners of the Roro dealership, Abe Saul and Lou T. Wright, said that the mower Ms. Buyer had purchased from Mowers R Us was not a mulching mower. It was a mower built before mulching was popular. Therefore, it would not perform the mulching task. It was designed merely to cut the grass. "Any merchant who has been in business even for one year should have known that mowers built before 1970 were not designed for mulching," Mr. Wright said. He showed Ms. Buyer where the manufacturing date appeared on the mower. "Manufactured in August 1969," it said on the plate with the serial number. "Also, mulching blades cannot be placed on these old mowers. Any mower dealer should know that too," Mr. Wright added. "However, this mower isn't bad. It can cut the grass without mulching it."

Ms. Buyer brought an action against Mr. Merchant and Mr. Facture in the Lucas County Ohio Common Pleas Court in Toledo, Ohio.

OBJECTIVE WRITING
9. Write three different discussions about your high school career. One discussion should present the experience in a negative manner. The second should attempt to persuade the reader that the experience was positive. Finally, write about your experience in a neutral manner, without any emotion. Compare the three discussions.

DRAFTING A FACTS STATEMENT
10. Draft a facts statement for our client, Ronnie Randall. Janice Kahn, the plaintiff, brought an action against Randall for intentional infliction of emotional distress. You should prepare your facts statement based on this excerpt from a deposition transcript, witness statements, and a police report. The facts statement will be included in a memo that discusses the issue of intentional infliction of emotional distress. For the purpose of this memo, intentional infliction of emotional distress is defined as follows:

An act by a person that is extreme and outrageous conduct, done with intent to cause another to suffer severe emotional distress, and which results in distress and emotional injury to another. The emotional injury must manifest itself with a physical problem.

Below is a portion of Janice Kahn's deposition transcript.

Q. What were you doing when the accident occurred?
A. Working in my garden. I planted tomatoes, green peppers, carrots, and broccoli.
Q. Where is your garden located on your property?
A. In the front, near the street. It is next to a brick wall. I can't see the garden from my house.
Q. What direction were you facing in your garden?
A. North.
Q. Does that direction face the street?
A. No.
Q. What do you usually do in your garden when you work?
A. Weed it.
Q. What were you doing in your garden when the accident occurred?
A. Weeding it.
Q. Where is the street in relation to your garden?
A. About five feet.
Q. Where do your children generally play?
A. In the backyard.
Q. Where were your children playing on the day of the accident?
A. They were playing t-ball in the front yard.

Q. Were you watching your children at the time of the accident?
A. Yes. I could see them.
Q. Did you see the accident occur?
A. Sort of.
Q. Did you or did you not see the accident?
A. I saw my son, who is 11 years old, on the ground covered with blood, and blood all over the front of the Cadillac.
Q. Did you actually see the driver strike your son?
A. No. But I know Ronnie hit him. I saw my son next to Ronnie's car. I heard him swerve.
Q. Did you know the driver?
A. Yes.
Q. How did you know him?
A. We met at a state fair. We dated for 10 years. I broke up with him two weeks before the accident.
Q. Did he know your son?
A. He knew my son was the most important person to me, and he tried to kill him to pay me back for dumping him.
Q. Are you accusing the driver of intentionally striking your son?
A. Yes. He wanted to get back at me, so he hit my boy.
Q. What happened to your son on the day of the accident?
A. He sustained head injuries and several broken bones. He can't play t-ball for the rest of the season, and we had to cancel our vacation to the Dells because he's been hurting so much.
Q. Was he conscious when you first saw him after the accident?
A. He was awake, but I thought he was dead at first. He had blood everywhere. I knew the driver, Ronnie, was drunk when he hit him. He wasn't even looking where he was going. He always swerves down our street to get my attention.
Q. Did your son speak to you right after the accident?
A. Barely. I told him that Ronnie was speeding and trying to run him down on purpose. I was horrified to see the blood and the broken bones. I couldn't move and I was so angry at Ronnie because I knew he did this on purpose.
Q. Did you go to the doctor after this accident?
A. I went by ambulance with my son to the doctor. His doctor looked me over and said I was suffering from shock. Since then, I haven't been able to sleep or eat. I have nightmares about the accident. I throw up every day.
Q. Have you seen a doctor for your complaints?
A. Yes. She said that they are related to the accident. I just keep thinking back to that day when the neighbor told me that Ronnie intentionally turned the wheel to hit my boy.
Q. Was your son able to move after the accident?
A. Slightly. He looked just like our neighbor's son did after Ronnie hit him with his car two weeks before at the same curve.

Police Report, State of Illinois

Ronnie Randall, the driver of a 1993 Cadillac, was cited for driving while under the influence of alcohol and/or drugs, reckless driving, and driving with a suspended license. I will ask the prosecutor to consider either reckless assault charges or vehicular homicide, depending upon the condition of the boy. I tested Randall for alcohol intoxication. His blood/alcohol level was .11. Randall struck another boy, Tommy Albert, at the same site two weeks earlier. He was cited for reckless driving for that accident and drunk driving. As I arrested Randall, he said that he was daydreaming during the accident and that he did not mean to hit the child. There were no skid marks. The street was dry.

The little boy's mother, Janice Kahn, was working in her garden about five feet from the accident scene at the time of the accident. Her son, Billy Kahn, was playing a game in the street.

Witness Statement

Two days before the accident, Rhonda Albert, a neighbor of Janice Kahn, heard Randall say that he planned to get even with Kahn after Kahn broke off her 10-year relationship with Randall. Albert saw the car strike Kahn's son. According to Albert, after the car struck the boy, Randall got out of his car and said "Oh, my God. I didn't mean to hit him. Is he OK?" Albert could smell alcohol on Randall's breath.

Witness Statement

Rebecca Mark saw the driver, Ronnie Randall, turn the car toward Kahn's son.

Review of Facts Statements

4. Now that you have reviewed the facts for the *Janice Kahn* case and have drafted a statement of your own, read the following statements of facts. Determine which facts statement is best. List any errors you find in any of the statements.

A. The plaintiff, a single mother, and the defendant, her ex-boyfriend, are involved in a lawsuit. The plaintiff alleges in her deposition that the defendant was driving recklessly and intentionally struck her son with his car. The defendant's motive was to pay her back for ending their relationship. He tried to kill her son for this reason. As a result of the accident, the plaintiff went into shock and suffers from insomnia, loss of appetite, nightmares, and vomiting.

B. The plaintiff was working in her tomato garden located in the front of the property about five feet from the street. She could see the children playing in the front yard. She did not see the driver, Ronnie Randall, hit her son with his Cadillac but did see blood on the front of the Cadillac and on her son, who was on the ground.

The plaintiff dated Randall for 10 years and had just ended their relationship. She states that Ronnie hit her son to pay her back for ending their relationship. Two weeks before, Ronnie had hit a neighbor's son at the same curve.

The plaintiff states that her son was covered with blood, able to move slightly. He suffered head trauma and broken bones.

416 CHAPTER 21 / FACTS

The plaintiff is suffering from shock after seeing her son. She remembers a neighbor telling her that Ronnie intentionally turned the wheel to hit her son.

The plaintiff is unable to eat or sleep, has nightmares, and vomits daily.

C. Janice Kahn is bringing an action against Ronnie Randall for the intentional infliction of emotional distress. Her son was recently hit by Ronnie Randall's car on the street in front of the Kahn home. At the time of the injury, Kahn was working in the front yard near her son. Her son went into the street and Randall hit him. At the time of the accident, Randall was legally drunk and driving with a suspended license.

Randall had previously told Kahn's neighbor, a Ms. Albert, that he was going to get even with Ms. Kahn over the breakup of their 10-year relationship. He also told Ms. Albert that he knew that Ms. Kahn's son was very important to her.

Since the accident, Kahn has been unable to eat or sleep properly. She vomits daily and often has nightmares about her son's injury. She has stated that Mr. Randall often drives by her home in an erratic fashion and on another occasion hit a neighbor's child. Kahn feels that Randall hit her son intentionally. Kahn did not see the injury take place but was at her son's side immediately after the injury. Kahn also says that Randall never slowed down until after he hit her son.

D. On August 12, 1998, Janice Kahn filed a lawsuit against Ronnie Randall for intentional infliction of emotional distress stemming from an accident involving Kahn's 11-year-old son.

On July 8, 1998, Janice Kahn was weeding her tomato garden while her children played t-ball a few feet away from her in the street. As she worked, Kahn heard a car swerve. She looked up to see her son, covered in blood, lying on the ground in front of a Cadillac, driven by Ronnie Randall.

Two neighbors witnessed the accident. Rebecca Mark saw the driver, Ronnie Randall, turn the car toward Kahn's son. Rhonda Albert also saw the car strike Kahn's son. According to Albert, after the car struck the boy, Randall got out of his car and said, "Oh, my God. I didn't mean to hit him. Is he OK?"

Albert could smell alcohol on Randall's breath. Police tested his blood/alcohol level and found that it was .11. Police cited Randall for drunk driving, speeding, and reckless driving.

After police arrived, an ambulance took Kahn and her son to the hospital, where he was treated for head injuries and broken bones. The doctor who treated Kahn's son told Kahn that she should be treated for shock. Since the accident, Kahn has been unable to sleep because of nightmares about the accident. She vomits daily. Her doctor said that the vomiting and nightmares are the result of the accident.

The driver of the car involved in the accident was Kahn's former boyfriend. They had dated for 10 years; however, Kahn broke off the relationship about two weeks before the accident. Kahn stated in her deposition that she believes Randall intentionally struck her son to pay her back for ending the relationship.

Also, two days before the accident Albert heard Randall say that he planned to get even with Kahn after Kahn broke off her 10-year relationship. However, the police report stated that Randall said that he was daydreaming during the accident and that he did not mean to hit the child. Since the breakup, Kahn has seen Randall often swerve down the street in front of her home. Two weeks before the accident, Randall hit Rhonda Albert's son with his Cadillac at the same curve.

SYNTHESIZING CASES AND AUTHORITIES

CHAPTER OVERVIEW

You will learn about the methods of synthesis used in a memo. Synthesizing authority requires finding a common theme from two or more sources that ties together the legal rule. Cases are synthesized because it is hard to find a single decision that articulates the precise rule of law required for a memo. Often one case holding will expand another, so the two holdings can be combined, or synthesized, to reflect an accurate statement of the law.

You will also become adept at synthesizing statutory authority as well as combining case law and statutes. Statutes should be given the highest regard in the hierarchy of authority. If you find case law that applies or interprets a statute, synthesize the statute and the case holding.

A. SYNTHESIS

Synthesis is the bringing together of various legal authorities into a unified cohesive statement of the law. The process of synthesizing authority requires finding a common theme or thread that relates to the various legal rules and tying the holdings to that unified theme. Discussing related decisions and statutes separately in a memo makes your points sound more like a list than an integrated, well-thought-out whole. Synthesis adds analytical insight to your legal documents and makes reading them easier.

▼ What Is the Process of Synthesizing Legal Rules?

Enacted law that emanates from more than one statute section must be synthesized under a common legal principle to promote cohesiveness and to add your analytical viewpoint to the memo. We synthesize cases and enacted law because memos and opinion letters are organized by legal issue and not by cited references. Frequently, more than one source of primary authority addresses a particular legal issue. The synthesis of related legal principles enables you to compare and to contrast the legal rules easily as well as to demonstrate how factual applications differ and to show how legal rules expand or contract. Often enacted law and case law are synthesized because the case law applies the statute or interprets the extent to which the statute can be applied.

▼ Why Do We Synthesize Legal Authority?

The legal issues form the framework for the memo discussion. The synthesized authority groups the legal holdings together to address the issues raised.

The following example demonstrates how one case defines an easement in gross and then another case explains how an easement in gross is retained. Both cases discuss easements in gross, yet one expands on the other. The facts on which the example is based are as follows:

> Robert and Jan Murray live in Evanston and are building an addition to their house on Ashland. There is eight feet between their house and their neighbor's, Mrs. Brown's, house. The properties are adjoining. A driveway does not separate the houses, and they cannot be accessed by an alley. The Murrays' contractors and construction workers must enter Mrs. Brown's property to work on the addition. Mrs. Brown is not very pleased that workers are entering her property. The Murrays came to our office wondering whether they should purchase an easement from Mrs. Brown, their neighbor.

EXAMPLE

Should the Murrays purchase an easement in gross from Mrs. Brown? An easement in gross, sometimes called a personal easement, is a right in the land of another, without being appurtenant to or exercised with the occupancy of the land. *Willoughby v. Lawrence,* 116 Ill. 11, 4 N.E. 356 (1886). It belongs to the easement holder independent of his ownership or possession of any tract of land and does not benefit the possessor of any tract of land in his use of it. *Schnabel v. County of DuPage,* 101 Ill. App. 3d 553, 428 N.E.2d 671 (1981). The Murrays are building an addition to their house. They want to have a right to use the adjoining land to perform the construction of their addition. They do not need an easement, which would be appurtenant to the estate. The interest that the Murrays have in Mrs. Brown's land is personal and would not benefit either tract of land. Therefore, the Murrays can purchase an easement in gross from Mrs. Brown that would permit the workers to enter the Brown property.

B. TYPES OF SYNTHESIS

▼ What Are the Four Methods of Synthesizing Authority?

As we discussed previously, synthesizing primary authority requires finding a common theme that is used to unify all of the sources related to the issue. The common legal theme can be developed by classifying the applicable precedent into categories. There are four basic ways to combine and to analyze legal rules to render a coherent distillation of the law:

1. **Primary authority** can be grouped by rule of law found in the text of the decision or in the statute or constitution.
2. Synthesis can be focused around the **reasoning** that a judge uses as the basis of the synthesis.
3. The various **facts** from different cases can form the foundation of the synthesis.
4. The **causes of action** are the last category of case synthesis.

In your writing you will synthesize primary authority by grouping related legal rules. All the examples focus on this method of synthesis. Detailed instruction as to how to synthesize various sources of case law, case law combined with statutory authority, as well as two sources of statutory authority follow.

C. STEP-BY-STEP PROCESS TO SYNTHESIZING LEGAL RULES

The most effective synthesis of legal rules follows conscientious case briefing and careful reading of enacted law. Case briefing requires conforming a decision into set categories: citation, procedure, issue, facts, holding, rationale, disposition. (See Chapter 18.) The following steps take you through the synthesizing process.

1. *Brief decisions.* Once you have carefully and meticulously briefed all of the decisions that you plan to use in your memo, you can establish categories of legal precedence to make comparing and contrasting decisions easier. It is far simpler to compare and to contrast seven holdings from briefed decisions than to flip through photocopies of authority.

2. *Outline the problem.* The next step is to formulate the analytical outline of your letter or memo and to pinpoint the issues and subissues that must be addressed to fully explore the memo topic.

3. *Relate research to legal issues raised.* Organize the primary authority by relating the research findings to the issues raised by the problem. Remember: Legal writing is never organized around your sources of authority but around the issues raised by the problem. After pinpointing the legal issues that will be explored, decide on the general rule relating to that point of law.

4. *Under each issue, organize your primary sources by hierarchy of authority.* Enacted law comes before common law, constitutions come before statutes, newer case decisions interpreting statutes come before common law cases, higher court holdings come before lower court holdings, and newer case holdings are more relevant than older holdings on the same point of law from the same court.

5. *Compare and contrast holdings and statutes.* Using the case briefs that you prepared and the notes you made from the plain reading of the enacted law, compare and contrast the holdings and statutory texts.

6. *Formulate a statement of the law.* Your statement should incorporate all of the primary sources that will be used under the subissue heading. Ask yourself: What are the similarities and differences between the various cases and statutes? How do the facts differ? What do the documents have in common?

7. *Correct Bluebook citation.* Remember that you must attribute the authority for any legal statement, even if it is a clause, using the proper Bluebook citation.

D. EXAMPLES OF CASE SYNTHESIS

This example demonstrates synthesizing the holdings from two legal decisions. A problem and two fictitious legal decisions are provided below on which case synthesis is performed.

PROBLEM

Mr. and Mrs. Black wanted to have a chair and a loveseat made to match the living room in their new home. The Blacks searched for weeks at various local furniture retailers for a furniture style and fabric that they liked but were unsuccessful. Finally, the Blacks went to a fabric sale at Fabric Retailers and found the upholstery fabric of their dreams. The Blacks purchased 50 yards of the fabric of their dreams to make sure that they would have enough for any project. Mr. Black called all of the furniture retailers in the area to inquire whether customers can have furniture covered in their own material. Finally, Comfy Furniture said that they permit customers to bring in their own material to cover upholstered furniture ordered from Comfy. The Blacks hurried over to Comfy with the 50 yards of fabric and placed an order for a chair and a loveseat using their own fabric. The price agreed on was the base price of $500 for the chair and $800 for the loveseat. Mr. Blaine, of Comfy Furniture, was their salesperson. Mr. Blaine said that the fabric was ideal for the styles selected because it required no matching. He also offered that there was plenty of material, that 30 yards is adequate for a job of this nature. The fabric was a small paisley print, with the right side having a lovely sheen and vibrant coloration. The Blacks placed the order on July 7, 1998. They were planning a family reunion for Thanksgiving and felt that ordering in July would give them plenty of time to completely decorate their living room. The new pieces would provide plenty of seating for the family reunion. The Blacks indicated to Mr. Blaine that they needed the furniture for the reunion. Mr. Blaine asserted that the furniture would be ready by September 15. The Blacks gave Comfy Furniture a deposit of $1,000. The loveseat and the chair were delivered to the Black home on September 10, but the furniture was upholstered with the fabric's reverse side showing. The Blacks were devastated.

The legal issue is whether the Blacks are entitled to damages for the breach of the contract to upholster the furniture.

The legal principle surrounding this problem is the expectation interest in a contract. The expectation interest is the expectation of gain from the performance of the contract. The damages are assessed to give the nonbreaching party the measure of gain that he or she would have received if the contract was performed as agreed. Sometimes special or consequential damages are awarded in addition to the expectancy interest.

CASE A

The Cahill family ordered a sofa from the Acme Furniture Company in red tapestry, on June 1, 1998, due to be delivered in six weeks, on July 15, 1998. The Cahills paid $600 for the sofa at the time of the order. After 10 weeks, Acme delivered a gold sofa to the

Cahill home. The Cahills called Acme to complain, and Acme picked up the sofa with the promise that it would be reupholstered in red. The sofa was delivered in green six weeks later. In the meanwhile, the Cahills decorated their living room to match the red sofa. After the sofa was delivered in green, 16 weeks after the initial order, the Cahills sued Acme for breach of contract and for damages resulting from the breach, which included the cost of redecorating their living room to match the red sofa. The legal rule is that the nonbreaching party can only collect damages to recoup the expected gain from the contract if performed as agreed. The nonbreaching party cannot receive damages for expenses incurred that were not in contemplation at the time the contract was formed. The Cahills are entitled to damages for the upholstering of the sofa in the incorrect color and are entitled to compensation for the loss of the use of their sofa for 16 weeks as well as the cost of a new red sofa.

CASE B

Jane Smith ordered a new car from Lunar Motors on June 1, 1998. The Lunar coupe in black was ordered, but the salesperson suggested that the gray floor model, which was used only for demo drives, would represent a $300 savings off the sticker price of the Lunar coupe. Ms. Smith agreed to purchase the floor model for $12,700 rather than pay $13,000 for the special-order car. The salesperson once again asserted that the floor model was new, was used only for demo drives, and had only 5 miles on the odometer. Ms. Smith returned to Lunar Motors on June 3, 1998, paid the $12,700 for the gray floor model Lunar coupe, and drove home. While driving home, Ms. Smith noticed that the car veered dramatically to the left. Ms. Smith took the car to her mechanic, who reported that the car was in an accident previously and had been repaired, but the frame was bent in such a manner as to distort the alignment. Ms. Smith contracted to and expected to receive a new, undamaged car with mileage and wear and tear due to demo drives. Ms. Smith did not contract to receive a damaged car. The salesperson asserted the car was like new. The holding of the court is that the nonbreaching party is entitled to the gain expected from the performance of the contract as agreed, and if the contract is not performed as agreed, the nonbreaching party is entitled to receive the benefit that she would have received if the contract had been performed as agreed. Ms. Smith is entitled to a complete refund of the $12,700 she paid for the car plus the daily cost of the loss of the use of the automobile to be tabulated by the fair market rental value per day of a Lunar coupe.

To synthesize the holdings from the fictitious cases, you would find a common theme that ties together the rules of law from both decisions. Basically, both cases hold that the nonbreaching party in a contract is entitled to receive the benefit of the deal that would have been received if the contract had been performed as agreed. First, craft a general statement of the law. Then, mention the legal rules from Case A and Case B as they pertain to the general statement of the law.

EXAMPLE

Are the Blacks entitled to damages compensating them for the breach of the contract to reupholster the loveseat and the chair? Damages are assessed in a breach of contract action (to give the nonbreaching party the measure of gain that he would have received if the contract had been performed as agreed) in a very specific manner. The nonbreaching party can collect damages to recoup the gain expected from the contract only if the contract had been performed as agreed. *Case A*; *Case B*. If the contract is not performed as agreed, the nonbreaching party is entitled to the benefit he would have received if the contract had been performed as agreed. *Case B*. The nonbreaching party cannot be compensated for expenses incurred that were not in contemplation at the time the contract was formed. *Case A*. In the alternative, the nonbreaching party can be compensated for expenses incurred that were in contemplation at the time the contract was formed. *Case A*. In our problem, the Blacks contracted to have the chair and loveseat upholstered in paisley fabric with the correct side showing. The furniture was upholstered with the wrong side of the fabric showing. When ordering the furniture, the Blacks stipulated that they needed the pieces for a family reunion and that the pieces would provide the necessary seating. The Blacks were without their furniture because of an error of Comfy Furniture, and the need for the seating was mentioned at the time of the contract formation. The Blacks should receive the gain they expected from the performance of the contract as agreed as well as compensation for the expense of providing alternative seating for the family reunion based on the rental cost of chairs.

An ineffective case synthesis based on our hypothetical problem would be as follows.

> Are the Blacks entitled to damages from Comfy Furniture for breach of contract? In *Case B,* the court held that "the nonbreaching party is entitled to the gain expected from the performance of the contract as agreed and if the contract is not performed as agreed, the nonbreaching party is entitled to receive the benefit that she would have received if the contract had been performed as agreed." *Case B*. The Blacks were the nonbreaching party and anticipated a loveseat and a chair to be upholstered in paisley with the correct side showing. Therefore, the Blacks are entitled to be compensated by a damage award to put them in a position as if the contract had been performed as agreed.

Are the Blacks entitled to be compensated for not having adequate seating for the family reunion? *Case A* holds that the non-breaching party cannot receive damages for expenses incurred that were not in contemplation at the time the contract was formed. *Case A*. The Blacks alerted Mr. Blaine, the salesperson, that the couches were needed for a family reunion at Thanksgiving. The Blacks indicated that the additional seating provided by the chair and the loveseat would be necessary at the reunion when ordering the furniture. Since the need for the seating, to be provided by the furniture, was in contemplation at the time the order was placed, the Blacks should be compensated for not having adequate seating at the time of the reunion; the damages should be measured by the cost of providing alternative seating.

This example, although clear and coherent, does not synthesize the decisions and unify the concepts articulated in the cases. Each holding is addressed separately, although one holding relates to the other and the authority is presented more as a list than as a cohesive unit.

When you have found a relevant statute for a problem, give it the highest regard, because statutes on point govern before case law. (See Chapters 1 and 2.) Generally, synthesize statutes separately from case law holdings. However, if you find cases that interpret and apply the relevant statutes, synthesize the statute text with the application found in case law. Always apply the plain meaning rule to statutes. The plain meaning of the statute text is derived from a reading of each word at its face value.

The problem below illustrates the synthesis of a statute and a case.

PROBLEM

FACT PATTERN

On August 7, 1998, our client, Jane Howard, obtained an $800 loan from Rough & Tough Pawn Shop, using her grandmother's engagement ring as collateral. Howard agreed to make monthly payments on the loan for a minimum of 13 1/2 months. After 12 months, Rough & Tough had the right to sell the ring and to refund Howard the difference between her outstanding debt and the price received for the ring.

On September 11, 1998, Howard received a postcard from Rough & Tough stating that its shop and its assets will be sold to Able Pawn. The postcard also stated that Able would assume the business of Rough & Tough, including the items pawned and the loans outstanding. The postcard alerted Howard to pick up the ring and to pay off her note by September 29, 1998, if Howard wanted to reclaim her property. Howard decided to continue to make her monthly payments to Able Pawn, where her loan would be transferred.

On October 1, 1998, Able Pawn was robbed and all of the jewelry was stolen, including Howard's ring. The premises were protected by a security alarm system and a guard dog. The jewelry was sold to Village Jewelers in Lincoln Park.

ISSUE

The issue to be examined is whether Rough & Tough had authority to sell its interest in Howard's ring.

STATUTORY AUTHORITY

The applicable statute is from the Pawnbrokers Regulation Act, 205 ILCS 510/10 (1992).

> *Sale of Property.* No personal property received on deposit or pledge, or purchased by any such pawnbroker, shall be sold or permitted to be redeemed or removed from the place of business of such pawnbroker for the space of twenty-four hours after the delivery of the copy and statement required by Section 7 of this act required to be delivered to the officer or officers named therein; and no personal property pawned or pledged shall be sold or disposed of by any such pawnbroker within one year from the time when the pawner or pledger shall make default in the payment of interest on the money so advanced by such pawnbroker, unless by the written consent of such pawner or pledger.

RELEVANT CASE LAW

This decision interprets and applies the relevant statute, so the statute and the decision should be synthesized.

<u>*JACOBS v. GROSSMAN*</u>
310 Ill. 247, 141 N.E.2d 714 (1923)

DUNCAN, J.

This case is brought to this court on a certificate of importance and appeal from a judgment of the Appellate Court for the First District, affirming a judgment of the municipal court of Chicago in favor of the appellee and against appellant in the sum of $330. Appellee, Minnie Jacobs, on April 8, 1921, began an action of replevin in the municipal court of Chicago against appellant, Harry Grossman, a licensed pawnbroker, to recover possession of a diamond ring delivered by herself to appellant to secure the payment of $70 borrowed from him. A replevin bond was given for $800, and a writ of replevin issued. It was returned April 12, 1921, served but no property found. Appellee then filed a count in trover, alleging possession of the ring of the value of $400 and the conversion of it by appellant. The case was heard before the court without a jury.

On June 3, 1919, appellee placed in pawn with appellant, a licensed pawnbroker doing business at 426 South Halsted Street, Chicago, the ring, and received thereon the sum of $70. Interest on the loan was paid to June 7, 1920. The pawn ticket issued to appellee contained this statement, "This office protected by the Chicago Electric Protective Company," and described the location and name of the pawnbroker as "Metropolitan Loan Bank, 426 South Halsted St." The ticket further described the goods pawned, the amount loaned, and the time of redemption. Between October 7 and 10, 1920, appellant sold all his interest in whatever pledges he had to Jacob Klein, another duly licensed pawnbroker at 502 South Halsted Street, for the sum of $16,000 or $17,000, which represented the principal sums loaned on said pledges with interest thereon. The pledges were sold by appellant to Klein upon the express understanding that the pledgors might redeem from Klein in the same manner as they could from appellant, had he not sold his interest in the pawns. It was admitted that Klein is a reputable business man, and it was also conceded by appellant that no notice was given by him, either expressly or impliedly, to the appellee of the transfer of her property. On January 8, 1921, the pawnshop of Klein was entered by four armed robbers. The robbers ordered the clerks employed there to hold up their hands, and they forcibly took from a safe a large number of articles, including the diamond ring in question of appellee, which has never been recovered.

There is an unimportant dispute in the record evidence as to whether appellee or her sister, after the sale of appellant's business to Klein, had called on Klein and secured an additional loan upon a diamond ring other than the one in question. The Appellate Court found that the evidence on this point showed that appellee's sister, and not appellee, was involved in that transaction. Appellant admits in his reply brief that he does not rely in any way on this testimony to show actual notice to appellee of the change in the possession of the pledge in question. As to the other material facts above set out, there is no dispute between the parties.

Counsel for appellant relies for a reversal of the judgment on two propositions: First, that a pawnbroker is bound only to use ordinary care for the safety of the pawner's property, and, if the property is lost or destroyed without the negligence of the pawnee, then he is not liable; second, that a pawnbroker has the right to assign or sell to another his interest in an article pledged to him.

A pawn is a species of bailment which arises when goods or chattels are delivered to another as a pawn for security to him on money borrowed of him by the bailor. It is the pignari acceptum of the civil law, according to which the possession of the pledge passes to the creditor, therein differing from a hypotheca. It is a class of bailment which is made for the mutual benefit of the bailor and bailee. All that is required by the common law on the part of a pawnee in the protection of the property thus entrusted to him is ordinary care and diligence. Consequently, unless a failure to exercise such care and diligence is shown, a pawnee is not answerable for the loss of the article pledged. 30 Cyc. 1169; *Standard Brewery v. Malting Co.*, 171 Ill. 602, 49 N.E. 507. This is an elementary principle, and there can be no question as to the accuracy and correctness of appellant's first proposition.

But the question arises as to whether or not appellant was guilty of negligence in transferring the interest of the pawner without giving her any notice of such transfer. Appellant's duty to her was to safely keep and protect the property pledged. It was a legal obligation on his part to appellee, from which he could not relieve himself by transferring the pledge to another without her consent. Appellee relied upon him to keep and protect her property where it would be reasonably safe, and he had in substance assured her by the language on the ticket that her property was insured or safeguarded. He violated this duty or obligation to her by transferring the possession of her property to another, to be kept at another place, which the evidence does not show to be protected by a protective company, and without giving her notice of such custody and transfer.

Whatever may be the right of the parties in a bailment for the mutual benefit of the bailor and the bailee, it is unquestionably the law that the parties may increase or diminish these rights by stipulations contained in the contract of bailment. 30 Cyc. 1167; *St. Losky v. Davidson*, 6 Cal. 643. The sum and substance of appellant's contract was that he would keep appellee's property at his office or shop described as aforesaid, and which was protected as aforesaid. The pawning of the ring by appellee under the circumstances imposed a personal trust upon appellant to personally keep the property at his shop and under the assurance of protection as aforesaid, and he could not at his will, without the consent of appellee, transfer the possession and custody thereof to another without such consent. The rule is stated in 3 R.C.L. 112, that any attempt on the part of the bailee in an ordinary simple bailment of a pawn to sell, lease, pledge, or otherwise part with the title or possession of the bailment, constitutes a conversion in every case where the bailment can be properly regarded as a personal trust in the bailee.

There is another controlling reason for holding that appellant is liable for the loss of the ring, and for holding that he could not transfer the possession of the article pawned to him to another and escape liability for a conversion. Section 10 of the Pawnbroker's Act (Smith-Hurd Rev. St. 1923, c. 107 1/2) provides, in part, as follows:

> No personal property pawned or pledged shall be sold or disposed by any such pawnbroker within one year from the time when the pawner or pledger shall make default in the payment of interest on the money so advanced by such pawnbroker, unless by the written consent of such pawner or pledger.

Appellant claims that the proper interpretation of this statute is that it prohibits the sale of an article, including the interest of the pledger or pawner as well as his own, and does not refer to a sale of only the interest of the pawnbroker or pledgee. The statute is not subject to such construction. It should be construed to mean what it says: That the property must not be sold or disposed of by the pawnbroker without the written consent of the pledgor. The statute does not confine itself to a sale, but also forbids any disposition of the same without consent as aforesaid. It cannot be seriously disputed that appellant did dispose of the property without the consent of appellee, within the meaning of the foregoing section of the statute.

The judgment of the Appellate Court is affirmed.

Judgment affirmed.

SAMPLE SYNTHESIS

Does Rough & Tough have the authority to sell its interest in Howard's ring? Unless the pawner gives written consent, no pawned property shall be sold or disposed of by any pawnbroker within one year from the time the pawner defaults in the payment of interest on the money advanced by the pawnbroker. 205 ILCS 510/10 (1992). Where a pawnbroker neglected to give notice of the intent to sell his interest in a pawner's diamond ring and neglected to receive written consent for such sale, the pawnbroker lacked authority to transfer his interest in the ring to another. *Jacobs v. Grossman*, 141 N.E. 714, 715 (Ill. Ct. App. 1923). Although Rough & Tough gave Howard notice of its intent to sell the shop and its assets, R & T failed to obtain Howard's written consent to sell her ring. Therefore, a court will probably find that Rough & Tough lacked the authority to sell its interest in Howard's ring to another pawnbroker.

The above example synthesizes the statute and the *Jacobs* case around the issue of a pawnbroker's authority to sell its interest in a pawned item without the consent of the pawner. Notice how the statute is mentioned first because its authority ranks higher than the case. The *Jacobs* case follows the statute because the holding is more detailed on the issue of a pawnbroker's duty to give notice before selling his interest in the pawner's ring and the facts are similar to Jane Howard's situation. Two sources of primary authority, a statute and a case, are used together in this sample synthesis because both sources relate to a single legal issue.

▼ How Do You Synthesize Two Sources of Statutory Authority?

Often you must use two or more sections of a statute in conjunction to explain the legal rule completely. Sometimes definitional provisions are located in one section and the applicable code section is located in another. (See Chapter 6 for a more detailed explanation of enacted law.)

Facts: Mr. Thomas was arrested on charges of domestic battery. He punched his wife in the face three times and broke her nose. Mr. and Mrs. Thomas live in Illinois, but they are living apart.

Issue: Whether the Illinois domestic battery statute applies to an estranged husband and whether punching is considered battery.

This problem requires you to use two statutory provisions. One section defines the relevant terms, and the other section details actions that constitute domestic battery. The statutory definition of family and household members as pertaining to domestic battery follows.

725 ILCS 5/112A-3(3) (1994):

"Family or household members" include spouses, former spouses, parents, children, stepchildren and other persons related by blood or marriage, persons who share or formerly shared a common dwelling and persons who have or allegedly have a child in common.

The domestic battery statute at 720 ILCS 5/12-3.2 (1994):

(a) A person commits domestic battery if he intentionally or knowingly without legal justification by any means:
(1) Causes bodily harm to any family or household member as defined in Subsection (3) of Section 112A-3 of the Code of Criminal Procedure of 1963, as amended;
(2) Makes physical contact of an insulting or provoking nature with any family or household member as defined in subsection (3) of Section 112A-3 of the Code of Criminal Procedure of 1963, as amended.

Sample synthesis using two statutory provisions:

We must determine whether the domestic battery statute, 720 ILCS 5/12-3.2 (1994), applies to married couples living apart and if so, whether Mr. Thomas, an estranged husband, committed domestic battery by punching his wife. The domestic battery statute applies to family members. "Family members" is defined to include "spouses formerly sharing a common dwelling." 725 ILCS 5/112A-3(3) (1994). "A person commits domestic battery if he intentionally or knowingly without legal justification by any means:
(1) Causes bodily harm to any family or household member. . . ." 720 ILCS 5/12-3.2 (1994). Since Mr. Thomas is a spouse who formerly shared a common residence with his wife, he is a family or household member, and the domestic battery statute is applicable. Mr. Thomas punched his wife in the face three times, which caused her nose to break. The facts do not state that his mental capacity was altered by inebriation or severe mental illness, so his actions can be deduced to be intentional. The facts also do not indicate if Mr. Thomas was provoked to commit battery by extreme jealousy. It appears that there was no legal justification for the bodily harm inflicted on Mrs. Thomas by Mr. Thomas. Although Mr. Thomas is a spouse formerly sharing a common dwelling with Mrs.

Thomas, he is a family member and is governed by the domestic battery statute. By punching his wife, breaking her nose, and causing her bodily harm, Mr. Thomas committed domestic battery.

CHECKLIST: SEVEN STEPS FOR EFFECTIVE SYNTHESIS

1. Brief your authority.
2. Outline the problem.
3. Organize the primary authority.
4. Under each issue, organize your primary sources by hierarchy of authority.
5. Compare and contrast the case holding and statutory text.
6. Formulate a statement of the law that incorporates all of the primary sources that will be used under the subissue heading.
7. Attribute the authority for any legal statement by using the proper Bluebook citation.

PRACTICE POINTER

When synthesizing authorities, always cite to every source that you use. Often the information gathered from the authority is not from the first page of the decision. You must use pinpoint cites to indicate from exactly where within the decision the information is obtained. Also, often you will use authorities more than once. This calls for subsequent citation format. Rely on Bluebook Rule 10.9 for guidance on short citation method when citing cases subsequently.

CHAPTER SUMMARY

Learning to synthesize authority is a mechanical process at first. Brief the cases and summarize the statutory authority. Insert the applicable authority in your outline by grouping together related statements of the law. Draft cohesive statements of the legal authority that you grouped together. Cite all authority accurately even if string citations are needed or if two separate clauses in a single sentence are each supported by a different authority.

As you become more adept at synthesis, you will see that your writing is smoother and less redundant. Synthesizing authority lets you write in one voice rather than awkwardly switching back and forth between your words and the words of the court.

KEY TERMS

causes of action
facts
primary authority

reasoning
synthesis

EXERCISES

SHORT ANSWER EXERCISES

1. Why do we synthesize authority?
2. What are the four basic types of synthesis?
3. What are the steps required to synthesize legal rules?

APPLICATION EXERCISES

4. Read the following fact pattern and cases carefully. Draft a paragraph in which you synthesize the holdings of the cases. The issue that you will address is provided as well. Remember that proper synthesis requires you to relate the authority to a common legal theme. The problem's issue will guide you in synthesizing the authority.

Facts

On November 29, 1997, Michael Jones purchased a used truck from Grimy's Auto and Truck Service. At the time of the purchase, Grimy's stated that the engine was completely overhauled and consisted of rebuilt and reconditioned parts, that all parts were guaranteed, and that invoices for all new parts would be provided. On November 13, 1998, after using the truck for almost one year, Jones discovered that several engine parts were not rebuilt or reconditioned and that other engine parts were defective. These defects caused the truck to break down, resulting in lost wages and lost profits for Jones. Jones made repairs to the truck on November 13, 1998, December 13, 1998, and December 16, 1998. Jones did not attempt to return the truck and did not notify Grimy's that the truck was defective. The truck is currently disabled in Columbus, Ohio. Jones wants to sue Grimy's for damages for breach of contract.

Issue

Whether Jones continued to use the truck for more than a reasonable time after noticing the defects and failed to properly reject the truck and to notify Grimy's as to the defects.

Case A

A buyer of goods must alert the seller as soon as he discovers that the goods are not as agreed on. A buyer must rescind a sales contract as soon as he discovers the breach or after he has had a reasonable time for examination. The buyer waives the right to rescind a contract for the sale of goods by continuing to use allegedly defective goods for more than a reasonable time.

Case B

To meet the requirements of an effective rejection, the buyer must reject the goods within a reasonable time and reasonably notify the seller.

5. Read the following fact pattern and cases carefully. Draft a paragraph in which you synthesize the holdings of the cases. The issue that you will address is provided as well.

Facts

Robert and Jane Moore live in Evingston and have to repair the gutters on their house. There is eight feet between their house and their neighbor's. The properties are adjoining; the neighboring Kandler house is north of the Moore house. The Moore's contractors and carpenters must enter the Kandler property to work on the gutters on the north side of the house. Mrs. Kandler is not very pleased that workers are entering her property. The Moores came to our office to find out what they should do. The Moores specifically asked if they should obtain an easement to grant them a right of way on Mrs. Kandler's property to make the repairs.

Issue

What legal access would allow the contractors and carpenters, repairing the gutters on the Moore house, to enter the adjoining property belonging to Mrs. Kandler?

Statutory Authority

Ch. 12 §99: If the repair and maintenance of an existing single-family residence cannot reasonably be accomplished without entering onto the adjoining land, and if the owner of the adjoining land refuses to permit entry onto that adjoining land for the purpose of repair and maintenance of the single-family residence, then the owner of the single-family residence may bring an action in court to compel the owner of the adjoining land to permit entry for the purpose of repair and maintenance where entry will be granted solely for the purposes of repair and maintenance.

Case Y

The need to enter the land of an adjoining property for the purpose of making repairs to one's own property should not mandate that an easement be acquired. An easement grants a right of way, but only the landowner can create an easement. The adjoining landowner may view the repairs as a nuisance and would not grant the easement. Sometimes repairs must be performed on a single-family residence that require entering the adjoining land. Statute Ch. 12 §99 was created to avoid the need to obtain an easement to enter adjoining land when the sole reason for the right of way is to make repairs on a single-family residence.

THE IRAC METHOD

CHAPTER OVERVIEW

The IRAC chapter focuses on the writing style used for the discussion portion of the memo. IRAC is an acronym for Issue, Rule, Application, Conclusion. These are the building blocks of a memo's discussion. You will learn to identify issues and applicable legal authority. You will also learn how to extract the legally significant facts and apply them to the relevant law to draw substantiated conclusions. You will learn to identify effective IRAC use by dissecting discussions and labeling the IRAC components, and you will learn to draft IRAC sequences as well.

A. PURPOSES OF IRAC

▼ What Is IRAC?

IRAC stands for Issue, Rule, Application, Conclusion. IRAC is the architectural blueprint for the discussion portion of a legal memorandum. It gives legal writing continuity and clarity and organizes the contents of the discussion. IRAC provides legal support and analysis for the issues posed by the problem and guides the writer toward a well-supported conclusion.

IRAC benefits both the writer and the reader because the components are essentially a checklist designed to ensure that the discussion is analytically well thoughtout and that it contains the necessary legal authority. IRAC is very important because it lets the reader see the particular legal point being addressed, the relevant legal rule, the application of the law to the facts, and the conclusion. It is formula writing in the same way that formula movie romances, westerns, and thrillers are. The predictability of the IRAC format enables the reader to obtain the information quickly.

B. IRAC COMPONENTS

Each IRAC sequence is composed of an **issue,** which is really a legal element or component; the **legal rule** or **holding** from a case or statutory authority; the **application,** which is a demonstration of how the legal authority applies to the problem that you are writing about; and the **conclusion,** the final assessment of how the rule applies to the facts of your problem.

▼ What Does an IRAC Paragraph Look Like?

This fact pattern forms the basis of the IRAC paragraph example.

On August 7, 1998, Ms. Howard went to Rough & Tough Pawn Shop in Chicago to obtain a loan using a diamond ring as collateral. Rough & Tough loaned Ms. Howard $800, and she agreed to pay $75 per month for a total of 13 1/2 months. Ms. Howard knew that she would have to pay off the balance of $1,025 in 12 months because at that time Rough & Tough would have the right to sell the ring. On September 11, 1998, Ms. Howard received a postcard from Rough & Tough stating that it was selling the shop and all of its assets to Able Pawn. Mr. Sam Able would assume the business of Rough & Tough, including all pawned items and outstanding loans. On the bottom of the postcard was a notice stating: "If you want your item, please pick it up by September 29, 1998, and pay off your note by September 29, 1998." Because Ms. Howard did not have the money to pay off the note, she decided to pay Able Pawn the $75 per month once the loan was transferred in the sale. In October 1998, Able Pawn was robbed and all the jewelry, including Ms. Howard's ring, was stolen. Able Pawn had a security alarm system and a guard dog to protect the property, but the robbers were able to circumvent these obstacles.

We will work through the following sample IRAC paragraph, based on the Howard fact pattern, and its components to illustrate how to draft an IRAC paragraph.

(**I**) Whether a bailment for the mutual benefit of Rough & Tough and Howard existed? (**R**) A pawn is a form of bailment, made for the mutual benefit of bailee and bailor, arising when goods are delivered to another as a pawn for security to him on money borrowed by the bailor. *Jacobs v. Grossman*, 141 N.E. 714, 715 (Ill. Ct. App. 1923). In *Jacobs*, the court found that a bailment for mutual benefit did arise because the plaintiff pawned a ring as collateral for a $70 loan given to him by the defendant. *Id.* (**A**) In our problem, Howard pawned her ring as collateral to secure an $800 loan given to her by Rough & Tough. (**C**) Therefore, Howard and Rough & Tough probably created a bailment for mutual benefit.

Note that the first sentence of the IRAC paragraph is a statement of the issue that will be examined in the paragraph. The issue is narrowly defined and focused on one of the analytical elements of the problem. The rule of law, the next component of the paragraph, provides the legal basis for the analysis of the issue. Then, it is appropriate to discuss some of the facts of the cited case if these facts help explain how the legal rule can be applied to your facts. Notice that everything that comes from an opinion is given citation credit.

The most important component of the IRAC paragraph is the application portion. The application is where you use the facts of your problem to demonstrate, but not to conclude, why the legal rule should apply to the issue posed. This is the legal analysis. After you let the facts speak for themselves by demonstrating how the legal rule applies to the scenario at hand, you draw a conclusion. The conclusion answers the issue posed. The issue is the question being examined in the discussion, and the conclusion is the answer.

This example illustrates how the conclusion responds directly to the issue:

Issue: Whether a bailment for the mutual benefit of Rough & Tough and Howard existed.

Conclusion: Therefore, Howard and Rough & Tough probably created a bailment for mutual benefit.

1. Issues

The question presented is the overall legal **issue** that will be resolved in the memo. A **subissue** in the IRAC paragraph is a point or query that must be addressed to substantiate one legal element of the problem. When analyzing and writing about a legal problem objectively, it is often important to address subissues in the order that they must be resolved to support legal analysis. For example, the general rule for arson in Illinois is the malicious burning of the dwelling house of another. The question presented for a memo on arson would be:

> Whether Mr. Smith committed arson by intentionally burning down his brother's factory.

The subissues addressed in the IRAC paragraphs would be:

> Whether there was a malicious burning.
> Whether the factory is a dwelling house.
> Whether the factory of Mr. Smith's brother constitutes the property of another person.

The subissues form the **topic sentences** of the IRAC paragraphs. They provide the analytical steps that you must take in your thought process and your legal reasoning to resolve the overall issue posed by the problem, the question presented. The topic sentences in the IRAC paragraph introduce the legal element in question that needs to be resolved to complete the steps necessary to thoroughly examine the problem and to determine a response to the question presented.

▼ What Is the Difference between the Question Presented and the Issues in IRAC Paragraphs?

The question presented is the overall problem that must be resolved in the objective memo. The question presented for the Howard fact pattern is:

> Whether Ms. Howard has a claim against Rough & Tough or against Able Pawn Shop for the value of her ring.

The subissues are determined by the legal elements or tests involved in the problem. The elements are discussed individually along with the relevant legal rule. There is a certain logical order when presenting the elements. Let the legal rules guide you in establishing the order of the subissues. Notice that each issue centers on a single step of the legal analysis necessary to fully examine the question presented.

The subissues that form the topic sentences of the IRAC paragraphs in a memo addressing Ms. Howard's problem would be as follows:

> The first issue is, what type of relationship does a pawner and a pawnee have?

What property rights do Ms. Howard and Rough & Tough Pawn have when they enter into a mutual bailment?

Can Rough & Tough Pawn transfer its interest in Ms. Howard's property to Able Pawn?

Did Rough & Tough Pawn receive the proper consent for the transfer of the ring from Ms. Howard?

Is Rough & Tough liable for the loss of Ms. Howard's property after transferring its interest to Able Pawn?

Is Able Pawn liable for the theft of Ms. Howard's property while it was in its possession?

All of these queries are really elements that must be addressed, step by step, to resolve the question presented.

Each of the subissues will be a topic sentence of the IRAC paragraph highlighting the analytical focus of the legal discussion in that paragraph. Each issue is a step in the thought process required to thoroughly prove all of the underlying elements necessary to address the question presented.

Notice how one issue statement logically leads into the next. A good test to see if your discussion is well organized is to write down all of your issue statements from your IRAC paragraphs. If the issue statements flow logically, one to the next, then the organization of your discussion will be logical.

To analyze the problem thoroughly, a number of issues must be examined in the discussion. To make the analysis logical, the issues must be examined in a certain order.

2. Rules of Law

The **legal holding** or **rule,** or synthesized compilation of the pertinent legal rules, follows the issue at the beginning of the IRAC paragraph. (For an in-depth discussion of the process of synthesizing authority, see Chapter 22.)

A rule of law is the court's holding or a synthesis of various courts' holdings on the same point. A rule also can be a statute and the legal elements laid out by the statute. A synthesis of a statute and a case applying or interpreting the statute also constitutes a rule.

In our IRAC example, note that the first sentence is the issue, and the second sentence is the legal rule.

Issue:	Whether a bailment for the mutual benefit of Rough & Tough and Howard existed.
Rule, followed by pinpoint citation:	A pawn is a form of bailment, made for the mutual benefit of the bailee and the bailor, arising when goods are delivered to another as a pawn for security to him on money borrowed by the bailor. *Jacobs v. Grossman,* 141 N.E. 714, 715 (Ill. Ct. App. 1923).

When organizing the discussion, first discern what issues are to be addressed, then find the pertinent mandatory authority that addresses the issues raised. Do not write the discussion around the authority, but make the authority address the issues. To demonstrate clearly how the authority supports or addresses the issues raised, discuss the pertinent facts of the cited case after you state the case's holding or legal rule. This is particularly helpful when the holding is very broad. You must demonstrate that the cited case truly supports the premise discussed in the IRAC paragraph.

▼ Why Is Citation Important?

Citation is an essential component of the rule portion of the IRAC paragraph. You must always give proper credit in Bluebook format to any statement made that is not wholly your own. Any legal principle or authority must be attributed to its source. Proper attribution of authority tells the reader where you obtained the legal principle that supports the discussion. Most important, the cite tells the reader whether the authority is primary mandatory authority, primary persuasive, or secondary authority. A cite also provides information without including the information in the discussion's text. For example, you could write a holding as follows:

> The state of Kimberly Supreme Court held in 1983 that individuals have a right to privacy. *Jones v. City of Moose,* 121 Kim. 12, 13 (1983).

A much more effective version of the same holding to include in the rule portion of the IRAC paragraph is:

> Individuals have a right to privacy. *Jones v. City of Moose,* 121 Kim. 12, 13 (1983).

The citation itself provides the information about the court, its jurisdiction and level, and the year. The text need not repeat this information. Citations are valuable sources of information about the legal authority presented in the rule component of the IRAC paragraph.

3. Application of the Law to the Problem's Facts

▼ How Do You Use the Legally Significant Facts?

Think of the legal rule as a test or a series of elements requiring certain facts to be used to support the outcome of the test. The facts used are **legally significant facts** because they bear legal significance as to the outcome of an issue. Our arson example mentioned at the beginning of the chapter illustrates this point.

THE ARSON HYPOTHETICAL

John Smith lived in Arkville. John Smith's brother, Richard Smith, lived in Barkville Estates. Richard Smith owned a factory in downtown Barkville. John Smith was consumed by a jealous rage over his brother Richard's success and intentionally and maliciously burned down the factory in Barkville. The question to be examined is whether John Smith committed arson by intentionally and maliciously burning down his brother's factory.

The general rule for arson is the malicious burning of a dwelling house of another. This general rule would be the legal authority used in the rule portion of the IRAC paragraph.

An IRAC paragraph on this topic would be as follows:

Issue: Whether John Smith committed arson by burning down his brother's factory.

Rule: Arson is the malicious burning of a dwelling house of another. 9 Stat. §§21, 23 (1976).

Application: John Smith burned down the factory of his brother, Richard Smith. John Smith's actions were intentional and malicious. Richard resides in Barkville Estates.

Conclusion: John Smith did not commit arson because he burned down his brother's factory, not his brother's residence or dwelling house.

The **application** lays a factual foundation on which the conclusion can be based. The facts are selected because each fact illustrates a legal point related to your rule of law: the malicious act, the intentional burning down of a building, the use of the building—whether it serves as a residence or dwelling house or whether it serves another purpose. The rule indicates which facts you should examine. Once you lay the factual foundation by using the problem's facts to illustrate how the law should apply, you draw a conclusion.

4. Conclusion

The **conclusion** resolves the issue posed at the beginning of the IRAC sequence. The conclusion should reflect directly the issue posed. If you remove the rule and the application portions of the IRAC paragraph, the issue and the conclusion should read as if they are a question and an answer. The conclusion generally restates the issue and includes the basis for the answer. The arson example with John Smith illustrates the role of the conclusion.

Issue: Whether John Smith committed arson by burning down his brother's factory.

Conclusion: John Smith did not commit arson because he burned down his brother's factory, not his residence or dwelling house.

Notice how the conclusion responds directly to the issue posed. The conclusion focuses directly on the question raised at the beginning of the IRAC sequence. Each element of the discussion is resolved before addressing the next element or issue.

PRACTICE POINTER

Always test to see if your conclusion is focused on the issue raised by reading the issue at the beginning of the IRAC sequence, then reading the conclusion. If the issue and the conclusion read like a question and a reasoned answer that responds directly to the question posed, then you have adequately resolved the issue raised.

CHAPTER SUMMARY

IRAC—standing for Issue, Rule, Application, Conclusion—provides the structure for the legal discussion. The IRAC structure provides a checklist for you to make sure that you have included all of the necessary components in the discussion and supported every premise with legal authority. Because it follows a predictable pattern, IRAC permits the reader to obtain information quickly. Mastering the IRAC format requires practice, which involves rereading and revising your work. Once you feel comfortable with the IRAC format, you should be confident that the discussion portions of your memos are logically ordered and analytically complete.

KEY TERMS

application	legal holding
citation	legal rule
conclusion	legally significant facts
IRAC	subissue
issue	topic sentence

EXERCISES

SHORT ANSWER EXERCISES

1. What does "IRAC" stand for? Define each component.
2. Why do we use the IRAC format?
3. What is a legally significant fact?

DIAGRAMMING IRAC COMPONENTS

4. Diagram the IRAC components of each paragraph in the discussion section. Note where the writing digresses from the IRAC format.

DISCUSSION

To be successful in a claim against Rough & Tough or Able Pawn, Ms. Howard would have to prove that Rough & Tough was liable for the loss of her ring. First, for an action against Rough & Tough, she would have to show that the company had no right to transfer her pawned property without her written consent. Illinois Pawnbrokers Act, 205 ILCS 510/7 (1992). If pledged property was transferred without written consent of the property owner, the pawnbroker can be held responsible for loss or theft of pawned property because the property was in his safekeeping and was transferred illegally. *Jacobs v. Grossman,* 141 N.E. 714, 716 (Ill. Ct. App. 1923). Rough & Tough did not get a written consent for the transfer of Ms. Howard's property. In its defense the company could claim that written correspondence without the written consent would be enough to inform the pawner of the transfer of her property. Second, for an action against Able Pawn, Ms. Howard would have to show negligence in its care of her pawned ring. Illinois courts have ruled that in bailment for mutual benefit, the ordinary care or diligence that one would give to one's own property would be adequate to avoid negligence. *Id.* at 715; *Bielunski v. Tousignant,* 149 N.E.2d 801, 803 (Ill. Ct. App. 1958). Mrs. Howard would have to prove that a security system and a guard dog would not be ordinary care and diligence. In his defense Mr. Able could argue that these were sufficient to be considered ordinary care and diligence. For a claim against Village Jewelers to be successful, Ms. Howard would have to establish that she held good title to her property because a thief cannot convey good title to stolen property. *Hobson's Truck Sales v. Carroll Trucking,* 276 N.E. 89, 92 (Ill. Ct. App. 1971). Village Jewelers, which purchased the ring from the robbers, could not have good title to Ms. Howard's ring. Ms. Howard probably could have a successful claim against Rough & Tough and Village Jewelers. She probably would not be able to prove Able Pawn negligent in the care of her ring.

Does a pawnbroker have the right to transfer pawned property or interest in that property without written consent of the pawner? Pawned property cannot be transferred within a year from the pawner's default without written consent of the pawner. Illinois Pawnbrokers Act, 205 ILCS 510/7. One Illinois court ruled that a pawnbroker had no right to transfer the plaintiff's pledged diamond ring to another pawnbroker within a year of the plaintiff's default of her loan, without written consent of the pawner. *Jacobs,* 141 N.E. at 716. In our situation, Rough & Tough sold its shop and assets to Sam Able within two months of Ms. Howard's pawning her grandmother's engagement ring. Because the sale occurred within a year of Ms. Howard's transaction with Rough & Tough, the company had a legal obligation under the Illinois statute to require a written consent for the transfer of her property. Also, the statute states that the time period for requirement of written consent for transfer of pledged property is established from the time of the pawner's default. 205 ILCS 510/7. Our client has not defaulted, and she deserves at least all of the rights offered by the statute to a pawner who is in default. Rough & Tough did send Ms. Howard a postcard notifying her that it had sold all the pawned items and outstanding loans, including her ring, but it did not get her written consent for the sale of her property. Rough & Tough did not have the right to transfer Ms. Howard's ring without her written consent, and the sale of her property was probably not a legal sale.

Is a postcard sent to a pawner by a pawnbroker sufficient notice for the transfer of pawned property? Personal pawned property cannot be sold by a pawnee within one year from the time the pawner has defaulted in the interest payment unless the pawner has given written consent. Illinois Pawnbrokers Act, 205 ILCS 510/7. The statute uses a definite and clear term: "written consent." Ms. Howard did not default, and she would have at least all of the rights of a pawner that did default. Therefore, the pawnbroker was required to receive her written consent before transferring her property. A postcard with written notice of a sale of pawned property is not a written consent by the pawner and would probably not be sufficient notice to constitute a legal sale.

5. Diagram the IRAC components of each paragraph in the discussion section. Note where the writing digresses from the IRAC format.

FACTS

The Blacks came to us with the following problem and want to know what type of damages they are entitled to.

Mr. and Mrs. Black wanted to have a chair and a loveseat made to match the living room in their new home. The Blacks searched for weeks at various local furniture retailers for a furniture style and fabric that they liked but were unsuccessful. Finally, the Blacks went to a fabric sale at Fabric Retailers and found the upholstery fabric of their dreams. The Blacks purchased 50 yards of the fabric to make sure that they would have enough for any project. Mr. Black called all of the furniture retailers in the area to inquire whether customers can have furniture covered in their own material. Finally, Comfy Furniture said that they permit customers to bring in their own material to cover upholstered furniture ordered from Comfy. The Blacks hurried over to Comfy with the 50 yards of fabric and placed an order for a chair and a loveseat using their own fabric. The price agreed on was the base price of $500 for the chair and $800 for the loveseat. Mr. Blaine, of Comfy Furniture, was their salesperson. Mr. Blaine said that the fabric was ideal for the styles selected because it required no matching. He added that there was plenty of yardage because 30 yards is adequate for jobs of this nature. The fabric was a small paisley print, with the right side having a lovely sheen and vibrant coloration. The Blacks placed the order on July 7, 1998, because they were planning a family reunion for Thanksgiving and felt that that date would give them plenty of time to completely decorate their living room. The new pieces would provide plenty of seating for the family reunion. The Blacks indicated to Mr. Blaine that they needed the furniture for the reunion. Mr. Blaine asserted that the furniture would be ready by September 15. The Blacks gave Comfy Furniture a deposit of $1,000. The loveseat and the chair were delivered to the Black home on September 10, but the furniture was upholstered with the fabric's reverse side showing. The Blacks were devastated.

ISSUES

Whether the Blacks are entitled to damages from Comfy Furniture for incorrectly upholstering their furniture.

Whether the Blacks are entitled to damages from Comfy Furniture for the expense of decorating their living room to match the furniture they did not receive in the agreed on condition.

DISCUSSION

Are the Blacks entitled to special damages from Comfy Furniture for the cost of the redecoration of their living room? An Illinois Appellate Court decided that the nonbreaching party should be put back in the position that they were in when the contract was formed. *Kalal v. Goldblatt Bros.*, 368 N.E.2d 671, 673 (Ill. Ct. App. 1977). The Blacks stated their intention at the beginning concerning the fabric, the redecoration of the living room, and the family reunion. This fact was a part of their original position. The living room was redecorated. The furniture was delivered; however, the fabric was incorrect. Therefore, the Blacks have a right to recover consequential damages for the cost of the redecoration of their living room because the end result was not achieved: correctly upholstered furniture, newly redecorated living room to match, and sufficient seating for the reunion. The conditions of the original contract were not met, and there was a breach of contract as embodied by the incorrectly upholstered furniture.

Under contract law, what damages are the Blacks entitled to pursue? Damages for breach of contract should place the plaintiff in a position he would have been in had the contract been performed. *Kalal*, 368 N.E.2d at 671. The plaintiffs in *Kalal* received a sofa that had been reupholstered in the wrong fabric after numerous delays, during which they had chosen three different fabrics in succession. *Id.* The court held that the defect could be remedied by the cost of reupholstering the sofa in the proper fabric. *Id.* at 674. The Blacks' sofa and loveseat were improperly upholstered. Comfy Furniture upholstered their furniture with the reverse side of the fabric showing. Therefore, they were entitled to damages equal to the cost of upholstering their furniture correctly. However, the Blacks' situation is distinguished from *Kalal* in that their furniture was delivered before the date set in the contract, and it can be argued by Comfy that there was time to remedy the defect before their target date of Thanksgiving.

Are the Blacks entitled to compensation for the loss of use of their furniture? The question of compensation for loss of use of the furniture was considered by both parties in *Kalal* to be appropriate since the plaintiffs in the case were without their furniture for several months while waiting for it to be reupholstered. *Id.* The Blacks have been similarly inconvenienced in that they, too, have been without the use of their new furniture. Thus, they are entitled to compensation for the loss of use of the furniture. However, it can be argued by Comfy Furniture that the furniture in the *Kalal* case was used and had been removed from the home for the purpose of reupholstering it. *Id.* In the present case, the furniture was new and had never been in the Blacks' home, and Comfy may argue that the Blacks did not actually suffer loss of use of the new furniture.

Are the Blacks entitled to damages for the expense of decorating their living room to match the furniture they did not receive in the agreed on condition? The redecorating of the living room in *Kalal* was not in the contemplation of either party at the time the contract was executed. *Kalal,* 368 N.E.2d at 671. Subsequently, the court held that the only damages that were recoverable for breach of contract are limited to those that were reasonably foreseeable and were within the contemplation of the parties at the time the contract was executed. *Id.* at 674. By the express terms of the Uniform Commercial Code, the court cannot follow tort theories to award damages. The legislative history of the U.C.C. indicates that contractual disputes should apply to the findings of the court. *Moorman Mfg. Co. v. National Tank Co.,* 435 N.E.2d 443, 453 (Ill. 1982). The Blacks only told Mr. Blaine that they needed the furniture to be completed in time for a family reunion. Comfy knew that the Blacks were under a time constraint for the delivery, but apparently there was no communication regarding the redecorating of the living room. With regard to Comfy Furniture, the redecorating of the Blacks' living room was an unforeseeable event, and consequently they would not be held responsible for the expense. Because the fact that the redecorating of the living room was unforeseeable, it was not included within the terms of the contract. Therefore, Comfy only breached the express terms of the contract. The Blacks probably will not be awarded compensatory damages.

APPLICATION EXERCISES

6. Write an IRAC paragraph using the following information. You need not include all of the information. The issue is whether the plaintiff can show that his attorney's failure to attend hearings was excusable neglect. A number of the text blocks below contain statements of rules. Other text blocks include legally significant facts. In some paragraphs, conclusions have been drawn for you. Combine the rules where necessary and form an IRAC paragraph for the issue.

> Fed. R. Civ. P. 60(b) provides for relief from judgment if plaintiffs can show that a mistake was made or that there was excusable neglect on the part of their attorney.

> Rule 60(b) is an extraordinary remedy, granted in only exceptional cases. *Harold Washington Party v. Cook Cty. Illinois Democratic Party,* 984 F.2d 875 (7th Cir. 1993).

> In this case, the plaintiff's attorney, Mark Adly, missed four court-set

status hearings. He failed to appear. He failed to answer motions. Court status hearings are routinely held every three months.

Adly claims he did not have any notice of the hearings. Adly knew status proceedings normally were held. He attended depositions in this matter. Court records show that he was sent notices of the hearings to the address Adly says is correct.

"Excusable neglect may warrant relief under Rule 60(b)." *Zuelzke Tool & Eng'g v. Anderson Die Casting,* 925 F.2d 226 (7th Cir. 1991). In this case, the defendant relied on a third party who told them to refrain from further action because efforts were being made to have the defendant removed as defendant. *Id.* at 228. Anderson did not answer any complaints or file any pleadings. *Id.* The lack of response led the court to enter a default judgment against the company. *Id.* at 229. The district court refused the motion to vacate, saying that the defendant had voluntarily chosen not to control its fate in the litigation. *Id.*

7. Review the following paragraph. Note the issue, the rule, the application of law to facts, and the conclusion.

An important factor in determining whether a funeral home is a nuisance is the suitability of its location. "Funeral homes are generally located on the edge of purely residential but not predominantly residential areas." *Bauman v. Piser Undertakers Co.,* 34 Ill. App. 2d 145, 148, 180 N.E.2d 705, 708 (1962). A carefully run funeral home may be located on a property zoned for business at the edge of a residential neighborhood. *Id.* The funeral home in this case is located in a predominantly rural area. It is outside the boundary lines of the Up and Coming Acres subdivision. It is a lawful business located on a parcel zoned for business. The funeral home is in a suitable location.

8. Read the following facts carefully.

Mr. and Mrs. Mortimer reserved the party room at Harvey's Restaurant and gave Harvey's a $500 deposit. Their party was scheduled for November 3, 1998. Mrs. Mortimer sent the invitations out on October 1, 1998. The Mortimers agreed to the quoted price of $62.50 per person. The purpose of the event was for Mr. Mortimer to establish relationships with current and prospective legal clients.

On October 20, 1998, Mrs. Mortimer called Harvey's to confirm party details. She was informed that the party room was under demolition and could not be used for the party. Mrs. Harvey offered to lower the price to $57.50 per person and reserve a portion of the dining room. Although she believed these arrangements were not suitable, Mrs. Mortimer agreed to use the dining room since the invitations were sent and many people accepted.

Mrs. Mortimer ordered lump crab meat as an appetizer for the party. A waitress told Mrs. Mortimer that imitation crab meat was used when Mrs. Mortimer inquired about the crab's unusual crunchiness.

The Mortimers want to sue Harvey's for breach of contract and believe that they relied to their detriment on this contract. They assert that Harvey's failed to notify them of the changes in a timely manner, consequently preventing them from making other arrangements. Additionally, the Mortimers want to know if they have a cause of action for the substitution of imitation crab meat for genuine.

The following is a portion of a memo relating to one of the issues raised by the Mortimers. Read the paragraphs carefully and revise in IRAC format. Remember that each IRAC sequence can span more than one paragraph (for example, paragraph 1—issue and rule; paragraph 2—application and conclusion).

Did the Mortimers suffer a loss of business because of Harvey's Restaurants's promise of the entire party room? The Mortimers can argue that a false representation surrenders the restaurant's interest. "When parties enter into a contract for the performance of the same act in the future they impliedly promise that in the meantime neither will do anything to harm or prejudice the other inconsistent with the contractual relationship they have assumed. . . . If one party to the contract renounces it, the other may treat the renunciation as a breach and sue for damages at once." The restaurant can argue that the contract did not cover the entire performance but was modified; therefore, no harm was done to the contractual relationship. *Pappas v. Crist,* 233 N.C. 265, 25 S.E.2d 850 (1943).

The Mortimers can argue that "damages are not speculative merely because they cannot be computed with mathematical exactness, if, under evidence they are capable of reasonable approximation." *Hawkinson v. Johnston,* 122 F.2d 724 (8th Cir. 1941). The "rainmaking" potential was minimized because of the restaurant's failure to supply the room contracted for.

The restaurant would argue that the "period for which the damages can be reasonably forecast or soundly predicted in such a situation must depend on the circumstances and evidence of the particular case." *Id.* at 727. Therefore, the Mortimers can only quantify the number of RSVPs, not the number of rejects due to the smaller room.

24

OUTLINING AND ORGANIZING A MEMORANDUM

CHAPTER OVERVIEW

In Chapters 19-23, you learned about the components of a legal memorandum as well as some drafting pointers. This chapter teaches you how to organize the discussion section of your memorandum. You are shown some outlining techniques. (These are suggested techniques only. You may have a technique of your own that works well. Feel free to use it.) In this chapter, you also learn how to draft thesis paragraphs for your discussion.

A. PURPOSE OF OUTLINING

The key to a well-organized memo is a well-drafted outline. **Outlining** allows you to organize your discussion easily so that it is smooth and cogent. An outline ensures that you cover all of the legal rules and apply all of the legally significant facts to those rules.

B. STEPS TO OUTLINING

The outline should be done in two stages, each of which consists of a number of steps. In the first stage, you compile a **list of legal authorities,** which includes the names of and the citations to authorities, a note about the legally significant facts presented in any case, and a statement that summarizes each authority's significance to the issues presented in your research problem. See Illustration 24-1. In the second stage, you arrange the discussion sections concerning each issue and, in some cases, arrange each paragraph. See Illustration 24-2.

ILLUSTRATION 24-1.   List of Authorities

1. **Crane Rev. Stat. §808 (Williams 1994):**   A civil battery occurs when one individual touches another individual without his or her consent and a physical injury occurs.

2. *Eve v. Scott,* **State of Crane Supreme Court:**   A contact between a nonconsenting individual with an object such as a bat thrown by an offender is sufficient to be a touching within the context of the civil battery statute because the object would be an extension of the offender's body. (primary binding)

3. *Wayne v. Robert,* **State of Crane Supreme Court:**   A person intends his or her conduct when he or she undertakes an action with a knowing mind.

4. *Hawes v. Jackson,* **State of Crane Supreme Court:**   If a person consents to the touching, a battery has not occurred.

ILLUSTRATION 24-2. Outline of Discussion

Element or Subissue 1
    Issue: Did a touching occur?
    Rule: Objects are extensions of body parts
        Contact with an object can be touching (*Eve*)
    Application of law to facts: Bucket contacted McMillan
    Conclusion: A touching occurred
Element or Subissue 2
    Issue: Did Mann intend to hit McMillan?
    Rule: A person intends an act when it is done purposefully (*Wayne*)
    Application of law to facts: Mann purposefully threw the bucket
        at McMillan and said she intended to strike her
    Conclusion: Mann had intent
Element or Subissue 3
    Issue: Did McMillan consent to touching?
    Rule: If a party consented to the touching, no battery occurred.
        (*Hawes*)
    Application of law to facts: McMillan did not consent
    Conclusion: A touching without consent as in this case can be a
        battery
Element or Subissue 4
    Issue: Did McMillan suffer the requisite physical injuries as a
        result of the contact?
    Rule: Physical injuries must result from contact for battery (Statute)
    Application of law to facts: McMillan sustained cuts and eye irri-
        tation from bucket and sand contact
    Conclusion: McMillan had requisite physical injuries

---

1. Steps in Compiling a List of Legal Authorities

1. Draft the statement of the facts, the questions presented, and the conclusions.
2. Research your issues.
3. Read the cases.
4. Brief the authorities as discussed in Chapter 18. Once you have briefed the authorities, you will write a holding for each case. These holdings should be used in your list of authorities. These holdings will summarize the significance of the authorities. If the holdings are well written, they will incorporate important facts derived from the authorities.
5. Write a summary statement for each statute or other noncase authority you plan to cite.
6. Prepare a list of each of the relevant authorities. Note that not all authorities will be relevant. Include only those that help you to determine the law involved in your case. For your list, include the name of the authority. If the authority is a case, list the holding

or summary statement of the significance of the authority. Note the complete citation. It is also helpful to list whether the authority is a primary binding, primary persuasive, or secondary authority.

Now review Illustrations 24-1 and 24-4. Illustration 24-1 is a list of the significant authorities for the memo in Illustration 24-3. Illustration 24-4 is a list of authorities for the memo in Illustration

ILLUSTRATION 24-3.   Memorandum: McMillan Battery Action

MEMORANDUM

To: William Mark
From: Ivy Courier
Date: November 7, 1998
Re: McMillan Battery Action

QUESTION PRESENTED
Did an actionable battery occur when Mann intentionally struck McMillan with a bucket, without McMillan's consent, causing McMillan to suffer physical and monetary injuries?

CONCLUSION
Mann's intentional striking of McMillan with a bucket and sand was an actionable battery.

FACTS
Our client, Mary McMillan, a 36-year-old bank teller, wants to bring an action for battery against Carol Mann, a 36-year-old mother, who threw a metal bucket filled with sand at McMillan at a local park. While McMillan sat on a park bench, she teased Mann's 7-year-old son. Mann did not like this teasing and threw a bucket filled with sand at Mary. Sand landed in McMillan's eyes while she was wearing soft contact lenses. As a result, McMillan's contacts had to be replaced. The bucket also cut McMillan's eye and cheek. She had stitches in both places. McMillan asked Mann to pay for her doctor bills and for the new contacts. Mann refused and added, "I'm not sorry. I meant to hurt you."

DISCUSSION
The issue presented is whether Mann's intentional touching of McMillan with a bucket rather than her person is an actionable battery. A battery is the intentional touching of another without consent, which causes injury. Crane Rev. Stat. §808 (Williams 1994). A touching can occur when an object rather than an individual's body contacts the other party. *Eve v. Scott; Wayne v. Robert.* In this case, Mann intentionally struck McMillan with a bucket without

ILLUSTRATION 24-3. *Continued*

McMillan's consent and that touching resulted in injuries. Therefore, a battery occurred.

The threshold issue is whether a touching occurred when the bucket struck McMillan. A contact between a nonconsenting party and object rather than the actor's body can be a battery. *Eve v. Scott*; *Wayne v. Robert*. In *Eve*, one person hurled a baseball bat at another person, resulting in injuries. The court found that the baseball bat was an extension of the person and that a contact between the bat and the nonconsenting person met the requirement of a touching under the Crane battery statute. In this case, Mann threw the bucket at McMillan, and the bucket contacted her face. Following the reasoning in the *Eve* case, the bucket would be an extension of Mann's body, and the contact between McMillan and the bucket would be considered a touching under the civil battery statute.

Next, the question to consider is whether under the statute Mann intended to touch McMillan when she struck her with the bucket. A person intends his or her conduct when he or she undertakes an action with a knowing mind. *Wayne v. Robert*. In the *Wayne* case, one co-worker, Robert, aimed a golf ball at the face of another co-worker, Wayne, and deliberately struck Wayne in the face. Following a bench trial, the judge found that Robert aimed a shot at Wayne with the purpose of striking him. *Wayne*. In McMillan's case, Mann aimed the bucket at McMillan purposefully trying to strike her. Mann later told McMillan that she deliberately threw the bucket at her. McMillan probably will be able to establish that Mann had the statutory intent.

The next factor to consider is whether McMillan consented to the contact. If a person consents to the touching, a battery has not occurred. *Hawes v. Jackson*. In our case, McMillan did not consent to Mann's throwing of the bucket at her face. Therefore, McMillan did not consent to any contact.

Finally, the question is whether McMillan suffered physical injuries. A battery occurs only if a plaintiff sustains physical injuries as a result of the touching. Crane Rev. Stat. §808 (Williams 1994). McMillan sustained cuts on her face and eye irritation as a direct result of the bucket striking her face and the sand flying out of the bucket into her eyes. McMillan will be able to show that she sustained physical injuries as a result of the contact with the bucket.

24-5, which follows the pattern of the outline in Illustration 24-2. To see the actual outline for the memo in Illustration 24-5, see Illustration 24-7. Each of the statements listed in each outline of authorities was derived from a holding found in a case brief prepared for the memos. A summary statement for the statute also was included in the list.

ILLUSTRATION 24-4.   Outline of Authorities

1. 42 U.S.C. §2000e (1998): The term "employer" means a person engaged in an industry affecting commerce who has fifteen or more employees for each working day in each of twenty or more calendar weeks in the current or preceding calendar year.

2. Zimmerman v. North American Signal Co., **704 F.2d 347 (7th Cir. 1983):** Salaried workers or full-time workers counted as employees for every day of the week on the payroll whether they were present at work or not. Hourly paid workers are counted as employees only on the days when they are actually at work or days on paid leave. (primary binding)

3. Musser v. Mountain View Broadcasting, **578 F. Supp. 229 (E.D. Tenn. 1984):** "Current calendar year" is the year of discrimination. (primary persuasive)

4. Wright v. Kosciusko Medical Clinic, **791 F. Supp. 1327, 1333 (N.D. Ind. 1992):** "Each working day" is literal and must be a day on which an employer conducts normal, full operations. (primary persuasive)

5. Norman v. Levy, **767 F. Supp. 144 (N.D. Ill. 1991):** Part-time workers counted only on the days that they actually work. (primary persuasive)

6. Knight v. United Farm Bureau Mut. Ins. Co., **950 F.2d 377 (7th Cir. 1991):** The "economic realities" of the relationship between an employer and his or her worker must be weighed by applying five factors: (1) the amount of employer control and supervision over employee, (2) the responsibility for the operational costs, (3) the worker's occupation and the skills required, (4) the form of compensation and benefits, and (5) the length of the job commitment. *Knight,* 950 F.2d at 378. Control is the most important factor. *Id.* Knight is an insurance agent, is not permitted to sell insurance for any other companies, is required to attend weekly staff meetings in the office, and works a specified number of hours in the office (primary binding). *Knight,* 950 F.2d at 378. Company provided supplies and paid for business expenses. *Id.* Essential to company operation. *Id.* Paid commissions with no deductions. *Id.* Knight not an employee.

7. Mitchell v. Tenney, **650 F. Supp. 703 (N.D. Ill. 1986):** The "economic realities" of the relationship between an employer and his or her worker must be weighed.

8. Vakharia v. Swedish Covenant Hosp., **765 F. Supp. 461 (N.D. Ill. 1991):** When an employee is economically dependent on an employer, the court is likely to find employment relationship. Plaintiff in *Vakharia* was a physician dependent on the hospital for business. *Id.* at 463. (primary persuasive)

ILLUSTRATION 24-5.   Memorandum: Sex Discrimination Case

MEMORANDUM

To: Wallace Maine
From: Thomas Wall
Date: November 15, 1998
Re: Sex Discrimination Case against Whole In One No. C98 CIV 190, G12399990

QUESTIONS PRESENTED
    1. Under Title VII, was Whole In One an employer when 14 people, including 3 full-time and 11 part-time workers, worked on any one day for 24 weeks and when 10 full-time employees were on the Whole In One payroll?
    2. Under Title VII, was Walker an independent contractor rather than an employee when she worked exclusively for Whole In One, paid taxes quarterly rather than through deductions, and worked with limited company supervision?
    3. Under Title VII, was Radiant an independent contractor rather than an employee when she worked with limited company supervision using company supplies and equipment and had taxes and medical deductions taken from her salary?

CONCLUSIONS
    1. Whole In One was an employer. Under Title VII, an employer has at least 15 employees working for 20 or more weeks during the relevant year. Salaried employees are included in this number for each week they are on the payroll, while hourly workers are only counted on the days they actually work. In 1998, the year of the alleged discrimination, 14 workers, 3 full-time and 11 part-time people, worked for Whole In One on any day during the 24-week restaurant and golf season. However, 10 full-time workers were on the payroll. As these part-time workers are only counted on the days that they work, the number of part-time individuals included in the count of employees is 11 for each day of the 24-week season. Because full-time workers, however, are counted for each day of a week that they are on the payroll, all 10 of Whole In One's full-time workers would be included in the count of employees. In total, Whole In One had 11 part-time workers and 10 full-time workers "working" for 20 or more weeks during the relevant year, bringing the total count of employees to 21. Therefore, Whole In One was an employer under Title VII.
    2. Walker was an employee. The Seventh Circuit will weigh five factors to determine whether she was an independent contractor or an employee for this Title VII lawsuit. The primary focus will be on

ILLUSTRATION 24-5. *Continued*

the company's control of Walker. Although Walker worked from home, set her own hours, and had an impact on her commission pay, the company controlled her work by reviewing and revising it, restricting Walker's employment opportunities, and providing supplies for her. Therefore, the company exerted control over Walker and she would be considered an employee.

3. Radiant was probably an employee. To determine whether she was an employee or independent contractor for this Title VII lawsuit, the court will focus on five factors, primarily the amount of control the company exerted over Radiant's work. Whole In One provided Radiant with an office, supplies, a two-year contract, and additional training. Whole In One paid her regularly and deducted taxes from her salary. Although Whole In One did not actively supervise Radiant's work on a daily basis, she still worked in the company offices and was under the control of Whole In One. Therefore, the court probably will find that Radiant was an employee.

FACTS

Victoria Radiant and Karen Walker, two former Whole In One Enterprises workers, brought a federal sex discrimination lawsuit based on Title VII against our client, Whole In One Enterprises, owned by Nancy and Craig Black. The lawsuit, filed in the U.S. District Court for the Northern District of Illinois, stems from the dismissal of the two women by the Blacks during 1993.

The Blacks own Whole In One Enterprises, which operates a miniature golf course and restaurant in Glenview, Illinois. During the 24-week 1998 restaurant season, 10 people worked full-time and 14 people worked part-time for Whole In One. However, no more than 14 people worked on any one day. Of those 14 people, only 3 were full-time employees. The other full-time employees regularly took days off during the summer restaurant and golf season.

Among the full-time workers was Karen Walker, who worked as a public relations director for Whole In One. Walker responded to an ad that said that "an employer" sought an individual to perform public relations work. Whole In One hired Walker without a contract and prohibited her from working for other firms. However, Walker worked from home and set her own hours. Whole In One required Walker to attend weekly staff meetings at the company offices, where Whole In One would review and revise Walker's work. The company supplied Walker with paper, pencils, stamps, and telephone service and paid for her life and health insurance. Whole In One did not withhold taxes from Walker's commissions.

Victoria Radiant, who had a two-year employment contract with the company, provided marketing services to Whole In One from October of 1996 until she was fired in 1998. Although Radiant worked in the company office, Whole In One management rarely supervised

ILLUSTRATION 24-5. *Continued*

her work. The company paid for her continued education, provided her with bonuses, and deducted taxes from her weekly salary.

APPLICABLE STATUTE

The term "employer" means a person engaged in an industry affecting commerce who has fifteen or more employees for each working day in each of 20 or more calendar weeks in the current or preceding calendar year. 42 U.S.C. §2000e(b) (1998).

DISCUSSION

This memo first will address whether Walker and Radiant can successfully establish that Whole In One was an employer within the meaning of 42 U.S.C. §2000e(b) (1998), commonly called Title VII. Next, the discussion will focus on whether Walker can establish that she was an employee protected by Title VII. Finally, the memo will explore whether Radiant was an employee protected by Title VII. If Whole In One was not an employer, then the Title VII claim will be dismissed. If the court finds that neither individual is an employee, the individual's claim will be barred.

I. Was Whole In One an Employer under Title VII?

Before a federal court can consider Walker's and Radiant's claims, the plaintiffs must establish that Whole In One was an employer under the definition established in Title VII. An employer is "a person engaged in an industry affecting commerce who has fifteen or more employees for each working day in each of 20 or more calendar weeks in the current or preceding calendar year." 42 U.S.C. §2000e(b)(1998). The focus of this discussion will be how to calculate whether 15 employees worked for Whole In One on each working day in each of 20 or more calendar weeks and how to determine which year's employment records are relevant. The Seventh Circuit has held that full-time employees are "working" each day of a week during a week for which they are on the payroll, but part-time workers are counted only on the days that they actually work. *Zimmerman v. North American Signal Co.,* 704 F.2d 347 (7th Cir. 1983). In 1998, the year of the alleged discrimination, 14 workers, 3 full-time and 11 part-time people, worked for Whole In One on any day during the 24-week restaurant and golf season. In addition, 10 full-time workers were on the payroll. Based on the counting method established in *Zimmerman,* these figures indicate that Whole In One had at least 15 employees working for each working day in each of 20 or more calendar weeks. Therefore, Whole In One was an employer under Title VII.

The central focus of this discussion will be how to calculate the number of employees. First, the relevant year must be determined.

ILLUSTRATION 24-5. *Continued*

The statute states that the time to be considered is "20 or more calendar weeks in the current or preceding calendar year." 42 U.S.C. §2000e(b)(1998). The current year of the discrimination was 1998. Because the statute specifies "or," the preceding year, 1997, also is relevant. However, in a persuasive decision a Tennessee district court held that the "current calendar year" is the year in which the alleged discrimination occurred. *Musser v. Mountain View Broadcasting*, 578 F. Supp. 229 (E.D. Tenn. 1984). If the court follows *Musser,* the employment records from 1998 would be relevant because Whole In One fired Walker and Radiant in 1998.

The phrase "each working day" must be clarified. "Each working day" should be taken literally and must be a day on which an employer conducts normal, full operations. *Zimmerman,* 704 F.2d at 353; *Wright v. Kosciusko Medical Clinic,* 791 F. Supp. 1327, 1333 (N.D. Ind. 1992). Whole In One operated the golf course and restaurant seven days a week. Therefore, Whole In One must have 15 employees working on all seven days of a week to be considered an employer under Title VII.

The final issue is who should be counted on each of the working days. The Seventh Circuit has determined that a salaried or full-time employee is counted as working for every day of the week that he or she is on the payroll, whether or not he or she was actually at work on a particular day. *Zimmerman,* 704 F.2d at 347. However, part-time workers are counted only on the days that they actually work. *Id.*; *Wright,* 791 F. Supp. at 1327; *Norman v. Levy,* 767 F. Supp. 144 (N.D. Ill. 1991). In 1998, the year of the alleged discrimination, 14 workers, 3 full-time and 11 part-time people, worked for Whole In One on any day during the 24-week restaurant and golf season. As these part-time workers are only counted on the days that they work, the number of part-time individuals included in the count of employees was 11 for each day of the 24-week season. Because full-time workers, however, are counted for each day of a week that they are on the payroll, all 10 of Whole In One's full-time workers should be included in the count of employees. In total, Whole In One had 11 part-time workers and 10 full-time workers "working" for 20 or more weeks during the relevant year, bringing the total count of employees to 21. Therefore, Whole In One was an employer under Title VII.

II. Are Walker and Radiant Employees or Independent Contractors?

If the plaintiffs can show that Whole In One was an employer, the court still must determine whether Walker and Radiant were employees entitled to Title VII protection or independent contractors. To determine whether an individual is an independent contractor or an employee, the "economic realities" of the relationship between an employer and his or her worker must be weighed. *Knight*

ILLUSTRATION 24-5.   *Continued*

v. United Farm Bureau Mut. Ins. Co., 950 F.2d 377 (7th Cir. 1991); *Norman,* 767 F. Supp. at 144; *Mitchell v. Tenney,* 650 F. Supp. 703 (N.D. Ill. 1986). The Seventh Circuit will weigh five factors to determine the economic reality of the relationship: (1) the amount of control and supervision the employer exerts over the worker, (2) the responsibility for the costs of the operation, (3) the worker's occupation and the skills required, (4) the method and form of compensation and benefits, and (5) the length of the job commitment. *Knight,* 950 F.2d at 378. Control is the most important factor. *Id.* When an employer controls a worker in such a manner as to make that worker economically dependent on the employer, the court is likely to find that an employment relationship exists. *Vakharia v. Swedish Covenant Hosp.,* 765 F. Supp. 461 (N.D. Ill. 1991).

The *Knight* case involved an insurance agent who was not allowed to sell insurance for any other company and who was required to attend weekly staff meetings in the office and work a specified number of hours in the office. *Knight,* 950 F.2d at 378. The insurance company provided Knight with supplies and paid for business expenses. *Id.* These agents were trained by the insurance company and were crucial to the company's continued operation. *Id.* Knight was paid on commission and did not have taxes deducted. *Id.* Knight also was free to leave the company and work elsewhere. *Id.* Based on these facts, the *Knight* court failed to find that the agent was an employee.

Although Walker's work situation was factually similar in many ways to that of the plaintiff in *Knight,* the *Knight* case can be distinguished based on the nature of the occupations. Knight worked in the insurance sales field. Most often, individuals who work in such positions are independent contractors rather than employees of a company. In addition, the Seventh Circuit indicated in the dicta of the *Knight* case that it might have found that Knight was an employee. *Id.* at 381.

In contrast to *Knight,* the U.S. District Court for the Northern District of Illinois found that control of an individual's livelihood could establish an employment relationship. *Vakharia,* 765 F. Supp. at 461. The plaintiff in *Vakharia* was a physician who was dependent on the hospital for business. *Id.* at 463. The district court found that this individual depended on the hospital for patients and that when the hospital reduced the number of patients it assigned to the plaintiff, the plaintiff's livelihood was affected. *Id.* The court held that when an employer has this type of control over an individual's livelihood an employment relationship may be established.

The facts in our case are similar to the facts in the *Vakharia* case. In our case, Whole In One barred Walker from working for other companies and required that she attend weekly staff meetings at the company offices, where Whole In One would review and revise

ILLUSTRATION 24-5. *Continued*

Walker's work. Because Walker was barred from working for other individuals and was required to attend these meetings where Whole In One would revise her work, it seems that Walker could establish the central element of control necessary to prove an employment relationship. In addition, these facts show that Walker, like the plaintiff in *Vakharia,* was economically dependent on her employer, Whole In One. Therefore, an employment relationship should be established.

However, the plaintiffs will be able to show more than control. They will be able to establish that Whole In One bore the cost of the operation of the business. Whole In One supplied Walker with paper, pencils, stamps, and telephone service and paid for her life and health insurance. These facts indicate that Whole In One was responsible for the cost of Walker's services to the company. Therefore, it would help to establish that Walker was an employee.

The factors that would mitigate the establishment of an employment relationship, however, are that Walker worked from home and set her own hours and Whole In One did not withhold taxes from Walker's commissions. Despite these factors, the court is likely to focus on the control Whole In One had over Walker and is likely to find that she was an employee rather than an independent contractor.

III. Was Radiant an Employee or an Independent Contractor?

Whether Radiant was an employee again turns on the amount of control Whole In One exerted over Radiant's work. The court will focus on the same factors established in *Knight* to determine whether an employment relationship exists. *Knight,* 950 F.2d at 378. Control will be the key factor the court will consider. *Id.* Radiant had a two-year employment contract with the company to provide marketing services. Whole In One also provided her with an office, supplies, and additional training. The company paid her regularly and deducted taxes from her salary. Based on these facts, the company exerted control over Radiant. Therefore, the court is likely to find that Radiant was an employee of Whole In One.

2. Organize Issues

After you have prepared a detailed list of authorities, you are ready to organize your issues and to determine each of the legal elements that your memo should address. Each legal theory is defined by several factors called **elements.** You can think of the elements as pieces of a puzzle. You must consider each element before you complete your discussion. You can think of your discussion of these elements as a discussion of the subissues of the questions presented. Your discussion of some of these subissues will be cursory; some elements can be discussed in a single sentence. Most subissues, however, will be discussed in one or more paragraphs, generally organized in the IRAC (Issues, Rules Application, Conclusion) format discussed in Chapter 23.

In-Class Exercise or Review

Review the list of authorities in Illustration 24-1. Each authority is followed by a summary statement, usually the holding if it is a case.
Next, review the outline of the discussion in Illustration 24-2.

▼ What Steps Should You Follow in Preparing Your Outline of Each of the Issues?

The first step in organizing your outline is to write a **thesis paragraph.** This is the first paragraph of your discussion. It is a summary of the legal issue you plan to discuss. In the thesis paragraph you introduce the issue, define the applicable rule of law, introduce each legal element, apply the legally significant facts to the rule of law, and provide a short conclusion, usually one sentence long.

3. Draft a Thesis Paragraph

The best format for the thesis paragraph is the IRAC format. (For a full discussion of this format, see Chapter 23.) The first sentence of a thesis paragraph introduces the overall issue presented in the memo. The second sentence explains the rule of law. The next sentence applies the rule of law to the facts of your case, and the final sentence states a conclusion. A general outline for a thesis paragraph, then, is:

1. Introduce the legal issue or question presented.
2. Summarize the legal rule for the question presented and each legal element to be discussed.
3. Apply the legally significant facts to the legal rule.
4. Conclude.

Review the thesis paragraph in Illustration 24-6, which is the first paragraph of the discussion section of the memo in Illustration 24-3. The first sentence introduces the issue: whether a battery occurred when Mann struck McMillan with the bucket. This sentence mirrors the question presented. See Illustration 24-3. The second sentence is the rule of law. In this sentence you introduce each of the legal elements or factors that will be discussed. In the *McMillan* case, the elements are touching, intent, lack of consent, and resulting physical injury. Each of these elements is discussed separately in the

ILLUSTRATION 24-6. Thesis Paragraph

The issue presented is whether Mann's intentional touching of McMillan with a bucket rather than her person is an actionable battery. A battery is the intentional touching of another without consent which causes injury. Crane Rev. Stat. §808 (Williams 1994). A touching can occur when an object rather than an individual's body contacts the other party. *Eve v. Scott; Wayne v. Robert.* In this case, Mann intentionally struck McMillan with a bucket without McMillan's consent and that touching resulted in injuries. Therefore, a battery occurred.

succeeding memo paragraphs. A thesis paragraph should introduce the reader to as many legal elements as possible in the thesis paragraph. The third sentence of this thesis paragraph is the application of the law to the facts. In this sentence, you explain to the reader the relationship between the relevant law and the facts of your case. In Illustration 24-6, the fact that Mann struck McMillan with the bucket without McMillan's consent was applied to the rule of law stated in the second sentence. The final sentence is a conclusion. This sentence explains to your readers your view of how the law and facts relate to each other. In the *McMillan* case, the writer concluded that a battery occurred.

OUTLINE OF THESIS PARAGRAPH FOR McMILLAN CASE

1. Introduce the battery issue or question presented.
2. Summarize the legal rule: battery is the intentional touching of another without consent that results in physical injury; touching can be with an object.
3. Apply the legally significant facts to the legal rule: touching occurred when bucket struck McMillan.
4. Conclusion: battery occurred.

Next, read the sample thesis paragraph below.

Before a federal court can consider Walker's and Radiant's claims, the plaintiffs must establish that Whole In One was an employer under the definition established in Title VII. An employer is "a person engaged in an industry affecting commerce who has fifteen or more employees for each working day in each of 20 or more calendar weeks in the current or preceding calendar year." 42 U.S.C. §2000e(b)(1998). The focus of this discussion will be how to calculate whether 15 employees worked for Whole In One on each working day in each of 20 or more calendar weeks and how to determine which year's employment records are relevant. The Seventh Circuit has held that full-time employees are "working" each day of a week during a week for which they are on the payroll, but part-time workers are counted only on the days that they actually work. *Zimmerman v. North American Signal Co.,* 704 F.2d 347 (7th Cir. 1983). In 1998, the year of the alleged discrimination, 14 workers, 3 full-time and 11 part-time people, worked for Whole In One on any day during the 24-week restaurant and golf season. In addition, 10 full-time workers were on the payroll. Based on the counting method established in *Zimmerman,* these figures indicate that Whole In One had at least 15 employees working for each working day in each of 20 or more calendar weeks. Therefore, Whole In One was an employer under Title VII.

An outline for the thesis paragraph above might look like the following example.

THESIS PARAGRAPH

Issue: Is Whole In One an employer?

RULE

Under Title VII, an employer has at least 15 employees working for 20 or more weeks during the relevant year. 42 U.S.C. §2000e(b) (1998). (**first element**) Salaried employees are included in this number for each week they are on the payroll (**second element**), while hourly workers are only counted on the days they actually work. (**third element**) *Zimmerman* (primary binding).

APPLICATION OF LAW TO FACTS

In 1998, Whole in One had 14 workers, 3 full-time and 11 part-time people, on any day during the 24-week season. Ten full-time workers were on the payroll. Part-time workers are only counted on the days that they work; they number 11 for each day of the 24-week season. All 10 full-time workers are counted each day of a week. In total, Whole In One had 11 part-time workers and 10 full-time workers "working" for 20 or more weeks during the relevant year, bringing the total count of employees to 21.

CONCLUSION

Therefore, Whole In One was an employer under Title VII.

The outline and thesis paragraph in the above example introduce multiple subissues or legal elements. Each of these elements is discussed fully in the sample memo contained in Illustration 24-5. The thesis paragraph, however, introduces the reader to the elements and provides a preview of the elements that will be discussed.

4. Determine Which Element to Discuss First

The next step is to determine which element to discuss first. If a legal claim has a **threshold issue** or **element,** it should be discussed first. A threshold issue is an issue that, if decided one way, would eliminate any further consideration of the legal claim. For example, in a breach of contract case, you must decide first whether a contract was formed before determining whether a breach occurred. Because courts sometimes change current law or approach legal claims differently than expected or than the law provides, you should fully discuss all subissues or elements, even if your threshold issue would dispose of the legal claim.

For the memo in Illustration 24-3, the touching is the threshold issue. If Mann did not touch McMillan, then McMillan could not bring an action for battery. Therefore, this issue must be considered first.

5. List of Elements or Subissues

Next, make a list of the elements or subissues to discuss. In the *McMillan* case, the elements list might be as follows:

touching
intent
lack of consent
physical injury

6. Add Authority

Now add the authority or authorities that relate to each element:

touching (*Eve; Wayne*)
intent (*Wayne*)
lack of consent (Statute)
physical injury (Statute)

7. Refine Issues

You might refine the issues so that they include facts from your case or incorporate further questions that are raised by the issues. For example, the issue of touching involves a secondary question of whether contact with an object rather than a person is a touching sufficient to constitute a battery. Your new list might be as follows:

touching (*Eve; Wayne*)
    object rather than person (*Eve; Wayne*)
intent (*Wayne*)
lack of consent (Statute)
physical injury (Statute)

8. Arrange the Order of Elements

Now arrange the order of the elements. Touching is the threshold element or subissue, so you should discuss it first. The order of the other issues is a value judgment. If one or more elements can be easily discussed in a single sentence, often it is best to consider them after the threshold issue. If none of the elements is a threshold issue, then consider those elements that can be discussed easily first.

9. Organize into IRAC Paragraph

After you have determined the order of the elements, organize each element or subissue into an IRAC paragraph. Introduce the issue, present the rule, apply the law to the facts of your case, and conclude. For the *McMillan* memo, the discussion outline for each element might be as shown in Illustration 24-2, page 451. Review Illustration 24-2 and compare it to the text of the memo in Illustration 24-3. The discussion is derived entirely from the outline and follows it closely.

C. EXAMPLE OF OUTLINING

You should follow this same process for more complicated issues. The memo shown in Illustration 24-5 discusses several complicated issues and subissues. Review the discussion of the question of whether Whole In One is an employer, section I on pages 457-458.

1. After you review the thesis paragraph, make a list of the elements. Your list of elements might be as follows:

Person

Engaged in industry affecting commerce

15 or more employees for each working day in each of 20 or more calendar weeks in current or preceding calendar year

2. Refine this list. Next to the element to which the authority relates, note the relevant authority from your list of authorities. Some authorities will relate to multiple elements. In such a case, note that authority next to each of the elements to which it relates. Now your list might read as follows:

Person (42 U.S.C. §2000e(b))

Engaged in industry affecting commerce (42 U.S.C. §2000e(b))

15 or more employees for each working day in each of 20 or more calendar weeks in current or preceding calendar year (42 U.S.C. §2000e(b)); *Zimmerman v. North American Signal Co.*, 704 F.2d 347

(7th Cir. 1983); *Musser v. Mountain View Broadcasting*, 578 F. Supp. 229 (E.D. Tenn. 1984); *Wright v. Kosciusko Medical Clinic*, 791 F. Supp. 1327, 1333 (N.D. Ind. 1992); *Norman v. Levy*, 767 F. Supp. 144 (N.D. Ill. 1991)

It is better to list the full name of the authority next to the element rather than the number of the authority because the numbers might be confusing later.

3. Your list of elements, however, should be revised again. Often, as in this case, the authorities will guide you as to how to further delineate the elements. Several authorities noted in the above memo focus on the word *employees* and indicate that different types of employees are counted differently for the purpose of the statute. For example, full-time or salaried workers are counted for each day that they are on the payroll, while part-time workers only are counted on the days that they are actually at work. Add this distinction to your list of elements. Now rewrite your list as follows:

Person (42 U.S.C. §2000e(b))

Engaged in industry affecting commerce (42 U.S.C. §2000e(b))

15 or more employees

— part-time: *Zimmerman v. North American Signal Co.*, 704 F.2d 347 (7th Cir. 1983); *Wright v. Kosciusko Medical Clinic*, 791 F. Supp. 1327, 1333 (N.D. Ind. 1992); *Norman v. Levy*, 767 F. Supp. 144 (N.D. Ill. 1991)

— full-time: *Zimmerman v. North American Signal Co.*, 704 F.2d 347 (7th Cir. 1983); *Wright v. Kosciusko Medical Clinic*, 791 F. Supp. 1327, 1333 (N.D. Ind. 1992); *Norman v. Levy*, 767 F. Supp. 144 (N.D. Ill. 1991)

Each working day in each of 20 or more calendar weeks current or preceding calendar year (42 U.S.C. §2000e(b)); *Zimmerman v. North American Signal Co.*, 704 F.2d 347 (7th Cir. 1983); *Musser v. Mountain View Broadcasting*, 578 F. Supp. 229 (E.D. Tenn. 1984); *Wright v. Kosciusko Medical Clinic*, 791 F. Supp. 1327, 1333 (N.D. Ind. 1992); *Norman v. Levy*, 767 F. Supp. 144 (N.D. Ill. 1991)

4. Note that one case defines the relevant year while another explains the phrase "each working day." Review the outline of elements below.

Person (42 U.S.C. §2000e(b))

Engaged in industry affecting commerce (42 U.S.C. §2000e(b))

15 or more employees (determining the number of employees)

— part-time: *Zimmerman v. North American Signal Co.*, 704 F.2d 347 (7th Cir. 1983); *Wright v. Kosciusko Medical Clinic*, 791 F. Supp.

1327, 1333 (N.D. Ind. 1992); *Norman v. Levy,* 767 F. Supp. 144 (N.D. Ill. 1991)

— full-time: *Zimmerman v. North American Signal Co.,* 704 F.2d 347 (7th Cir. 1983); *Wright v. Kosciusko Medical Clinic,* 791 F. Supp. 1327, 1333 (N.D. Ind. 1992); *Norman v. Levy,* 767 F. Supp. 144 (N.D. Ill. 1991)

Each working day in each of 20 or more calendar weeks (*Wright v. Kosciusko Medical Clinic,* 791 F. Supp. 1327, 1333 (N.D. Ind. 1992))

Current or preceding calendar year (42 U.S.C. §2000e(b)); *Musser v. Mountain View Broadcasting,* 578 F. Supp. 229 (E.D. Tenn. 1984)

5. Now you are ready to arrange the order of each of the elements. Determine if any of the elements should be discussed first. For the above memo, the threshold issue is how to determine whether Whole In One had 15 or more employees.

6. After you have determined the order of the elements, organize each element or subissue in an IRAC paragraph. For the above discussion, the outline of each element might be arranged as follows:

Element or Subissue 1
  Issue: For which year is the number of employees relevant?
  Rules: The current calendar year or preceding year (42 U.S.C. §2000e (1998)); the "current calendar year" is the year of the discrimination (*Musser*)
  Application of law to facts: Discrimination occurred in 1998
  Conclusion: 1998 is the relevant year

Element or Subissue 2
  Issue: What does the phrase "each working day" mean?
  Rule: "Each working day" is literal: a day of normal operations (*Zimmerman; Wright*)
  Application of law to facts: Whole In One operated the golf course and restaurant seven days a week
  Conclusion: Therefore, Whole In One must have 15 employees working on all seven days of a week to be considered an employer under Title VII

Element or Subissue 3
  Issue: Who should be counted as employees each day?
  Rule: Salaried or full-time employees counted for every day of the week that they are on the payroll (*Zimmerman*); part-time workers counted only on the days that they actually work (*Zimmerman; Wright; Norman*)
  Application of law to facts: In 1998, 14 workers, 3 full-time and 11 part-time people, worked for Whole In One on any day during the 24-week season. Eleven part-time workers counted on the days that they work. Ten full-time workers counted for each day of a week. In total, Whole In One had 11 part-time workers and

10 full-time workers "working" for 20 or more weeks during the relevant year, bringing the total count of employees to 21. Conclusion: Therefore, Whole In One was an employer under Title VII.

Review this outline and compare it to the text of the memo in Illustration 24-5. The outline closely parallels the discussion concerning Whole In One.

PRACTICE POINTER

If your outline is well drafted, your writing of the discussion will flow from it easily.

D. MULTI-ISSUE MEMORANDUM

If you have a multi-issue memorandum, you will use many of the same techniques discussed above.

▼ How Do You Organize a Multi-Issue Memorandum?

1. Determine how many issues you will discuss. Often an attorney will help you make this determination. Decide which issue should be discussed first. Again, consider whether there is a threshold issue. In the memo above, the first issue is whether Whole In One is an employer. If Whole In One is not an employer, then Title VII will not apply and the later issues do not need to be addressed. Therefore, this issue is the threshold issue and should be placed first. However, you should still discuss the later issues even if you determine that the first issue would be decided in a manner that would dispose of a case. Courts are unpredictable and might decide the issue differently than you did.

2. Determine the legal elements you will discuss and a logical order for this discussion.

3. Prepare a detailed outline of the discussion. For each issue, note each legal element you will address, the authority related to that element, and the legally significant facts applicable to that element.

4. Write a thesis paragraph. For a multi-issue memo, such as on Whole In One, introduce the issues and explain the rules of law in the thesis paragraphs that introduce each issue. Your organization for a multi-issue memo might be as follows:

Thesis Paragraph
   Introduce all legal issues or questions presented
   Conclusions

Thesis Paragraph for Issue or Question Presented #1
   Introduce the legal issue or question presented
   Summarize the legal rule for the question presented #1 and
      each legal element to be discussed
   Apply the legally significant facts to the legal rule
   Conclusion

First Legal Element or Subissue
   Introduce the legal element
   Summarize the legal rule
   Apply the legally significant facts to the legal rule
   Conclusion

Second Legal Element or Subissue
   Introduce the legal element
   Summarize the legal rule
   Apply the legally significant facts to the legal rule
   Conclusion

Thesis Paragraph for Issue or Question Presented #2
   Introduce the legal issue or question presented
   Summarize the legal rule for the question presented #2 and
      each legal element to be discussed
   Apply the legally significant facts to the legal rule
   Conclusion

First Legal Element or Subissue
   Introduce the legal element
   Summarize the legal rule
   Apply the legally significant facts to the legal rule
   Conclusion

Second Legal Element or Subissue
   Introduce the legal element
   Summarize the legal rule
   Apply the legally significant facts to the legal rule
   Conclusion

5. Use headings to introduce new issues. Use transitions to guide the reader from one issue to another and one paragraph to another.

Illustration 24-7 is an outline of the Whole In One memo shown in Illustration 24-5.

Once you complete your outline, you are ready to begin writing your discussion. Follow your outline and use the applicable law and the facts from cases when they are useful. Illustration 24-8 reprints the last paragraph in Illustration 24-5 and the original outline for

ILLUSTRATION 24-7. Multi-Issue Outline

Thesis Paragraph
  Introduce issues
    Whether Whole In One is an employer under Title VII
    Whether Walker is an employee under Title VII
    Whether Radiant is an employee under Title VII

Heading: Issue 1 or Question Presented 1
    Introduce issue: Was Whole In One an employer under Title VII?
    Rules: **(A)** Under Title VII, an employer has at least 15 employees working for 20 or more weeks during the relevant year. (42 U.S.C. §2000e(b) (1998)) (**first element or subissue**) **(B)** Salaried employees are included in this number for each week they are on the payroll. (**second element or subissue**) **(C)** Hourly workers are only counted on the days they actually work. (**third element or subissue**) *(Zimmerman)* (primary binding)
    Application of law to facts: In 1998, Whole In One had 14 workers, 3 full-time and 11 part-time people, on any day during the 24-week season. Ten full-time workers were on the payroll. Part-time workers are only counted on the days that they work; their number is 11 for each day of the 24-week season. All 10 full-time workers are counted each day of a week. In total, Whole In One had 11 part-time workers and 10 full-time workers "working" for 20 or more weeks during the relevant year, bringing the total count of employees to 21.
    Conclusion: Therefore, Whole In One was an employer under Title VII.
  First Legal Element or Subissue:
    Introduce subissue: Which is the appropriate year for counting workers?
    Rules: **(A)** Under Title VII, an employer has at least 15 employees working for 20 or more weeks during the current calendar year or preceding year. (42 U.S.C. §2000e(b) (1998)) **(B)** The "current calendar year" is the year of the discrimination *(Musser)*
    Application of law to facts: Discrimination occurred in 1998.
    Conclusion: 1998 is the relevant year.
  Second Legal Element or Subissue
    Introduce subissue: Is "each working day" literally interpreted?
    Rule: "Each working day" is literal: a day of normal operations *(Zimmerman; Wright)*
    Application of law to facts: Whole In One operated the golf course and restaurant seven days a week.
    Conclusion: Therefore, Whole In One must have 15 employees working on all seven days of the week to be considered an employer under Title VII.

ILLUSTRATION 24-7.   *Continued*

Third Legal Element or Subissue

   Introduce subissue: Who should be counted?

   Rules: (**A**) Salaried or full-time employee counted for every day of the week that he or she is on the payroll *(Zimmerman)* (**B**) Part-time workers counted only on the days that they actually work *(Zimmerman; Wright; Norman)*

   Application of law to facts: In 1998, 14 workers, 3 full-time and 11 part-time people, worked for Whole In One on any day during the 24-week season. Eleven part-time workers counted on the days that they work. Ten full-time workers counted for each day of a week. In total, Whole In One had 11 part-time workers and 10 full-time workers "working" for 20 or more weeks during the relevant year, bringing the total count of employees to 21.

   Conclusion: Therefore, Whole In One was an employer under Title VII.

Thesis Paragraph to Introduce Issues 2 and 3

   Issues 2 and 3

      Introduce issues and elements: Are Walker and Radiant employees or independent contractors?

      Rules: (**A**) "Economic realities" of the relationship between an employer and his or her worker must be weighed. *(Knight; Norman; Mitchell)* Five factors to determine the economic reality of the relationship: (1) the amount of control and supervision the employer exerts over the worker, (2) the responsibility for the costs of the operation, (3) the worker's occupation and the skills required, (4) the method and form of compensation and benefits, and (5) the length of the job commitment. *(Knight)* (**first element**) (**B**) When an employee is economically dependent on the employer, an employment relationship exists. *(Vakharia)* (**second element**)

      Application of law to facts: Walker worked from home, set her own hours, received pay on commission. Company controlled her work by reviewing and revising it, restricting Walker's employment opportunities, and providing supplies for her.

      Conclusion: Therefore, the company exerted control over Walker, and she would be considered an employee.

      Application of law to facts: Whole In One provided Radiant with an office, supplies, a two-year contract, and additional training, paid her regularly, and deducted taxes from her salary. She worked in company offices under the control of Whole In One.

      Conclusion: Therefore, the court probably will find that Radiant was an employee.

ILLUSTRATION 24-7. *Continued*

Reintroduction of Issue 2: Was Walker an employee or an independent contractor?

  First Legal Element or Subissue

    Introduce subissue: What factors will the court weigh to determine economic realities?

    Rule: "Economic realities" of the relationship between an employer and his or her worker must be weighed. *(Knight; Norman; Mitchell)* Five factors to determine the economic reality of the relationship: (1) the amount of control and supervision the employer exerts over the worker, (2) the responsibility for the costs of the operation, (3) the worker's occupation and the skills required, (4) the method and form of compensation and benefits, and (5) the length of the job commitment. (*Knight.* Facts: Knight worked in the insurance sales field, traditionally an independent contractor setting.)

    Application of law to facts: Walker worked from home, set her own hours. Received her pay on commission. Company controlled her work by reviewing and revising it.

    Conclusion: Walker was an employee.

  Second Legal Element or Subissue

    Introduce subissue: Was Walker economically dependent on Whole In One?

    Rule: When an employee is economically dependent on the employer, an employment relationship exists. (*Vakharia.* Facts: A physician dependent on the hospital for business establishing employment relationship.)

    Application of law to facts: Similar facts for Walker. Whole In One barred Walker from working for other companies.

    Conclusion: Because Walker was barred from working for other companies, employment relationship existed.

    Reintroduction of Issue 3: Was Radiant an employee or an independent contractor?

    Rule: Five factors weighed, primarily control of her by the company. *(Knight)* See also the Rules discussed below the thesis paragraph introducing Issues 2 and 3. There is no need to discuss the Rule in as much detail in Issue 3 as in Issue 2.

    Application of law to facts: Whole In One provided Radiant with an office, supplies, a two-year contract, and additional training, paid her regularly, and deducted taxes from her salary. She worked in company offices under the control of Whole In One.

    Conclusion: Therefore, the court probably will find that Radiant was an employee.

ILLUSTRATION 24-8. Writing from an Outline

Outline

> Issue 3: Was Radiant an employee or an independent contractor?
> Rule: Five factors weighed, primarily control of her by the company. *(Knight)* See also the Rules below the thesis paragraph introducing Issues 2 and 3. There is no need to discuss the Rule in as much detail in Issue 3 as in Issue 2.
> Application of law to facts: Whole In One provided Radiant with an office, supplies, a two-year contract, and additional training, paid her regularly, and deducted taxes from her salary. She worked in company offices under the control of Whole In One.
> Conclusion: Therefore, the court probably will find that Radiant was an employee.

Paragraph Drafted from Outline

III. Was Radiant an Employee or an Independent Contractor?

Whether Radiant was an employee again turns on the amount of control Whole In One exerted over Radiant's work. The court will focus on the same factors established in Knight to determine whether an employment relationship exists. *Knight,* 950 F.2d at 378. Control will be the key factor the court will consider. *Id.* Radiant had a two-year employment contract with the company to provide marketing services. Whole In One also provided her with an office, supplies, and additional training. The company paid her regularly and deducted taxes from her salary. Based upon these facts, the company exerted control over Radiant. Therefore, the court is likely to find that Radiant was an employee of Whole In One.

---

that paragraph. Once you have completed your draft, compare the draft to the outline to ensure that you have incorporated all of the components in your outline and that your text matches your outline organization.

CHAPTER SUMMARY

Outlining is an important component of legal writing. It helps you organize the discussion section of your legal memorandum. To outline a legal memorandum, first draft a list of legal authorities. Second, arrange the discussion sections concerning each issue and, if necessary, arrange each paragraph of the memorandum.

The list of legal authorities should include the names and citations to the authorities, a note about the legally significant facts contained in the authority, if any, and a statement that summarizes the significance of the authority.

The legal issues of the discussion should be organized in the IRAC format discussed in Chapter 23. Each element of a legal issue should be addressed in this format.

Before you can begin writing your memorandum, you must organize your thesis paragraph. The thesis paragraph is the first paragraph of your discussion. It summarizes the legal issues you will discuss in the memorandum. This paragraph also should be organized in IRAC format, if possible.

You have been shown how to draft questions presented, issues, conclusions, brief answers, facts statements, and discussion sections. In addition, you have been taught how to synthesize authorities and how to use a legal writing convention called IRAC.

KEY TERMS

elements
list of legal authorities
outlining

thesis paragraph
threshold issue

EXERCISES

SHORT ANSWER EXERCISES

1. How do you organize a thesis paragraph?
2. How do you compile a list of legal authorities?
3. How do you determine which element to discuss first?
4. What format should each paragraph take?

HOMEWORK EXERCISES

5. Review the following memo. Prepare an outline based on this memo. (This is the reverse of the process you would normally use.)

MEMORANDUM

To: Margaret Sterner
From: Marie Main
Date: January 28, 1998
Re: *Harris v. Sack and Shop*

QUESTION PRESENTED

Is Sack and Shop, a grocery store, liable for injuries sustained by Harris, a store patron who slipped on a banana peel that had been on the grocery store floor for two days?

BRIEF ANSWER

Probably yes. Sack and Shop, a grocery store, probably will be liable based on negligence for injuries sustained by Harris, a store patron who slipped on a banana peel that had been on the grocery store floor for two days.

FACTS

Our client, Sack and Shop Grocery Store, is being sued for negligence by Rebecca Harris.

Harris went to the store to purchase groceries on July 8, 1998. While she was in the produce section, she slipped on a banana peel that had been left on the floor by a grocery store employee. The employee had dropped it on the floor two days earlier and had failed to clean it up after a patron asked him to do so.

Harris sustained a broken arm and head injuries as a result of the slip and fall.

DISCUSSION

The issue presented in this case is whether Sack and Shop Grocery Store was negligent when Rebecca Harris slipped in the store's produce section. A grocer will be found negligent if a store employee breached the store's duty of reasonable care to its patrons and, as a result of that breach, the patron was injured. *Ward v. K Mart Corp.*, 554 N.E.2d 223 (Ill. 1990). In *Ward,* the grocery store employee failed to clean up a banana peel for two days and that peel caused a patron to be injured. Similarly, in our case Sack and Shop failed to remove the banana peel. Therefore, Sack and Shop is likely to be found liable for the injuries Harris sustained.

The first element to consider is whether Sack and Shop owed a duty of reasonable care to Harris. A grocery store owes a duty of care to any patron. *Ward,* 554 N.E.2d at 226. Harris was a customer in the store. Therefore, Sack and Shop owed her a duty of care.

The next question to consider is whether Sack and Shop breached its duty of reasonable care to Harris. A store will be found to have breached its duty of reasonable care to a patron if a store employee fails to properly and regularly clean the floor of the store. *Olinger v. Great Atl. & Pac. Tea Co.,* 173 N.E.2d 443 (Ill. 1961). In *Olinger,* the store was found liable because a store employee failed to clean the floor for one day and a patron slipped on a substance on the floor. 173 N.E.2d at 447. No one had told any store employee about the slippery substance. *Id.* at 447. Nonetheless, the Illinois Supreme Court found the store liable, saying that the store employees had sufficient time to notice the substance if they had used ordinary care. *Id.* In our case, Sack and Shop's employee had two days to clean the floor before Harris fell. In addition, a customer had placed the store employee on notice of the banana peel. Therefore, Sack and Shop breached its duty of care to Harris.

The plaintiff, however, still must establish proximate cause, that is, that the injury resulted as a natural consequence of Sack and Shop's breach of its duty. A store owner's failure to clear debris from a store floor, resulting in injury to a patron who slipped on the floor, was found to be the proximate cause of the patron's injuries. *Id.* at 449. In this case, Sack and Shop's failure to clean the peel from the floor was a breach of its duty of care to

Harris. This breach resulted in injury to Harris. Sack and Shop's breach will be found to be the proximate cause of Harris's injuries.

The final element that must be established is that the plaintiff, Harris, suffered injuries. Harris sustained a broken arm and head injuries as a result of the slip and fall. Therefore, she will be able to show that she was injured.

CONCLUSION

Sack and Shop owed Harris a duty of reasonable care. The store is likely to be found to have breached that duty of reasonable care because an employee failed to remove a banana peel from the grocery store floor during the preceding two days. The injuries Harris sustained were directly caused by a slip on a banana peel. Therefore, Sack and Shop is likely to be found liable to Harris.

6. Write a thesis paragraph for this discussion section.

FACTS

Drake Industries has been leasing warehouse space at 2700 North Bosworth Avenue, in Chicago, Illinois, from the owner of the building, Michael Martin. Drake began leasing space from Martin beginning January 1, 1969, at $700 per month until the lease expired on December 31, 1980.

Martin offered a new lease to Drake on November 25, 1980, to be signed and returned by December 31, 1980. The new lease began January 1, 1981, and expired on December 31, 1995, and the rent increased to $850 per month, payable on the first of each month. Drake never signed or returned the new lease, but did pay the increased rent amount during the term of the unsigned lease ending December 31, 1995. Since then, Drake has continued paying $850 on the first day of each month. On August 15, 1996, Martin requested that Drake surrender the premises. Drake came to your firm to find out what type of tenancy he has and whether Martin gave Drake the proper notice to quit the premises.

DISCUSSION

Is Drake Industries a holdover tenant? A holdover tenancy is created when a landlord elects to treat a tenant, after the expiration of his or her lease, as a tenant for another term upon the same provisions contained in the original lease. *Bismarck Hotel Co. v. Sutherland,* 92 Ill. App. 3d 167, 415 N.E.2d 517 (1980). In *Bismarck,* defendant Sutherland's written lease expired. Bismarck presented her with a new lease that included a rent increase. She began to pay the increase but did not sign the new lease. Sutherland could not be a holdover tenant since the terms of the old lease were not extended to the terms of the new, unsigned lease. Drake Industries was offered a new lease in 1980 that included a rent increase. Since the terms were different from the original lease, Drake could not be considered a holdover tenant.

It is the intention of the landlord, not the tenant, that determines whether the tenant is to be treated as a holdover. *Sheraton-Chicago Corp. v.*

Lewis, 8 Ill. App. 3d 309, 290 N.E.2d 685 (1972). When a landlord creates a new lease and presents it to the tenant, it is clear that it was his intention that a new tenancy was created. *Holt v. Chicago Hair Goods Co.,* 328 Ill. App. 671, 66 N.E.2d 727 (1946). Martin presented Drake with a new lease to sign in November 1980, with new terms beginning January 1, 1981. It was never his intention to hold over the same lease from 1969. Therefore, Drake was not a holdover tenant and has never been one. 735 ILCS 5/9-202 (West 1993) could not apply to Drake. Martin could not demand double rental fees from Drake when it remained in possession of 2700 North Bosworth after the written lease expired on December 31, 1980.

Is Drake Industries a year-to-year tenant? When the payment of rent is annual, there arises a tenancy from year to year, even if the agreement provides for a payment of one-twelfth of the annual rental each month. *Seaver Amusement Co. v. Saxe et al.,* 210 Ill. App. 289 (1918). The terms of the 1969 written lease would have to have said "$8,400 a year rent, payable in monthly installments of $700" for it to have been considered a year-to-year lease. Since the terms of the 1969 lease only provided for monthly payments and not a yearly rental rate, Drake was not a year-to-year tenant. 735 ILCS 5/9-205 (West 1993) does not apply at all to Drake. Martin would not be required to tender 60 days' notice in writing to terminate the tenancy.

Is Drake Industries a month-to-month tenant? A month-to-month tenancy is created when a tenant remains in possession of the premises after a lease expires under different terms of tenancy. *Bismarck Hotel,* 92 Ill. App. 3d at 168, 415 N.E.2d at 517. By paying Bismarck's increased rental amount, different terms of the tenancy were established, so Sutherland's tenancy was considered month to month by the court. Drake remained at 2700 North Bosworth after its lease expired in 1980 but began paying the increased rent to Martin under the new terms of the unsigned lease. This established different terms of tenancy, so Drake has been a month-to-month tenant since 1980.

What type of tenancy is created under an oral lease? When a tenant goes into possession of real estate under an oral leasing agreement for a term over one year at monthly rental, the agreement is voidable under the Statute of Frauds. The most that the tenant in possession can claim is that the leasing is from month to month and that the landlord can terminate the tenancy by providing 30 days' notice in writing to the tenant. *Creighton v. Sanders,* 89 Ill. 543 (1878). Charles Creighton had an oral agreement to lease a house from Patrick Sanders for a five-year term. When Creighton ceased paying rent, Sanders gave him a written notice to quit the premises. Creighton maintained that he had a five-year lease, but the most the court allowed was that he was a month-to-month tenant, based on the parol lease. When Drake never signed or returned the new lease in 1980, he entered into a parol lease agreement with Martin. Martin cannot hold Drake to any terms of that lease because the tenancy was for a duration of 15 years, well over the one-year limit under the Statute of Frauds. The most Martin can claim is that Drake is a month-to-month tenant.

What type of notice is necessary to vacate the premises? Under 735

ILCS 5/9-207 (West 1993), notice to terminate a month-to-month tenancy must be given in writing 30 days before termination before any action for forcible entry and detainer can be maintained. Drake said that on August 15, 1996, Martin "requested" that Drake surrender the premises. An oral request may not be sufficient and Drake may maintain that proper notice has not been made and it need not surrender the premises by September 15, 1996. A forcible entry and detainer action could not be entered and maintained and Drake need not surrender the premises until proper notice has been given.

7. Review the discussion section above and draft a list of authorities. Then draft an outline of the discussion section.
8. Review the discussion section below and draft a list of authorities. Then draft an outline of the discussion section.

Are the Blacks entitled to special damages from Comfy Furniture for the cost of the redecoration of their living room? An Illinois Appellate Court decided that the nonbreaching party should be put back in the position that they were in when the contract was formed. *Kalal v. Goldblatt Bros.,* 368 N.E.2d 671, 673 (Ill. Ct. App. 1977). The Blacks stated their intention at the beginning concerning the fabric, the redecoration of the living room, and the family reunion. This fact was a part of their original position. The living room was redecorated. The furniture was delivered; however, the fabric was incorrect. Therefore, the Blacks have a right to recover consequential damages for the cost of the redecoration of their living room because the end result was not achieved: correctly upholstered furniture, newly redecorated living room to match, and a new living room look for the reunion. The conditions of the original contract were not met, and there was a breach of contract as embodied by the incorrectly upholstered furniture.

Under contract law, what damages are the Blacks entitled to pursue? Damages for breach of contract should place the plaintiff in a position he would have been in had the contract been performed. *Kalal,* 368 N.E.2d at 671. The plaintiffs in *Kalal* received a sofa that had been reupholstered in the wrong fabric after numerous delays, during which they had chosen three different fabrics in succession. *Id.* The court held that the defect could be remedied by the cost of reupholstering the sofa in the proper fabric. *Id.* at 674. The Black's sofa and loveseat were improperly upholstered. Comfy Furniture upholstered their furniture with the reverse side of the fabric showing. Therefore, they were entitled to damages equal to the cost of upholstering their furniture correctly. However, the Blacks' situation is distinguished from *Kalal* in that their furniture was delivered before the date set in the contract, and it can be argued by Comfy that there was time to remedy the defect before their target date of Thanksgiving.

Are the Blacks entitled to compensation for the loss of use of their furniture? The question of compensation for loss of use of the furniture was considered by both parties in *Kalal* to be appropriate since the plaintiffs in the case were without their furniture for several months while waiting for it to be reupholstered. *Id.* The Blacks have been similarly inconvenienced in that they, too, have been without the use of their new furniture. Thus, they are entitled to compensation for the loss of use of the furniture. However, it can be argued by Comfy Furniture that the furniture in the *Kalal* case was used and had been removed from the home for the purpose of reupholstering it. *Id.* In the present case, the furniture was new and had never been in the Blacks' home, and Comfy may argue that the Blacks did not actually suffer loss of use of the new furniture.

Are the Blacks entitled to damages for the expense of decorating their living room to match the furniture they did not receive in the agreed on condition? The redecorating of the living room in *Kalal* was not in the contemplation of either party at the time the contract was executed. *Kalal,* 368 N.E.2d at 671. Subsequently, the court held that the only damages that were recoverable for breach of contract are limited to those that were reasonably foreseeable and were within the contemplation of the parties at the time the contract was executed. *Id.* at 674. By the express terms of the Uniform Commercial Code, the court cannot follow tort theories to award damages. The legislative history of the U.C.C. indicates that contractual disputes should apply to the findings of the court. *Moorman Mfg. Co. v. National Tank Co.,* 435 N.E.2d 443, 453 (Ill. 1982). The Blacks only told Mr. Blaine that they need the furniture to be completed in time for a family reunion. Comfy knew that the Blacks were under a time constraint for the delivery, but apparently there was no communication regarding the redecorating of the living room. With regard to Comfy Furniture, the redecorating of the Blacks' living room was an unforeseeable event and consequently they would not be held responsible for the expense. Because the fact that the redecorating of the living room was unforeseeable, it was not included within the terms of the contract. Therefore, Comfy only breached the express terms of the contract. The Blacks probably will not be awarded compensatory damages.

LETTER WRITING

CHAPTER OVERVIEW

This chapter explains letter writing basics, such as format and types of letters. It provides examples of a variety of letters you might use in practice.

Letter writing is one of the basic tasks you will perform as paralegals. Most letter writing conventions apply to legal correspondence in much the same way as they do to other business communications. Paralegals should be aware of the components of basic letters as well as some special rules for legal communications.

A. BASICS OF LETTER WRITING

Letter writing is done in much the same way as any other legal writing. You plan it, draft it, and revise it. In planning your communication, you must determine your audience and outline what you plan to say to your reader. When revising the letter, use proper grammar and consider any revisions that would make the letter clearer. Proofread your letter.

▼ What Formats Are Used?

Letters may be drafted using a variety of formats. Firm style or personal taste generally determines the format of your letters. The formats are **full block, block, modified block,** and **personal style.**

In a full block letter, you do not indent the paragraphs. The paragraphs, the complimentary close, and the dateline are flush left. See Illustration 25-1. For block format, all paragraphs and notations are flush left, except for the date, the reference line, the complimentary close, and the signature lines, which are just right of the center of the page. See Illustration 25-3. In a modified block style letter, the first line of each paragraph is indented about five characters. See Illustration 25-6. In a personal style letter, often written to friends, the inside address is placed below the signature at the left margin.

B. COMPONENTS OF A LETTER

1. Letterhead and Headers

A letter is divided into several sections: the date, the name and the address of the addressee called the inside address, a reference line, a greeting to the addressee, the body of the letter, and the complimentary closing.

You should draft the first page of a letter on firm letterhead. The **letterhead** is the portion of the firm's stationery that identifies the firm, generally the attorneys, and sometimes the firm's paralegals. It usually includes the firm's address and its telephone and facsimile numbers. Additional pages should not carry the firm letterhead but should be placed on matching paper with a **header** on each page. The header identifies the letter and is generally placed

ILLUSTRATION 25-1.   Full Block Letter

[1]Fuzzwell, Cubbon and Landefelt
888 Toledo Road
Ottawa Hills, Ohio 43606
(419) 535-7738

[2]November 7, 1998

[3]Via Federal Express

Mr. Stuart Shulman
Navarre Industries
708 Anthony Wayne Trail
Maumee, Ohio 45860

[4]Rc: Settlement of <u>Kramer v. Shulman</u>

[5]Dear Mr. Shulman:

[6]I have enclosed a copy of the settlement agreement that we drafted and that has been signed by Mr. Kramer. Please sign the agreement and forward it to me at the above address by November 30, 1998.

If you have any questions, please feel free to call me at 535-7738.

[7]Sincerely,

Mara Cochran
Legal Assistant

[8]cc: Randall Fuzzwell
[9]Enc.
[10]MAC/wlk

1. Letterhead
2. Date
3. Recipient's address and method of service
4. Reference line
5. Greeting
6. Body of the letter
7. Closing
8. Carbon copy notation
9. Enclosure notation
10. Initials of drafter/typist

---

on the top right side of the page. A header includes the name of the addressee, the date, and the number of the page:

Cheryl Victor
November 15, 1998
Page Two

2. Date

The **date** should be placed at the top of the letter just below the firm's letterhead. The date is one of the key components of a letter concerning any legal matters. Date the letter with the same date as the date of mailing. This date can be crucial in determining a time line in a legal proceeding. Timing in sending documents and correspondence is often important in legal transactions and litigation matters. Therefore, be careful to include the date of mailing rather than the date of writing the letter. For example, if you prepare a letter on July 4 after the last mail pickup, you should date the letter July 5 because that is the date it would actually be mailed. This may seem like a purely technical distinction if you put the letter in the mail on July 4. However, some court cases and negotiations turn on the date of mailing.

3. Method of Transmission

If the letter is being sent by a method other than U.S. mail, it should be indicated on the top of the address and then underlined as follows:

Via Facsimile and U.S. Mail
Cheryl Victor
Vice President
Arizona Money Makers
1000 Tempe Road
Phoenix, Arizona 85038

This notation should start at least two lines below the date. See Illustration 25-1.

4. Inside Address

The next part of the letter, the **inside address,** should contain the name of the person to whom the letter is addressed, the individual's title if he or she has one, the name of the business if the letter is for a business, and the address.

5. Reference Line

The **reference line** is a brief statement regarding the topic of the letter. For example, if the letter concerns a contract for the sale of a particular property, your reference line would say:

Re: Sale of 2714 Barrington Road, Toledo, Ohio

Some firms and corporations ask that the reference line contain a client number, claim number, or case number, so investigate your firm's style.

PRACTICE POINTER

If possible, review letters in a file written by the assigning attorney. Note the attorney's style for the reference line and follow it.

---

6. Greeting

In general, your **greeting** depends on how familiar you are with an individual. An individual whom you do not know should be addressed as "Dear Ms. White." If you know an individual well, you may address that person by first name. If you are uncertain whether to address the individual by first name, use a title and the individual's last name. If you are addressing a letter to a particular person, such as the custodian of records, but you do not know the person's name, try to determine the person's name. If necessary, call a company or agency to determine the appropriate recipient for the letter. Your letter is more likely to be answered quickly if it is addressed to the appropriate person rather than "To whom it may concern."

7. Body of Letter

The **body** of the letter follows the greeting and should begin with an opening sentence and paragraph that summarizes the purpose of the letter. Draft the body of the letter carefully. Outline the letter before writing it to be sure that you address all of the necessary points. List each point you want to cover. For Illustration 25-1, your outline might read as follows:

1. enclose settlement agreement
2. ask for signature and return date
3. ask addressee to call if he has questions

Consider your audience. If you are writing to a layperson who is unfamiliar with the law, explain any legal terms you use. However, do not provide any legal opinions. If you are addressing your letter to an individual who is familiar with the law, such as a judge, a paralegal, an in-house counsel, or an attorney, you do not need to explain such terms. To do so might be considered condescending.

8. Closing

End your letter with a **closing** in which you invite a response, such as "Please do not hesitate to call if you have any questions," or thank the addressee for assistance, such as "Thank you in advance for your cooperation." Finally, end the letter with a complimentary closing such as "Sincerely," "Very truly yours," or "Best regards" placed two lines below the final line of the body of the letter. Place your name four lines below the closing to allow for a signature. Include your title, that is, paralegal or legal assistant.

Do not provide legal advice in your letter or represent yourself as an attorney. Ethical codes and state laws prohibit paralegals who are not licensed to practice law from providing legal opinions or from representing themselves as attorneys. To avoid any confusion or possible misrepresentation, include your title after your name when you write a letter.

9. Copies to Others and Enclosures

If you are copying a third party on the letter and want the original addressee to know this, note it with a "cc" at the bottom left margin of the letter following the closing. The cc indicates **carbon copy** sent to the person listed. (Although photocopies have replaced carbon copies, cc is still used.) Indicate to whom a copy of the letter was sent as "cc: Mike Sterner." See Illustration 25-2. If you do not want the original addressee to know that you copied a letter to another person, note on the draft or file copy "bcc," which means **blind carbon copy.** That notation should only appear on the draft or file copy of the letter and not on the recipient's letter.

The next notation is for enclosures, such as court orders, contracts, or releases. Place the abbreviation **Enc.** or **Encs.** at the bottom left margin of the letter. See Illustration 25-1.

Finally, the letter should note your initials in all capital letters as the author of the letter and then the initials in lowercase letters of the person who typed the letter. If your initials are RAS and the typist's are HVS, then the notation under the enclosure or cc notation would read RAS/hvs.

C. TYPES OF LETTERS

Paralegals write letters to clients to confirm deposition dates, meeting dates, hearing dates, or agreements. These letters are called confirming letters. Other letters provide a status report of a case or summarize a transaction. Some letters accompany documents, such as those for document productions, contracts, or settlement

ILLUSTRATION 25-2.   Letter Confirming Deposition

Law Offices of Sam Harris
2714 Barrington Road
Findlay, Ohio 45840
(419) 267-0000

January 28, 1999

Ms. Karen Dolgin
2903 W. Main Cross Street
Findlay, Ohio 45840

Re: Deposition of Robert Harrold
    Harrold v. Sofer

Dear Ms. Dolgin:

This letter is to confirm our conversation today in which you stated that you will present the plaintiff, Robert Harrold, for a deposition at the law office of Sam Harris, 2714 Barrington Road, in Findlay, on March 18, 1999, at 2 p.m. This deposition is being rescheduled at your request because the plaintiff had a family commitment set for February 15, 1999, the date originally set for the deposition.

If you have any questions or additional problems, please feel free to call me at (419) 267-0000, extension 608.

Best regards,

Craig Black
Paralegal

cc: Sam Harris
    Wally Sofer
CMB/klm

---

releases. These are called transmittal letters. Still others are requests for information. Some letters explain the litigation process to clients. See Illustration 25-3.

1. Confirming Letters

Confirming letters reaffirm information already agreed to by you and the recipient. It is a good practice to follow up any conversation with a client or an opposing attorney or paralegal with a confirming

ILLUSTRATION 25-3.   Letter Concerning Deposition Schedule

Law Offices of Sam Harris
2714 Barrington Road
Findlay, Ohio 45840
(419) 267-0000

January 28, 1999

Wally Sofer
Chief Executive Officer
1000 Hollywood Way
Houcktown, Ohio 44060

> Re: Deposition of Wally Sofer
>   <u>Harrold v. Sofer</u>

Dear Mr. Sofer:

This letter is to advise you that you are required to submit to a deposition by the plaintiff's attorney at 10 a.m. on March 1, 1999, at the law office of Karen Dolgin, 2903 W. Main Cross Street in downtown Findlay. During this deposition, the plaintiff's attorney will ask you questions related to the above-referenced court case, and you will provide answers while under oath and in the presence of a court reporter. Mr. Harris also will be present to represent you during the deposition.

Mr. Harris and I would like to meet with you at least once before the deposition to discuss your case and this important part of your case.

I will call you Wednesday to schedule an appointment next week to prepare for your deposition.

Please bring any accident reports, citations, or other documents that relate to the accident if you have not already provided them to our office.

I look forward to speaking with you this week.

Sincerely,

Craig Black
Paralegal

cc: Sam Harris
CMB/klm

---

letter that summarizes the conversation, any agreements made, or any future acts to be accomplished. See Illustration 25-2. For example, after you discuss a document production with a client and set a meeting date to review the records, send a letter summarizing the conversation. Such confirming letters provide you with a reminder of the conversation and allow anyone who reviews the file later to know what you and the client discussed should you be unavailable.

If opposing counsel has agreed to produce documents or provide a witness for a deposition at a particular time, write a confirming letter to the opposing counsel summarizing these facts and asking to be contacted if there are discrepancies. Whenever a deposition is rescheduled or continued, it is imperative that a confirming letter be sent to avoid future discovery disputes. Whenever your client is deposed, send him or her a copy of the deposition for review. A sample of such a letter is found in Illustration 25-4.

2. Status Letters and Transaction Summary Letters

Often you will be asked to provide a **status report** of a case, especially to insurance companies and other clients. See Illustration 25-5. These letters provide clients with an overview of the current activities in a court case, transaction, or other legal matter.

Transaction summary letters often follow a business transaction such as a real estate closing. In these letters, you summarize a transaction.

In other letters, you will **request information,** often from the custodian of records. See Illustration 25-6.

Often you will be responsible for coordinating document productions. Illustration 25-7 shows a sample **transmittal letter** to a client concerning a request to produce documents.

Many letters will be written to accompany documents, releases, and checks. See Illustrations 25-8 and 25-9.

3. Demand Letter

A **demand letter** is a letter that states your client's demands to another party. A common letter paralegals write is a demand letter that seeks to collect debts. Such a letter may need to comply with the requirements of your state's fair-debt collection laws. See Illustration 25-10.

In a demand letter, you should include the fact that your firm represents the creditor or other client, as well as the client's desire for full payment of the claim. Specify the amount demanded or state the action sought, and ask the debtor either to make payment or to contact your office within a certain number of days. Then state

ILLUSTRATION 25-4.   Letter Enclosing Deposition Transcript

Law Offices of Sam Harris
2714 Barrington Road
Findlay, Ohio 45840
(419) 267-0000

July 11, 1999

Mr. William Gary
709 Franklin Street
Findlay, Ohio 45840

Re: Deposition on July 8, 1999

Dear Mr. Gary:

Enclosed is a copy of the transcript of your July 8, 1999, deposition. Please review the transcript carefully and note any statements that were incorrectly transcribed. You may not rewrite your testimony, but you should note any inaccurate transcriptions. You may correct the spelling of names and places. If you find any serious mistakes, please call me to discuss these problems.

When you review the deposition, please do not mark the original transcript. Instead, note any discrepancies on a separate sheet of paper. Please note the page and line of any discrepancies. I will have my secretary type a list of the discrepancies, and we will discuss these changes before we send them to the court reporter. These changes must be received by the court reporter within 30 days; therefore, I would appreciate your prompt review of the transcript and would like to review your changes by July 30, 1999. If we fail to provide the changes to the court reporter within 30 days, we will forfeit your right to correct the transcript and any inaccuracies will be part of the record.

If you have any questions, please do not hesitate to call me.

Thank you for your cooperation in advance.

Best regards,

Benjamin Harris
Paralegal

Enc.
BSH/jas

ILLUSTRATION 25-5.   Status Report Letter

Cosher, Cosher and Snorer
960 Wyus Boulevard
Madison, Wisconsin 53606

June 12, 1999

Mr. Cal L. Medeep
Pockets Insurance Company
10 Wausau Way
Wausau, Wisconsin 54401

Re: Kelsey v. Cocoa
   Your claim number: C100090888

Dear Mr. Medeep:

This letter is to provide you with a status report concerning the progress of the above-referenced matter. To date, we have requested that the plaintiff answer interrogatories and requests for admissions. I sent a copy of these requests to you about a week ago. The plaintiff is required to answer these requests within 30 days. We will send you a copy of the plaintiff's answers as soon as we receive them. We are scheduled to depose the plaintiff on September 1, 1999.

The plaintiff's attorney is scheduled to depose a representative of Oreo Company on October 13, 1999.

At this time, the court has not scheduled a settlement conference, but is likely to do so before the end of the year.

Please feel free to call if you have any questions.

Sincerely,

Karen Thompson
Legal Assistant

KLT/yml

ILLUSTRATOIN 25-6.   Request for Information

Cosher, Cosher and Snorer
960 Wyus Boulevard
Madison, Wisconsin 53606

August 12, 1999

Sarah Rachel
Custodian of Records
Federal Deposit Insurance Corp.
9100 Bryn Mawr Road
Rosemont, Illinois 60018

Re: Freedom of Information Act Request

Dear Ms. Rachel:

Based on the Freedom of Information Act, 5 U.S.C. § 552 et seq., I am requesting that your agency provide copies of the following:

Each and every document that relates to or refers to the sale of the property located at 2714 Barrington Road, Glenview, Illinois, 60025.

The documents should be located in your Rosemont, Illinois office.

Under the act, these documents should be available to us within ten days. If any portion of this request is denied, please provide a detailed statement of the reasons for the denial and an index or similar statement concerning the nature of the documents withheld. As required by the act, I agree to pay reasonable charges for copying of the documents upon the presentation of a bill and the finished copies.

Thank you in advance for your cooperation in this matter.

Sincerely,

Carolyn Wentworth
Paralegal

CAW/dag

ILLUSTRATION 25-7. Request to Produce Documents

Carthage, Katz and Kramer
1001 B Line Highway
Darlington, Wisconsin 53840

February 28, 1999

Ms. Karen Taylor
Carrots and Critters Corp.
1864 Merrimac Road
Sylvania, Ohio 43560

Re: Carrots and Critters v. Rabbits and Rodents

Dear Ms. Taylor:

Enclosed please find a request from the defendants asking you to produce documents. The date scheduled for the production of these documents is April 1, 1999. Some documents may be protected from disclosure because they may contain confidential trade secret information, and others may be protected because they are communications between you and your attorney or the result of your attorneys' work. We must respond in writing by March 25, 1999, in order to raise any of these claims.

As we must review the documents to determine whether any documents are protected, we should compile the documents no later than March 15, 1999. This will allow us time to review, to index, and to number each document.

I will be available to assist you in gathering documents to respond to this request. I will call you this week to schedule an appointment.

If you have any questions, please feel free to call.

Sincerely,

Eileen Waters
Paralegal

Encs.
EDW/jnn

ILLUSTRATION 25-8.   Letter Accompanying Document

David, Randall & Henry
1600 Thirteenth Street
Wilmette, Illinois 60091

March 4, 1999

Eve Lillian
Lake County Recorder of Deeds
18 N. County Street
Waukegan, Illinois 60085

Re: 1785 Central Street
    Deerfield, Illinois 60015

Dear Mrs. Lillian:

Enclosed please find two original quit claim deeds, one dated December 30, 1998, and one dated January 2, 1999, relating to the above-referenced property. Both deeds have been marked "exempt" from state and county transfer tax. A check for $50.00 to cover the recording fees ($25 each) is enclosed. Please record these deeds at once and return the originals to Karen Smith at the 1785 Central Street address.

Thank you for your assistance.

Sincerely,

Jennifer Lauren
Legal Assistant

Encs.
cc: Karen Smith
JML/jch

the action that the firm will take if the demand is not met within the specified time period.

CHECKLIST: RULES FOR LETTER WRITING

1. "Never give legal advice" is the first rule of letter writing for paralegals.
2. Be informative.
3. Consider your audience. If you are addressing a client, do so courteously and at a level that the client will understand. If you were asked to answer a client's questions, be sure that you do. You should always be respectful to the addressee.

ILLUSTRATON 25-9.   Letter Accompanying Check

Hellman & Fernandez
Central and Carriage Way
Evanston, Illinois 60202

April 22, 1999

William German
Chicago Bar Association
124 Plymouth Court
Chicago, Illinois 60611

Re: Commercial Real Estate Contract Prepared by the Real Property
     Law Committee

Dear Mr. German:

Enclosed please find a check for $30.00 to cover the mailing fees and
the cost of a copy of the Real Estate Contract referenced above. Please
send me a copy of the contract at your earliest convenience.

Thank you for your cooperation.

Sincerely,

Thomas Taylor
Paralegal

Enc.
cc: Rachel Kramer
TCT/ear

---

4. Choose your words carefully. You want to make certain that your
   words express what you intend.

CHAPTER SUMMARY

Letter writing is an essential part of your daily routine as a paralegal.
Most letter writing conventions apply to legal correspondence in much
the same way as they do to other business communications. However,
paralegals should be careful about dating letters concerning legal matters. Letters should be dated with the date of mailing, which may or may
not be the date of drafting.

   A letter should contain a date, the name and address of the addressee,
a reference line, a greeting to the addressee, the body of the letter, and
the complimentary closing.

ILLUSTRATION 25-10.   Demand Letter

Law Office of Sam Harris
145 Water Street
Madison, Wisconsin 53606

April 1, 1999

Carolyn Wehre
889 Barrington Road
Middleton, Wisconsin 53608

Re: Furniture Crafters Account 4155

Dear Ms. Wehre:

Our office represents Furniture Crafters in the collection of the $468.00 debt due on the above referenced account. Furniture Crafters requests that you pay the full amount of the debt, $468.00, immediately.

You must pay this amount in full or contact our firm at the above telephone number or address within seven days. If we do not hear from you within seven days, we will proceed to court in this matter.

Sincerely,

Marcia Bottoms
Paralegal

MAB/hvs

Confirming letters reaffirm information already agreed to between you and the recipient. Status letters provide an up-to-date review of the process of a pending matter. Transaction summary letters explain particular transactions. Letters also are written to accompany documents, such as releases and checks, or to state your client's demands to a third party, such as for payment.

As with any written document, letters should be outlined, written, and then rewritten if necessary.

KEY TERMS

blind carbon copy (bcc)	confirming letter
block letter	date
body	demand letter
carbon copy (cc)	enclosure line
closing	full block letter

greeting
header
inside address
letterhead
modified block letter
personal style letter

reference line
requests for information
status report
transaction summary letter
transmittal letter

EXERCISES

SHORT ANSWER EXERCISES
1. What are the basic components of a letter?
2. What is a reference line?
3. How do you indicate that you are sending a copy of a letter to another person?
4. How do you indicate that you want someone to receive a copy, but you don't want the addressee to know that the other person received a copy of the letter?
5. What are confirming letters?
6. What is a status report letter?
7. What are transmittal letters?
8. What are demand letters?
9. Should you provide a legal opinion in a letter?

LETTER WRITING EXERCISES
Prepare the following letters as if you were a paralegal with the law firm of Snorer, Hackett and Blank, 1000 Madison Way, Madison, Wisconsin 53606. Addressee names are identified for you, but you may supply each one's address yourself.

10. Write a letter to Madison Insurance Corporation explaining that your law firm will be representing Carol White for a lawsuit against its insured, Harold Watson, stemming from an automobile accident that occurred on September 1, 1997. The Madison claims adjuster is Howie Mark. Harold Watson's insurance policy number is 1280. You once had a difficult time dealing with Mr. Mark and Madison Insurance in the past, so you send your letter by certified mail. Enclose a copy of the police report. Send a blind copy to your client. You write it at 5 P.M. on December 24. You realize that December 25 is a holiday and that mail will not go out until the next day.
11. Your firm represents a client, Karen Taylor, who sustained a neck injury during an automobile accident between Carter McLaughlin and Robert Carroll. Write a letter to Dr. Wendell Martin asking for a detailed report concerning the present and future medical problems of that client. Dr. Martin is an orthopedic surgeon. Indicate that you have a signed release from the client to enclose.
12. Your firm represents Margaret Weston in a divorce case. Write a short letter to her informing her of the final hearing date in her divorce

case. The date is June 16, 1999, in Lucas County Domestic Relations Court, 900 W. Adams Street, Toledo, Ohio 43602.

13. Your client needs to give testimony at a deposition on November 15, 1999, at 10 A.M. at your offices. Please draft a letter asking William Hesse to be at the deposition. Explain to him that you will meet with him in advance to discuss his testimony.

14. Your firm has just settled a case involving Karen Douglas and your client, the Wentworth Industries in Morristown, New Jersey. The case was settled for $88,000. The Wentworth corporation paid Douglas for injuries she sustained when she fell at a Mexican hotel. You do not want to admit any liability in your letter or admit any ownership interest in the Mexican hotel, the CanCan. You merely want to tender the check to Douglas in full satisfaction of any claims she or her husband have against Wentworth. You also have the signed settlement agreement to send her and the court dismissal of the action.

APPENDICES

SHEPARDIZING AND CITE CHECKING

▼ What Is Cite Checking or Shepardizing, and When Is It Done?

The meaning of the term *cite checking* varies. Often, the meaning depends on the particular attorney asking you to complete the project. For some attorneys, cite checking includes three components:

1. ensuring that the cited authority in fact states what the brief or memorandum tells the reader the authority states and that the correct authority is cited;
2. making certain that the citation is placed in proper Bluebook format or style; and
3. checking that the authority is still current and valid law.

When some attorneys ask you to cite check your research results, they only want you to complete the final component of the cite checking process. Others may want you to complete all three tasks or just two of the three procedures.

For the first stage, you might consider using the following process:

1. Review the brief and the citation.
2. Read the cited authority.
3. Ask yourself a series of questions:
   Does the cited authority say what the brief or memorandum states that it says?
   Should quotes be placed around the text in the brief or memorandum?
   Is the correct page number for the citation listed?

What is the correct case name?
What court decided this case?
What is the date of the decision?
What is the parallel citation?
4. Make certain that you note the correct court.

For stage two, consult Appendix B. For stage three, refer to the cite checking checklist that follows.

Cite Checking Checklist

1. Make a list of the cases, statutes, rules, or other authorities you need to cite check.
2. To be thorough, search cases in all of the following sources or services: *Shepard's* (hardcopy, online, or CD-ROM), Auto-Cite, KeyCite, and LEX-CITE.

Shepardizing Cases in Hardcopy Materials Checklist

1. Determine which *Shepard's* series is the appropriate one to consult. Is the case in the federal or state citators? Should you consult the regional rather than state citator?
2. Review the front cover of the most current pamphlet that accompanies the *Shepard's* citations to determine what volumes should be reviewed for your cite check.
3. Gather each of the volumes and supplements mentioned on the cover.
4. Find the appropriate reporter section in each volume.
5. Locate the volume number listed in bold. Check the top corner of the page until you find pages encompassing your volume number.
6. Find the page number.

Shepard's Online Checklist for Cases

1. For LEXIS, click on the *Shepard's* button and type in the citation.
2. On the Internet, follow the directions.

Auto-Cite Checklist

1. Access LEXIS.
2. Click on the Auto-Cite button or line under the services window. Type the citation.

KeyCite Checklist

1. Access WESTLAW.
2. Click on the KeyCite button. Then type in the citation.

LEXCITE Checklist

1. Access LEXIS.
2. Select the appropriate library.
3. Select the appropriate file.
4. Type **LEXCITE**, and then type the citation in parentheses.

Shepard's **CD-ROM Edition Checklist**

1. Select the proper CD-ROM and place it in the drive.
2. Type in the citation you want to Shepardize.
3. You will receive the *Shepard's* display of the citation.
4. If you do not have the citation, you can enter the name of the case and the CD-ROM scrvice will display the case for you.

BLUEBOOK CITATION

The Bluebook is the guide to citation form for all legal documents, whether office memos or Supreme Court briefs. The Bluebook, formally known as the *Uniform System of Citation, Sixteenth Edition,* governs because of convention and tradition rather than by the mandate of the state legislature. Other forms of citation have been developed, like the University of Chicago Maroon Book, but the Bluebook is so entrenched in custom and usage that it is hard to replace. New forms of citation are emerging due to the advent of nonproprietary cases in which the case is not attributed to a publisher. Generally, the Bluebook is the bible for citation format for all legal personnel. If ever in doubt as to citation format, rely on the Bluebook.

▼ What Is a Citation?

A citation is really an address indicating where the cited material can be found so that anyone reading your document can find the material if he or she wants to. The abbreviations must be consistent so that everyone knows what they mean. We rely on a similar convention with street addresses and postal abbreviations. The abbreviation for avenue is Ave.; the postal abbreviation for New York is NY.

▼ What Documents Are Cited?

Any source of authority that you discuss in any legal document is cited. Any concept or idea that is not your own must be cited; this is called attributing authority to your ideas. Citing credits the source from which the idea or legal rule came. It also tells the reader where he or she can find the original source. Citations are used for all authority, whether it is primary authority like a case or a statute, or secondary authority like a treatise or a law review article. Also cited are looseleaf services, practitioners' materials, and newspaper articles.

The Bluebook has two citation formats, one for briefs and memos and the other for law review articles. Paralegals rely on the brief and memo format for citation.

▼ What Are the Components of a Citation?

Generally, the components of a cite are the name of the particular document, the volume or title where the document is located, the name of the publication that contains the document, and the specific page, section, or paragraph where the document is found. Also included is the year that a case was decided or the publication date of a book or volume of statutes. For example:

Jacobs v. Grossman, 310 Ill. 247, 141 N.E. 714 (1923)

The name of the document is the case name, *Jacobs v. Grossman.* Parallel citations are given in the example so that you can find the case in both sources, the official reporter that is always mentioned first and the unofficial reporter, mentioned second. The first number preceding the reporter abbreviation is the volume number of the reporter. Next is the reporter abbreviation and then the page number where the case begins in the reporter. The year that the case was decided is included in parentheses. Bluebook **Table T.1** lists reporter abbreviations.

Using the Bluebook takes practice. The Bluebook is organized by rules. Each rule details the citation format for each type of document. The index is very helpful in finding specific references to the citation format for an individual document like a statute, an administrative regulation, or a law review article.

The following portion of the appendix provides examples of the materials mentioned in the book and sample cite formats based on the Bluebook. These examples will help you navigate your way through the Bluebook. If the illustration here does not provide adequate information, you can turn to the Bluebook rule mentioned to obtain more detailed treatment.

▼ How Are Slip Opinions Cited?

Slip opinions are cited according to Bluebook **Rule 10.8.1**. You should provide the docket number, the court, and the full date of the most recent disposition of the case.

slip opinion cite: Gillespie v. Willard City Bd. of Educ., No. C87-7043 (N.D. Ohio Sept. 28, 1987)

with page cite: Gillespie v. Willard City Bd. of Educ., No. C87-7043, slip op. at 3 (N.D. Ohio Sept. 28, 1987)

▼ How Do You Cite a State Case?

Cite a state case according to Bluebook **Rule 10**. The first example below shows the citation for an Illinois case cited in a brief prepared for an Illinois Supreme Court case. The second example shows the same case cited in a brief to the United States District Court for the Northern District of Illinois.

Ill. Sup. Ct. brief: Thompson v. Economy Super Marts, 221 Ill. App. 3d 263, 581 N.E.2d 885, 163 Ill. Dec. 731 (1991)

U.S. Dist. Ct. brief: Thompson v. Economy Super Marts, 581 N.E.2d 885 (Ill. Ct. App. 1991)

When you use a state decision in a memorandum or a brief, always include the regional citation. See Bluebook **Table T.1**. If you are citing a state case to a state court in which the case was decided, provide both the official citation, if one exists, and the regional citation, as the first example above shows. Always list the official citation first. When you cite a state case in a memorandum addressed to a federal court or to a court of a state different from the state that decided the case, include only the regional citation as the second example above shows. If you are using only the regional citation, remember to place the abbreviation for the deciding court in parentheses. See Bluebook **Rule 10.4**.

Some states now have adopted so-called public domain citations as their official cites that should be cited in accordance with **Rule 10.3.1**. These cites are designed to allow readers to find the case in a computerized system that does not rely on commercial publishers. Cites to commercial reporters such as West's may be used to augment public domain citations.

The public domain format is as follows: case name, followed by the year of the decision, the deciding court, and the sequential number of the decision. To cite to a specific portion of the decision, you may add a reference to the paragraph.

Public domain citation: State v. Kienast, 1996 S.D. 111 ¶ 2.

▼ How Do You Cite Decisions Found in the *Federal Reporter* or the *Federal Supplement*?

Bluebook **Rules 10.1–10.6** and **Table T.1** provide detailed coverage of the citation format for cases from the *Federal Reporter* and the *Federal Supplement*. The case name is placed first and underlined. Next, place the volume number. The reporter abbreviation is next. For the *Federal Reporter*, the abbreviation is "F." The number of the series, second or third, should be placed next to the "F." For the *Federal Supplement*, the reporter is abbreviated "F. Supp." The page number follows the abbreviation for the reporter. Next, place an abbreviation denoting the appropriate court and the date of the decision. Be certain to include a geographic designation for the district courts.

> *Federal Reporter* **case:**   Zimmerman v. North Am. Signal Co., 704 F.2d 347 (7th Cir. 1983)
>
> *Federal Supplement* **case:**   Musser v. Mountain View Broad., 578 F. Supp. 229 (E.D. Tenn. 1984)

▼ How Do You Cite a Decision Contained in the *Federal Rules Decisions* Reporter?

The abbreviation for the *Federal Rules Decisions* is F.R.D. A case would be cited according to Bluebook **Table T.1**, as follows:

> Barrett Indus. Trucks v. Old Republic Ins. Co., 129 F.R.D. 515 (N.D. Ill. 1989)

▼ How Do You Cite a U.S. Supreme Court Case?

Once a U.S. Supreme Court case is published in an advance sheet of the *U.S. Reports,* the *U.S. Reports* citation, and only the *U.S. Reports* citation, is the proper citation. Do not include parallel citations. See **Rule 10** generally and specially see **Rule 10.4** and **Table T.1**.

> **correct:**   Erie R.R. v. Tompkins, 304 U.S. 64 (1938)
>
> **incorrect:**   Erie R.R. v. Tompkins, 304 U.S. 64, 58 S. Ct. 817, 82 L. Ed. 1188 (1938)

However, if a Supreme Court opinion has been published in the *West Supreme Court Reporter* but yet not in the *U.S. Reports,* the *Supreme Court Reporter* citation should be used. See **Table T.1**.

If a Supreme Court opinion has not yet been published in *U.S. Reports, Supreme Court Reporter,* or *U.S. Reports, Lawyers' Edition,* then you should cite to *United States Law Week.* See **Table T.1**. The court designation, U.S., should be placed in the parentheses with the full date. See Bluebook **Rules 10.4** and **10.5**. The citation would read as follows:

> UAW v. Johnson Controls, 59 U.S.L.W. 4209 (U.S. Mar. 20, 1991)

▼ How Do You Cite a Decision Reported on WESTLAW?

Rule 10.8.1(a) explains how an unpublished decision found only on either WESTLAW or LEXIS should be cited. For WESTLAW, first provide the name of the case and underline it. The next part of the citation is the docket number. In the example that follows, that number is No. 82-C4585. The next part of the citation is the year that the decision was issued. Next, indicate "WL" for WESTLAW and finally the WESTLAW number assigned to the case. In the parentheses, place the date.

WESTLAW example: Clark Equip. Co. v. Lift Parts Mfg. Co., No. 82-C4585, 1985 WL 2917 (N.D. Ill. Oct. 1, 1985)

▼ How Do You Cite a Decision Reported on LEXIS?

For LEXIS citations, first state the name of the case, the docket number, the year of the decision, the name of the LEXIS file that contains the case, and the name LEXIS to indicate that the case is found on LEXIS. Next place the date in parentheses.

LEXIS example: Barrett Indus. Trucks v. Old Republic Ins. Co., No. 87-C9429, 1990 U.S. Dist. LEXIS 142 (N.D. Ill. Jan. 9, 1990)

If a decision is published in a hardcopy reporter, you should not use the WESTLAW or LEXIS citation.

▼ How Do You Indicate a Page or Screen Number for the Case?

An asterisk should precede any screen or page numbers. See **Rule 10.8.1.(a)**.

WESTLAW screen no.: Clark Equip. Co. v. Lift Parts Mfg. Co., No. 82-C4585, 1985 WL 2917 at *1 (N.D. Ill. Oct. 1, 1985)

LEXIS screen no.: Barrett Indus. Trucks v. Old Republic Ins. Co., No. 87-C9429, 1990 U.S. Dist. LEXIS 142 at *1 (N.D. Ill. Jan. 9, 1990)

▼ How Do You Cite Internet Resources?

Rule 17.3.3 covers Internet sources. Only rely on Internet resources if there is no other way to obtain the material, because Internet resources are transient in nature. Cite as:

Karin Mitra, Information v. Commercialization: The Internet and Unsolicited Electronic Mail, 4 Rich. J.L. & Tech. 6 (Spring 1998) ⟨http://www.richmond.edu/jolt/v4i3/mitra.html⟩.

▼ How Do You Cite Federal Statutes?

Always cite to the official statutory compilation. The first entry in the citation is the title number, then the abbreviation for the statutory compilation, and then the section or paragraph number. Bluebook **Rule 12** details all of the various rules pertaining to citing statutes and codes, state or federal. Always cite to the year of the code's compilation, not the year that the particular statute section was enacted. For example:

12 U.S.C. §211 (1988)

If a code section is well known by a popular name, then include the name in the citation. For example:

Strikebreaker Act 18 U.S.C. §1231 (1988)

You may rely on an unofficial version for updating purposes. All of the following are citations to the identical statute.

> 26 U.S.C. §61 (1988)
> 26 U.S.C.A. §61 (West 1988 & Supp. 1994)
> 26 U.S.C.S. §61 (LEXIS-NEXIS 1998)

As with the U.S.C., the year included in the citation is the year that the code volume was published, not the year that the statute was enacted. In the U.S.C.A. example above, the first year mentioned, 1988, is the year that the particular volume of the code was published; the second date, 1994, is the year of the pocket part supplement that updates the code volume. The publication date is printed either on the title page of the bound volume or on the back of the title page.

▼ How Do You Cite a Section of a Constitution, Federal or State?

Bluebook **Rule 11** outlines the citation format. The United States Constitution citation refers to the particular article, section, and clause being used. For example:

> U.S. Const. art. II, §2, cl. 1

This cite is used when you are referring to the body of the Constitution. A special citation format is required when you are referring to an amendment. For example:

> U.S. Const. amend. II

State constitutions are indicated by the name of the state in the Bluebook abbreviated format. **Table T.1** indicates the accepted state name abbreviation; this is not necessarily the postal abbreviation. For example, the state of Washington's postal abbreviation is WA, but the Bluebook abbreviation is Wash. A section of the Washington state constitution would be cited as follows:

> Wash. Const. art. I, §2

Years or dates are not included in citations to constitutions, state or federal, that are current. Parenthetical notations after the citation indicate the year a constitutional provision was repealed or amended. An example is the Eighteenth Amendment to the U.S. Constitution prohibiting the sale of liquor. The Twenty-First Amendment later repealed this. Bluebook **Rule 11** provides the following example using the Prohibition amendment:

> U.S. Const. amend. XVIII (repealed 1933)

▼ How Do You Cite to a Legislative History of a Statute?

Bluebook **Rule 13** details the citation format for all of the components of the legislative process: the bill, the committee report, the debates, and transcripts of the hearings.

▼ How Are the *Code of Federal Regulations* and the *Federal Register* Cited?

Rule 14 of the Bluebook details the citation format for administrative and executive materials, which include the *Code of Federal Regulations* and the *Federal Register.* Title 21 of the C.F.R. part 101 from 1992 is cited as:

21 C.F.R. pt. 101 (1992)

If you were citing to Title 21 of the C.F.R. §101.62 from 1993, it would be written as:

21 C.F.R. §101.62 (1993)

A *Federal Register* entry from volume 58, beginning on page 26121, from April 30, 1993 would be cited as:

58 Fed. Reg. 26121 (1993)

As you can see, the specific calendar date is not cited, just the year.

▼ How Do You Cite to a Legal Dictionary?

The information for the correct citation format for dictionaries is found in **Rule 15.7** of the Bluebook. For example:

Ballentine's Law Dictionary 1190 (3d ed. 1969)
Black's Law Dictionary 712 (6th ed. 1990)

▼ How Are Legal Encyclopedias Cited?

Bluebook **Rule 15.7** discusses legal encyclopedias. A citation to the discussion of easements would be as follows:

25 Am. Jur. 2d Easements and Licenses §93 (1966 & Supp. 1993)
28 C.J.S. Easements §18 (1941 & Supp. 1993)

▼ How Do You Cite to *American Law Reports?*

This is found in **Rule 16.5.5** of the Bluebook.

William B. Johnson, Annotation, Locating Easement of Way Created by Necessity, 36 A.L.R.4th 769 (1985)

▼ How Do You Cite to a Law Review or Law Journal?

Bluebook **Rule 16** indicates the citation form for a law review article, as follows:

> Thomas W. Merrill, Property Rules, Liability Rules, and Adverse Posses-
> sion, 79 Nw. U. L. Rev. 1122 (1985)

The abbreviation for the journal name is found in **Table 13** of the Bluebook. A legal newspaper is cited according to **Rule 16.4**:

> David Bailey, Call for Video Reenactment of Jury Rejected, Chi. D. L.
> Bull., Nov. 1, 1993, at 1

▼ How Do You Cite the Restatements?

Bluebook **Rule 12.8.5** indicates that the Restatements are cited as follows:

> Restatement (Second) of Contracts §235 (1979)

Note that the year is the year that the Restatement section was adopted. This information is given on the title page of every volume of the Restatements. When you are citing to a comment that follows the Restatement section, **Rule 3.5** of the Bluebook applies. For example:

> Restatement (Second) of Contracts §235 cmt. a (1979)

▼ How Do You Cite an Ethics Rule Found in the *ABA Model Code of Professional Responsibility*?

The rules for citation of ethics codes are found in Bluebook **Rule 12.8.6**. Rule 1.10 of the *ABA Model Code* would be cited as follows:

> Model Code of Professional Responsibility Rule 1.10 (1992)

▼ How Do You Cite an ABA Ethics Opinion?

The rules for citation of ethics opinions are contained in Bluebook **Rule 12.8.6**. For example:

> ABA Comm. on Professional Ethics and Grievances, Informal Op. 88-
> 1526 (1988)

▼ How Do You Cite the Various Federal Rules?

Cite the federal rules in accordance with Bluebook **Rule 12.8.3** as follows:

> Fed. R. Civ. P. 56
> Fed. R. Crim. P. 1

Fed. R. App. P. 26
Fed. R. Evid. 803

The local appellate court rules also are cited based on the same rule.

7th Cir. R. 1

INDEX